THE NORTHERN HEMISPHERE

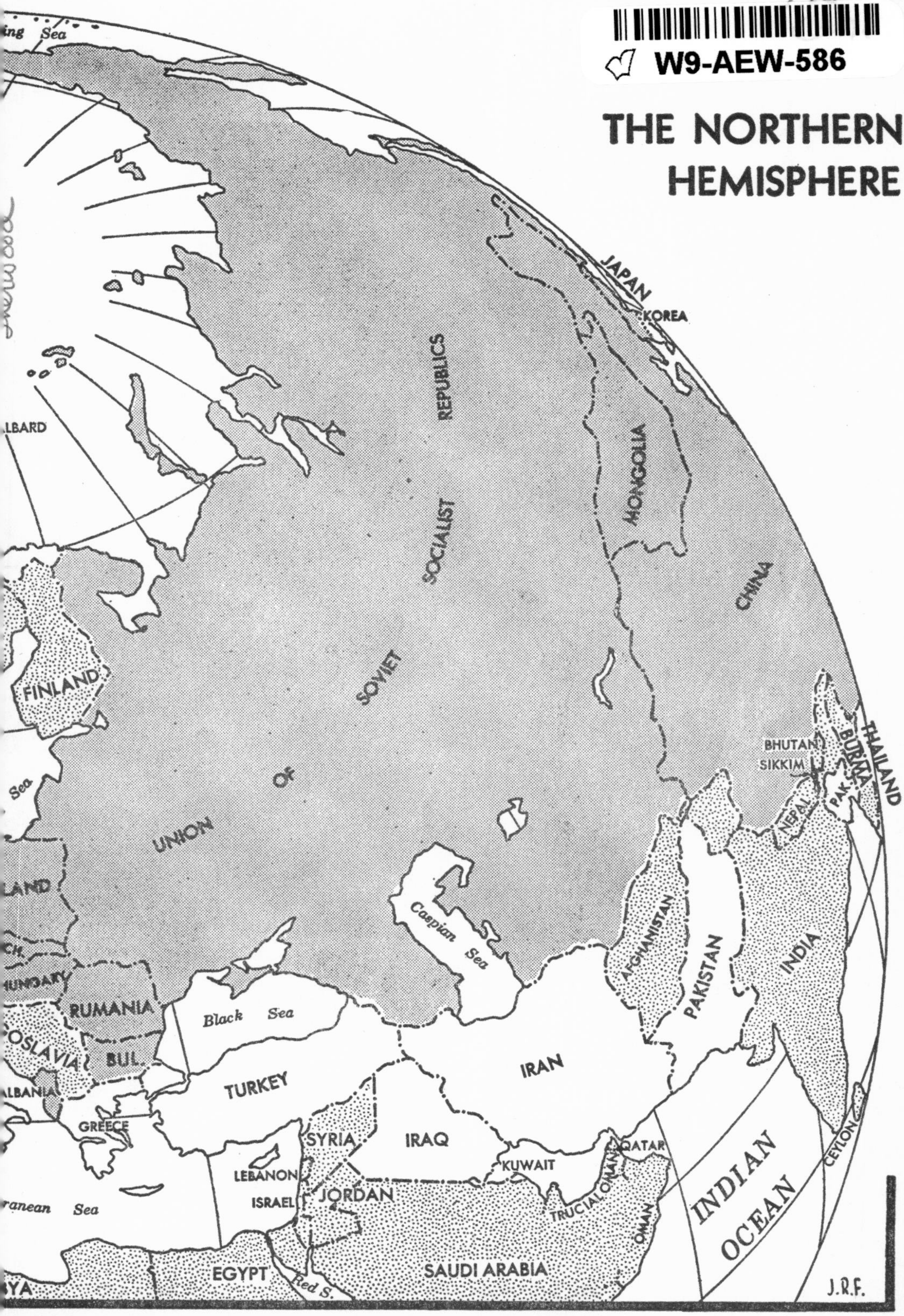

The "West": NATO and Baghdad Pact Nations

U.S.S.R., China, and Satellite Nations

PRINCIPLES of POLITICAL GEOGRAPHY

BY

Hans W. Weigert
GEORGETOWN UNIVERSITY

Henry Brodie
DEPARTMENT OF STATE

Edward W. Doherty
DEPARTMENT OF STATE

John R. Fernstrom
GEORGETOWN UNIVERSITY

Eric Fischer
GEORGE WASHINGTON UNIVERSITY

Dudley Kirk
THE POPULATION COUNCIL, INC.

New York: APPLETON-CENTURY-CROFTS, Inc.

6111-4

Library of Congress Card Number: 56-9859

PRINTED IN THE UNITED STATES OF AMERICA

Introduction

1

This study of political geography is not an ordinary textbook. The subject is both in the field of political science and of geography, and being both it must be analytical in all its aspects; for the attempt to show the interrelationship and the blending of political and geographical factors in power relations is analytical in nature. The result is a book which confronts the reader with the facts and problems of political geography, stating the facts and posing the problems without, however, attempting to find easy answers for the latter. It aims, above all, at making the reader realize the importance and magnitude of the problems that arise from the interrelationship of political and geographical factors. The emphasis on problems accounts for our statement that this volume is not an ordinary textbook.

It is not a well-paved and easy road that we propose to travel in our effort to link the two realms of geography and of man's political authority and organization within his natural environment. The view, and the review, of this relationship is characterized and complicated by the dominant fact that the realm of political geography is subject to constant change and fluctuation. We have become used to the phrase that ours is a "shrinking world." In no phase of history has this shrinking process progressed as rapidly as in our time. In this rapid revolution of change, instability has become a main characteristic of our political world. The factor of instability renders the task of exploring the synthesis of political activity and natural environment both difficult and challenging. The rapidity with which the shrinking process progresses creates a cultural lag, for man, in the words of Vilhjalmur Stefansson, "has learned to change the face of nature but not to change his own mind." We have been trained to interpret the laws of nature as they reveal themselves in our natural environment, but with this knowledge we have not acquired the wisdom to discern the relationship and the conditioning effects of natural environment and man's political behavior within it. The wisdom of the Bible still rings true (St. Luke, XII: 54-56):

> And He said also to the crowds: "When you see a cloud rising in the west, you say at once, 'a shower is coming,' and so it comes to pass. And when you see the south wind blow, you say, 'there will be a scorching heat,' and so it comes to pass. You hypocrites! You know how to judge the face of the sky and of the earth; but how is it that you do not judge this time?"

2

Aware of the problems and difficulties awaiting the student of political geography who is not afraid of taking a hard look at its realities, the authors of this book found themselves in full agreement on one basic issue of organization: they decided in favor of a functional rather than regional approach to political geography. Only in Part 3, on "The Economic Factor in Political Geography," did it appear advisable to stress regional groupings. Mindful of the uneasy balance of political power that is the product of varying geographical and economic conditions, the authors follow the regional approach in the part mentioned to provide a useful assessment of the aggregate economic capabilities characteristic of certain major countries and regions.

It is not our intention to present the reader with all the politico-geographical facts of each country, or of all political groupings, on the globe. Such encyclopedic enumeration of facts and figures, available from many published sources and providing a helpful tool in our task, is not enough if one tries to penetrate to the roots of the subject. The functional approach, as we see it, does not supply the reader with easy answers to the manifold problems in our field. Nor does it try to illuminate each and every scene where political geography has a legitimate place. It does, however, tend to sharpen our geographical "view," or what has been called "geographical sense," of the world's scene. It undertakes to forge the tools with which the political geographer applies general functional findings to whatever political area he desires to bring into focus.

3

That this book is the common labor of six authors requires an explanation. The borderlines which separate our subject from other related fields, as for instance economic geography and demography, are often extremely thin and difficult to define. Thus the student of political geography is often compelled to step beyond the narrow confines of his realm. The necessity to deal with problems requiring specialized skill and background convinced us that the co-operation between a number of authors with complementary fields of study and interest in the general area of political geography would result in a more definitive and constructive product than one man's labor could create. On the other hand, this book is not a mere symposium. The target of our common venture was a uniform and integrated work. The authors have made a conscientious effort to write their contributions in close co-ordination. To achieve this task it was essential that they subscribe to certain basic principles or to what might be called a common philosophy in their treatment of political geography. The reader will detect this "philosophy" in and between the lines of our book. It is essentially a devotion to objective analysis. It is also to be found in the absence of a negative quality (for which the pseudo-science of geopolitics has rightly been criticized), namely of partisan politics: the authors have no political axes to grind. That their target of ideal integration has not always been reached seems to be the price one must pay in the endeavor to produce teamwork. The critical reader will discover easily that the authors' attempt at reaching uniformity in their presentation has not been carried to the extreme, and that no effort was made to suppress their individualities and to harness their style and general approach to their specific problems. Whether or not they have succeeded in traveling safely the hazardous path between the devil and the deep blue sea is for the reader to discover.

4

This book presents its material in three main parts, following an introductory section on the meaning and scope of political geography. These distinguish between the spatial, the human and cultural, and the economic factors in political geography. This final part does not attempt to be a substitute for a text in economic geography but is limited to the discussion of those economic factors in power relations the understanding of which we consider essential to the study of political geography. Their absence from a book of this kind would make our approach to political geography impractical and unrealistic.

In order to identify the responsibilities of the individual authors it may be stated that Mr. Weigert has served as general editor with responsibility for the over-all organization of the book and the integration of its various sections, and that Mr. Fernstrom has undertaken the cartographical work. In particular, Part 1 (The Spatial Factor in Political Geography) has been prepared by Mr. Fischer and Mr. Weigert (Fischer, pp. 26-208; Weigert, pp. 3-25, 209-290); Part 2 (The Human and Cultural

Factor in Political Geography), by Mr. Kirk, Mr. Fischer, and Mr. Weigert (Kirk, pp. 291-341; Kirk and Weigert, pp. 342-382; Weigert, pp. 383-404; Fischer, pp. 405-439; Weigert, pp. 440-445), and Part 3 (The Economic Factor in Political Geography) by Mr. Brodie and Mr. Doherty (Doherty, pp. 449-566; Brodie, pp. 567-712).

It is inevitable that in spite of our endeavor to avoid when possible the discussion of temporary developments, certain findings and statements in this book, as well as details of the political maps, will have become obsolete by the time this book is published. Therefore, it should be noted that the authors have considered events only until early 1956.

Most of the authors are associated with work for the United States Government, and all of them have at some time been in public service. For this reason it is pointed out that our book presents the thinking of the authors as private citizens only and does not reflect the views of the government agencies with which they are, or have been, connected. Our materials are based on open sources and no use whatsoever has been made of classified documents.

The authors wish to express their sincere thanks to Professor Kirtley F. Mather, who, as Editor of the Century Earth Science Series, guided us with patience and wisdom; to Mrs. Claire Brogan, who bore the main burden of typing and retyping our manuscript; to Mrs. Mary Dyer, who helped us greatly in editing some of our chapters; to Richard P. Joyce who contributed generously in the preparation of the index and to Mrs. Joyce T. Lutz who typed the index; last but not least, we feel obligated to mention gratefully the long and (mostly) silent sufferings of our wives, who had to endure the labor and birth pains surrounding this effort.

H.W.W.

Contents

PART 3

The Economic Factor in Political Geography

List of Maps

Part

1

THE SPATIAL FACTOR IN POLITICAL GEOGRAPHY

CHAPTER 1

The Meaning and Scope of Political Geography

POLITICAL GEOGRAPHY AND HUMAN GEOGRAPHY

Political geography is a legitimate child of human geography. Both deal with the interplay of physical and human factors, with the interrelationship between earth and man. Both try to discover and explain the influences of the physical world on human society and the limitations it puts on human activities; they deal with diverse manifestations of a symbiosis of nature and man.

The life patterns revealed in this symbiosis are the subject matter of human geography. Out of the study of human geography evolves a better understanding of human groups within their natural environment, of civilizations formed and grown in a variety of environments, and of the physical causes which influenced this growth.[1]

It is, perhaps, the roots of human groups in their natural environment that most influence their development. These are, however, not the only formative factors in human society. Historical and sociological motivations, as well as cultural influences, cannot be discounted. Yet to be rooted in a natural and cultural landscape and environment is the essence of life to the individual and to the group. The roots are manifold; so strong and interwoven is their net that man and his natural environment are inseparable. Human geography, in its many manifestations, draws its

[1] P. W. J. Vidal de la Blache, *Principles of Human Geography* (London, 1926), p. 19.

inspiration from this complex symbiosis. It focuses our attention on man and his environment, on man as a geographical factor, thus growing beyond descriptive narrative. Human geography evolves as a discipline whose primary target is "the study of human society in relation to the earth background." [2] As such it ranks alongside of other social sciences whose common purpose is to study the structure and behavior of human society.

By this definition of the scope of human geography we have, by implication, excluded geographical speculations which are not borne out by scientific research. Numerous concepts have been developed over the last fifty years. These range from "environmental determinism," which postulates a causal relationship between the characteristics of the earth and the activities of man, to modified theories of "possibilism," which grants man and human groups a number of possible choices among the limits set and the opportunities offered by the physical environment. In a philosophical vein and in lofty language the concept of "possibilism" was expressed by Alexis de Tocqueville: [3]

> I am aware that many of my contemporaries maintain that nations are never their own masters here below, and that they necessarily obey some unsurmountable and intelligent power, arising from anterior events, from their race, or from the soil and climate of their country. Such principles are false and cowardly; such principles can never produce aught but feeble men and pusillanimous nations. Providence has not created mankind entirely dependent or entirely free. It is true that around every man a fatal circle is traced beyond which he cannot pass; but within the wide verge of that circle he is powerful and free; as it is with men, so with communities.

These theories of determinism and of possibilism, developed mainly by geographers in Europe, especially in Germany and France, were also accepted readily by several geographers in the United States. Later a healthy reaction occurred, primarily based on the realization that although significant changes in the physical environment will often strongly condition human affairs, a positive determinism cannot be demonstrated in a relatively stable environment. The general concept commonly accepted today is "that the physical character of the earth has different meaning for different people: that the significance to man of the physical environment is a function of the attitudes, objectives, and technical abilities of man himself. With each change in any of the elements of the human culture the resource base provided by the earth must be re-

[2] C. L. White and G. T. Renner, *Human Geography, An Ecological Study of Society* (New York, 1948), pp. V, VI.

[3] *Democracy in America.*

evaluated." [4] We shall re-examine these ideas later, when distinguishing between political geography and geopolitics.

Political geography, a subdivision of human geography, is concerned with a particular aspect of earth–man relationships and with a special kind of emphasis. It is not the relationship between physical environment and human groups or societies as such that attracts us here but the relationship between geographical factors and political entities. Only where man's organization of space and historical and cultural influences upon geographical patterns are related to political organizations, are we in the realm of political geography. In contrast to the "natural regions" of physical geography, the area units of political geography are those of states and nations. To determine how these organizations are influenced by and adjusted to physiographical conditions, and how these factors affect international relations, is the aim of political geography.[5]

POLITICAL GEOGRAPHY AND GEOPOLITICS

Since all political landscapes are man-made, they are subject to continuous fluctuations. The politico-geographical realities of today may easily become the myths of tomorrow, and vice versa. Geography, it has been said, does not argue—it simply is. When we examine the changing relationships of territory and people, either within a state or between states, we are confronted with artificial, because man-made, structures. The analysis and evaluation of the problems of political geography are definitely not in the realm of natural science.

Our approach to a field in which physical geography, political science, and economics meet should be distinguished from the school commonly identified as "geopolitics." The latter goes beyond the objective study of politico-geographical factors and is an applied pseudo-science with very questionable objectives. As such, it has an axe to grind. The French geographer Demangeon correctly labeled geopolitics "a national enterprise of propaganda and teaching." At the point where geopolitics becomes a philosophy (or rather pseudo-philosophy) of geographical determinism, meant to justify the political aims of a specific nation, the curtain is drawn which separates it from our field of studies.

The philosophical basis of geopolitics is rather crude. It tries to draw its strength from an identification of state and individual. Like any other

[4] P. E. James, *American Geography, Inventory and Prospect* (Syracuse, 1954), pp. 12, 13.

[5] *Cf.* W. Fitzgerald, *The New Europe* (New York, 1945), p. 1.

living being, the state is endowed with a will and even with passions of its own. Like man himself, the state goes through the stages of birth, growth, maturity, aging, and death.[6] Hence, as seen through the glass of a "philosophy" of geopolitics, there are in the lives of states "laws" of growth and "laws" of decay. Out of these concepts grow terms which readily become political slogans, such as "Sense of space," "Folk without space," or the one which proved most effective as justification of German and Japanese expansionism, "Living space."

At the risk of somewhat oversimplifying the issues, it can be said that the basic difference between political geography and geopolitics exists in the emphasis on the effect of geography on the dynamics of states and nations. The radical representatives of the German geopolitical school held that geographical factors so entirely determine growth and decline of states that no room is left for a course which contradicts the alleged geographical commands. From a concept which looks upon geography as the inalienable cause of human events, it is but one logical step to a political philosophy that claims for itself the right to predict the course determined by geographical factors, and thus to lead statesmen and soldiers alike in the making of strategic decisions. Hence it is not surprising to find the German geopoliticians proclaiming that geopolitics "is the geographical conscience of the state." But the factors of change and fluctuations which daily write anew the map of the world belie the pretensions of a narrow determinism. More realistically and more modestly than the prophets of geopolitics, most students of political geography hold that geography does not determine but merely conditions the course of states. Geography is but one of many tangible and intangible features which form the pattern of a state. A significant note to this concept of political geography has been added by French geographers who stress the possible modification of geographical features as a result of man's technological achievement.[7]

[6] W. G. East, "The Nature of Political Geography," *Politica* (1937), p. 259. It should be noted that not only Germans have inclined toward this biological outlook. The French geographer Ancel (see the preface to his *Geopolitique*, 1936) and the American geographer Van Valkenburg (*Political Geography*) were equally impressed. "The thesis," R. Hartshorne (in *American Geography* [Syracuse, 1954], p. 185) writes, "has been widely criticized not only because of a lack of demonstration that the life processes of any state have led inevitably to the characteristics that can be called old age and ultimately to dissolution, but, even more fundamentally, on the grounds that it is false to reason from a superficial analogy between a biological organism and a social organization operated by men, since men collectively through successive generations are at no time older than their predecessors."

[7] In our efforts to distinguish between geopolitics and political geography, a note of caution is in order which is due to the semantics of the term *geopolitics*. Both terms

To the reader who has been taken in by the fading glamour of the catchword "geopolitics," this brief attempt to distinguish between geopolitics and political geography may appear superficial in view of the amazing fascination which geopolitics evoked during, and following, World War II. To a large extent American interest in, and preoccupation with, geopolitics dates from the time of Hitler's military victories. American acceptance of geopolitics perhaps resulted from the actual and seeming successes of the German grand strategy by what then appeared to be a doctrine and science on which the Germans could claim to have a monopoly.

It is not without irony that even before Americans looked with anxious fascination upon German geopolitics, its German monopolists conveyed to their own countrymen the idea that geographers and statesmen in Britain and the United States, and even in France, had mastered the principles and application of geopolitics much more skillfully than was true in Germany. In a symposium by the editors of the *Journal of Geopolitics,* published in 1928, as well as in many editorials, General Karl Haushofer sadly commented that geographers like Mackinder and Curzon in Britain, Semple and Bowman in America, and Brunhes and Vallaux in France had not only understood the teachings of Friedrich Ratzel, the father of political geography in Germany, much better than the Germans themselves but had also succeeded in utilizing these lessons "for the sake of power expansion." [8]

To Haushofer and his school, it was a matter of serious concern that German leadership, both in the German Foreign Office and the General Staff, excelled in geographic ignorance and overemphasis on legal training. Hence the necessity to create a new "science" for would-be statesmen and conquering generals, a borderline science with a practical political purpose. Borrowing heavily from the disciplines of "geography, history, and politics," it would supply statesman and officer alike with the necessary tools for making political and strategical decisions.

While the godfathers of geopolitics in Germany cited with admiration and envy the achievements of political geographers in the Anglo-American countries, to convince their countrymen that a thorough revision of geo-

---

are frequently used interchangeably and it cannot, therefore, be assumed that the use of the word *geopolitics* is in itself indicative of the author's subscribing to the beliefs of geographical determinism.

[8] *Bausteine zur Geopolitik* (Berlin, 1928), p. 61; see also, in rebuttal, I. Bowman, "Geography vs. Geopolitics," in H. W. Weigert and V. Stefansson, eds., *Compass of the World* (New York, 1954), pp. 40-53. Bowman branded Haushofer's philosophy of power as "utterly dishonest."

graphic thinking and training was overdue in Germany, the early victories of the German war machine prompted a similar train of thought in America. As one American geography professor put it in 1943: "The airplane has created a new geography of the world. Axis leaders knew this several years ago and have been taking advantage of it, but few Americans are yet really aware of it." [9] Believing that the Germans were more than a step ahead of Americans in supplying statecraft and strategy with tools from the realm of geography, the American proponents of geopolitics argued, even as the Germans, that it was high time to learn from the enemy and to make geography fashionable by calling it geopolitics. Thus the American vogue in geopolitics had its roots less in the discovery of a new (German-grown) branch of political geography than in nebulous conceptions and in the realization that the study and application of geography in America was in anything but a perfect state. Viewed against this historical background, the struggle between political geography and geopolitics can be seen in its proper perspective. Much less than a competition between two clearly discernible schools of human geography, it reflects in Germany the efforts, during the ill-fated latest phase of German totalitarianism, to use, and often abuse, geography as a political device to justify acts of aggression and expansion. At the same time, the awareness, in this country, of weaknesses in our own arsenal of geographical knowledge and training led to often nebulous and misguided attempts to bring geography into focus by dressing it as geopolitics. If one visualizes the theme of geography versus geopolitics against the historical setting of the years surrounding World War II and the ideologies underlying its power struggle, we shall not fail to realize the temporary nature of the vastly overblown controversy. This realization should make easy the return to the less glamorous but more solid grounds of political geography.[10]

[9] Actually, the history of World War II teaches the opposite to be true and shows the German and Japanese High Commands as prisoners of a fatally mistaken Mercator world view which caused them to misjudge completely the geographical relationship of the United States to the rest of the world; *cf.* R. E. Harrison and H. W. Weigert, "World View and Strategy," in Weigert and Stefansson, *op. cit.*, pp. 74-89.

[10] For a more detailed discussion of German geopolitics, see H. W. Weigert, *Generals and Geographers* (New York, 1942); R. Strauss-Hupé, *Geopolitics* (New York, 1942); E. M. Walsh, "Geopolitics and International Morals," in Weigert and Stefansson, *op. cit.*, pp. 12-40; I. Bowman, "Geography vs. Geopolitics," *Geographical Review* (1942), pp. 646-658; and Weigert and Stefansson, *op. cit.*, pp. 40-52. See also the discussion between M. A. Junis and J. O. M. Broek, "Geography and Nationalism," *Geographical Review* (1945), pp. 301-311. All of these authors try to explain and to debunk the strange phenomenon of geopolitics in Germany as they saw it from the United States and hampered by the fact that their critical evaluation was undertaken during

Despite its obvious fallacies, geopolitics in Hitler Germany flourished as one of the main roots of a philosophy which almost succeeded in becoming a powerful political reality. The British historian H. Trevor-Roper has highlighted geopolitics as understood and practiced by Hitler in an analysis which we quote in order to emphasize the challenge of Hitler's brand of geopolitics: [11]

Hitler, like Spengler, saw history as a series of almost geological ages, each characterized by a special "culture" and separated from the others by crucial periods of transition in which the old era, the old culture, gave way to the new. There had been the ancient era of Mediterranean culture, the medieval era of frustrated Germanic culture, the post-Renaissance era of wicked capitalist culture dominated by the maritime powers; and now at last—did not all the omens show it?—that era had in turn reached its fatal period and must be replaced by a new. But what would this new era be? Whose culture would dominate it? How would it be brought to birth out of the dying convulsions of the old?

To all these questions Hitler had thought out his answer. The new era would be a "geopolitical" era, for the conquest of space had rendered the old maritime empires obsolete—that was why he could afford to "guarantee" the irrelevant British Empire. It would be dominated—the geopoliticians had said so—by whoever dominated the mass of Central and Eastern Europe. That might, of course, mean the Russians, who were more numerous, powerfully organized under a totalitarian genius whom he admired, and already there. But Hitler did not want it to be the Russians: he wanted it to be the Germans; therefore, in answer to the third question, he declared that it would come about not by a natural economic process but by a violent change, a crusading war of conquest and colonization, a war of giants in which he, the demiurge of the new age, would by sheer human will power reverse the seeming inevitability of history and plant upon conquered Eurasia that German culture which would dominate the world for the next thousand years.

Such was the vast, crude vision which inspired Hitler's demonic career—the vision for the sake of which he had revolutionized and rearmed Germany, ruthlessly and cunningly solved all intervening problems, created an elite of mystical crusaders, and now, in June 1941, suddenly launched what would be for him the ultimate, the only relevant campaign: the Armageddon that was to decide, not petty questions of frontiers or governments, but the whole next era of human history.

One further note of warning appears necessary. It would be a serious mistake if we minimized the dangers, to American thinking, of a geopolitical doctrine and ideology so firmly rooted in German soil. It would

---

World War II when another Iron Curtain separated Hitler Germany from the Free World. It is therefore indispensable for a better and unbiased understanding of German geopolitics to consult a "critique and justification" of geographic science in Germany during the period from 1933 to 1945, written in 1941 by a ranking German geographer, Carl Troll, who had been an uncompromising foe of National Socialism (*Annals of the Association of American Geographers* [1949], pp. 99-135; translated and annotated by Eric Fischer).

[11] "Hitler's Gamble," *Atlantic Monthly* (September, 1954), p. 42.

indeed be fallacious to argue that the issue of geopolitics versus political geography is purely academic in America for the reason that geopolitics was, after all, a German product and not exportable to America. That in a few exceptional cases American writers and students of geography had been unduly influenced by concepts of geopolitics, it could be argued, should not detract from the fact that America is no fertile ground for the alien credo.

However, a comparison between the basic ideas of German geopolitics and of the American creed of Manifest Destiny (extending into Theodore Roosevelt's era) rampant between 1830-60, shows that the German mind has no monopoly on the kind of argumentation typical of geopolitics. Although the two concepts were conditioned by their different environments, it appears that similar centrifugal forces have cast them off—similar, but not identical, for Manifest Destiny, if one disregards some of its more radical proponents, was in its original pronouncements not based on militarism. The manifest destiny of the American Republic was to expand over the continent of North America by peaceful process and by the force of republican principles of government. Yet the similarities are striking. Geopolitics, with its basic concept of "Living space," and Manifest Destiny alike embraced expansionism as a biological necessity in the lives of states and justified it by the conception of the state as an organism. Both fed on the theory of "economically integrated large space areas." Even as the idea of an economically integrated Central Europe (Mitteleuropa) was part and parcel of German geopolitics, so the territorial expansion of the United States westward, southward, and northward became a battlecry of Manifest Destiny and found its theoretical justification in the principle of geographical unity. In their arguments, the proponents of Manifest Destiny embraced geographical determinism and vague geopolitical concepts of "natural" frontiers. These played a role in the discussions in 1846 over the Oregon question and recurred during the Mexican war. They found their strongest expression in the geopolitical beliefs of Lincoln's Secretary of State, William H. Seward, beginning in 1860 with his speech in St. Paul, Minnesota, in which he envisioned the peaceful expansion of the United States over the whole continent of North America as the fulfillment of the will of Providence. After the Civil War, Seward's geopolitical ideas revolved around an even greater American empire. They included the strategic islands in the Caribbean, Cuba, and Puerto Rico. Looking forward to possessions in the Atlantic and Pacific, he made plans for a canal route through Nicaragua by ensuring transit rights in the treaty of 1867; he hoped that the

United States would annex the Hawaiian islands; he favored the annexation of Canada. As the lone lasting result of his expansionist endeavors he was able to show only the acquisition of Alaska from Russia.[12]

With the naval historian Alfred Thayer Mahan, expansion overseas was added to the credo of American Manifest Destiny geopolitics which, except for Seward's dreams, had remained essentially continental. Mahan's influence went far beyond the American scene. It is difficult to say whether it was more instrumental in promoting Manifest Destiny concepts in the United States, leading her toward world power through sea power, or whether it was strongest in stimulating German expansionism, based on geopolitical teachings in which Ratzel, influenced by Mahan, had pointed to the sea as an important source of national greatness. The concept of space, so essential since Ratzel and so distorted and overdrawn since Haushofer and his disciples, was also a keynote of Manifest Destiny, beginning with the purchase of Louisiana by Jefferson. Coupled with large-space concepts we find in latter-day German geopolitics an unhealthy contempt for the rights of the small states which stood in the way of the expansionist drive of their large neighbors. In a similar vein, Henry Cabot Lodge stated, in truly geopolitical fashion, that small states had outlived their worth in the progress of the world. Even the racial and cultural superiority slogans, which should not be charged to the gospel of German geopolitics but which were, however reluctantly, accepted and adopted by Haushofer and his group during the Third Reich, have their counterpart in the pronouncements of the most radical prophets of Manifest Destiny in the United States. For example, Burgess foresaw the establishment of a new Christian order through a world dominion of Anglo-Saxons. The "philosophical" basis of his prediction was the concept that the Teutonic nations, including those considered Anglo-Saxon in culture and population, were alone equipped to assume leadership in the formation and administration of states and that they therefore had not only the right but also the duty to subdue other nations and to force organization upon "unpolitical populations." [13]

Both concepts, then, have in common the popular use of environmental, especially spatial, factors for the justification of power-political, expansionist aims. Since their similar creeds mushroomed in different periods of history and in different national and natural environments, dissimilar-

[12] F. Parella, *Lebensraum and Manifest Destiny,* MA thesis, Georgetown University, pp. 88-101; our discussion of the relationship between German geopolitics and Manifest Destiny is based on this thesis.

[13] J. W. Burgess, *Political Science and Comparative Constitutional Law,* Vol. I (Boston, 1890), pp. 30-39, 44-46.

ities are obvious. But the most important distinguishing fact is that basic concepts of geopolitics in Germany became the official policy of Hitler's Third Reich, whereas Manifest Destiny was never adopted as an official policy by the United States; it never went beyond the stage of a popular conviction.[14] Yet the readiness with which it was absorbed by the public and by many in positions of power should give us pause. The history of the Manifest Destiny movement in the United States should warn us not to disregard as irrelevant the pseudo-philosophy of geopolitical schools abroad, on the theory that this brand of geopolitics was typical only of the half-forgotten Third Reich in Germany.

THE IMPACT OF CHANGE AND STABILITY

Although statistics and other evidence can be assembled to serve the study of political geography, we must not lose sight of the fact that its realm is affected by constant change and fluctuation. In the first place, the physical environment itself, the geographical framework within which the destinies of states and nations unfold themselves, is changing every day. Changes in climate, for instance, and the resulting effects on vegetation, have affected man's adjustment and consequently his civilizations, although the degree of these influences is still an open question.[15] At least as significant is the fact that man's response and adjustment to his environment has, throughout history, undergone constant change and evolution. Man, organized in social and political groups, has learned increasingly to adapt himself to the conditioning effects of geography. He has countered more and more successfully the influences of geographical factors by making the best use of the opportunities offered him by his environment. He has gone farther, and by what has been described as "geographical surgery," he has molded the landscape to fit his needs or wants.

At the same time, it should be remembered that the manner and degree of human adjustment to the natural environment follows no uniform pattern. Rather, human societies, whether primitive social groupings or highly developed modern states, have always varied in their reaction to their environment. To account for the basic differences between nations in their response to environment requires an examination of sociological and psychological characteristics which are beyond the province of geography. However, an awareness of these factors helps us to realize that

[14] Parella, *op. cit.*, p. 103.

[15] *Cf.* E. Huntington, *Mainsprings of Civilization* (New York, 1945); White and Renner, *op. cit.*, pp. 240, 241.

geographical influence is but one of many conditioning factors; geography does not act as an "agent of determinism."

While "man has found it easy to change the face of nature, he has found it difficult to change his own mind" (V. Stefansson). It has become a truism to speak of our shrinking world, yet man individually and collectively, has proven his inability to adjust his thinking and ideas to the changes that have taken place in environmental conditions. The more mankind has succeeded in overcoming barriers of terrain and distance, thus erasing isolation and bringing about a closely-knit society of nations, the less unity has the "one world" of ours produced. It is this cultural lag which is a major cause of political instability in our time. One main reason for the cultural lag can be seen in the difficulties we encounter when we attempt to adjust political realities and ideals to the continuous change in the relationship between man and his natural environment. Clearly the study of political geography concerns itself with the description and analysis of the features of instability and change which permeate the pattern of relations between earth and state. That necessitates continuous re-examination and re-evaluation of only seemingly established facts in the spatial relationship between states and political organizations.

We shall deal on many occasions with the changes that have altered the face of the earth and we will find again and again that these changes have affected vitally the lives of nations and the power relationships of every state in war and peace. It does not matter whether they are the result of physical processes or of the activities of man himself. The latter include changes that are man-made, such as canals, or man-caused, such as the depletion of forested lands or of natural resources, as well as those that indirectly result from technological progress. The full impact of these transformations, which in our time have succeeded each other more rapidly and have shaken the foundations of the globe more terrifyingly than in any other epoch of history, defies human imagination.

We can think of no better illustration of the magnitude of the problem of comprehending the changes which our planet is continuously undergoing than the words spoken in 1827 by the great German poet Johann Wolfgang von Goethe. With prophetic imagination he envisaged geographical surgery which would alter the face and structure of the earth and thus revolutionize the relationships of nations. These are Goethe's reflections as expressed in a conversation with his secretary, Eckermann:

> . . . a passage through the Isthmus of Panama has been suggested. Other points have been recommended where, by making use of some streams that flow into the Gulf of Mexico, the end may be perhaps better attained than at Panama.

All this is reserved for the future, and for an enterprising spirit. So much, however, is certain, that if they succeed in connecting the Mexican gulf with the Pacific Ocean, innumerable benefits will come to mankind. But I doubt whether the United States will pass up the opportunity to get control of this undertaking. I predict that this young state, with its decided westward course, will, in thirty or forty years, have occupied and peopled the whole tract of land beyond the Rocky Mountains. Along the entire coast of the Pacific, which nature has endowed with the most capacious and secure harbors, important cities will gradually arise, for the furtherance of much trade between China and the East Indies and the United States. In that case, it will become desirable and even indispensable that a more rapid communication be maintained between the eastern and western shores of North America, both by merchant-vessels and by men-of-war, and far superior to the tedious, unpleasant, and expensive voyage around Cape Horn. So I repeat, it is absolutely indispensable for the United States to effect a passage from the Mexican gulf to the Pacific Ocean; and I am certain that the United States will accomplish it.

Would that I might live to see it!—but I shall not. I should like to see another event—a junction of the Danube and the Rhine. But this undertaking is so gigantic that I doubt the possibility of its completion, particularly when I consider our German resources.

And third and last, I should like to see England in possession of a canal through the Isthmus of Suez. Would that I could live to see these three great works. It would be well worth the trouble to last some fifty years more. . . .

This is indeed the future in retrospect. Viewed through the glass of an imaginative observer of the world's stage, a scene unfolds which has become so obvious a reality in our day that we fail to grasp easily the changes which these geographical surgeries have caused. They have not only altered our physical world but have transformed basically the power relations of the great national states. To foresee the potentialities and possibilities of change in state-earth relationships, as Goethe did, is an even more vital task today than it was 150 years ago. "Is not the crisis of today, which penetrates into every human activity and almost every larger thought, essentially geographical in origin?" Halford J. Mackinder, an outstanding British geographer, raised this question in 1935. He tried to answer it by emphasizing the elementary facts of our shrinking world. Mankind, he suggested, has suddenly become world-conscious and has taken fright. The nations have run to their homes and are barricading their doors. They have realized that henceforth they must live in a closed system in which they can do nothing without generating "repercussions from the very antipodes." To grasp the world-wide scope of modern geography and the pattern of interrelationships which is still growing in complexity is one thing. To apply the lessons of this geography, so that they will be accepted by statesmen and nations, is altogether different. Man finds it easier to change the face of nature than to change his own mind.

Although we have emphasized the role of change, which precludes an easy explanation of how geographical factors change the course and destinies of nations, we must now equally stress certain basic geographic characteristics that possess the quality of stability. They have remained unchanged throughout history, and an understanding of these unchangeable geographical features is indispensable to statecraft and military strategy. Historical geography verifies that the cost of geographical ignorance, one facet of which is lack of appreciation of these unchangeable factors, is immeasurable. Also immeasurable is the cost of geographical ignorance due to lack of understanding of changes in the environment and their effect on power relations. Especially eloquent are those instances where nations fell because of their failure to grasp the size of enemy territory and of the manpower of their foes. Such ignorance explains the downfall of the Greeks when attacked by Persia, the Jews in their struggle with the Assyrians and Babylonians, and the ultimate defeat of Napoleon and Hitler in the vast expanses of Russia. If we discount the often remarkable changes in the structure of smaller powers occasioned by geographical surgery, as in the case of Egypt (Suez Canal) or Colombia and Panama (Panama Canal), the physiographic foundations of state power will in most cases remain unchanged. Foreign policy and military strategy will have to accept these foundations as basic; ignorance of these factors, both at home and abroad, can prove to be fatal.

It is a truism that the history of Britain since the Norman conquest and her political and military decisions have been clearly based on her island fortress position; her world power in the Victorian age and the decline of this power since the advent of the submarine and the airplane are linked to this geographical fact. In contrast, the geographical position of France has always been one of extreme vulnerability. Her exposure to invasion has always tempted her neighbors, like the Hapsburgs, who laid an iron ring around France and later invaded her territory when her internal stability collapsed in the turmoil of the French Revolution. The utter insecurity of France because of geographical location—in contrast to the security which, until yesterday, characterized the location of the British Isles and of the United States—is documented on every page of her history. To counteract it, France has always been forced to establish, often at high expense, a friend in the rear of her most dangerous enemy, so that if war came the enemy would be compelled to fight on two fronts.[16] Thus the alignments of France with Sweden, Poland, and Turkey to check the expansion of the Holy Roman Empire and, after the First World War,

[16] C. Petrie, "The Strategic Concept of Modern Diplomacy," *Quarterly Review* (1952), pp. 289-301.

the creation of the Little Entente in Germany's backyard to meet a future German threat, go back to the simple facts of her regional location *vis-à-vis* her neighbors. Similarly, Germany's strategy in war and peace since the nineteenth century has been dictated by awareness of weakness stemming from her open frontiers in East and West. Statesmen like Bismarck who knew their geography designed a foreign policy for Germany to insure her against war on two fronts; criminal dilettantes at the helm of Germany, like Hitler, disregarded this basic policy and led their people into disaster by attacking their neighbors on all fronts.

These examples can be multiplied, and later we shall discuss the factors of size, shape, and location in more detail. They serve here merely as illustrations of stable geographical features which in the past have conditioned internal and external policies of states and which are likely to affect the same decisions in the present and in the future. We must view a country against this background of geographical fundamentals in order to understand its role within the concert of nations.

THE NEW FRONTIERS

The study of fluctuating frontiers, boundaries, frontier zones, and "no man's lands" is a most important field for the student of political geography. The day seems to be distant when nations will have become so interdependent that separating frontiers will be allowed to wither away. Until such time, the study of frontiers remains a vital prerequisite for the understanding of the internal conditions of a state and nation as well as of the international relations of states.

"The Old Europe is gone. The map is being rolled up and a new map is unrolling before us. We shall have to do a great deal of fundamental thinking and scrapping of old points of view before we find our way through the new continent which now opens before us." These prophetic words, spoken by Field Marshal Jan Christian Smuts before the Empire Parliamentary Association in November, 1943, deserve a much broader application. The old *world* is gone and we must find our way through the new continents across new frontiers.

It is impossible to describe with any degree of stability the contours of political boundaries. In studying problems of boundaries and frontiers, the focus is therefore on instability, expansion, and retraction. We must visualize two radically different world maps of political boundaries: one based on the boundaries which are internationally recognized, and the other whose lines of demarcation are in dispute, even though they may be affirmed in legally-recognized treaties. The boundaries on this latter map reflect the extension of national power by aggressor states.

The new political map of the world that is unrolling before us is indeed so basically different from the map of, for instance, about fifty years ago that a comparison of the boundaries of existent "independent" states speaks for itself. Nothing illustrates the fluctuating foundations of political geography better than the fact that in 1902 the number of "independent" states in the world was forty-seven and that, in 1952, it had increased by thirty-seven to eighty-four. The following list records these relatively new additions to the family of nations. However, in tracing their contours on the map we should remember that their inclusion in the list does not reveal, and in fact does in some cases cloud, the vital issue of whether these states have by their legal recognition achieved true independence or, if so, will be able to maintain it.

In the Americas, two: Canada, Panama.

In Europe, ten: Albania, Austria, Bulgaria, Czechoslovakia, Finland, Hungary, Iceland, Ireland, Poland, Yugoslavia.

In Africa, three: Egypt, Libya, South Africa.

In Asia, twenty-two: Afghanistan, Australia, Burma, Cambodia, Ceylon, India, Indonesia, Iraq, Israel, Jordan, Korea, Laos, Lebanon, Outer Mongolia, Nepal, New Zealand, Pakistan, Philippines, Saudi Arabia, Syria, Viet Nam, Yemen.[17]

The end is not yet in sight, as is illustrated by no less than three territories (Morocco, Tunisia, and the Sudan) winning independence during the first quarter of 1956. Referring to the more than 500,000,000 people of Asia now living in territories which have achieved national recognition since 1945, the Secretary-General of the United Nations wrote in 1951 that "one-fourth of the population of the world has gained independence within the span of only six years. The pressure of other dependent peoples toward freedom and equality has become much stronger since the war and continues to increase."

THE STUDY OF STATE-EARTH RELATIONSHIPS

Although the limits that distinguish political geography from other fields of human geography cannot be clearly defined, we secure a firmer basis for our study if we realize that we are primarily concerned with the relationship between the state and its natural environment. Territory

[17] *Cf.* H. W. Briggs, "New Dimensions in International Law," *The American Political Science Review* (1952), pp. 680 f.

and people are the foundations of the state, but they are much more than that because the complex interrelationship between the two molds the structure of the state into what distinguishes it from other state organizations. The physical environment blends with the manifold tangible and intangible features which characterize a nation, and out of this legion of mosaic stones emerges the picture of a state with an individuality of its own.

The study of political geography deals with the internal geographical factors which contribute to the state's individuality and, at the same time, with the geographical factors which condition the external relations between states. In a "closed system in which any major action within a state system must generate repercussions from the very antipodes" (Mackinder), any attempt to differentiate between the two sets of geographical factors creates a highly distorted picture. The patterns of internal and external political geography are complementary.

If we then explore the geographical situation of a state, or what is often even more important for the understanding of international power relations, the geographical situation of a number of states bound together by ideological and other bonds, we must probe their main geographical characteristics. Among the most important, we may list *size* (in combination with related factors such as productivity of the land, accessibility through communications, and climate); *location* (distinguishing between the regional location of a state and the world location of a state); and the influence which *shape* and *topography,* in particular the impact of land and sea, have on national and international power.

Although the violent fluctuations affecting areal differentiation of the earth's political entities prevents the construction of a pure science system of political geography, its study offers one significant advantage compared to evaluation by regional or other factors of geography. This advantage is one of technique. Statistical and other evidence needed for the appraisal of the world's political units can be gathered only within political boundaries. Even where the available data are compiled by international agencies, they are nevertheless classified by national units; a population census, for instance, cannot be obtained for a natural or cultural region.

In spite of its man-made and often irrational and fortuitous qualities, the state structure of the world, like its physical structure, offers therefore a rationale for geographical analysis and interpretation. The presence of a political boundary is as significant a geographical factor as are soil, relief, or climate. One illustration is the "railway state" organized by Japan in southern Manchuria. When Russia, in 1905, transferred to Japan control of the Southern Manchurian Railways, coal and iron mines, and a narrow strip of land, 700 miles long but only 100 square miles in area, Japan transformed this zone into a new political entity in which industries, villages, and towns mushroomed.[18] Similarly, the Soviet Union in 1954 stepped up its plans to assist Communist China in the development of a new industrial base in North China, which, with the help of railway construction, would draw Northern China, Inner Mongolia, and Sinkiang closer to the Soviet orbit.

If we thus focus our attention on a political territory within the confines of its boundaries, we will understand what distinguishes the study of political geography from that of regional geography. Political geography deals with the human and physical texture of political territories, whereas regional geography concentrates on the features which together create a physical and human landscape,[19] achieving, both physically and humanly, the characteristics of regional uniformity.[20]

It is important to remember that the "political territory" which we have in mind as the basis of politico-geographical investigation does not need to be identical with or limited to a state area and its internal political subdivisions. International relations and politics are shaped by the existence of political units and regions which bind together, sometimes firmly but more often loosely and on a very temporary basis, a number of individual states professing to share national and economic interests and ideologies. Within such political areas, there always exist both unifying factors and elements of disunion and diversity. To explore both and to arrive at a balanced view of a political region composed of sovereign states with common interests is part of the endeavor of the political geographer. Here we must distinguish between areas whose physical geography alone justifies their study in terms of political unity or disunity, and others which as the result of alliances or international agreements have been forged into political areas with characteristics of their own to complement those of the component states. In the first category belong such "units" as Latin America or South East Asia, "Western Europe," the Eastern European satellites bloc, the Balkan countries,[21] or such a political grouping as the new British dominion of Central Africa consisting

[18] East, *op. cit.*, pp. 254, 267; but compare the remarks, on p. 19, on the political geography of zones not identical with political territories.
[19] *Ibid.*
[20] White and Renner, *op. cit.*, pp. 638-657.
[21] See Hartshorne, *op. cit.*, pp. 186, 187.

of Northern and Southern Rhodesia and Nyasaland.[22] To the second group would belong units such as the NATO countries, or the wide expanse of nations extending from Pakistan to the Philippines which are committed to the South East Asian Collective Defense Treaty (SEATO), or the political realm of the United Nations.

POLITICAL GEOGRAPHY AND RELATED FIELDS

The close relationship of historical geography and political geography is evident. The political geography of today will be the historical geography of tomorrow. A sound evaluation of politico-geographical factors is impossible without consideration of historical factors and fluctuations. Essentially, the boundary line between the two is one of emphasis only. We are concerned with those facts and events of history and politics which can be described as "geography set in motion," but which have not yet become petrified sufficiently to permit us to appraise them mainly from a historical viewpoint.

More important than the distinction between historical and political geography is the intrinsic value of historical geography to the student of its sister discipline. For while history may not repeat itself, it is equally true that geographical factors repeatedly influence the destinies of nations. To follow the pattern of geographical influences historically facilitates the task of the political geographer in exploring the relationship of state and earth as it exists today and may evolve in the future. We must, however, re-emphasize that what in the early stages of human history appeared as unchangeable physical facts have been, with more and more rapid revolution, altered by human action. Whether we consider major accomplishments of geographical surgery, through inland canal systems, or the opening of new territories through railroad and highway construction, or the clearing of forests and the resulting effect on the conservation of moisture, and thereby fertility, in many regions, we will always discover new documentations of human action modifying the physical environments. Alongside such changes we must consider the development and exploitation of natural resources, as well as the settlement of empty spaces, in particular the phenomenal effects of colonization policies of the major powers—all factors which contribute to affect earth-state relationships.

These changes and their impact on history remind us that we would

[22] See pp. 186, 706.

be seriously mistaken in taking for granted that the geographical factors which conditioned earth-state relations in a given area in the past will have the same conditioning effect today. At the same time, the appraisal still holds true by which a British geographer, more than thirty years ago and before the advent of modern aviation, summed up the relative significance of the permanent factors of geography and the man-made changes of the earth's surface: "Real as are all these modes in which human action has modified the influence of physical factors, they are obviously but trifles in comparison with the natural forces which they to a slight extent counteract. The Alps have lost their mystery, but they still form a barrier which must be crossed: they affect the cost of every parcel of goods conveyed into or out of the valley of the Po. Civilized enterprise may seek out new localities in which valuable products can be made to grow; but the steady working of the great natural forces still determines climate, with all its boundless effects on human history. Man may drain and plant, redeeming a little space here and there from barrenness or from malaria: but all he has done or even can do is infinitesimal beside the influence of the North Atlantic drift, which is only one fraction of the world's system of ocean currents." [23] Thus it becomes imperative for the student of political geography to view his scene through the glass of historical geography; the lessons of the past which explain the conditioning effect of a country's geography on its inhabitants will often—not always—illuminate the clouded scene on today's stage.

To illustrate the close bonds between historical and political geography, enough examples could be cited to fill a voluminous book. The one example we select should lead us to evaluate in retrospect the internal and external geography of the United States over a period of less than one hundred years.

In his message to Congress on December 1, 1862, Abraham Lincoln spoke of the "Egypt of the West." He defined this region as "the great interior region bounded east by the Alleghenies, north by the British dominions, west by the Rocky Mountains, and south by the line along which the culture of corn and cotton meets. . . . A glance at the map shows that, territorially speaking, it is the great body of the Republic. The other parts are but marginal borders to it . . . [it] being the deepest and also the richest in undeveloped resources. . . And yet this region has no seacoast —touches no ocean anywhere. . . . [Its people] find their way to Europe by New York, to South America and Africa by New Orleans, and to Asia

[23] H. B. George, *The Relations of Geography and History*, 5th ed. (New York, 1924), p. 19.

by San Francisco." What Lincoln thus described as the great body of the Republic, the Egypt of the West, is the same Middle West which since his day has been destined, by the strength of the natural wealth of its broad plains, to play a pivotal role in the internal political geography of the United States. To emphasize the decisive part which the Middle West has always played in national politics would be to stress the obvious. More involved are the problems which confront us if we view the Middle West, that region that "has no seacoast—touches no ocean anywhere," as a factor in the external political geography of this country, both in retrospect and from the ramparts of the atomic age. When Lincoln addressed Congress in 1862, this heartland of the Republic was indeed safe in its splendid inland isolation. It did not need to fear attack from without as long as it wisely refrained from stepping beyond its ideal natural frontiers. It is this historical geography of the United States which accounts for an isolationism deeply and justly rooted in the country's geography of yesterday and therefore a live and a powerful force in our national and international policies until yesterday.

At the height of the last World War, Bernard De Voto,[24] himself no isolationist, summed up the atmosphere of the Middle West by saying that

> it is so deep in the vastness of the American continent that it cannot believe in the existence of salt water. Still less does it believe that beyond the oceans there are other peoples or that what happens to such peoples in any way affects what happens to the Middle West. It knows the marginal borders of its own province, the States east of the Alleghenies and west of the Rockies; for they also belong to its political system. But its awareness stops there, somewhere inland from tidemark. In its own province it lives an intensive local life, remarkably integrated, absorbing, so rich that it instinctively judges all other variants of American life to be less substantial. If the rest of America is insubstantial, Europe and Asia and Africa are phantoms or perhaps rumors. The Middle West is indifferent to them, even skeptical. Like blizzards and droughts, foreign nations and foreign wars are temporary and peripheral. When they require action we will take action—temporarily and on the periphery. We will take action as militia rising to repel a raid, minutemen dropping the plow in ignorance of whence the raid came and why, and returning to the plow doggedly uninterested in any reasons or causes that have made us soldiers, killed our neighbors, and burned our crops.

De Voto, after thus evaluating the frame of mind of the Midwestern heartland as he saw it conditioned by its natural environment, ventured to predict that the geographical foundations which had shaped the political climate of the Middle West in the past would remain the same

[24] *Harper's Magazine,* June, 1943.

in the future. Even as these lines are written, it appears premature to pass final judgment on the correctness of these predictions:

> Some day the fighting will stop, the war will, temporarily, be over. On that day, with a high and singing heart, with the relief of long-impounded energies coming back to their own at last, the Middle West will pick up its interrupted pattern. It will resume its way of life. It will turn toward the fundamental valley of the Mississippi, away from the oceans, earthward from the planes which its own sons fly on great circle courses across its own sky to all the continents of the globe. It will turn back to the only reality it recognizes and let the rest of the world fade out beyond the margins of its consciousness.

John Smith, in his *Generall Historie of Virginia, New England, and the Summer Isles,* in 1624, memorably phrased an enduring truth: "Geography without History seemeth a carcasse without motion, a History without Geography wandreth as a Vagrant without a certain habitation." And W. Gordon East, in an inspiring book,[25] succinctly defines the bond between history and geography in these words: ". . . in studying the inescapable physical setting to history, the geographer studies one of the elements which make up the compound, history: he examines one of the strands from which history is woven. He does not assert foolishly that he can detect, still less explain, all the intricate and confused patterns of the tapestry. He does assert, however, that the physical environment, like the wicket in cricket, owing to its particularities from place to place and from time to time, has some bearing on the course of the game." And "Since history must concern itself with the location of the events which it investigates," it must continually raise, not only the familiar questions "Why?" and "Why then?" but also the questions "Where?" and "Why there?" It is primarily to the solution of the latter questions that geography can contribute, "for it has been Nature, rather than Man, hitherto, in almost every scene, that has determined where the action shall lie. Only at a comparatively late phase of action does Man in some measure shift the scenery for himself." [26]

As in the case of historical geography, it seems of relatively little importance to define the boundaries which separate our field from other areas of human geography. Studies in social, cultural, economic, and military geography as well as in demography are legitimate parts of our explorations of politico-geographical patterns. Without a discussion of the factors accounting for population growth and decline, the picture of a state area or the comparison of such regions remains colorless. With-

[25] *The Geography Behind History* (London, 1938).
[26] *Ibid.,* pp. 13 and 15.

out a description of the economic resources of a nation, its strength or weakness, internally and in relation to other powers, cannot be understood.[27] This volume, therefore, includes in its chapters an analytical treatment of economic factors which form an essential part of the intricate pattern of political geography (in spite of the fact that some of them appear to be but indirectly related to geography). Without an appraisal of the geographical foundations of military strength, as expressed in land-, sea-, and air-power, the political area as such remains an empty shell. And the manifold manifestations of social and cultural geography, whether they are ethnic, linguistic, or religious in nature, form in a mosaic the characteristics of a political region whose people in their tangible and intangible ways of life account for innumerable features of the region not to be described in terms of physical geography. We cannot escape the necessity of including these various patterns in our analysis, but we must not, by overemphasizing them, lose sight of our principal target. We will have to be careful not to be led astray by psychological patterns of behavior only remotely related to a subject which, although political, still remains essentially geographical.

There is a fashionable temptation to speculate on the "character" of nations and to relate it to their natural environment. We find such distinctions as "Latin realism," "French ingenuity," "English tenacity," "German discipline," "Russian mysticism," and "American dynamism."[28] Actually the concept "national character" is part and parcel of a way of thinking typical of the age of nationalism. Its generalizations and oversimplifications are, from a scientific viewpoint, worthless, the more so as they are usually made with the faulty assumption that the character of nations has the quality of stability.[29] No safe formula has been found by which distinguishing personality traits governing the behavior of nations can be measured. It seems more likely that "those nations endanger world peace which, having the necessary demographic and eco-

[27] The blending of political and economic geography is well illustrated by the change of a book's title to *An Outline of Political* (instead of *Economic*) *Geography* because, as the author pointed out in 1941, some of its chapters lay less stress on the relative economic resources of the great world powers, and more on the question of the political organization of the world (J. F. Horrabin, *op. cit.*, XI).

[28] A typical example is A. Siegfried's *The Character of Peoples,* English translation (London, 1952).

[29] C. J. Friedrich, *Constitutional Government and Democracy* (Boston, 1941), p. 23; see also the critical essay by G. J. Pauker, "The Study of National Character Away from that Nation's Territory," in *Studies in International Affairs* (Cambridge, Mass., June, 1951).

nomic resources, are governed by men for whom maximization of power is the supreme value, than that the danger comes from 'national character.' The threat came from Frenchmen led by Napoleon at one time, from Germans led by Hitler, Italians by Mussolini and Japanese by their militarists at another time, from Russians and Chinese governed by Communist Politbureaus at present."[30] It must therefore be concluded that no useful purpose in the exploration of politico-geographical factors will be served by the introduction of such nebulous features as "the character" of nations.

Although this warning appears necessary to avoid the introduction of sociological and psychological considerations which are but loosely, if at all, related to the realm of political geography, it would be equally fallacious to take too narrow a view of the geographical confines of the study of political geography. Its scene is not necessarily, and not limited to, the political area of a state or of interrelated states. Looking beyond shifting political boundaries, we will profit from exploring connections between physical environment and national groups or nations as distinguished from states. Political geography, if limited to the study of landscapes affected by the activities of a state or of states, would produce incomplete and often distorted pictures. As especially a number of French geographers have emphasized, the structure and the activities of states within their natural setting can be better evaluated if we include in our studies the nation and such national groups which account for the strength or weakness of a state. The political boundary of a state represents therefore no boundary for our explorations. The ethnic, linguistic, religious affiliations of national groups are not altogether halted by political boundaries. In many respects the cultural landscape, which is formed by zones of religion, of language, or of ethnic relationships, even of common denominators of literacy and illiteracy, acquires the characteristics of a political landscape. As such it belongs to the domain which the student of political geography will have to explore.[31]

[30] Pauker, *op. cit.*, p. 99.

[31] Q. Wright, *The Study of International Relations* (New York, 1955), undertakes in a chapter on "Political Geography" a critique of what he claims has been the hope of some geographers that because of the apparent permanence of geographical conditions, geography might become the master science of international relations. He states, correctly, that this hope seems to be in vain. We agree with his conclusion that political geography, in order to develop a general theory of international relations, must be combined with demography and technology as well as with "social psychology, sociology, and ethics." In other words, it contributes, together with other equally significant disciplines, to the understanding of internal and external power relations.

CHAPTER 2

Size

SIZE—A BASIC FACTOR IN POLITICAL GEOGRAPHY

Political geography deals with the political organizations of men on the face of the globe. As the globe has only a limited surface, the division of this surface between political units—their size—becomes a basic factor. Some geographers have shied away from recognizing size as a basic factor in political geography.[1] There is however, no escape from the fact that political units are of different size and that their political behavior is in part determined by the size of their territories as well as the size of other, especially of adjacent, political units. In order to understand political behavior, it is therefore necessary to evaluate the size of the political unit.

"SPACE" IN GEOPOLITICS

In the terminology of geopolitics, it became fashionable to talk of space (*Raum*) rather than of size. This concern with space had become, even before the Haushofer school achieved prominence, a veritable obsession of many German geographers who felt that Germany had too little "living space" (*Lebensraum*). The proponents of geopolitics were convinced that British and American geographers had come to take for granted the spatial advantages of their countries and were apt to overlook the importance of space for other countries. However, this dichotomy between German and Anglo-Saxon political geographers should not be

[1] R. Hartshorne, "Functional Approach in Political Geography," *Annals of the Association of American Geographers* (June, 1950), p. 99.

overrated.[2] It was an American geographer, Ellen Churchill Semple, inspired by Ratzel and in full agreement with what was to become the gospel of the Haushofer school, who wrote: "... for peoples and races the struggle for existence is at bottom a struggle for space." [3] On the other hand, not all students of political geography in Germany succumbed to the emotional connotations of the geopolitical school and some continued to use the term *space* (*Raum*) as a synonym for territory, stressing the intimate connection of state and territory.

The emphasis on "space" in Germany can be traced to Friedrich Ratzel, but in his writings it has not yet the character of a slogan and of a political battle cry which it acquired with Haushofer. The concepts of space and size are not entirely interchangeable, because space is boundless and is therefore not mathematically measurable, while size is determined by known dimensions. Geographic space, however, implies a definite location and an area of a certain size. There is also the mystical and emotional connotation which clouds the meaning of "space" in geopolitical literature. Because the term *space* can equally be used both loosely and literally, it is possible to use it vaguely and still with the pretension of accuracy. From this ambiguous use the mystical connotation of the terms *space* and *living space* evolved. For this reason, we prefer the use of the term *size,* even where it would be possible to speak of *space,* and shall thus, aware of the semantic implications, use the term *space* only cautiously and where it has a definite meaning.

MOTIVATION FOR EXPANSION IN SPACE

The size of political units varies within rather wide limits. For a number of states the available space within these limits seems too confining. One of the motivating impulses in man, though not necessarily the dominant one, is the "will to power." [4] Individuals, becoming leaders of nations, often try to exert their "will to power" through enlarging the power of their nations; in the international sphere the will to power expresses itself in the desire to dominate large areas. Even where this motivation can be discounted, the fact remains that nations generally strive to improve their living standards, or at least try to maintain them despite a growing population. From the geographer's point of view, there are three possible ways to accomplish such a goal. One is to utilize space within a

[2] See pp. 7 f.

[3] *Influences of Geographical Environment* (New York, 1911), p. 188.

[4] The German philosopher Nietzsche built a philosophical system around the assumed pre-eminence of this psychological trait.

country's boundaries which was heretofore unused. However, the possibilities of internal colonization are limited, unless the colonization is accompanied by technological progress and a corresponding expansion of communications. Internal colonization is therefore often possible only in connection with the second method, intensification of available space. This second method has been used in all of the great periods of human history, from the time when Egyptians and the nations of Mesopotamia united to devise their grand river regulations and irrigation canals to our modern period of industrialization and urbanization. But nations and their leaders have at many times also tried the third alternative and have often preferred to reach the desired goal by expanding their territories through war, by taking the lands of their neighbors and expelling or exterminating the inhabitants, or forcing them to work for their conquerors.

This third method of maintaining and improving living standards seemed the only one available to nomadic herdsmen in times of drought or when a major population increase and the consequent increase in number of their cattle forced them to migrate or to expand. In nomadic society there is generally little or no unused space available; intensification of animal husbandry is generally impossible on the nomadic level of civilization and technology. Conquest as alternative to starvation thus appears as the only solution. In our time, nomadism as a power factor has practically disappeared. However, expansion of territory through conquest never was limited to nomads. Whether under the slogan of "conquest for living space" or with some other justification, it has remained the most usual weapon in the struggle to maintain or to improve living standards. Because conquest, even if undertaken for the sake of escaping starvation, results in increased power, conquering nations have often gone much farther than can be justified by their original aims. Successful conquerors are led from one goal to the next. Hitler the conqueror, and Communism the conquering ideology are embodiments of age-old phenomena.

THE WORLD STATE

The theoretical extreme limit of size which a political unit can attain would be a state embracing the entire world. Whether such a state would still belong to the legitimate field of investigation for the political geographer is an academic question. However, the problem has some meaning in historical geography, if applied in a restricted sense to such world powers as the Roman Empire, the ancient Chinese Empire, and possibly such empires as the Incan and Mayan empires. These occupied what indeed was at their time known as the entire world, or what appeared worth conquering, thus excluding inhospitable regions, thinly settled by despised barbarians. Today the known world coincides, for all practical purposes, with the whole surface of the globe. Thus size can never be valued absolutely but only in relation to the conditions prevailing in a given period.

POLITICAL UNITS WITHOUT TERRITORY

On the other end of the scale from world statehood are political units without any territorial extent. It is open to question whether such a unit can accurately be named a "state"; most political geographers, however, will regard a discussion of the geographic problems surrounding such organizations as the League of Nations or the United Nations as within the scope of their interests. Actually in such organizations the idea of the global state and of political bodies without space meet and merge into one.

THE PAPAL STATE

The organization of the Roman Catholic Church presents another interesting marginal problem. There is nothing comparable in any other religious organization, not even in the often compared state of the Dalai Lama in Tibet. The Pope, as head of the Roman Catholic Church, is also the head of a state in central Italy. His temporal power goes back to the days of the declining Roman Empire. In 1871, the Papacy lost its worldly dominions and these were not restored until 1929, when the Church and Mussolini concluded the Lateran Treaty. Since then the Pope has ruled again as spiritual head over the Catholics of the world from the tiny, independent state of the Vatican City.

HISTORICAL REMNANTS

The Papal state can be regarded also as a historical remnant. In Germany, until its occupation by Napoleon's armies, many tiny ecclesiastic states existed. Very often the secular territory of an archbishop, bishop, or abbot was looked upon as the indispensable basis for his spiritual dominion. All these ecclesiastic and feudal states have disappeared. Only the Papal state remains.

Other historical size-power anachronisms include the still-used power-suggestive titles of emperor, or king of kings by rulers of such countries as Ethiopia, Iran, and Annam. Equally disproportionate in terms of size, at least, is the position of Taiwan-based Free China among the Big Five, those states which alone exert veto power in the United Nations.[5]

EVOLUTION OF STATE POWER AND THE FACTOR OF SIZE

In general, military and economic power, size of territory, and rank are commensurate. There are states whose size has remained constant, but whose power has grown in spite of the lack of territorial growth. These are the countries whose spaces have been filled with people, as in Argentina; or countries in which new resources have been discovered and their use organized for the good of the country, as in Mexico and other countries with exploitable oil resources; or in countries such as Canada and the U.S.S.R. which succeeded in transforming prairies into wheat lands and in extending northward their limits of agricultural activities. There are again other nations which, established for many centuries within their present boundaries, have maintained the size of their territory to the present day. Denmark and Switzerland have almost exactly the same size as they had five centuries ago, although their populations have multiplied. Whereas once her territory was sufficiently large, populous, and rich to warrant a significant position in European or even world affairs, Switzerland's political power potential today has significance only because of the defensive possibilities of its mountains, and Danish statesmen in the 1930's liquidated their military establishment completely because, within the country's small territory, it did not seem possible to defend it against aggressors. Both Denmark and Switzerland still rank as important members of the European community of nations, but only because of their high cultural standing and strong economic position, not because of the size of their territory or population.

REMAINDERS OF SMALL FEUDAL STATES

Feudal states still exist in Europe essentially in the same form as centuries ago. Some of these are tiny sovereign monarchies such as Monaco (370 acres), and Liechtenstein (62 square miles). Some are republics, such as San Marino (38 square miles), and Andorra (191 square miles). In India, scores of such small feudal states have disap-

[5] The island of Taiwan (13,890 square miles) is about twice the size of Massachusetts (7,867 square miles) or New Jersey (7,522 square miles). Its population, in 1950, totalled 7,647,000 which equals that of Texas (263,513 square miles).

peared only since the country gained independence in 1948 and merged them into princely federations. Others are administered centrally. Even after this consolidation process, the Saurashtra Union has a territory of only 21,062 square miles in spite of the fact that it succeeded not less than 222 states, including dwarf states of several acres. The Patiala and East Punjab States Union is still smaller (10,099 square miles). However, a new reform program proposes to wipe out these remnants. Among other, centrally-administered, territories, such small states as Tripura (4,049 square miles) have not completely lost their identity. Within Pakistan a few states, such as Chitral (4,000 square miles), Swat (1,000 square miles), and Khairpur (6,050 square miles), have retained approximately the same position they had under British rule.

In contrast to the consolidation process under way in India and Pakistan, we find in the Malayan Peninsula native, essentially feudal sultanates. These have successfully resisted consolidation in their effort to protect themselves from Chinese and Indian immigrant communities such as have become majority populations in other parts of the Peninsula. In Europe, the complicated pattern of close to one hundred dwarf states which once constituted the political map of Germany, has changed radically since Napoleon I erased most of these states from the map. A few managed to survive into the period of the Third Reich and were then finally incorporated into larger political units. It was their very smallness that contributed to their preservation for such a long time; their smallness was also a factor in the preservation of anachronistic feudal features. The smallest modern state which is more than a feudal remnant is Luxembourg (999 square miles), which is distinguished for its iron ore deposits, its highly-developed steel industry, and its dense population of 290,000. Despite its small size, and due to its economic and constitutional development, Luxembourg has been able to preserve its independence, but only as a partner of other states in customs and economic unions. At present it is one of the three members of the Benelux combination, Belgium and the Netherlands being the other partners.

FEUDAL STATES OF LARGER SIZE

Where feudal states of larger size have carried over into the twentieth century, we can generally observe a process of transformation or breaking up into smaller units. In India, the more progressive princely countries, such as Mysore and Travancore, survived in but slightly changed form. The largest and strongest feudal princely state, that of the Nizam of

Haidarabad, became a victim of the Indian transformation. This process is not limited to Asia. It is paralleled by what happened two decades earlier in Europe when the semi-feudal Austro-Hungarian monarchy of the Hapsburgs broke up in the turmoil of the defeat of the central powers in 1918. The semi-feudal nature of the Hapsburg realm is obvious from the fact that in spite of parliamentary institutions it was still regarded as the personal estate of the emperor.

CITY-STATES

Historically of great importance, and by far the most notable of all small states, are city-states. Greek city-states formed the geographical basis of the political philosophy of Aristotle and Plato, who extolled the advantages of the small state. The failure of the Greeks to develop political power on a scale commensurate with the wide sphere of their cultural influence is in part due to their inability to free themselves from the

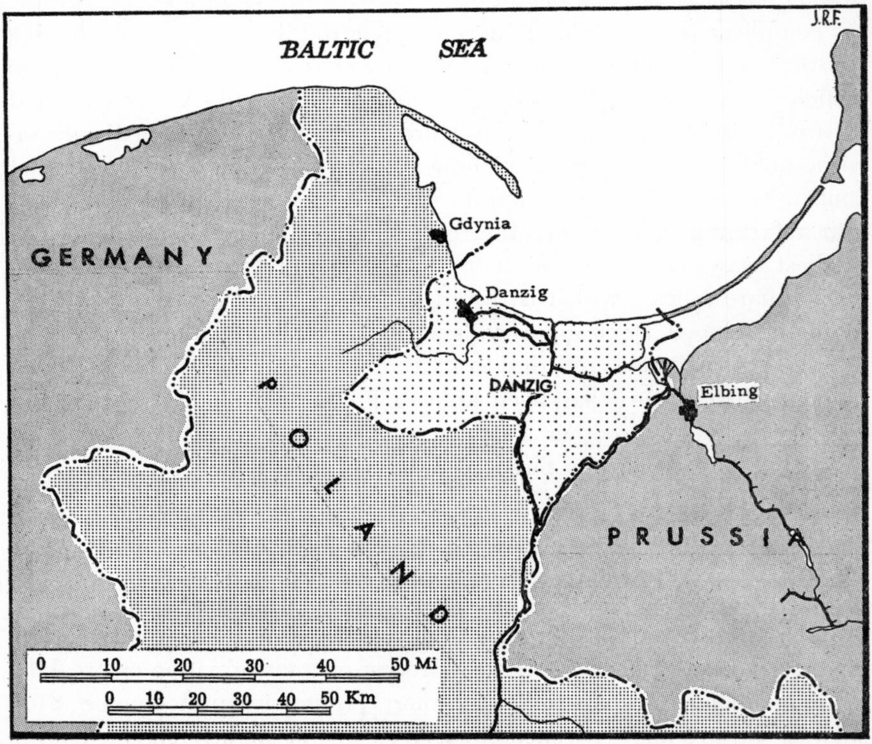

FIG. 2-1. Danzig—1919-1939.

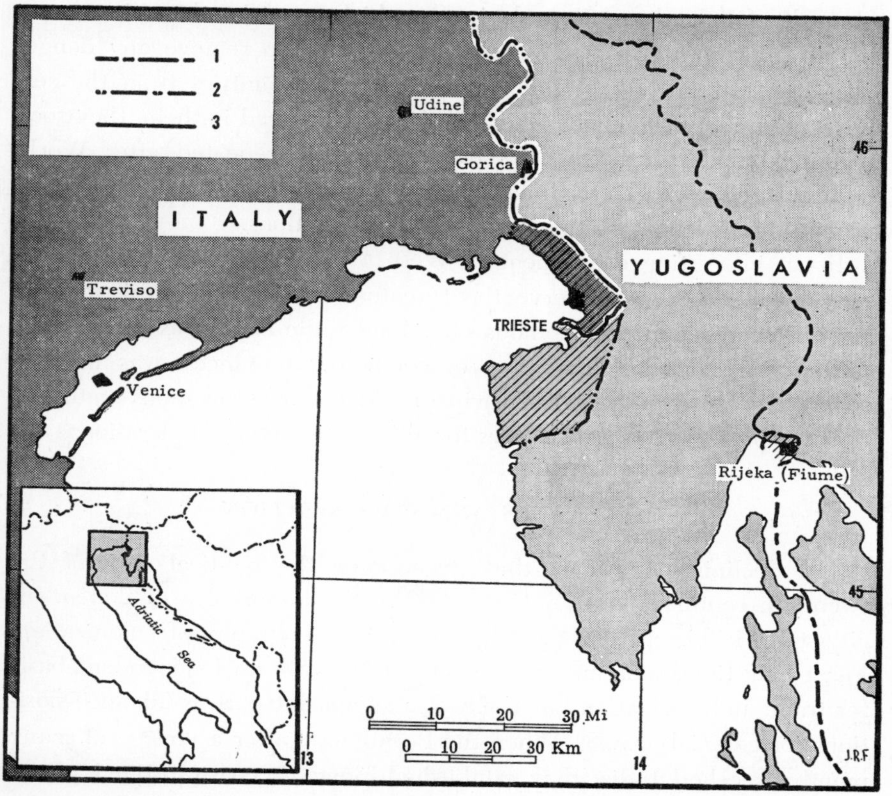

FIG. 2-2. Short-lived City-states at the Head of the Adriatic Sea: (1) boundary after World War I; (2) boundary after World War II; (3) boundary in 1955.

limitations of the city-state concept.[6] We can trace city-states in various parts of the world, in Phoenicia and Greece, in India, in some American Indian areas, and in medieval Germany and Italy. Among many German city-states, only Bremen and Hamburg have survived as constituent members of the German Federal Republic. In spite of their great historical importance, city-states have largely disappeared as sovereign states.

In recent years attempts have been made to revive small-sized city-states, the express purpose being to avoid creating a state which could exert power of its own. Danzig (708 square miles) (Fig. 2-1) and Fiume (8 square miles) (Fig. 2-2) were set up after World War I in order to give their overwhelmingly German and Italian populations freedom from

[6] Semple, *op. cit.*, pp. 195-196.

the rule of Poland and Yugoslavia, for which countries the cities served as main harbors. Their smallness was expected to remove any danger that they would ever be able to cut off these countries from the sea. When these city-states did not fulfill the hopes placed in them, they soon disappeared. Nevertheless, the experiment was repeated after World War II in Trieste. The turbulent history of this experiment illustrates the manifold problems resulting from such constructions.

In an interesting experiment in West Africa, British colonial rule is making an effort to preserve the threatened unity of Nigeria by the establishment of an autonomous city. Lagos, the capital as well as the port of the Nigerian federation of conflicting provinces, was in 1953 separated from the Western Provinces and given autonomous status, in order to preserve its vital services for all members of the federation.

CITY-STATES AND COLONIZATION

The declining power of the city-state on the political map of the twentieth century should not overshadow the importance of dependent city-states in historical geography and in the geography of colonization. For a long time, such autonomous city-states with an independent basis for trade and navigation have played a significant part as advance positions for colonial growth. When the Portuguese, after a voyage of many months, reached India, they established along its coast fortified places which were destined to carry on trade with the hinterland during the long periods between visits of the fleets. These Portuguese factories in India were in the medieval tradition of the Italian factories in the Levant.[7] They eventually grew away from their distant places of origin and as a result of various sociological factors and of the ability of the colonizers to mix with the native population, a distinctive non-Indian national feeling developed, at least among the Goanese, the native inhabitants of the largest of these city-colonies. The new India, growing into the role of an independent nation, has become apprehensive about what she considers an outdated continuation of Portuguese colonial rule on Indian soil (Fig. 2-3).

While only Goa, with its population of about 700,000, appears to have developed a distinctive individuality of its own, we find along the Indian

[7] The Italian cities Venice, Genoa, and Pisa founded autonomous colonies in Palestine, in Syria, and on Cyprus, and in the Byzantine Empire at the period of the Crusades.

Fig. 2-3. Portuguese and French (1954) Colonial Holdings in India.

Coast other city-colonies, small fragments of Portuguese territory which, as remnants of trading stations in India, have ironically survived the greater empire of Britain.[8] Other, and more significant, examples are the endangered British gate-city to China, Hong Kong, the Soviet Union's

[8] W. G. East and O. H. K. Spate, *The Changing Map of Asia* (London, 1950), p. 152.

ice-free harbor in Manchuria, Dairen,[9] and the British guardian of the south entrance to the Red Sea, Aden. The Hong Kong situation, in particular, is one of instability in the light of constant and growing tensions. Pressure for a plebiscite may eventually revert the crown colony to China; its population which had totalled 850,000 in 1931 and which as a result of the influx of refugees from China was estimated in November, 1952, at 2,250,000, included only a total of 13,000 British subjects of European race.[10]

Thus, while the balance of power between the major Asian and European nations has maintained the city-colony beyond other forms of dwarf states, these, too, tend to disappear gradually from the political scene. Some city-states have served as the basis for larger colonies and states, as Rome did in ancient times. Bombay has expanded into one of the largest provinces, now states, of India; the little city-colony of New York, because the entrance gate, to a powerful state of the Union. This trend toward larger political units is evident if one compares the distant past with the present. Athens, Sparta, Corinth, Tyre, and Sidon in ancient times, and Venice, Genoa, and Pisa in the Middle Ages, ranked as big powers. Today, no nation with so small a territorial basis could be regarded as a great power. Even such states as Portugal or the Netherlands, though great powers in the sixteenth to eighteenth centuries, could not play an analogous role today.

The discrepancy in size of territory in these instances is much more striking than the discrepancy in size of population. Athens in the 4th century B.C. finally succumbed to the Macedonian territorial state. However, it might be fairly doubted whether Athens (including its dependent island cities in the Aegean, or even without them) was the inferior in population of the two powers. Throughout Greek-Roman antiquity [11] in the Mediterranean area, the majority of the free population lived in city-states. Probably only since the time of the declining Roman Empire has the population of territorial units grown, while that of the cities, with few exceptions, proportionately shrank.

[9] Dairen was returned to China in May, 1955.

[10] *The Statesman's Yearbook, 1955,* p. 238; *Focus* (November 3, 1953), Hong Kong.

[11] It should be noted in passing that antiquity and the Middle Ages had also their overlarge states, such as the Persian, Roman, and Mongolian Empires. Nobody, so far, has based on the disappearance of such empires (which embraced most of their known worlds) a theory of a trend to a proliferation of independent smaller states.

THE METROPOLITAN CITY

Far into the nineteenth century urban populations constituted a small proportion of the world population. The rapid growth of the modern city, which made the largest of them more populous than some medium-sized nations, has not found a political expression in the international field. Paris, London, or New York have a larger population than Norway, Denmark, Switzerland, or Uruguay—greater New York even more than Belgium, the Netherlands, Portugal, or a majority of the Latin American or Arab nations. Historically, such metropolitan areas sometimes have been given the status of provinces or member states. Berlin became one of the Prussian provinces, Vienna one of the nine constituent states of the Austrian federative republic. Neither can be called a genuine city-state. Still less is this true of Washington, D.C., of the City of Mexico, or of Canberra, the capital of Australia.

All this points to the conclusion that under modern conditions the growth of metropolitan areas is rather a function of the development of the country than an independent phenomenon. However, while the growth of metropolitan areas is a function of a growing country (as in the doubling of the population, in ten years, of the twin cities of Delhi and New Delhi), the decline of a nation is not necessarily indicated by a decline of population in its main cities. Only in extreme cases does such a development occur, such as in the case of Vienna and Istanbul. Both had been capitals of empires of 30 to 50 million inhabitants and both went down in World War I. Both cities lost up to 25 per cent of their population, with Vienna becoming the capital of the new Austria with a population of 6½ million, and Istanbul becoming the main port city of a country of 12 million.

THE SUPER POWERS

The global scene of our time is dominated by the emergence of the United States and the Soviet Union as super powers. Both extend over large continental areas and both have expanded beyond these boundaries. The forms of these expansions are manifold. As in the case of the Soviet satellites, they may have taken shape by forcing smaller states to accept the leadership of the super state in a manner differing only to a small degree from outright subjugation. In contrast, the acquisition of military bases overseas plays an important role in the security situation in which the United States finds itself. This is an unimportant form of expansion in the Soviet Union.[12]

REGIONAL ORGANIZATIONS

In the face of the power exerted by super states, smaller states have increasingly attempted to safeguard their independence and to increase their influence by drawing together in unions, regional organizations, or federations. Some of these, such as the Pan-American Union, also embrace one of the big states, the smaller members hoping thereby to influence their big neighbor's policies. Other organizations, as for instance those of the Colombo Plan[13] or of the Arab League, try to keep out of the U.S.S.R.-United States disputes. Regional organization of smaller powers are not all-inclusive, however. We find a number of states which have remained uncommitted to some larger organization, in each case for peculiar reasons. Austria, for instance, was occupied by four powers until 1955 and was given no freedom of choice; nor can she join any organization now as the result of the terms of the Peace Treaty which reinstated her sovereignty. Israel cannot join any organization without making her partners unwilling supporters of Israel's unresolved war with the Arab bloc. Sweden, Finland, Switzerland, and Eire try to remain independent and uncommitted to any bloc. The vast majority of states, however, are in one form or another partners in some political grouping of continental size.

The significance of this trend is not challenged by the important fact that some of these supra-national organizations are far from being stable. It is probable that their size and membership will change rapidly in the near future. What connections will the Sudan make after attaining sovereignty? Will the Gold Coast join the British Commonwealth as a dominion? How long will the Union of South Africa remain a member of that commonwealth? How long will these small nations that are trying to maintain a neutral attitude be able to pursue that policy? Above all, will the Soviet Union and the United States be able to win over to their power combinations and to their causes member states of the other bloc? In any case, the emergence of political bodies of continental size has to be accepted as permanent, even though their structures and the extent of their boundaries are and will remain subject to change and fluctuation.

[12] The vital role of the strategic base net along the American perimeter of defense in the security picture of the United States is discussed in detail in Chapter 15.

[13] See pp. 286-290.

CONSOLIDATING AND DISRUPTIVE FACTORS IN THE EMERGENCE OF MODERN STATE SYSTEMS

The industrial revolution of the nineteenth century and modern colonialism have supported the emergence of large state structures. The British Empire, the Russian Empire of the Czars, and the Soviet Union have no equals in size in the past. The United States and France are not far behind. Canada and Brazil are about to organize and penetrate their wide unoccupied spaces as the United States did a century earlier. Some states, however—Germany, Italy, Yugoslavia, Rumania—became large through the consolidation of several small states. Such consolidations are seldom primarily effected for the sake of greater economic efficiency, as has often been the case in the industrial field. It is true that the customs union was the pacemaker for German national unity, but at the same time Italy accomplished her national unity and still has not succeeded in welding her territory into a uniform economic unit. The problem of the impoverished south, the Mezzogiorno, plagues Italy continuously. In the unification of Germany and Italy and in some more recent cases, it was not the consideration of economic efficiency, but the irrational power of modern nationalism which was the driving force.

Modern nationalism which has become effective since the French Revolution has not only contributed to enlarging the size of many political units, it has also been a disruptive force. This was the case in the nineteenth century in Europe and the same trend is evident in the twentieth century in other continents. The breakup of the Hapsburg and Ottoman empires, of the Scandinavian and the Dutch-Belgian unions is followed by that of India and the creating of an Indian Union; Pakistan, Ceylon, Eire, Burma, the Arab states, preferred to establish themselves as independent states, though they had to forego the many economic advantages of belonging to large empires. The creation of Israel is another illustration of this recent trend toward national states, however small.[14] It is still more significant that the Soviet Union felt it necessary to create autonomous national states, even though the autonomy was in many respects only make-believe. Although the Soviet Union could suppress these autonomous states, even as she has curtailed their function, to do so might well mean that she would deprive herself of much of her appeal to the colonial nations of Asia and Africa. A new organization of Africa is in the making and it is possible, if not likely, that the large African

[14] The area of Israel is 8,048 square miles.

colonial empires will be replaced by some smaller national or pseudo-national political bodies before the twentieth century draws to an end.

Size is a variable factor in the life of states and there is no uniform trend toward larger or smaller states. There is no optimal size for states, not in our time nor in any period of the past. There have been, however, very few instances when leaders of nations have regarded their country as being too large; the Gladstonian Liberals in Great Britain in the 70's and 80's of the nineteenth century are the only well-known case. Striving for larger size is, on the other hand, a common historical phenomenon.

TERRITORIAL AGGRANDIZEMENT AS PRIZE OF WAR

It is typical of the high value placed on the size of states that territory is almost invariably the prize in a conflict between nations. Even in those cases in which a war broke out for reasons other than conquest, or in which the attacked nation won the victory, the victor commonly asks for expansion of his territory. The United States entered the war with Spain in 1898 because of the feeling that the strengthening of any European position in the Americas would be intolerable, and not for reasons of territorial aggrandizement. The war resulted, however, not only in the temporary occupation of Cuba, but in the annexation of Puerto Rico and even of the remote Philippines, which in no way had been an object of contention. Belgium in 1914, the Netherlands in 1941, would have been content to be left alone in the conflict of the great powers; nevertheless, at the end of the World Wars, they demanded, and obtained, territory from defeated Germany. In many cases such demands are disguised as compensation for damages suffered. The case of Bismarck who, after Prussia had won the war of 1866, persuaded the King of Prussia to conclude a peace treaty with Austria without territorial cessions (in order to insure Austrian neutrality in the coming conflict with France) is a rare exception to this general rule. In a power bloc as large as the Soviet orbit which includes many contending nationalities, we find such internal territorial changes benefiting one partner at the cost of another. The Ukrainian Republic within the U.S.S.R. has a total area of 232,625 square miles, of which not less than 25 per cent was acquired after World War II from Soviet satellites: Eastern Galicia, 34,700 square miles, from Poland; Subcarpathian Ruthenia, 5,000 square miles, from Czechoslovakia; Northern Bukovina and part of Bessarabia, 8,000 square miles, from Rumania. In February, 1954, the Crimean peninsula (10,000 square miles) which had lost its autonomous status at the end of World War II

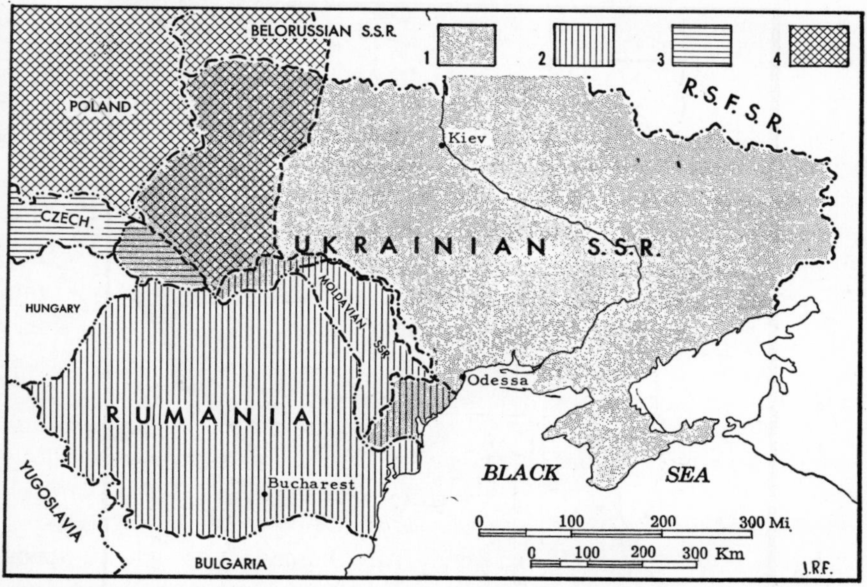

Fig. 2-4. The Ukrainian S.S.R. (1955): (1) present Ukrainian territory; (2) pre-World War II Rumania; (3) pre-World War II Czechoslovakia; (4) pre-World War II Poland.

because of the alleged co-operation of its people with the Germans, was incorporated into the Ukrainian Republic (Fig. 2-4).

An important motivating power for territorial aggrandizement is the prestige with which size endows a country. The mere fact of size gives to a state a certain standing in the community of nations. The occupation of the western Sahara by Spain, or the claims of Chile, Argentina, and other countries to Antarctic wastes, spring partly from this source. If the large state is united in one continuous territory, this factor gives to its citizens a feeling of security and importance. Being removed from contact with other nations, a deceptive feeling of independence, protection, and security develops, especially among persons who live in the interior. Out of this feeling grows a powerful concept of "splendid isolation" which clearly has its roots in geographical ignorance.

THE MAP AS A CAUSE OF GEOGRAPHICAL MISCONCEPTIONS

A contributing factor to the growth and survival of these geographical misconceptions is the map: the average school atlas depicts a student's own country, his own continent, in larger scale than other countries and

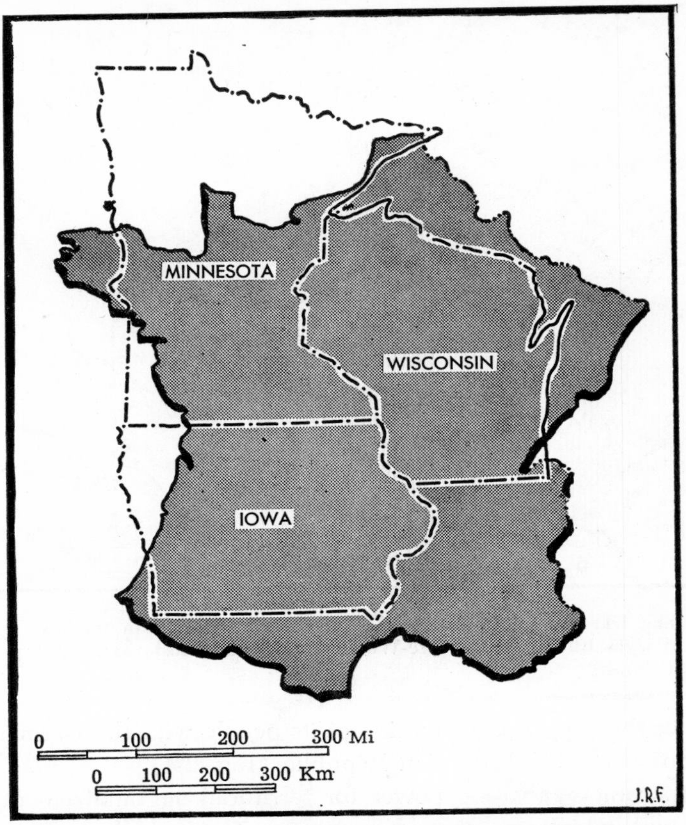

Fig. 2-5. Comparative Size of France (superimposed on Minnesota, Iowa, and Wisconsin).

continents. Independent countries are given more prominence than even large constituent parts of still larger states. Many people have the impression that France is a very large country, while actually it is about the size of Minnesota, Wisconsin, and Iowa combined (Fig. 2-5). On most maps showing individual continents, Europe is presented in larger scale than Asia, although non-Soviet Europe is only slightly larger than India (Fig. 2-6). It is seldom realized that Brazil with its 3,288,000 square miles is larger than the 2,977,000 square miles of the United States, and that both together are still much smaller than the Soviet Union (8,700,000 square miles). (See Fig. 2-7.)

This reference to the map as a primary cause of common misconceptions of size factors would be incomplete without mentioning the misuse of the (in many respects extremely valuable) Mercator projection as largely

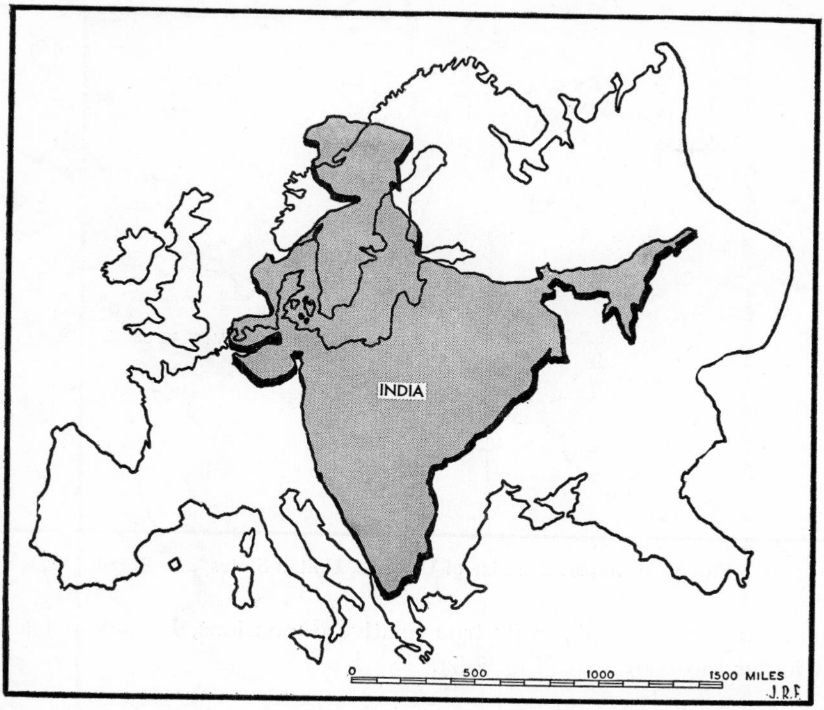

FIG. 2-6. India and Europe at the Same Scale.

responsible for such errors. Although it shows true compass directions and therefore is still the ideal map for ship navigators, the Mercator map has serious shortcomings. Except in the vicinity of the Equator, it does not even pretend to show the correct relative size of the land areas of the globe. The nearer one comes to the North Pole, or to the South Pole, the more distorted are the factors of size as shown on the Mercator map.[15] Richard E. Harrison, with European geographers, has called attention to the elementary, yet to most of us surprising fact that on a Mercator world map Greenland appears larger than the continent of South America. But when shown in its true relative size, we discover that it is only about one tenth of the area of South America. An even better example (Fig. 2-8) is offered by Ellesmere Island, northwest of Greenland. On a Mercator world map with its typical distortions in the polar regions Ellesmere Island appears to be almost as large as Australia. Actually, when it is

[15] R. E. Harrison, *Maps*, 2nd ed. (Consolidated Vultee Aircraft Corporation, 1943), p. 7; R. E. Harrison and H. W. Weigert, "World View and Strategy," in H. W. Weigert and V. Stefansson, eds., *Compass of the World* (New York, 1945), pp. 74-88.

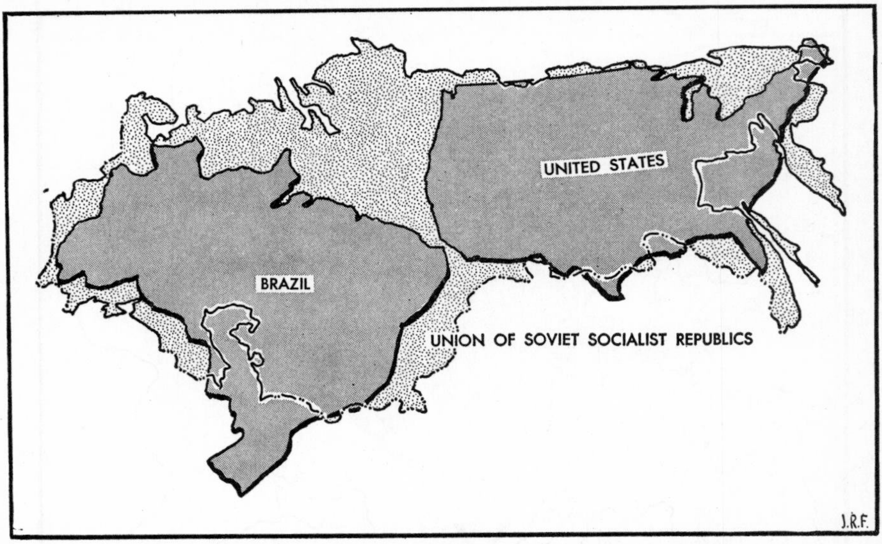

Fig. 2-7. Comparative Size of U.S.S.R., United States, and Brazil.

shown beside Australia in its true relative dimensions, Ellesmere Island dwindles to dwarf size (Fig. 2-8).

THE VALUE OF SIZE AS A SECURITY FACTOR

It is obvious that size is an important factor in the determination of economic and political power. However, whether it evolves as an asset or as a liability depends on many factors. In a general way, it can be stated that size tends to be an asset to military power. Only a large country, such as the Soviet Union in World War II, can trade space for time and win, after retreating—voluntarily or by necessity—for hundreds of miles. The time needed for the enemy's advance is used to build up new industries, to train new troops, and to prepare a counteroffensive. Only in very large countries can areas still be found which are sufficiently remote from enemy bases to be relatively safe from air attack. Only in a large territory can an air raid warning system function efficiently. On the other hand, large size, coupled with other factors, can pose serious problems to military strategy; for instance, outlying parts of a large country, if thinly populated and if lacking adequate communications lines, are difficult to defend—a problem Russia experienced in the war with Japan in 1904 to 1905. For similar reasons, the defense of Alaska is a problem to military planning in the United States.

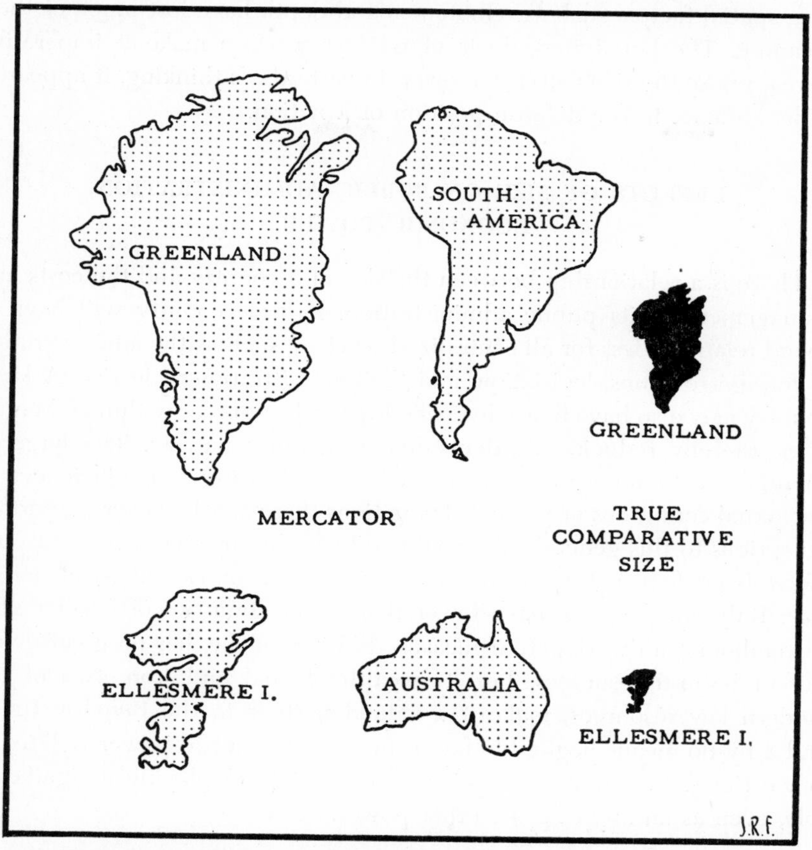

FIG. 2-8. Effects of Projections on Appearance of Size: Greenland, South America, Ellesmere Island, Australia (after R. E. Harrison).

In a country of small size, this factor always is negative if contemplated in terms of external security. If invaded, even if ultimately on the winning side, the small country will suffer damages affecting its entire territory, whereas a large country, even if forced to accept defeat, may still retain large areas untouched by the direct effects of war.

We must always be aware that evaluations of size factors with reference to military planning and security can not lead to more than observations of a very general nature. This note of caution has never been more timely than in our age of potential hydrogen bomb warfare. The development of thermonuclear weapons, and the problem of radioactive "fall-out," have shattered our concepts of security. In a territory of small size, there will no longer be left any areas of refuge or safety. But even for areas of larger size, spatial factors such as remoteness and depth have lost much of their meaning. The horrifying effects of nuclear warfare make it imperative to reappraise the size factor wherever, in yesterday's thinking, it appeared to be an asset to the defense position of a nation.

EFFECTS OF SIZE ON PUBLIC ADMINISTRATION, ECONOMIC POWER

There is a relationship between the size of a country and the costs and management of its public administration. A large country will have to spend relatively less for all centralized services, such as the administration of foreign relations, legislation, and the administration of justice. A large country may also have more diversified natural resources within its boundaries, thereby reducing its dependency on other nations. The larger a country the better are its chances of approximating self-sufficiency. In the actual conditions of present-day nations there are, however, important exceptions to this general rule. Spain and Czechoslovakia have more, and more diversified, natural resources than many countries of much larger size; Italy and Norway have fewer than other countries of smaller size. Luxembourg, a dwarf state if measured by size alone, has no great diversity of natural resources, but its wealth of coal and iron, two of the modern key resources, make it a valued partner in the Benelux Union and a by no means negligible factor in West European power politics in peace times. In war its small size prevents it from playing a significant role, even as an ally of some other power.

SIZE AND POPULATION

The most important factor tending to offset the importance of mere size is population. A thinly populated, sprawling country is handicapped by the necessity of maintaining costly transportation organizations; whereas efficiency is easily attained by much smaller countries having similar population figures. On the other hand, the needs of a large population may tax too heavily the resources of a country and weaken its influence among the nations of the world. Only in this case would we speak of overpopulation. India and Egypt are cases in point. Densely populated Belgium is, without its colonial empire, a small country of 12,000 square miles, but it is culturally, economically, and even militarily of much greater importance than, for instance, larger Austria (32,375 square miles) or Bulgaria (42,796 square miles). That Ethiopia, a country one and a half times the size of France, is of almost negligible influence and power, is due not only to the scarcity of its population of 11 million but also to its relative cultural backwardness. Cultural and technological underdevelopment are factors which can hardly be measured, but their influence can nevertheless offset completely the influence of large size.

Apart from the actual numbers of people, their distribution within a state is of decisive importance. A striking example is Canada which has areas of relatively dense population but also other extensive areas which are for all practical purposes uninhabited. Not the map picturing the size of Canada but one showing the distribution and density of its population of 14,000,000 explains its political geography (Fig. 2-9). This shows clearly that Canada's settled areas are along the southern, American border, and that they are separated into two groups by the large uninhabited Laurentian wilderness. Each of these groups is divided again into two areas of dense population, separated in the western provinces by the thinly populated areas of the Canadian Rocky mountains, and in the eastern provinces by the thinly settled hill country of southeastern Quebec. Nevertheless, it would be erroneous to think of Canada as a group of four loosely connected areas strung out north of the 42° parallel. The unpeopled spaces between the populated areas are like the tissues in the human body between the vital organs. Frequently the sparsely settled areas have yielded unexpected natural resources and have thus offered new possibilities of development. A Canada without its hold over these spaces would not reach the Arctic Ocean except at a few points, its role among the world powers would be altogether different.

Similar conditions exist in other areas. The Australian Commonwealth (Fig. 2-10), if it included only the well-settled coastal areas would be only a number of barely connected, hardly defensible small settlements. Australia is at present a rather influential power because of its continental size (2,975,000 square miles), despite its small population. Comparable in population (8,500,000 in 1951) as well as in cultural and technological development to Belgium (8,700,000 in 1951), its size among other factors gives it a different weight in international affairs. As in the case of Canada, the recent discovery of mineral resources (in particular uranium and oil), in hitherto "empty spaces," has had a profound effect on Australia's internal and external political geography.

Among the major regions of "empty spaces" the Sahara with an area of over three million square miles is certainly as much an anecumene as

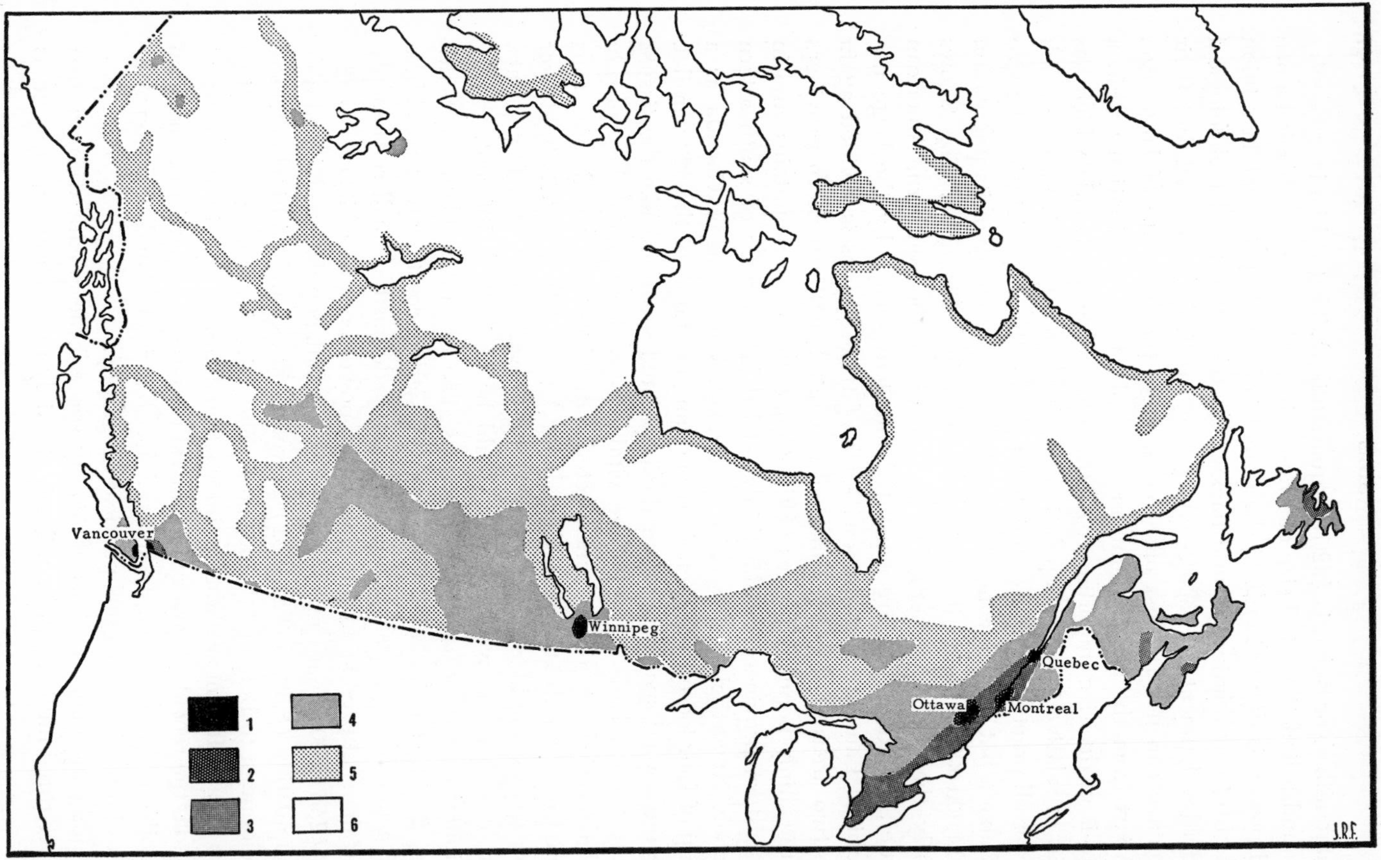

FIG. 2-9. Canada: Population Density per Square Mile: (1) over 500; (2) 250-500; (3) 100-250; (4) 50-100; (5) 5-50; (6) under 5.

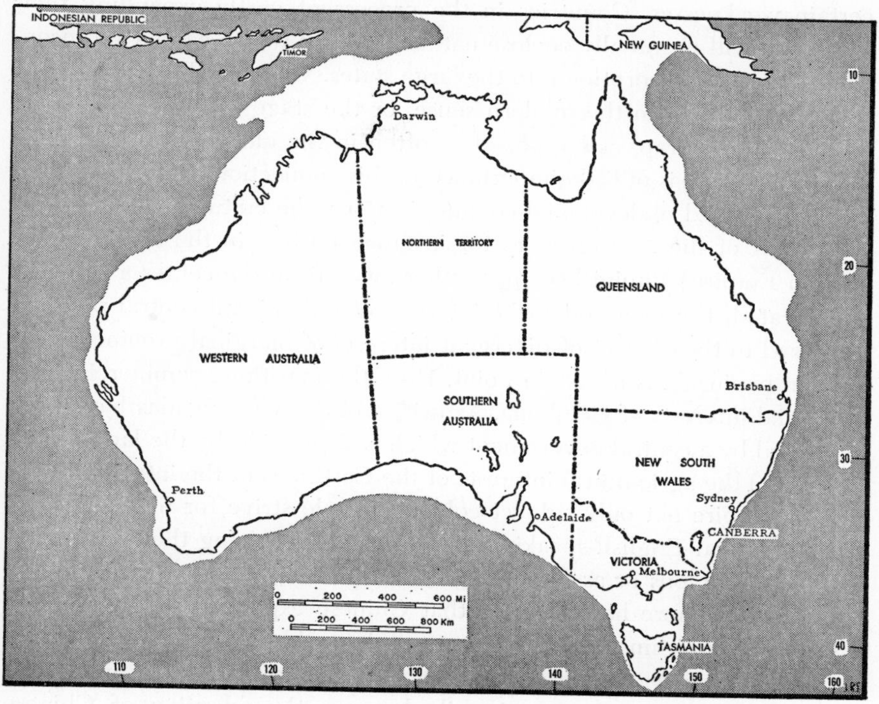

Fig. 2-10. Australia (Continental Shelf: unshaded water portion).

is the ocean. However, without its firm grip on the Sahara the French African colonial empire would lose much of its compactness and defensibility.

The political map may grossly mislead the unwary by showing size without the necessary qualifications. Political geography cannot rely on the political map alone; the physiographic map, presenting deserts, mountains, swamps, virgin forests, lakes, and large rivers has to furnish the necessary qualifications and limitations for the evaluation of size; the population maps and maps of resources are other indispensable adjuncts. Location, another limiting factor, will be discussed in another chapter in more detail.

THE RISKS OF OVEREXPANSION

It is obvious that small countries are susceptible to pressure from large and powerful nations, but the size of large nations does not exempt them from pressure. It is less obvious, perhaps, but large size itself entails certain weaknesses. Countries in the process of vastly expanding their territories will eventually enclose national groups which cannot be reconciled with their absorption into the large states. Whether this is a national minority problem in the modern sense, or the stage for the rebellion of an ambitious satrap, as happened so often in the old empires on Indian and Iranian soil, is of little importance in this connection. In former times, due to slow and undeveloped communications, the cultural influence and the power of the core area (as for instance Latium in the center of the Roman Empire) diminished the farther away from the center a province was located. But even today the interests of a dominant central province may lead to the neglect of divergent interests of marginal provinces. The Iberian peninsula is a case in point. Here the maritime, commercial, and industrial interests of Catalonia, Asturia, and the Vascongadas have been neglected by a central government which is dominated by the land-locked vision and the agricultural interests of the Castilians of the interior. In the British Empire not only subject colonial people strive for independence, but peripheral English-speaking areas aim at increasing their independence as dominions or as loosely federated partners of equal standing.

Owen Lattimore has shown [16] that Chinese expansion finally reached a zone of diminishing returns, where people could no longer be converted to the Chinese way of life—to adopt the language, houses, and social system of the conquerors—primarily because the adoption of Chinese agricultural methods in arid areas proved unprofitable. There was even a strong incentive, in these areas, for the Chinese immigrant to become a herdsman and to become "barbarized" by accepting the way of life which went with nomadic herding. As a result, Chinese political rule in such areas did not last long. Lattimore also traced a corresponding limiting trend for the Russian expansion in Inner Asia.

PSYCHOLOGICAL AND CULTURAL FACTORS RELATED TO SIZE

Large countries breed often a mental attitude which is inimical to an understanding of foreigners and may ultimately lead to fatal mistakes in dealing with other nations. It is not necessarily narrow-mindedness and stress of the particular local interests, it is a geographically induced and unavoidable lack of ability to understand others. Even in the shrinking

[16] O. Lattimore, "The New Political Geography of Inner Asia," *Geographical Journal,* Vol. 119 (March, 1953), and more in detail for the Chinese, *Inner Asian Frontiers of China,* American Geographical-Sociological Research Series, No. 21, 1940.

world of today it holds true that part of the population never has the opportunity to come in contact with foreigners, or only with a few individuals. The mass of the population, therefore, do not develop real understanding of foreign thinking and attitudes. Strange as it may appear, the larger a country, the less diversified tend to be its foreign contacts. The United States is an extreme example, with only two countries as direct neighbors. The number of Americans who are continuously aware of conditions in a foreign country, even of Mexico or Canada, is very small. Both these countries are sorely neglected in most of the textbooks on American history used in American schools and the small space and time allowed to matters Canadian or Mexican in the average local newspaper or radio station illustrates the lack of interest, in the United States, in the affairs of the two neighboring nations. However, radio and television and especially the fact that millions of Americans have served overseas during and since the war have prompted a greater awareness of, and interest in, foreign affairs.

In contrast, Switzerland borders on four countries, Hungary on five, while the U.S.S.R. borders on nine, and the British Empire through its colonies on many more. There is hardly a Swiss or Hungarian who is not aware in one way or another of happenings in two or even three foreign countries. There are none who live farther away from a foreign country than sixty-five miles. Cultural interaction is pronounced, knowledge of foreign languages—the best means of cultural contact—much more widespread than in the United States. Thus we find that lack of cultural contacts, as a natural consequence of the large size of a country, causes the outlook of its citizens to be often more parochial than is true in countries of small size. Again this general observation is not without exception.

An oddly similar parochial outlook exists in many small countries where the citizens live under the illusion that their co-nationals have done more than their share for world civilization. It is a distorted perspective which sees things close to home as much larger than remote ones. Most history books of small countries depict national inventors, artists, and writers as people of international fame, while actually their contributions may be unknown abroad.

In internal politics the size factor has important ramifications, especially in large countries where the normal concentration of political activities in the capital usually results also in drawing most of a country's cultural activities toward the political center. Such concentration is apt to promote the development of a provincial, if not backward, outlook among the population in regions remote from the cultural and political nucleus. Sometimes we find, as a usually healthy reaction, the growth of several and competing cultural centers. Again the size of the country is a significant conditioning factor in this process. The multiplicity of cultural centers in the numerous capitals of politically divided Germany in the fifteenth to eighteenth centuries, in Italy from the thirteenth to the eighteenth century, or in the many states of India at several periods, as compared with the overwhelming concentration of intellectual, artistic, and scientific activity in Paris, Madrid, Peking, or Tokyo are illustrations. A modern example of a deliberate attempt to avoid what was considered undesirable political and cultural concentration in one capital is the Union of South Africa. South Africa has two capitals, the legislative in Cape Town, and the administrative in Pretoria. Even in a federal state like the United States, cities such as New York, Washington, Boston, and a few others tend to draw all cultural activities into their orbit. A French geographer, Jean Gottman, observed that an American "megapolis," four hundred miles long and populated by thirty million persons in not more than a half-dozen states, influences thinking, fashions, manner of speech, and social relations, as well as political concepts. "Although dependent upon the rest of the nation for food and communication, this megapolis is becoming an area 'outside' of the United States, just as Amsterdam, Naples, Rome, and to a degree, London and Paris are entities." [17]

SIZE FACTORS IN INTERNAL POLITICAL GEOGRAPHY

Large or small size of a country plays an important role in shaping a country's internal political geography, especially in regard to internal divisions of states. When the French Revolution abolished the historical provinces, and organized rational, but artificial administrative subdivisions (*departments*), it was decided that the size of each unit should be determined by the consideration that each citizen should be able to visit the seat of the administration and to return to his home on the same day, after having attended to his business. The development of modern communication forms has since rendered this basis for the size of the *departments* meaningless. That they have survived, and that France's internal political geography is still basically unchanged, shows how well these units became established in French life. Ratzel in his time stressed the point that it is much easier to change internal borders than international

[17] *New York Times,* January 25, 1953.

ones, and gave a great number of examples.[18] It seems remarkable, therefore, how seldom such changes of interior boundaries occur, and then usually only under revolutionary or other unsettled conditions. In France, after World War II, when everything seemed unsettled, it was decided to replace these *departments* by larger administrative units, more in tune with technological advances and the need for larger economic grouping. However, before action was taken, life had reverted largely to the accustomed ruts and nothing was done.

It can be observed that within states subdivisions tend to be larger the thinner the population is spread. The western provinces of Canada, the northeastern subdivisions of the U.S.S.R., the southern regions of Algeria, are some of the best known examples. Such large subdivisions are characteristic of areas that lacked a dense indigenous population in the first stages of colonization. The western states of the United States were carved out of immense territories, such as the Northwest Territory and the Kansas Territory. In Brazil, a similar administrative pattern of more recent date is evident, following the progress of colonization. In the normal trend of consolidation, boundaries, local loyalties, and the pattern of administration become crystallized and no further subdivisions take place, or they occur only under extraordinary conditions, as in the separation of West Virginia from Virginia during the Civil War when these two states adhered to the Union and to the Confederacy respectively. Size as such is no sufficient motive to prompt the breaking-up of administrative units. Neither California nor Texas are expected to split into two or more states because of the large size of their territories. Thus the different size of subdivisions bears and maintains the imprint of conditions which prevailed when they were formed or which shaped them during a revolutionary period. The formative influence may have been that of railroads as when the mountain states were formed or that of carts and pack animals as when the New England states were colonized. The need for defense against sudden attacks across borders accounts for the creation of *marches,* that is, larger territorial units than the usual units such as counties or dukedoms. Relics of such medieval *marches* in England are the large counties along the Scottish and Welsh borders; similar *marches* existed in Eastern Germany, and survived as large political subdivisions to the end of World War II. They are the historical basis of the independent state of Austria.

Smaller political subdivisions are, generally, easier to change than large

[18] F. Ratzel, *Politische Geographie,* 3rd ed. (Munich, 1920).

ones. They command fewer emotional loyalties and in many states their functions are not important. As a rule, it has been easier to create new counties than to change state boundaries. It is true that local loyalties exist also in counties, but they exert influence only when they coincide with material benefits.[19] With the development of modern communications these cases have become rather infrequent.

On the other hand, larger units have increasingly come into being because they alone were able to cope efficiently with the complicated problems of modern economic life. The Tennessee Valley Authority is perhaps the best-known example of a large territorial unit created without replacing traditional state boundaries. The New York Port Authority is another example. In the international field the Caribbean Commission is one of several examples. It unites American, British, French, and Dutch possessions for explicitly defined social, economic, and cultural purposes.

None of these examples proves convincingly that there is a trend toward larger administrative units. In the Soviet Union the Communists replaced the large administrative divisions, the *gubernivas* and their subdivisions, the *volosts,* by *oblasts* and *rayons.* Industrialization and the increased need for political and economic administration and control led to a decrease in the size of these new subdivisions as compared with the subdivisions of Czarist Russia. This is another example showing how a revolution can overthrow traditional forms no longer fitted to modern conditions. While in the first decade of the Soviet state the boundaries of these *oblasts* and *volosts* remained flexible, the number of such transformations shows a decreasing trend as the U.S.S.R. acquires traditional values of its own.

Contradictory tendencies toward increasing and decreasing size can even be observed in the size of cities, despite the undeniable world-wide trends toward urbanization. Only a few years ago there seemed to be no question that cities were growing and that incorporation both of formerly rural areas and adjoining cities constituted a general and inevitable trend. Where older communities retained their separate existence, even if surrounded by a growing metropolitan area (such as Highland Park and Hamtramck in Detroit (Fig. 2-11), or Brookline in Boston), this was regarded as a temporary delay, which could be explained by special sociological factors. Even the actual shrinking of some cities by war destruction, as in Germany, or by revolutionary change, as in the case of Vienna

[19] Changes of voting districts, the so-called gerrymandering, does not quite belong in this category, as in many ways voting districts do not have a separate life or any function except during election time.

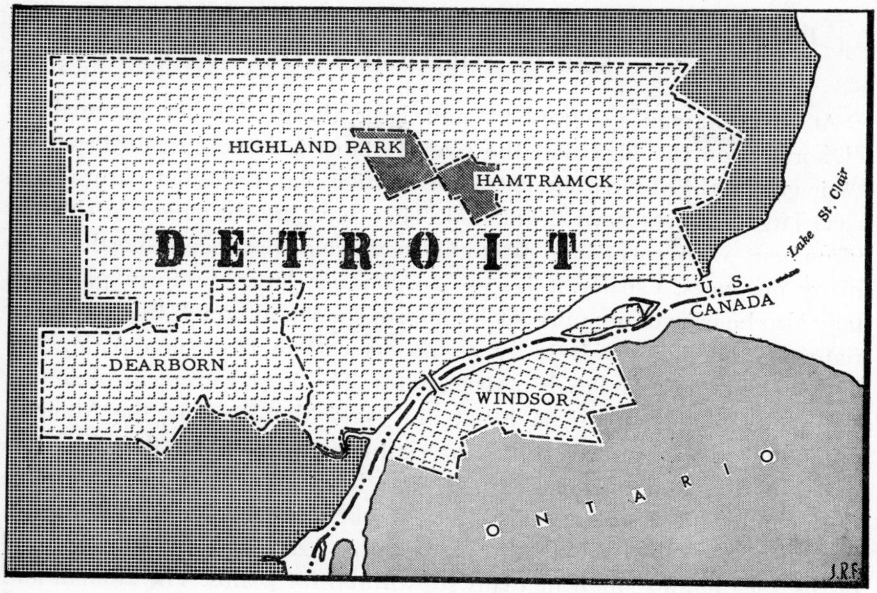

FIG. 2-11. Encircling Growth of Metropolitan Area: Detroit.

which lost its position as the capital of a great power, seemed not to contradict the general trend. This belonged in the same category as the destruction of Pompeii and St. Pierre by volcanoes, of Yokohama by earthquake. Only recently, and especially pronounced in England after the destruction caused by World War II, the construction of satellite towns around metropolitan agglomerations has set in. In most other countries such a tendency is still in the discussion stage. However, we witness in the United States a novel and recent trend by which suburbs are developing their own community life. Distance from the city centers, overcrowding of public transportation, lack of parking space, and so on, are the tangible causes. The development of suburban shopping centers and cultural facilities leads to the gradual transformation of "dormitory towns" into communities fulfilling all administrative and sociological functions of the cities. It is interesting to observe that, while this development goes on, larger territorial units are created for certain functions better served on a broad metropolitan basis. Such functions may be public services, as telephone, water, sewage, fuel distribution, or sanitary provisions. The United States' Census recognized the latter development in 1950 by establishing metropolitan areas and thus supplementing the census data usually obtained only along lines of incorporated city limits.

PHYSIOGRAPHIC FACTORS IN THEIR INFLUENCE ON THE SIZE OF POLITICAL UNITS

At first German geographers and later those of other nationalities elaborated on the idea that the size of states is largely conditioned by their geographical environment. On extensive plains without natural barriers large empires have developed. They have mushroomed in this environment with surprising rapidity; they have also been shortlived in many instances. Clearly it is easy to conquer large, uniform plains; it may also be easy to organize such uniform spaces, although this statement requires qualification. It is by no means certain that such plains will eventually be consolidated in large states. The East European plain and the Indo-Gangetic plain have not only seen the Russian, the Maurya, and the Mogul Empires, but also centuries of political division. The plains of the Sudan and of Inner Asia have supported large empires during relatively short periods only. No such empire has ever arisen in the Mississippi lowland. In the case of the Aztec state of Mexico, and of the Inca empire, high plateaus substituted for plains. The Roman and the Persian Empires are instances of large and long-lasting empires which did not develop around nuclei of large plains.

There are regions, especially in mountains and on islands, where small natural units such as valleys or basins tend to provide a good frame for small political units. These may be political units of secondary importance, such as the minute cantons of Switzerland, twenty-two of which co-exist in an area not larger than Massachusetts and New Hampshire combined. Or these units may be independent countries, such as the small states of the Himalayas, the Alps, or formerly of the Caucasus. Large conquering nations from the surrounding lowlands have been able occasionally to conquer these mountains, but the periods when these mountains belonged to large states were short in comparison with their long histories as small independent states. However, the Rocky Mountains and associated mountain systems will warn the political geographer to seek in these physiographic conditions more than a single favorable condition. In the mountainous American West not even the political subdivisions have tended to be small.[20] Of the ten independent republics of South America, three are small countries; however, only one of the

[20] Semple, *op. cit.*, p. 95, speaks of "28 different Indian stocks . . . between the Pacific coast and the eastern slope of the Sierra Nevada and Cascade Range," but she speaks neither of states, nor can her historical statement be used as an argument in political geography.

three, Ecuador, is a mountain country; neither Uruguay nor Paraguay are in the Andes.

It has been said that the existence of small or large political units is a function of physical geographic factors. This statement can be maintained only in a very generalized and qualified form. Latin America seems to present a good case for such a contention. Many small political units exist in the islands and the mountainous isthmus of Central America; several medium-sized states are in the Andine West; the only two large states are in the eastern plains of South America. Even the mountainous Central American islands are not entirely politically united. The partition of Hispaniola between Haiti and San Domingo may find some justification in both human and physical geography. However, this is largely a result of historical accident. History rather than physical geographic conditions will explain the irrational mosaic of the political map of the Lesser Antilles, or the division of tiny St. Martin between the Dutch and French. It may be said that the nature of small islands, like that of secluded mountain cantons, makes it easier to administer them as units than as parts of larger units. But no conclusion is warranted as to whether this unit should be an independent state, an autonomous region, or an administrative unit on the same level as other similar units.

Even such a limited dependency of the size of political units on physical geographic conditions can be established only for certain periods. The Greek islands were independent kingdoms in the time of Homer, they are not even administrative units today. It is undeniable that technological progress has made possible the consolidation of larger states, and within states, of larger divisions, leading to more efficient political and economic administration. Nevertheless, to establish a connection between technological progress and a trend promoting units of increasing size is possible only with numerous qualifications, as has been shown above. Despite technological progress there are also strong tendencies in the opposite direction. The size of political units and structures is shaped by the action and counteraction of all these diverse forces.

CHAPTER 3

Shape

CONTIGUOUS AND NONCONTIGUOUS STATE AREAS

While few people will question the political significance of the size of a state, many more will be in doubt as to whether its shape deserves special attention. The shape of a state is in many respects a haphazard characteristic without much significance. However, in other respects, shape has a definite meaning. An obvious example is the distinction between states which have a contiguous area and those which have not. The average educated person might be inclined on first sight to regard a state possessing a contiguous area as the normal form, and noncontiguous state territories as inherently weak. He will probably remember states consisting of noncontiguous areas (Fig. 3-1) because they are anomalous. Pakistan, with its outlier in East Pakistan, and Germany between 1919 and 1939, with its outlier in East Prussia, will come to mind. The latter has not survived, and was during its existence a continuous source of irritation and complaints. The soundness of the Pakistan solution has still to stand the test of history.

These two examples are widely known. Perhaps it is also still remembered that an attempt was once made to create the new state of Israel with several non-contiguous areas and that this attempt miscarried from its beginnings. Forgotten, except by a few specialists, are other conflicts such as those connected with the Portuguese area—often called an enclave —of Cabinda, north of the Congo mouth. As a result of the creation of the Congo state, Cabinda was separated from the main Portuguese colony of Angola.

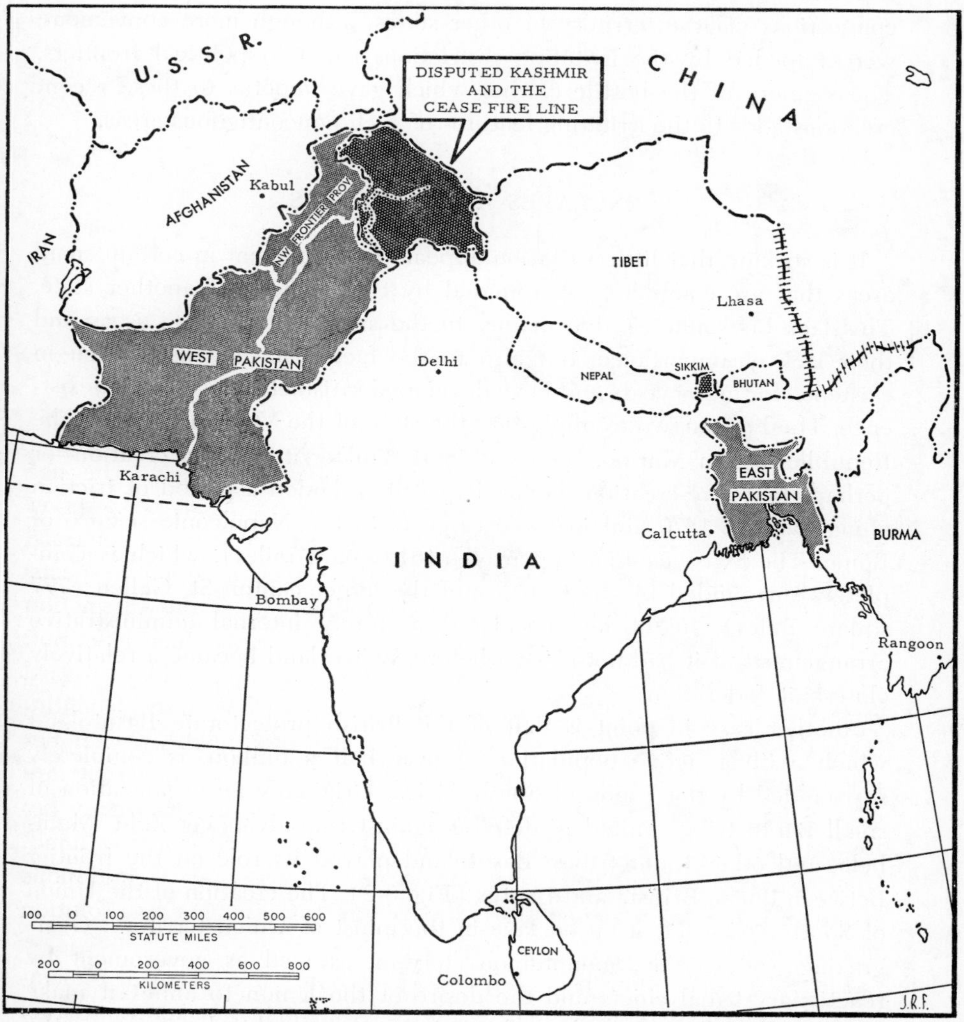

FIG. 3-1. Pakistan: A Non-contiguous State Area.

The German and Pakistan examples of noncontiguous territories have in common the fact that communication between their disconnected parts is possible by sea, that this connection is devious and slow, and that land connections via the territory of other states, although more convenient, were impeded by the irritating restrictions usual to political frontiers. The memory of the hostile clashes which gave impetus to these recent creations adds to the irritating features of such noncontiguous areas.

ENCLAVES AND EXCLAVES

It is striking that little irritation appears to be present in certain small areas that are completely surrounded by the territory of another state. This lack of conflict is due mainly to the smallness of these areas and their lack of importance, but also to the fact that they have been in existence for many years and have developed satisfactory ways of co-existence. The best known examples are the state of the Vatican City and the Republic of San Marino, both within Italian territory. The creation—or perhaps better re-creation—of the Papal State ended a period of friction going back to 1870 and in some respects to the Napoleonic seizure of Rome. The Swiss canton Appenzell (161 square miles), which is completely surrounded by the territory of the larger canton St. Gallen (777 square miles), might be considered a purely internal administrative arrangement, if it had not existed before Switzerland became a relatively close-knit federation.

Another case in point is that of the British protectorate Basutoland which, with a native population of over half a million, is completely surrounded by the Union of South Africa. Originally an organization of small Bantu tribes united in defense against the advancing Zulu, Matabele, and other Kaffir tribes, Basutoland played its role on the frontier between Boers, British, and Bantus (Fig. 3-2). The creation of the Union of South Africa left it an enclave in the midst of Union territory. Overgrazing, soil erosion, mountainous terrain, as well as government by reactionary tribal chiefs and the desire of the Union to annex it make the future of this unusual configuration rather doubtful. Similar is the position of Swaziland (with a population of close to 200,000), also a British protectorate. Although it borders with Portuguese Mozambique for a short distance, it is for all practical purposes an enclave and at the mercy of the Union of South Africa. The "Apartheid" segregation policy of the Union of South Africa government is increasingly changing the political map of this country into a checkerboard of white-man territory

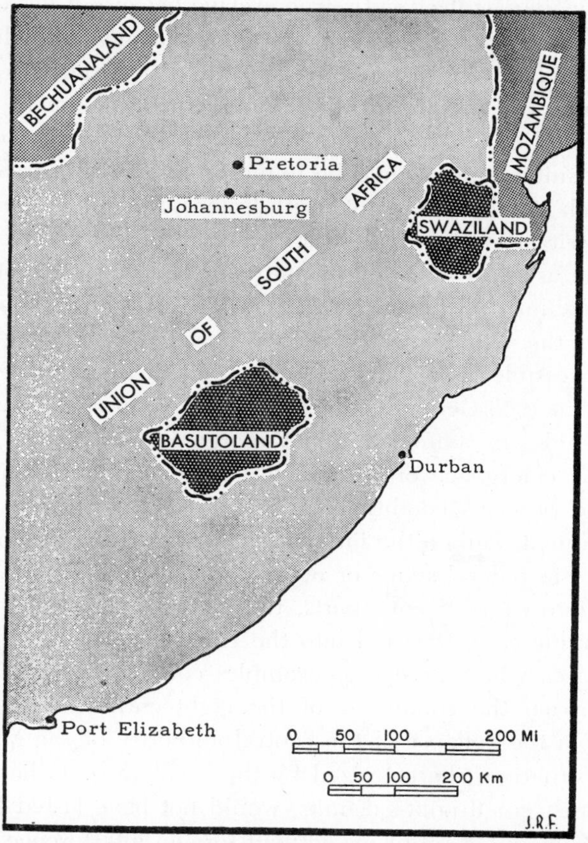

FIG. 3-2. Basutoland: An Enclave in the Union of South Africa.

and reserves and compounds of the native population. By strict regulations which require travel documents for African males who wish to move from district to district, or who want to leave their reserves, or want to enter a proclaimed labor area, the separation of white and native within the Union has been accomplished to a point where, internally, the native territory is composed of noncontiguous enclaves which are firmly and centrally supervised by the central government.

Other enclaves, because of their small area and the lack of international friction involved, are likely to escape notice. Within Swiss territory, Germany owns the tiny enclave of Büsingen east of Schaffhausen, and Italy the enclave of Campione on Lago di Lugano. Spain retains the enclave of Llivia in the Pyrenees. Even the tiny Portuguese possession of

Damão, its main part itself not a true exclave because it lies on the coast, includes two outlying territories, Dadara and Nagar Aveli, which are true enclaves in Indian territory and are separated from Damão by approximately six miles of Indian territory. A modern development is the Swiss airport of Basel which is an enclave near the French city of Mulhouse. Because no suitable area could be found on Swiss soil a treaty was concluded which left the sovereignty with France, but ceded the area for the airport to Switzerland in every other respect. Still less known because not recognizable as exclaves of one country or enclaves of another are the areas of Jungbluth and of the Kleine Walser Tal. They belong to Austria and seem on the map connected with it; however, due to high mountains they are accessible from Austria only via Germany territory. After the "Anschluss" in 1938 Germany annexed these two areas to Bavaria, which move was only an administrational reorganization under the circumstances. The emergence of Austria as an independent country in 1945 restored the previous conditions.

More frequent than on the international scene is the fragmented shape of provinces in federal states or other political subdivisions. In its fragmentation into some twenty parts, the German state of Braunschweig was an extreme case. It lasted into the Hitler period. India before 1948 is another area where numerous examples could be found. Here British rule had frozen the conditions of the eighteenth century, which had resulted from the collapse of the central authority of the Moghuls. This anarchical situation, characterized by the breakup of India into a crazy quilt of mostly small political units, would not have lasted long if India could have solved her problems without foreign interference. Baroda was split into five major and some thirty minor parts, some of them still surviving as exclaves of Bombay in the Saurashtra Union. Cases of fragmentation can be found elsewhere, even in countries that are generally and rightly regarded as uniform. In Spain the area of Ademuz is an outlier (in the province of Teruel) of the province of Valencia. In England, Dudley, a town of Worcestershire, is an outlier within Staffordshire.

Exclaves of one political unit are not necessarily enclaves in another—they do not always result in a perforated outline within the map of another political unit. It is not so in the case of East Prussia or of East Pakistan. On the other hand, the existence of enclaves does not necessarily imply that they are exclaves of another state. The City of the Vatican and San Marino are completely surrounded by Italian territory; they are true enclaves without being exclaves.

Two outstanding examples of enclaves in recent history are the cities of Berlin and Vienna, the latter until recently occupied by troops of the Western powers, and in part by Russian troops which also occupied the surrounding country while in Berlin the satellite East German state rules one half of the city and the surrounding country. Public services are common to both parts of these cities, and in Vienna the boundary was invisible most of the time for the natives. Throughout this period, Vienna remained still the capital of Austria and the Austrian government and parliament had their seat there. Vienna exerted also in other respects its central function. It was an exclave only for the Western occupying forces. As such it had the further anomaly that two airfields constituted tiny exclaves some distance from the city, administered by the British and Americans respectively.

West Berlin comes closer to the concept of a genuine exclave,[1] both for the occupation forces and for the (West) German Federal Republic. As its contacts with the surrounding territory have been more and more restricted, the boundary of West Berlin has become a true international boundary (Fig. 3-3).

Within provinces, counties, and so forth, perforation frequently results from the autonomous administration granted to urban centers in the midst of rural areas. This last feature is seldom noticed by the observer not directly concerned with local municipal problems and is hardly regarded as an anomaly. It may date as far back as those other truly anomalous configurations on the international map, but now such features emerge continuously as natural by-products of modern economic and political developments. Under the law of the Commonwealth of Virginia, settlements become incorporated cities with administration distinct from that of the county as soon as they attain a certain size. Similarly exclaves and enclaves have developed quite recently in rapidly growing metropolitan areas by incorporation of noncontiguous pieces of land for public utilities, or by the resistance of old established communities against incorporation (Fig. 2-11, p. 55).

In contrast to these developments are some exclaves which originated far back, in history in some cases several centuries. They are relics of what have become obsolete political concepts: princes acquired territories for their states in the same manner in which they would have acquired private property. As a result a political unit, like an estate or a farm, might consist of several unconnected parts. Like modern farmers, sover-

[1] G. W. S. Robinson, "West Berlin: The Geography of an Exclave," *Geographical Review*, Vol. 43 (October, 1953), pp. 541-557; P. Schöller, "Stadtgeographische Probleme des geteilten Berlin," *Erdkunde*, Vol. 7 (March, 1953), pp. 1-11.

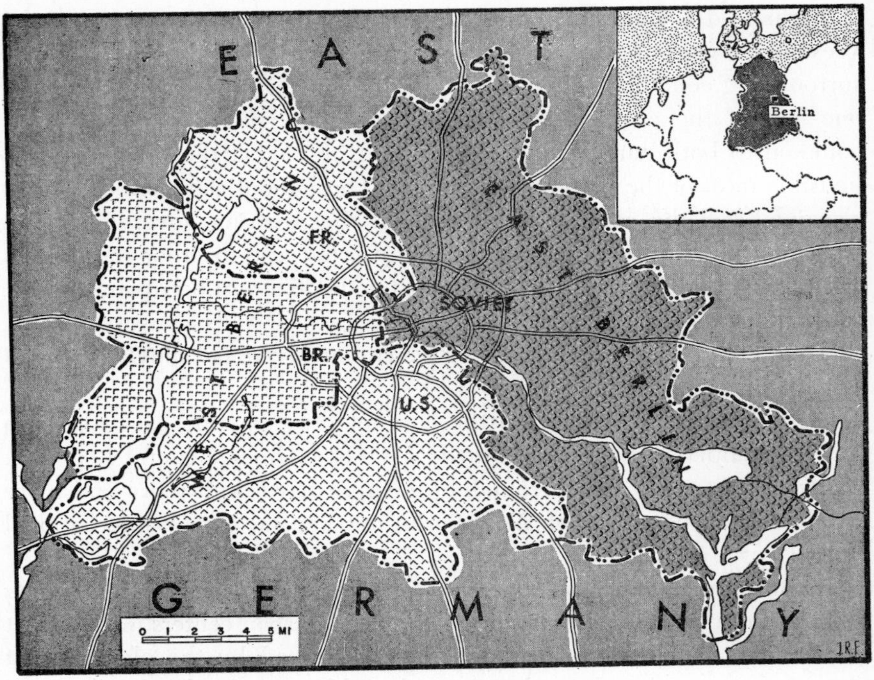

Fig. 3-3. Berlin: An Exclave.

eigns of such states might try to accomplish contiguity as a convenience, but not as a matter of principle. Under feudal conditions traveling from one property to another across "foreign territory" did not involve passports or, necessarily, customs. In other cases noncontiguous areas have been acquired by chance heritage, or in order to get a foothold in an area which was desired because of its richness. In time, a deliberate policy of acquiring connected territories was pursued. An example in the United States is the Western Reserve in present northern Ohio, belonging once to Connecticut. In Europe, history records many such incidents: e.g. the Hapsburgs, counts in northern Switzerland, became dukes of Austria far to the East. This acquisition was a by-product of the elevation of the first Rudolf to the royal throne and of the need to replace the domain lost during the preceding period of anarchy. The descendants of Rudolf I worked consciously to build a land bridge between Austria and their Swiss dominions. Carinthia and the Tyrol were acquired, but a gap remained and the Swiss territories were finally lost. More fortunate were the Hohenzollerns of Brandenburg who acquired outlying territories on the Rhine and in East Prussia by inheritance in the seventeenth century; they succeeded in forming a contiguous state territory extending from the Rhine to Memel after two centuries of struggle.

In the feudal age in Europe or India, or wherever a comparable stage existed, political allegiance was a personal matter and not a territorial one. The Germanic tribes and heirs of their legal concepts carried this idea to an extreme. Every person carried the laws of his origin with him. The same idea was modified in the system of "capitulations," according to which Europeans in many states of Asia and Africa, even if born there, could be tried only before the authorities of their country of origin. Only twenty years ago a map of Asia would show large areas where the sovereignty of the countries was not complete because of the extraterritorial status of foreigners. In the Byzantine Empire and later in Turkey it was customary for communities of non-Islamic faith to live in separate quarters under autonomous administration (*millet*). Following this custom, the privilege of living together was given to merchants coming from the same city, from Venice, Pisa, or Genoa. These quarters maintained their own separate laws and were often surrounded by a wall. They became a kind of territorial enclave. Turkey never relinquished sovereignty over such areas as did China and India over the factories of Portuguese, Dutch, and other Western European powers. Here finally the transition from the personal to territorial status was completed and enclaves developed.

The establishment of such extraterritorial trading posts signifies the beginnings of modern European colonial imperialism. These colonies distinguish modern empires, except the Russian Empire, from ancient empires in that they are characterized by a fragmented shape. Fragmentation of this kind comes clearly into focus when colonies shake off their colonial bonds and become independent partners. Then the manifold problems of dependent outlying possessions are superseded by the problem of equal rights under different conditions. This has led to the breaking away of the American republics from England, Spain, and Portugal, and in our time threatens with dissolution the British Commonwealth of Nations in many parts of the world.

The nineteenth and twentieth century concept of nationalism has had a strong influence in changing the shape of many states as well as in determining what constitutes a desirable or undesirable shape. Two major instances of fragmented shape are mentioned above, East Prussia and East Pakistan. If the concept of nationalism were applied consistently to shaping of state territories it could become of immense importance in federal states such as those of the Soviet Union. But despite the Soviet's proclaimed adherence to the principle of national autonomy, economic advantages of contiguous areas weighed heavier in shaping the federated autonomous and constituent republics. Even the subordination of Nakhitchevan to the noncontiguous Azerbaijan Soviet Republic does not really contradict this fact, as Nakhitchevan is a mountain canton having little contact with neighboring Soviet Armenia.[2]

ISLAND STATES

In a looser sense, noncontiguous states are also those states the territory of which is composed partially or entirely of islands. Where such islands are coastal islands, or clearly belong to one group, as do the four main islands of Japan, lack of contiguity of the political area is hardly felt. Where islands are no more than—usually—three miles distant from the mainland or each other, they are legally contiguous, because they are still within the so-called territorial waters. Norway, with its numerous coastal islands, offers a good illustration.[3] Groups of islands such as the Tonga Islands, the Hawaiian Islands, the Azores, and many others also form obvious units, although the distance between individual islands may be scores of miles. It does not matter whether such groups have a history of political unity—as do the Hawaiian Islands and the still functioning kingdom of the Tonga Islands—or whether they have attained political unity only since they were "discovered"—as have the Cape Verde Islands and the Azores.

Large bodies of intervening water constitute a problem which is aggravated if other sovereignties are actually nearer to the outlying area than the country to which it officially belongs.

The long-drawn discussions concerning statehood for Hawaii and Alaska are an example. Though other issues, such as the racial composition and political party inclinations of the inhabitants may be the main cause for delay in extending statehood, these factors would not carry weight in a contiguous area. On the other hand, the Azores are regarded by Portugal as an integral part of the mainland. France even regards northern Algeria as part of metropolitan France.

[2] A few small autonomous oblasts, those of the Adyge, Cherkess, and Nagornot-Karabakh, are enclaves in other administrative units. The two national Okrugs, the Aginskoye Buryat-Mongol and the Ust-Ordyn Buryat-Mongol, are actually exclaves of the Buryat-Mongol autonomous Soviet Socialist Republic.

[3] Norway, like all the Scandinavian countries, claims a belt of five nautical miles as territorial waters.

THE FACTOR OF COMPACTNESS

In countries which include island territories and yet constitute a fairly compact unit—such as Great Britain, Japan, the Philippines, and to some extent Greece, Denmark, and Norway—contact between islands or between island and mainland may be easier than between adjacent parts of the continental territory. Intercourse was never difficult across the Aegean Sea between the Greek Islands and Greece. Even continental parts of Greece are today in many cases more easily accessible by boat than by mountain trails or winding roads. Similar conditions exist in the Japanese Islands, where contacts across the Inland Sea are easy and were so before the age of railroads. Yeddo, the northernmost island, though separated by the narrow Strait of Hakodate, was joined to the other islands very late because, among other reasons, navigation across the strait was difficult under the frequently adverse weather conditions. On the other hand, intercourse over land routes becomes a difficult problem in countries where deserts take the place of a dividing ocean. Such deserts are the Sahara between French North Africa and the Sudan, and the Inner Asian deserts between Russia proper and Turkestan. In these areas maps which do not stress physical features are misleading. Physical factors play a part in much smaller countries over short distances. Until a few years ago, Vorarlberg, the westernmost province of Austria, could not be reached directly from the rest of the country when snow blocked the pass route over the Arlberg. Similarly, the canton Tessin was separated from the rest of Switzerland when the St. Gotthard pass was closed. In all these cases only modern communications have rendered the apparent compactness a reality. Powerful governments had also in other cases to develop and protect communications across difficult terrain such as mountains, forests, and deserts. However, only constant vigilance and investment of capital can keep open such routes.

CIRCUM-MARINE STATES

Under such conditions it would hardly be justifiable to overlook the role of sea transportation in defining the idea of a compact state. It makes understandable the fact that circum-marine states can have a fundamental compactness. We can envisage the ancient Roman Empire as a compact unit, with the Mediterranean Sea as an integral part, if we take into consideration that sea lanes in general were more efficient in antiquity than land routes, until the Romans built their military road-net. If we

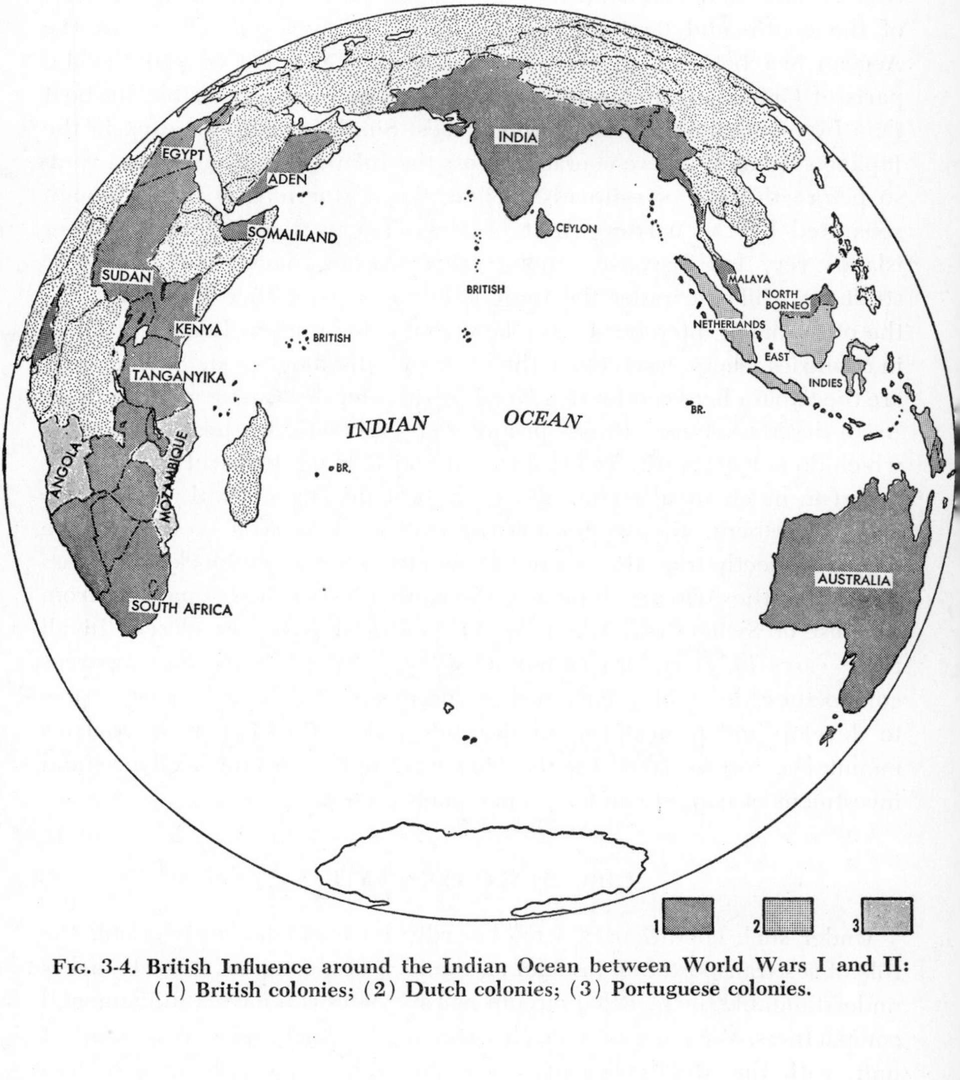

Fig. 3-4. British Influence around the Indian Ocean between World Wars I and II: (1) British colonies; (2) Dutch colonies; (3) Portuguese colonies.

insist on regarding only the terra firma as constituent part of the Roman Empire, one of the oddest shaped territories would emerge. The same is true for other circum-marine empires, such as the former Swedish empire around the Baltic Sea, and the Turkish empire around the Black Sea and eastern Mediterranean. In this category belong even countries of shape as familiar as the British dominion around the Irish Sea, and in the Middle Ages the British realm on both sides of the British Channel. In modern times such circum-marine empires have become rare. The British domination, between the two World Wars, of most coastal territories around the Indian Ocean is the most recent example, especially if one regarded the Dutch and Portuguese colonies, though nominally belonging to foreign independent states, as practically at the disposal of the British (Fig. 3-4). Today this circum-Indic empire is rapidly dissolving, and the dominions, despite their official ties to the Commonwealth, are apparently less closely bound to the policy of the United Kingdom. Their territory is not as unquestionably at Britain's disposal as those Portuguese and presumably also Dutch foreign colonies once were. The only true circum-marine state of today is Indonesia, a state around the Java Sea (Fig. 3-5). Its peculiar character is underlined by the lack of railroads and highways on all islands except Java. Indonesia is dependent upon sea lanes.[4]

SHAPE AFFECTED BY A STRATEGIC BASES CONTROL SYSTEM

These circum-marine empires have been superseded by a different type of control based on the possession of skillfully selected and strategically distributed bases.[5] The Mediterranean became a British sea as the result of a combination of these bases with political controls. Britain acquired Gibraltar in 1704, the Maltese islands in 1800, and Cyprus in 1878. These footholds were augmented by two powerful political supports—political control of Egypt from 1882 to 1936, fortified by the military base in the Suez Canal zone, and "a skilful diplomacy which produced allies and neutrals within the Mediterranean basin." [6] These factors are what made the Mediterranean a British sea in the nineteenth century, not territorial possessions along the Mediterranean shore. In the post-World War II world, the growing threat of airpower and submarines has altogether

[4] W. G. East and O. H. K. Spate, *The Changing Map of Asia* (London, 1950), p. 217.

[5] See also pp. 70, 157.

[6] W. G. East, "The Mediterranean: Pivot of Peace and War," *Foreign Affairs,* Vol. 32 (1953), p. 623.

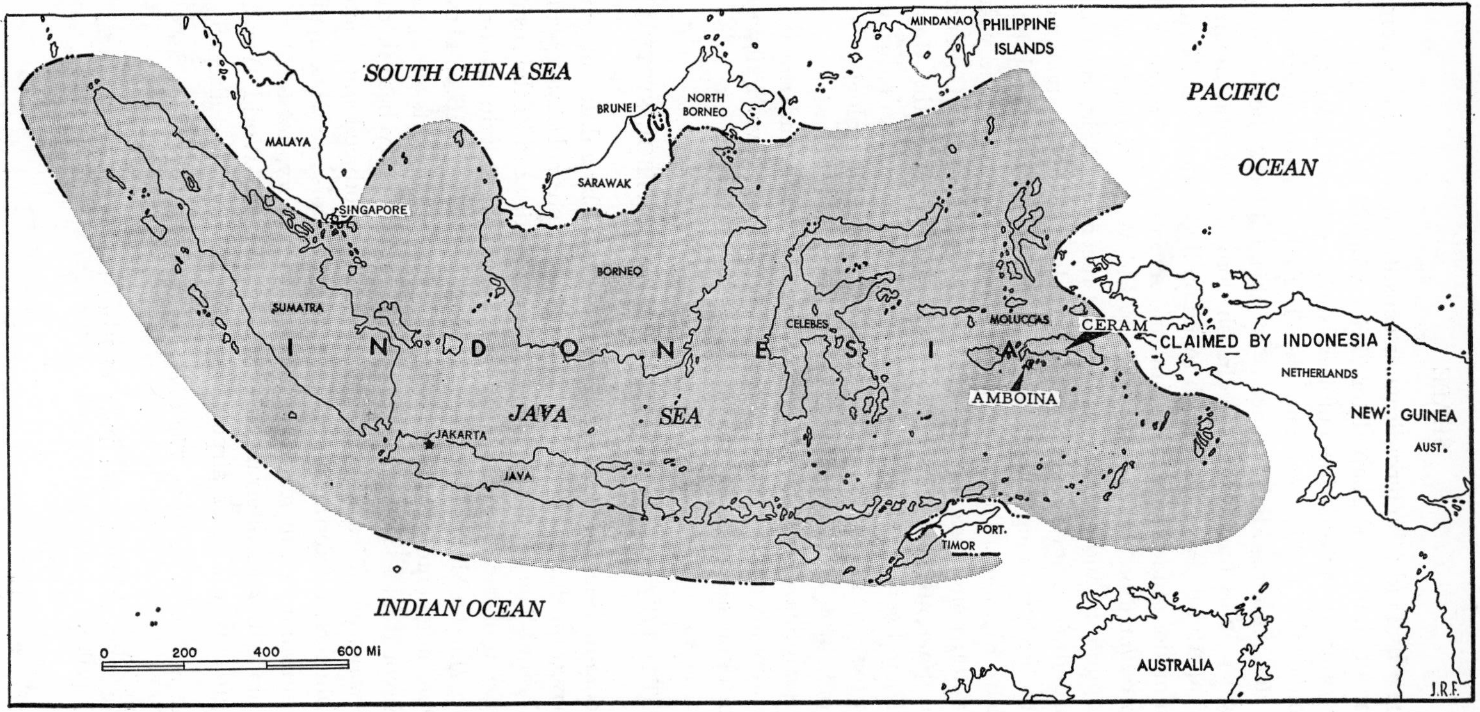

FIG. 3-5. Indonesia, an Example of a Contemporary Circum-marine State.

changed the role of the Mediterranean area, especially of the Mediterranean-Red Sea route, in world affairs. In recognition of these basic changes, we witness today the evolution of a new circum-Atlantic power combination of the NATO countries in which the United States and Britain are the main partners, and which is based on a broad European and African defense. The American Mediterranean, the Caribbean Sea, is dominated by the United States from Puerto Rico, the Virgin Islands, Guantanamo on Cuba, Panama, and the leased bases on Trinidad, in British Guiana, on Jamaica, the Bahamas, Antigua, and St. Lucia (Fig. 3-6). An American Pacific dominion is taking shape, with Okinawa and the bases on the Philippines as westernmost outposts. The Soviet Union has tried to create a Baltic dominion, more in the form of the older empires, occupying all coasts from Leningrad to Rügen, but also using the bases concept by the acquisition of Porkkala-Udd on the Finnish coast, which, however, was returned to Finland in 1956.

THE VALUE OF SHAPE

Political and military geographers have tried to blame certain unhappy events in the history of some countries on the shape of their territories. In recent decades it was fashionable to compare such states as France and Czechoslovakia and explain the relative stability of the French state by its compact, almost pentagonal shape, and blame the endangered position of Czechoslovakia on its elongated form.

Even if it were possible to separate the factors which make for the stability or instability of France and Czechoslovakia, and to isolate the influence of shape in itself, this influence would still need explanation. There was a time when French kings felt that their country was surrounded by Spanish-Hapsburg possessions and that in order to break the threatening encirclement it would be advisable to acquire territory in Italy, which would indeed create a tongue-like extrusion from the compact area of France, but would make encirclement more difficult. Similarly, the Czechs felt that a compact Bohemian state (plus Moravia) would be in constant danger because of being surrounded by the territories of two German-speaking countries, Germany and Austria, whereas the odd-looking eastern extension through Slovakia and Podkarpatská Rus would provide territorial contact between the main part of their country and a friendly power (Rumania), bring their territory into close proximity to another potential ally against Germany (U.S.S.R.), and give them a long boundary with another Slavic state (Poland).

FIG. 3-6. The Caribbean Sea: An American Mediterranean.

It seems fair to state that shape in itself has little meaning, but that it has to be taken into consideration as one factor which, together with other factors, constitutes the political geography of a country.

The problem of shape is especially devoid of meaning if it is regarded as a problem of geometrical shape. The claim that a compact and, ideally, a circular shape is the best for the safety of a country is a theoretical deduction without confirmation in experience. The only meaningful question is, whether and in how far the political shape parallels certain natural features and factors of human geography. Chile and Norway have an extremely elongated shape, more so than Czechoslovakia, but both have displayed a persistency and stability of shape less subject to changes throughout the centuries than the compact outline of France. Before World War II the idea of boundaries along natural features was much used and misused; recently it has been too much discounted. Norway, Chile, an island state such as Iceland, or a mountain state surrounded by deserts such as Ethiopia or Yemen, are largely congruent with a natural geographical region—Norway and Chile to a slightly lesser degree. Where Norway reaches in the southeast across the mountains, it includes all Norwegian-speaking areas. Czechoslovakia did not attain this unity, its physiographic features almost nowhere being congruent with the areas of languages and nations in this area. For this reason, and only for this reason, its elongated shape is so vulnerable. The same problem of vulnerability has arisen in Spain, and for the same reason, although it is an outstanding example of adaptation to physiographic features. Spain had to wrestle with repeated attempts at dismemberment in its Catalonian and Basque provinces. Its human geography does not fit its theoretically perfect shape.

"FORWARD POINTS OF GROWTH"

A shape often regarded as a handicap to the economic development and military safety of countries is that involving an area connected with the bulk of a country only by a narrow neck of land. Such shapes have been compared with peninsulas and promontories. An outstanding example of such a shape, and of its almost perennially endangered position is that part of Sinkiang known as Chinese Turkestan. For long periods this area was connected with the main bulk of the Chinese Empire only by the narrow corridor of semidesert Kansu between the desert of Gobi and the mountains of Tibet. Some geographers have spoken in this connection of a prorupted shape.[7] At one time, long ago, this area

[7] C. L. White and G. T. Renner, *Human Geography* (New York, 1948), p. 588.

was acquired by China as a base for further westward penetration. German geographers, and not only those of the geopolitical school, spoke therefore in this connection of *Wachstumspitzen*—"forward points of growth." They compared such forms with the shoots of plants, or even with the advance force of an army. Thus, instead of indicating weakness, it appears that such "proruptions" may under certain conditions signify an aggressive vitality. If one looks at the former Chinese forward points of growth through Chinese glasses, from China's core area, one understands how, under changed political conditions, such areas can become political liabilities and economic liabilities as well. This is especially true in the absence of rail and road communications, without which overland outposts can scarcely be an integral part of a core area. Sinkiang (which has twice the area of France but a population of only about four million) illustrates the withering-away of the "forward point of growth" when an expanding neighboring power (the U.S.S.R.) drives its railroad and highway net closer to the disputed area, in an effort to expand.

The case of Kashmir has been interpreted as an illustration of a "forward point of growth or aggression" being established against the resistance of a competing power, in this case Pakistan. It may well be that this is rather an attempt to hold on to a "point" which has high emotional value and might serve as a sensitive observation post in an area where Pakistan, the U.S.S.R., Chinese Sinkiang, and Afghanistan meet. As a *Wachstumspitze,* the value is probably very small, because communication from Pathankot, the nearest important station of India, to the valley of Kashmir leads across extremely high, roadless passes that are closed by snow many months of the year.

The tiny princely state of Sikkim (2,745 square miles; population in 1951, 137,000; *cf.* Fig. 3-1) offers another example of how such a "forward point of growth" degenerates into a proruption which is hard to defend. Pointing like an arrowhead toward Tibet (470,000 square miles; population about three million), the Himalayan mountain state dominates the main trade route between India and Tibet and thus is the gateway to Tibet. From here the British made their successful attempts to win entry into Tibet. Today its demographic composition, linguistically and religiously closely related to Chinese-held Tibet, makes it a weak point in the Indian perimeter. On the other hand, the example of the prosperous and democratic Indian protectorate may make itself felt in poverty-stricken Tibet. The successful agrarian and tax reform in Sikkim, which superseded absolute rule and oppression by autocratic landholders, provides

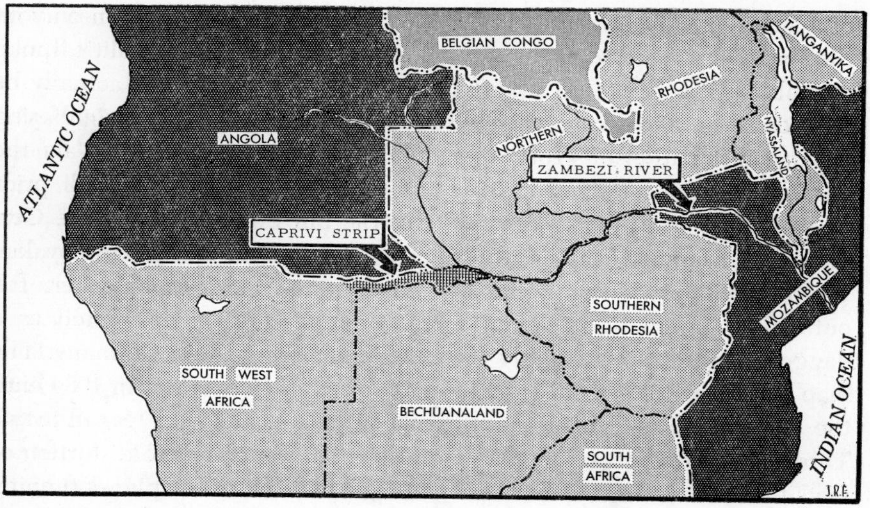

Fig. 3-7. Portuguese and German Expansion in Central Africa.

arguments against Communism in the ideological struggle over the future of Tibet.

In some instances, proruptions have been intentionally created for purposes of aggression. Several examples of this are the so-called Caprivi strip, which extends as a narrow strip from the northeastern corner of Southwest Africa—a German colony, when it was devised—to the Zambesi river; Portuguese Mozambique expanded inland along the Zambesi at about the same period in order to meet Portuguese colonization advancing from the Angola West African coast (Fig. 3-7); the narrow coastal landscape of Tenasserim, a southern extension of the then British Burma toward the northward-growing Malay States and Straits Settlements offers another illustration; the Alaskan panhandle, recording the Russian advance toward California, is an example from America.

In each of these cases the *Wachstumspitze,* the forward point of growth or of aggression, lost its essential character at the time when the core area and its people underwent basic changes, or when their outlook toward the forward point was reversed. The Alaskan panhandle is an illustration; its quality as a *Wachstumspitze* vanished when Russia lost interest in American expansion.

All these examples should make it abundantly clear that the same shape may indicate an area of weakness or a forward point of growth or even of aggression. The answer cannot be found by focusing attention only on the shape of a political region. Configurations which on the political map resemble a *Wachstumspitze* may be not only a relic, but may actually be the result of a flanking or encirclement movement of a neighboring expansionist nation or group of nations. This is best illustrated by the unhappy spatial relationship in which Czechoslovakia found itself prior to 1939 in regard to Germany and Austria, but especially after the Germans had occupied Austria, thus closing the pincers on Czechoslovakia. To the uninformed, or politically misinformed German onlooker, the outflanked or almost encircled small country could be presented as a dagger pointing threateningly toward the encircling Nazi Germany. The map published in General Haushofer's *Journal of Geopolitics* in 1934 with the caption "Ein Kleinstaat Bedroht Deutschland" (A Small State Threatens Germany) offers a good illustration of a complete distortion of facts by abusing the map as a weapon. The umbrella of airplanes fanning out from the alleged *Wachstumspitze* of Czechoslovakia brought home to the Germans, fed by the geopolitical propaganda of the Third Reich, what seemed to be an imminent danger of German cities being bombed by the air force of Czechoslovakia. Haushofer did not stop to think of how the same map, with a reversed air-umbrella, would impress the citizens of the small nation which was watching helplessly while the ominously progressing flanking expansion of the Third Reich reached out for more and more *Lebensraum* (living space) (Fig. 3-8).

Clearly the mere shapes of Czechoslovakia and Germany on the political map of Central Europe do not supply the answer to the question of whether and where in their spatial relationships forward points of aggression can be detected. The answer can be found only if one weighs the manifold historical, cultural, ethnic, and economic factors which have contributed to the spatial relationship of neighboring nations and have become crystallized, even temporarily, in what the map reveals as odd-shape relations. It should be added that the study of mere physical expansion deals with but part of the problem. The policy of flanking or encirclement can be carried out by means of physical expansion or by the conclusion of treaties or alliances.[8] The case of Czechoslovakia is not an unusual one. Historical geography supplies many similar illustrations of basic changes of the political map as the result of flanking movements of expanding powers. The Mongolian advance on India, the Roman drive toward western Germany show the aggressor nations in

[8] N. J. Spykman and A. A. Rollins, "Geographic Objectives in Foreign Policy," *American Political Science Review* (1939), p. 394.

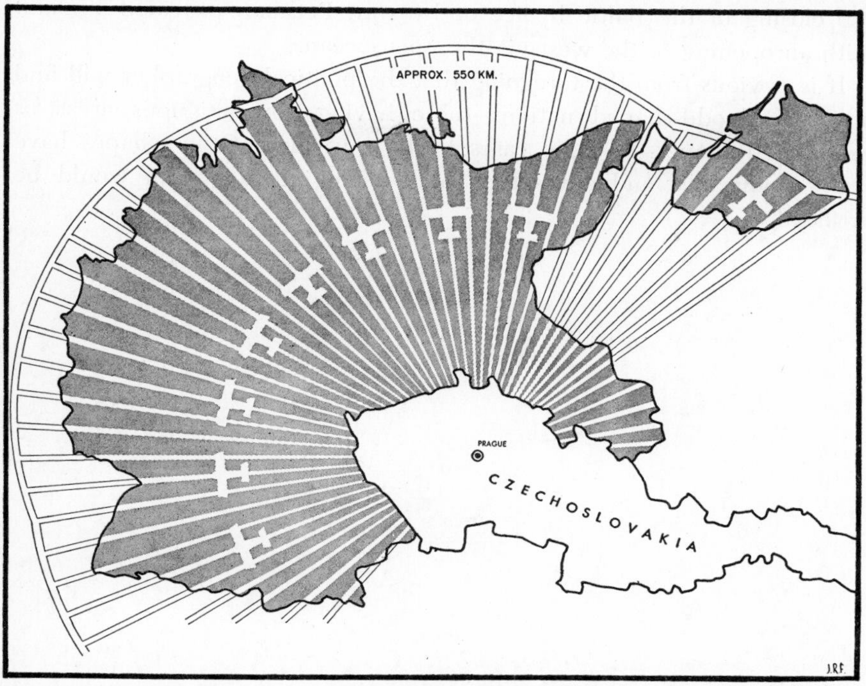

FIG. 3-8. The Map as a Weapon of Geopolitics: Czechoslovakia, a "Threat" to Nazi Germany.

their flanking operations against the attacked nations, just as classical encirclement moves can be seen in the drives of Carthage, and later Rome, against the Iberian peninsula, and of the Romans against the Germans.[9]

If a forward point serves the purpose of establishing contact with another area it is called a corridor. Such corridors have been established by Colombia and Bolivia in order to win access to the Amazon and the Parana rivers. Neither of these corridors so far has attracted much traffic. Far more important, both politically and economically, was the Polish corridor, designed to serve as a real corridor between landlocked Poland and the sea in the period between the two World Wars. A large part of Poland's overseas traffic passed through this corridor to Danzig and Gdynia, as well as some traffic which would have gone more directly over land routes but thereby would have had to cross foreign territory. A similar function was served by the Finnish corridor of Petsamo, which opened a route to the fishing grounds of the Arctic Sea. In the event of

[9] O. Maull, *Politische Geographie* (Berlin, 1925), p. 96.

the closing of the Baltic by ice or by war, Petsamo provided Finland with an opening to the west via the open ocean.

It is obvious from the foregoing that the political geographer will find a study of odd-shaped nations—those having noncontiguous areas or extenuated shapes—in some cases fairly rewarding. Other shapes have little significance and any effort to fit them into a system would be artificial.

CHAPTER 4

The Nature and Functions of Boundaries

BOUNDARY LINES AND BOUNDARY ZONES

We have discussed political units under the tacit assumption that they were bordered by sharp, definite boundaries. This is a condition which applies at present, at least in theory, to most political boundaries. Yet it is in sharp contradistinction to conditions which existed in most of Europe in the past and in some non-European continents into the twentieth century. Frontier zones, belts of no man's land, and even overlapping sovereignties were then the rule. A rather extensive literature [1] deals with the development of boundary lines out of such zones or related vague features. Somewhat less attention has been paid to the development of boundary lines from old property, especially field boundaries. The Romans

[1] No complete list of publications on this subject shall be given. Among the more important are S. B. Jones, *Boundary-Making* (Washington, 1945); P. de Lapradelle, *La Frontière* (Paris, 1927); O. Lattimore, *Inner Asian Frontiers of China* (New York, 1939); S. W. Boggs, *International Boundaries* (New York, 1940); K. Haushofer, *Grenzen* (Berlin, 1927); O. Maull, *Politische Geographie* (Berlin, 1925); J. Ancel, *La géographie des frontières* (Paris, 1927); R. Hartshorne, "Geography and Political Boundaries in Upper Silesia," *Annals of the Association of American Geography*, Vol. 23 (1933), pp. 195 ff.; E. Fischer, "On Boundaries," *World Politics*, Vol. 1, No. 2 (January, 1949), pp. 196-222; G. N. Curzon of Kedleston, *Frontiers*, 2nd ed. (Oxford, 1908); J. Sölch, *Die Auffassung der natürlichen Grenzen in der wissenschaftlichen Geographie* (Innsbruck, 1924); Thomas Holdich, *Political Frontiers and Boundary Making* (London, 1916); C. B. Fawcett, *Frontiers* (Oxford, 1918); A. E. Moodie, *Geography Behind Politics*, Ch. 5, "Frontiers and Boundaries" (London, 1947); A. Melamid, "The Economic Geography of Neutral Territories," *Geographical Review*, Vol. 45 (July, 1955).

in the time of the republic used the plow to draw the boundary (limes) of a newly founded colony or city. With the development of the Roman city-state into a territorial state the concept of strict delimitation spread and became basic in Roman law. Though these problems will be mentioned, wherever pertinent, the main interest in this chapter is not the historical development of the boundary line, but rather the description of the presently existing boundary lines, their functions and problems. A later chapter will deal with boundary zones in the political conflicts of nations today. Although we maintain that there is a basic difference between boundary lines and boundary zones, we shall not insist on regarding as boundary lines only the mathematical line of one dimension. For all practical purposes a wooden barrier, having a width of a few inches, a grassy path between fields, having a width of a few feet, or even a lane cut into a forest, having a width of a few yards, are boundary lines. Boundary zones exist only where the space between two countries is wide enough to permit man to live within it, either actually or potentially. In lands that are inhabited by sedentary populations, this distinction is satisfactory. In the rapidly shrinking areas of nomadism, this distinction between boundary zones and boundary lines may lead to border incidents, or at least account for a gradual transition from a zone to a line. It is sufficiently accurate to serve as definition.

There is another difference between the boundary line and the boundary zone. The latter is almost always a feature which has developed from the conditions of contact between adjacent countries. In the few cases where a boundary zone has been determined by law, actually three internationally recognized units exist, sharply divided from each other by boundary lines. An example of this is the zones of the Pays de Gex and of Haute Savoie surrounding the Swiss canton of Geneva, which are outside of the French customs boundary and subject to Swiss military occupation in wartime, though in all other respects being genuine parts of the French republic.

On the other hand, a boundary line is always a legally established and defined feature, though its legality may not have found recognition in international law. The United States has declared that it does not recognize the incorporation of the three Baltic States, Lithuania, Latvia, and Estonia, into the Soviet Union, nor does it recognize several other boundaries drawn after World War II. Nevertheless, these boundary lines exist and function as instituted by Soviet action and Soviet law, unaffected by international recognition or nonrecognition. The boundaries of the Baltic

States function today as internal, or purely administrative boundaries, and have been changed in some parts.

TYPES OF BOUNDARIES

We have, therefore, to distinguish several types of boundaries: (1) boundaries that are recognized in international law, as is normal with most boundaries; (2) boundaries that are recognized only by some countries, especially by both adjacent countries. (*a*) This may be the result of a shift of the boundary without altering its legal character. The eastern boundary of Poland and the northeastern boundary of Rumania are such boundaries. (*b*) On the other hand, the boundaries of the Baltic countries are regarded by the United States as *de jure* international boundaries, but are *de facto* and according to the legal concept of the Soviet Union internal boundaries. The practical effects of such a nonrecognition are very restricted, and will pertain to passport procedures, immigration practice, and similar functions. The term "disputed boundaries" is correct for these boundaries, but applies in general usage rather to (3) *de facto* boundaries, the legality of which is not recognized by one of the adjacent countries. Parts of the Ecuadorian-Peruvian boundary and of the Indian-Chinese boundary belong in this category. Often the two adjacent countries claim two different lines as correct, of which only one exists *de facto* (the disputed boundary), while (4) the other can be found on maps but has no counterpart in the field. Such a fictitious boundary is the boundary between Germany and Poland as it existed before 1939 and is still regarded by the nations of the West as legally valid until such time as a peace treaty may change it (Fig. 4-1). Most American maps show this line and designate the territory west of it as under Polish administration. On Polish maps, and on maps printed in countries which are emotionally less involved in this conflict, this boundary has disappeared.

Both the *de facto* and the claimed boundary may be recognized or not by third powers, strengthening thereby the legal and political position of one of the contesting countries, but not immediately affecting the material situation. In Trieste from 1946 to 1954 there existed three boundary lines (*cf*. Fig. 2-2). One, claimed by Italy, incorporated the whole territory of Trieste, including areas administered by Yugoslavia. *De facto* this is an internal boundary. Another part of the boundary line divided Yugoslav territory from that administered by Great Britain and the United States, though claimed by Italy. A third boundary, which separated the

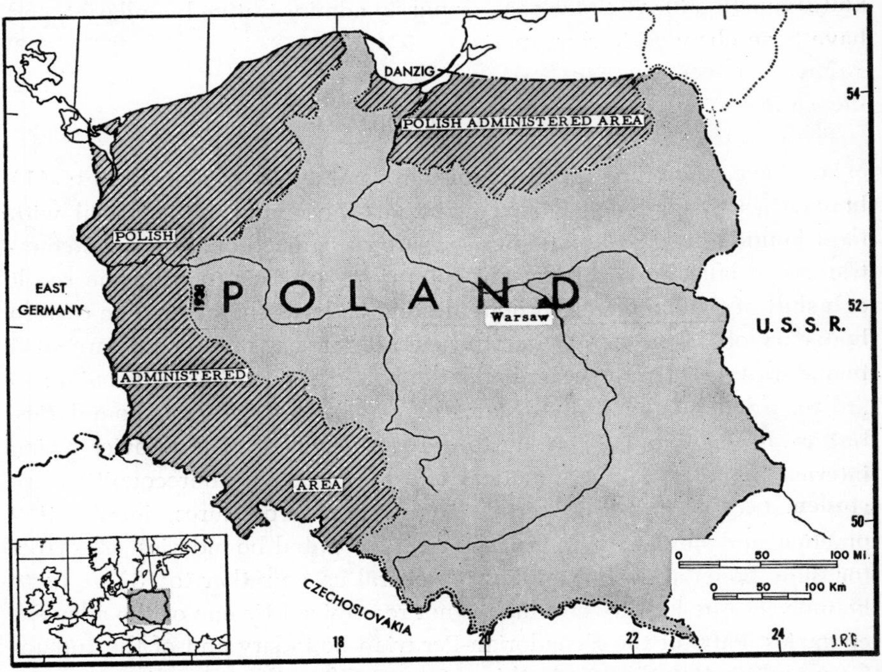

FIG. 4-1. The Boundaries of Poland since World War II.

same territory from Italy, was a *de facto* boundary, but with a different status in the eyes of the different powers. The occupying powers regarded it as a fully recognized international boundary. The Yugoslavs agreed to its designation as an international boundary, but claimed it as their own and not that of a Free Territory of Trieste. The Italians finally regarded it at best as a temporary *de facto* demarcation line which has no legal standing as boundary. In the same category belongs the 38th parallel in Korea which served as a *de facto* boundary from 1945 to 1951; all participants regarded it as a temporary solution, an armistice line rather than a boundary.

Claimed (fictitious) boundaries are also those on the Antarctic continent; [2] but it can hardly be said that they run through a foreign territory as all claims are equally theoretical and none fully recognized internationally (Fig. 4-2). The United States has not recognized the claims of several states on Antarctic territories. Great Britain, Australia, New Zealand, France, Norway, Argentina, and Chile have made such territorial claims

[2] *Cf.* L. Martin, "The Antarctic Sphere of Interest," H. W. Weigert and V. Stefansson, eds., *New Compass of the World* (New York, 1949), pp. 61 ff. (71-73).

and fixed by proclamation exact boundary lines. Those of the five first-named countries have been mutually recognized, while in the case of the Palmer Peninsula, where Britain, Argentina, and Chile are established, these three countries continue to dispute their mutual claims.

These Antarctic sectors have their counterpart in the Arctic. Here, however, it is not the discovery of uninhabited territories which forms the basis of claims, but an extension of the areas of the countries surrounding the Arctic Sea. Though in a different form and more or less assertive, Canada, Denmark, Norway, and the Soviet Union rely on the "sector principle" (*cf.* Fig. 5-4, p. 126). Only the Soviet Union went so far as to fix the boundaries of its Polar possessions in accordance with the sector principle, by decree of April 15, 1926.[3]

The sector principle serves as a good illustration of the intimate relationship which exists, particularly in the realm of boundary problems, between basic concepts of international law and political geography. The student of political geography is concerned mainly with the definition of the area between the base line which links the meridians of longitude marking the limits of its frontiers in the east and in the west, and which extends as far north as the final intersection of those meridians in the Pole: this is the geographical definition of the sector principle as primarily a geometric method to measure the geographical extent of a sovereignty claim in the Arctic. To understand the legal, or quasi-legal, foundation of this principle one has to turn to basic principles of international law. The sector principle, legally, is an expression of basic concepts of sovereignty resting firmly upon geographical foundations, or supposed to rest on them. Sovereignty over a territory presupposes normally that a state exercises authority over certain territory. Normally, this authority is established and maintained by what is called "effective occupation." In extension of this principle, attempts have been made to establish sovereignty by contiguity; this concept has been used mainly to determine if islands which are relatively close to the shores of a country should belong to the country controlling the shores in virtue of their geographical location. The sector principle represents a further expansion of the contiguity principle.

If one realizes these features of international law which are at the bottom of the sector principle, it is not difficult to find that a basic difference exists between the Arctic and the Antarctic in regard to the sector

[3] E. Plischke, "Sovereignty and Imperialism in the Polar Regions," reprinted in H. and M. Sprout, *Foundations of National Power,* 2nd ed. (N. Y., 1951), pp. 727, 729.

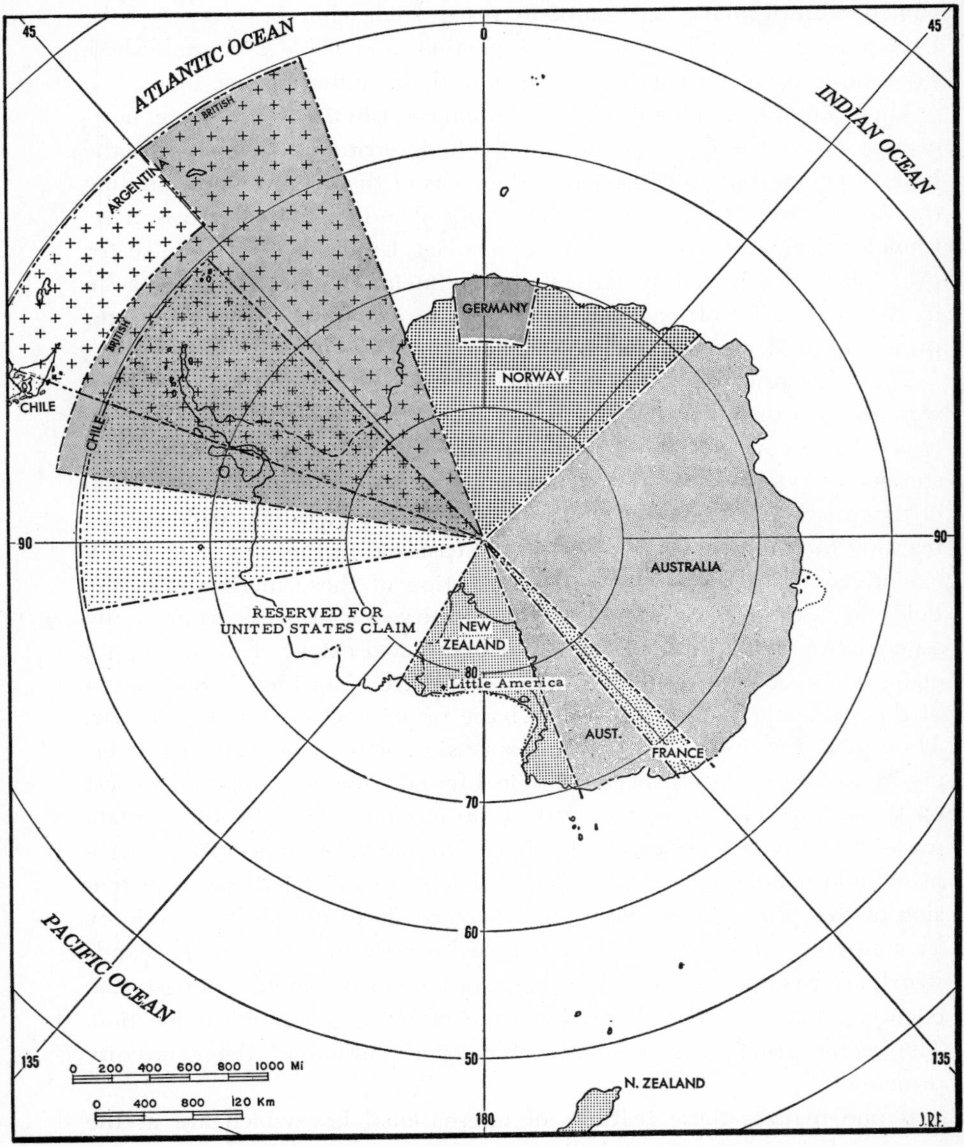

Fig. 4-2. Antarctic Claims.

principle; for this principle, as an extension of the contiguity concept, does not make sense in the South Polar regions.

Here we deal with a continent detached from any other and separated from other lands by broad expanses of water from the territories that are acknowledged to belong to claimant states. "Inasmuch as there are no 'contiguous' territories extending into this area, as Canada and Russia extend into the Arctic, these Antarctic sector claims must rest upon a different theory from the Arctic principle." [4]

The United States has subscribed always to the theory that "effective occupation" is required as the basis of a claim of sovereignty over newly-discovered lands, including Polar lands.[5] The technological achievements of our times lend support to the concept that the principle of international law under which "effective occupation" is a prerequisite for the acquisition of "title" over a territory merits validity also in the Arctic and Antarctic.

THE FUNCTIONS OF BOUNDARIES

There is a real gradation in the effective functioning of a boundary from serving as an almost absolute barrier through several stages to the purely theoretical function of a claimed boundary. The barrier function is best exemplified in the Iron Curtain around the countries of the Soviet Bloc at present. It is, however, not an absolute barrier. There are not only those refugees who escape; more important is that trade is being carried on all the time. There are sensitive areas where countries bordering the Iron Curtain are not completely identified with either East or West, such as Finland and Iran. A big hole appears where until 1955 the Iron Curtain crossed Austria, a country that had retained its unity despite the fact that parts of it lay behind and others in front of the Iron Curtain. It thus appears that the Iron Curtain has not achieved, and, at least as long as peace can be preserved, is unlikely to achieve the strength of the walls which Japan and China erected around their borders from the seventeenth to the nineteenth century. We know, however, that even at the time of the most perfect seclusion of Japan, the tiny Dutch foothold in the harbor of Nagasaki was sufficient to maintain a certain osmotic exchange. Japanese artistic influences filtered into the West, as did Western medical knowledge into Japan, to mention only two important features.

[4] Hackworth, *Digest of International Law* (1940), p. 461. The official positions of Argentina and Chile are in conflict with the above and their claims are based in part on the contiguity concept; at best, a geological but certainly not a geographical contiguity can be claimed in this case.

[5] Miller, "Rights Over the Arctic," *Foreign Affairs* (1925), pp. 49-51.

Boundaries are often closed for certain functions only. Barriers to immigration or to the import of merchandise are more frequent than those to emigration and exports. The closing of the American border to liquors in the era of Prohibition is well remembered. Newspapers and books are sometimes excluded from crossing a border. Such barriers may be absolute or may be partial. Under the so-called quota system a certain merchandise may be allowed across the border in specified quantities only, or prohibitive customs may reduce the quantities which would come in without such taxation. The high value of a currency may act as a deterrent. It is obvious that the restricting influence of all such factors can vary in wide degrees. The system of immigration quotas in the United States is based on a general principle, the proportion of resident alien-born from each country at a given date. In practice, this law opens the borders to any average Englishman, but closes it to the majority of prospective immigrants from many other countries such as China or Italy.

Though almost all degrees of exclusion may be found, there is no international boundary which does not constitute an obstacle of some kind. Legal systems differ even between countries very close to each other in sentiment and practice. No two countries have the same system of taxation. Unavoidably, the teaching of history in schools has slightly different emphases. Allegiance is required to a specific flag. The American-Canadian boundary is an example of such a minimum function which still, in many tangible and intangible ways, has a separating effect.

It is obvious that such international boundaries do not have a much different function than do certain internal boundaries, especially those between the states of the United States. In other countries internal boundaries may mean less. In the United States state boundaries have stronger separating functions than county boundaries or city boundaries; still less important is the function of boundaries of townships or city wards. However, there is no boundary which is not separating some feature, no boundary without function.

The modern state is characterized by the great number of functions it exercises, functions distinguishing it in all its constitutional forms from its earlier predecessors, especially the feudal state. This multiplicity and the complexity of organization related to it is one of several reasons why accurate, linear boundaries become necessary, and are now the rule.

BORDER ZONES

The status of border territories has been more and more defined and transitional border zones have almost disappeared from the map, even in South America where they were the rule along the borders only fifty years ago. Also the number of undemarcated boundaries is rapidly shrinking, though as a matter of course not as fast as the number of undelimited boundaries or unallocated territories. The only sizeable land area under this last category would be—and this only for official American opinion—the Antarctic continent. There are a few more undelimited areas in the Arabian peninsula, along the land boundaries of China, and those of Thailand. Not quite in the same category are disputed areas, such as Kashmir, the southwestern corner of Ecuador, and a few others of minor importance at present. Among the undemarcated boundaries are several African boundaries, such as most boundaries of Ethiopia, or the boundary between the French and Spanish Sahara, Libya, and others.

Even if a boundary has been agreed upon, the old separating zone must not disappear. There is still the little known and little exploited forest between Brazil and its neighbors to the north and west, the desert between Libya and its neighbors, and the high mountain belt between Burma and its neighbors. It is, however, the agreed boundary line, and no longer an unpassable belt of forest, desert, or swamps which minimizes the danger of border clashes. An interesting example is offered by the Rub'al Khali (Fig. 4-3), the Empty Quarter of Southern Arabia, which serves as frontier or boundary zone between Saudi Arabia to the north and west and the Trucial emirates, Oman and Hadramaut, to the east and south. In 1913 Turkey and Great Britain agreed to a boundary through unknown areas. This boundary still appears on some maps, though the outbreak of World War I prevented ratification of the treaty and Saudi Arabia never recognized its validity. This was still no matter of concern for Britain until Bertrand Thomas in 1927 and St. John B. Philby the following year crossed this desert. From this moment the dwindling barrier character of the Rub'al Khali became obvious. However, Saudi Arabia felt strong enough to press its claim only after it had granted oil concessions to the Arabian-American Oil Company (Aramco), hoping thereby to force the United States to back her claims. The recent conflict over the Buraima oasis between Saudi Arabia and Oman, the claims of both the tiny but oil-rich Sheikhdom of Qatar and of Saudi Arabia have highlighted a developing dangerous situation in this desert

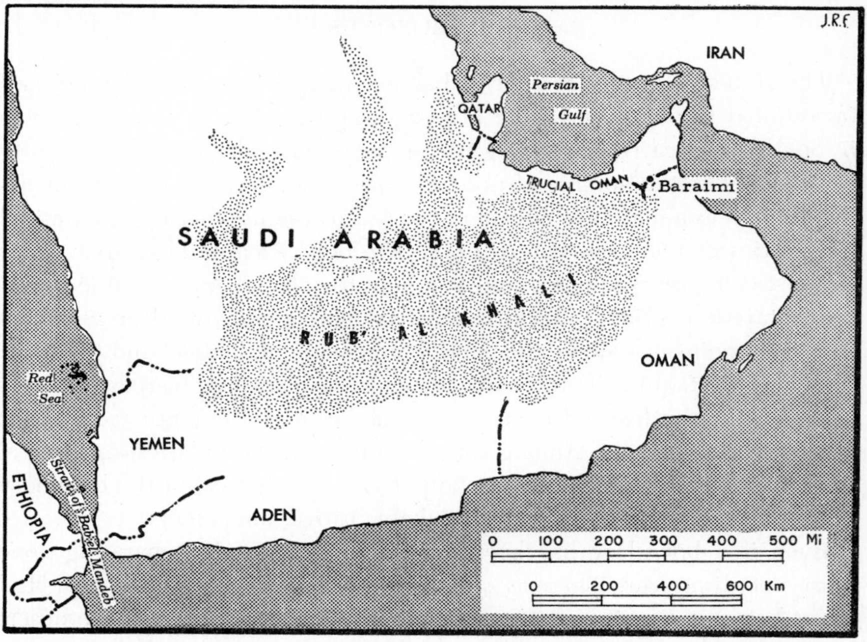

Fig. 4-3. Rub'al Khali, "The Empty Quarter" of Southern Arabia.

area.[6] Without the establishment of boundary lines, bloody conflicts may become more and more frequent.

A similar situation existed in the north of the Arabian peninsula. Since World War I boundaries have gradually been established and largely demarcated between Saudi Arabia and its neighbors, Jordan, Iraq, and Kuwait. In two places, where no agreement could be reached, two neutral zones between Saudi Arabia on the one side and Iraq and Kuwait on the other are policed by both adjacent powers. They are themselves bordered by definite lines and owe their continued existence not as much to their barrier character as to rivalry and jealousy. They are more closely related to buffer states or condominiums than to frontier zones of a primitive character. A much discussed area is the tribal area or the frontier region of the North West Frontier, an area included by the international boundary between Afghanistan and Pakistan and the administrative boundary

[6] A. Melamid, "Political Geography of Trucial Oman and Qatar," *Geographic Review,* Vol. 11, No. 3 (April, 1953); and the same author: "Oil and the Evolution of Boundaries in Eastern Arabia," *ibid.,* Vol. 11, No. 4 (April, 1954).

of the North West Frontier Province proper, the Durand line of 1893. The British gave only a minimum of administration to this area.[7]

The only other surviving zones lie between India and Tibet in the high uninhabited mountains of Himalaya and Karakorum, and between China and Burma in the broken plateaus inhabited by Shan tribes. Both adjacent countries claim sovereignty over each of these zones and some day some delimitation will have to take place. During the nineteenth century many countries agreed to draw boundary lines through such unexplored boundary zones. Such boundaries were drawn on the conference table and either used assumed physical features or geometrical lines as boundary lines. Assumed physical features were selected as a rule in South America, geometrical lines more frequently between European colonies in Africa and occasionally in other continents. This method has been denounced as artificial and arbitrary. However, it is often unavoidable. Geographers refer to this type of boundaries as "antecedent" boundaries, antecedent to actual occupation or even exploration.[8] It cannot be denied that this method resulted in especially unfortunate results in regions of densely settled, somewhat advanced civilizations, though the area might have been unexplored by Europeans. Some of the boundaries of Thailand and of the western Sudan belong in this category. This applies only to densely populated areas, and fortunately they were a minority. One should, furthermore, keep in mind that in most of these instances the only alternative was either to defer delimitation until demarcation on the ground should become possible, or to designate some suspected physical feature. To defer delimitation would actually mean to wait until interest in the hitherto unknown area materialized and friction evolved. This way has rarely been selected, and where it has, results were unfortunate.

UNDEFINED BOUNDARIES

The history of the boundaries of Afghanistan throughout most of the nineteenth century is an example of frictions which a not clearly defined boundary line may cause. The Russian-Afghan-British-Indian relations were in a state of nearly open conflict throughout the second half of the nineteenth century; the temporary weakness of Russia and world-wide political activity enabled a settlement of the boundary conflict in the

[7] There is a large literature on this area starting with G. N. Curzon of Kedleston, *Frontiers* (Oxford, 1907). The latest review is by J. W. Spain, "Pakistan's North West Frontier," *The Middle East Journal,* Vol. 8, No. 1 (1954), pp, 27-40.

[8] R. Hartshorne, "Suggestions on the Terminology of Political Boundaries," abstract, *Annals of the Association of American Geography,* Vol. 26 (1936), p. 56.

eleventh hour. However, the solution along the Afghan-British-Indian boundary proved workable only as long as the British power in India stood on solid foundations. Instead of the usual boundary line to which all state functions extend, three lines were established. This resulted in the creation of two boundary zones of which only that adjacent to India was administered effectively. Even here not all state functions were exerted. Another zone adjacent to Afghanistan was not administered but was supervised by the British. Since Pakistan has taken the place of India, Afghanistan has voiced more vocal claims than ever before for this area, which is inhabited by Pushtu-speaking tribes; Pushtu is the language of the ruling group of Afghanistan (*cf.* Fig. 3-1, p. 59).[9]

The undefined boundary between Ethiopia and Italian Somaliland opened the road to the war of 1935, when both parties advanced into no man's land and clashed at Ual-Ual.

DEMARCATION OF BOUNDARIES

Designation of unexplored physical features such as water partings, mountain crests, and rivers, has caused many conflicts in South America. The Argentine-Chilean conflict was ended by arbitration of the British monarch who assigned the disputed territories to the contestants. The conflict area was described in detail by the British geographer-statesman [10] who was engaged in investigating the topographic background. In this case it had been agreed that the boundary should follow "the highest crest which may divide the waters" (Fig. 4-4). Unfortunately, and unknown at the time of the agreement, the highest crest and the water-parting do not coincide for a distance of many hundreds of miles. The final award found a compromise solution.

A river was designated as the boundary between French Guiana and Brazil, another, the St. Croix river, between Maine and the adjacent provinces of Canada, both rivers no longer identifiable [11] when settlement advanced and fixation of the boundary became necessary. The nonexistent "northwestern corner of the Lake of the Woods" on the Minnesota-Canada boundary (Fig. 4-5) required at least sixteen additional conventions [12] until all the questions were resolved which arose from the original peace treaty formulation.

[9] See p. 394.
[10] Holdich, *op. cit.*
[11] Jones, *op. cit.*, p. 200.
[12] Boggs, *International Boundaries,* pp. 47-50.

FIG. 4-4. The Argentine-Chilean Boundary.

On the other hand, none of the geometrical lines in Africa has led to serious conflicts. It was possible in several cases to create a satisfactory boundary by means of exchange of territory and other adjustments. The Congo State (*cf.* Fig. 7-6, p. 186) originally established as a quadrangle, at present has a river boundary with French Central Africa, rivers and lakes as boundaries with most of the British areas, and very irregular boundaries with the Portuguese possessions, the latter created by exchange of territories.[13]

Because each boundary is a result of human selection and action,

[13] *Ibid.*, p. 186.

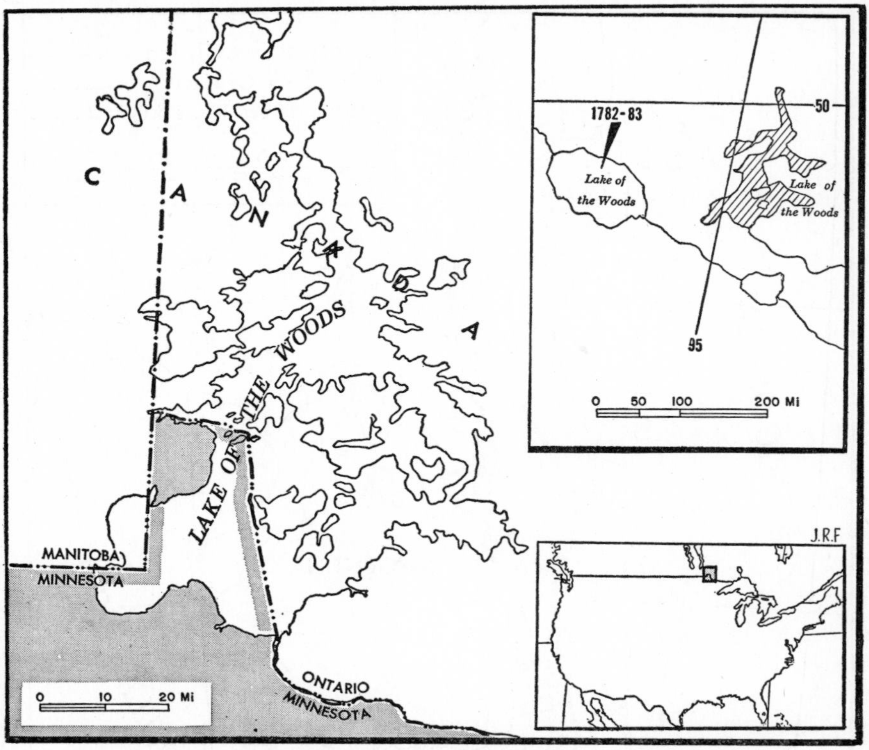

Fig. 4-5. The Minnesota-Canada Boundary: Large inset shows location of Lake of the Woods, as used at Paris 1782-83. The lake in its true position is cross-hatched. After Boggs, *International Boundaries*.

boundary lines are always artificial throughout.[14] A boundary between states can exist only where and if man establishes a boundary. Boundary-making is done generally in several steps, which Stephen B. Jones[15] distinguishes as delimitation and demarcation. Some authors[16] distinguish three steps: (1) allocation of territory in general terms, (2) delimitation, and (3) demarcation. Only demarcation, though actually only the last step, will be considered here. This is the work of the surveyor in the field, directed by a commission composed of the diplomatic representatives of the two states concerned, sometimes accompanied or even headed by one or several neutrals. The agreement which has been made

[14] Maull, *op. cit.*, p. 143, was apparently the first to stress this point.

[15] *Op. cit.*, p. 5.

[16] Boggs, *International Boundaries;* and A. Hall, "Boundaries in International Relations," in G. E. Pearcy and R. H. Fifield, *World Political Geography* (New York, 1948), pp. 521-524.

at some conference table as to the site of the boundary has to be transferred into the landscape. Whoever has observed the slow, painstaking work of a surveyor fixing the limits of private property, will not be surprised to learn that demarcation of state boundaries takes months or even years, not counting delays due to disagreement. Mountains may be unscalable, but they are generally less difficult to demarcate than water-boundaries. A meandering river with its continuously shifting banks and changing channel is a much more difficult problem. Even a stream confined by rocks to a definite channel poses demarcation problems. Boundary markers can not be put in the middle of a stream, but must be set on the banks and serve only as indicators from which to look for the actual boundary. Thousands of soundings had to be made to determine the *thalweg* of the St. Croix river on a short stretch.[17] Decisions of a peace conference or boundary conference to use villages as boundaries may sound very simple. This may result, however, in dividing the adjoining fields of a single proprietor or in a boundary with many protruding corners or irrational vagaries.

Generally boundaries have been demarcated by carefully surveyed intervisible markers. In the once valueless, now oil-rich but featureless desert in Arabia behind the town of Kuwait the desert is strewn with tar barrels deposited by sheiks as local landmarks.[18] On some boundaries, where roads or railroads cross them, roadblocks are not uncommon. Sometimes a path is cut through forest and bush, a grass strip left between fields, or even a fence erected along the whole length of a boundary. This is usually regarded as a last resort, if for no other reason than because of the high cost of erection and maintenance. The Great Chinese Wall and the Roman Limes are unrivaled today. The so-called Teggart Wall on the northern border of Palestine, an electrically laden wire fence, was a last attempt by the British to keep undesired intruders out. This was due to the explosive situation in the last years of the mandate. Such fences, only shorter ones, have been erected where boundaries cut through towns, such as through Italian Fiume and its Yugoslav suburb Susak before 1940, today reunited as Rijeka, or even along the United States boundary with Mexico through the city of Laredo. The minefields along large stretches of the "Iron Curtain" are less visible but more vicious barriers.

All these devices, however, follow predetermined boundaries. They make the boundary visible, but do not establish it. Demarcation is the

[17] Jones, *op. cit.*, p. 117.
[18] *The Economist,* March 28, 1953, p. 882.

legitimate process to make a boundary visible. Sometimes demarcation follows allocation of territory and its more detailed delimitation on the conference table as soon as possible. That is often the case after wars when territories are shifted from one sovereignty to another. Hartshorne [19] speaks of superimposed boundaries and contrasts them with antecedent boundaries which were established long before the land was actually taken possession of, or even before it was known.

"NATURAL" AND "ARTIFICIAL" BOUNDARIES

Many political geographers have fought against the popular distinction between artificial and natural boundaries.[20] The latter are supposed to follow natural features such as mountain ranges, rivers, or deserts, the artificial ones being created by man without regard for physical features. Actually all boundaries are made by man. Whether or not the boundary followed or could follow a natural feature depended on many different circumstances. It has been suggested that such boundaries should rather be called "naturally marked" [21] or "borrowed from nature" (*naturentlehnt*).[22] They are often opposed to straight-line boundaries. The cause for the selection of straight-line boundaries may be ignorance of the topographical features, as is true of many of the claimed boundaries in the Antarctic continent. In other instances, such features as linguistic affinities, popular loyalties, or existence of communication lines, seemed far more important than the course of a river or a mountain crest. There is little reason to call this latter type more artificial than a diplomatically selected mountain boundary which perhaps cut off alpine pastures from the villages which used them. This happened when the Austro-Italian border was drawn after World War I separating German-speaking South Tyrol from North Tyrol; and it was claimed that the coincidence of a high mountain crest with a parting of waters and strategic favorable circumstances made it a perfect "natural" border. The same happened in the Carpathians between Poland and Czechoslovakia and a similar situation was described for an old established border, that following the Pyrenees.[23]

Interest in boundary problems as a geographical problem was first

[19] "Geography and Political Boundaries in Upper Silesia," *loc. cit.*

[20] Sölch, *op. cit.;* Hartshorne, "Suggestions on the Terminology of Political Boundaries," *loc. cit.;* Jones, *op. cit.*, pp. 7-8.

[21] D. Whittlesey, *The Earth and the State* (New York, 1944), p. 5.

[22] R. Sieger, "Zur politisch-geographischen Terminologie," *Zeitschrift der Gesellschaft für Erdkunde,* Vol. 52, No. 3 (Berlin, 1917-18).

[23] D. Whittlesey, "Trans-Pyrenean Spain, The Val d'Arran," *Scottish Geographical Magazine,* Vol. 49 (1933), pp. 217-228.

awakened by Ratzel. Living and writing in Germany, he knew thoroughly the problems and artificial character of the boundaries of the German states. Indeed, they were to a large degree a product of the Napoleonic period and their delimitation was mainly a result of considerations which had nothing to do with geography or historical tradition, but aimed to give every prince a state of carefully balanced size and taxable income. Nevertheless, these artificial boundaries have disappeared only since World War II in many parts of Germany and some still survive.[24]

Often the term artificial boundary is used as the equivalent for bad boundary. Jones [25] has shown in a very great number of examples that any boundary may be good or bad according to the difficulties inherent in the type of boundary as well as in the circumstances of the time. While mountain ranges are generally regarded as good boundaries, the international commission appointed to fix the boundary between Turkey and Iraq in 1921 agreed unanimously that the Jabel Sinjar should be allocated as a unit.[26] This mountain chain in a semidesert is practically a group of oases on both sides of the range, remote from any other permanent settlement.

In conclusion, "there are no intrinsically good or bad boundaries . . . all international border lands are potentially critical. A boundary may be stable at one time, unstable at another, without a change of a hairsbreadth in its position." [27]

BOUNDARIES MARKED BY PHYSICAL FEATURES

Because of the widespread preference for such naturally marked boundaries, those physical features shall be briefly reviewed which are most often quoted and used for such purposes, especially mountain crests, water partings, and rivers. Mountain crest boundaries exist in all continents with the exception of Australia. It has been noticed that the perhaps oldest group of political boundaries, the boundaries of the historical eighteen provinces of China, in general follow mountain crests or traverse other sparsely populated zones; only occasionally do they utilize rivers.[28] But even in New Guinea the boundary between the Australian territory of Papua and the trusteeship territory, the former

[24] F. Metz, *Südwestdeutsche Grenzen* (Remagen, 1951).
[25] *Op. cit.*, pp. 121-162.
[26] *Ibid.*, p. 98.
[27] *Ibid.*, p. 3.
[28] H. J. Wood, "The Far East," in W. G. East and O. H. K. Spate, *The Changing Map of Asia* (London, 1950), p. 268.

German New Guinea, was placed on the central mountain axis of the island. Where a sharp crest exists and where it coincides with the parting of waters, such a boundary line is of the most stable and satisfactory type. The mountains often have formed an uninhabited and mostly unused zone between two countries long before a boundary line was established. One of the few surviving examples of such a state exists in the Himalayas between India and China. Frequently mountain valleys and high pastures have been slowly included in the economic system of the adjacent areas and the actual boundary line developed gradually. Such boundary lines do not necessarily coincide with the crestline—it may be practical to reach high pastures by means of a mountain-crossing pass; or, people living on one side may have used, and be entitled to, areas on both sides of the crest; or, a common economic way of life may bring together a population living on both sides of the crestline. The usual small-scale map is misleading because it cannot show small but significant deviations. Thus the Pyrenees, often cited as a perfect mountain boundary of this type, separate France and Spain only on part of the actual boundary.[29]

In mountain ridges which lack sharp, continuous crests, it can be shown that the boundary line is usually a late development, developing from an original frontier zone. The mountains may not even be the primary frontier zone, which may be dense forests.[30] Bohemia, often called a mountain fortress, is surrounded by rather low mountains, mostly short ridges with gaps between them. One of them, the Ore mountain (Erzgebirge to the Germans, Krušne Hory to the Czechs), is devoid of the original forest cover, and it appears that the very old boundary deviates almost throughout its whole length from the rather sharp divide between the gentle north-western Saxonian slope and the steep escarpment leading into the interior of Bohemia. The boundary is located on the gentle northwestern slope, though it is evident that this slope constitutes the lesser obstacle to penetration. However, it was not the desire for tillable land or political expansion which brought man onto the mountain, but the quest for precious minerals. Mining attracted settlers into the mountains and the need of timber and charcoal for the mines is responsible for the disappearance of the forests. The boundary line, however, became stabilized in general where the miners from both sides met.

In general, it still holds true that virgin forests, uninhabited mountain

[29] Whittlesey, "Trans-Pyrenean Spain, The Val d'Arran," *loc. cit.*

[30] At least one recent author denies entirely the protective function of the Bohemian mountain rim, J. A. Steers, "The Middle People: Resettlement in Czechoslovakia," *Geographic Journal,* Vol. 102 (January, 1949).

ridges, swamps and deserts fulfill their function as natural boundary zones, as, for instance, is still the case in the undefined deep boundary zones which separate the border of Sinkiang from Tibet and the similarly inaccessible 1800-mile-long border which separates Tibet from India, Sikkim and Bhutan. At the same time, it is true for many areas that the intensification of agriculture, technological progress, the improvement of communication systems, and the spreading population have narrowed the extent of no man's land serving as boundary zones. Forests have been cut down or taken under management. Regular policing has extended far into the largest desert of the world, the Sahara. Permanent meteorological and a chain of radar stations are ringing the Polar regions. Swamps have been drained, as happened to the Bourtanger Moor on the German-Dutch border. Under a five-year plan presented in 1952, the U.S.S.R. intends to drain about 25,000 square miles, or an area roughly the size of Connecticut, Massachusetts and Delaware combined, in the Pripet marshes in Byelorussia and the Ukraine, with the goal of adding about nine million acres of fertile peat soil lands to the Soviet cultivated area.

RIVERS AS BOUNDARIES

In many cases preference has been expressed for rivers as boundaries. Boggs [31] and Jones [32] have shown the difficulties arising from the use of rivers as boundaries. Most boundary conflicts between states of the United States have been caused by river boundaries.[33] Also the international boundary disagreements of the United States have been concerned with rivers. There was the question concerning the course of the St. Croix river which had been designated as the boundary between the state of Maine and the Canadian Maritime Provinces, and there are the continuing problems which the continuously shifting Rio Grande has created at the Mexican border since it was adopted as boundary in 1848. An agreement in 1934 settled most, but not all controversial points. The conflict over the use of the waters of the Colorado river by California and diminution of their volume for Mexico is not strictly a boundary problem.

In Kashmir, a similar controversy lent strength to the claim of Pakistan for a boundary which would give to that country control over waters it needs for irrigation. This type of conflict becomes a genuine boundary case if a river which is necessary for irrigation is used as a boundary

[31] *International Boundaries,* pp. 179-182.
[32] *Op. cit.,* pp. 108 ff.
[33] See map, Jones, *op. cit.,* p. 109.

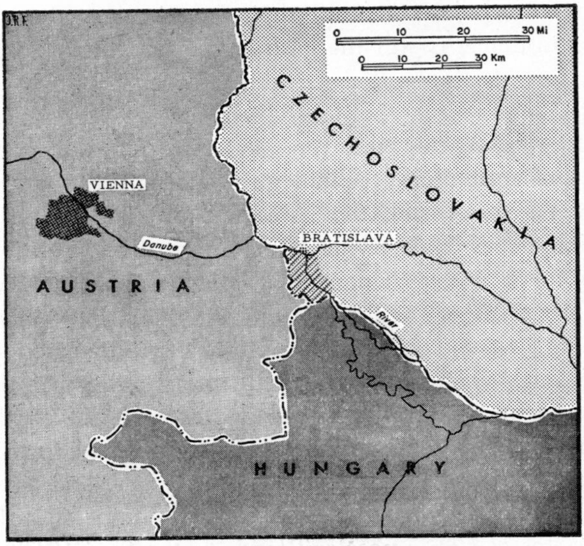

Fig. 4-6. The Bratislava Bridgehead on the Danube.

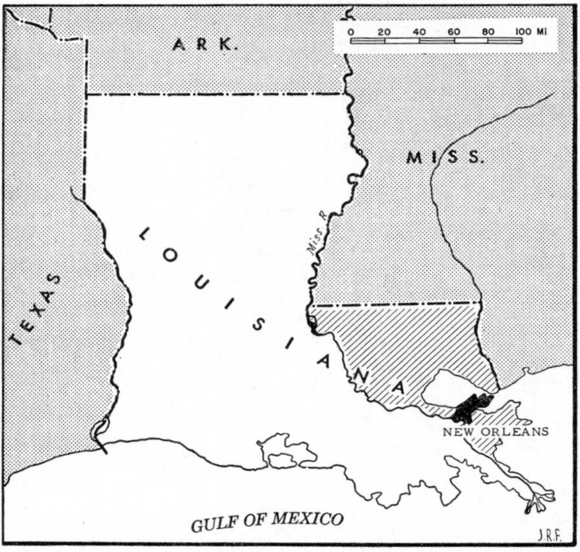

Fig. 4-7. The Louisiana Extension on the Mouth of the Mississippi.

line, as is true of the Jordan river between Syria and Israel. To the use of waterways for navigation, irrigation, and flood control, recently has been added their use as a source for power. In all these cases not only the management of the river along the border, but that of tributaries far away may influence its usability.

It appears that rivers are less manageable as boundaries than any other feature. Any tampering with them, even the construction of badly needed flood dykes, influences the opposite, foreign shore and possibly affects areas farther downstream. To leave a river alone is not practicable, because of the general tendency of rivers to undercut portions of their banks, silt up channels, or shift their beds. Only common management in a friendly spirit can minimize the frictions resulting from the separating boundary function.

Actually, rivers unite rather than divide the opposite banks. River basins are essentially units and the unifying function of a drainage basin is in many cases indistinguishably joined to the separating function of the divides. Historians and political geographers have long recognized the essential unity of the Paris basin of the Seine river, of Bohemia, of the Danubian basin, the Vistula basin, the Amazon basin, the Gangetic plain, and many others. On the other hand, where river boundaries have been established there is frequently the desire to create at least a bridgehead on the most important crossing point. The Bratislava bridgehead on the Danube (Fig. 4-6) and the Louisiana extension across the lower Mississippi (Fig. 4-7) may suffice as examples.

Many attempts have been made to unite entire river basins for the purpose of flood control, irrigation, and power development. By the inclusion of the whole river basin in such a scheme, these projects differ basically from international river regulation agreements for navigable rivers such as have been devised for the Danube and the Rhine. In this context the spectacular success of the Tennessee Valley Authority (TVA) project comes to mind (*cf.* Fig. 18-3, p. 579). But the achievements of the TVA reveal both the potentials and limitations of this type of river basin control project, especially if one tries to use the TVA example as a yardstick for other river and flood control plans. In the case of the TVA it was possible to overcome gradually the reluctance of a number of states within the Union which gave up some of their state rights in favor of the interstate agency.

Since the TVA came into existence, dozens of "TVA's" have been planned within the United States and abroad; scores of missions from foreign countries have studied the American TVA and American experts have explored the possibilities for similar projects in foreign countries. However, while the economic advantages achieved by the TVA in many respects are impressive, no other attempt to imitate this project has been successful and political obstacles have proved too formidable to be overcome. This is primarily true for projects in internationally disputed areas as along the Jordan river or in the area of the principal rivers of the Indus Basin which provide water for irrigation in Pakistan and originate in, or flow across India, Kashmir, or Jammu.[34] In spite of the often-expressed hope that the execution of such river basin projects would result in significant economic advantages to all contestant powers and would pave the way for political reconciliation, political issues have maintained their priority as a separating factor. It appears that such ambitious projects can be undertaken successfully only if the international situation between the interested nations is on a firm and peaceful basis. Even within the United States objections to unification raised by local and special interests have proved to be a most formidable obstacle. Neither the Missouri Basin nor the Columbia Basin Authority have developed beyond the blueprint stage. Most of the international projects have not even entered the blueprint stage, and some of them, though entirely sound and important from the economic point of view, are at this time not more than speculations in the harsh light of political realities.

OCEANIC BOUNDARIES

A special type of water boundaries are the oceanic boundaries of all states bordering the sea. The shoreline is often regarded, especially for statistical purposes, as the boundary of a country. The definition of the shoreline may lead to difficulties, particularly on low coasts adjacent to shallow seas with high tides. Should the mean water level, the average low-water mark, or the mark at spring tide be regarded as the boundary? Different countries have claimed each of these lines. More important, however, is the claim of most nations to sovereignty over their territorial waters. This is a zone of water several miles wide. A majority of countries, among them countries which in 1950 registered four-fifths of all commercial shipping tonnage, claim a zone three miles wide.[35] Another almost 10 per cent of commercial tonnage was registered in Scandinavian countries which claim a four-mile limit. The remaining countries are by no

[34] See p. 97.

[35] S. W. Boggs, "National Claims in Adjacent Seas," *Geographical Review,* Vol. 41 (1951), p. 202.

means negligible, as they count among them the Soviet Union which claims a twelve-mile belt.

The United States, on September 28, 1945, proclaimed that it would regard the "natural resources of the subsoil and the sea bed of the continental shelf beneath the high seas but contiguous to the coasts of the United States as appertaining to the United States, subject to its jurisdiction and control" (*cf.* Fig. 5-3, p. 125). This assertion of rights, which is based on the geological unity of the shelf and the adjacent land, received legislative sanction by the Outer Continental Shelf Act of August 7, 1953.[36] A number of states, most of them in the Americas and around the Persian Gulf, have followed the American example and claimed certain rights over the continental shelf. Australia followed suit in 1953, by proclaiming sovereignty over her entire continental shelf reaching in places more than two hundred miles off her coast. The Japanese were thus precluded from fishing for pearl shell in the waters off Australia's northern coast. Countries such as Chile, Peru, San Salvador, and Honduras have substituted for the claim to the continental shelf a claim to a two hundred-mile zone. All these countries border the Pacific Ocean—except the north coast of Honduras—and the continental shelf under any definition would be of insignificant width. Many countries have established special purpose claims of different width, ranging from the six miles claimed for customs and coastal defense by Poland, to a security zone of at least three hundred nautical miles around the Americas proclaimed by the Consultative Meeting of Foreign Ministers of the American Republics at Panama on October 3, 1939.[37] The present situation is confusing and gives rise to international conflicts in many oceanic boundary areas. The International Law Committee of the United Nations is therefore attempting to clarify the problems involved by emphasizing that a coastal nation exercises sovereignty over the continental shelf, but subject to the principle of the freedom of the seas.

In reviewing such claims, boundary lines emerge which can not be demarcated but which are nonetheless real. Boggs has shown [38] that except in the rare instance of a straight coastline, it is not easy to be definite as to where a line should be drawn. Bays,[39] islands and rocks, even curva-

[36] See Boggs, "National Claims in Adjacent Seas," *loc. cit.*, pp. 185-209.

[37] Department of State Bulletin, Vol. 1 (1939), pp. 331-333.

[38] In several publications, among them in *International Boundaries*, pp. 178-85, and "Delimitation of Seaward Areas under National Jurisdiction," *The American Journal of International Law*, Vol. 45 (April, 1951), pp. 240-266.

[39] Boggs, "National Claims in Adjacent Seas," *loc. cit.;* and A. L. Shalowitz, "The Concept of a Bay as Inland Waters," *The Journal*, Coast and Geodetic Survey, Department of Commerce, No. 5 (June, 1953), pp. 92-99.

tures of the coastline justify different points of view. If two islands of different sovereignty are closer together than six miles, the definition of the median line is by no means simple. Even an interior boundary, such as that in Lake Michigan between Michigan and Wisconsin, took long-drawn litigation and investigation and finally a decision of the Supreme Court in 1936 to define the line. Presumably this boundary had been well described in preceding legal acts which were, however, shown capable of different interpretation under the actual conditions of a complicated coastline. The situation is particularly difficult if two adjacent countries claim a different width of their territorial waters. Boggs has tried successfully to develop methods to find the best line.[40] Whether these will be adopted in international law seems questionable, at least as long as the present tension remains.

Even less clear is where the continental shelf ends. The usual definition of the continental shelf as the area less than a hundred fathoms deep and adjacent to dry land is only a rough approximation. In some cases, such as the cited example of Chile, the slope of coastal mountains is continued below the ocean surface and there is, geographically, no continental shelf. In other cases, the gradual slope may reach much farther than the hundred-fathom line before the sharp declivity of the continental slope starts. Rarely will continental slope and continental shelf join in such a sharp break that it could be called a line. Even the determination of the hundred-fathom line, though possible with modern means of echo soundings, would be a tedious job. We do not even know how stable this line is.

DIVIDING LINES

A review of maps shows that all these various lines have seldom been mapped. Occasionally, however, we find simple lines, often geometrical lines, dividing sovereignties over islands or in narrow seas. Most of these lines are used as a convenience by the cartographer. Some, however, have or have had international legal meaning, such as the line separating Alaska from Siberia (Fig. 4-8), the line dividing the islands belonging to Indonesia and the Philippines, or the now obsolete but famous dividing line of the Papal decision and the Treaty of Tordesillas between the Spanish and Portuguese overseas empires. The Alaska-Siberian boundary was established by the purchase treaty of 1867, by which the United States acquired Alaska. It consists of two straight lines joining at an obtuse angle in Bering Strait. The north-south aligned part follows the

[40] Boggs, "Delimitations of Seaward Areas Under National Jurisdiction," *loc. cit.*

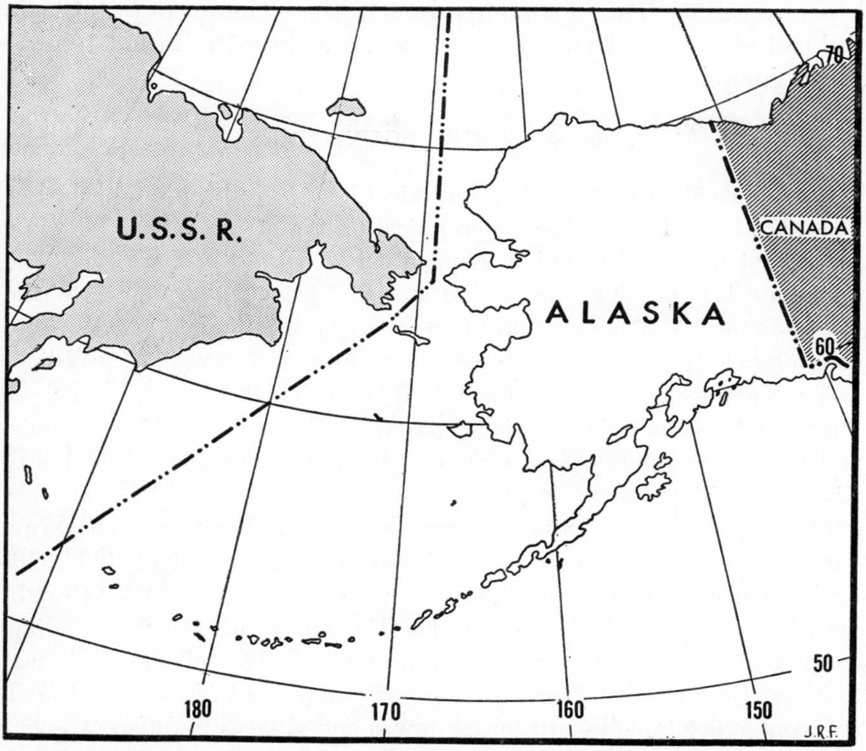

Fig. 4-8. The Geometrical Line as Boundary: Alaska-Siberia.

meridian 168° 58′ 5″ west of Greenwich and is not problematic. The northeast-southwest aligned part connects the southern terminus of this line in 65° 30′ northern latitude with a point about halfway between the westernmost of the Aleutian Islands and the Soviet Komandorskie Islands in 54 degrees north latitude, 170 degrees east longitude. It never was agreed whether this line is part of a great-circle line or a rhumb line, probably because no practical dispute arose. It was adopted as part of the defense perimeter of the Americas at the conference in Rio de Janeiro in 1947 and was defined there as a rhumb line.[41] This Alaskan-Siberian boundary line appears on many maps not as a true political boundary, which it is, but as part of the International Date Line. This is the line where ships—and presumably airplanes—crossing the Pacific Ocean westward skip a whole day, or if bound eastward, start the past twenty-four

[41] The Treaty was published and the pertinent article 4 is most accessible in F. O. Wilcox and T. V. Kalijarvi, *Recent American Foreign Policy* (New York, 1952), p. 210.

hours over again. This line follows the 180° meridian except in this area and east of New Zealand, where it deviates eastward to include several island groups.

GEOMETRICAL BOUNDARIES

It is no accident that where geometrical lines have been established as boundary lines, lines of the geographical grid were preferred. They are the easiest to establish. Other geometrical lines exist but are rare. The boundary between California and Nevada from Lake Tahoe to the Colorado near Mohave city, and that between Arizona and Mexico from the Colorado to Nogales are straight lines but not geographical grid lines and as such are rather exceptional. Still less common are curves, such as the parts of a small circle which separates Delaware from Pennsylvania, and that which limited the former German, later Japanese concession of Kiaochao (Tsingtao).

It is too little realized that many of the winding boundaries shown on our small-scale maps are often a series of very short, straight lines. This may surprise many people, because we are inclined to regard straight lines in the countryside as unnatural. We expect rivers to be winding, coasts to have bays and promontories, and the edges of natural forests to be far from straight. However, new boundaries are often agreed upon at a conference table by attributing towns and villages to different sovereignties. These local boundaries are often boundaries between fields and, as often as not, are straight lines.[42] In other cases a winding line is divided by the surveying field party into short straight stretches to make it practicable.

In Africa and between the states of the United States straight lines originally were nothing more than temporary demarcation lines. In the United States such boundaries have often degenerated into exclusively administrative lines. Different laws, especially different state tax systems, liquor laws, and so on, keep them in the consciousness of their citizens. In a few instances they have won emotional values comparable to European boundaries—the Mason-Dixon line and, internationally, the 49th

[42] Only one interesting illustration will be mentioned to show the interplay of man-made features and natural features and their influence upon local boundaries. In eastern and southeastern Wisconsin "in general the small rectangular" woodlot is predominant, following the lines the surveyor has drawn dividing the quadrangle. But in central Wisconsin "the rectangular land survey shows only rarely in the present woodland cover. . . . Slope and rock outcrop are much more critical in aligning the woodland location." L. Durand, Jr., and K. Bertrand, "Forest and Woodland of Wisconsin," *Geographical Review,* Vol. 45 (1935), p. 270.

parallel. Eisenhower has denounced the shopworn use of the slogan of the "unfortified boundary." He did not intend, thereby, to minimize the value of this boundary, nor would it be possible or desirable to erase the connotation of pride in this boundary from the American consciousness. Americans, who are often impatient of geometrical boundaries in other continents, are often unaware that forty-seven of their states [43] have such geometrical boundaries and that disputes between the states over such boundaries have been far less frequent than, especially, those over river boundaries (Fig. 4-9).[44]

The straight line has definite advantages over a winding line that follows some physiogeographic feature. This occurs in deserts, where land values are practically nil. It is very expensive and difficult, if not outright dangerous, to follow some winding hill range or dry wadi bed. It may be quite simple to draw a straight line. A curious incident was settled in 1952 between Italy and Switzerland. The boundary at one place in the high mountains crossed a glacier. Demarcation by stones on the glacier was possible, but the moving glacier continuously displaced these boundary markers. Finally a straight line was adopted which needed for fixation only two intervisible markers on the firm rock on both sides of the glacier.[45]

This does not imply that geometrical boundaries are always and everywhere preferable. Apart from other problems they are not even always easy to demarcate. The 49th parallel is a ready example, especially as its demarcation was undertaken in a spirit of good will and neighborliness. A parallel is, however, a curve and as such not very convenient in the field. Instead of following such a curved line, the boundary commission followed the sensible procedure of fixing only the boundary markers in the astronomically correct position on the parallel and drawing straight lines between them. It is easily recognizable that such straight lines are the chords of an arc and shorten not only the distance but cut off small pieces of land actually north of the 49th parallel.[46] Jones has shown that the area involved is not large but neither is it negligible.[47] Probably not very often can such a spirit of compromise be expected.

[43] South Carolina is the only exception.
[44] See Jones, *op. cit.*, p. 109.
[45] Convention of Martigny, July 4, 1952.
[46] Jones, *op. cit.*, p. 154.
[47] *Ibid.*, p. 157.

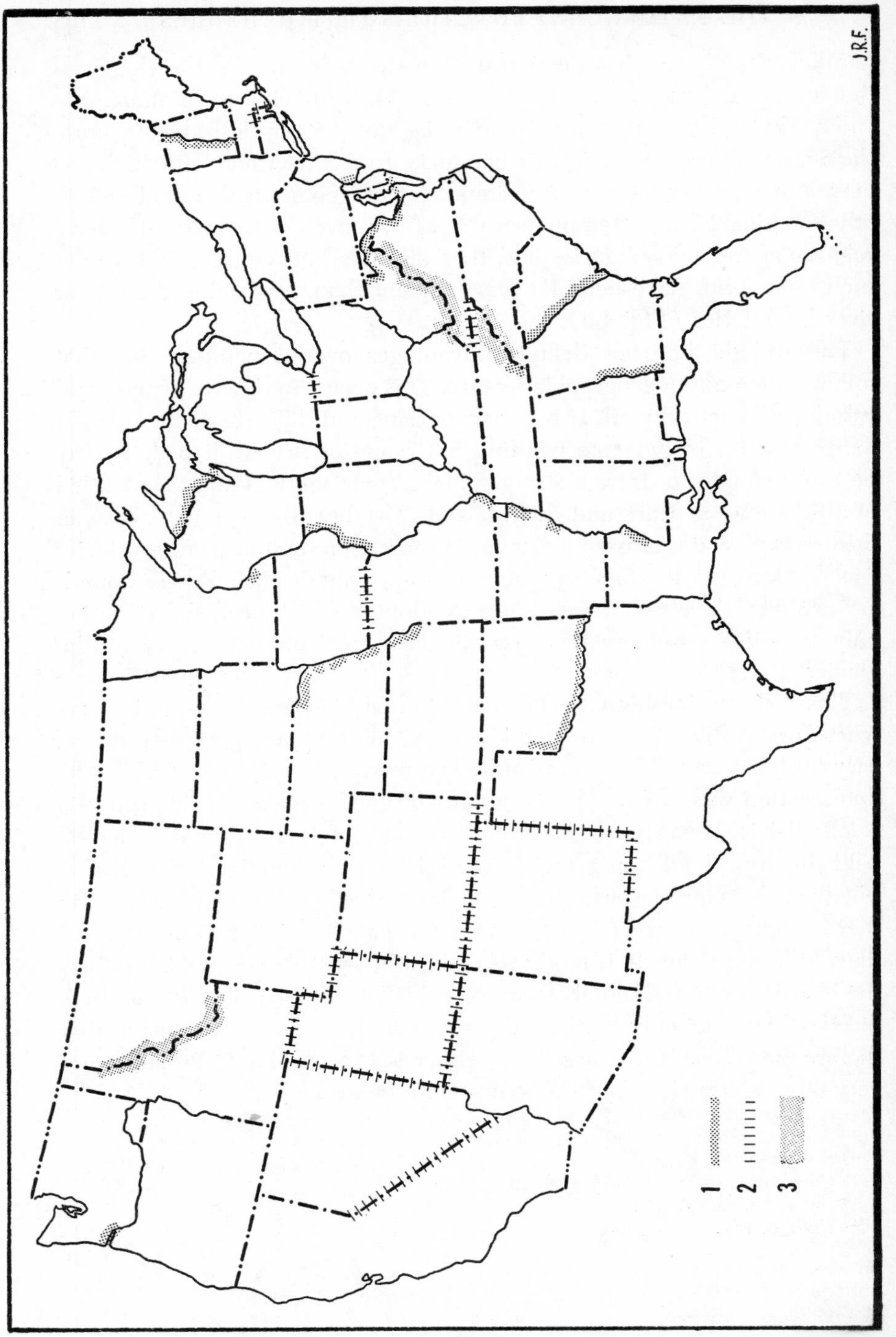
J.R.F.
1
2
3

BOUNDARY CHANGES

An unfortunate quality of political boundaries is that they are so difficult to change. The longer a boundary exists the less flexible become economic ties of the frontier regions to their respective hinterland. Administrative practices and legal systems become ingrained in the life of almost every person, as in the case of inheritance or marriage laws and customs. Emotional values and questions of prestige are added. Still it is not clear why boundaries should remain unchanged while man and all his institutions change. It has been shown [48] that there are, indeed, occasions when a boundary becomes obsolescent, loses part or all of its functions and its international status. Such was the case when Italian and German princely states joined to make a unified or federal state. Created as property boundaries of feudal powers, these boundaries crisscrossed the landscape in such an irrational way, especially in Germany, that they could not fulfill their function in a modern state. They degenerated until after World War II they lost all meaning and were no longer a serious obstacle for the redrawing of the internal German map.[49] Only Bavaria remained mainly within its prewar boundaries. However, such a change of international boundaries is rare without resort to war. It is somewhat more often found in internal boundaries, where a peaceful change in the location of a boundary can often be effected. The growth of modern metropolitan cities shows the frequency of such changes on a low level, but also the obstacles which exist even on this level.

International boundary changes are usually effected by violence. The 38th parallel in Korea is the most recent example of an unsatisfactory boundary resulting from war. However, when the 38th parallel boundary was established, following World War II, it was not thought of as a boundary line of any duration, but as a momentary demarcation line between the occupying forces of the Soviet Union advancing from the north, and the Americans advancing from the south.[50] No natural features would have commanded immediate recognition as outstanding, as shown by the widely divergent suggestions for regional boundaries which had been advanced under peaceful conditions.[51] Old administrative boundary

[48] Fischer, *loc. cit.*, p. 208.

[49] Metz, *loc. cit.*

[50] S. McCune, "The Thirty-eighth Parallel in Korea," *World Politics*, Vol. 1 (January, 1949), pp. 223-225.

[51] Review of such suggestions, especially by the Russian geographer V. T. Zaichikov in 1947 and the German geographer H. Lautensach in 1942, by S. McCune, "Geographic Regions in Korea," *Geographical Review*, Vol. 39 (October 21, 1949), pp. 658-660.

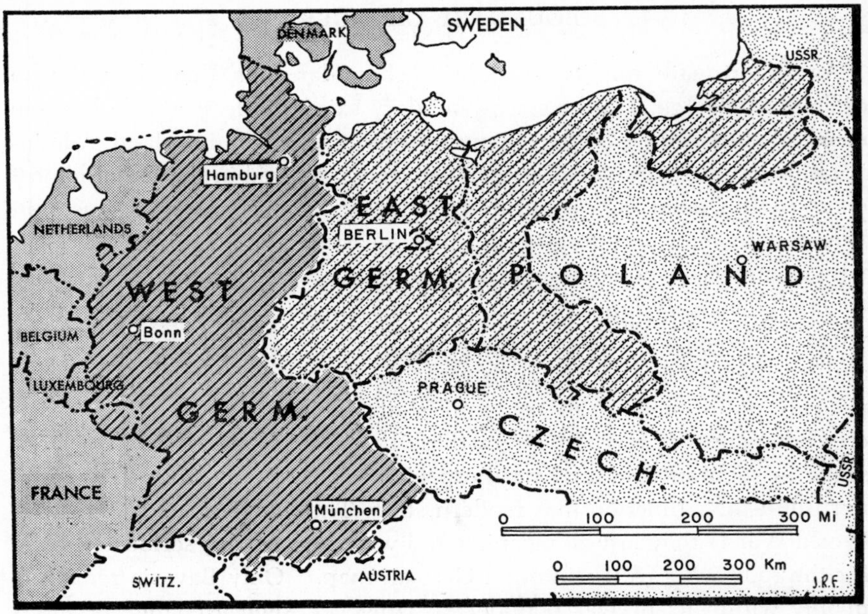

FIG. 4-10. Germany Divided (1955).

lines offered another alternative. In the light of experience in Europe it must be doubted whether any of these alternatives was preferable. The Oder-Neisse line follows physical features. The boundary line between Eastern and Western Germany follows pre-existing administrative boundaries. Both have been denounced vehemently. If so far they have not played the same unfortunate role as the 38th parallel, this is hardly to be attributed to intrinsic merits but rather to political circumstances. The violation of the 38th parallel could be expected to lead to a conflict between minor powers, South and North Korea only; as a matter of fact, despite the activities of the United Nations, and especially of American troops, the war remained localized. In Germany any clash over the boundary would have meant the immediate outbreak of another World War.

It is to be regretted that immediate independent negotiations for a boundary to replace the temporary 38th parallel demarcation line, were not entered into. Again the German example is significant (Fig. 4-10). Despite all protests there is a strong possibility that the Oder-Neisse line will remain for some time. Even more ominous is the gradual crystallization of the boundary between the two Germanies. The establishment and development of two totally different economic, ideological, and political systems can no longer be extinquished by a political act of reunion. The allegiance of the two economies to two different systems is leading to many competing developments in industry and elsewhere which can not coexist in a reunited Germany. A youth educated and indoctrinated by a Communist regime will speak a language which, despite the same vocabulary, will have little meaning in the West. The longer the boundary continues to exist the more difficult it will be to erase it.

It has been suggested that it is easier to change boundaries that have not had time to crystallize—to become associated with prestige, historical traditions, or material interests.[52] Geometrical lines as boundaries through unknown territory correspond best to these conditions. They may, therefore, for the purpose of a preliminary division fulfill the purpose. Danger arises if they are allowed to crystallize before a necessary adjustment can be accomplished. Such a danger line is the boundary partitioning the Ewe tribe in Africa between French and British sovereignty and kept by both powers despite all protests by the Ewes themselves. In the same area, namely Togoland and the Gold Coast, an early adjustment made possible the reunion of two other tribes, the Dagomba and Mamprusi in 1946.[53]

The 38th parallel is no longer used as a boundary in Korea. The new demarcation line, the armistice line of 1953, has replaced it at least temporarily. This line follows ridges and associated physical features for large stretches. It is based on the results of the fighting, and has been proved by its history as a strategically acceptable boundary. Who would state, however, that this one factor is so preponderant as to make it a "good" boundary? At least it does not coincide with any of the lines suggested previously.[54]

[52] Fischer, *loc. cit.*, p. 203.
[53] G. Padmore, *The Gold Coast Revolution* (London, 1935), pp. 153-154.
[54] See McCune, "The Thirty-eighth Parallel in Korea," *loc. cit.*

CHAPTER

5

The Impact of Boundaries

THE BOUNDARY AS FUNCTION OF THE STATE

Whether we like it or not, we are living in a period when the state is assuming more and more functions. Americans, traditionally, do not like it. Population increase, technological progress, especially development of communications, progressive differentiation and stratification of social groups, increase of population groups of proportionally greater mobility, rising standards of living, and need for raw materials from all over the world, have combined to make life more complicated. They have forced more functions upon the state because the individual or even the small integrated group is no longer capable of performing them, and is also incapable of existing without them. At the same time people are becoming more and more conscious of the omnipresence of the state, its functions, and its institutions. We have become accustomed to the national mail service. Today we write and receive more Christmas cards than all the correspondence our great-grandfathers had in a whole year, or perhaps in a lifetime. We use money coined and printed by the government. But in many other respects we regard government as irksome or as an unavoidable nuisance.

Boundaries are national institutions and fulfill functions that a hundred or more years ago were unthought of.[1] Some of the functions, such as high tariffs, are asked for by interested groups of the citizenry. Others are demanded by considerations of national welfare, such as the exclusion

[1] An almost complete list of functions is given by S. W. Boggs, *International Boundaries* (New York, 1940), pp. 9-10.

of diseased animals. Some functions are simply taken for granted, and are hardly noticed by the great majority of citizens. The average citizen is little concerned with the fact that on the other side of the border different laws and customs regulate the punishment of crime, inheritance of property, and many other things. When he attempts to cross a boundary, however, many functions are felt and resented as restrictions of his freedom and independence. That a passport is necessary to cross most boundaries, that a tourist can take out of a country only certain items, and similar boundary restrictions are resented by the average traveler. These are, at least potentially, sources of friction.

To remove these boundary frictions two solutions seem possible: diminution of the functions of boundaries until they finally disappear, or redrawing of boundaries. Theoretically the first way seems the better; in practice, it is the second solution which is almost exclusively aimed at.

We must start with the admission that the complete abolition of international boundaries is a utopian concept at present. Apart from practical difficulties, as long as nationalistic ideologies are so deeply ingrained and are still increasing in many parts of the world, the chances for "One World" seem very remote indeed. Realistic advocates of gradual diminution of boundary functions look to results of their work with satisfaction only if they take a very long-range view. It must be realized that the current trend of development goes rather in the opposite direction and it may be that to keep boundaries functioning within traditional limitations is sometimes beyond practical possibilities.

DIMINISHING FUNCTIONS OF BOUNDARIES

Still, it is possible to draw a long list of functions which have been suspended for the benefit of international organizations, thereby relieving international boundaries of some of their functions. The most far-reaching undertakings in this respect are truly world-wide in purpose, such as many of the functions of separate committees of the United Nations. Some of the most successful of such organizations antedate the United Nations and even the League of Nations. The Red Cross, founded in 1859, is still outside the United Nations, as is a late-comer, the World Council of Churches of Christ.[2] Their effect on boundary functions may be small or intangible; however, the Red Cross has been able to send rapid help across boundaries in disaster areas without regard of boundary restrictions, and the recent assembly of the Council enabled Church func-

[2] Founded 1948.

tionaries who would have been excluded by law, to come to the United States. Some older institutions have become special agencies of the United Nations, such as the Universal Postal Union,[3] the International Court of Justice,[4] and the International Labor Office; [5] but most of these international organizations have originated as special agencies of the United Nations. The United Nations Educational, Scientific, and Cultural Organization, the Food and Agricultural Organization, the International Monetary Fund, and the World Health Organization are the best known.[6] Others, aiming at common standards in certain aspects of life, are continuously added. Only recently a World Meteorological Organization,[7] and a few years earlier an International Telecommunications Union,[8] have been founded. These two agencies are remarkable because they include among their members all states of the Soviet bloc.[9]

Even where common standards are accepted by several nations or all nations concerned, the member nations will often continue to perform their functions differently. For instance, the same standards adopted in educational matters do not necessarily lead to the different states administering them similarly. Yet such agreements gradually lead to the simplification of functions which eventually are no longer irritating and sources of friction in their differences. Sometimes the diminution of boundary irritations is not always obvious in the disappearance of functions; their effects are intangible but not less real.

OBSOLESCENCE OF BOUNDARIES

It seems easier to conclude international agreements between two or a few states than to make multination agreements. Agreements between the United States and Canada about the utilization of the waters of the Great Lakes, or between the United States, Great Britain, France, and the Netherlands concerning economic co-operation in the Caribbean region come to mind. However, it should not be overlooked that regional pacts may carry with them the danger of substituting a larger and stronger organization for several smaller and weaker ones. There is the danger of making some boundaries less obnoxious by strengthening the outer bor-

[3] Founded 1874.
[4] Created 1945 as successor to the Permanent Court of International Justice.
[5] Founded originally 1919, reorganized 1944, accepted into the U.N. 1946.
[6] Founded between 1944 and 1948.
[7] Founded 1951.
[8] Founded 1934.
[9] For a complete list of organs, special agencies of the U.N., and other international organizations see *The Statesman's Yearbook*, 1953.

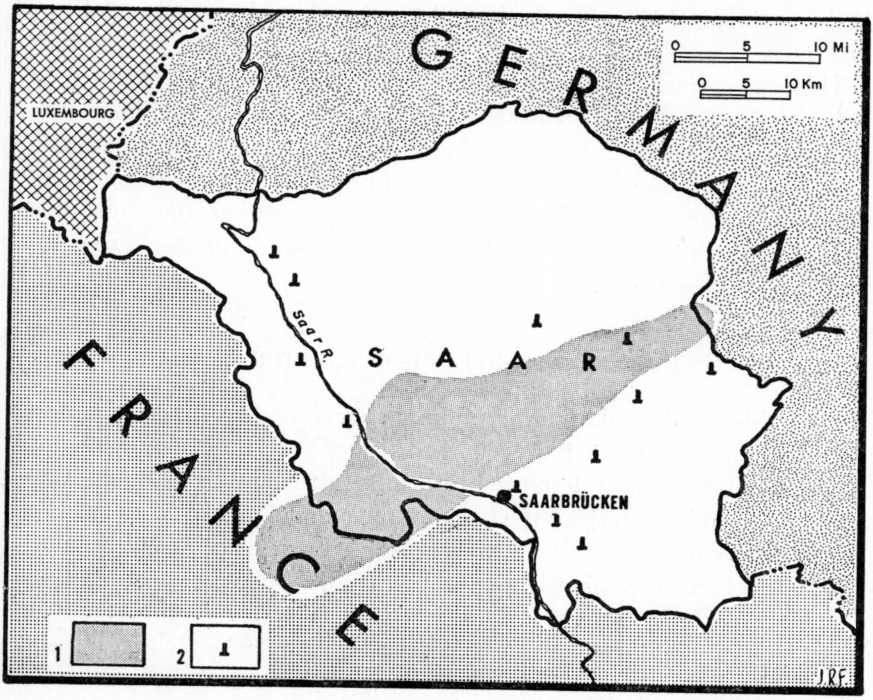

Fig. 5-1. The Saar: Coal and Steel Industries: (1) coal field; (2) steel mills.

ders of the regional organization. Such development occurred when the continuously quarreling, but rarely fighting, small German and Italian princely states were replaced by a strong Germany and Italy. Their wars endangered Europe and finally the world. Similarly, we can discern that the replacement of the Arab states by a well-organized league would certainly end the petty squabbles between them, but might strengthen them for a great war.

So far it is easier to show for internal than for international relations that obsolescence of boundaries may be a way of progress. The development of the Ruhr industrial area across the boundaries of the Prussian provinces of Westphalia and Rhineland led to the organization of the Ruhr Planning Authority in 1920.[10] After Germany's defeat in 1945 the road was open to unite the two Prussian provinces in one state. Similarly two cities, the Free City of Hamburg and the Prussian city Altona were, with several smaller communities, reorganized as a land (state) under the

[10] For a detailed discussion of the Ruhr as an integral part of the European economy, see N. J. G. Pounds, *The Ruhr* (Bloomington, Ind., 1952), pp. 237-239.

Hitler regime in 1938, after the boundaries had lost almost all sociological functions.

There are some slight indications that the increasing interdependence between the Saar area and France and the old-established close cultural and social connections between the Saar and Germany are tending to make the boundaries gradually obsolete (Fig. 5-1). Should these boundaries lose further economic and sociological functions they would be reduced to political and national ones, and a solution of the vexing Saar problem may be easier.

UNCONTESTED BOUNDARIES

Desirable as the taking-over of boundary functions by international organizations may be, it is largely a matter of future developments and, therefore, still outside of the field of political geography. On the other hand, political boundaries have been redrawn on a large scale all the time, mostly under pressure by the stronger country and very rarely by mutually satisfactory agreements. Conquest is still the main factor in boundary changes. We have to accept as a fact the phenomenon that there are strong forces working for change of existing boundaries. It is tragicomic that a stronger country often justifies its expansion with the argument that for its own protection it needs border areas belonging to a weaker neighbor. If boundaries remain unchanged this may be caused by the absence of forces which work for change. Although Americans will immediately be reminded of the United States boundary with Canada, it should be stressed that stability due to absence of these forces is rather the exception than the rule. It has been pointed out [11] that the line separating the United States from Canada is generally referred to as "the boundary," while the line separating this country from Mexico is called "the border." It is believed that the distinction stems from the fact that there has been more friction between the United States and Mexico than with Canada. There has also been more lawlessness on both sides along the southern line, which the word *border* suggests. We may translate it into our terminology by saying that there has been less pressure against the invisible but rigid boundary, causing conflicts and violation of laws, than against the southern border, creating along the latter a zone in which the repercussions are felt.

[11] W. P. Webb, *The Great Frontier* (New York, 1952), pp. 2 ff.

BOUNDARIES UNDER PRESSURE

More significant than the absence of forces is the presence of conflicting forces which exert pressure against the boundary from opposite sides. Working singly, either would tend to displace the boundary; operating in opposition, they tend to neutralize each other. The attempt has been made to define international boundaries as the continuously changing line where the pressure from two adjacent political bodies attains a momentary balance.[12] Last, but not least, there are strong forces at work to preserve established boundaries. Before discussing these two types of forces, those working for change and those working for stability, it is necessary to point out some features of boundaries which are characteristic for a zone of varying width adjacent to a boundary. This zone is commonly called the frontier.

FRONTIER AND INTERIOR

It has become common usage to speak of frontiers or frontier zones in two different meanings. One is the frontier as a border area without exact delimitations, usually preceding the delimitation and demarcation of a boundary. This use of the term in the designation of the western frontier of the United States is well known. We have seen in a preceding chapter that this type of frontier has almost disappeared. We are here concerned with the second type of frontier: the zone which extends inland from a boundary line and generally merges gradually with the interior of the country. Small countries, of course, have no interior in the sense that there is an area where the influence of the frontier is not felt at all. However, even in such a tiny country as Israel the difference between the frontier and the interior is apparent. The inhabitants of the villages on the border are not only in daily danger of life by raids across the frontier, but they also resent the seemingly unconcerned behavior of the big-city dweller. However, measured by standards of other countries, these same city dwellers are acutely aware of boundary problems, if for no other reason than the space they occupy in the daily news.

In large countries the dwellers of interior areas are unaware of and indifferent to boundary problems. The Middle West of the United States, once the "frontier" par excellence, has become the prototype of a country where people do not know anything of foreign countries, are not interested in them, and do not want to have anything to do with them. Appar-

[12] J. Ancel, *Géographie des frontières* (Paris, 1938).

ently this type of isolationism is receding; it is still enough of a life force to illustrate our point.[13]

In this connection, mention may be made of the fact that the very size of the country and the basic difference of psychological attitudes in regard to border problems between the people of the Middle West are, for instance, the people of the Eastern Seaboard regions, account for the fact that "in the United States the word *frontier* . . . becomes a concept with such wide ramifications and so many shades of meaning that it cannot be wrapped up in a neat definition like a word whose growth has ceased and whose meaning has become frozen. It is something that lives, moves geographically." [14]

FRONTIER PSYCHOLOGY

Willingly or not, people living near a boundary have their lives shaped by its influence one way or the other. In past periods border provinces received greater autonomy because it was impossible to defend them against a sudden attack if their authorities had not enough power to do so of their own accord. There are many examples where the population of a border area was organized in a permanent semimilitary organization, called a "march" in Europe. The Cossacks, along the Russian and Ukrainian frontiers, were organized against Turkey and the Tatars and are perhaps the best known. Their semimilitary autonomy survived to the Bolshevist revolution. Austria, another medieval "march," has survived as a separate body politic, but its citizens are still unsure how far they have developed a separate national awareness. At times they liked to think of themselves as Germans because of their German language and certain traditions; but every time they come in close contact with the Germans, they feel vividly the differences in their way of life.[15]

Inhabitants of frontier zones are in many cases conscious of the fact that they live in an exposed situation. This is not only true in half-civilized environments such as the Frontier Province of Pakistan and Afghanistan, but people of Lorraine and Alsace feel the neighborhood of a potential attacker very strongly. It is not incidental that some of the most nationalistic, but also most gifted political leaders of France came from this politically-conscious frontier. Many similar cases can be cited. One may suffice.

[13] See pp. 21-23.
[14] Webb, *op. cit.*, pp. 2 ff.
[15] There exists a voluminous literature on this problem. See especially H. W. Weigert, *Generals and Geographers* (New York, 1942), pp. 115 ff., and the book of the chancellor Schuschnigg, *Drei Mal Österreich* (Innsbruck, 1938), written before Hitler's conquest of Austria in 1938.

The population of Finnmark and Troms, the two northernmost provinces of Norway, suffered most heavily from war destruction in World War II because of their proximity to the Russian border. Now they are more conscious than ever that they would be the first victims of a violent East-West conflict.

EFFECTS OF THE FRONTIER ON ECONOMIC LIFE

The endangered frontier situation is brought home to people also in regard to their freedom of movement. Not only the boundary itself but military installations and regulations affecting so-called defense areas restrict this movement. This leads also to restrictions hampering the economic life of such a region. Market towns, which normally would be in the center of an agricultural area, may have a lopsided trading area. In general, because of boundary restrictions, a city close to a boundary will be cut off from "natural," that is, nearby, customers by the boundary. Less normal, but still quite frequent, is the city that because of differing prices and money values has a trading area across the border larger than in its own country. During the last few years we have seen how in Berlin people from the western sectors of the city flocked into East Berlin because of the lower exchange value of the East Mark; [16] later this trend was reversed when wares became scarce and the people from the Soviet sector came into West Berlin to purchase things unavailable in the East. Eventually movement in both directions slackened because of the political difficulties put in its way [17] (*cf.* Fig. 3-3, p. 64). On a smaller, but instructive scale it was shown that new businesses concentrated at the points of crossing from one to the other zone, while at the same time established businesses —barbers, grocers, cobblers, and others—located along the boundary but away from the crossings, had to close up because many of their customers could not reach them across the street, or at least could not pay the prices in a different currency.[18] What happened, dramatically, in Berlin within a short period and in a small area is but an illustration of what occurs in one or the other form along almost any boundary. Even if economic conditions on both sides of a boundary are approximately equal, prices on the same level, and boundary formalities at a minimum, the unavoidable formalities will influence the mutual movement.

[16] P. Schöller, "Stadtgeographische Probleme des geteilten Berlin," *Erdkunde*, Vol. 7, No. 1 (1953), p. 6.

[17] G. W. S. Robinson, "West Berlin, The Geography of an Exclave," *Geographical Review*, Vol. 43 (October, 1953), p. 549.

[18] Schöller, *loc. cit.*

Movement occurs not only in the form of trade, but also in commuting from the place of residence to the place of work. Some boundaries make commuting of this kind impossible or difficult; others invite it. Mexicans come across the border as seasonal labor and their heavy influx has created the problem of the so-called "wetbacks." On the Canadian border, especially in the Detroit area where social conditions on both sides of the border are similar, the problem of commuting across the boundary is of insignificant proportions. French mines and industries located in France, but along the Belgian and the Saar borders have attracted labor from across the border (*cf.* Fig. 5-1). There is a zone close to the border where daily commuters live; in a second, slightly overlapping zone we find commuters who return home only over the weekend; a third zone, that of seasonal migrants, is not distinctive, partly because of their small number in this particular area, and partly because their habitation can not be localized so distinctly.[19] We do not have comparable data for the French side of the border. It can only be assumed that there also a subzone of factories and mines which employ daily commuters can be distinguished from another wider, but overlapping zone with weekly commuters. Similar conditions exist on other boundaries.

FRONTIERS AND MEANS OF COMMUNICATIONS

Among the factors emphasizing the dividing function of the boundary is, in many cases, a country's communications system, the extension of which is halted by the boundary. Railroads often have their terminals at some distance from the boundary, or have more restricted service across it than in the interior. Good roads may deteriorate near the boundary into badly maintained secondary roads and trails. Even internal boundaries may have similar effects. The eastern Rhode Island-Massachusetts boundary was superimposed as a straight line on an area which had already developed irregular road and subdivisional patterns. Though roads may not be affected in this case, services such as gas, electricity, and water end abruptly at the border. School districts may have an inconvenient shape.[20]

There are, however, frontiers where the opposite effect occurs. On heavily fortified boundaries, military roads, built for heavy loads, form a dense net close to, and occasionally lead to, the very boundary where

[19] R. Capot-Rey, *La region sarroise* (Nancy, 1934).

[20] E. Ullman, "The Eastern Rhode Island-Massachusetts Boundary Zone," *Geographical Review,* Vol. 29 (1929), pp. 41 ff.

they terminate. Before World War II the Italians pursued such policy on their European boundaries, and extensive road-building preceded their attack on Ethiopia.[21] Another illustration is the six thousand-mile trans-Siberian railway which was pushed to completion in 1904, mainly for the purpose of defense. Military considerations also account for other railroad developments in Soviet Asia after World War II. Another influence of boundaries can be observed along every administrative boundary. People in small towns or on dispersed farms have business to transact with authorities, as for instance the tax collector, the courts, the school board, or the county agent. They will visit the seat of the local government more or less regularly and, on the occasion of these visits, do their shopping. The administrative centers therefore attract the population even if other towns may be in closer proximity.

THE FRONTIER AND ITS IMPACT ON LOCATION AND INDUSTRIES

Frontier zones are to a certain degree at a disadvantage as far as their economic activities are concerned. A new boundary is a strong deterrent to new investments and may even cause some industries to migrate farther inland. However, mines, primary agricultural production, industries dependent upon raw material, and in general industries whose histories and needs are closely linked with their geographical location cannot easily move away from boundaries. Other industries are less intimately wedded to a certain location, especially defense industries, and will be transferred to safer locations inland, especially when war or danger of war moves the frontier too close for comfort. Well known is the example of the Soviet Union, where whole industries have been moved east from the western frontier zones into the Volga region, behind the Urals, and into Asia. This movement reached its climax in the years of World War II. It seems to have slowed down considerably since then, partly, no doubt, because the satellite states have largely taken over the boundary functions of the western provinces, partly also because of the difficulties of this wholesale migration. In the United States, a trend can be observed to establish new critical defense installations far inland, in the Tennessee valley, in the deserts of the western plateaus, but nowhere near the borders or coasts, which can be easily reached from across the sea. In comparison, Sweden,

[21] D. Whittlesey, "The Impact of Effective General Authority Upon the Landscape," *Annals of the Association of American Geography,* Vol. 25 (1935), pp. 85 ff, has described the formation of defense zones or shells.

lacking large spaces remote from boundaries such as exist in the United States, has effected a transfer of critical, especially aircraft, industries to underground locations offering relative safety against attacks from the air. The Swedish example emphasizes the limitations, in aerial warfare, of a policy bent on establishing and transferring industrial plants inland and far from coasts and borders, since these locations do not necessarily deter an aggressor striking from the skies.[22]

CROSS-BOUNDARY INFLUENCES

Hardly any frontier has escaped being influenced from across the boundary. The influence may be only a few words of the foreign language helping to shape the local dialect, or a few borrowed habits in custom and food. It may lead to a more or less pronounced bilingualism, to likes or more often dislikes of the neighbor, to rare or frequent intermarriages, or at least to knowing more than one way of life. Frontier people, consciously or not, willingly or not, absorb some of the ways of their neighbor.[23] Or they retain and cling to older customs which have disappeared elsewhere, developing a cultural lag in areas remote from centers of a different and often more rapid cultural growth. The gaucho of the Argentinian Pampa has in some respects customs similar to those of his neighbors across the frontier in Bolivia, Paraguay, or Uruguay—customs which have disappeared from the vicinity of Buenos Aires. Sometimes such similarities across a frontier are remnants of former political alignments. Nobody will doubt that California is American in its way of life despite the Spanish-Mexican atmosphere suggested by some missions, churches, or place names. But few people realize that water rights in California, and elsewhere in the southwest, are still governed by law derived from Roman law in its Spanish-Mexican tradition and not by the Anglo-Saxon common law.[24]

CONTINUATION OF FEATURES ORIGINATING FROM BOUNDARIES NO LONGER IN EXISTENCE

However the frontier man may differ from his co-national in the interior, he will also differ from the people across the boundary, even if he should belong to the same linguistic or other minority group. This is due to his

22 See p. 189.
23 Boggs, *op. cit.*, p. 10, speaks in this connection of osmosis.
24 Whittlesey, "The Impact of Effective General Authority Upon the Landscape," *loc. cit.*, p. 54.

necessary adjustment to the economy and administration of the state of which he is a citizen. Economic activity, however, shapes the cultural landscape so deeply that, should such an international boundary cease to exist, many former features tend to persist.

One such feature which tends to persist are trade areas. In theory, a town of a certain size will dominate a more or less circular or hexagonal trade area. Such circular areas of different radii overlap according to size and extent of services offered by various urban areas. Political boundaries tend to distort such trade areas and these distortions disappear only some time after the disappearance of the political boundary. This is true also of the road and railroad systems. Although roads and railroads can be built quickly, it is seldom done as fast as is technically possible. Certain reminders of an old boundary may survive for centuries. The street plan of many German cities west of the Rhine and south of the Danube is still determined by the original location of the walls and main streets of the Roman castle on the site of which the city developed, while north and east of the ancient Roman boundary other patterns prevail.

Also psychological factors may be very persistent. The open, optimistic, neighborly ways of the American West are an inheritance of frontier days, where life would have been impossible without the unorganized but very efficient help of the neighbors. On the other hand, the aggressive nationalism of the French of Lorraine reflects a frontier mentality of an altogether different kind in this much-fought-over country.

In regions which have been fought over through long periods we often find that the contest has been instrumental in forcing certain characteristics upon the frontier population which distinguish them, in spite of their linguistic and religious bonds, from their neighbors.[25] The Saar is an illustration of a frontier area whose population has been wooed by French and Germans. As elsewhere under similar conditions, we find here nationality traits reflecting consciousness of a frontier situation which is precarious and, at the same time, offers opportunities for bargaining on a political and economic plane.[26]

IMPRINT OF THE BOUNDARY UPON THE LANDSCAPE

A boundary becomes more ingrained in the landscape and in the ways of the people the longer it exists. This, and not special topographic fea-

[25] *Ibid.*

[26] C. C. Held, "The New Saarland," *Geographical Review,* Vol. 41 (1951), esp. pp. 603 ff.

tures, is the main reason why old established boundaries seem often so much better than newly established ones. It has been asserted that if boundaries retain their locations through centuries, or reassume them when displaced, this is in itself a proof of the peculiar fitness of their location. That may be true in a few instances. Usually, however, it is the very existence of the boundary which shapes the human landscape and makes it advisable to retain old boundary sites or to readopt them. This is also the factual background for the argument for "historical" boundaries, specious in some cases, but very real in others. On the other hand, a new boundary, however artificial, acquires separating features of its own by prolonged existence.[27] Boundary-makers, especially those of the Versailles and St. Germain, Trianon and Neuilly treaties of 1919, have often been accused of geographical ignorance, of imperialistic greed, or of callous disregard of the popular wishes. Some of these accusations may be well founded. However, it should not be overlooked that every new boundary cuts through some older unit, requires adjustments, and will thereby cause a painful transition for some groups. In areas of old boundaries such birth pains are forgotten; they may even never have been felt painfully because boundaries had so few functions in former centuries. The human, if not the physical landscape has changed since the boundary was established. If there are valid reasons for a boundary change there is no way out of the dilemma; both the retention of the old or the creation of a new boundary will hurt.

THE PRESTIGE FACTOR

These factors of human geography, developed over a lengthy period, are a force working for preservation of an existing boundary. This force may in some cases be only one of several factors and in itself not very strong; it is, however, closely connected with nongeographical conditions, such as questions of prestige. Prestige has often hindered agreement by nations on boundary changes, even if they did not inconvenience the one partner and brought obvious advantages to the other. Only where the factor of prestige does not enter into the picture are such arrangements possible. It was possible in 1927 for Belgium to give up an area of 480 square miles of the Congo in return for a cession by Portugal of (Fig. 5-2) little more than one square mile near Matadi in the estuary of the Congo[28]—an area of uncrystallized boundaries. But it seems impossible

[27] G. Weigand, "Effects of Boundary Changes in the South Tyrol," *Geographical Review,* Vol. 40 (July, 1950).

[28] *The Statesman's Yearbook,* 1953, p. 807.

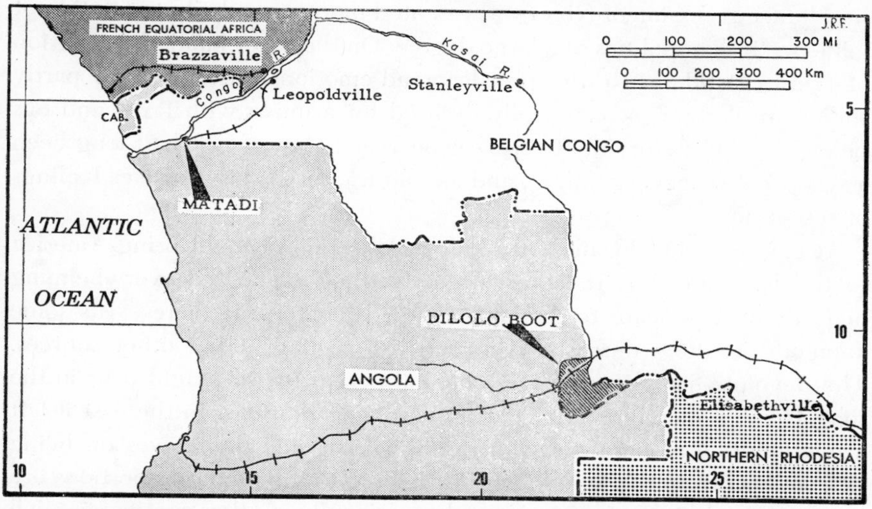

FIG. 5-2. The Congo Territory: Exchanges Between Belgium and Portugal.

for Austria to give up the almost-exclave of Jungbluth, containing a hamlet in mountainous terrain.[29] Other exchanges in colonial regions have been effected, hardly noticed in the metropolitan area and hardly realized by the natives of the area. Once a territory has acquired an emotional value, no economic *quid pro quo* can satisfy. When Switzerland needed the headwaters of a tributary of the Rhine, the Val di Lei, for a power plant, it was possible to reach an agreement over this uninhabited tiny area concerning use and indemnities, but not concerning the transfer of the sovereignty from Italy to Switzerland. If boundaries of a lower order, that is, not international boundaries, are to be corrected, however, such rectification is no longer uncommon though by no means easy.

EMOTIONAL ATTACHMENT

It is difficult to distinguish between questions of prestige and true emotional attachment based on long common history, memories, or symbolical values. The Italian people have easily forgotten the loss of Savoy, which was ceded to France as the price for Napoleon III's help in bringing about the unification of Italy in the war with Austria. Savoy was the home of the kings of Italy, but was not Italian in language or tradition. In most parts of Italy the identification with the dynasty was never strong. The

[29] See p. 63.

simultaneous cession of Nizza was resented more strongly, but still did not influence Italian politics to a large degree. On the other hand, the question of Trieste is still one to stir up widespread emotions. Trieste is only partly Italian-speaking, is economically ill-fitted for a union with Italy, and has belonged to Italy for only twenty-seven years. However, it had long been a symbol of success or failure, and any attack on its status evokes feelings of resentment.

At one time the slogan "Fifty-four forty or fight" could bring America to the brink of war. It is forgotten. Nothing binds the overwhelming majority of Americans to the once claimed territory. If there exists some antagonistic, often unreasoned anti-British feeling, it has other sources. The Revolutionary War and the colonial period is still fought over in the schools and remembered at Fourth of July celebrations. In the east it left a few tangible monuments. Many Americans pride themselves on being descendants from the fighters of this time. Yet no boundary questions are involved. In contrast, in Europe, and occasionally in other continents, such historical memories are usually somehow connected with boundary problems. This makes boundary changes, except by war, extremely difficult.

COASTAL BOUNDARIES

Despite all these forces working for the *status quo* there are, on almost every boundary, also forces which work for change. Stability, stronger or weaker pressure, and actual change result from the interaction of all these forces. There is hardly any boundary the stability of which is absolute. Problems exist even at boundaries such as coasts which by their very physical nature seem destined for stability. We have referred briefly to the proclamation by the United States that it would regard the continental shelf as pertaining to the United States.[30] We have mentioned in the same place that other states took this as an occasion to expand their claims seaward. In one case, that of Australia, the motive is to keep the Japanese fishermen away, a very understandable desire in view of the events of the last war, but a one-sided act subject to challenge at some future moment. The issue of the ownership of the submerged lands was settled, at least temporarily, by act of Congress of May 22, 1953. This act gives ownership to the coastal states within a zone of three miles between the low-water mark and the outer limit of the coastal waters, and ten and a half miles along the coasts of Florida and Texas (Fig. 5-3). It does not apply to tidal land—the zone lying between mean high and mean low water

[30] See p. 101.

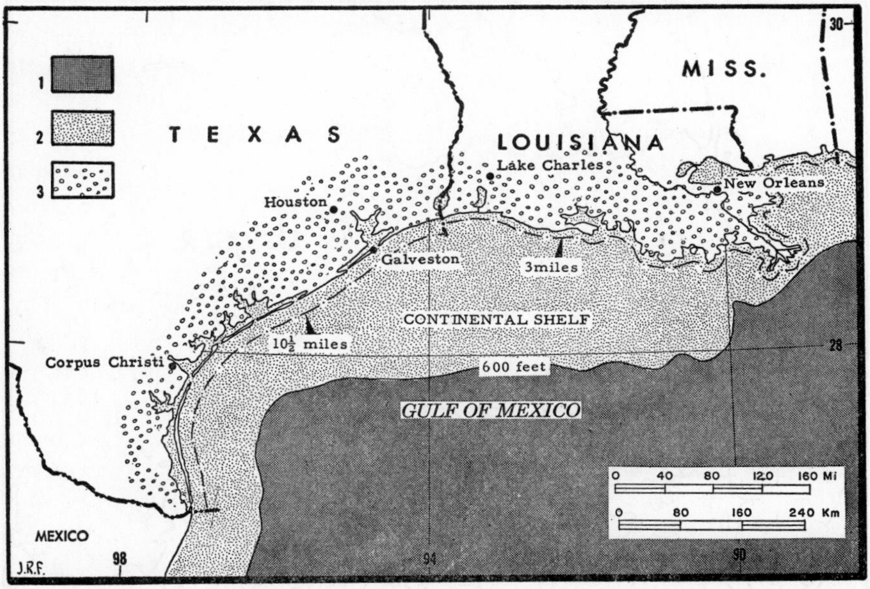

FIG. 5-3. State Boundaries in the Continental Shelf: Louisiana (3 miles), Texas (10½ miles): (1) High Seas of Gulf of Mexico; (2) Continental Shelf; (3) Salt Dome Oilfields.

which is submerged only temporarily generally twice a day. Fishing rights have played a considerable role in the development of the concept of territorial waters. France has retained two tiny islands off the coast of Newfoundland—Saint Pierre and Miquelon—as bases for its fishing fleet, and until 1904 clung to the right, acquired by the Treaty of Utrecht in 1713, for its fishermen to land on the coast and dry their catch within definite periods. France still retains fishing rights within the territorial waters. Similarly, American rights, cause of many recriminations, were fixed—and curtailed—only in 1910. Fishing rights in territorial waters and conflicts arising therefrom have also contributed to acerbate the relations between Japan and Russia.

One would hardly expect the coast circling the Arctic Ocean to be the stage for similar problems. Actually, nowhere else have coastal powers extended their claims so far seaward as here. Starting in 1927, the Soviet Union proclaimed the sector principle, claiming sovereignty over all the sea, including undiscovered islands, in a sector with its base on the coast extending from Murmansk to the Chukchee Peninsula and having its apex at the North Pole. The United States government has never recognized the validity of this legal construction, although all other powers

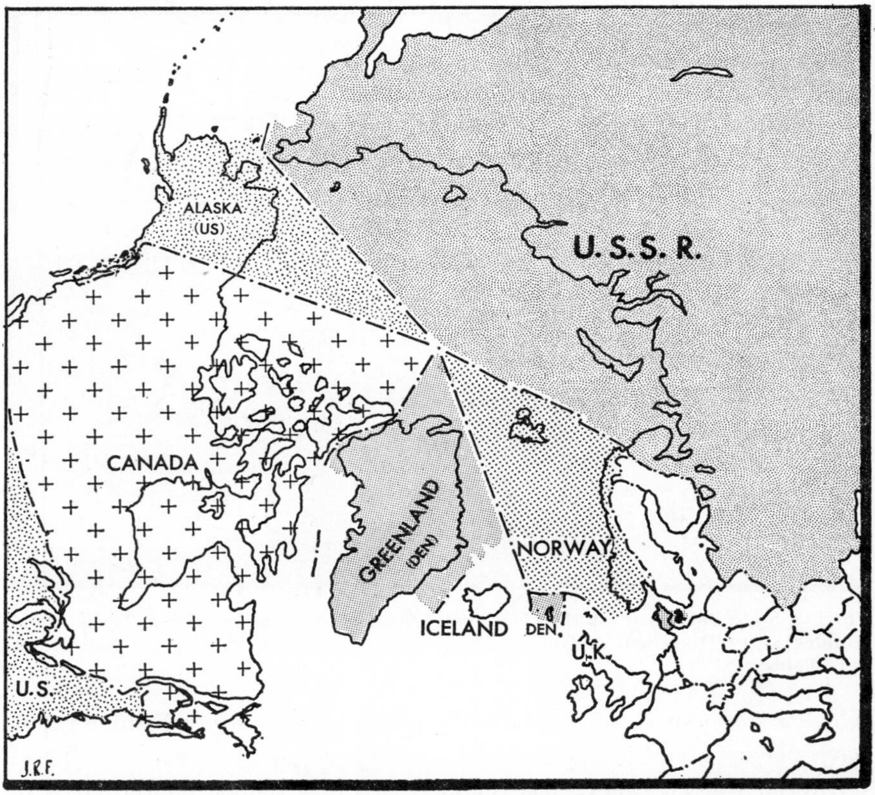

Fig. 5-4. The Sector Principle in the Arctic Ocean.

having interests in the Arctic or Antarctic have recognized it [31] (Fig. 5-4).

Coasts are not only a basis for expansion, they are also open to all kinds of intrusion. It has been said that coastal peoples have a wider horizon, are more influenced by foreign thought than people inland, not excluding those on land boundaries. There is a difference, however, between different types of coasts. Steep, rocky coasts; straight, sand-dune girded coasts on shallow waters and mangrove-grown tropical coasts may be practically inaccessible. High mountains a short distance behind the coast may restrict the influences coming from overseas. They may also force the coastal population to look for their livelihood on the water. Phoenicia and Greece are the classical examples; Norway, Iceland, and to a certain degree Japan, the modern ones. However, not every population takes to the sea. Neither the Indians of California nor the Araucanian Indians of Chile

[31] See pp. 82-84.

ever became seafaring, though confined by mountains and sea to an inhospitable narrow strip of land.

All these Pacific Indians remained culturally secluded because they never were able to reach an opposite coast.[32] Phoenicians and Greeks brought home cultural achievements from many coasts. There is no doubt that any accessible coast is open to varied influences, while land borders are open only to influences from one neighbor.

The negative factor in such accessibility is that coasts are open also to military invasions. Great Britain has been invaded by Celts, Romans, Anglo-Saxons, Danes, Norsemen, and French with results still to be found in the British demographic, linguistic, and cultural heritage. With the great outburst of European activity in the period of the Renaissance and overseas explorations, Europeans invaded the coasts of all other continents. Following invasion, the course of development depended on physiographic factors in the other continents, political and demographic conditions in the European homelands, and cultural levels of the non-European countries. Escarpments and rapids in rivers kept the European explorers on the coasts of Africa, whereas the accessible St. Lawrence and Mississippi led the French rapidly into the interior of America. A low level of civilization of the indigenous population kept the Europeans between mountains and sea in eastern Australia, while the advanced civilization of Peru and Mexico lured the Spaniards across tremendous mountain barriers. Few Frenchmen were available for the penetration of North America, while the coastal string of British colonies soon became the basis for westward migration on a broad front. In the highly civilized Asian countries, colonies along the coasts remained either purely commercial bases—Hongkong and Macao are relics on the coast of China—or became bases for political domination but not mass immigration. In India, Indonesia, the Philippines, and Burma this process has run its full course; political domination has vanished, but not without leaving a deep cultural imprint.

An interesting example of a country with coastal boundary is offered by Palestine. Invasions from all directions have penetrated into this country. Invasions from north and south usually passed through, using this poor and small country as a corridor between sea and desert to more alluring goals in the great river valleys. To the nomads from the east, however—warlike but small tribes—it appeared a "country flowing with milk and honey." From Abraham to the Arabs these intruders settled there. Less

[32] German geographers have a special term, *Gegenküste,* which recently has found entry into English-language geographical writing.

successful have been the intruders from the sea, Philistines as well as Crusaders. Their latest successors are the Jews, whose state in its configuration resembles that of its historic predecessors with its domination of the coastal plain and odd-shaped extensions inland.

As mentioned before, the successful resurrection of long-abolished boundaries has been regarded as proof of their location in a geographically favorable location. Such a statement can not be maintained as a general rule. The example of Palestine (*cf.* Fig. 7-7, p. 192) demonstrates its fallacies especially clearly, but also shows the extent of its validity. The eastern boundary of Palestine has been the edge of the desert time and again. However, this desert boundary shows a continuous change, depending upon the mutual strength of nomads and settlers, as well as upon the changes of climatic conditions, expressed in a series of moist or dry years. In western Palestine invaders from the sea could penetrate the plains, while the natives, pushed into a defensive position, held on to the high plateaus. Saul and David held the Judean plateau against the Philistines; but at the same period the Jebusites still maintained their stronghold on the least accessible part of the plateau, Jerusalem and Mount Zion.

BOUNDARIES AND POPULATION PRESSURE

It would be strange if ancient boundaries, even those that served well in the past, would fit equally well into modern conditions. Hardly any of the human conditions have remained unchanged. Almost everywhere, population, its increase and its pressure, has undergone basic changes. Again Palestine—indeed, all the countries of the Fertile Crescent—offers a good example. In the steppe and desert, living room is sparse. Nomadic tribes have to migrate as soon as their herds have eaten all edible food in one locality. They can return to the same place only after the pasturage has had a long period of recovery. They need, therefore, much space. If the tribe increases, it has to increase its herds or starve. Increased herds need more pasture. Soon the size limit is reached and quarrels with other tribes over pasture follow. Each tribal group alone is small and not able to conquer the fertile land of the settlers. This land lures them, however, and finally many tribes unite to conquer the settled land, originally to convert it into pasture, usually ending by becoming sedentary themselves. Akkadians and Aramaeans, Hebrews and Chaldaeans, Elamites and Hyksos, all repeated the same story. Mohammed united the Arabs with a religious idea and his successors led the Arabs farther afield than any of the preceding waves of nomadic conquerors had been able to penetrate.

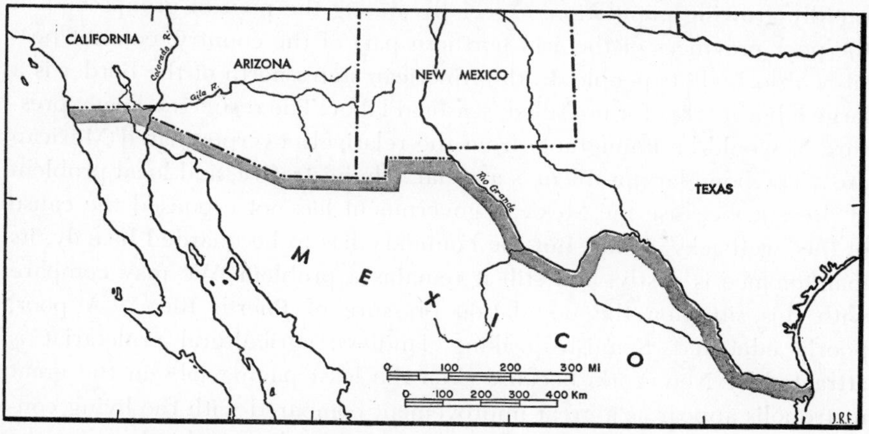

Fig. 5-5. The United States-Mexican Boundary.

The same story is repeated in all the steppe and desert countries of the world, and in other primitive societies. Overpopulated Pacific Islands sent their surplus population to people uninhabited islands. The Maoris reached New Zealand only a short time ahead of the white man.

Under conditions of technological progress countries can occasionally absorb part or all of a population increase. England at the time of the industrial revolution is the classic example. But the Greeks, in the period of their largest cultural progress, sent out scores of colonies. The early medieval German tribes, at the time when they were adopting the more productive three-field agricultural rotation, and had started using the iron ax for clearing the forest, were pushing into the sparsely settled Slavic countries to the east.

Population pressure is still one of the most powerful forces causing emigration, immigration, and conquest to win "Lebensraum." This urge to obtain new living space can be abused dishonestly, as it was by Hitler and Mussolini who, at the same time clamored for new space for their population surplus and initiated a program for a more populous nation at home. This can not disguise the fact that population pressure is a real problem. In this chapter we do not deal with the question of whether population pressure can be relieved by other measures than boundary changes; here it must suffice to point out that population pressure still accounts in our time for major boundary problems.

An American problem is that of the "wetbacks" on the southern boundary between the United States and Mexico [33] (Fig. 5-5). Mexico with its

[34] See p. 377.

rapidly growing population, especially among the poorest groups and in the poor provinces of the arid northern part of the country, can not possibly absorb all its people. In the American states north of the border is a large labor market for unskilled, seasonal labor. The result is a heavy pressure of would-be immigrants from the relatively overpopulated Mexican area. The boundary problem is a social, administrative, and local problem at present, because the Mexican government has not espoused the cause of the "wetbacks" so far. But the boundary has to be guarded heavily, its maintenance is costly, and still it remains a problem. We may compare with this situation the population pressure of Puerto Rico.[34] A poor, poorly educated, Spanish-speaking, landless, agricultural proletariat is attracted by New York, because even the least paying jobs in the great metropolis appear as a great improvement compared with the living conditions at home. There is no international boundary to hinder or make difficult migration or to threaten international complications. That does not eliminate the problem. It pushes the boundary problem, that of an administrative boundary, into the background, and emphasizes the problem of social and racial discrimination and adjustment.

BOUNDARIES AS SOCIAL DIVIDES

Even social boundaries may be mapped. Occasionally a street is a very distinct boundary between a "restricted" area and one peopled by a racial minority. However, such boundaries have less staying power than international ones.

Under the racial policy of the Union of South Africa the native Bantus are theoretically confined to reservations which have insufficient resources. The Bantus are forced to migrate into the mines and compounds of the South African gold fields or, less often, to farms to find their living. In order to maintain the artificial social order the Union is forced to strengthen its segregation policy. Enclaves or neighboring areas which do not conform to the South African pattern are an actual or potential threat to the social order of the Union. This has already led to the practical annexation of South-West Africa, despite the protest of the United Nations. There is also a mounting pressure for incorporation of the British protectorate in Basutoland, Swaziland, and Bechuanaland (*cf.* Fig. 3-2, p. 60), and for expanding the Union to the Rhodesias.

Social boundaries of the kind existing in the United States can, politically and sociologically, be highly disturbing, and the social boundaries

[33] See p. 377.

in South Africa which are the expression of the *Apartheid* principle may contribute at some future date to explosive developments affecting African lands far beyond the boundaries of South Africa. Population pressure, more than ever before, affects boundary structures seriously. It was population pressure, combined with an open-door policy of the British colonial administration, which led to mass immigration of Indians into Burma, Ceylon, and the Malayan Peninsula; into the latter Chinese came in even greater numbers (*cf.* Fig. 10-3, p. 378). World War II and its aftermath has stopped this migration, and forced many Indians, especially from Burma, to flee their new home. India and Ceylon are in negotiation about the repatriation of a large part of the Indians. But in Malaya the creation of a plural society can no longer be undone.[35]

STABILITY OF BOUNDARIES OF SPARSELY-POPULATED AREAS

We can not neglect the fact that boundaries between areas of rapidly increasing population and areas of sparse population are threatened in their stability. A case in point is the relationship of Australia to the over-populated lands of Southeast Asia and of Japan. We may agree with Griffith Taylor's assertion that "the empty lands" of Australia are a burden to the Commonwealth rather than an asset, and their vast potentialities exist only in the mind of the ignorant booster.[36] Although he estimates that Australia could, mainly in the southeast, sustain twenty million people under the present standard of living, he admits that with the lower standards of Central Europe this number could be doubled and trebled. At present only seven million are living there. Thus it may still, for a long time, appear an empty continent to the overcrowded Asian nations.[37]

The villages of France have been depopulated by the combined effects of low birth rates and migration to the cities. Gradually Italian and Spanish immigrants are taking the place of the Frenchmen who are moving into the cities. As long as the cultural attraction of France is strong enough to absorb these humble immigrants, this process is healthy and is not likely to cause friction. However, should France no longer be able to assimilate the immigrants, and large Italian and Spanish-speaking areas develop on the French side of the boundary, the boundary

[35] J. Morrison, "Aspects of the Racial Problem in Malaya," *Pacific Affairs,* Vol. 22 (December, 1949). The official census of 1947 showed that the Federation of Malaya had a population of 4,908,000. Of this total the Malays made up 49.5 per cent, the Chinese 38.4 per cent, and the Indians 10.8 per cent; see also pp. 379, 380.

[36] G. Taylor, *Australia,* 6th ed. (London, 1951), p. 477.

[37] On immigration to Australia, see p. 375.

will become less secure despite its location along the high ranges of Alps and Pyrenees.

ECONOMIC REASONS FOR BOUNDARY OBSOLESCENCE

Population is not the only factor for change. Significant changes which affect the economic structure of a country are likely to affect its boundary structure as well. The development of commercial cities and later of a capitalistic economy has been responsible to a large degree for the obsolescence of the ill-defined boundaries between small feudal principalities. This process has been going on since the Renaissance, when in Italy a few powerful cities, republics, or city states, some ruled by military dictators called *condottieri*—Venice and Florence, as well as Milan or Ferrara—established viable territorial states reaching beyond their city limits. This happened in France at approximately the same period, when autocratic kings deprived the nobility of their actual rule and left them only titles and income, but no power. The unification of France in administrative respects was not complete as long as the kings retained the feudal system of levying tolls on many stations along the main trade routes. The French Revolution opened the way for the transformation of the artisan and merchant citizenry into a capitalistic society by sweeping away also these internal boundary-like obstructions together with other obsolescent institutions. A continuous boundary around France was established, indicating not only a common political allegiance but also economic uniformity.

This process has not yet come to an end. Economic and technological development has made the economic position of the small and weak countries rather precarious. Immediately after World War II, three small countries, Belgium, the Netherlands, and Luxembourg, agreed to enter into an economic Union, Benelux.[38] Although the implementation of the Union is proceeding at a much slower pace than was anticipated,[39] it has become a reality. Larger unions of the European countries have proceeded even more slowly, especially if seen with the impatient eyes of many Americans who recognize the advantages of such international groupings on an economic plane but are too distant to appreciate the numerous intangible

[38] The agreement was entered into in September, 1944, became effective in October, 1947, and the common customs tariff was activated on January 1, 1948.

[39] Among the retarding factors the following are worth mentioning: (*a*) Belgium's situation after World War II was much better than that of the Netherlands, which had to overcome the loss of its colonial empire and had to repair the severe damage caused by the opening of the dykes by the Germans during the war; (*b*) Belgium, Luxembourg, and the Netherlands were in many ways competitive economic systems; (*c*) the mentality of the Belgian and Dutch nations differs in many ways of life.

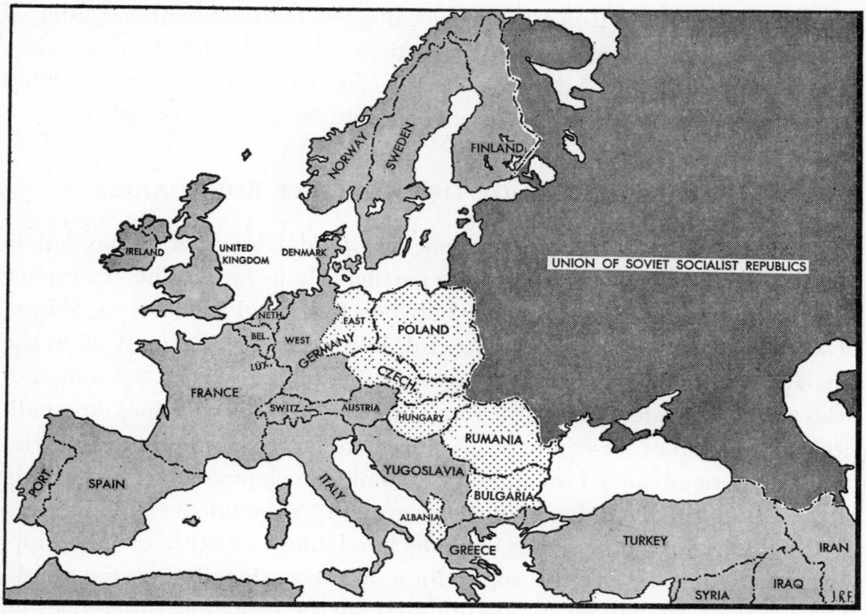

Fig. 5-6. The Satellite Countries of Eastern Europe.

factors which the unifying process has to overcome. Another important development in Western Europe was the conclusion of the European Coal and Steel Community [40] preceded by the Organization for European Economic Co-operation (1947), and the European Payments Union (1950).

OBSOLESCENCE OF BOUNDARIES IN THE SOVIET ORBIT

From an altogether different political, social, and ideological point of view, the Communist regime in the Kremlin has embarked on an integration program aimed at drawing closer to the Russian center the satellite countries of Eastern Europe (Bulgaria, Albania, Rumania, Hungary, Czechoslovakia, Poland, and East Germany [Fig. 5-6]). Under this program, the requirements of the U.S.S.R. were to dictate the food production and the industrial output (including expansion and relocation of industries) within these countries. This long-range policy has affected in many ways the boundary system within the Soviet orbit. Economically, it has expedited the withering-away of economic boundaries within the Soviet sphere of interest, while tightening the same boundary against the

[40] The Treaty, proposed by French Minister for Foreign Affairs Schuman, was signed on April 18, 1951 and instituted on August 10, 1952.

West. Politically, the Iron Curtain has affected both external and internal boundaries; for the same Soviet regulations which strangled the freedom of movement of citizens desiring to visit countries of the West prevented them from traveling freely from one satellite country to the other.[41]

OTHER INSTANCES OF OBSOLESCENT BOUNDARIES

Outside of Europe the obsolescence of feudal boundaries has led to large-scale territorial reorganization, particularly in India. The emergence of the new international boundary between India and Pakistan should not obscure the revolutionary, yet peaceful disappearance of almost all of the small princely states and of thousands of miles of boundaries. Such boundaries often separated areas still retaining the social and economic conditions of a feudal order—some tiny, some quite large—from other territories of much more advanced social and economic development, areas standing at the threshold of modern industrial growth. Although the political importance of these boundaries had declined under British overlordship, local laws, differing systems of taxation, and occasionally varying conditions of access to markets, tended to increase the economic differences on the two sides of these boundaries. On the other hand, the reorganization of the internal political geography of India was found to have significant consequences in the economic field. In the western hemisphere, the attempts of Argentina to eliminate the customs boundaries between itself, Chile, Bolivia, and Uruguay point to analogous developments.

Differential economic growth changes the value and the functions of boundaries in other respects also. For instance, from the viewpoint of Egypt, it has at times been possible to regard the boundary between Egypt and the Sudan with equanimity. Modern hydrological developments, such as the construction of dams, reservoirs, and flood control projects, have made the Egyptians more and more aware that their agriculture depends entirely on the water supply systems originating in the Sudan. It has been said succinctly that Egypt "lives on borrowed water," and it is for this reason that the goal of Egypt's policy now is to control the Sudan, preferably by eliminating the boundary between this area and Egypt.

Interest in the southern and southeastern boundaries of what is now Saudi Arabia has been dormant for centuries (*cf.* Fig. 4-3). Oman, Ha-

[41] How difficult it is even for a totalitarian regime such as the Soviet Union to keep an Iron Curtain truly intact is evidenced by the fact that between 1950-54 not less than 1,800,000 people, or 10 per cent of East Germany's population, fled to West Germany! (See also p. 362.)

dhramaut, and the smaller sheikhdoms were looking toward the Indian Ocean, the tribes of Inner Arabia were concerned with the west and north. The wide desert between them was of little concern to anyone. The discovery of oil has changed the picture. Saudi Arabia now asserts its sovereignty over the "Empty Quarter," in order to be able to lease its suspected hidden oil treasures to oil companies.

In this instance modern economic developments often have the effect of forcing neighboring countries to break up a vaguely delimited border area by definite boundary. In contrast, established boundary lines can become an obstacle to efficient management of mines under modern subsurface exploitation conditions and as a consequence, new boundary agreements will be effected between two adjacent countries. Occasionally in such instances, the new subterranean boundary changes agreed upon will deviate from the surface boundary. This was the arrangement in the salt mines of Hall and Reichenhall at the Austrian-German boundary and in some coal mines north of Maastricht at the German-Dutch boundary.

Expansion of industry leads to the quest for new markets, new sources of raw materials, and new areas of capital investment. The acquisition of new markets and new sources of raw materials by colonial expansion and imperialistic conquest has been responsible for the disappearance of many boundaries. The independence of quite a few states has been undermined or impaired by their dependency on foreign capital for development of their industrial potential. Thus the existence, side by side, of states on a different level of industrial and technological development has led in some cases to conquest, in others to a change of the boundary function.

THEORIES OF ORGANIC GROWTH OF STATES

The conditions of differential population growth, population pressure, differential economic and technological development and the influence of all these factors upon the political fate of countries attracted attention very early, and led to the organic theory of the state. Friedrich Ratzel developed this theory and applied it to human geography.[42] He was the first to popularize the idea that "there are boundaries which change so fast, e.g., boundaries of expanding peoples that it is possible to speak directly of migratory boundaries. . . . The apparently rigid boundary is only the stoppage of a movement." [43]

[42] The first chapter of F. Ratzel's *Politische Geographie* (München and Berlin, 1897), is called: "Der Staat als bodenständiger Organismus" (The State as Organism tied to the Soil).

[43] *Ibid.* (3rd ed. by E. Oberhummer), p. 386.

Ellen Churchill Semple, Ratzel's best known American disciple, expressed the same thought in the sentence: "As territorial expansion is the mark of growth, so the sign of decline is the relinquishment of land that is valuable or necessary to a people's well-being." [44] She exemplifies this idea among other examples by saying: "Japan's recent aggression (referring to the Russian-Japanese war of 1904/05) against the Russians in the Far East was actuated by the realization that she had to expand into Korea at the cost of Muscovite ascendancy, or contract later at the cost of her own independence." [45]

Ratzel described the change of boundaries in the spirit of the scholarly observer. So did Miss Semple. Some of Ratzel's followers, however, tried to use such geographical observations as guide for political action. They could refer to statements of the master,[46] quoted here in the translation by Miss Semple: "The struggle for existence means a struggle for space." [47] Thus emerged geopolitics.[48] Its leading exponent, Haushofer, has incorporated such ideas in many articles and in his book on boundaries.[49] He writes: "we recognize the boundary through empirical observation as an organ, a living being, destined either to shrink or to push outward, not rigid, in no case a line—in contrast to the theoretical concept . . ."

The French geographer Ancel, an outspoken foe of German geopolitics [50] and of the use of pseudogeographical arguments as base for claims for natural boundaries,[51] nevertheless arrives at a concept which does not differ basically from that of the geopoliticians. He states that "a boundary is a political isobar which indicates the momentary equilibrium between two pressures." [52] Like those he means to criticize, he overstresses the factors working for change and neglects those working for stability. He also overlooks the fact that the pressure exerted from one or both sides upon a boundary may not result in a dislocation of the boundary, but in the change of its function. As important as such a change of function may

[44] E. C. Semple, *Influence of Geographic Environment* (New York, 1911), p. 163.

[45] *Ibid.*, p. 66.

[46] F. Ratzel, *Der Lebensraum* (Tübingen, 1901), p. 157. Ratzel, however, was speaking of plants and animals and only by implication of man.

[47] Semple, *op. cit.*, p. 170.

[48] General problems of geopolitics (versus political geography) are discussed on pp. 5 ff. Here we are concerned with boundary problems as seen through the glasses of geopolitics.

[49] K. Haushofer, *Grenzen* (Berlin-Grunewald, K. Vowinkel, 1927), p. 13.

[50] J. Ancel, *Géopolitique* (Paris, 1936).

[51] J. Ancel, *Manuel géographique de politique Européènne,* Vol. I: "L'Europe Centrale" (Paris, 1936), pp. 12 ff.

[52] J. Ancel, *Géographie des frontières* (Paris, 1938).

be, it is not always visible on a map, and because of its gradual nature is not even always realized immediately by the frontier people themselves.

IDEOLOGICAL JUSTIFICATIONS OF EXPANSION

Concepts which helped the conquering white man to forget lingering pangs of his conscience have found their expression in slogans such as "the White Man's burden," or "Manifest Destiny." [53] Though it was denounced later as hypocrisy, at one time hundreds of thousands of Englishmen honestly believed that it was their moral duty, burden though it was, to expand the boundaries of the British Empire to include the poor pagans, to educate them to an industrious life, and to administer their lands according to the West's advanced concepts.[54] In 1900, a great majority in the United States believed in their divine destiny to spread American civilization westward.[55]

The communist ideology, also, is a messianic doctrine, bent on "improving" the whole world. While in the psychological make-up of many of the Soviet elite the lust for power is stronger than the belief in their apostolate, there can be little doubt that among some of the leaders and certainly within the ranks of communist youth a deep conviction in the messianic destiny of communism exists.

There are probably very few wars of conquest in which the ideological factor is absent. Very often, as in the Soviet example, it can not be separated from other motives. Some historians and political scientists are inclined to neglect this ideological factor. Marxian philosophy is inclined to stress the economic causes and to neglect or to minimize as superstructure, if not as outright fraud, ideological reasons. In some cases it may be impossible to come to an agreement. If one primitive tribe raids another, it may be impossible to refute the claim that the underlying cause is the opportunity to loot, while it appears that the tradition of the nation does not accept the young man into the community as a full-fledged member before he has proved his courage and valor in a fight. The human trait of aggressiveness has been investigated thoroughly in respect to the individual since Freud drew attention to it as basic; its significance as motive power in international relations is still rather obscure. Fortunately, it is not necessary in this connection to prove or disprove the claim that certain

[53] See pp. 10-12.

[54] D. Whittlesey, *The Earth and the State* (New York, 1944), pp. 127-128.

[55] Although a popular slogan since the 1840's, "manifest destiny" was clearly endorsed by a majority of the voters as late as the presidential elections of 1900. From then on it lost rather quickly its unsophisticated appeal; see also pp. 10-12.

ideological motives are superstructures according to Marx and his followers, or sublimations according to Freud and his school, or primary facts.

Ideologies are subject to change. The feudal economic and political order was possible and secure only as long as undeveloped transportation allowed and even forced every small area to lead an isolated existence; as long as social stratification was regarded as willed by God; and as long as loyalty was regarded as a purely personal bond. The feudal order disappeared long ago, but remnants have existed into the twentieth century. Until 1918 the Prince of Liechtenstein was sovereign in his tiny country, but subject to the Austrian Empire in his other much larger estates. Polish noblemen were simultaneously subjects of the Austrian Emperor and the Russian Czar. Similar conditions survived in India until 1947. In general, however, the territorial state replaced the feudal state all over the world wherever it existed.

TERRITORIAL STATE BOUNDARIES AND NATIONAL STATES

Our concept of boundaries is essentially still that of the territorial state, inherited from the concept that the state belongs to the ruler. Much confusion has been created in our minds by the unrealized fact that this concept does not fit present conditions. Men regard themselves no longer as primarily subjects of a lord. The development of the democratic idea was insolubly connected with that of the nation. Men are emotionally bound to their nation and feel that they owe allegiance to it. The national state has replaced the territorial state in the minds of men. It has not yet replaced the territorial state and its boundaries on the surface of the earth. Fortunate is the country where state and nation coincide as is the case in the United States and in most American republics. In Europe, however, and more recently in Asia and Africa, nation is more and more identified with a common language.[56] Minorities develop a double allegiance. As long as in their system of values allegiance to the state, to the people with whom they share common traditions, takes precedence over allegiance to the people who speak the same language, the inherited framework of the territorial state is adequate. Switzerland in Europe is the best example of this order of values. The overwhelming majority of Swiss are first Swiss, and then German, French, or Italian. As a consequence the boundaries of Switzerland have not changed in this age of nationalism.

[56] See Chapter 11 on the Political Geography of Languages.

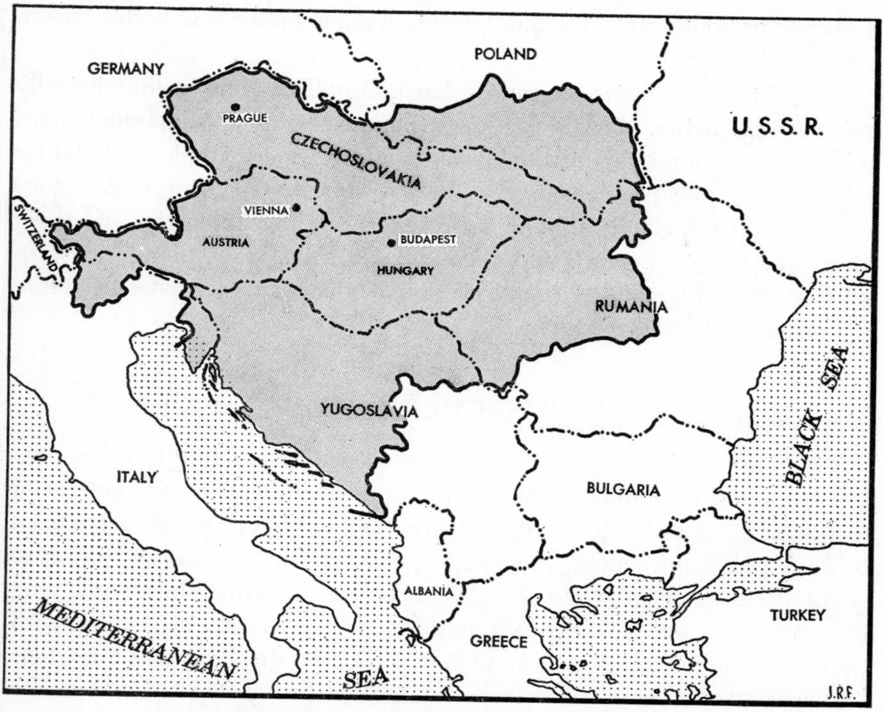

Fig. 5-7. The Break-up of the Hapsburg Empire after 1918.

Another outstanding example of a state that has won the allegiance of its citizens of foreign tongue is the United States. Despite individual defections of German-speaking Americans during both World Wars, and despite the widespread suspicions against "hyphenated" Americans during World War I, the American community has stood the test of time. Actually most immigrants desire for themselves or at least for their children to become Americans not only in allegiance, but also outwardly by adoption of the English language of the majority. A favorable condition is also that non-English speaking groups do not as a rule occupy contiguous territories in the United States.

In many cases, from the time of the French Revolution to the most recent claims of Franco for Gibraltar, and of Afghanistan for the Pushtu-speaking areas, the linguistically uniform national state could not be fitted into borders created under different conditions. Wars and revolutions followed. Boundaries were changed, either by unification, as in Germany and India, or by breakup of large states, such as the Hapsburg (Fig. 5-7) and the Ottoman Empires, or by conquest of border areas, such as Alsace-

Lorraine or Southern Tyrol and Trieste, to name only a few better-known examples.

Linguistic boundaries are rarely sharp. Usually a zone of linguistically mixed areas exists. Nor do language boundaries as a rule follow lines which for economic or other reasons would be more convenient. Hitler tried to solve this problem by two devices; first, by asserting that in case of irreconcilable claims, that of the "higher race," meaning that of ethnic Germans, had to prevail; and secondly, by transfer of populations. In other words, the stability of a traditional boundary was regarded more important than other factors.

IDEOLOGICAL GROUPINGS

While the strife for national boundaries is still spreading to other continents, a new evaluation of boundaries is developing as a concomitant of a changing order of values. For an increasing number of people allegiance to some political ideology—democracy, communism, or fascism—seems to stand first in their order of values. With Hitler and Mussolini this striving to unite in one state ideologically-uniform people was not reconciled with traditional national values. The policy of the two dictators was a mixture between extreme nationalism and the attempt to regroup nations on the basis of their adherence to fascist ideologies.

Present-day alignments follow not only ideological groupings, but have tremendously changed the function of boundaries. Czechoslovakia's boundaries—with two small exceptions—may be the same as before 1939. However, the boundary between Czechoslovakia and Western Germany has become a part of the Iron Curtain and almost all traffic has stopped across it. Barbed wire barricades on all roads have replaced the old simple signs announcing the existence of a boundary. On the other side, with the progressing integration of Czechoslovakia into the Soviet economic bloc, the boundaries of Czechoslovakia with the U.S.S.R., Poland, and Hungary are losing some of their functions. We have mentioned this process before in its economic aspects which lead to the creation of large economic units in Eastern as well as in Western Europe. With the creation of the Soviet bloc the boundaries lose also some of their political and military functions. Soviet troops may not actually cross the boundary into Czechoslovakia; they could do so in case of need without provoking an international conflict.

Perhaps even more significant, education on both sides of the boundary is organized along the same lines. The Russian language is being taught so thoroughly that engineers and probably other professional people in the future should have no difficulty in exerting their skill in other countries of the Soviet orbit without preparatory adjustment. The legal systems are rapidly shaped after a uniform pattern. The Russification program which at present sweeps through the lands of the Soviet orbit would, if continued radically, gradually erase the cultural distinctions within the large family of nations of the Soviet Union and its satellite nations.

In the tearing-down of cultural boundaries which characterize the Soviet system, the religious differences that were factors in the conflicts between Roman-Catholic Czechs and Poles on the one side, Russians and Ukrainians on the other side, would, according to Soviet planning, gradually decrease and make way for the uniformity of materialistic-Marxian philosophy.

This development in the communistic ideological orbit is not matched in the democratic world. Here the trend to unification has found its expression, as pointed out before, in weakening certain boundary functions in the economic and military-political realms. Here the ideological factor has played a subsidiary role, not vigorous enough to modify strong economic considerations. In the United States, tariff questions and immigration restrictions are regarded by many as of such overriding importance that their ideological repercussions are hardly taken into consideration. If, nevertheless, a democratic community of states is emerging, it is mainly as a result of resistance to the fascist and communist pressures of the last two decades. Such a state lacks the cohesion which religious communities have achieved occasionally in the past.

CONCLUSIONS

We arrive, therefore, at the conclusion that human progress and natural changes are continuously at work to change the functions of boundaries and their value for the bounded areas. Demographic, economic, and ideological developments interact in this process. Nevertheless, boundary changes occur only at intervals and usually as the result of wars, conquest, or revolution. There are strong forces, economic, historical, and ideological, which work for stability. Stability does not mean absence of change; it includes change of function. An existing boundary may not only acquire new functions, it may also gradually lose functions to the point, if not of complete vanishing, of being reduced to the performance of unspectacular functions, as in the case of internal boundaries which do not give cause for armed conflicts.

CHAPTER

6

Political Core Areas, Capital Cities, Communications

INTERIOR ZONES AS "CORE" AREAS

Interior areas form as a rule the main body of a political unit. Only in small political units of elongated form do we find territories consisting mainly of frontier zones. Whereas frontier zones play a definite and specific role in the political geography of any country, interior areas differ widely and can not in their manifold ramifications be discussed as units which share the same characteristics. Large parts of the interior are of interest to the political geographer only insofar as they add bulk to the political unit, either in size or in population, in raw materials or in finished products, in distance or in diversity. There are, however, parts of a political unit, usually parts of its interior, which have special significance for the body politic. These parts are called core areas.

THE CORE AREA IN REGIONAL AND POLITICAL GEOGRAPHY

In regional geography the core area is usually considered that part of a region in which the characteristic features of a region can be observed best because they prevail over other incidental features. Thus the core of the Middle West corn belt is in areas where other types of agriculture do not play a significant role and where industry also is dependent on or serves largely this particular form of agriculture. Hog raising, slaughterhouses, and farm machinery factories are characteristic of the corn belt.

A political core area is somewhat different. Within its often relatively small area is concentrated the political power of a state or of a secondary political unit.[1] What happens in the core area has ramifications far beyond the area itself.

THE CAPITAL

For a preliminary identification of the core of a political unit it is generally sufficient to identify the capital city.[2] The capital city contains the central executive organs of a political unit and commonly other central institutions, judicial, legislative, educational, and cultural. A differentiation should be made between those institutions closely connected with the function of a capital and those that are in an area irrespective of whether the capital is there. On the other hand, these latter features may provide the explanation for the location of many a capital in a specific area.

RELATIONSHIP OF CORE AND CAPITAL AREA

A significant interrelationship exists between the core area of a country and the location of its capital. But, as is pointed out above, to focus on the capital city of a country provides only a preliminary identification of its core area. In the following discussion an attempt is made to trace certain general trends as they reveal themselves in the comparison of capital and core areas. Sometimes the two are identical. Sometimes the initial selection of a place as site of the capital results in the consequent growth of a political, and in some cases also of an economic core area. In other instances we find that a new political and economic core area develops at a distance from the capital area. Then the problem arises inevitably as to whether intangible factors, such as tradition and prestige, prove strong enough to maintain the capital location at its original place, or whether the centripetal forces of the core area are stronger and will eventually result in the shift of the capital to a new site. The following discussion is limited to a few outstanding examples that are treated in terms of political geography only. The reader who wishes to study the role of capital cities on a broader plane and in its historical and cultural impacts is referred to the stimulating treatment of this subject by A. J. Toynbee in *A Study of History*.[3]

[1] D. Whittlesey, *The Earth and the State* (New York, 1944), pp. 2 and 597, define the core or "nuclear" core as "the area in which or about which a state originates."

[2] W. G. East, in his essay on "The Nature of Political Geography" (*Politica*, 1937, p. 273), defines therefore the core, or as he calls it, nuclear region, as the one "which, lying around the capital, contains the major endowment of the state in respect of population, resources and political energy."

[3] A. J. Toynbee, *A Study of History*, Vol. VII (New York, 1954), pp. 193-239.

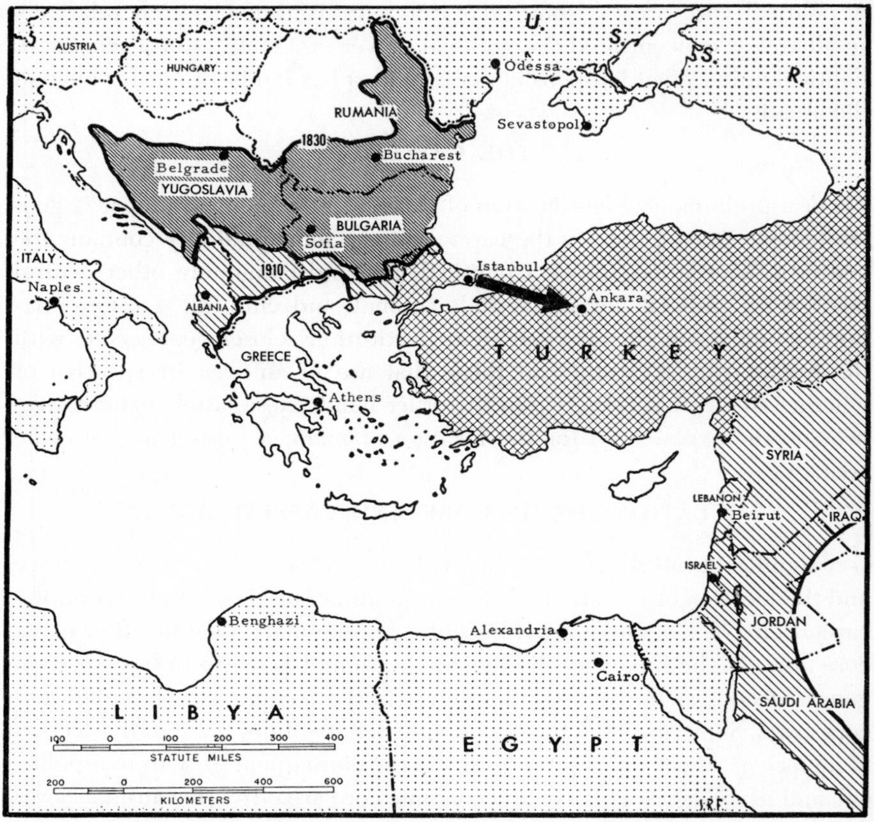

Fig. 6-1. The Shifting Core of Turkey.

SHIFT OF CAPITAL: TURKEY

In contrast to the situation prevailing during World War II when the Soviet government, for purely military reasons, evacuated Moscow and made Kuibyshev the temporary capital, we observe in Turkey the genuine shift of a capital from Istanbul to Ankara where the government of Kemal Ataturk moved it. A provincial city began immediately to develop as a focal point for the Turkish Republic [4] (Fig. 6-1). This shift can only in part be explained by what appeared to be an arbitrary decision of the government to remain in Ankara, even after the emergency that had caused the shift had passed. The real reason for the shift must be seen in the fact that the Straits and Istanbul had lost many of the factors that had

[4] See E. Fischer, "Southern Europe," in G. W. Hoffman, ed., *A Geography of Europe* (New York, 1954), pp. 463-465.

made them the core of the old Ottoman Empire. They were no longer in a central position for Turkey (Fig. 6-1). After the loss of the European provinces Istanbul's bridge position was of no peculiar value. The important trade between the Black Sea countries and the Mediterranean since antiquity came to an almost complete standstill when the Bolshevist Revolution had replaced a wheat-exporting Russia by a Soviet state striving for autarchy. Istanbul had never been a manufacturing center. It had been a gathering point for all the nations of the Ottoman Empire and had a very strong Greek element. This had been an advantage for the Ottoman Empire, which used Turks as soldiers and governors but filled many administrative positions with Greeks and Armenians. This national composition made Istanbul unfit to serve as the core of a national Turkish state. When Ankara was chosen as its capital, a number of favorable factors contributed to the development of a new core. It was in the approximate center of the state, in an area of pure Turkish population. To this were added the governmental functions, and gradually some industry, and railroad and road connections were established in all directions.

LACK OF IDENTITY BETWEEN POLITICAL CORE AND CAPITAL: THE GROWTH OF WASHINGTON, D.C.

We find in the example of Istanbul and Ankara almost all of the features which are the characteristics of a political core. These stress the degree to which a capital can serve as the indication of a political core. However, not every capital is the real core of a country. Newly-founded capitals may need a long time to attract other than purely governmental functions. An outstanding example is the development of Washington. It is obvious that in a federal state the functions of the federal government are of less importance than in a centralized state. Therefore, the influence of the governmental functions in creating a political core area is less in a federal state. Washington's growth as a political center was retarded by these factors, until during World War I, and later, especially under the New Deal, the functions of the federal government grew in size and importance. Never before had the central direction of the armed forces played such a role. Furthermore, because of the relatively small influence American naval or military power exerted upon relations with other countries, the actual influence the United States exerted abroad had little to do with a power-backed foreign policy. This influence originated rather from the growing economic power of the United States and because it had become the principal haven for immigrants. Consequently, the area of highest political power, the political core, was not centered in the capital but in the area of the most intensive economic activity, in the coastal belt extending from southern New England to Baltimore. This was also the area where many products of other regions converged for export, where the immigrants landed and a large proportion of them stayed, and where the population was the densest.

STABILITY OF CAPITAL LOCATION IN THE LIGHT OF POLITICAL CHANGES

One major reason for the original selection of Washington as the capital site was its central location between the northern and southern states. With the expansion of the United States westward and, at the same time, with the rapid increase of population in the north, Washington lost this locational advantage. Yet no shift of the capital was contemplated because a capital has the tendency to remain in the place where it was founded. This is partly a matter of convenience and the costs involved in the abandonment of buildings designed for special purposes with the resulting necessity of erecting new ones; mostly, however, it is due to tradition and prestige. Rome, Jerusalem, and Mecca are prime examples. Mecca has nothing to recommend it except its religious significance. It is at present only the second capital of Saudi Arabia and shares the capital position with the more centrally located Riyadh. Mecca emerged from periods of obscurity several times in its long history for no other apparent reason than the intangible impact of its tradition. It is a moot question whether Rome would have been selected as the capital of an Italian national state except for its tradition as the seat of the Roman Empire and the Papacy. In these eighty-odd years since it became the capital of Italy it has increased in stature, but not solely by reason of the concentration of government functions. It became one of the foci of the Italian railroad system, though Milan and perhaps some other cities are rivaling its importance in this respect. Subsequently Rome has become a seat of industry, but there is still little indication that it may become the center of an industrial district, as are Turin and Genoa.[5]

Still more significant is the case of Jerusalem. The capital of the revived

[5] According to official Italian statistics, Rome's population has more than doubled since 1921, when it was 692,000. It has increased ten times since 1850, when it was 175,000. It totaled 1,791,000 in 1954, and is approaching the 2,000,000 mark which it reached at the height of the Roman Empire when it was the political, economic, and social capital not only of the Mediterranean areas but likewise of the western world, including a Transalpine annex extending to the Rhine and the Tyne.

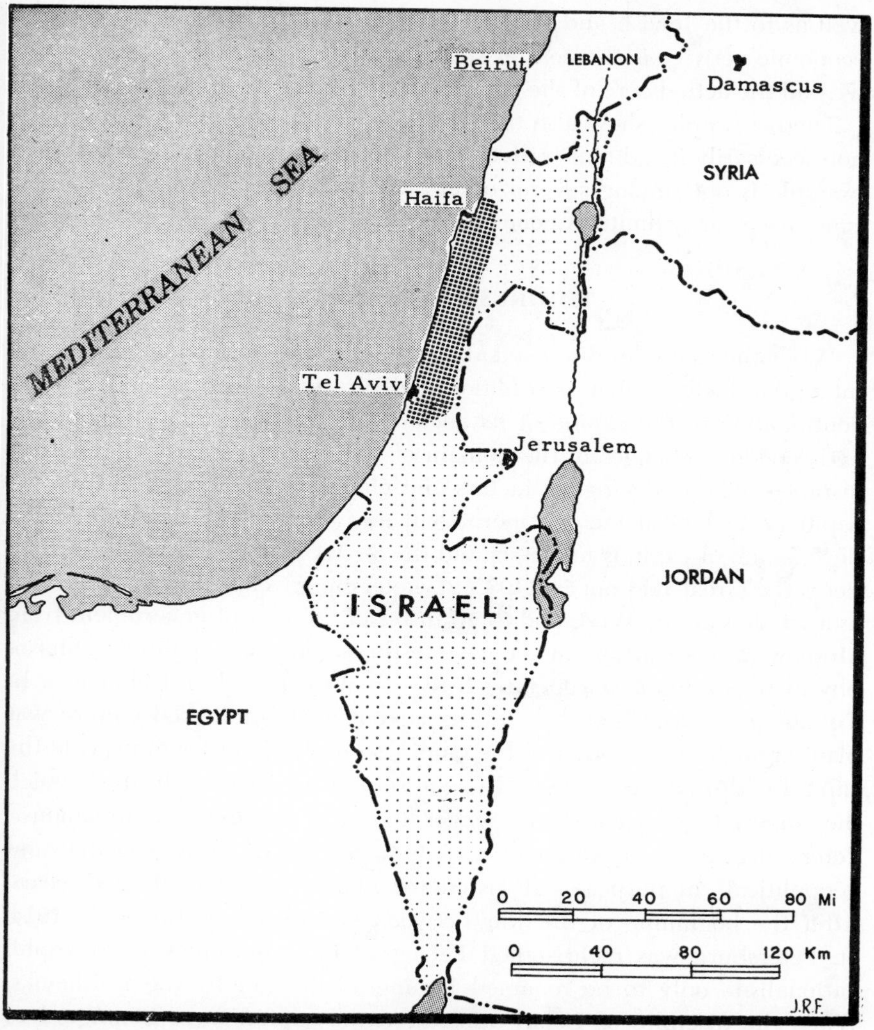

FIG. 6-2. The Core Area of Israel.

Jewish state of Israel is located in the new part of the city, which has no real tradition. Its historical prestige is derivative. It is located on the tip of a salient, surrounded on three sides by hostile Jordan territory, cut off from possible trade routes and even from a local trade area. Industry is little developed and that in existence is an artificial growth fostered for political reasons. To speak of Jerusalem as a core area is only possible in a psychological sense because of the emotional appeal to the Israelis as well as to the Jewish and to the Christian world outside. The center of economic activity is the coastal strip between Haifa and Tel Aviv; here we find the actual core of the country (Fig. 6-2).

These examples show also that the core area of a country or a state is not necessarily its administrative center nor its area of origin. The Italian example is one among several others which demonstrate that a country is not necessarily limited to one core area.

THE RUSSIAN CAPITALS

While the examples discussed above point to the stabilizing influence of intangible factors, such as tradition and prestige, which account for the continuation of the capital at its ancient site in spite of drastic political and economic changes in the domain of the country, we find in contrast instances where ideological factors and changes motivated a shift of the capital. Ideological factors, more than any other, have determined the designation of capitals in Russia and the Soviet Union. The capital which Peter the Great laid out in 1703 (St. Petersburg) close to the Baltic Sea as a window to the West, and the transfer of the seat of government from Moscow in the heart of Russia, gave testimony of a new political philosophy in Russia intent on opening Russia to Western cultural influence. In Toynbee's words,[6] "the seat of government of a landlocked empire was planted in a remote corner of the empire's domain in order to provide the capital with easy access by sea to the sources of alien civilization which the imperial government was eager to introduce into its dominions." Peter's decision was, as Toynbee puts it succinctly, both "spiritual and geopolitical" in purpose.[7] It lasted for more than two hundred years. After the beginning of the war between Germany and Russia in 1914, St. Petersburg was rechristened Petrograd in an outbreak of Slavophil nationalism, only to be renamed Leningrad in 1918 by the Bolsheviks. When the disciples of Lenin transferred the capital from Leningrad to Moscow, they were motivated not only by the more conveniently located site for the administrative capital of the Soviet Union as a whole; they also intended to symbolize the break, culturally and power-politically, between the Soviet empire and the West.

[6] *Op. cit.*, Vol. VII, p. 221; see also pp. 222, 223; 690-691.
[7] *Ibid.*, p. 238.

THE "NATURAL" CORE: CENTRAL AND PERIPHERAL LOCATION

In some countries (such as France and Portugal in Europe, Argentina, Uruguay, and Chile in South America, and many others) there exist relatively simple conditions favoring the development of the core area. Paris is the undisputed center of French intellectual and social life; Paris and the Ile de France have been France's political center for many centuries; Paris is by far the largest city of France. Furthermore, the main industrial and mining districts of France are practically adjoining. All this makes the north and northwest of France together with Paris the core area of this country [8] (*cf.* Fig. 6-7, p. 159). This also indicates that a core area is not necessarily in the center of a country, though such a location undoubtedly favors the development of a core area.

Peripheral location of a core area is especially frequent among seafaring nations. Lisbon in Portugal, and London in the British Isles are examples. Where the adjacent sea represents one major field of economic activity of a nation, such a location of a capital and core area may be even more significant than a central position.

LATIN AMERICAN CORE AREAS

Slightly different is the case of those South American countries that were mentioned before. Their capitals and the core areas surrounding them are the points of entry into these countries and still mirror the history of colonization (Fig. 6-3). In general it is true that other parts of a country are the less advanced the farther they are from these points. In the areas of old Indian civilizations, the capitals of Spanish vice-royalties and audiencias, and later of the independent states, tended to replace old Indian centers, or at least to stay in the areas of population agglomeration. These core areas are still surrounded by areas of very sparse population. Thus Quito, Bogotá, and Mexico City became capitals of Ecuador, Colombia, and Mexico.[9] In Peru, Lima, the city near the port of entry, became predominant over the older capital, Cuzco, situated centrally in the densely inhabited Indian highland. However, in the other countries, in Brazil, Argentina, Chile, Paraguay and Venezuela, and in almost all of the Central American countries, the capitals are the center of the only, or

[8] Whittlesey, *op. cit.*, p. 429. His discussions of other capitals are scattered throughout the book.

[9] P. E. James, *Latin America* (New York and Boston, 1942), p. 4.

FIG. 6-3. Population Centers of South America.

the predominant, population cluster and the boundaries, with only few exceptions,[10] are laid in the extremely sparsely populated zones.

STATE CAPITALS IN THE UNITED STATES

It is interesting to compare with this development the history of many of the thirteen original states of the United States. The capitals and core areas of the thirteen states were originally the points of entry, and, therefore, with the exception of Hartford, Connecticut, port cities. When the territories of the states filled up, the capitals moved in many cases to some central location in the state. It is rather an exception that Boston, because of its predominance in the small Commonwealth of Massachusetts, retained its capital position. Neither New York nor Philadelphia continued as capital cities. Annapolis, still the capital of Maryland, is rather atypical. It certainly does not indicate the core area of the state.

INDIA AND AUSTRALIA

In India the shift of the capital from Calcutta to New Delhi in 1911, the creation for this area of a separate status resembling that of the District of Columbia by the Government of India Act in 1935, and the sudden and tremendous increase of population of the twin cities Delhi and New Delhi after 1941, all signify the progress from a British colony, ruled from across the sea, to a self-governing political body and final independence.[11] Here the political power can no longer be exerted from the periphery.

In Australia, the realization that the interests of a federated state would be better served by a capital near the anticipated population center of the country than by one in a peripheral location led to the selection of Canberra instead of one of the coastal state capitals when the six colonies formed the Commonwealth in 1901 (*cf.* Fig. 2-10, p. 49).

BRAZIL AND ARGENTINA

In Brazil, quite similar considerations have prompted plans to shift the capital from Rio de Janeiro on the coast to a central inland location. The new site has been blueprinted on the watershed between the Amazon and the Parana, in a region rich in mineral resources and coffee plantations; but it remains to be seen whether the growth and concentration of eco-

[10] *Ibid.*, James names the boundaries between Venezuela and Colombia, Colombia and Ecuador, and Peru and Bolivia as the only ones which run through population clusters.

[11] O. H. K. Spate, *Geography of India and Pakistan* (London, 1954), pp. 491-493.

FIG. 6-4. Brazil: Shift of Capitals.

nomic interests in the interior will prove strong enough to unseat Rio as capital [12] (Fig. 6-4). Such a change is characteristic of a dynamic and growing new nation and is not without historical precedent in Brazil. Brazil's first capital was Salvador, located near the easternmost point of land in the state of Bahia. Salvador was founded in 1510 and remained the capital of Brazil until 1792, when the shift of economic interests southward led to the selection of Rio as capital, about midway along the coastline.

In contrast to the changing fortunes of the political and economic core areas in Brazil, Argentina's capital, Buenos Aires, has maintained its rank since 1580, showing a phenomenal growth in the last 150 years (1800: 30,000; 1950: 3,445,000). The vision and geographical sense of Don Juan

[12] In this connection, it is interesting to compare the population growth of Rio de Janeiro from 1,787,000 in 1940 to 2,600,000 in 1954 with that of São Paulo, during the same period, from 1,323,000 to 2,500,000.

de Garay who resettled the deserted town of Nuestra Señora Maria de Buen Aire in 1580 accounts for Buenos Aires' safe position as the country's core over the centuries, for he understood that not gold and silver but the agricultural wealth of the city's hinterland assured its future. Although his party consisted of only 66 persons, de Garay drew plans for a metropolis large enough to house 4,000,000 inhabitants.[13]

SPAIN

The political function of Madrid accounts predominantly for its position as the core of Spain. This is an especially striking example that the political core does not necessarily coincide with the economic core or a central population cluster. Areas of higher economic importance, denser population, and, even more significant, very old tradition of political importance, are ruled from this center. These other areas are handicapped by their excentric and more or less isolated location, and by their different languages (Basque, Catalan) or dialects (Andalusia, Asturias, Galicia). These factors would hinder any attempt by such areas to become the political core of Spain. The most they could strive for, and for which all except Andalusia challenged the core area in the Civil War, is some status of autonomy. In this they have been thwarted. The only principal area which, on the strength of firmly embedded traditions, retained its independence from Madrid and Castile is Portugal.

CHINA

If potential core areas are more equally balanced, the outcome may be different. In China three core areas have been the seat of capitals [14] (Fig. 6-5) the Wei valley, the Yangtse valley, and northeast China. The Wei valley, where Sian (today called Changan) is located was placed most favorably in a China which neither included all of South China nor large parts of the coasts. Capitals in the Yangtse valley were characteristic for periods when the north was either lost to inner-Asiatic conquerors or the south could assert its preponderance for other reasons. Hankow and Nanking have been capitals in the past and again for short periods in the seesaw battle of opposing forces in twentieth century China. Nanking as capital has not only historical associations but as a harbor city symbolized also the connection with the western powers. Places still farther away, on Formosa or even the important city of Canton, have never been nor are likely to become more than local centers. In the north Peiping (Peking)

[13] F. A. Carlson, *Geography of Latin America* (New York, 1952), p. 153.

[14] W. G. East and O. H. K. Spate, *The Changing Map of Asia,* 2nd ed. (New York, 1953), pp. 270-272.

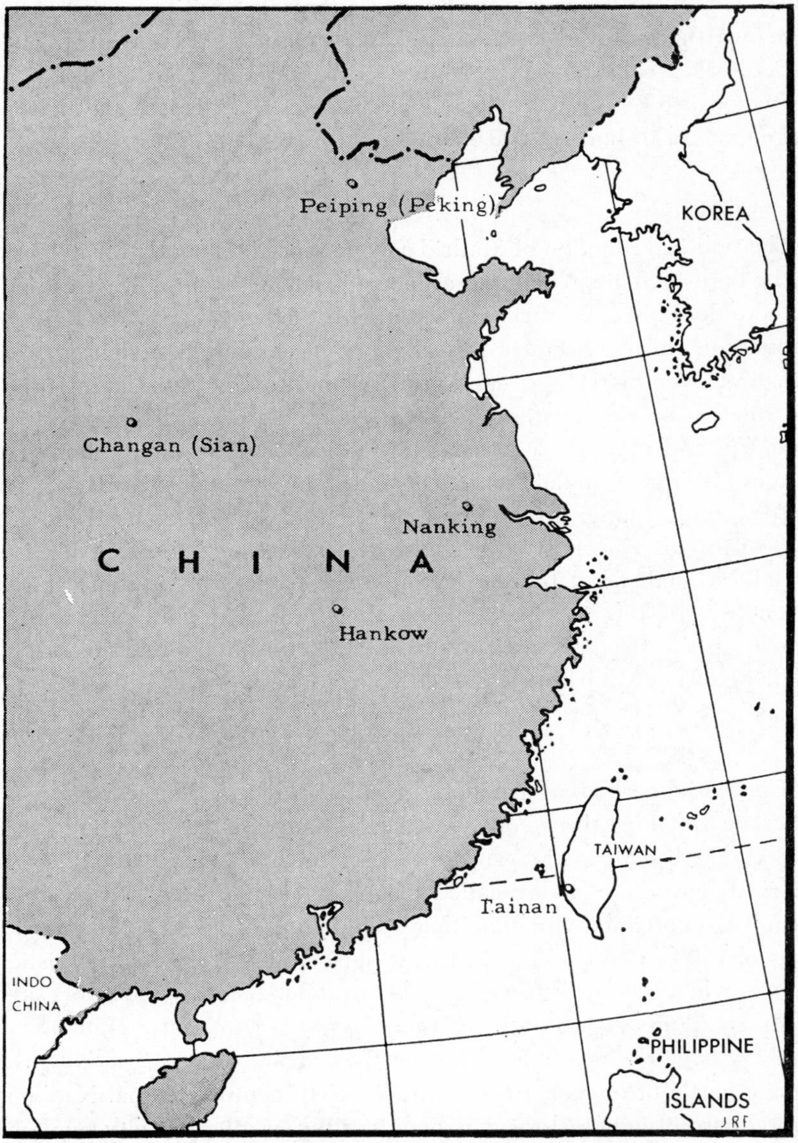

FIG. 6-5. Capitals of China.

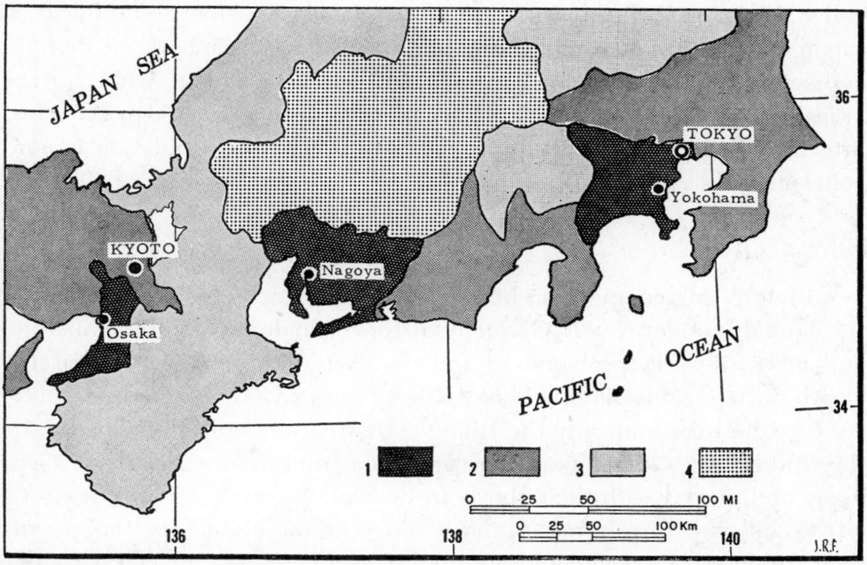

FIG. 6-6. Core Areas of Japan according to Population Density per Square Kilometer: (1) over 625; (2) 210-625; (3) 130-210; (4) 70-130.

represents the opposite principle to that represented by Nanking. At all periods it emphasized the predominance of Chinese interests in Central Asia and the prevalence of influences originating there or working through Central Asia, as at present from Soviet Asia. This is the more remarkable, as Peking is not located on a geometrically straight route to Central Asia, but on a dominant point of the circuitous route which leads from China to Central Asian centers without having to cross a desert. This location makes Peking a convenient capital for a Communist China. Chinese westernization had caused industrial centers to mushroom in the coastal cities, Shanghai, Canton, and Nanking. The direct result of the new industrial developments in the north and in regions which are accessible to the Soviet borders has been that the older industrial centers along the coast of southeastern China have practically ceased to function.[15]

JAPAN

In Japan, the transfer of the capital in 1868 from Kyoto, for many centuries the country's major city in the west, to Tokyo or, as it was then

[15] C. M. Chang, "Five Years of Communist Rule in China," *Foreign Affairs* (1954), pp. 98-110 (109); see also R. Murphy, "The City as a Center of Change: Western Europe and China," *Annals of the Association of American Geographers* (1954), pp. 349-369 (360-361).

called, Yedo, on the shores of Yedo Bay in the east, symbolized the end of Japan's feudal isolation and the nation's readiness to embark on its new course as a world power [16] (Fig. 6-6). In the Kwanto plain, with its twin cities of Tokyo and Yokohama, in a core area of only 5,000 square miles, fifteen million people or less than one-fifth of Japan's population is now concentrated.

GERMANY

An interesting competition between rival core areas for the location of the capital is under way in Germany. It is overshadowed by the numerous and more pressing problems of today's East-West struggle but is still clearly recognizable. Throughout many centuries Germany had no political core, and economically the Rhine core area was only ill-defined.[17] In the Middle Ages kings and emperors came from different parts of Germany and moved with their courts from castle to castle and from city to city. When the Hapsburgs established a semi-inheritance of the crown, their residence, Vienna, could not qualify as a core area for Germany because of its excentric location.[18] When in the nineteenth century the kings of Prussia succeeded in uniting Germany, their capital Berlin dominated Prussia politically, while the lower Rhine valley around Cologne and Düsseldorf and the Ruhr area had many characteristics of a true economic core area but lacked political tradition. In the German Empire politically favorable conditions tended to strengthen Berlin's position. Not only did its administrative functions increase strongly with the centralization culminating under Hitler; a railroad net focusing in Berlin was constructed; more and more banks established their main offices in the capital, and many flexible industries gravitated to Berlin in spite of its rather inconvenient location in the northeast of the Reich. Today, despite all that has happened, Berlin is still regarded as the "natural" capital of Germany. It may be made the capital again as soon as Germany is reunited. Therefore, attempts are made [19] to prove the continuing core function of Berlin, even though its location in present Germany would be very close to what is now the Polish boundary on the Neisse and Oder rivers (*cf.* Fig. 4-10, p. 108).

[16] G. B. Cressey, *Asia's Lands and People,* 2nd ed. (1951), pp. 210-216 (map); East and Spate, *op. cit.,* pp. 298, 299; see also Toynbee, *op. cit.,* Vol. 7, pp. 220-221.

[17] R. E. Dickinson, *Germany* (Syracuse, N. Y., 1953), *passim.*

[18] Today, Vienna's role as the core of Austria, is illustrated by the fact that one-fourth of its population of 7,000,000 is concentrated in the capital.

[19] Institut für Raumforschung, Bonn (ed.), *Die unzerstörbare Stadt* (Cologne-Berlin, 1953).

When the question of the seat of government for West Germany was decided, Bonn won over Frankfurt. Frankfurt is much more centrally located between north and south and is an important communications center; it is also the center of an economically important district. Frankfurt even has a political tradition as the long-time coronation city of the First Empire and the seat of its impotent diet. For all these reasons it was feared that if Frankfurt were made temporary capital it might become a serious rival for Berlin after reunion. Bonn, on the other hand, was clearly a placeholder for Berlin. A small university town without much economic activity, adjacent to but outside of the Cologne-Ruhr area, it could not seriously threaten Berlin's expected reappearance as capital.[20]

LOCATION OF CAPITALS NEAR FRONTIERS

Some political geographers have noted the position of several capitals near a frontier of conquest or also near an endangered frontier. Berlin, Vienna, and Peking have been named in this connection. Location near a frontier may have been an advantage in an era of slow communications. It is a distinct disadvantage in the era of mobile and air warfare. So far only the Soviet Union and Turkey, have removed their capitals permanently from an endangered frontier to a safer place; in other cases the factors favoring permanence, especially ideological factors, have defeated those favoring change.

THE EFFECT OF COMMUNICATIONS NETS ON CORE AREAS

A core area as an area where the political power of a state is concentrated requires the means to make its influence felt in the other parts of the political body. It needs a well-developed communications net. Students of transportation geography have been primarily concerned with the economic aspects of communications; the political and power aspects have been treated only incidentally. Without a properly developed system of communications the prolonged existence of a territorial state—as opposed to a tribal territory, a feudal agglomeration, or a city-state—is almost impossible. It is a common characteristic of most ancient states that they were strung out along rivers—the Nile, Tigris, Euphrates, Indus, Wei, and Hoang-ho. It was much later that ocean shipping was developed enough to allow the existence of coast-based or circum-marine states. The Athenian and the Roman empires are the best known examples, although older

[20] See also p. 156.

ones, like the Cretan and Carthaginian, have existed. Roads, designed from the beginning for military purposes and administrative efficiency, were built in the Persian Empire, and brought to a stage of perfection in the Roman Empire unequaled until modern times. The flagstone trails and canals of the Chinese Empire and the roads of the Incas should also be mentioned in this context.

Compared with these long-lived and well-organized empires most other great states of the past have been either short-lived, such as the Mongolian Empire, or they were so loosely organized and their communications systems so disintegrated that their activities as consolidated units in relation to other powers evolved only in rare instances and after long periods; the medieval states of France or Germany are good examples. Or they had to be reconstructed periodically because of the continuous process of disintegration—such a state was the Assyrian kingdom, whose kings were continuously on the warpath in order to exact overdue tributes, subdue rebellious vassals, and re-establish their control. This type of empire has survived in a few instances into the twentieth century. To the very eve of the conquest by Italy, the rulers of Ethiopia were wont to send tax-gathering and punitive expeditions into such outlying areas as the Ogaden and Kaffa. Sinkiang, formerly called Chinese Turkestan, had to be reconquered time and again. It has been estimated that out of about 2,000 years of Chinese rule, this control was effective only approximately 425 years.[21]

The significance and importance of paved roads for the stability of states has changed only slowly since antiquity. The compass, sea charts, and nautical instruments, together with developments in ship designs, enabled not only the great discoveries since the sixteenth century, but also the establishment of far-flung colonial empires. Besides these forms older ones persisted and until the second half of the nineteenth century Russian rule in Siberia, and also Canada's development, were based on river navigation by small vessels, supplemented by portages.

Hard-surfaced roads—the *chaussées* of the French (Fig. 6-7)—railroads, canals, and ocean highways are among the indispensable bases of the modern state. The twentieth century has added the internal-combustion engine and its use in the automobile and the airplane.

This short historical review permits the conclusion that small states are far less dependent on internal communications than are large ones. Within

[21] O. Lattimore, *Inner Asian Frontiers of China*, American Geographical Society Research Series No. 21, 1940, p. 171.

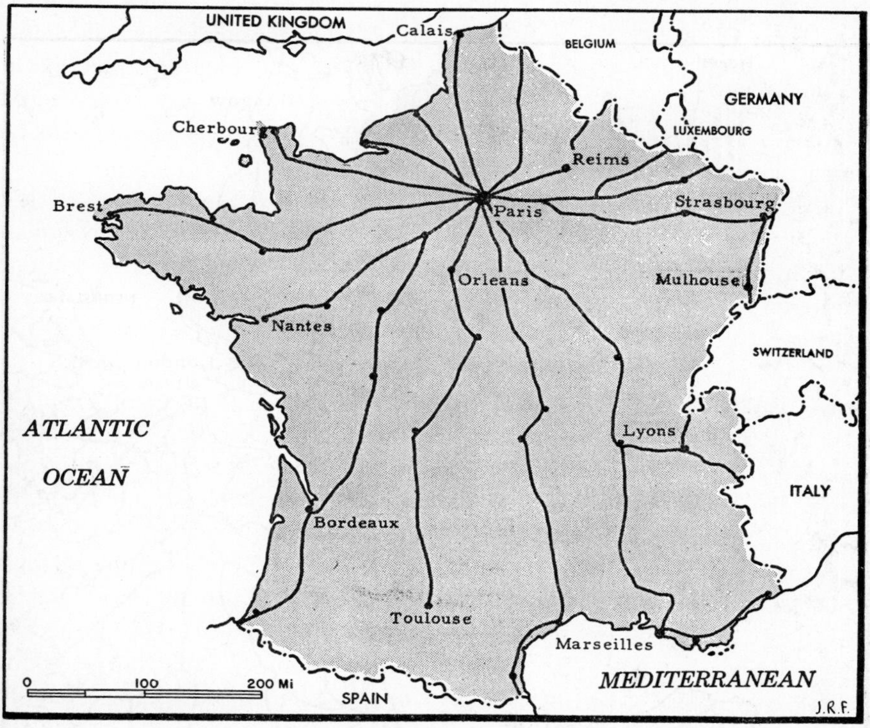

FIG. 6-7. Post Roads of France.

the latter, the political core is strong only if it is served adequately by communications. We must distinguish between the economic and political functions of the communications net within a core area and those connecting it with other parts of the body politic. In the Ruhr area, in England's "black country," in the area extending between Baltimore and Boston, the road, railroad, and in places the canal net is very dense; indeed these areas could not exist as economic centers without this highly developed transportation network. On the other hand, Madrid in Spain, or Ankara in Turkey, are in the centers of a radiating pattern of roads, railroads, telegraph and telephone lines, but there is hardly a network, except the normal communications network within the big city.

It is not incidental that the first important rail line in Russia linked St. Petersburg and Moscow. The return of Moscow to its role as seat of the government and political core was heralded by the construction of railroads to the Volga cities; "they soon established the pattern of radiat-

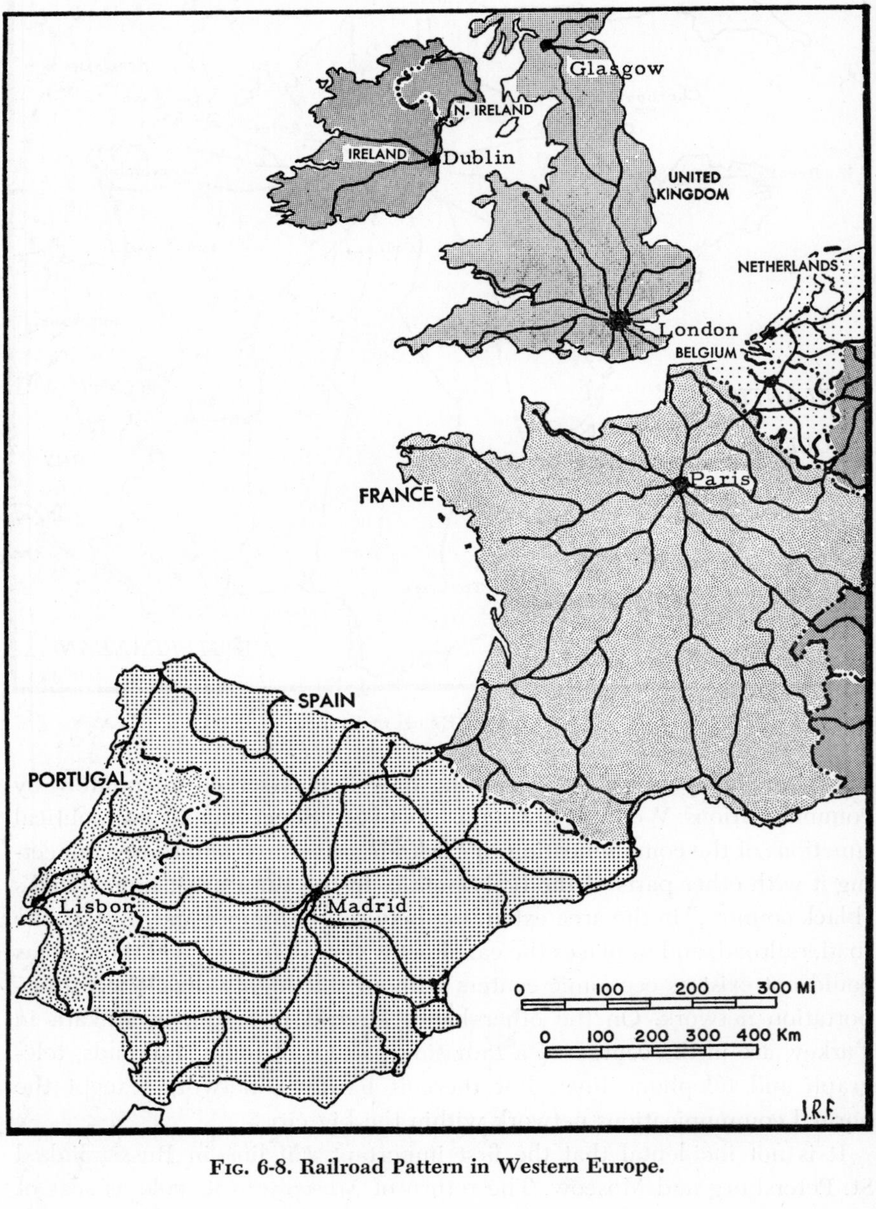

Fig. 6-8. Railroad Pattern in Western Europe.

ing lines centered at Moscow which became the dominant feature of the pre-revolutionary railroad geography of the country." [22] The continuous extension of the railroad network by the Soviet government, especially the slowly proceeding eastward extension, has not altered Moscow's role as the main hub of the Soviet Union (*cf.* Figs. 15-1, 15-2, pp. 476, 478). Moscow's core quality is further emphasized by its strategical location within the economic core area fed by the principal inland canals of the Soviet Union: the Mariinsk system, the Moscow Canal, and the White Sea-Baltic Canal (see Fig. 8-7, p. 238).

The radiating communications pattern is characteristic for a political core area. A highly centralized country like France or Great Britain shows this pattern in perfect form (Fig. 6-8). Berlin and Vienna are in the center of radiating communications which, however, are no longer congruent with the new political map. When after World War I new states emerged, their political problems were aggravated by the incongruence of the political and the communication patterns, that is, the lack of a communication system focusing upon the new political centers. A severe case of maladjustment because of an inherited communication system developed in Czechoslovakia (Fig. 6-9). The railroads and roads of Moravia and even of large parts of Bohemia had been constructed for easy traffic with Vienna. Some of the main lines by-passed Prague, the capital, at a short distance. Slovakia's railroads and roads focused on Budapest, the capital of Hungary, and were only tenuously connected with Moravia and Bohemia. In Yugoslavia the situation was even worse. In order to travel from the capital, Belgrade, to some parts of the country detours were necessary which more than doubled the actual distance. In both cases, but especially in Yugoslavia, the problems of federalism, and of provincial autonomy versus centralism, were aggravated by these conditions.

In underdeveloped countries the extent of backwardness is clearly reflected in the communications net. Neither Brazil nor Colombia has a railroad or road pattern radiating from Rio de Janeiro or Bogotá (*cf.* Fig. 22-2, p. 674). Both countries have suffered from recurring revolts originating in economically advanced, but politically not well integrated, outlying areas. Repeatedly São Paulo, Rio Grande do Sul, Medellin, or Barranquilla refused to accept the policy decreed at the political center. Large parts of the Amazonian lowlands belong still only nominally to Brazil, Bolivia, Peru, or Colombia. Some of their Indian tribes have never heard the name of the country to which they supposedly belong. The advent of the air-

[22] T. Shabad, pp. 82-92 (83).

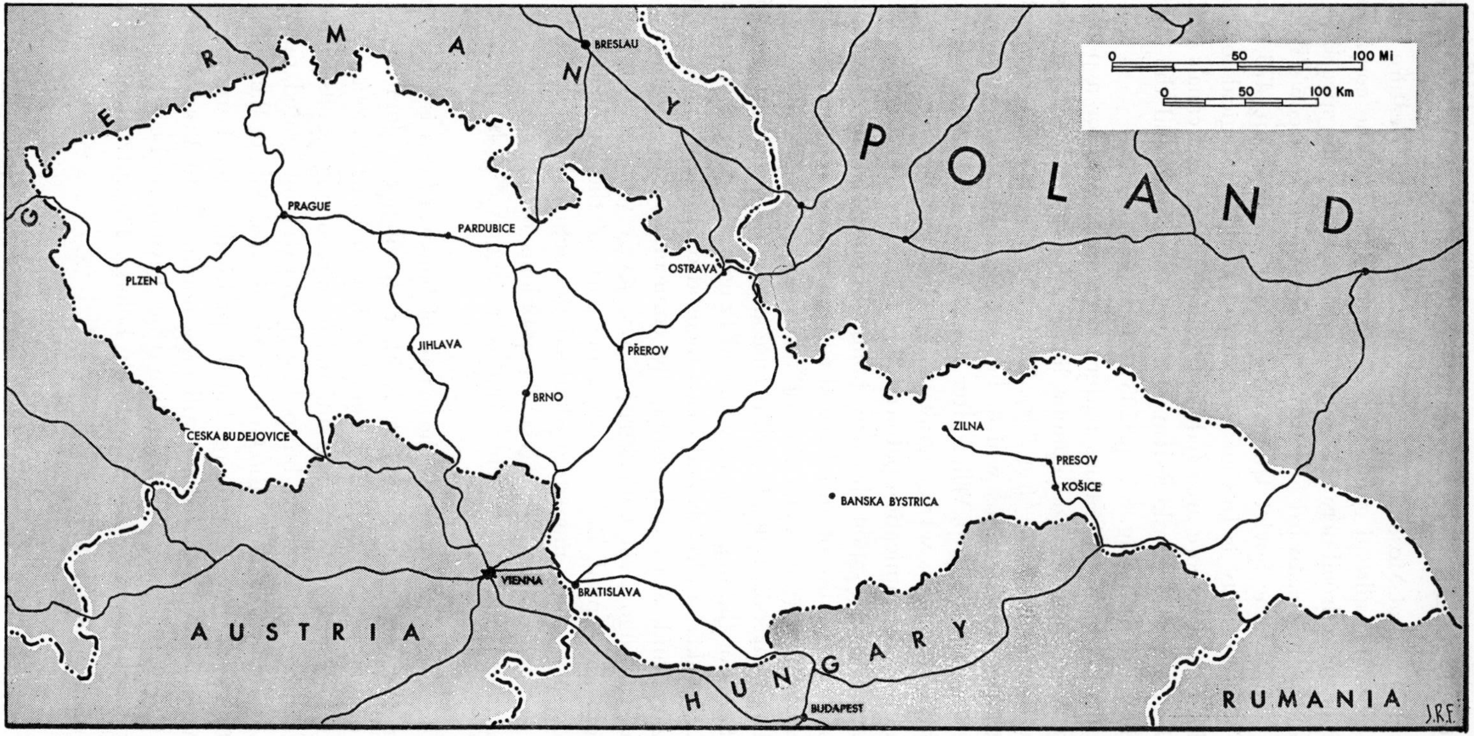

FIG. 6-9. Ineffective Rail-net of Czechoslovakia at the Time of Its Formation.

plane has, however, strengthened the influence of the central authority.

Generalized maps, as small-scale maps necessarily are, sometimes give only an inadequate picture of the actual conditions. On a small-scale map France seems to be covered with a web of lines, with Paris clearly in the center. Adequate provisions for direct connections between the provincial centers apparently exist. But this picture is deceiving, because the traffic on most of these lines is slow, trains are infrequent, and through-trains are not everywhere available. A road map shows the generally better quality of the roads focusing on Paris and the secondary character of most others. Similar maps of Germany would not easily and unmistakably reveal the political core of the country. They would indicate several centers, among them Cologne, Halle and Leipzig, Frankfurt am Main, all of them as prominent as Berlin. The first three places are also in the midst of a very dense local pattern, the sign of an economic concentration, while an analogous pattern is absent from the Berlin area, indicating its predominantly political role. A similar picture emerges on a communications map of Italy. The dense network in the Turin-Milan-Genoa triangle, and in a second triangle, Verona-Venice-Bologna, is clearly distinguished from the radial pattern of Rome, which is the political core.

In the United States, Chicago is far more important in terms of its communications pattern than Washington. Cleveland, New York, Philadelphia, Omaha, and several other places are at a par or ahead of Washington. Somewhat different is the pattern in Great Britain. London, being a great economic center as well as the political core, dominates Great Britain's communications system.

SHIPPING LANES AND CORE AREAS

The picture would be incomplete without the shipping lanes. Once one includes them in the consideration, the routes between ports of the United Kingdom are not very prominent. However, the shipping lanes and also the air routes from other countries lead to a number of British ports and, though London is the most frequented, the general pattern is not that of focusing on London (Fig. 6-10). Rather Great Britain as a whole appears as the core of the Commonwealth. It may be useful to distinguish between several types of routes radiating from the ports of the United Kingdom. There are those which serve only or primarily commercial interests. The routes to the United States and most of the routes to the European continent belong in this category. Other routes serve both political and economic interests and it would be difficult to separate those

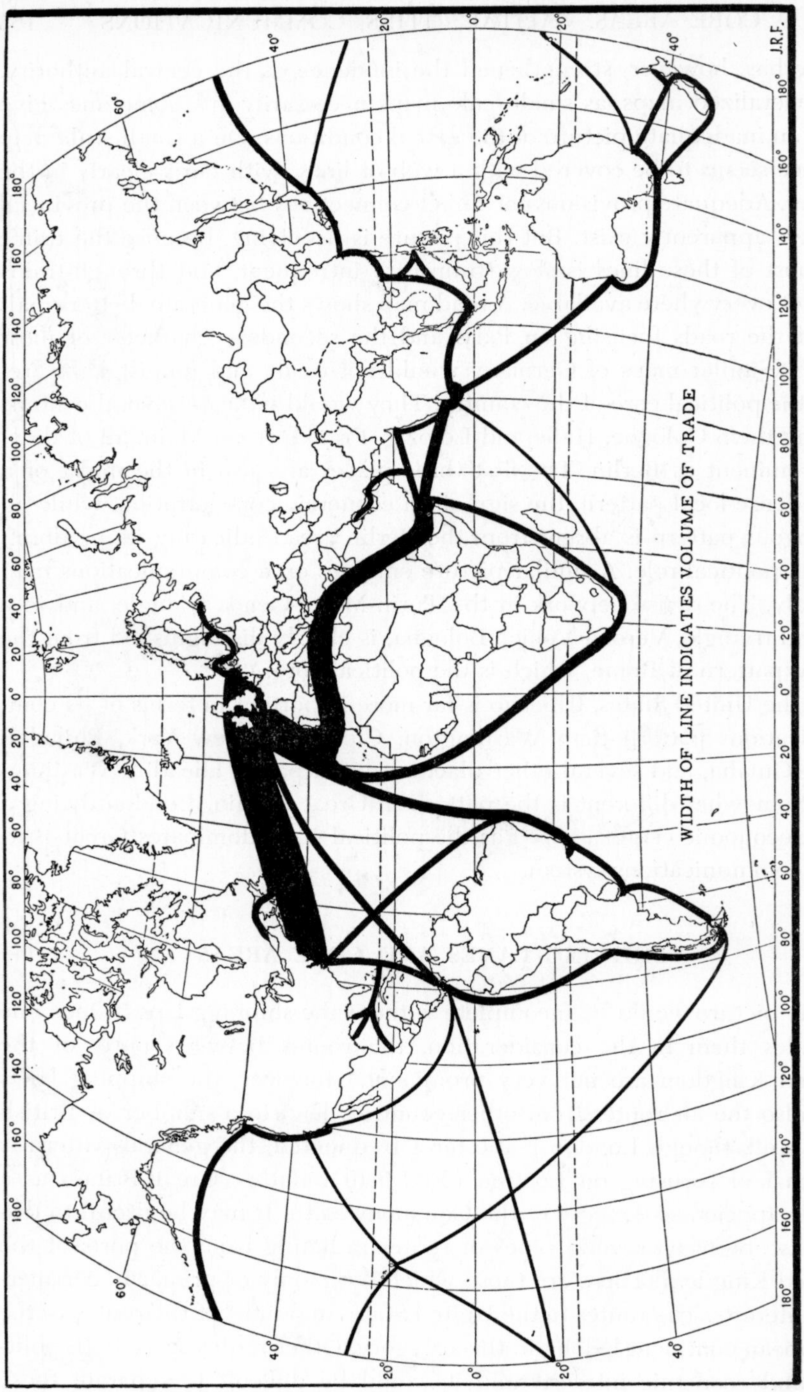

FIG. 6-10. Shipping Lanes Radiating from United Kingdom Ports.

functions. The routes across the Atlantic to Bermuda and Canada exemplify such a composite function, with the economic function prevailing. The route through the Gulf of Biscaya, the Strait of Gibraltar, the Mediterranean Sea, and the Suez Canal to Southern and Eastern Asia and Australia has often been called the lifeline of the Commonwealth, stressing thereby its political function. The alternate line around the Cape has had its phases of strength and weakness; it showed strength especially when political considerations made it appear safer than the Suez Canal route.

Another group of routes would never have come into existence if not for political reasons, though economic interests may be served. The economic functions, however, are clearly incidental. This is especially obvious in the case of analogous shipping services of other powers. Why should a French line extend to Madagascar, Martinique, or Guadeloupe, a Portuguese to Angola, a Belgian to Matadi on the mouth of the Congo, if not because of the political affiliations of these countries? The fact that there is no regular established service between Portugal and Goa or Macao is anomalous.

On the other hand, a number of world routes are frequented by vessels under many flags and are thereby of major importance in international trade relations. Such routes are the transatlantic routes from the ports of Western Europe to North America and also to South America. The Mediterranean and Suez Canal route is a main artery. So is the route through the Panama Canal, which is also of greatest political and military significance for the United States. When the construction of the Panama Canal was undertaken, President Theodore Roosevelt sent the American fleet on a world cruise. Its first lap was from the Atlantic Coast around Cape Horn to the Pacific Coast of the United States, demonstrating thereby the feasibility—and the disadvantages—of this world sea route and the strategic-political importance of the Panama route.

The construction of major canal systems leads inevitably to significant dislocations of economic and political core areas. We can anticipate such changes and dislocations within the United States and Canada upon completion of the St. Lawrence Seaway (Fig. 6-11). Involving expenditures of about $300 million to provide a 27-foot deep channel from the Atlantic to Lake Ontario, the Seaway is scheduled to be completed in 1958. The bitter and long fight which preceded the agreement between the United States and Canada was a vivid illustration of the hopes and fears expressed by competing coastal and port areas in the two countries. For instance, the port director of Milwaukee, the waterborn foreign commerce of which totaled in 1953 only 35,000 tons, has estimated it to rise, after 1958, to

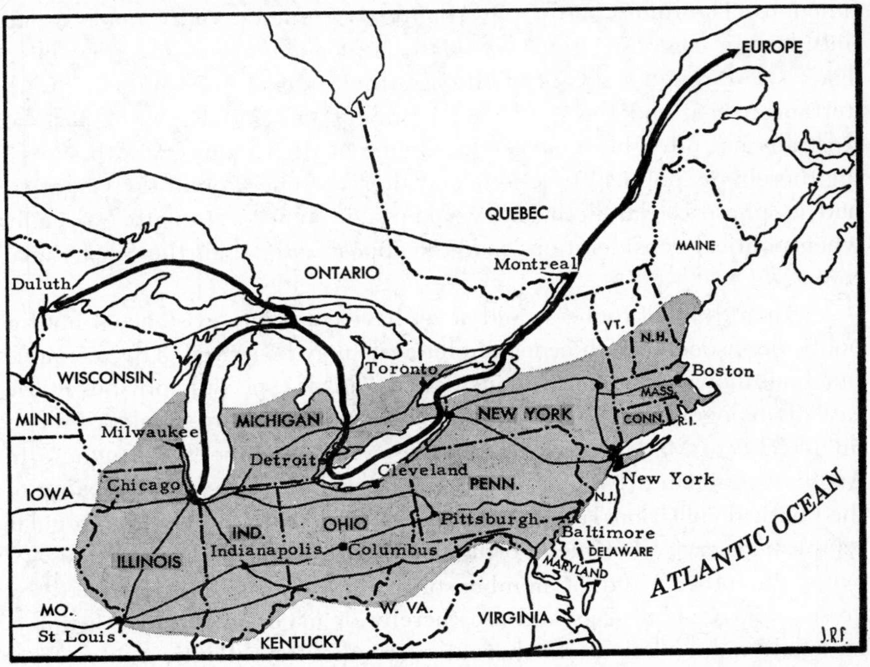

FIG. 6-11. **The St. Lawrence Seaway and the American Manufacturing Belt.**

over a million tons annually, while the port director of New York fears a loss of about 3,500,000 tons a year, one-sixth of the port's foreign commerce in general cargo and grain.[23]

The Seaway may also prevent the "American Ruhr" (Detroit's automobile industries, Chicago's farm equipment plants, Milwaukee's heavy machinery industries) from losing its economic core area rank as the result of the dwindling of its iron ore reserves in the mines at the head of the lake system around Lake Superior. With the completion of the Seaway iron ore from Labrador, Quebec, and foreign sources could be supplied, and at competitive prices. The serious blow which the Seaway may deal to the railways in the eastern part of the United States should also be mentioned. The future changes in the location and strength of economic core areas which can be envisaged as the result of the St. Lawrence Seaway construction may also make themselves felt in the internal political geography of the United States and its competing political cores.[24]

Maritime routes are to a certain degree flexible. They can be relocated

[23] *The Economist,* August 28, 1954, pp. 663-4. See also below, pp. 588, 589.
[24] See pp. 170, 171 on the development of a political core area in California.

at short notice. Submarine warfare forced ships to change their course continuously. Large vessels, with their independence of weather conditions and greater capacity for provisions, can afford direct travel without use of ports-of-call. On the other hand, they are restricted to fewer harbors. Nor can the largest ocean liners use the great inter-oceanic canals. Venice, once a political and economic center of a far-flung organization, is unable to serve modern shipping because of its shallow lagoon. No large seagoing vessels are able to sail up the Potomac. But this development has not affected the role of Washington as a political core.

AIR COMMUNICATIONS

Air communications have resulted in significant shifts, though none to the present moment have affected the standing of political cores and hardly of secondary political units. Alaska and Hawaii have been brought in closer contact with the continental United States, although, at the writing of these lines, statehood has not yet been granted to either of them.

SIGNIFICANCE OF RAILROAD SYSTEMS

Least flexible are land communications. It is for this reason that certain roads and railroads have acquired great political significance. The Soviet —formerly Russian—empire in Asia would be impossible in its present form without its strategic railroads (*cf.* Fig. 15-2, p. 478). The Trans-Siberian railroad linked the Far East to the distant core; it initiated the Russification of wide areas; it enabled the penetration of Manchuria and paved the way for influence in China. The Turkestan railroad enabled, accompanied, and secured the Russian domination of Central Asia. A spur from this railroad into the oasis of Merw alarmed the British rulers of India. The Turksib railroad, connecting the Turkestan and Trans-Siberian railroads and paralleling the Chinese boundary, was a powerful instrument in bringing Russian economic, social, and political influence to Sinkiang, the most remote of the provinces of China.

The dependence of Russia, and later of the Soviet Union, on supplies from its western allies during both World Wars led to the construction of the Murmansk railroad in World War I and the Trans-Iranian railroad in World War II. The first of these two lines acquired a critical importance for Finland and caused the Soviet Union to insist on the cession of sparsely inhabited, climatically adverse areas which appeared to the Soviets in too-close, threatening neighborhood to the railroad. The construction of the Trans-Iranian railroad threatened to destroy the shaky independence of this country, which was occupied by forces of the allied Powers.

Perhaps in no other part of the world have railroads played such a political role as in the Near and Middle East. The short railroad from the Russian boundary to Tabriz signalized one step in the repeated attempts of Russia to win control of Persian Azerbaijan.

The Republic of Turkey (*cf.* Fig. 8-19, p. 284) for a long time, was hesitant about allowing railroad construction by foreign syndicates. Its reluctance was due to the realization that generally investment of foreign capital in undeveloped countries has resulted in making such countries dependent upon the lending country. Investment in railroads—or port installations—has been in many cases the main instrument by which control of an area could be obtained, and the railroad lines were built more in the interest of the lending than in that of the borrowing country. In pre-World War I Turkey, the Trans-Anatolian and the Baghdad railroads were constructed to facilitate German expansion southeastward to the Persian Gulf. British capital succeeded in building a railroad from the Gulf to Baghdad, bringing lower Mesopotamia under Anglo-Indian influence and paving the way for the creation of post-war Iraq as a British mandate.

With the Hedjaz railroad, Turkey attempted to counteract foreign interference in what it considered its own sphere of influence. Sultan Abdul Hamid II appealed to the religious feelings of the Mohammedans in order to promote the construction of a railroad which would facilitate the pilgrimage to the holy places of Islam. Thus he was able to keep foreign capital out and to build a railroad which allowed him to send troops to Hedjaz and on to Yemen, thus by-passing the Suez Canal. However, it was too late to strengthen the ties of these remote areas with the political center.

MEASURES AIMED AT REDUCING THE INFLUENCE OF THE POLITICAL CORE

In discussing the relationship of the core to its outlying parts we have also to consider constitutional problems. In a compact country of some size the political core in some respects may be compared with the center of gravity in a physical body. While all parts of the body have weight, they exert pull upon other bodies through this center of gravity. The decisive difference is that in nations and countries the core generally has more weight than any other comparable part of the body politic. However, in many instances this is hardly reflected in the organization of the state. Democratic parliamentary countries allow the core area as much but not more representation than any other area with a comparable population. Nevertheless, the impact of the agglomeration of people in the capital, and of a central bureaucracy, exerts a special influence. Several devices have been tried to avoid or to reduce this influence. The French moved their parliament to Versailles on different occasions to remove it from the influence of the "street mob." In the United States the creation of a federal district apart from the large cities has fulfilled its purpose for a long period; but more recently Washington, D. C., as the seat of the national power, has tended to attract great numbers of people, institutions, central offices of unions, and so on. In several of the forty-eight states the same device has been used. Annapolis in Maryland, Lansing in Michigan, Springfield in Illinois, Harrisburg in Pennsylvania, and Sacramento in California are cases in point. At least in the last two examples a development comparable to that of Washington, D. C., has set in. The American example has been imitated elsewhere, in Canberra, the capital of the Australian Commonwealth, in Toronto in Canada, and in Brazil with the designation of a Federal District, though in this country so far nothing has been done to move the government.

In other countries an attempt was made to split the central organization between several cities. The Netherlands has the seat of the court and some central organs in The Hague, while the parliament convenes in Amsterdam. In the Union of South Africa the parliament has its seat in Capetown, the government in Johannesburg, and the Supreme Court in Pretoria. In Switzerland the seat of the government rotated between Zurich, Basel, and Lucerne. Despite a long tradition this arrangement was finally abandoned; however, the distinction between the economic core in and around Zurich and Lucerne and the political core in Berne remained alive.

COMPETITIVE CORE AREAS IN OUTLYING REGIONS

For countries endowed with large-size territories, the opening-up of new lands in the outer regions and population growth often leads to the development of new core areas that compete with the older areas economically, without necessarily growing into a competitive political core except in certain matters of internal politics. California, in its position within the United States and among the western states of the Union, is an interesting case in point (Fig. 6-12). California has become an important

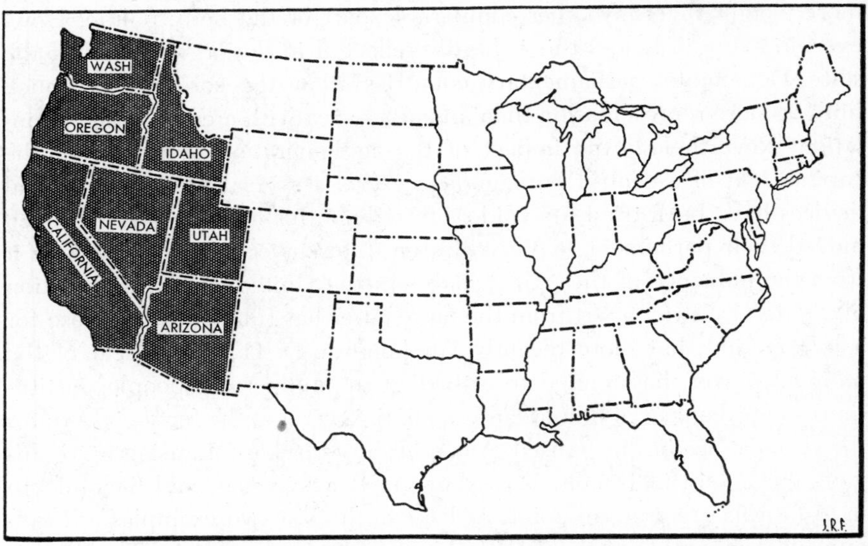

Fig. 6-12. The West Coast Core Area of the United States Centered on California.

economic core area of the West Coast which includes, in addition to California, the two coastal states of Oregon and Washington and the four "mountain states" of Idaho, Utah, Nevada, and Arizona. With a total population of more than eighteen million, this area has come to represent a clearly defined economic bloc within the economy of the country. This fact of course has not led to a weakening of the political structure of the Union but has brought about a strengthening of the specific political interests and viewpoints of this area in national politics, as for instance in the question of United States policy toward Asia. It is also interesting to note that the development of an economic core area within California, far from having found its final center of gravity, is still in a state of fluctuation. The center is shifting from the north to the south. In 1900 only one-fifth of California's population was to be found in southern California; at present its share is more than one-half. The congested area of San Francisco had to pay the price for its geographical disadvantages in the competition with the metropolitan areas of Los Angeles and San Diego, which nature had endowed with more ample "living space" and less fog—factors which attracted especially the new aircraft industries.

The growth of the new core area in California finds significant expression in the rise of its electoral votes. Their number in a state is based on the state's representation in Congress, which again is based on the state's relative gain or loss in population during a decade. California has pushed its electoral vote up farther and faster than any other State in the Union. After the 1940 census it boosted the figure from twenty-two to twenty-five. After the 1950 census, California gathered in seven more—half of the fourteen-vote increase registered by all the states. The election of Richard M. Nixon to the office of Vice President in the Eisenhower Administration underscored the importance of the California secondary core area in the internal political geography of the United States.

CHECKS AND BALANCES IN FEDERAL STATES

Another device by which the influence of the core area can be balanced consists of giving to less populous areas a stronger representation in the parliament and government. This is done especially in federal states. In the United States, Canada, Australia, and in Europe in Switzerland, each of the component federal states has legal representation in one chamber, thus giving more weight to thinly settled rural states. In some of the forty-eight states of the United States the "unit system" accomplishes a similar end. The frequent victory, in Georgia, of a numerical minority of conservative rural voters over a progressive city population has had repercussions for the entire United States.

THE POLITICAL CORE IN TOTALITARIAN COUNTRIES

The less democratic a country is, the more pronounced is the impact of the political core. In absolute monarchies or in dictatorships the core literally rules over the other parts. Although the Nazi party in Germany or the Fascist movement in Italy originated outside the political core and the capital, the victory of totalitarianism brought about the concentration of power in Berlin as well as in Rome, where the "march on Rome" climaxed the Fascist victory. In other countries also the final success of revolution has been marked by the fall of the capital. This is true of almost all the numerous Latin American revolutions, and also of the pattern of revolutions in Europe. The more than two years of civil war in Spain ended with the conquest of Madrid, and the Bolshevik regime came into the saddle with the conquest of Leningrad and Moscow. The years of civil war which followed did not change the outcome. Neither the Ukrainian breadbasket nor the vital Donets industrial and mining area ever competed with Moscow as fountainheads of the central political power.

COLONIALISM AND CORE AREAS

As mentioned before, in colonial empires the metropolitan area as a whole has to be regarded as the political core. It has been noted by several authors that colonial dependencies are not necessarily located in other continents. The Amazonian forests and their little-developed tribes are typical colonial areas for Brazil, Bolivia, Peru, and Colombia. So are the cold areas of Patagonia and Tierra del Fuego for Argentina and Chile, the Tundra regions for Canada, Lapland for Norway and Sweden. Chinese Turkestan (Sinkiang) was a colonial overland possession of China. Constitutional or legal definitions do not always reflect the actual conditions prevailing in a dependent area in relation to the main body. In some cases such areas are treated like the usual administrative divisions. In other cases they are administered as "territories." That is the way in which the United States administers the undeveloped parts of Alaska together with its civilized fringe.

None of these areas is officially recognized as a colony. The term "colony" has become unfashionable, and designations such as Overseas France or Overseas Portugal have replaced it. For the political geographer the varying terminology is more confusing than helpful. However, there is a great variety in the degree of dependency. The Dominions are only in a very loose connection with the British core. India has led the way toward a still looser connection, abrogating the symbolic bond of the common crown and declaring itself a republic. Ireland and Burma actually left the Commonwealth.

The constitution of the Soviet Union includes an article which grants to the full-fledged Soviet republics the right to secede. History has yet to prove if this "right" exists on paper only. What has become a reality in the British Commonwealth, has so far remained an empty promise in the Soviet Union.

The Soviet Union has established a whole hierarchy of dependencies from the national okrug through the national oblast and the autonomous soviet republic to the sixteen constituent soviet republics. It allows the satellite people's republics to be designated as independent states, although in fact they are less free than many parts of the British Commonwealth, especially the Dominions.

RELATIONS BETWEEN DEPENDENCIES AND CORE AREAS

It is very difficult to bring the dependencies of Great Britain under a comprehensive system. Almost every area is somewhat differently placed from all others. There are crown colonies, administered by London-appointed officials, and naval bases such as Gibraltar under strict military rule. In a crown colony there may be an advisory body, wholly or partially elected, and elected by white settlers only or by natives. There are different types of self-governing colonies, protectorates where native rulers and native administration govern, guided by British advisers. Some dependent areas are not dependent on London, but on one or the other of the Dominions.

Although the colonial structure of other powers—French, Belgian, Portuguese, or Dutch—is much simpler, they all represent an attempt to organize large areas, scattered over at least two continents, not because they form a natural geographic physical unit, but from a core which dominates by political means. Whatever the economic motives for acquisition and retention of colonies, the political factor is in the end decisive.

There is another group of dependent areas, those territories designated as Mandates by the League of Nations after World War I, and as Trusteeships by the United Nations. Theoretically their overriding loyalty should go to the United Nations. However, though certainly an object of study for the political geographer, the United Nations are no political body and lack any organized area of their own, therefore also any core area. Actually all the trust territories are dependent on the core areas of their administering nations.

CHAPTER 7

Location

INTERACTION OF STABLE AND CHANGING CONDITIONS AFFECTING THE IMPACT OF LOCATION

For a century the United States was on the periphery of the world; only in the last generation has it moved to the center of the stage and, on a world-wide basis, has become a core area. Similarly it is a generally accepted notion that until the discovery of America, the British Isles lay on the very edge of the known world, but that thereafter they were at the world's center for the next four centuries. In regard to their relations with the European continent a British historian has pointed out that "to invade Britain was singularly easy before the Norman Conquest, singularly difficult afterwards . . . safe behind the Channel . . . no invasion hostile to the community as a whole has met with even partial success owing to the barrier of the sea. But . . . ancient Britain was peculiarly liable to invasion for geographic and other reasons." [1]

From a geographical point of view one should express the same thought slightly differently: although the location of a place on the earth is fixed, the political value and implications of this location are continuously changing. It is this interaction of stable and changing conditions which is at the basis of political geography. People have been fascinated by the apparent stability of the "well-grounded earth," as it was called three thousand years ago by Hesiod. They are apt to look at geographic locations and their relations without taking account of changes in time.

It is the function of the political geographer to point out this integration

[1] G. M. Trevelyan, *History of England,* Vol. 1 (Garden City, N. Y., 1953), pp. 14 ff.

of time and space factors and to be aware of the time-conditioned elements which affect his findings. Certain politico-geographical statements or, in the true sense of the word, "views" have had great poignancy at one time, but were relevant for a short period only. Others have kept their validity over long periods. Both types of statements are of interest, but should not be confused. Confused thinking on basic concepts of location in political geography, affecting not only the ordinary citizens but statesmen and military strategists alike, is only due to the failure to distinguish properly between the time-bound validity of a politico-geographical concept and its, in many cases only seemingly, timeless application. Such misinterpretation of spatial relationships in location can distort, and has distorted the outlook of international relations which forms the basis of the foreign policy of the great powers.

LANDLOCKED AND INTERIOR LOCATION

One of the most persistent concepts of political geography is concerned with the location of countries in close contact with the sea or far away from it. This is the long-range basis of the Heartland theory [2] which must be seen as a special, period-bound example of the politico-geographical conditions of landlocked or interior location which have been tested by History time and again. In antiquity a landlocked Macedonia remained dependent upon Athens, until Philip, the father of Alexander the Great, conquered the coastal cities. It is generally believed that landlocked locations are a serious disadvantage to the state concerned. This is correct in many respects; however, in a strictly strategic sense a landlocked position may provide a nation engaged in war with the advantage of the "inner line." Given a system of good communications, a well-developed system of intelligence, and good armies under able leadership, a country can use its interior location to shift troops from one front to another and thus win victories by local superiority. Frederick of Prussia, Napoleon, and also the Bolsheviks during the Civil War of the Revolution made the best use of location factors of interior location which, except for the advantages they offered in war strategy, were highly disadvantageous.

The disadvantages of interior location are manifold, particularly in that a landlocked country is deprived of the opportunity to have direct contact with any country except those with which it has common boundaries. This is still true, although it must be realized that the great advantages which

[2] For a discussion of the relationship of Heartland expansion to marginal lands and narrow waterways, see pp. 113 ff.

the seafaring peoples enjoyed over those of the interior lands before the full establishment of mechanical transport on land and in the air are no longer as distinctive as was the case only fifty years ago. But even though the progress of technology has aided greatly in the utilization of diversified land areas and in establishing continuity and compactness of the territory, the fact has not been altered that every country remains dependent on one or all of its neighbors. Modern industrialization and modern commerce with their dependence on a great variety of raw materials have rather sharpened this relation.

BOUNDARIES AND NEIGHBORS

The question has been raised as to whether it is more favorable for a country to border with many or with few other countries. Experience has shown that the fact that the United States has only two neighbors has simplified many problems. Germany, in contrast, has suffered from the fact that it has had to deal with a great number of neighbors. It requires a very skillful handling of foreign affairs to maintain tolerable relations with neighboring countries of different, often contradictory interests. The situation is aggravated by the fact that a coalition of several of these neighbor countries is always a possibility. Bismarck, himself a master in the diplomatic game of coalitions, confessed that during his chancellorship he was continuously plagued by the "nightmare of coalitions." Hitler thought himself strong enough to neglect this possibility and led a potentially victorious Germany into catastrophe.

For a landlocked state, to have only very few neighbors may equally be a great disadvantage. The extreme case of a country with only one neighbor, which would mean that it is completely surrounded, is seldom found in recent history. The Boer states offer as close an example as possible. Save for a short boundary in remote terrain with an undeveloped Portuguese colony, the two Boer states, Transvaal and the Orange Free State, were at one time completely surrounded by British territory (Fig. 7-1). In the ensuing struggle the Boers succumbed. However, in this struggle even the remote connection with Portuguese Laurenço Marques was of great value.

BUFFER LOCATION

To be placed between only two states is a location which seriously affects the power position of any state but especially of a weak one. At best it becomes a buffer state. Its continued existence depends on the

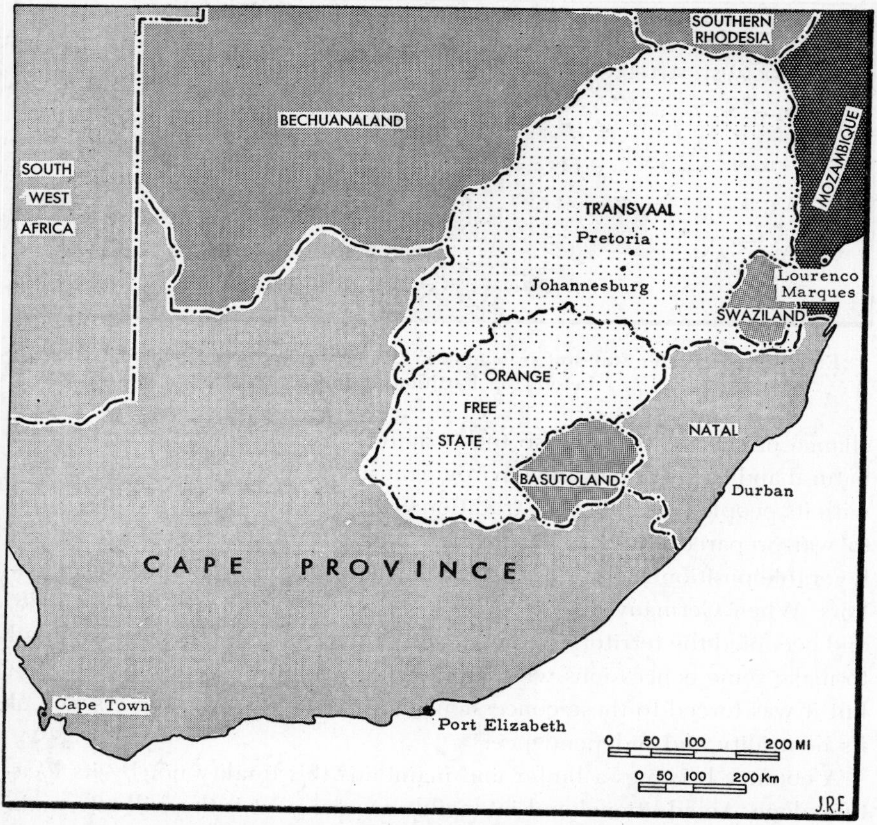

Fig. 7-1. The Boer States in Relation to British and Portuguese Territories.

agreement between the two neighbor states or at least on stable relations between them. Persia, Afghanistan, or Siam in the first years of the twentieth century are examples. All three states owed their continuing independence not so much to internal strength, but to treaties between Britain and Russia, and Britain and France, based on the desire to keep the other power out of the respective area and still to maintain good relations with this power (Fig. 7-2). A similar agreement, in this case between three powers—Britain, France, and Italy—kept the independence of Ethiopia intact for some time (Fig. 7-3). When France and Britain were no longer ready or able to wage war for Ethiopian independence, and when Italy was ready to risk friendly relations with these powers, Ethiopia became a victim of Italian expansion in 1935. If buffer countries become strong enough to be able to defend their independence themselves with some

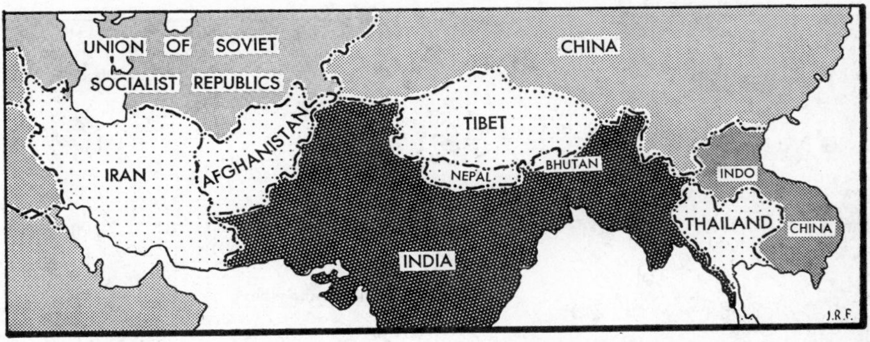

Fig. 7-2. The Buffer States of Iran (Persia), Afghanistan, and Thailand (Siam) before the Partition of India.

chance of success, they cease to be buffers. Switzerland, favored by its natural and easily defensible environment in the midst of high mountains, with its people cherishing the tradition of liberty, with its economy geared to war-preparedness, can hardly be called a buffer state. However, its favorable position is also due to the fact that it has four competing neighbors. When Germany annexed one of these neighbors, Austria, in 1938, and occupied the territory of the second, France, in 1940, Switzerland had to make some concessions which might have compromised its neutrality; but it was forced to these concessions in order to preserve the essence of its neutrality and independence.

A country becomes a buffer and maintains this quality not by its location alone. An additional and intangible requirement is the will to remain independent despite powerful neighbors. Finland, between East and West, is a splendid example of such a buffer state determination. In contrast, the chain of states from Poland to Bulgaria were consolidated by the U.S.S.R. in a bloc organization, and virtually ceased to be independent states when a relatively large sector of their population, after 1945, was blinded by the might of the Soviet Union and did not regard national independence a supreme value. They exchanged their status as buffer states, which they had maintained in the period between the two World Wars, for that of satellites.

Not all buffer states are landlocked; neither Iran, nor Thailand, Finland, or before their inclusion in the Soviet bloc Poland, Rumania, or Bulgaria can be called landlocked in the strict sense of the word. However, the coasts of most of these states are on an inland sea, the exit of which to the open ocean is practically closed. Iran's coast is very remote from the settled centers of the country, separated from them by high mountains and

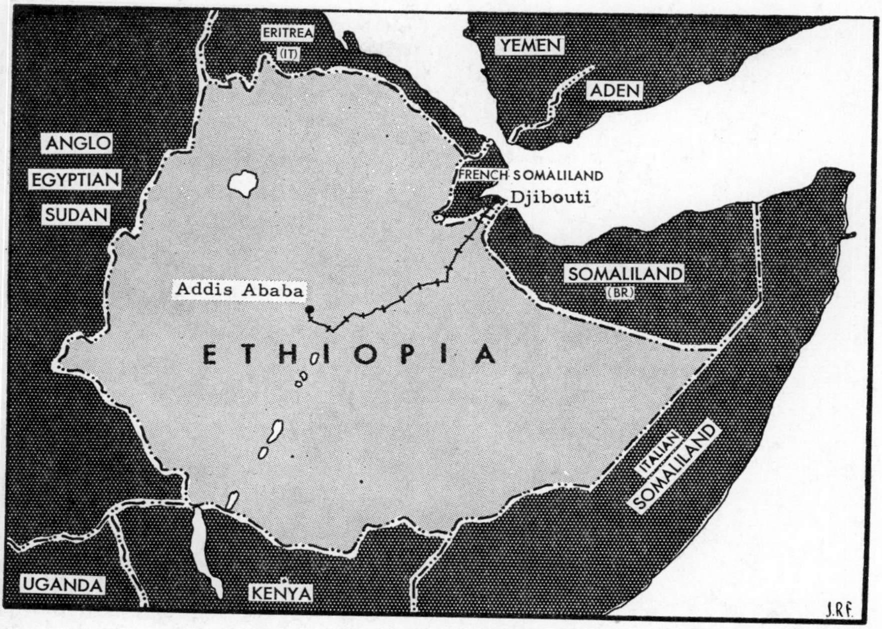

Fig. 7-3. The Buffer State of Ethiopia before 1935.

hot deserts. If it were not for the very short coastal stretch near the mouth of the Shatt el Arab, Iran despite its many hundred miles of seacoast would be a maritime state only in name.

A peculiar situation develops if a country is penned in between a large neighbor country and the *anecumene*. In this context the ocean can not be regarded as part of the *anecumene* as the navies of all countries are free to approach all its coasts. Thus the above description could with slight qualification apply to Portugal which, in the past, in a typical buffer-state position between the larger neighbor Spain, and a British dominated sea, and in the true spirit of independence, retained its freedom against repeated onslaught. Like the ocean much earlier, now deserts and the Arctic are beginning to loose their true character as *anecumene*. It is doubtful whether Greenland and Iceland, with their back to the Arctic, and Lybia, with its back to the Sahara, will retain this character much longer. Perhaps Oman and Hadramaut in Southern Arabia are the last perfect examples. In the not too distant past such countries as England, Japan, or the Philippine Islands were in this position. And Ireland, Australia, and New Zealand are accommodating themselves to new relationships under our very eyes.

Fig. 7-4. Boundary Conflicts in South America: the Acre dispute; Bolivia's lost access to the sea.

"BACKDOOR" AREAS

The classical example of a basically landlocked country is Russia and its successor the U.S.S.R. Its Arctic coast and especially its harbors of Murmansk and Archangelsk have often been called Russia's backdoor. That designation does not refer as much to the difficult access from the sea, as to their remote distance from the core areas of the U.S.S.R., indeed from any economically significant part of the country. Large, almost uninhabited, and inhospitable areas of virgin, swampy forest, the *taiga,* and moss-covered wind-swept cold steppe, the *tundra,* separate the few coastal settlements and a few mining districts from the rest of the country.

FIG. 7-5. Bolivia to the Sea via Brazil: (1) existing railroad; (2) proposed railroad; (3) highway link.

In South America every country except Uruguay has such boundaries, remote, difficult to reach through tropical forest or over towering mountains. Though, seemingly, the exact location of these boundaries could not be of great value to these countries, their national pride and the hope of finding hidden natural resources hindered them from compromise. The remoteness of these boundaries also prevented their exact delimitation and demarcation and thus caused many conflicts. Brazil, Bolivia, and Peru quarreled over the Acre territory when wild rubber rendered this hitherto unknown area a country of great potential value (Fig. 7-4). Peru, Colombia, and Ecuador for similar reasons competed for the Oriente, an area which in addition gives access to the Amazon. Bolivia and Paraguay went to war over the Chaco. Bolivia, for economic reasons, and reasons of prestige, wanted access to the Rio Parana. This would be a typical inconvenient backdoor through steaming, practically uninhabited tropical forests to an undeveloped river port far inland and to an outlet to the sea on the other side of the continent. It would still be a valuable gate to the outer world, as the main entrance from the Pacific Ocean is firmly in the hands of Peru and Chile. The corridor to the ports of Tacna and Arica, once owned by Bolivia, was lost in the Pacific War of 1884 and seems beyond hope of recovery (Fig. 7-4). In 1955, Bolivia at last took a step in easing its landlocked position, when a highway-railroad link between Brazil and Bolivia was completed (Fig. 7-5).

Even in densely populated European states such as Portugal, the Netherlands, Norway, Sweden, and Finland, all of which front the sea, the backdoor areas are in thinly inhabited inland areas. Much less frequent is the country facing inland with its coast containing the backdoor. Such is Yugoslavia. Though the interests of its coastal population are definitely bound up with fishing and shipping, the main bulk of the country and its population has little contact with this coastal area. Rugged, karstic mountains are a powerful barrier to settlement and communications.

Neither Chile nor Peru have significant interests on or across the sea. But Chile is, nonetheless, a coastal country, looking toward the sea, while for Peru the interior is as important as the coast. In Europe, Belgium's land boundaries are much more important than its short coast. The one great Belgian harbor, Antwerp, is accessible only through the Scheldt river, the mouth of which Belgium shares with the Netherlands.

THE URGE TO THE SEA

It is understandable that interior states try to reach the open sea. History is full of conflicts between interior states and coastal powers blocking their road to the sea. Ethiopia has been cut off from the sea by Italian, British, and French colonies since the second half of the nineteenth century (*cf.* Fig. 7-3, p. 179). Only their rivalry kept it from losing its political independence, while economically its underdeveloped condition made it less vulnerable to economic pressure. Thus it faced the dilemma of whether to remain undeveloped and fall prey for this very reason to more highly developed countries sooner or later, or to slide into economic dependency in the course of its own progress. Many factors contributed to Ethiopia's involvement in the ideological world conflict, to its conquest by Italy, and finally to its liberation. Together with its freedom, Ethiopia won the coveted exit to the sea (*cf.* Fig. 7-3, p. 179).

A much older and still lasting struggle for free access to the sea is that of Russia and, since 1917, the Soviet Union.[3] Interior location is, in Russia, usually assumed under the implied or acknowledged supposition that the ice-barred Arctic coast does not have any practical value. Even today, this assumption can be accepted as correct in a general way despite the progress which the Soviet Union and Canada have made in the utilization of the Arctic Sea and coast by means of icebreakers, aviation, and weather stations. This utilization has been favored by recent climatic changes. In the last half century the Arctic Ocean has become warmer and the ice

[3] R. J. Kerner, *Russia's Urge to the Sea* (Berkeley, Calif., 1942), and his chapter on "The Soviet Union as a Sea Power," in H. W. Weigert, V. Stefansson, and R. E. Harrison, eds., *New Compass of the World* (New York, 1949), pp. 104-123.

border has receded, making navigation and living conditions possible in some formerly closed areas. Whether this climatic amelioration will remain a permanent feature we do not know. In any event, certain technical advances, such as the use of radio, radar, and aviation for ice reconnaissance, the use of strong icebreakers, and so on, will further contribute to the utilization of the Arctic. In terms of strategy both the U.S.S.R. and Canada are interested in strengthening their control of the Arctic coast (*cf.* Fig. 8-11, p. 252). Whether this effort will bear economical fruit in time of peace remains to be seen, despite the spread of settlement north, which goes forward on a small scale and at great cost.[4] We shall discuss developments in the Arctic "Mediterranean" later in greater detail.[5]

Located originally in a secluded forest area of Eastern Europe, the state of the princes of Moscow developed near the source of several rivers, flowing to different seas. Much of Russia's history can be understood if we see it as a continuous struggle, kindled time and again by the urge to the sea. In earliest times this urge was limited to attempts to utilize the navigable rivers. The first time Russia reached the sea it was at the Arctic Ocean and this proved to be of very limited value, both because of the inhospitable and remote nature of the sea, and of the long and difficult access to the coast from the interior. Only since World War I has Murmansk been connected by a railroad with the interior. Gradually, several seas were reached: in the southeast, in 1557, the Caspian Sea at Astrakhan; in the east, in 1635, the Sea of Okhotsk; in the west, about 1700, the Baltic Sea at St. Petersburg (today Leningrad); in the south, in 1713, the Sea of Azov and through it, in 1783, the Black Sea. All these exits proved unsatisfactory. Either they led into enclosed seas, such as the Baltic and the Black Sea, or over immense, almost uninhabited stretches, as to the Pacific Ocean. Although the frontages at the sea have expanded, they have remained basically unsatisfactory. The Soviet Union, as the heir of Russia, has established itself as the paramount, hardly challenged power in the Baltic, Black, and Caspian Seas, but still the exits from the first two seas are in foreign hands,[6] and the Caspian Sea has no outlet. Therefore the pressure is still mounting, also and significantly in directions where not

[4] The fact that the North American nations lag behind the U.S.S.R. in Arctic research and development should not detract from their achievements in recent years. To mention one significant development, two American and one Canadian icebreakers navigated in the fall of 1954 the Northwest Passage leading from the Atlantic Ocean to the Beaufort Sea, thus laying the groundwork for the development of the mineral and biological resources in the Canadian North, of which the vast iron ore deposits in northern Labrador are most important.

[5] See pp. 246 ff.

[6] See pp. 242 ff.

even a limited success has been achieved so far, as across Iran to the Indian Ocean. The recurrent pressure on Turkey to deliver the Straits into Soviet hands and the pressure on the Scandinavian States and Denmark to open free access to the Atlantic cannot be explained by Communist ideology or temporary constellations (*cf.* Fig. 8-7, p. 238); they are inherent in the disabilities of a landlocked position. A further means to combat the disadvantages due to landlocked position is the canal system of the U.S.S.R. which permits small navy vessels to go from the Arctic Ocean to the Baltic Sea, and from the Baltic Sea to the Black Sea.

In general each coastal state has potential contact with all other coastal states of the globe, that is, with more than 90 per cent of all independent states. In situations where it appeared impossible to establish a route to the sea over a country's own territory, occasionally the substitute of a free harbor was chosen, sometimes with shipping privileges secured on a river. Czechoslovakia owned and still owns free harbors in Hamburg and Szescszin (the former Stettin), Austria in Trieste, and Yugoslavia potentially in Salonica, a commentary on the above-mentioned inaccessibility and remoteness of her own coast (see pp. 33, 198 ff.). But only Czechoslovakia has the right to dispatch ships or barges on an internationalized river to these ports. Though few rivers have been put under an international regime to secure access to the sea from interior states, these few are of importance, and among them, of primary importance, the Rhine. Switzerland has a growing Rhine merchant fleet, based on Basel, and even a few seagoing vessels. Both France and Germany built canals from the Rhine through their own territory to national harbors; nevertheless, for both countries the Rhine traffic on the internationalized river to its mouth in Dutch territory has always remained of greater interest than the canal traffic to the Rhône and Marne or the Ems and the port of Emden.

The Danube has always played a lesser role. Several reasons account for this, among them the geography of the rapids which alternate with sections of shallows and sandbars, its mouth in the closed-in Black Sea, and the little-advanced economic conditions of much of its drainage basin. Political causes have contributed to this stagnant condition. Until 1914, and to a lesser degree from 1919 to 1938, an international organization controlled the Danube. The post-1945 conditions for a while cut the river in two parts. Gradually navigation along the whole river has been resumed, first by Yugoslav shipping. Lately Austrian and German ships were admitted in parts of the Soviet area, but the eastern Danubian countries form a separate international organization completely dominated by the Soviet Union.

When the Congo State (Fig. 7-6) was founded, Britain tried to hinder the creation of this new political body by inducing Portugal to reassert century-old claims to the whole West African coast from a point north of the mouth of the Congo. In 1785, the Portuguese had established a fort at Cabinda, about thirty miles north of the mouth of the Congo. The French explorer de Brazza reached the Congo near what is today Brazzaville and claimed the northern bank of the lower Congo for France. Finally at the Congo Conference in Berlin, 1884 to 1885, an agreement was reached which left the newly-founded Congo State, the present Belgian Congo, with an outlet to the sea on the northern bank of the Congo River, conceding the southern bank and the territory of Cabinda to Portugal, and most of the western bank of the lower Congo farther inland to France. This outlet proved to be so unsatisfactory when a railroad to the port of Matadi was to be constructed, that in 1927 Belgium exchanged with Portugal 1350 square miles of inland territory for only one square mile near Matadi (*cf.* Fig. 5-2, p. 123).

As it turned out, the southeastern corner of the Belgian Congo became the most valuable part of the colony because of its rich mineral resources.[7] Transportation to the coastal port of Matadi is very inconvenient because of the necessary transloading several times between river and rail and because of the long distance. Thus, despite the tariff advantages which this all-Belgian line offers, the Portuguese railroad through Angola and to the port of Benguela and the connection with British Rhodesia could tap a large part of the traffic going to either distant South Africa or to the Portuguese East African port of Beira.

In most of these cases the railroad outlets were constructed with mutual agreement and to the mutual advantage of the powers concerned. However, where such arrangements are unfeasible, the blocked state may force an unwilling neighbor by territorial annexation or by boundary readjustments to supply the railroad outlet. The best known example is that of the South Manchurian Railroad and the Chinese Eastern Railroad to Dairen. Here Czarist Russia forced upon China an outlet to the ice-free sea, only to lose it to the stronger power of Japan.[8]

The new British dominion of Central Africa, formed as recently as 1953 and including Northern Rhodesia, Southern Rhodesia, and Nyassaland

[7] The Congo produced in 1954 more than 50 per cent of the Free World's uranium, 80 per cent of its cobalt, 70 per cent of its industrial diamonds, 8 per cent of its copper, and 8 per cent of its tin.

[8] R. B. Johnson, "Political Salients and Transportation Solutions: as Typified by Eastern North America and Manchuria," *Annals of the American Association of Geographers,* Vol. 39 (March, 1949), pp. 71, 72.

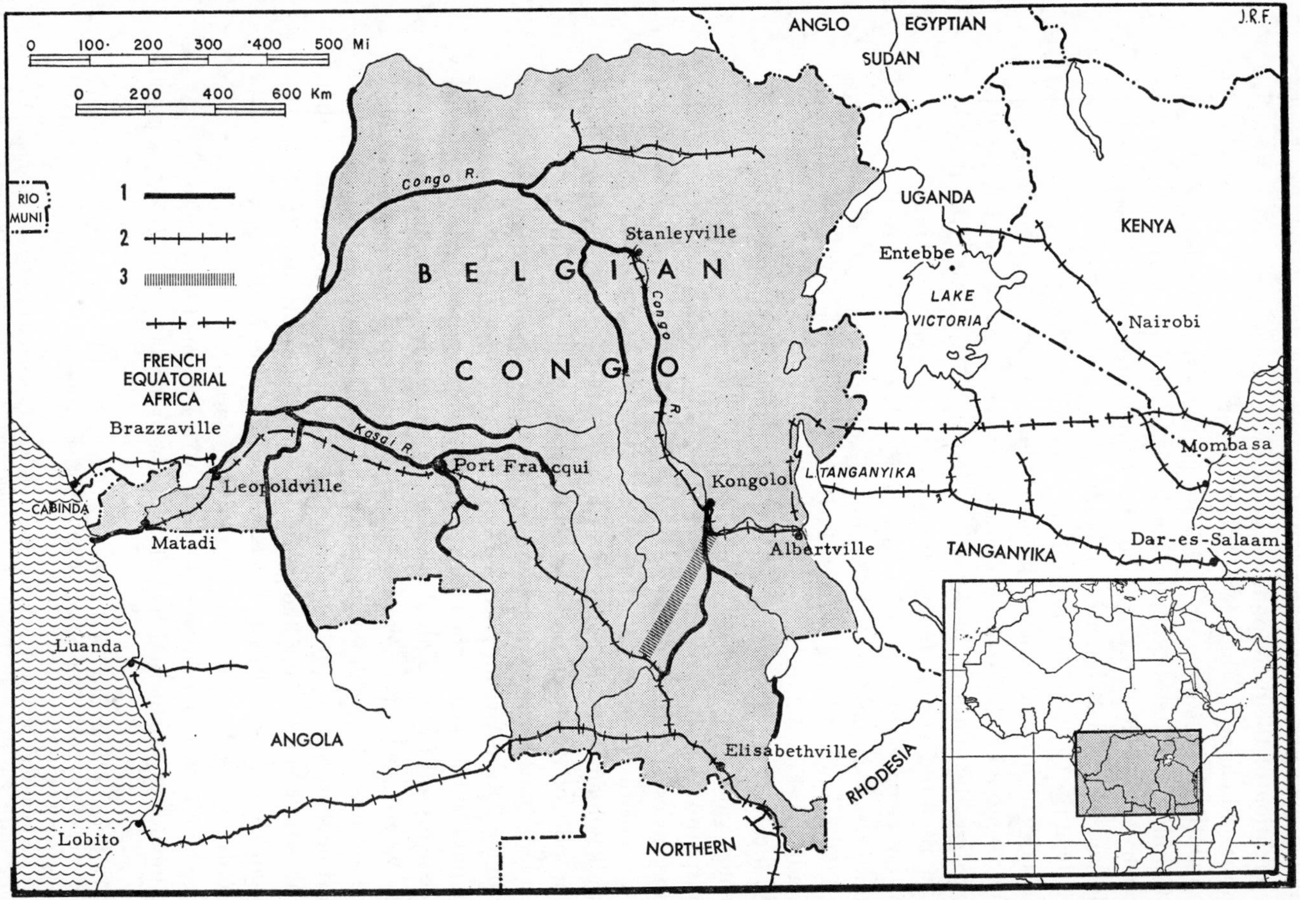

FIG. 7-6. Central Africa: Railroad Competition between Belgium, Portugal and British Rhodesia. (1) Navigable waterways; (2) existent railways; (3) railroads under construction; (4) proposed railroads.

(*cf.* Fig. 23-1, p. 690) is also a landlocked area. Most of the conventional political maps do not depict clearly its landlocked quality as they show Central Africa as well as the British Mandate of Tanganyika and the Union of South Africa in the same color. The Union of South Africa has made major efforts to extend its ideology and its economic system over this area. It is in a position to exert strong economic pressure since it is the main customer of the Central African territories and because the main railroad link leads into the Union. Thus the railroad into Portuguese Mozambique to Beira and even by way of Katanga to Angola wins political importance. The river-links to the sea, the Zambesi and its tributary the Shire—the latter the only direct outlet of Nyassaland—are obstructed by cataracts and are without sufficient depth during the dry period.

How important a river can be as outlet, if it has no obstacles to navigation, is shown by the Paraguay and Plata rivers. They are for Bolivia potentially an important outlet to the sea, and function as such for Paraguay. An even more striking example is the Amazon. Although it involves long transport from a Peruvian Pacific port by way of the Panama Canal, Peruvian shippers find this river route a more convenient, cheaper, and faster way for bulk wares than the difficult and tedious transport of wares across the high Andes and through the steaming forests to the Oriente of Peru (*cf.* Fig. 22-2, p. 674).

The Great Lakes are drained by the St. Lawrence River but the barrier of the Niagara Falls has enabled other routes to compete as shipping outlets. Through the Illinois River ships pass to the Mississippi. Through Georgian Bay and the Ottawa River, and from Lake Erie through the Mohawk and Hudson rivers, they go to New York. Gradually canals and railroads have replaced the ancient portages. The struggle for the St. Lawrence Seaway (*cf.* Fig. 6-11, p. 166) is only one phase in the age-old struggle to direct the area around the Great Lakes inland or outward to the Sea, to use a favorable coastal position to dominate, or at least to exploit this area of interior position. This struggle for the domination of the Great Lakes' traffic has become quite complex. At one time it was sufficient to occupy a coastal station like Manhattan Island or Montreal to assure control of the access to the Great Lakes. Today a combination of transportation improvements and economic inducements is necessary to secure for any port a share in this profitable traffic.[9]

[9] See also pp. 165, 166 on the role of the St. Lawrence Seaway in the development of economic core areas in the United States.

SEA POWER POSITIONS AND EXPANSION INLAND

The domination of large continental areas has been attempted many times by sea powers. In the past the occupation of a coastal island or of a headland was sometimes sufficient to assure complete domination of the hinterland. Phoenicians, Greeks, medieval Italian cities, the Portuguese, Dutch, French, and British succeeded each other in this type of locational struggle. Few relics of such sites exist today. The British crown colony of Hongkong is probably the most important. However, its function has changed. It no longer dominates China by its trade, but has become the main point of contact between China and the West. At one time Port Arthur in Russian hands assumed a similar position in regard to Manchuria. Portuguese Macao, the Portuguese colonies on the Indian coast, and international Tangier in Morocco have become fossils without important functions.

Other somewhat similar places, especially in Africa, became the starting points for expansion inland. Mombasa in Kenya and Bathurst in Gambia have retained their protected location on an island close to the coast, resembling the location of Manhattan Island. So did Lagos in Nigeria on an island in the lagoons, and Dakar in French West Africa at the tip of a peninsula. Their present functions, however, are no longer the same as in the past. These places are no longer the trading posts of a foreign power, assuring an economic stranglehold on the hinterland. With the strengthening and political consolidation of the hinterland these coastal sites have become the trade outlets of what in most cases has become a politically integrated area. Bombay and Calcutta in India also come to mind. Certain of these coastal towns have become the capitals of their territories. More indicative of the real situation are the capitals that have been transferred to inland cities, as to Nairobi from Mombasa or to New Delhi from Calcutta, stressing thereby the politically subordinated position of the harbor town.

A similar process, though under slightly different conditions, took place in the United States towards the end of the colonial period. As the original colonies expanded, capitals also were moved inland from the first coastal settlements, from New York to Albany, from Philadelphia to Harrisburg, from Jamestown to Richmond, from Charlestown to Columbia, and from Savannah to Atlanta. Of course, these cities were from the beginning the centers of European agrarian settlement as well as trading posts for the overseas trade. Dutch New Amsterdam, today's New York, bears the closest resemblance to the African examples.

LOCATION AND NATIONAL SECURITY

A related modern problem concerns the advisability of removing industrial and political centers from frontier zones for security reasons. Political shifts resulting from such a relocation can not be assessed at the moment, as most such plans have not progressed beyond the blueprint stage. Examples of the past show the military and economic implications of such shifts, but do not reveal much about their influence on politico-geographical conditions. The history of World War II offers several examples of countries trying to relocate industries in areas considered safe, or relatively safe, from enemy action and remote from the frontier zones which were, or seemed to be, more exposed to enemy interference, especially by air power. In line with this kind of strategy, the Soviet Union withdrew and re-established important industries behind the Urals and in Western Siberia during World War II in order to protect them from conquest or destruction by the German invader.

The new tools of atomic and biological warfare provide mankind with means of total destruction which stagger the imagination and render hopeless the task of rewriting the location pattern of a country in order to create areas of "safety."

Actually, none of the great powers seems to have been able to work out a new locational pattern for the purpose of meeting the threat of atomic warfare. It is true that in countries like the Soviet Union and the United States industrial planning in recent years has attempted to refrain from making the country as a whole dependent on one or a few vital industrial production centers. But except for this, preoccupation with the urgent problems of the day has militated against the carrying out of radical plans for protecting areas of high concentration of population and industry. So-called "ribbon developments" along the lines of a grid of transportation and communication lines [10] or plans to set up small detached production units instead of a cluster of industries and to assure these units of uninterrupted transportation have remained in the blueprint stage. According to newspaper reports in smaller countries with a more simply arranged and highly concentrated industrial location pattern, such as Sweden, plans have been executed successfully to protect strategic industries by relocating them underground.

[10] E. H. Hoover, *The Location of Economic Activity* (New York, 1948), p. 296.

LOCATION ALONG NARROW MARINE STRAITS

Another type of dominating location has survived without much change in function, namely, location along an indispensable route, a route which cannot be by-passed, especially along narrow marine straits. Istanbul and vicinity along the Straits (Bosporus and Dardanelles), Copenhagen on The Sound (*cf.* Fig. 8-7, p. 238), Singapore at the Straits of Malacca, Aden at the entrance to the Red Sea, and Gibraltar at that to the Mediterranean have been vital points for centuries and are still so. The Straits and The Sound are in the hands of relatively minor powers, Turkey and Denmark, but other powers are vitally interested in their free use. Among the interested powers, Russia, and now the Soviet Union, has ranked first for about two centuries. This fact accounts for the continuous pressure put by this power on the two smaller nations. Great Britain controls the three other places mentioned and draws part of its strength as a world power from this fact. The same is true for the interoceanic Panama Canal, controlled by the United States.

The Suez Canal (*cf.* Fig. 8-8, p. 240), in 1954, has ceased to be a British zone of influence and direct power. With the exodus of the British garrison, to be completed in 1956, Egypt will reach one of the goals of her national ambition. The Suez Canal remains an international waterway open to all peaceful navigation. Only the future can tell what role it will play in a serious international crisis in which Egypt may have to take sides. In 1954, the new power position of Egypt in the Canal Zone was illustrated by the fact that she was in a position to continue, in spite of the disapproval of the United Nations, her blockade measures against Israel, in regard to which a state of war continued to exist.

Turkey, or Egypt, or Denmark cannot help but be interested in these passages because of their location astride them. In contrast, Gibraltar, Singapore (*cf.* Fig. 8-5, p. 232), and Aden are so important only because they have been transformed deliberately into strongpoints for the protection of what has been called a vital artery of the British Empire.[11] In the hands of weak powers, they would lose much of their importance.

It is the general area along the waterway which is important, not a specific point. The straits of Gibraltar (*cf.* Fig. 8-8, p. 240) were dominated in the past from Cádiz and not Gibraltar, those of Malacca from the city of Malacca and not from Singapore. In both cases distant, but not

[11] C. B. Fawcett, "Lifelines of the British Empire," in Weigert-Stefansson-Harrison, *op. cit.*, pp. 238-249 (244).

too distant bases sufficed for a strong naval power to control the actual narrow passage. In the same manner the United States supplements its hold on the Panama Canal by its bases in the Caribbean area (*cf.* Fig. 3-6, p. 79), such as the Virgin Islands, Guantanamo on Cuba, and the leased bases on Trinidad and other British islands. Similarly the broad connection between the Atlantic and Indian Oceans south of South Africa is controlled from rather distant bases on the coast of the Union of South Africa, especially Simonstown.

Harbors, strategically well-located as they may be, if they are in the hands of powers without a strong navy have little actual value for the domination of these waterways. Neither Spanish Ceuta nor neutral Tangier along the Strait of Gibraltar, nor French Djibouti at the exit of the Red Sea, nor any of the many potential island bases around the Caribbean Sea, nor the Portuguese Lourenço Marques in South Africa, nor the Indonesian Medang at the Straits of Malacca are comparable to, for instance, Gibraltar. The city of Hormuz which once dominated the entrance into the Persian Gulf has found no successor. It is the peculiar combination between naval power and mercantile opportunities that makes sites alongside straits so important and that explains why their fortunes change with the passage of time and changes in world conditions.[12]

NARROW PASSAGES ON CONTINENTS

Narrow passages for traffic exist also on the continents. Where long mountain chains cross whole continents, pass routes across these chains are of decisive importance. As a rule they cannot be controlled from positions at some distance, but only alongside or astride such passages. Afghanistan is the country of the Khyber Pass, the most important pass leading from India to its Asiatic neighbor states. Included in this pass region are also a few less important nearby passes, which all together form this unique pass zone. The unifying force of this route has proved strong enough even in the present contest of the great powers to preserve Afghanistan as a political unit.

Similarly Switzerland grew up around the St. Gotthard Pass and gradually included some nearby passes. It is significant that Switzerland is also one of the few multinational states which have withstood so far the infection of nationalism. East of Switzerland, Austria developed as a pass state in the Middle Ages and after a spectacular development in the Hapsburg

[12] For an elaboration of this topic and its strategical implications see pp. 227 ff.

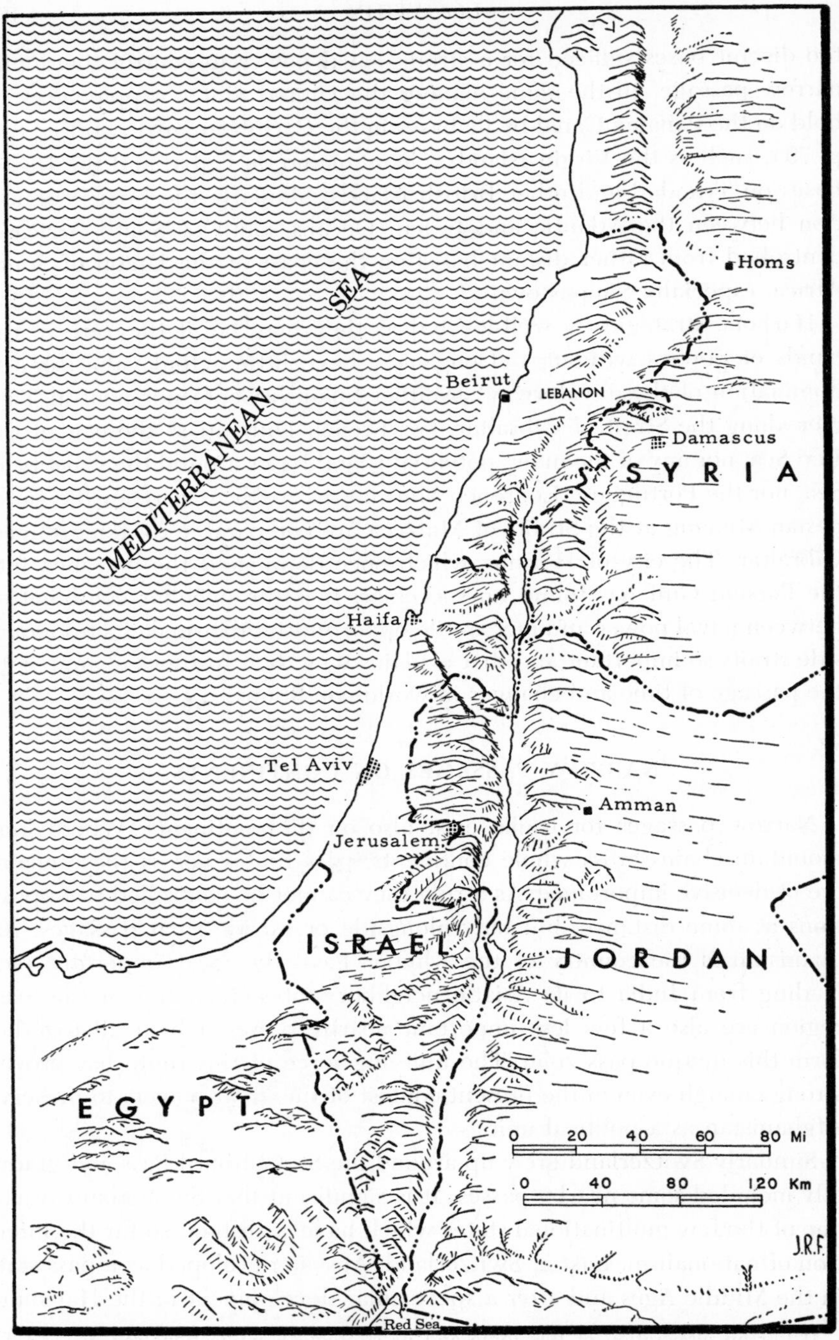

FIG. 7-7. The Palestine-Syria Corridor.

Empire is reduced again to an Alpine pass state. The analogous pass state of the western Alps, Savoy, disappeared not quite a century ago after an existence of many centuries. The autonomy, acquired for the Val d'Aosta in 1945, is a weak aftermath. In contrast it should be noted that in the long chain of the American Cordilleras no pass state has developed. The Republic of Panama, of recent birth, comes closest to this concept.

Location around a pass does not by itself signify independence, or even different development of a region. Quite the opposite, such pass areas are much sought after and coveted by adjacent countries in the plains. The easier the route through them, the easier they fall prey. The Iroquois were able to base their federation on the gap of the Mohawk valley through the Appalachians, but this political body did not exist very long. Many others never became the center of states. One such gap, which has long been a cradle of conflict—the area around Trieste—either belonged to some strong state or was divided between two of them. It was too important to be left to the control of the local inhabitants, and too wide and open for them to preserve their independence against other strong powers. There are other such pass regions. One of the most fateful in European history is the gap between the southern end of the Urals and the northern end of the Caspian Sea which opens into the steppes of Central Asia. Too broad and flat to be defensible, it proved to be definite enough to channelize movement of nomadic tribes. Time and again Huns, Magyars, Tatars and many others broke into Europe, and occasionally mass movements in the opposite direction also occurred. However, the Russian peasants migrated into Siberia in numbers of many hundreds of thousands not through this gate but over low passes farther north in the Urals. Today this region, though not very far from the geometrical center of the Soviet Union, is still a region off the main roads.

The same fateful role which the Ural-Caspian gate plays in European history was assigned to the Palestinian-Syrian corridor in the history of the Near East (Fig. 7-7). It is a narrow piece of cultivable land between the Arabian desert and the Mediterranean Sea connecting Egypt with the mountains of Asia Minor and the fertile plains of Iraq. Nomads and other peoples, forced to migrate, have used it since prehistoric times. Merchants and other peaceful travelers followed. Armies trod the corridors under obscure leaders or under world-famous generals and kings from the Ramses and Alexander to Napoleon and Allenby. A number of nations have tried to make their home in this corridor and defend themselves in its narrow confines and its rugged hills and mountains. Recurrent wars and annihilating catastrophes were their repeated fate.

A much broader corridor that time and again played a role of fateful importance in European history is the western continuation of the broad Russian Plain through Poland, Northern Germany, Belgium, and into western France. Cultural influences, tribes and nations, commerce and armies have moved through this corridor. Large rivers cross it, and at the few points where these rivers can be crossed, important cities have sprung into existence. In its narrowest part—in Flanders—the meeting of diverse influences has created one of the centers of European civilization. Here also an unusually large number of famous battlefields can be found.

Parallel to this corridor there is another south of the Alps, the Po valley. However, the great centers of civilization are neither west nor east of it, but Rome to the south and the French and German core areas to the north of it. The stream of east-west movement in the corridor was crossed by a more important one on the points where routes over the Alps and the Appenines open. The great centers tend to lie on such cross routes.

ISTHMUSES

Isthmuses, those narrow pieces of land which connect two continents or larger land masses, look on the map like natural corridors. Only detailed maps show that this is rarely the case. The Isthmus of Panama, or even the whole of Central America, have never served as a corridor between North and South America. High rugged mountains and the unhealthy climate of the lower parts account for this. It is still debated whether the two pre-Columbian high civilizations of the Mayas and the Incas had any contact over this land route. The Pan-American highway system is still incomplete.[13]

Other isthmuses, like that of Kra at the base of the Malayan peninsula (*cf.* Fig. 8-5, p. 232), are only slightly favorable for the movement of men and goods. Cultural influences and invaders entered the Greek Peloponnesus and the Crimea, to name only two examples, as often across the narrow sea as through the isthmuses which connect these peninsulas with the mainland.

More important than the negative function of isthmuses as land routes is the fact that the narrow waist of an isthmus is a minor obstacle for crossing from sea to sea. The construction of canals only accentuates a pre-existing favorable condition. The canals of Suez and Panama are the two main examples.

[13] See Fig. 22-1, p. 670.

ISTHMUSES AND CANALS: SUEZ AND PANAMA

The Suez Canal (*cf.* Fig. 8-8, p. 240) cuts through the only isthmus which is a major historical highway. This canal separates the Eurasian and African landmasses, connecting the Mediterranean at Port Said with the Red Sea at Suez over the short distance of about one hundred miles. This short cut which obviates the necessity of transloading has completely replaced the old land route from Alexandria to the Red Sea, as well as that from the Syrian ports to Basra at the Persian Gulf. It has, thereby, increased the key position of Egypt and Sinai, and made Syria's position as an intermediary between East and West a matter of the past, impairing its standing among the countries of the Near East. During recent decades, however, the construction of pipelines from Iraq and Saudi Arabia to the Syrian and Lebanese ports has tended to return to Syria some part of its key position.

Constructed by the French, the Suez Canal has been under British control from 1875 to 1954, a period roughly contemporary with the flourishing of the so-called third British Empire. As long as India was an integral part of this Empire the Suez Canal was indispensable to it and has long been an important link in the "life line" starting at Gibraltar in the West and leading into the Indian Ocean at Aden. During and after World War II India, Pakistan, Burma, and Ceylon loosened their ties with Great Britain. As a result, the Canal, though still a valuable asset, is no longer the indispensable link. At the same time the development of air power has made the Canal vulnerable to enemy attack. With the transfer of the Canal to Egypt the Canal and the country on its banks is in the hand of the same power. Its control has strengthened the position of Egypt, both economically and politically.

The Panama Canal (*cf.* Fig. 3-6, p. 72) offers an interesting similar example. Though of equally great importance, the isthmus of Panama in the hands of weak and small nations, first Colombia, later of the Republic of Panama, was rather a cause of weakness for these countries. Like the Suez Canal, the Panama Canal has great importance for international commerce. Its role is even more significant than that of the Suez Canal because of its importance for the commerce and the political position of the United States. However, while the Suez Canal could justly be called a part of the life line of the British Empire, the cohesion of the United States would not be threatened without the Panama Canal. It enables the United States Navy to operate the American fleet in two oceans and to concentrate naval strength in the face of the greatest danger. Because of this hemispheric defense role of the Panama Canal, the United States has established bases for the protection of the Canal on the island approaches in the Caribbean and in the Pacific. This necessitated a change in its political relations to the areas concerned, which were either British colonies or independent states. It has strengthened the economic and political ties in all cases, but it has also evoked unfavorable repercussions. Some groups in the Republic of Panama could base their political prestige on the popularity of the fight against encroachment by the Americans. However, nowhere did the opposition take forms of open hostility comparable to that shown by the Greek majority on Cyprus since the British have shifted their Suez Canal installations to this island.

The Panama Canal was not the only canal site which has been considered by the Americas at one time or another. Canals have been proposed across Nicaragua, Honduras, and across Mexico's Isthmus of Tehuantepec. Probably earliest was the proposal to use the Atrato River and on the Pacific side the San Juan River. While this project never came near serious consideration, primarily because of geographical and technical difficulties, in all the other proposals political considerations were at least as important as the technical problems, and all were so intimately interwoven that they can not well be separated in the discussion. Perhaps the clearest case is that of the Tehuantepec project which would have put American forces, already deployed along the northern boundary of Mexico, into the southern frontier zone and would have deprived this country potentially of all direct contact with any other neighbor. What was tolerable and even to a certain degree an insurance for its independence for such a small country as Panama, would have been considered an impairment of its sovereignty by a larger country with the proud tradition of Mexico.

THE KRA CANAL PROJECT

The Kra isthmus on the Malayan Peninsula (*cf.* Fig. 8-5, p. 232) is the potential site of an interoceanic canal. Though plans for such a canal never have passed beyond the blueprint stage, their existence alone has been helpful for Thailand in its struggle to maintain its independent buffer position against France, Britain, and Japan. Opposed to such a canal were the local interests of Singapore and the larger interests of Great Britain, whose supervision of the traffic through the Strait of Malacca would be challenged. The construction of a canal through the Isthmus of Kra would shorten the route around the Malayan Peninsula by 600 miles and, therefore, despite canal fees, be a heavy competitor of the

Singapore route. The importance of Singapore is only about 150 years old. Before the advent of the Europeans in the sixteenth century and also later, as long as shipping preferred routes not too far from land, the route from the Indian Ocean to the South China Sea led this way. The route was dominated by a site farther north, that of the city of Malacca. When the Dutch came and ventured a direct route from the Cape of Good Hope across the Indian Ocean, the Sunda Strait and Batavia grew in importance. Singapore's importance was finally confirmed when the opening of the Suez Canal made the northerly straits the more convenient route to the Far East.

The minor importance of the Kra route, and that of the only other existing interoceanic canal, that of Kiel in Germany at the base of the Jutland Peninsula, is geographically caused by the fact that the saving in shipping time is relatively small compared with that brought about by the construction of the Suez and Panama canals. The latter obviate the necessity of circumnavigating a whole continent, the first two only of peninsulas.

PENINSULAS

The importance of peninsulas must be seen in their isolation potential caused by their semidetachment. This sometimes meant that these peninsulas remained culturally backward and politically of little importance. A striking example is that of the peninsula of Lower California, where isolation is aggravated by a desert or semidesert climate. As early as in pre-Columbian times it was inhabited by one of the most backward Indian groups and this backwardness, in relation to other parts of Mexico, has remained characteristic. Even in Europe some peninsulas, such as Cornwall, Wales, or Brittany, have been able to preserve their identity, even some remnants of a separate nationality, but have remained somewhat backward. Mountains, everywhere in the world favored as refuge areas, accentuate this function of peninsulas—and of islands—because there is no longer any other possibility of retreat.

In large peninsulas we speak of favorable conditions for development of separate nationalities and independent states such as Italy, Spain together with Portugal, Denmark, or Korea. However, this condition should not be overrated, as the long history of political divisions in Italy, the Iberian Peninsula, and even in Korea shows. The Balkan Peninsula, Arabia, and others never accomplished political unification.

However, due to the geographical accident that many peninsulas are continental protrusions reaching close to some other continent, historically the most important function of peninsulas has been that of steppingstones for migrations and invasions. From the prehistoric immigration of man into the Western hemisphere by way of the Chukotsk peninsula of northeastern Asia and Alaska, and into Europe by way of the Iberian Peninsula —and through the lowland between the Urals and the Caspian Sea—to the invasion of Europe by the Allies through the Italian Peninsula and Normandy there is a continuous stream of such movements. Oriental ancient civilization found its way west along the coasts of Asia Minor and Greece. This bridge situation has created a psychological and political attitude which is similar to the buffer-state psychology, but differs in that the political bodies on such peninsulas feel—rightly or often wrongly—much more secure, and very often culturally superior. Koreans, Greeks, Italians, and even Spaniards have displayed this feeling of superiority, and it has led, sometimes, to disastrous overestimation of their own political potentialities. Italy's dream of a *mare nostro* is only the last instance.

ISLAND CHAINS AND LAND BRIDGES

Much better steppingstones for cultural or migratory movements have been provided by island chains. As a rule, such island chains are open from all sides, thus inviting invasion at many points. In Japan, cultural influences have entered as well through the harbor of Nagasaki at the southern end as through Tokyo, situated roughly in the center of the chain. Land bridges, though mostly entered from the end, can be open to occasional invasion from the sides. People moving through such a corridor are confined to it by the accompanying mountains, sea, or desert. Thus they are open to attack from the flank by raiders striking from the desert or from the sea, who are accustomed and equipped to move through these inhospitable spaces. Syria and Palestine are the classical examples of such a corridor, attacked time and again by the wandering nomads of steppe and desert from the east, and from the west by seaborne invaders. The days of nomadic invaders are apparently past. However, modern Jews have followed the path of Philistines and Crusaders who, coming from beyond the Mediterranean, founded a state based on the coast, but like their predecessors are unable to control the entire width of the corridor.

SEACOASTS OF CONTINENTS

Seacoasts, depending on their physical character and configuration, are open to raid and invasion to a smaller or larger degree. Invasion across the sea is a powerful factor in the history of modern states. Almost all the states of the Americas, Australia, and New Zealand, as well as most of the colonies or semi-independent political bodies of Africa bear the mark of their maritime origin in the distribution of their populations, cities, religions, and cultural ties. Coasts, of course, differ greatly in terms of accessibility. The Atlantic coasts of North and South America are easily accessible and natural harbors are within easy distance of each other. On the other hand, many African coasts are exposed to heavy surf, have few natural indentations, and are backed by almost impenetrable, dense, wet forests. No seafaring nations grew up on any part of this coast. The factor of distance from other coasts, and especially from any opposite shore at a reasonable distance, contributed to render these coasts of West Africa a backwater of history. Even when the Europeans appeared, they occupied only a few coastal points and built forts where slaves were collected for shipment to America. The invaders were kept from penetrating inland by the forests, swamps, and diseases of the coastal plain, as well as by the slopes of the plateau and the cataracts of the rivers farther inland. The resistance of the natives could be discounted.

It is interesting to compare with these West African coasts those in East Africa in approximately the same latitude. The general character of the coast is similar, though there are a few more natural harbors in the east. The immediate hinterland is similarly uninviting. Well-organized native states nowhere reached to the coasts. However, West Africa remained apart from the currents of world history to the end of the nineteenth century, when the scattered trading posts finally developed into exploitation colonies where raw materials were developed systematically, native labor trained, and markets for European products found. In East Africa this condition had been reached almost one thousand years ago and mass colonization from overseas had even been attempted. The decisive distinguishing factor is that East Africa is close to coasts where seafaring peoples have developed. Since the times of the ancient Egyptians, traders and occasionally colonists have come continuously to these coasts. Though neither colonizing Arabs nor Europeans ever came in great numbers, the Arabs to the coast, the Europeans to the Kenya Highlands, they have won a firm foothold. Perhaps numerically strongest was the invasion of Madagascar by Malayans from the opposite shores of Indonesia. Though large, the Indian Ocean proved to be not too large to prevent its crossing by men in considerable numbers even before the age of the modern ship. Thus it was nothing specifically novel when the British founded their circum-oceanic empire around the Indian Ocean in the nineteenth century.

There are no shores which have no opposite shore, in geometrical terms. For practical purposes, however, the Pacific Ocean is so wide that neither Chile nor Peru have ever been influenced in their political thinking by the awareness of their opposite shore. The same is true of those shores of Eurasia and North America which face the Arctic Ocean. In the days of the "air age," this situation is changing rapidly and Americans have discovered to their discomfort how close is the opposite shore across the frozen sea for military aircraft. The importance of new locational factors in the Arctic regions is discussed in Chapter 8.

COASTS OF ISLANDS

What is true for the coasts of continents is equally valid for coasts of islands. The British Isles afford an example which is of interest in more than one respect. The close proximity of the European continent to the southeastern coast of Great Britain made this coast the repeated entrance for invaders and the earliest inhabitants were pushed northwestwards into the mountains. Vestiges of these subsequent invasions can be found in many peculiarities of the cultural landscape. But politically only the Irish in Eire have been able to shape the map, and to a slight degree the Celtic-speaking remnants in Wales and the Scottish Highlands. In Ireland the struggle between the invaders and the indigenous Celtic group is still going on. Despite the apparent victory of the Irish, it should not be forgotten that the English language is spoken by the majority and that it is far from decided whether it will lose or win ground in the coming decades.[14] Ireland's north, west, and south coasts and the western coast of Great Britain, facing the apparently endless ocean, were a coast without an opposite coast up to the time of Columbus. It was close enough to the European continent that Vikings could attack and even settle here. That remained an isolated instance. After the discovery of America the west coast of Great Britain lost this character of a back door, but the Irish western coast largely retained it.

ISLANDS AS AREAS OF REFUGE

Despite this threat of invasion due to their location, many islands have become refuge areas. The Irish in Ireland, the Ainos on Hokkaido, the aborigines in a Chinese Formosa, or the Singhalese on Ceylon are island peoples in areas of refuge and it is little realized that all these peoples

[14] See pp. 392 ff.

once occupied much larger areas. They have tended to develop special traits, or rather to retain older traits which have disappeared elsewhere. The language spoken by the people of Iceland is much closer to the Norwegian spoken a thousand years ago in Norway than is the modern Norwegian. The Eskimos of Greenland, until quite recently, were able to preserve old customs over many centuries. Islands have often, and partly because of these cultural peculiarities, retained a special political status even when conquered. Such conquests did not always come from culturally related nations nearby, but from countries far away. Malta, Cyprus, or Ceylon are bound to the British Isles under different constitutional forms; Madagascar belongs to France, although it is far from France as well as from any other French colony; Sicily has its separate status within Italy; Ireland, Iceland, Cuba, Santo Domingo have attained independence after centuries of foreign rule.

It would, however, be misleading to regard islands as refuge areas by their very location in the midst of the sea. Many islands are not refuge areas at all. Others are refuge areas not as such, but because their mountains have offered the sought-for protection. Ceylon, separated from India by a strait only some twenty miles wide, is an especially clear example. Here the primitive, dark-skinned, small Veddas live in the least accessible parts; the Singhalese have retreated to the mountains and the southern parts of the islands, while the northern half of the island was invaded by Tamils. They in turn were confined to dry, mountainous areas by Singhalese recovery. The latest to come were people from different parts of southern India and some Europeans. Like the Irish, the Singhalese seem to have succeeded in reasserting their preponderance on the island. However, Ceylon is a refuge area also in another sense. This is the only part of the Indian subcontinent where Buddhism remained the dominating faith. The historical background is reflected in its political status since 1948 as an independent nation, although retaining some ties to Great Britain as well as to India. While India was able to absorb mainland areas of very different background, such as those of the hill tribes, and gave up other areas to Pakistan only after prolonged struggle, it permitted Ceylon to go its own way. The geographic factors of insularity, of the physical qualities of the island, and of its prominent position on vital shipping lanes in the Indian Ocean account for Ceylon's being able to chart its own political course, independent of India.[15]

Another example of islands as the basis of independent statehood,

[15] B. H. Farmer in O. H. K. Spate, *Geography of India and Pakistan* (London, 1954), pp. 743 and 782.

although it has still to pass the test of history, is offered by the South Moluccas (also called the Spice Islands), where a secessionist "South Moluccas Republic" was established in 1950 (*cf.* Fig. 3-5, p. 70). Indonesia, which had gained independence from the Netherlands in 1949, recaptured the port of Amboina where the secessionist movement originated, but the rebels escaped to the island of Ceram and neighboring islands where they have continued to resist.[16] One important feature in the current struggle between Indonesia and the South Moluccas is the religious cleavage, since Indonesian nationalism was essentially a Javanese movement in its early stages, and as such closely associated with the Moslem religion, while the pagan population of Amboina and the neighboring islands, isolated from the main islands, had been converted to Christianity by the Dutch.[17] Afraid of mass immigration from overpopulated Java, the people of the South Moluccas have chosen to resist the substitution of Dutch by Javanese rule in their island refuges.

Another example is offered by Formosa. The native population was displaced and forced into the mountains by numerically overwhelming Chinese, and during the Japanese rule, by Japanese immigration. However, recently, even their hold on their mountain refuge seems to weaken. Numerically the situation appears hopeless. While the number of the 156,000 aborigines, reported in 1938, remains almost stationary, the Chinese population increased from 3,156,000 in 1905 to 5,747,000 (plus 308,000 Japanese) in 1938, and to 8,000,000, which is the estimate in 1955. More significant, Formosa now for the second time has become a refuge area for traditional China. The first instance occurred in the seventeenth century, after the Manchus had overrun the mainland, the second in our own time in the face of Communist rule on the mainland.

REFUGE AREAS ON CONTINENTS

The problem of the Formosan aborigines in a refuge area for a primitive group is not so much that of an island as a problem within an island. In that it is not different from the problems of other primitive groups, such as the Veddas in Ceylon, the Ainus in Hokkaido, the Dyaks in Borneo, the Igorots in Luzon, and many others. In all these instances mountains and forests rather than the islands themselves offered the refuge area both for culturally backward and for numerically weak populations. On the continents such mountain refuges and forest areas were sought out

[16] See Fig. 3-5, p. 70.
[17] See pp. 423 ff.

by small groups, and served in a few cases to shelter independent states.[18] Ethiopia and Nepal are the best remaining examples, or among highly civilized nations, Switzerland. More frequent are instances where such units have preserved some form of autonomous self-government under foreign domination. The autonomous Soviet republics in the Caucasus, or the Basque area in Spain are well-known examples. Less known is the case of the "Autonomous Region" which the Rumanian constitution of 1952 granted to a Hungarian minority in northeastern Transylvania. It seems significant that this autonomy was not granted to the majority of Hungarians within the confines of Rumania, but to these so-called Sziks (Szeklers) who form only about two-fifths of the Hungarian minority in Rumania, but have led a separate existence in their mountains since the tenth century. In the diet of Transylvania they formed a separate nation from the Magyars (Hungarians) until 1848.

It is improbable that a new state would arise today and receive its shape from such local conditions of topography. That states formed under primitive conditions in the protection of mountains and forests have been able to survive into the present is largely due to the power of tradition and to the national pride which prompts people to cling to every piece of land they have inherited, or even to the fact that divisive features in the landscape have developed because there was a boundary. In contrast, Poland offers an example of a nation with very strong national concepts and traditions but without the benefit of established boundaries fortified by physical features. The boundary changes which took place after World War II were the result of its precarious location between the U.S.S.R. and Germany and of its new status as a Soviet satellite (*cf.* Fig. 4-1, p. 82). Poland its industrial and agricultural base and its population were moved many miles westwards in a generally featureless plain. Only its southern mountain boundary along the Carpathians remained basically unchanged.

The classical example of a state whose boundaries seem to conform to a mountain configuration is Bohemia, the western part of the Czechoslovakian republic. The Slavic tribes, which coalesced to the Czech people in the early Middle Ages, settled in the treeless, fertile basin where they enjoyed the protection of the uninhabited, forested mountain rim. German colonists, moving east, by-passed this mountain fortress to the north or south, moving through more inviting plains. However, these conditions

[18] G. B. Cressey, *Asia's Lands and People*, 2nd ed. (New York, 1951), pp. 138-139; W. G. East and O. H. K. Spate, *The Changing Map of Asia*, 2nd ed. (New York, 1953), p. 278.

disappeared long ago.[19] The forests have been cleared in wide areas, the low mountains are no longer an obstacle for modern road or railroad construction, and German settlers penetrated over the mountains to the edge of the interior basin. Nevertheless, the medieval boundary on the crest of the mountains remained essentially unchanged throughout the centuries. When Hitler opened the world conflict and attempted to replace the historical boundary by a linguistic one, this spelled in the end only disaster for the Germans within this boundary. It appears that the present location of the boundary is essentially defined by history and by the different development which areas take on the two sides of a long-existing boundary, but that the location along ridges has lost all independent meaning.

THE ROLE OF DESERTS

The physical factors which seem least variable in determining the location of boundaries are deserts. The Sahara, the Gobi, the Rub' al Khali in Arabia determine the location of political bodies even in our day. The French colonies south of the Sahara are clearly different from the French-dominated areas north of the desert. The Atlas countries are predominantly settlement colonies, and areas of political domination, those south of the Sahara are colonies of economic exploitation. However, even this clear-cut divisive force of the desert may eventually come to an end under the impact of modern technical civilization. The oasis of Buraimi in the Rub' al Khali has become the object of a conflict between Saudi Arabia, from which it is separated by hundreds of miles of sandy desert, and Oman, from which it is separated by dry inhospitable mountains (*cf.* Fig. 4-3, p. 88). It is, however, in an area which may contain oilfields. Its importance for modern technological civilization, and at the same time the means which this civilization offers to overcome the desert, make this conflict significant. It is a sign that we may stand at the end of the period when deserts were a nearly insuperable factor. Whether air or surface motor transport will play the decisive role in this change can not be predicted.

Some people believe that the construction of railroads will be more important than motor or air transport. This idea is primarily advanced in France by the promoters of the construction of a Trans-Saharan railroad. In any case the time seems near when three so far quite disconnected

[19] J. A. Steers, "The Middle People; Resettlement in Czechoslovakia," *Geographical Journal,* Vol. 102 (January, 1949).

centers of power can be linked together. These areas of present and potential power concentration are the French North African territories (Morocco, Algeria, and Tunisia), the Central African Tchad, Ubangi, and Congo regions, and lastly the British East African colonies. Their linking would be of special significance since these regions are likely to play a primary role in a future conflict involving the defense of western Europe and the Near and Middle East against attack from the north and the east.

SEDENTARY AND NOMADIC WAYS OF LIFE

To the same degree as uninhabitable, or uninhabited, or at least unclaimed zones tend to disappear, nations of different ways of life become close neighbors. Thereby the causes of friction are greatly increased. Conflicts arising from different ways of life have existed since times immemorial. However, the essential features of ways of life have changed, too. One of the oldest and most frequent sources of conflict has been the conflict between the sedentary peasant and the nomadic herdsman. Encroachment of the land-hungry tiller on the steppe and pasture, and raids on the settlements by the easily moving nomads are a recurrent theme in all these border zones between "sown and desert." Within the last half century the roving herder has ceased to be a potential threat to the peasant settler in any part of the world. Motorized police patrols and airplanes have reduced this problem in the French Sahara to a mere police problem. In Arabia King Ibn Saud succeeded in settling large parts of the nomads by the shrewd employment of new political and religious ideas. In Central Asia, the Soviet policy of totalitarianism has changed drastically the ways of life of nomadic herdsmen. In North America, under different conditions, the once-roving Sioux, Apaches, and Comanches now live in reservations.

THE CONFLICT BETWEEN THE COMMUNIST AND THE FREE WORLD IN TERMS OF LOCATION

In place of these ancient problems new ones have arisen. Communist and non-Communist states must get along as close neighbors. While it was still possible after World War I to attempt to minimize frictions between Communism and the rest of the world by creating a *cordon sanitaire* around the Soviet Union, this solution has become obsolete today. The countries of South and East Asia are for all practical purposes close neighbors of Australia and New Zealand today, as are those of

North America, Asia, and Europe lying across the Arctic Ocean from each other. The danger of friction arising from such location in close proximity is great.

ADJACENT LOCATION OF LARGE AND SMALL NATIONS

Adjacent location of a small country and a large or strong one always influences their relationship. Whether the politics of the small country takes the form of more or less voluntary subordination to and accommodation of the stronger neighbor, whether it tries to find independence in coalition with several other small countries in a similar position, or in an alliance with a distant but strong country, or whether it chooses isolation and withdrawal from all problems of the community of nations, depends on many nonlocational factors and on their interplay with the implications of location. Mexico is a country that has tried different policies in its relations with its neighbor in the north—from invoking the sympathies of other relatively small Latin American states, to the more recent attempt to follow a course which avoids antagonizing the United States without letting the powerful neighbor actively influence Mexican internal political decisions. A great variety of attitudes is shown by the North European countries toward the Soviet Union. Finland is trying hard to accommodate its policy to the whims of Soviet policy, making it clear at the same time that she is not ready to pay the high price of becoming a satellite. Sweden tries to steer a more independent course. She is in a better locational position as she has no land boundary with the Soviet Union and takes encouragement from the not too conclusive fact that she succeeded in remaining neutral during both World Wars. Norway, on the other hand, chose an alliance with the great powers of the West. An attempt by Denmark made immediately after World War II to promote an alliance of the Scandinavian powers was met by failure.

The inland country blocked from access to the sea by other countries has been discussed in another connection. It remains to mention the less frequent situation in which a weak country is pinned between the sea and a strong but landlocked country. The Baltic republics did not remain free for long under such conditions. Another example is offered by the Netherlands. They are located across the mouth of the Rhine which, although not the only outlet to the sea for large parts of Germany, is by far the shortest and best. Skillful statesmanship, an obviously peaceful and sincere neutrality, willingness to fulfill all reasonable German wishes, and the preparedness to refuse any demands which would impair Dutch sovereignty made the Netherlands apparently secure throughout most of the nineteenth century and through World War I. Hitler, in World War II, upset these carefully developed balances.

It may be of minor importance whether two countries have a long or short common border; the fact that they border at all is of primary importance at least to the interested parties. In 1954, a flurry of excitement arose when a Soviet newspaper hinted that in the high Pamirs the Soviet Union had a common boundary with Kashmir, though in almost impassable terrain and for the length of a few miles only. This would deny China direct contact with Afghanistan. China, however, seems eager to retain its common boundary with Afghanistan (*cf.* Fig. 3-1, p. 59).

ADJACENT LOCATION AND CULTURAL, IDEOLOGICAL, AND OTHER DIFFERENCES

Sometimes countries of different cultural level face each other across the border, and these differences can create political problems. Usually the country of lower economic, technological, or cultural development will feel endangered, while the neighboring country may embark on a "mission" to bring the advantages of higher civilization to the underdeveloped neighbor. In the not too distant past this took the form of church missionary activity which in turn called for protection by state authority. In other instances merchants and planters maintained that by expanding their occupations they were spreading European civilization, lifting natives to a higher level by teaching them, or forcing them, into the habit of regular work. If they met with resistance they appealed to their national authorities and such disputes often ended in war and conquest. At present the repercussions of this policy are felt in quite different ways; they range from the relatively minor problems of the United States with its Indian wards to the serious Mau Mau revolution in Kenya. There are, however, instances where such conquest led to the acceptance of the former colonial subjects as equals. India may always have been spiritually the equal of Europe; today she is also an equal in economic methods and technological approach, even though much may still have to be done to spread technological achievements over the country. The Gold Coast and Nigeria may still harbor primitive tribes, but they are regarded as ready, or almost ready, to enter the Commonwealth as equals. There is still an expanding frontier of civilization, and even of white settlement in the interior of Brazil, in Canada, in Siberia, but this is no longer a question of war and conquest, but an internal problem of the countries concerned. For perhaps the last time a Christian power openly proclaimed its cultural mission as justification for conquest when Italy attacked Ethiopia in 1935.

The Soviet Union holds or at least proclaims that every extension of its control is a feat of liberation. From this point or view any such conquest, with whatever means accomplished, is justified as a part of inevitable and preordained progress. There is, however, a decisive difference between Communist conquest and other conquests accomplished under the slogan of civilization for backward nations. Amerindians, Siberian natives, negro tribes in Inner Africa, and even Ethiopians, though they cherished their own way of life, regarded Europeans as superior, at least in certain respects. The non-Communist world, on the other hand, considers its way of life not only equal but in many respects definitely superior to the Communist order. As participants in this struggle we may not claim impartiality. However, the Soviets acknowledge at least in some respects this superiority of the West, spurring on their workers to imitate and finally to improve American methods, concealing certain aspects of Western society from their subjects, keeping them away from Western literature and any contact with foreigners, showing by this method their actual evaluation of the attractive features of Western civilization which they could not denounce as inferior if free access to the knowledge of Western ways were possible.

Thus there exist not only politically enforced but very real though intangible boundaries which separate people and areas of different political ideology. Where there are conflicting ideologies each party is convinced of its superior way of life. Confusion between these two concepts is old. The ancient Greeks felt dimly that the disparity between their ways of life and those of the highly civilized peoples of the Persian empire was of another order than the gulf which separated their way of life from that of the illiterate primitive tribes of most of Europe. They recognized that Marathon was more than a military-political event, and that it decided for many centuries to come which type of civilization should be dominant in Europe. Nevertheless, they persisted in calling Persians, Egyptians, Babylonians, and others by the same deprecative name they used for Thracians, Numidians, and Celts—barbarians.

The main conclusion to be drawn from our discussion of factors of location in the realm of political geography is that location must be regarded as a basic factor which, certainly, can not be neglected, but which never can be considered alone. Its implications are changing continuously in response to other factors.

CHAPTER

8

The Impact of Location on Strategy and Power Politics

A. *The Heartland and the Rim Lands: A Study in Location*

Among the large-space concepts of location which fascinate the student of political geography, that of the Heartland has been most emphasized in recent times. It has received both enthusiastic and scornful reception. Often the disciples as well as the critics of the Heartland theory have been led astray by their unwillingness to recognize the factor of time and change that erodes this concept in so far as it affects any other concept of location in the fluctuating realm of political geography.

We propose to deal at some length with the Heartland concept and to investigate to what extent it has proved its long-range validity, and where in retrospect it appears to be depicting only a temporary situation. As a study in location, the interpretation of the Heartland, representing a significant philosophy of political geography, can serve to sharpen our thinking on factors of location in general.

INFLUENCE ON POLITICO-GEOGRAPHICAL THINKING

Although often misunderstood and loosely applied by armchair strategists, the Heartland theory has had nevertheless a profound influence on politico-geographical thinking in our time. In discussing what the British geographer Sir Halford J. Mackinder termed in 1904 as "the pivot region of the world's politics" (Fig. 8-1) and later described as the "Heartland"

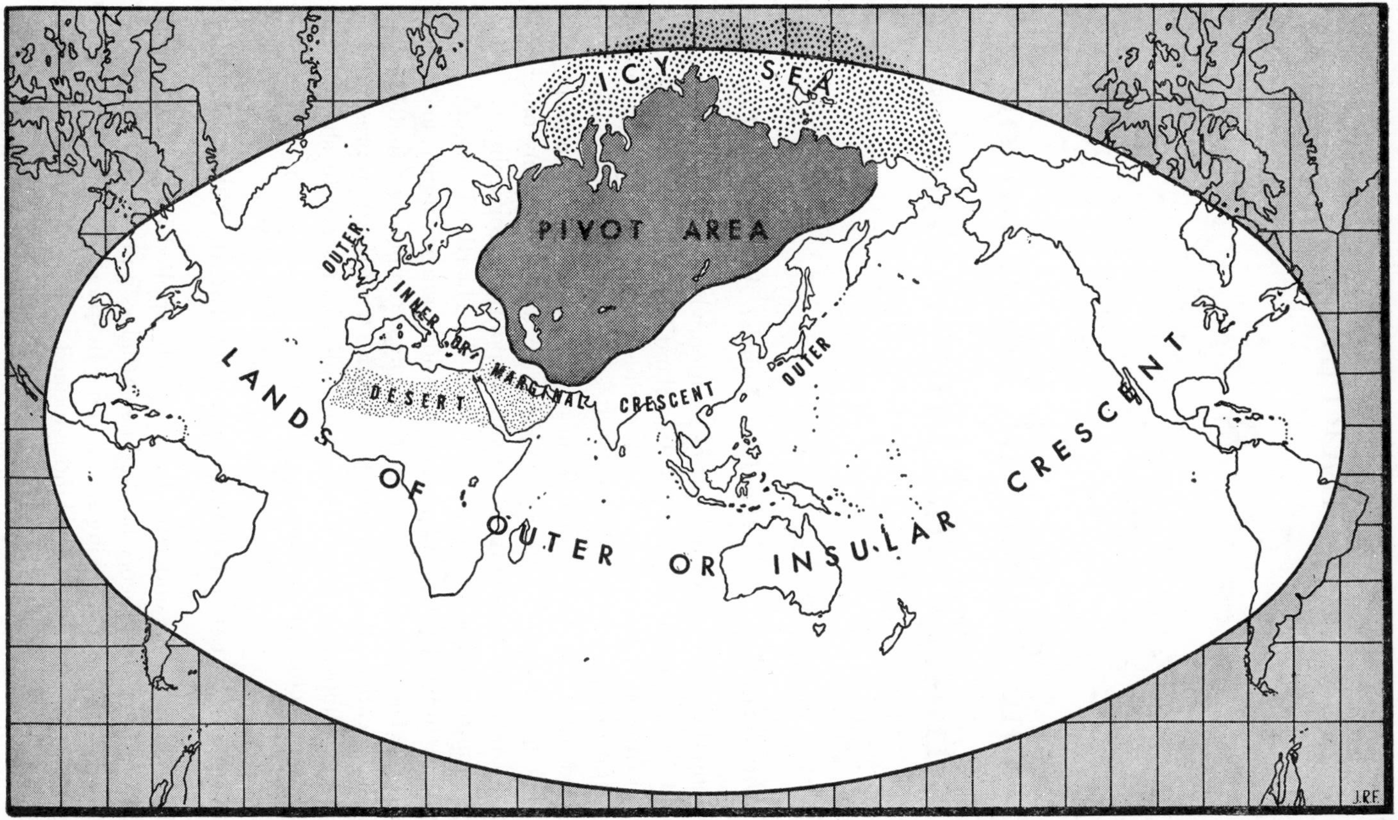

FIG. 8-1. Mackinder's Heartland (1904) (extended Mercator projection).

we shall observe the truly revolutionary changes of a world history in terms of geography set in motion. But while ten-dollar terms such as Heartland and World Island have been readily accepted in the dictionary of geopolitics, they share the fate of the American Security Sphere or of the American Perimeter of Defense in remaining hazy concepts when it comes to exact geographical definition and evaluation. We must be careful not to be found napping in the nineteenth century when we attempt to organize our "world view" and to define the political boundaries separating the globe's land and sea masses which really matter in world politics. We still like to visualize the political map of the world as a mosaic, the contours of which follow the boundaries of the national states. Quite naturally we feel uncomfortable when confronted with a novel map of the world on which the feeble boundary lines and the colors which distinguish the national states are minimized, with the emphasis placed on certain geographical regions which endow the powers controlling them with the very assets needed in the struggle for world power. In a constantly and rapidly shrinking political world, politico-geographical entities comparable to the American security sphere have achieved a new meaning due to significant changes in the realm of transportation and communication. The Heartland of Eurasia is therefore more than a dusty concept of the historical geography of the Victorian age.

THE HEARTLAND CONCEPT AND THE VICTORIAN SEA POWER AGE

The new world view evolved slowly. Mackinder, at the threshold of the new century, began to grasp the fact that the geopolitics of the Victorian age was no longer based on geographical realities. Only if we project Mackinder's concepts against the panorama of the Victorian age, with world politics revolving around Britain's successful struggle for control of the high seas and of the pathways of seaborne traffic, can we perceive the force of a new way of thinking in which land power outflanked sea power and new industrial powers were rising on the continent of Eurasia. These concepts loomed large enough to challenge the basic ideas of the political philosophy and the political geography of an age of sea power. The transition from a political philosophy revolving around the "age of sea power" concept to one stressing land power reflects a new look at basic factors of location.

In the United States, the political geography of the sea power age had long been dominated by the thinking of Alfred Thayer Mahan, an American naval officer. His work, *The Influence of Seapower Upon History, 1660-1783,* is one of the rare books which profoundly affected history. While his writings lack systematic organization, his political philosophy clearly preaches the gospel of the new American Imperialism drawing its strength from sea power, and a new Manifest Destiny based on America's future role as the leading maritime nation in the world—leading, because he envisaged the day when the United States would replace Britain in its rating as the world's supreme naval power. The oceans had become inland seas of the British Empire, and the trade routes of the world its life lines. The growing maritime power of the United States was to inherit these concepts. Coupled with this feeling there was a conviction that power based upon land and its overland transportation systems could never compete, either commercially or stategically, with movement by sea.[1] There is no doubt that Mahan's doctrines gave a lift to military and political planners throughout the world who readily adopted his formula for the achievement of world power through sea power. Even in Imperial Germany, under Wilhelm II, it kindled a hectic enthusiasm for what appeared to be a new shortcut for Germany to world power. It is not surprising to find that Germany's outstanding political geographer of these times, Friedrich Ratzel, who had received a practical geographical training in the United States, published a book called *The Sea as a Source of National Greatness* which was broadly influenced by Mahan's thinking.[2]

From the ramparts of England, Halford J. Mackinder agreed with the thinking of Mahan in one important aspect: he, too, could not help realizing that Britain had, in the twentieth century, lost its leading position of naval power and control of the seas. In 1901 Mackinder wrote in his *Britain and the British Seas:* "Other empires have had their day, and so may that of Britain. But there are facts in the present condition of humanity which render such a fate unlikely, provided always that the British retain their moral qualities . . . the whole course of future history depends on whether the Old Britain beside the Narrow Seas has enough of virility and imagination to withstand all challenge of her neighbor's supremacy, until such time as the daughter nations shall have grown to maturity."

But aside from agreeing on the future respective parts which Britain and the United States were to play in the struggle for naval supremacy,

[1] H. and M. Sprout, *Foundations of National Power,* 2nd edition (New York, 1951), p. 154.

[2] R. Strausz-Hupé, *Geopolitics: The Struggle for Space and Power* (New York, 1942), p. 245.

the basic concepts of political geography of Mahan and Mackinder have little in common. For it is exactly Mahan's exaltation of sea power which was challenged by Mackinder who, viewing the growing strength of Russia and Germany on the continents, became more and more alarmed by the challenge to sea power in a new age in which land power could outflank it and in which the mushrooming growth of industrialization and the extension of railroad nets on the continent were successfully competing with Britain's economic position in the world.

THE NEW ROLE OF ASIA

Mackinder's consciousness of the passing of the Victorian sea power age made him see Europe and its political geography as subordinate to Asia.[3] It is in Asia that land power and (as Mackinder did not anticipate originally) land-based air power have had their greatest opportunities to challenge established power positions in the world at large. The mobility of land power (not land power as such), in competition with the mobility of sea power, evolved as a decisive geopolitical feature of the twentieth century. By evaluating the competition and possible clash between sea and land power, Mackinder discovered the "pivot region of the World's politics": the Heartland of Eurasia. He did not hesitate to project the effects which an increasing mobility of military and economic power in this area is bound to have on the rest of the world. In 1904, he saw that "the century will not be old before all Asia is covered with railways. The spaces within the Russian Empire and Mongolia are so vast, and their potentialities in population, wheat, cotton, fuel, and metals so incalculably great, that it is inevitable that a vast economic world, more or less apart, will there develop inaccessible to oceanic commerce."

This pivotal area Mackinder projected as an organic unit within the world unit. Inaccessible to ships but covered with a network of railways, the continental basins of Eurasia are seen as the homeland of a new Russia which is successor to the Mongol Empire. From its central position, Russia can exert pressures on Finland, Scandinavia, Poland, Turkey, Persia, and India. The centrifugal force which drove the horse-riding nomads of the steppes westward and southward against the settled peoples of Europe is still a living force in the Russian Heartland. If ever it succeeded in expanding over the marginal lands of Eurasia, if ever it were able to use its continental resources for fleet-building, then,

[3] H. W. Weigert, *Generals and Geographers* (New York and London, 1942), pp. 115-139.

Mackinder felt, "the empire of the world would be in sight." And to leave no doubt about the direction of his fears, fifty years ago he added: "This would happen if Germany would ally herself with Russia."

CRITIQUE OF MACKINDER: THE HEARTLAND AS VIEWED OVER THE TOP OF THE WORLD

When Mackinder, at the close of the first World War, re-examined his original thesis in his famous address (called *Democratic Ideals and Realities*) to the peacemakers about to assemble in Paris, he found that his "thesis of 1904 still sufficed." He voiced this warning: "Who rules East Europe commands the Heartland; Who rules the Heartland commands the World Island; Who rules the World Island commands the World." It became much too smooth a slogan when it was dusted off in our day. Most of those who used it persistently were fascinated more by the general appeal of the slogan than by its geographic realities.

The Heartland of Europe and Asia had essentially the same frontiers in 1918 as Mackinder's "Pivot Area" of 1904. It comprised the vast expanse of the continental island basins of arctic and continental drainage which measure nearly half of Asia and a quarter of Europe, and which are inaccessible from the ocean. As a strategical concept, the Heartland includes all regions which can be denied access by sea power. Railways, growing and expanding inward, have changed its face continuously since 1904 and have tested Mackinder's thesis. Above all, the airplane has since upset the unstable balance between land and sea power; Mackinder greets it as an ally to land power in the Heartland.

The first World War Mackinder sees as the climax in the eternal conflict between continental land power and marginal power, backed and fed by sea power: "We have been fighting lately, in the close of the war, a straight duel between land power and sea power. We have conquered, but had Germany conquered she would have established her sea power on a wider basis than any in history, and in fact on the widest possible basis."

The third and final test of the Heartland formula was undertaken by Mackinder in the article, "The Round World and the Winning of the Peace," which he wrote in 1943 for *Foreign Affairs*.[4] To Mackinder, the test was positive; he found his concept "more valid and useful today than it was either twenty or forty years ago."

[4] *Foreign Affairs* (1943), pp. 595-605; in H. W. Weigert and V. Stefansson, eds., *Compass of the World* (New York, 1945), pp. 161-173.

Yet while the original concept of the Heartland remained basically intact, its frontiers were significantly revised. The revisions were required in order to accommodate certain major changes in the political geography of the world since 1904 and 1918. The territory of the U.S.S.R. remains equivalent to the Heartland. But there is one rather important exception. A vast area within the Soviet Union which begins east of the Yenisei River and whose central feature is the Lena River has now been exempted by Mackinder from the original Heartland. "Lenaland Russia" has an area of three and three-quarter million square miles but a population of only some six millions, in contrast to "Heartland Russia" which covers four and a quarter million square miles and has a rapidly growing population numbering one hundred and seventy millions.

Heartland Russia, backed by the natural resources of Lenaland, foreshadows greater power than the Heartland Mackinder envisaged in decades past. What earlier had seemed to be mere speculation had now grown into reality, and Mackinder could state as a fact that "except in a very few commodities the country is capable of producing everything which it requires." Again he views the open western frontier of the Heartland. His conclusion that "if the Soviet Union emerges from the war as conqueror of Germany, she must rank as the greatest land power on the globe" is slightly less emphatic than his vision of the approaching "empire of the world" (1904). Otherwise, the Britisher's view of the geopolitical relationship of Russia and Germany had remained unchanged.

Any attempt at a critique [5] of Mackinder's powerful generalizations should begin with the acknowledgment of our indebtedness to the man who did more in our time than anybody else to enlist geography as an aid to statecraft and strategy. The fundamentals of his closed-space concept stand so firmly today that we almost forget how revolutionary the concept was when first formulated forty years ago. The same observation applies to Mackinder's land power thesis which, appearing at what seemed to be the height of the Victorian sea power age, seemed shocking and fantastic to many in the English-speaking world. But in reviewing his thesis today, we should remember that it is the concept of a man who viewed the world from "England . . . that utmost corner of the West." Only a Britisher could have written as Mackinder did. Recognizing this and taking account of the technological changes which have surpassed even Mackinder's imagination, we should have sufficient perspective today to speak critically of the theory of the Heartland.

[5] *Cf.* H. W. Weigert, "Heartland Revisited," in H. W. Weigert, V. Stefansson, and R. E. Harrison, *New Compass of the World* (New York, 1949), pp. 80-90.

Fig. 8-2. Relationship of Heartland and North-America on the Azimuthal Polar Projection.

It is perhaps not incidental that the logic of Mackinder's Heartland seems to reveal itself best on a Mercator world map (such as Mackinder used when he first laid out his blueprint). Here the Heartland lives up to its name. We see it surrounded by a huge arc forming an inner crescent which includes Germany, Turkey, India, and China. Beyond the crescent of peripheral states, Mackinder envisaged an outer crescent which embraced Britain, South Africa, Australia, the United States, Canada, and Japan. Again the Mercator projection lent a helpful hand in constructing what seemed to Mackinder a "wholly oceanic" and "insular" crescent.

However, we find it difficult, if not impossible, to visualize this relation of the Heartland to a surrounding inner and outer crescent if we exchange the Mercator map for the globe or any azimuthal-equidistant map (Fig. 8-2). The concept of North America as part of a chain of insular powers distant from the Heartland now becomes a geographical myth. In terms of air-geography the Heartland and North America appear in destiny-laden proximity. As viewed over the top of the world, the Heartland assumes a location different from that which Mackinder assigned to it, plotting it from Britain, and with the destinies of Britain foremost in his mind. While time has verified Mackinder's concept of Russia's growing importance as a land power in a pivotal area, and while the political and military control of the U.S.S.R. over the Heartland and Eastern Europe are at present more firmly established than ever, the skyways of the Arctic Mediterranean give validity to a new way of regarding the geographical relations of North America and the U.S.S.R. The inaccessibility of the vast inland spaces of the Heartland became evident when the Heartland power was attacked by Germany in the west, where the Heartland opens itself to invasion. But seen from North America, and in terms of new communications reaching out from many points in the far-flung "perimeter of defense" line, inaccessibility and vastness no longer conceal the Heartland from us. It no longer lies behind an impenetrable wall of isolation.

In his article in *Foreign Affairs,* Mackinder seems to have made major revisions in his original concept of the relationship of the rest of the world to the Heartland. We have noticed that the original Heartland thesis remained basically unaltered, although the emphasis on the thinly populated Lenaland area has been toned down. But the surrounding crescents (and particularly North America as a member of the outlying insular power group) are viewed by the Mackinder of 1943 in a different light. This is significant. The original British view which left North America seemingly isolated and beyond the sphere of power zones directly linked with the Heartland, has now been replaced by an Anglo-American world view.

Has Mackinder thus silenced his critics? Those who questioned the validity of his thesis [6] stressed uniformly the pivotal importance of the densely populated regions of the marginal coast lands or rim lands. The overemphasis, however, on either inland or rim-land location neglects the complementary character of the two, as well as their constantly changing values. Mackinder understood these dynamics clearly. He re-examined and revised his appraisal of the relationship between interior and peripheral; he perceived from Britain that the peripheral felt, more than ever, the shadow of the continental land mass in its expansionist movement. Thus he projected a new vision of the Heartland in its relation to the surrounding zones. In doing so, he envisaged the geographic link between the Heartland and the Anglo-American world in a new light. From Mercator he turned to the globe. Around the north polar regions he hung a "mantle" of deserts and wildernesses. From the Sahara Desert, the mantle extends to the deserts of Arabia, Iran, Tibet, and Mongolia. From there it spreads out across the "wilderness of the Lenaland" to the Laurentian shield of Canada and to the subarid belt of the United States.

Thus he constructed what seems to be a new "pivot of history"; a zone including both the Heartland and the basin of North Atlantic. Thereby Mackinder reveals a new fulcrum of world power, and a new relationship between the Heartland and the outer world. The enlarged pivotal area of 1943 is made apparent by drawing a great circle arc from the center of the Yenisei River across the mid-ocean to the center of the Mississippi valley. The arc leads across the bridgehead of France, over the stronghold of Britain—"a Malta on a grander scale"—to the vast arsenal of the eastern and central United States and Canada. This North American-British-French-U.S.S.R. bloc comprises a power fulcrum of one billion people. It neatly balances that other thousand million in the monsoon lands of India and China. "A balanced globe of human beings. And happy, because balanced and thus free." [7]

THE BALANCE-OF-POWER FORMULA

This balance was too neat and perfect to be true. The power bloc within which Communist China and the Soviet Union are allied, has upset Mackinder's balance, if it ever was a reality. We shall not deal

[6] See especially N. J. Spykman, *The Geography of the Peace* (New York, 1944).
[7] Mackinder, "The Round World and the Winning of the Peace," *loc. cit.*

in detail with Mackinder's final balance-of-power vision, a world divided into two equal hemispheres of one billion human beings each, because it was from the beginning a structure built upon shifting sand. Like other neat balance-of-power formulas, it did not work, not because a North American-British-French-U.S.S.R. bloc appears utterly unrealistic at this time, but because one cannot, in terms of geographic realities and of human and natural resources, construe a balance-of-power formula which can be applied permanently to the world relationship of one major area, such as the Heartland. The relativity of power relations between human areas was demonstrated clearly in the history of Mackinder's own thesis. During the fifty years in which he was allowed to watch and revise his Heartland thesis, new pivot areas have evolved and still others are due to emerge. New areas and their peoples have come of age, and will continue to come of age. New lines of communication will transform international relations.

The revised Heartland concept of 1943 wisely acknowledged a significant geopolitical fact by including with the coast land of Europe the North American rim lands and central regions in the enlarged pivotal area. Since it is our purpose to clarify in terms of relative location the relationship between North America and the Eurasian continent by following Mackinder's changing vision of this relationship, we might emphasize the fact that his enlightened view still remained a view through British glasses. Britain is the vital link in his concept of the "Mid-Ocean" as the main artery making the United Nations bloc (without China) a life force. Does he not try to prove too much? Do not his own lessons of a phase of history in which land power (plus land-based air power) challenges the remnants of the Victorian age, guide us to additional routes which extend from North America to the Heartland?

NEW LINKS BETWEEN HEARTLAND, NORTH AMERICA AND NORTHERN ASIA

These routes do not touch Britain, although they touch, through Canada, life lines of the British Commonwealth of Nations. Mackinder's latest vision pushes the Lenaland and with it the whole of Soviet Asia into the background. This seems logical if one views the Heartland from the British Isles. However, a view of the Heartland from any place in North America exposes the fact that the mid-ocean avenue is by no means the only one connecting North America and the Heartland. The established sea lanes of the North Atlantic are and will probably remain the cheapest avenues; but, in years to come, traffic will mount on the new highways and skyways to the Heartland and to Western and Northern Europe across both the Alaska and the Greenland-Iceland bridges. While we are aware of the climatic barriers which always may hamper an American and Russian expansion northward and a large-scale colonization and land-utilization of their Arctic possessions, we can not eliminate the northern links from the blueprint of a new world view. These links are represented not only by skyways but also by new inland communications and by sea lanes, opened by weather stations, planes, and ice breakers.[8]

It has been suggested that such emphasis on the frozen, desolate lands of ice and snow which form the new frontier of contact between the Old and the New World is unrealistic because "the Polar Mediterranean and its surrounding territory represent the greatest inhospitable area on the surface of the globe." [9] Such criticism would be justified were it directed only at the loose thinking which indeed often ignores the physical obstacles to large-scale human settlement in the American and Russian Far North. However, the attempts at de-emphasizing the growing significance of these regions miss their target when it comes to a consideration of not only (admittedly limited) agricultural potentials but especially the vast mineral resources and, above all, the tremendous timber resources of the polar regions; the latter loom even larger in the light of developments in the field of wood and cellulose technology.

Of greater importance in the evaluation of the global picture of the Arctic regions is the strategic consideration.[10] In case of a military conflict between the United States and the Soviet Union, it is obvious that important military operations would take place north of 50° and a considerable portion, and possibly a decisive one, within the Arctic Circle. To emphasize that in spite of man's efforts to push northward everywhere, digging for mineral resources in the eternally frozen soil of the tundra and even growing barley beyond the timber line, the Polar territory remains essentially inhospitable to human settlement, is beside the point when it comes to locating the areas of paramount strategic importance on the world map. For wars are not necessarily fought and decided in densely populated regions, as is shown by the role of North Africa and New Guinea in the history of World War II. Strategic location can, and often does, outweigh population and resources in determining not

[8] See pp. 246 ff.
[9] Spykman, *Geography of the Peace*, pp. 56, 39.
[10] *Ibid.*, pp. 43-45.

only battle sites but the over-all importance of a region in a global picture. It goes without saying that the factor of strategic location would loom larger than ever in nuclear warfare. For this reason, the link between North America and Europe across the mid-ocean avenue is paralleled significantly by the links to the Heartland across the Alaska and the Greenland-Iceland bridges.

Similarly, it would be mistaken to view the geographical relationship between the Heartland and China too much in terms of sea communications. Of growing importance are the new inland roads, already either in operation or in the planning state, which together with new airways bring the Heartland gradually closer to China,[11] whose old front doors on the Pacific coast, in Hongkong and Shanghai, are disintegrating. One significant achievement in this development was claimed in the Soviet Union in November, 1954, when *Pravda* reported the completion of the easternmost section of the Baikal-Amur railroad from Lake Baikal to the Pacific near Khabarovsk.[12] Equally the growing net of Arctic air routes between North America and Japan and the Asian continent de-emphasizes a spatial relationship based in the not-so-distant past entirely on the link of Pacific sea lanes.

These connections, both actual and potential, disprove any construction based on an alleged position of North America as part of an outer crescent surrounding the Eurasian land mass or, as Mackinder postulated in 1943, based on a maritime link only, leading from the Heartland across France and the British Isles to the eastern and central United States and Canada. The new connecting links across the Arctic Mediterranean and its surrounding regions emphasize the fallacy of any world view focused on an alleged geographic isolation of the United States within the allegedly secure confines of an equally mystical "Western Hemisphere."[13] But they also stress the significance of the Heartland zone itself. The incessantly growing net of interior lines of communication—railroads, highways, inland canals, and airways across its skies—adds consistently to the strength of a Soviet Union endowed with the geographic advantage of a central position and growing interior lines of transportation.

Viewing this growing land power from a Britain whose empire, based on the control of the sea, he saw declining, Mackinder in his final appraisal found his thesis as sound, and as portentous, as ever; for "the Heartland—for the first time in history is manned by a garrison sufficient

[11] *Ibid.*, p. 42.
[12] *New York Times*, November 21, 1954.
[13] See pp. 258 ff.

in both numbers and quality." [14] He compared the Eurasian land mass, its central position and all its advantages of interior lines of communication connecting it with the regions which he had described as the "inner crescent," with the exterior lines of British naval power "running from Great Britain through the circumferential highway around the Eurasian rimlands." [15] The comparison did not favor Britain. The Heartland loomed larger than ever.

It looms large and is in close and increasing propinquity to the northern borders of North America, a propinquity which renders useless, because unrealistic, any attempt at picturing the Western Hemisphere in a state of remoteness and isolation as part of an outer crescent surrounding the Heartland. As a glimpse of the globe or any world map not inspired by Mercator makes clear, the two "mainlands" almost merge in their northern expanses. It is here that the land power and the land-based air power of the North American nations and of the U.S.S.R. are now maneuvering for positions in anticipation of a possible major conflict.

REASSESSMENT OF THE POSITION OF RUSSIA AND U.S.S.R.

Mackinder's new arrangement of the political map of the world—the Heartland itself, the marginal lands of the inner crescent, the lands of the outer crescent beyond that of the peripheral states—served (as we have seen) above all the purpose of reassessing in geographical terms the position of the Russian empire in the world at large; in political terms this reassessment was to serve as an eloquent warning to the Western world aligned with British sea power. It recognized as the signal geopolitical development of the young twentieth century the increasingly powerful position of Russia due to her central position and steadily growing communication system of railroads, highways, and inland canals. These interior lines of communication were seen as a rising challenge to powers relying on sea communication. On the other hand, it must be realized that the railroads of the U.S.S.R., while playing the major role in the transportation economy of the country, are still far from satisfactory,[16] in spite of the fact that the Soviet regime which inherited a network of 36,300 miles has since increased the railroad mileage to about 78,000 miles. But especially in Soviet Asia, the railway system is still skeletal in nature and the supply situation, especially from a military

[14] *Foreign Affairs,* July, 1953.
[15] Spykman, *Geography of the Peace,* p. 40.
[16] T. Shabad, *Geography of the U.S.S.R.* (New York, 1951), pp. 83-88.

point of view, of the far-flung corners of the empire—Central Asia, Eastern Siberia, and the Maritime Provinces—can be described as crucial [17] (*cf.* Fig. 15-2, p. 478).

THE RIM LANDS

In this comparison of geographical foundations of land power and sea power we are taught to distingush between interior lands inaccessible to navigation, and coast lands or, as they have also been called, marginal lands or rim lands, which are accessible to the shipmen, sailing from beach to beach and harbor to harbor round the west, south, and east coasts of the Old World, and sailing up its navigable rivers.[18] Nicholas J. Spykman has justly criticized Mackinder for oversimplifying the land power versus sea power conflict. The historical alignment, he pointed out, has always been in terms of some member nations of the European rim land with Great Britain against Russia in alliance with other members of the rim land; or it has been a conflict between Great Britain and Russia together against a rim land power which, as for instance France or Germany, dared to gamble for the domination of the continent. Hence Spykman's formula in critique of Mackinder's: "Who controls the *rimland,* rules Eurasia; who rules Eurasia controls the destinies of the world." [19]

There are a number of significant geographical factors which justify the attempt to classify, in terms of political geography, the marginal lands (or rim lands) as distinctive units differentiated in many ways from the interior lands that are inaccessible to sea power and form the basis of the Heartland. These regions have in common three major characteristics distinguishing them from the interior lands.

(1) With the exception of the Heartland's north, where west winds carry a considerable amount of rainfall across the plains as far inland as the Altai Mountains, the inland areas are at a disadvantage in regard to water supply as compared with the marginal lands which can count on reliable rainfall sufficient for agriculture.

(2) The marginal lands are centers of population density. It should also be noted that, within the Soviet Heartland region, the greatest concentration of population, agricultural and industrial concentration, and power potential is in the western regions of the inland area, close to the marginal lands.

[17] W. G. East, "How Strong Is the Heartland?" *Foreign Affairs* (1950), pp. 78-93, 87.

[18] *Cf.* C. B. Fawcett, "Marginal and Interior Lands of the Old World," in Weigert-Stefansson-Harrison, *op. cit.*, pp. 91-103.

[19] Spykman, *Geography of the Peace,* p. 40 ff.

(3) The marginal lands, in terms of political organization, lack the political unification and centralization of power which characterizes the Heartland power. They are broken up into a number of more or less independent national units which, however, strive in the face of aggression threats toward new forms of supranational unification.[20]

Thus we are led to that crucial cradle-of-conflict zone which extends along the western frontier of the Soviet Union and, continuing westward, forms in an irregular peninsula the center of the so-called continent of Europe. As seen from Moscow, or London, or Washington, the nations of this broad rim-land zone, while politically lacking uniformity and unification, share certain basic advantages due to their geographical rim-land position. To a large extent these account for the concentration and growth of their population and their agricultural and industrial wealth. They are the rim lands the control of which, it was claimed, endows the ruling power with control over Eurasia and, consequently, of the world. Marginal as these lands are to the Heartland, they must be viewed in their role of actual and potential extensions of the Heartland itself. We have seen how Mackinder developed his thesis along strategic considerations; sea power and land power required new appraisals based on geographic facts and new lines of communication. Thus the strategic Heartland became the region to which, under modern conditions, sea power can be refused access by a locally dominant land power.

In the light of this strategic concept, it becomes evident that certain marginal areas are needed to achieve the security objective of the Heartland, namely, to extend its perimeter to a line which would assure the Heartland of the exclusion of sea power. We shall note immediately that emphasis on the land power-sea power conflict meant even before the advent of air power a gross oversimplification, as it is the accessibility to both sea and land and the power deriving from it which gives the marginal regions growing importance. In the second half of the twentieth century, the impact of air power makes a new appraisal of the marginal lands mandatory, in their relationship to the Heartland as well as to other areas.

THE HEARTLAND AND EASTERN EUROPE

In attempting to define the major strategic areas forming the marginal lands to the west of the Heartland and having enough in common to be treated as entities, the political divide created by the Iron Curtain makes it necessary to distinguish between the regions of Eastern and Central

[20] Fawcett, "Marginal and Interior Lands of the Old World," *loc. cit.*

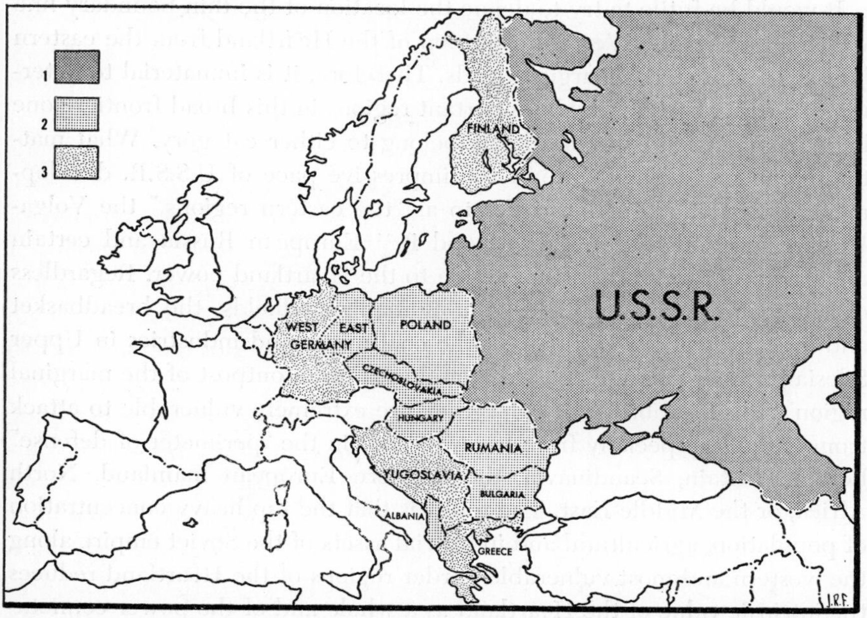

Fig. 8-3. Marginal Lands to the West of the Heartland: (1) U.S.S.R.; (2) satellites; (3) marginal lands.

Europe and the rest of Europe (Fig. 8-3). As was stressed previously, a major distinguishing factor between the lands of the interior and the marginal regions to the west of them is a negative one and one strictly related to political geography: whereas in the middle of the twentieth century the Heartland interior is a politically integrated unit fully controlled by the Kremlin, the countries of Eastern and Central Europe are characterized by the existence of politically conflicting structures, with both East and West attempting to mold them into a unified sphere. In political terms, this region includes Germany, Poland, Czechoslovakia, Rumania, Austria, Hungary, Bulgaria, Albania, and on their periphery, Finland, Yugoslavia, and Greece. It goes without saying that in this pivotal area of centuries-old clashes between the East and the West any attempt at visualizing this area as a political unit of some broader meaning defies proper geographical definition. Its typical state is one of fluctuation and transition; its human geography was rewritten many times in history as a result of wars and migrations sweeping westward and eastward. Yet, if only we apply the term *marginal area* in a broad sense, we can appreciate it as a large-space concept complementary to the interior lands of the Heartland.

It would be futile to try to define the location of the thin boundary line which separates the Western extension of the Heartland from the eastern border regions of the marginal lands. Therefore, it is immaterial to determine whether certain highly important regions in this broad frontier zone between Heartland and rim lands belong to either category. What matters is the fact that in spite of the impressive pace of U.S.S.R. development in what the Russians refer to as "the eastern regions," the Volga-Ural region and Soviet Asia beyond it,[21] European Russia and certain areas adjacent to it are indispensable to the Heartland power. Regardless of whether the Baku oilfields, the Rumanian oilfields, the breadbasket and industries of the Ukraine, or the coal mines and industries in Upper Silesia form an annex of the Heartland area or an outpost of the marginal region, their location is such that they are extremely vulnerable to attack from without, especially from bases located in the "perimeter of defense" belt, in Britain, Scandinavia, the Western European mainland, North Africa, or the Middle East. The result is that the top-heavy concentration of population, agricultural and industrial assets of the Soviet empire along the western and most vulnerable border regions of the Heartland reduces the intrinsic value of the Heartland as a whole and of the power connotations it implies.

The concentration of economic power and power potentials in the western fringe areas of the Heartland, which is still, in the second half of the twentieth century, a major characteristic of the Heartland power, has thus fully confirmed Mackinder's thesis that he "who rules East Europe commands the Heartland." At the same time, we must not lose sight of the marchlands along the eastern border of the Heartland. As in the case of Eastern Europe, to focus attention on the Heartland *per se,* with its central position in Eurasia, its physical inaccessibility from the oceans, its seeming security from attack due to the natural bastion provided by the frozen waters of the Arctic and the mountain ranges and steppes of Central Asia, leads to an underestimation of the rim lands in the east which play a significant role in linking the Heartland with the rest of the world. The conquests of Alexander the Great and of the Arabs remind us of the role of the marginal areas of Southwest Asia in historical efforts aimed at controlling the Heartland. Even more important was the challenge to the Heartland by the empire of the Mongols. Its nucleus of power located in the steppes of Mongolia, it broadened its basis to include, in the thirteenth century, China proper.[22] In reverse, and as seen from Moscow, the

[21] East, "How Strong Is the Heartland?" *loc. cit.,* p. 90.
[22] *Ibid.,* pp. 83, 84.

same marchlands, like those in Eastern Europe, provide stepping stones for the expansion of the Heartland power itself. Lenin's prediction that the road to Paris leads through China and India still rings ominously. The slow growth of railroads in Siberia and toward the Pacific coast as well as in Central Asia links the Heartland more and more with marchlands of great strategic portent, even more strategic in as much as the corresponding railroad system developed by China and linking its mainland with the outer regions remained (as, for instance, in the case of Sinkiang) utterly weak and vulnerable.

THE INTERRELATIONSHIP OF HEARTLAND AND MARGINAL LANDS

It must, therefore, be concluded that the study of location which the investigation of the Heartland and its physical qualities entails, while contributing greatly to the understanding of its strength, is not enough and is even misleading if it amounts to a preoccupation with the Heartland concept. In order to arrive at a balanced view, the study must be extended to include the marginal lands along all of the frontiers of the Heartland. In these regions where the Soviet sphere of expansion and influence is met and challenged by the "perimeter of defense" [23] organized by the Free World, it is frequently the concentration of populations and the wealth of resources, rather than geographical position by itself which accounts for their pivotal role. The combination of power based on the Heartland's central area and greatly increased control over vital parts of the marginal belt, not the central nucleus of the Heartland alone, would represent a unit which could challenge with a high degree of success the power position of the rest of the world. However, it must be realized that the impact of time and change, due to progress in technological achievement, is such that this formula holds good but in general terms and must be re-examined whenever makers of policy or planners of strategy put it to test at a given time.

B. *Strategic Implications of the Location of Marginal Seas and Narrow Waterways*

Marginal seas and narrow waterways occupy today, as in past history, a highly important position in the struggle for powers and rank high among the geographical foundations of political and military power. In

[23] See page 272 ff.

the present conflict between the Soviet orbit and the West, the evaluation of the opposing power systems makes it mandatory to understand the effect of the locational factors of marginal seas and narrow waterways on the respective powers—their geography granting decisive qualities of strength and weakness, qualities which have molded historical geography and which define political geography today. A glimpse at the map of water bodies does not always disclose easily power and control factors of the nations competing in these areas. The locational impact of these water bodies on the countries bordering them does not reveal itself on the map as clearly as is the case in regard to the factors of location which define the areal situation of a country and its relations to other countries across land borders. Their role becomes apparent only if projected against larger space configurations. Both the importance of the location concepts of these water bodies and the complicating factors which render difficult the appraisal of their geopolitical values make it appear advisable to discuss the major marginal seas and narrow waterways in some regional detail.

Stretching around the vast littoral of the Eurasian land mass, from Spitsbergen to the Kuriles, is a chain of islands and archipelagoes, some delimiting, others within a series of marginal seas and narrow waterways. These control vital sea communications of the world and are likely to be pivotal areas in any conflict between the two power blocs that is not immediately decided by atomic-thermonuclear weapons of air power. The marginal seas are peculiar to the Eurasian continent. The only similar instance of enclosed sea in the North and South American continent is that of the Caribbean Sea, which is defined by the Bahamas and the Antilles.

The significance of these marginal seas and the narrow straits within them cannot be overemphasized. So long as intermediate bases are maintained by the Free World in the coastal regions of Eurasia, they function as a *cordon sanitaire* around the expanse of the Soviet domain. Once this line of sea communications is breached by Soviet penetration, the entire peripheral strategy of the Free World would be endangered. The sea communications of the Free World are secure only if the seas through which they pass and the narrow straits on which they converge are secure. The potential threat of such penetration must not be seen in the possible rise of the Heartland power to the stature of a maritime power able to challenge Anglo-American naval supremacy, for geography is prohibitive to such development. Rather the threat is against the sea lanes from aircraft based in the Heartland itself and in satellite rim lands. Nicholas J. Spykman's observation still holds true: "there is no geopolitical area in the world that has been more profoundly affected by the development of air power than this one of the marginal seas." [24] The development of air power has not reduced the importance of these seas and communications focal points, but it has made them more difficult to defend. Besides the defenses located in the immediate vicinity of the waterway, it is now necessary to establish bases hundreds of miles away. A case in point is the entire Caribbean, which is now a part of the defensive perimeter of the Panama Canal.

In the period between the sixteenth and twentieth centuries it was possible to keep enemy ships and troops outside artillery range of a narrow waterway. This is no longer true, since aircraft can now make the waterway untenable even to the nation which controls it. Although that nation remains in a position to prevent enemy traffic from passing through it, hostile aircraft can render it too costly to send friendly ships through the channel. Early in World War II Britain did not dare to send its ships through the Suez Canal because of the threat of German air power. Such an air threat necessitates the maintenance of distant air bases to provide adequate aircraft interception. A discussion of these waterways and their distinguishing geographic characteristics enables us to see in true perspective the marginal problems of the Heartland power itself and equally those of the nations in the perimeter of defense zones.

THE GEOGRAPHICAL PATTERN

If a strip map were constructed extending from the northwestern North American coastline and the eastern Asiatic coastal area it would reveal a succession of marginal seas defined by an almost interminable chain of islands and archipelagoes (Fig. 8-4). This is particularly true of the immediate continental margin, where from the Arctic Circle to the Equator, and beyond, there is a regular repetition of the same simple geographical pattern. The continental mainland is separated everywhere from the open oceans by a succession of partly enclosed seas, each protected and easily defended on the Pacific side by curving peninsular and island barriers. These loop-like barriers, swinging toward the mainland at either extremity, not only define and separate the marginal seas but lead to a sequence of straits and narrows that have great strategic significance.

Beginning in the Alaska peninsula, and continuing through the Aleutians, the first arc ties in to the shore of Kamchatka, shutting in the Bering Sea and covering the most accessible entries into the Yukon and Anadyr

[24] Spykman, *Geography of the Peace*, p. 54.

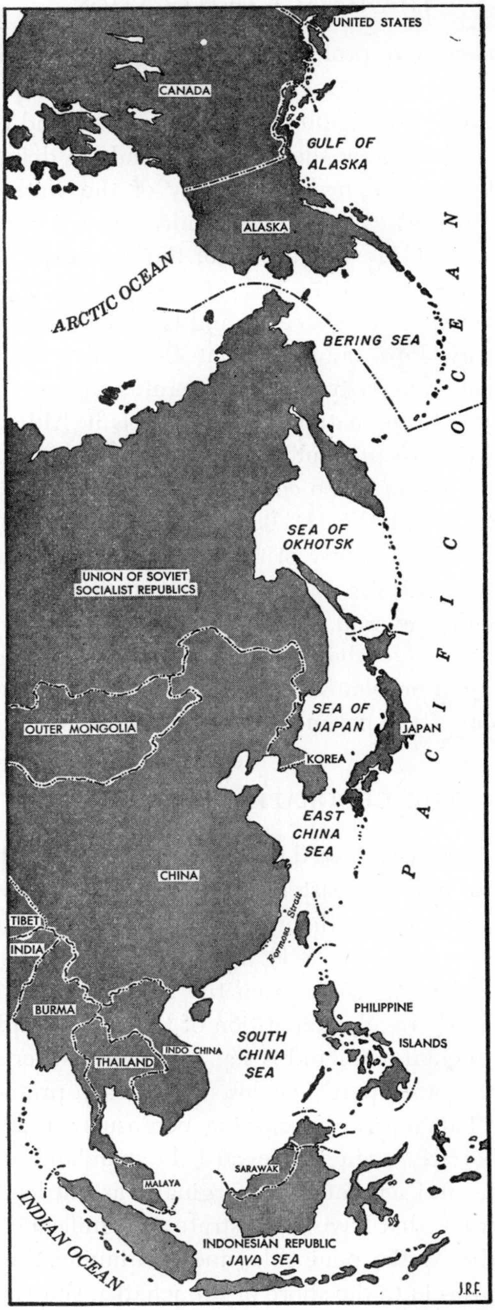

Fig. 8-4. Succession of Marginal and Enclosed Seas—from North America to the Indian Ocean.

valleys. Near the Alaskan end the United States has a strong naval base at Dutch Harbor, while the corresponding Russian base is at Petropavlovsk on Kamchatka.

The second unit in this pattern begins with the Kamchatka Peninsula and is continued without a break by the Kurile Islands, which follow a running curve and then tie in with the northeastern extremity of Hokkaido. The last of these islands, Paramushiro, is a northern Gibraltar in sight of Kamchatka. These islands are controlled by the U.S.S.R. and make of the Sea of Okhotsk a virtual Russian lake, controlling the northern access to the Amur basin.

The third arc begins with Sakhalin, which is separated by less than twenty miles from the continental coast, and extends southward for over seven hundred miles to the northwestern tip of Hokkaido. From this point Japan itself forms the outer arc, which at its southwestern extremity approaches within sixty miles of the Korean coast. Enclosed within this arc is the Sea of Japan. Mid-way along the continental shore is the Soviet naval base of Vladivostok, guarding the eastern terminus of the Trans-Siberian railroad and projecting Soviet naval power toward the chain of Japanese islands.

The fourth geographical unit can be traced from the Korean peninsula through Kyushu (part of Japan proper) and the Ryukyu chain which ties in to the island of Formosa. The enclosed China Sea has a secondary inner basin, the Yellow Sea, and two innermost recesses, the Gulfs of Chihli and Liaotung, behind the Kwantung Peninsula. This whole outer arc, nearly two thousand miles long, faces toward the entrances to Manchuria, the North China Plain, and the Yangtze Basin. Within this arc on the mainland is the port city and naval base of Shanghai. In the southern entry to the China Sea the Formosa Strait is narrowed further by the Pescadores. They are located within the United States perimeter of defense as defined in January, 1955.

The fifth repetition of this geographical pattern is drawn on a larger scale than its northern counterparts. Beginning with Formosa, an outer protective barrier runs through the Bataan Islands (part of the Philippines), Luzon, Mindoro, Palawan, Northern and Western Borneo, Billiton, Banka, and eastern Sumatra. The last swings in toward Malaya and thus completes the enclosure of the South China Sea while defining its southern entry through Malacca Strait. Singapore, Bangkok, Hanoi and Hong Kong all lie within this barrier. The area is honeycombed with shallows and treacherous waters which confine ships to well-defined sea lanes.

Thereafter, this configuration of marginal seas is lost in the Indian

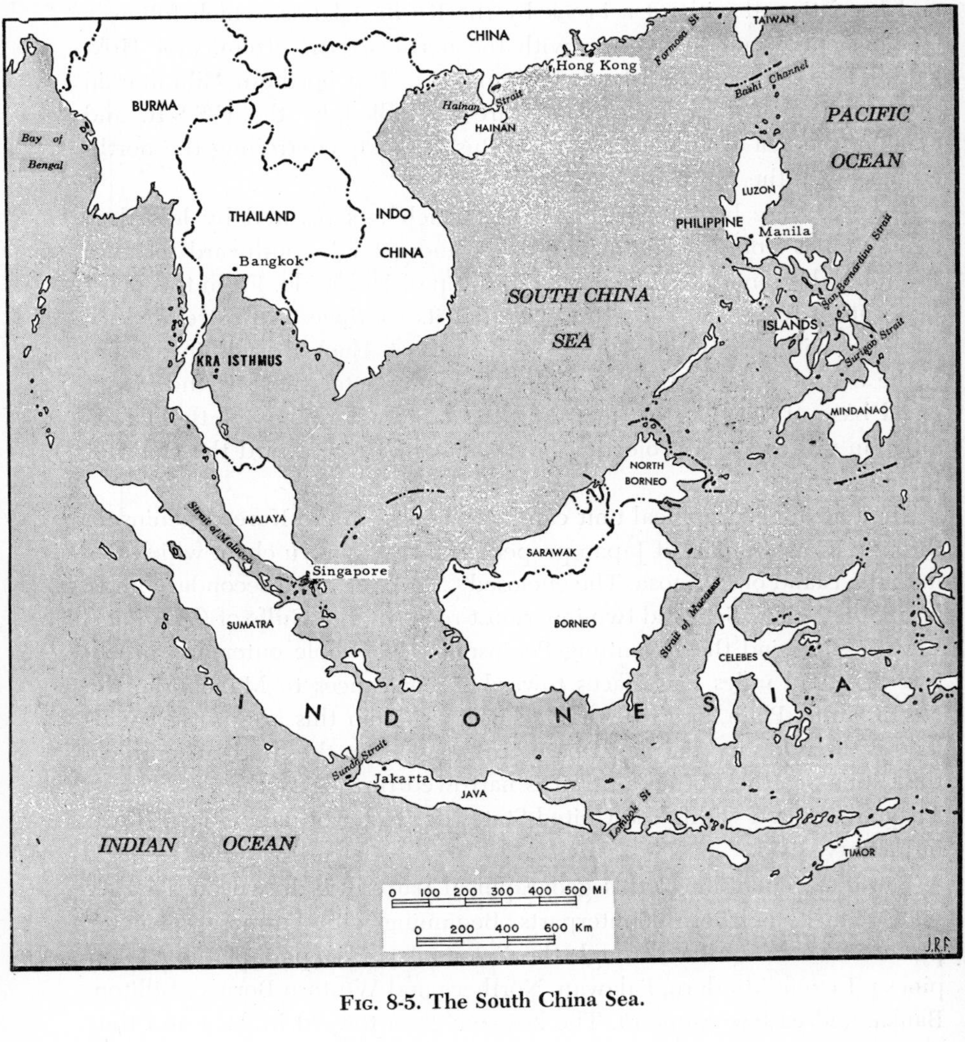

FIG. 8-5. The South China Sea.

Ocean (unless one considers the Andaman and Nicobar Islands chain as sufficient to define the contours of a marginal sea), only to reappear in a different pattern in the Middle East and Western Europe, in the Persian Gulf, the Red Sea, the Mediterranean Sea, North Sea, Baltic Sea, White Sea and the Barents Sea. With the exception of the Red Sea and the Persian Gulf all of these seas wash the shores of Heartland—or Heartland controlled—marginal territory; the North Sea in this sense is seen as forming a unit with the Soviet-dominated Baltic Sea. As marginal seas they have immediate importance in any effort by the Soviet Union to gain clear access to the open Atlantic, the Mediterranean, and the Indian Ocean. Such an effort would presuppose control, by the Heartland power, of the narrow straits which must be passed to reach the open sea.

Scattered along the chain of islands and archipelagoes in the Pacific and dotting the system of marginal seas in Europe and the Middle East are those focal points between land masses which provide egress from the interior or marginal seas. These straits and channels are not as numerous, however, as one might expect. In many instances where they do exist sea traffic is impeded or strictly channeled by the nature of treacherous shoals. A graphic illustration of the importance of deep straits occurred after the Battle of the Java Sea in 1942. All the deep exits from this sea were guarded by Japanese vessels, which sank or captured most of the Allied ships. The shallower craft were able to make the passage between Java and Bali Island (Bali Strait), and were able to escape the lone Japanese guard. But the larger ships that tried to escape through the Sunda Strait (between Sumatra and Java) and Lombok Strait (between the islands of Bali and Lombok in the Indonesian archipelago) encountered armed forces too large to evade or conquer.[25]

Most of the strategic waterways—the narrow passages—of the world can be divided into two general classes: those which are maritime highways between two of the great oceans; and those giving access to enclosed or semienclosed seas. In the first group are:

(1) The Mediterranean system, including the Strait of Gibraltar, the Sicilian Straits, the Suez Canal, the Red Sea, and the Strait of Bab-el-Mandeb. This is the vastly important water passage through the Eurafrican land mass to India and Southeast Asia—vitally important in the peripheral strategy of the Free World.

(2) The Panama Canal, connecting the Atlantic and Pacific Oceans, with its antechamber, the Caribbean Sea and the passages which connect

[25] E. G. Mears, *Pacific Ocean Handbook* (San Francisco, 1944), p. 43.

the latter with the Atlantic Ocean. Of these, the Windward Passage is of first importance.

(3) The waterways linking the Indian and Pacific Oceans (Fig. 8-5). These include the Strait of Malacca, Sunda Strait, and Singapore Strait, which provide access from the Indian Ocean to the South China Sea; San Bernardino Strait and Surigao Strait, which connect the South China Sea with the Pacific; Lombok and Macassar Straits, which connect the Indian Ocean with the Java and Celebes Seas; and Torres Strait, which connects the Arafura Sea to the Coral Sea.[26]

In the second category—passages providing access to enclosed seas or to seas which for all practical purposes are enclosed—are the following:

(1) The Turkish Straits, including the Dardanelles, the Sea of Marmara, and the Bosporus, which provide access to the Black Sea from the Mediterranean.

(2) The Straits at the entrance to the Baltic Sea. These are the Kattegat and Skagerrak, The Sound, and the Great Belt. The Kiel Canal is an alternate entrance to the Baltic Sea.

(3) St. George's Channel and the Irish Channel, which are the southern and northern entrances to the Irish Sea.

(4) The entrances to the Sea of Japan. These include the Tartary Strait, La Pérouse Strait, Tsugaru Strait, Tsushima and Shimonoseki Straits.

(5) The Strait of Ormuz, giving access to the Persian Gulf from the Indian Ocean.[27]

Perhaps still a third group of vital waterways can be distinguished in the narrow channels which pass between insular areas and the mainland. Certainly the most important of these is the English Channel. In addition, the Strait of Formosa connects the East and South China Seas, Hainan Strait separates the island from the mainland, Palk Strait separates Ceylon from the southern tip of the Indian mainland, and the Straits of Messina lie between Sicily and the Italian toe. The Strait of Bonifacio, between Sardinia and Corsica, and the Strait of Otranto, between Albania and Italy, have a secondary importance.

For the past century it has been Britain which has dominated the sea lanes and sea communications, but it must be stressed that, in the spring of 1956, the British naval and air base position between Aden and Australia appeared to be crumbling: Bombay passed from British control in

[26] G. F. Eliot, "Strategic Waterways," *United Nations World* (September, 1947), pp. 30-35.

[27] *Ibid.*

1950; the government of Ceylon requested in 1956 an early evacuation of the British base at Trincolamee; its air bases in Malaya are threatened by Communist infiltration; and Britain's control of Aden is under pressure both from within the colony and from Egypt, Saudi Arabia, and Yemen. Britain had established its domination of the sea lanes by seizing all but three of the strategic gateways or bottlenecks between the oceans. Of the remaining three, that at Panama remained in the friendly hands of the United States, while two others in the Indonesian archipelago—then held by the Netherlands—were also under friendly control. Controlling the strategic sea lanes in this manner, "not a ton of interocean shipping could move on the earth without going past British or United States points of naval control." [28] A globe-girdling chain of strategic naval bases was constructed to safeguard these points of control. Although constructed or acquired in days of the sailing vessels, the foresight in their selection made them equally valuable once steam and oil-powered vessels supplanted sailing ships. As already noted, the most severe challenge to their usefulness and the usefulness of the narrow waterways is to be seen in the ability of air power to neutralize them.

Today these narrow straits are still under the dominant control of Anglo-American naval power or of smaller nations friendly to, or even dependent on, that power. A discussion of these waterways will point this up although the precarious position of the British base net and the undermining effect of this weakness on the security of the United States and the free world as a whole must be kept in mind.

THE SEA OF JAPAN

Of the entrances to the Sea of Japan (Fig. 8-6) all except the Strait of Tartary and La Pérouse Strait are wholly controlled, on both shores, by American forces occupying Japan and South Korea. The northern shore of La Pérouse Strait is formed by the Russian island of Sakhalin. The Tartar Strait is wholly Russian, but ice closes it during a great part of the year. Despite the U.S.S.R. naval base at Vladivostok the Sea of Japan is effectively counterbalanced by the United States so long as occupation forces continue to remain in Japan and South Korea. Whether, and if so, to what extent, submarine warfare and the mining of port entrances would in a war necessitate a reappraisal of this situation is in the realm of speculation.

[28] G. T. Renner and associates, *Global Geography* (New York, 1944), p. 618.

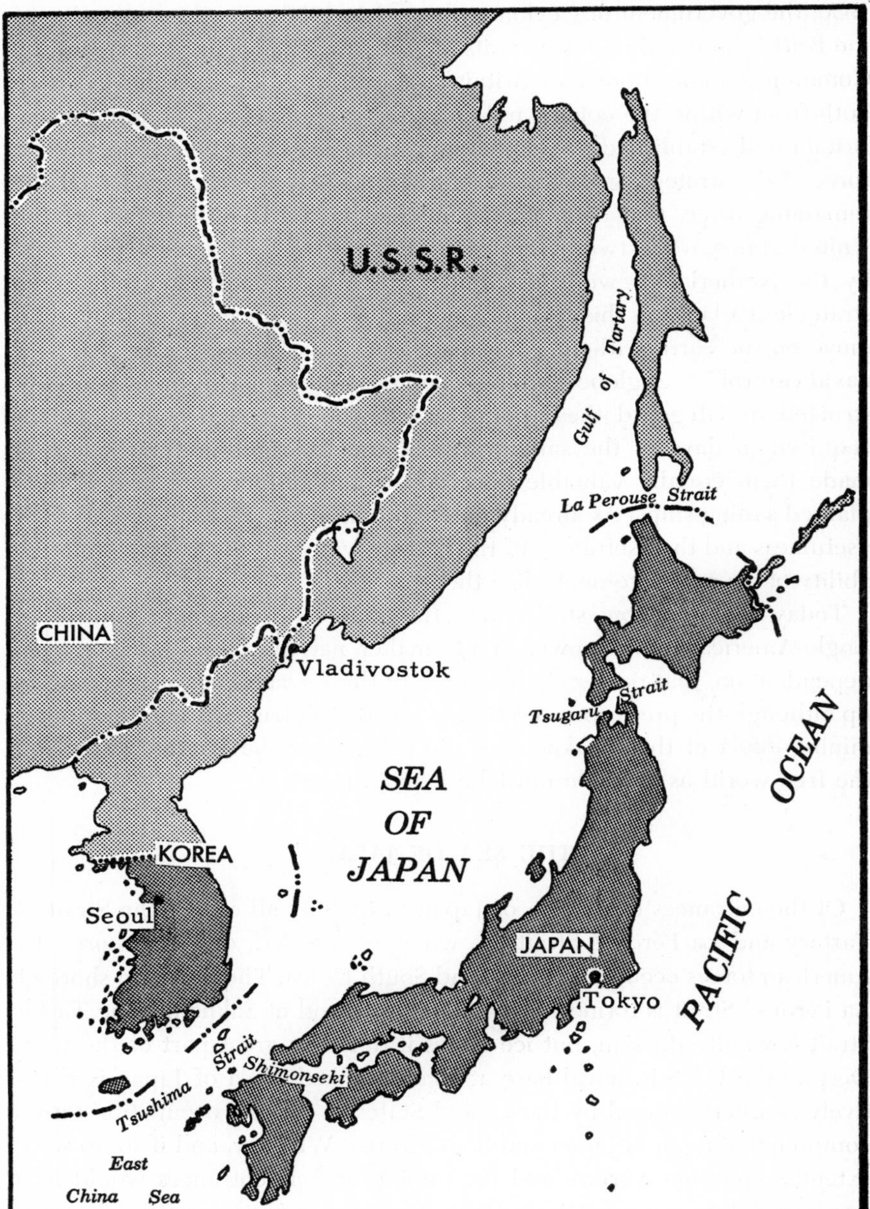

FIG. 8-6. Sea of Japan.

FROM INDIA TO THE PACIFIC

The waterways linking the Indian and Pacific Oceans are still dominated by British naval power at Singapore. In conjunction with United States naval forces in the Philippines the entire Southeast Asian series of narrow waterways is effectively dominated. The only immediate threat to Singapore is a Communist drive down the Malayan peninsula comparable to the successful Japanese thrust in the Second World War. The network of sea communications in this area is second only in importance to that of the Mediterranean. Not only is it the vital hub of communications between the Indian and Pacific Oceans, but also it controls communications extending north through the Formosa Strait to the Japanese Islands. The access of the maritime powers to all of Southeast Asia and a considerable part of the Far East thus depends on friendly control of this sea communications hub. The Bering Strait to the north, separating Alaska and eastern Siberia, is difficult of access both by sea and from the interior.

THE PANAMA CANAL AND CARIBBEAN AREA

This area is wholly controlled by the United States (*cf.* Fig. 3-6, p. 72). The Caribbean Sea is the key to the Panama defenses and includes three independent republics and possessions of the United States, Britain, France, and the Netherlands. As a practical matter, however, it is an American lake, dominated by sea and air power. The outer zone of secondary bases stretches from Exuma in the Bahamas to Antigua and St. Lucia in the Lesser Antilles, both leased bases. The inner zone of main defense covers an arc reaching from Guantanamo Bay on Cuba in the west to San Juan in the north and Trinidad in the southeast. On the western approaches, leased bases in the Galápagos Islands of Ecuador protect the canal from a distance of a thousand miles away. The canal is vital in the East-West communications of the entire free world, and as such is the only narrow waterway of great strategic importance in the North and South American continents. The rest of the world's strategic waterways are found in the marginal seas ringing the Eurasian land mass.

THE BALTIC SEA

Following the long coast line of the U.S.S.R., from the westernmost of its Arctic seas, the Barents Sea, and its southern annex, the White Sea which has become increasingly important as outlet of the Baltic-White

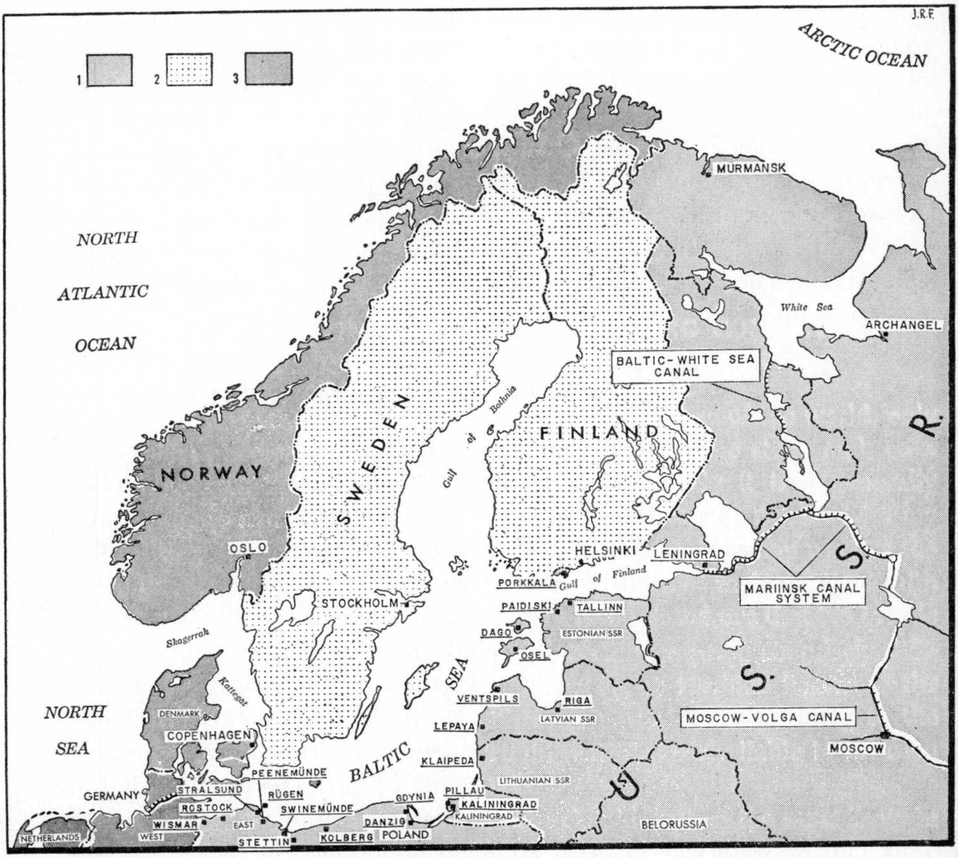

Fig. 8-7. The Baltic Arena and Its String of Soviet Military Bases: (1) Soviet bloc nations (Porkkala returned to Finland 1956); (2) neutral; (3) NATO bloc.

Sea inland waterway, we reach the Baltic Sea, Russia's window toward Scandinavia and the Atlantic (Fig. 8-7). Slowly but systematically, the Soviet Union has increased its direct control of the Baltic littoral which had been for a long time limited to the easternmost section of the Gulf of Finland. Ice-bound half of the year, the old Russian zone seemed too weak to assure the safety of Leningrad, the Soviet Union's second city. The Baltic States were incorporated in 1940. With their annexation, the Soviet Union organized new seaports which are more favorably located than is Leningrad's naval base, Kronstadt, which is icebound for five to six months: Tallinn, the main port of Estonia, is practically ice-free; the important port of Riga in Latvia is icebound for about three months, whereas the naval base of Libau is relatively ice-free. Farther south, the U.S.S.R. extended her Baltic power position through control of Memel in Lithuania and the port city of Kaliningrad, the former Königsberg, which is ice-free most of the year. In satellite Poland, the twin ports of what, after World War I, formed the Free City of Danzig and of Gdynia, as well as Szczecin (Stettin), not threatened by ice, are the natural outlets of the Vistula and Oder basins for the agricultural and industrial products of Poland, the western Ukraine, and Silesia. In 1955, the Soviet Union's grip around the Baltic included the coastline of satellite East Germany with its naval stations on the island of Rügen and at the port of Rostock. Its flanking expansion along the Baltic littoral ends in sight of the West German port of Lübeck.

This extension of Soviet Union control since the end of World War II has greatly improved its over-all defensive position as well as its potential role as an aggressor in the Baltic arena. On the other hand, the strength of NATO prevents further expansion and bars the Soviet Union from turning the Baltic Sea into a Russian lake from which its naval power, especially its submarines, could penetrate into the Atlantic. West Germany controls the ports of Lübeck and Kiel on the Kiel Canal which, in its length of fifty-three miles, cuts through Schleswig-Holstein and enters the Elbe river, fifteen miles east of Cuxhaven. Denmark, the natural goal of a Russian attempt to gain full control of the Baltic Sea and access to the Atlantic, still controls, through land fortifications, the strategically important island of Bornholm, and through mine fields, The Sound and the Belts. Sweden, in its important outlet to the North Sea, the naval base and port of Göteborg, shares with Denmark in the defense of the Kattegat. Sweden is not as exposed a Baltic Power as is Denmark. Its bases in Stockholm, Karlskrona, and on the island of Götland are a strong protec-

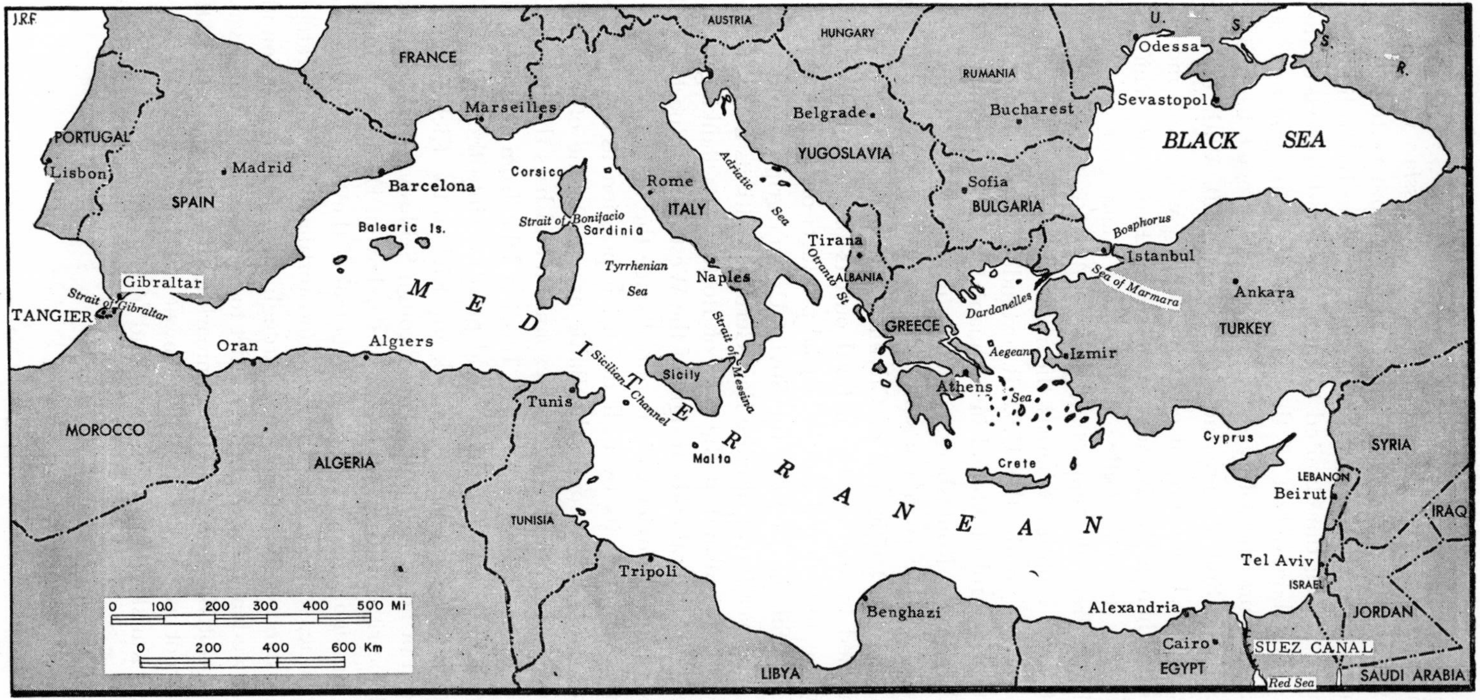

FIG. 8-8. The Mediterranean.

tion of its southern lands and have served as an effective deterrent to a challenge of Sweden's neutrality. Finland, on the other hand, in spite of the boundary changes effected after the Russo-Finnish war, is in a precarious position because of its close proximity to the Soviet Union's life-center of Leningrad. Its Åland islands which control the entrance to the Gulf of Bothnia have been neutralized. In conclusion, we find the Baltic arena a strategic area of great significance both to the Soviet orbit and the Free World. Seen from the standpoint of Soviet Union security, the Baltic defense line protects the vital agricultural and industrial concentrations between Leningrad, Moscow, and the eastern Ukraine and the increasingly important mining districts of Upper Silesia. In terms of aggression, the U.S.S.R. position along the Baltic coast could be seen as a stepping stone for Russian expansion into the Atlantic, with the consequent threat of dangerous submarine warfare against Allied shipping. Conversely, the location of NATO strength in its littoral member states and the strong position of Sweden produce a balance of power which halts further expansion by the U.S.S.R. and helps to maintain peace because the Free World occupies strategically favorable positions from which, in retaliation to aggressive moves by the Soviet Union, air blows or even an invasion could be started against vital industrial centers and communications lines in the European expanses of the Soviet Union.

THE MEDITERRANEAN NETWORK

The western entrance to the Mediterranean (Fig. 8-8) is commanded by the Gibraltar fortress, its British rule being vainly challenged by Spain. The narrow waist is dominated by the British fortress-island of Malta, and to some extent by the French base at Bizerte in Tunisia and the American air base at Wheelus Field at Tripoli. Sicily and other neighboring Italian islands are de-neutralized under the Italian peace treaty. The most critical control point in the Mediterranean vital passageway is the Suez Canal.[29] The concession of the joint-stock company which operates the canal does not expire until 1968, but since 1954 the canal is no longer under British control.[30] A possible alternative control point for the eastern Mediterranean is the British island of Cyprus and naval installations in the Iskenderon area of southeastern Turkey. However, the control over the last British-ruled bastion in the Middle East, Cyprus, appeared to be seriously

[29] A. Siegfried, "The Suez: International Roadway," *Foreign Affairs* (1953), pp. 605-618.
[30] See pp. 639, 640.

threatened in late 1955 by the mounting hostility of 400,000 Cypriotes of Greek descent, who were fighting for "self determination". Other narrow waterways of strategic value in this network are the Turkish Straits, the Strait of Otranto, the Strait of Messina, and the Strait of Bonifacio. The latter two are not of critical importance, but are available as convenient alternate ship routes.

However, such listing of the ramparts that guard the Mediterranean Sea would be misleading if we lost sight of the fact that the Mediterranean in its true power connotations, and as a "pivot of peace and war," [31] must be looked upon as a continuous waterway made up of two unequal parts, which until 1869 functioned separately—the Mediterranean proper and the Red Sea—tenuously linked at the isthmus of Suez.[32] It should be noted that the loss of Egypt as kingpin of the Middle East defense position has accentuated the critical defense position of the Western powers in the Middle East area as a whole, which is in sharp contrast to their firmly established security system in the Mediterranean arena itself.[33]

THE "GEOGRAPHICAL BLOCKADE" OF THE HEARTLAND POWER

The control of the sea communications throughout the maritime world and the network of intermediate bases counterbalance the power concentration in the Soviet-dominated Eurasian land mass.[34] We have stressed before that with only one or two exceptions the most vital narrow waterways are controlled by Anglo-American naval power. This naval dominance extends to most of the marginal seas as well. The immediate advantage to the Free World in this pattern of political geography is the complete accessibility by way of sea communications to the land area dominated by the Soviet Union. In contrast to the Eurasian land mass, the shores of the North and South American continents fall into the sea without a pattern of marginal seas or insular ramparts, which fact accounts for the vastly superior defense position of the American nations. Geography endows with great advantages powers whose naval strength, supported by air bases, controls the marginal seas and narrow passageways, as long as this control is not challenged successfully by naval and air power based on the Eurasian Heartland or rim lands under its control.

[31] W. G. East, "The Mediterranean: Pivot of Peace and War," *Foreign Affairs* (1953), pp. 619-633.

[32] *Ibid.*

[33] W. G. East, "The Mediterranean: Pivot of Peace and War," *loc. cit.*, pp. 631-633; see especially the observations on the alternative of a British defense-in-depth system in and around the Indian Ocean.

[34] See p. 214 ff.

This observation leads to the conclusion, borne out by history, that the Heartland power, even if succeeding in the establishment of a firm stronghold over the Eurasian marginal lands, will try to extend its perimeter of defense—or aggression—to include the marginal seas and narrow waterways off its shores. In its urge toward the open seas,[35] the Soviet Union, as formerly Russia, meets with formidable barriers: the Soviet Baltic lake is bottled by the Skagerrak and the Kattegat (*cf.* Fig. 8-7); her Black Sea outlet to warm waters is choked by the Turkish Straits; the Bering and Okhotsk Seas are fogbound and icebound a great part of the year; the Sea of Japan is subject to American naval power in Japanese bases; and the succession of Anglo-American naval bases along the whole of the insular rampart to Singapore would serve to nullify potential Soviet naval power ranging from Tsingtao, Shanghai, Vladivostok, and Petropavlovsk.

If one considers a possible break-out from this "geographical blockade," with the factors of geography foremost in mind, the two most likely areas are the Baltic and Black Seas. The former brings to the U.S.S.R. most of her imports, while the latter carries most of her exports to world markets. In both situations the Soviet Union is confronted with a narrow waterway which is subject to Anglo-American naval control. The acquisition, by the Soviet Union, of the Finnish coast beyond Viborg, her annexation of the Baltic states of Latvia, Estonia, and Lithuania and also of a strip of East Prussia which includes Kaliningrad, are evidence that the Baltic is to become, if it is not already, something of a Russian lake, its security threatened, however, by air power from the ring of bases which surround it. Furthermore, a concentration of Soviet naval power in the Baltic serves no great interest of the Soviet Union unless it can reach out beyond the Kiel Canal, The Sound, and the Great Belt to the North Sea and beyond.

A similar joining of rival naval forces would occur in the Aegean if the U.S.S.R. were ever successful in breaking out from the Black Sea through the narrow Bosporus into the Sea of Marmara, and from there through the winding channel of the Dardanelles into the Aegean Sea. Anglo-American naval power would appear to be highly sensitive to Russian intrusion on the eastern Mediterranean sea lanes, not to mention the neutralization of Turkey that would result from such a successful breaching of this geographical barrier. Hanson N. Baldwin stated the case clearly in saying that "geography is the Russian Navy's undoing" and that, even if the Dardanelles were to fall to Communist armies, the maze of islands in the

[35] See the comprehensive account by R. J. Kerner, "The Soviet Union as a Sea Power," in Weigert-Stefansson-Harrison, *op. cit.*, pp. 104-122; see also, F. Uligh, Jr., "The Threat of the Soviet Navy," *Foreign Affairs* (1952), pp. 444-455.

Aegean and the closed waters of the Mediterranean would make a sortie by Russian surface ships or submarines a desperate adventure.[36]

If one views the Baltic and Black Seas and their narrow passageways through the glass of the Heartland power that is trying to render the land mass itself and the marginal lands it dominates secure against attack from without, it is evident that they play as important a part in the security system of the Heartland complex as do the marginal lands adjacent to its borders. These marginal areas, as well as the western territories of the Heartland, are accessible at both ends from the sea. Any power equipped with the ships and with air cover to penetrate into the Baltic and Black seas would create a serious threat to the security of the Heartland-rim land structure as a whole. Clearly these marginal seas and their pathways loom large in the strategy of both the Soviet Union and the West. The case histories of the Black Sea and of the Baltic Sea, as well as those of the other marginal seas discussed, offer significant evidence that the appraisal of any security and power position remains incomplete unless the marginal seas, and their passageways, be given proper consideration. As a footnote to this general appraisal, it should be added that the strong emphasis on submarine construction in the Soviet Union—which, in 1955, was reported to have three hundred submarines in service—is clearly its attempt at partial solution of the geographical problems of the Heartland-rim land structure. In an appraisal of the geographical barriers which obstruct the Soviet Navy, Hanson W. Baldwin concluded in 1955 [37] that its construction program

> . . . will reach really dangerous proportions only if two or more of the following developments occur: (1) If Soviet long-range planes with an operational radius of at least 1,000 miles and a capability for effective attack upon shipping learn to co-ordinate their operations with Soviet submarines;
>
> (2) If Russia acquires new open-water naval, submarine and air bases on the coasts of Western Europe by land conquests (as Germany did in World War II);
>
> (3) If the industrial facilities of Soviet Siberia are strengthened so greatly as to be capable of the self-sufficient support of a very much more powerful Far Eastern Fleet;
>
> (4) If a breach in the Western Pacific island chain is achieved by Communist conquest or political action so as to provide Soviet Russia with a warm-water port fronting on the open Pacific.
>
> The Achilles' heel of Soviet Russia's deep-sea power today is her naval base complex. Her most important and best bases are bottled up in narrow seas; the few that give access to the open ocean are subject to the vagaries of Arctic weather and are vulnerable to atomic or conventional bombing attack by land-based or ship-based aircraft.

[36] "The Soviet Navy," *Foreign Affairs* (1955), pp. 587-604 (590, 591).
[37] *Ibid.*, p. 604.

Soviet Russia's naval might cannot be dismissed as a factor in her present global power. But it is not a major factor. Her submarine strength and in particular her minelaying capabilities deserve increasing respect. But it is still true today as it was in the days of the Tsars that if Russia is to challenge the United States or Great Britain for primacy upon the high seas she must, besides strengthening her maritime power with increased export trade, acquire warm-water ports fronting upon the open oceans of the world and expand her shipbuilding industry and the vast industrial complex to support it.

NARROW MARINE STRAITS IN THE ANTARCTIC

Our discussion of the strategically significant narrow passages would be incomplete without mentioning the increasingly important role of the Drake Passage between South America and Palmer Peninsula (Fig. 8-9), ominously important because of the vital role this passage would assume if in a future conflict passage through the Panama Canal or the Suez Canal, or through both of them, would be barred. In such a case ships would have to plough the Antarctic Seas on their way from the Pacific to the Atlantic, or on their way from the Atlantic to the Indian Ocean. The political geography of the Antarctic sphere of interest has come into the picture very late,[38] but the possible blocking of the passages through the Suez and Panama Canals has made the Drake Passage, between Tierra del Fuego and the Falkland Islands to the north and the outer reaches of Antarctica to the south, a potentially decisive strategic area. Many nations are now competing for sovereignty rights in the Antarctic arena. Argentina has established stations at both ends of the Drake Passage. Competing with Argentina are Chile, Great Britain (which, in 1908, set up her Falkland Islands Dependencies), and the United States, as well as other nations with more or less specific claims. Significant battles for the control of these Antarctic waters were fought in World Wars I and II when in both wars the Germans succeeded in playing havoc with Allied shipping in southern waters. Forewarned by the experiences of the two wars, Argentina, Chile, and Britain have established themselves in the Palmer Peninsula area and are competing in their sovereignty claims. The United States in 1955 completed a non-military Antarctic exploratory mission (the *U.S.S. Atka* expedition) and has good ground for sovereignty claims of its own in the Palmer Peninsula. The Soviet Union, in an ominous move late in 1955, announced plans to establish three bases near the South Pole. These plans could be interpreted as the possible beginning of a double flanking of

[38] L. Martin, "The Antarctic Sphere of Interest," in Weigert-Stefansson-Harrison, *op. cit.*, pp. 65-73 (65).

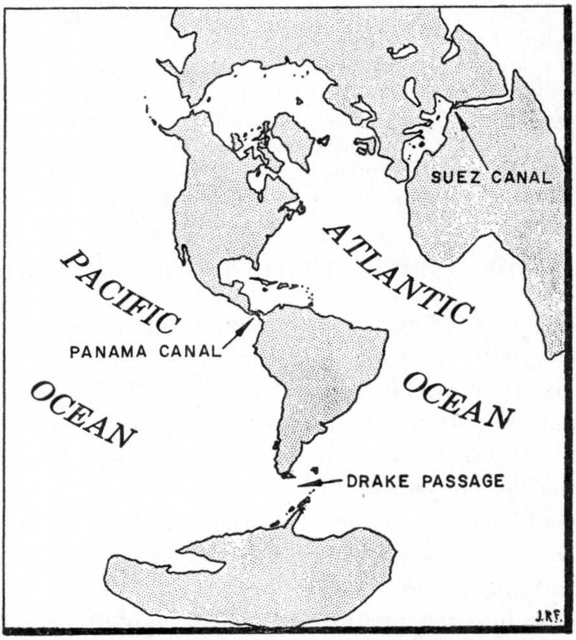

FIG. 8-9. Drake Passage in Relation to the Panama and Suez Canals.

Australia and New Zealand by the Soviet Union. It has been argued [39] that a considerable Communist air power might gain a foothold in Indonesia in the next ten to fifteen years, unless the influence of the Free World prevails. If the Soviet Union would establish Antarctic air bases, Australia and New Zealand would be vulnerable from the West, too. Forty nations will take part in the Geophysical Year, 1957-58, with the United States' expedition under the command of Rear Admiral Richard E. Byrd as a major participant. Time will tell whether and in what respects the objectives in the fields of pure science will be overshadowed by strategic, political, and economic developments in the vast and empty Antarctic arena.

LOCATIONAL FACTORS OF THE ARCTIC: THE ARCTIC MEDITERRANEAN

The Arctic Ocean is in actuality a part of the Atlantic Ocean whose littoral includes the land masses of the Northern Hemisphere. It has been rightly termed the Polar Mediterranean. When Vilhjalmur Stefansson

[39] *New York Times,* November 20, 1955.

coined this phrase in 1922, he defined it in terms which, if examined in retrospect, appear to be visionary: [40]

> A map giving one view of the northern half of the northern world shows that the so-called Arctic Ocean is really a Mediterranean sea like those which separate Europe from Africa or North America from South America. Because of its smallness, we would do well to go back to an Elizabethan custom and call it not the Arctic Ocean but the Polar Sea or Polar Mediterranean. The map shows that most of the land in the world is in the Northern Hemisphere, that the Polar Sea is like a hub from which the continents radiate like the spokes of a wheel. The white patch shows that the part of the Polar Sea never yet navigated by ships is small when compared to the surrounding land masses. In the coming air age, the. . . Arctic will be like an open park in the center of the uninhabited city of the world, and the air voyagers will cross it like taxi riders crossing a park. Then will the Arctic islands become valuable, first as way stations and later because of their intrinsic value—minerals, grazing, fisheries . . .

The Arctic Mediterranean is an excellent example of an area in which technological progress, especially in aviation, has caused far-reaching changes which make imperative a reorientation and a new evaluation of locational factors of the area. Because of these aspects of location, a review of some of them is necessary in order to appraise the new role of the Arctic in the relationships of the northern powers.

As the air age has developed, more and more attention has been focused upon the Arctic, for over the Arctic pass the great circle routes connecting the United States and Canada and the Far East in one direction and in the other direction linking the United States with Northwestern Europe. The great circle is the flyer's short cut, for the arc of a great circle is the shortest distance between two points on a sphere.

In laying out a great-circle course between New York and Moscow, or between Chicago and Peiping, the great-circle routes pass over the Arctic (Fig. 8-10). Until 1954, in most cases, the implications were more significant for military planning than in the field of commercial aviation. Prior to 1954 the airlines of commerce followed the longer courses of trans-oceanic flight in an effort to serve an optimum of population centers. Civil aviation succeeded late in 1954 in making the Arctic short cut to Europe a regular airline route. The Scandinavian Airlines initiated scheduled flights from Los Angeles to Copenhagen, with stops at Winnipeg, Canada, and Söndre Stromfjord, Greenland. The distance measures 5,085 nautical, or about 5,800 statute miles, being 465 nautical miles (535 statute miles) shorter than the trip by way of New York. The timetable calls for the eastbound polar flight to take about twenty-four

[40] "The Arctic as an Air Route of the Future," *National Geographic Magazine* (1922), p. 205 ff.

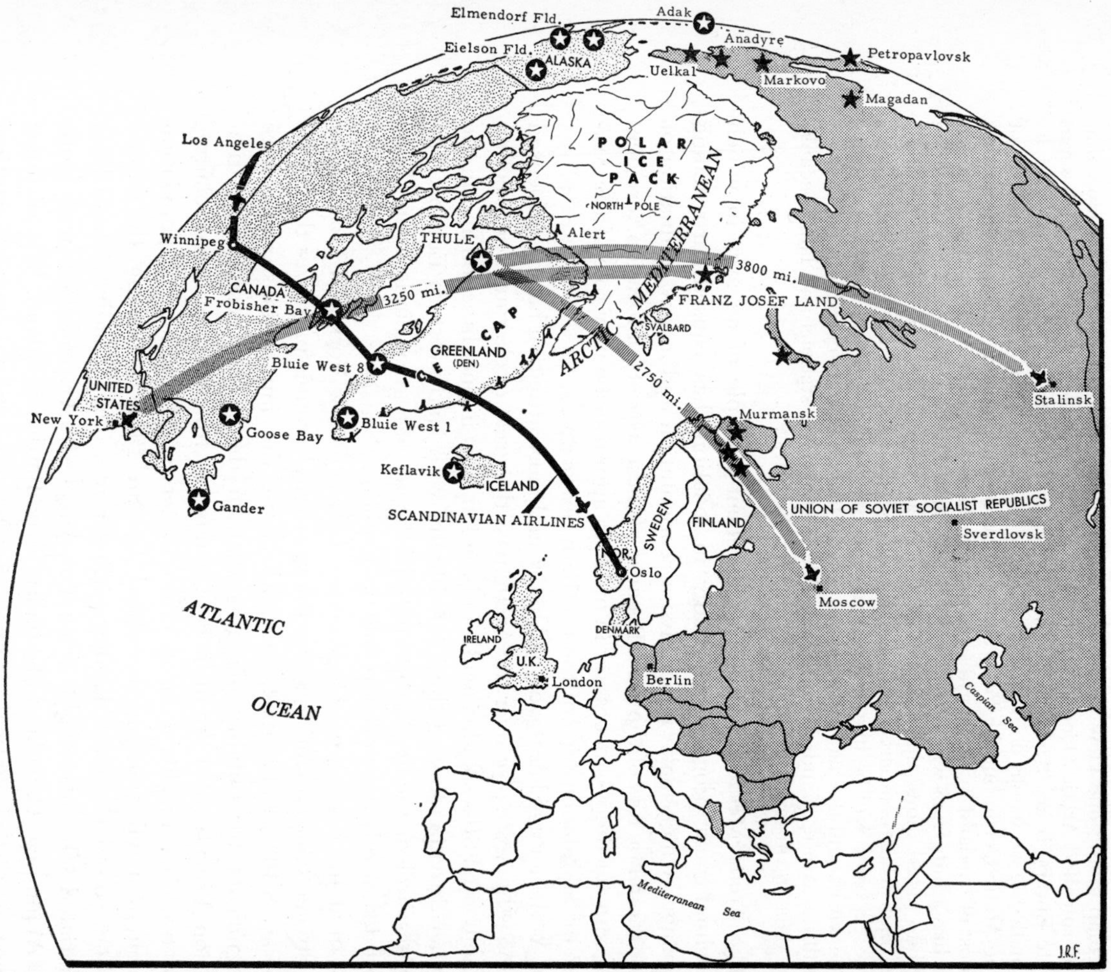

FIG. 8-10. Air Routes and Strategic Bases in the Arctic Mediterranean.

hours, a saving of three or four hours over the conventional route. This regular "over the top" service is likely to be the forerunner of many more such airline routes and it is reported that the Scandinavian Airlines has blueprinted a transpolar service from Oslo to Tokyo that would cut the run from fifty-three hours to twenty-four. This example shows the impact of new transpolar air routes in civil aviation upon peacetime relations of the nations which these routes are to link so much more speedily and, as a result, more firmly. The new links between California and the Scandinavian countries offer a good illustration of the radical changes in the locational relationships of "distant" countries as the result of the opening of new skyways above the Polar regions.

In terms of locational relations of the great powers we are still struggling to grasp the changes which Polar aviation has caused in the locational relationships of the powers of the West and East, by turning the Arctic Mediterranean and its frozen lands into a pivot area and strategic center. This concept reveals itself best on a north-polar version of a great-circle chart. With its great-circle projections, this is the kind of map the aviator needs. To him the idea of our Polar Mediterranean is familiar. To many navigators and to those who have grown up in the shadow of the Mercator projection (with the poles at infinity) this vision has appeared strange and almost inconceivable not so long ago. In terms of flying, the grouping of the nations around the Polar Mediterranean reveals the elementary truth that the direct route between any of these nations is in some northerly direction; on the cylindrical Mercator world map (with the poles lost in its open ends) the logical flight direction is seemingly east or west.

It is over this Arctic Mediterranean that air strikes upon the United States and retaliatory raids may be expected. Even the exchange of guided missiles would take place over the Arctic great-circle routes, not only because these offer the shortest distance, but also because the Arctic area is difficult to defend.[41]

The air distance from New York to Moscow is 4,675 miles by way of the Arctic. The air distance from San Francisco to Peiping by way of the Arctic is 6,600 miles, 3,000 miles shorter than the trans-Pacific route. These distances appear formidable, but this is not the distance aircraft would have to travel in the event of an East-West war, for the Arctic Mediterranean is being ringed with bases by both the United States and the Soviet Union (see pp. 249 ff.). The distance over the Arctic from the important

[41] J. W. Watson, "Canada: Power Vacuum, or Pivot Area?" in Weigert-Stefansson-Harrison, *op. cit.*, pp. 40-60.

United States base at Thule, Greenland, is only 2,752 miles to Moscow, whereas the nearest Soviet base at Rudolf Island, one of the Franz Joseph groups, is 3,800 miles distant from New York City.

This is a reflection of the greater depth of the United States from the pole as compared with the U.S.S.R. The core area of the Soviet Union is centered along the 55th parallel. It is 15 degrees closer to the pole than the United States core area, which is centered along the 40th parallel. However, it would be fallacious to conclude that this locational relationship gives North America a strategic advantage over the Soviet Union. It must be realized that the polar ice pack, and the advance positions it offers to all Arctic powers, puts the weapon-bearers of our time in closest proximity.

The polar ice pack, although it develops areas of open water, is a vast ice landing field; a field which also contains floating ice islands more stable than the pack of ice itself. The first of these ice floes was reported by the U.S. Air Force in 1946 and named T-1; subsequently, two more were located in 1950 (T-2 and T-3). According to Soviet claims their airmen had noted earlier the presence of these ice islands and established the identification of certain other floes in the sector claimed by the U.S.S.R. as "North Pole One, Two," and so on.

These islands may last for years and perhaps even for centuries. However, the islands discovered by the U.S.S.R. are not as large as the ones reported by the United States Air Force, and the Soviet Union has had to make the best of ice floes a mile or so in length and perhaps ten feet thick. Both the United States and the Soviet Union use the ice islands as bases of operations for their Arctic research.[42]

Another vast ice landing strip is the Greenland Ice Cap which is also a possible refueling base; uninhabited, with the exception of radar stations in the vicinity of Thule, the ice cap presents a good location for caching fuel. With the exception of the crevassed edges of the Greenland Ice Cap aircraft landings can be made almost anywhere, especially on its ice lakes. The strategic importance of this uninhabitable section of the world cannot go unrecognized and the long-term strategic implications are equally significant both for offense and defense. This was demonstrated during World War II when the Germans maintained a series of weather stations along the Greenland Coast. These weather observation stations in the North Atlantic "weather factory" for Northwestern Europe

[42] The dangerous overlapping of American and U.S.S.R. ice island zones is illustrated by newspaper reports in February, 1955, according to which the Soviet permanent research base North Pole Two has drifted eastward toward Greenland across Canadian waters.

enabled the Germans to forecast conditions to some extent over the British Isles.

Effective means and types of transportation have been sought since historical times to defend the Arctic and to exploit its resources. It has been the aim of many explorers to discover northern sea routes across the top of the Eurasian land mass, as well as the Northwest Passage, which has been sought for since 1610 as a short cut to Asia (Fig. 8-11). Discovery of such passages and the opening of new sea lanes have paralleled the development of skyways and contributed to the important change in the spatial relationship of the great Arctic powers. The use of a northwest passage from the Atlantic to Asia has lagged considerably behind that of the Northern Sea Route, which the Soviet Union initiated to cross the Arctic Sea from Murmansk through the Bering Strait. However, in 1954, United States and Canadian icebreakers succeeded in navigating the passage leading from the Atlantic Ocean to the Beaufort Sea.

By using more than a dozen icebreakers, several dozen freighters, and its own aviation patrol, the Soviet Union keeps its sea lane open nearly three months each year. In this way, it lifts a burden from the overworked Trans-Siberian railroad, enables the Soviet Navy to move between the Atlantic and the Pacific, and facilitates the all-out exploitation of the ex-Finnish nickel mines, the Vorkuta coal mines, and the Kolyma gold fields, along with the forest and other natural resources of Siberia.

These Arctic sea routes solve one phase of the problem of Arctic transportation. A second solution, and one which may increase in importance as an aid to the exploitation of the natural resources within the Arctic, is the use of tractor trains in winter, and during the short summer the use of barges on the inland waterways of the northward flowing rivers. Both methods are seasonably limited, however, and in spite of the high cost, aircraft are used increasingly even for transport of bulky goods in the Arctic regions.

In the face of the growing strategic importance of the Arctic Mediterranean, the competing powers have been forced to make the extension of the defensive and offensive capabilities of the Arctic an integral part of their over-all defense system. The Soviet Union is ringing the Arctic Sector with air and naval bases, and with radar and weather stations. Similarly, the United States, in co-operation with Canada and the nations of NATO—particularly Denmark, which owns Greenland—has set up air bases, weather stations, and a radar net along the coasts of Alaska and Labrador, in order to establish an Arctic line of defense. The Thule Air Base in Northwest Greenland is the key to the new strategy.

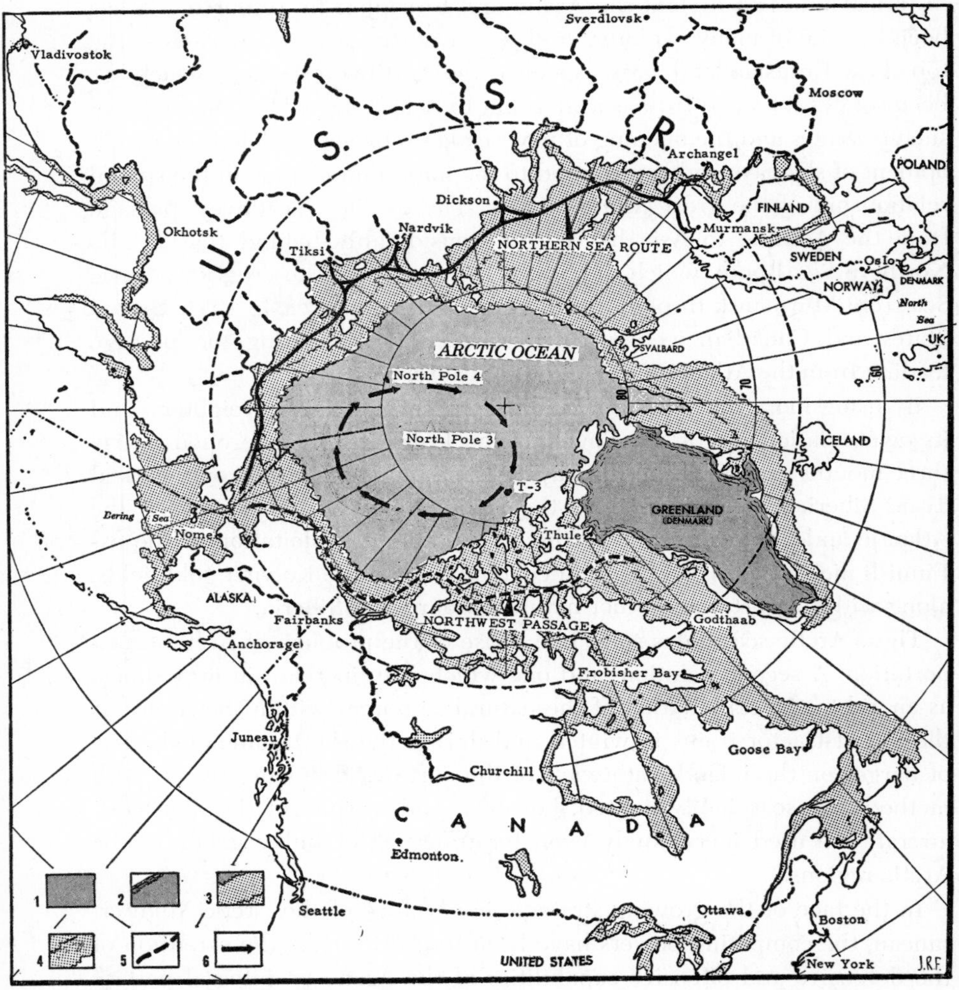

FIG. 8-11. Sea Routes and Bases in the Arctic Mediterranean: (1) permanent ice; (2) Greenland ice cap; (3) land-fast ice, summer; (4) land-fast ice, winter; (5) navigable sea routes; (6) general direction of ice island drift.

The Danish-American Agreement of April 27, 1951, under which the Thule defense area was developed, is worked out as a part of the North American defense of NATO. A concept of the present polar strategy is to build the interceptor and radar defenses as far north as it is possible to support them, and to build striking bases in the same areas from which to mount attacks if the need should come.[43] Its fulfillment will continue to depend on the close co-operation between the United States and its northern neighbors, Canada, Iceland, and Denmark, and on great expenditures of money to develop this northern defense perimeter.

This sketchy picture of the Arctic Mediterranean as an ominously important cradle-of-conflict area in which modern technology has changed radically the locational relationship of the Soviet Union and the North American powers would be incomplete without mentioning that the Arctic ice-cover provides also a camouflage for Soviet long-range submarines. Their range of operations could extend from bases within the Arctic to the trade routes of the Atlantic and the Pacific, to the very shores of the Canadian Arctic and, perhaps, even into Hudson Bay where they might launch guided atomic missiles. Submarines enabled by atomic power to cruise indefinitely under ice, and equipped with machines for cutting through when they wish to surface, might become a considerable threat to the northern defense of the American nations. This is only another illustration of the fact that, as a result of the development of new weapons of total warfare, the Arctic Mediterranean has grown greatly in importance as a pivotal area. Both the Communists and the Free World no longer look only east and west, but northward to the Pole and the danger that lies beyond.[44]

C. The "Western Hemisphere" and the United States "Perimeter of Defense"

THE "CONTINENTS" AND OTHER LARGE-SPACE CONCEPTS

"We think today in continents," wrote Oswald Spengler, the German philosopher of doom, in 1920; "but that is too little today. We must have the global, the imperial view." Since these words were written, political

[43] "Survival in the Air Age," Report by the President's Air Policy Commission (Washington, D. C., 1948).

[44] A. J. Toynbee paints a dark picture of the consequences which "the approaching conquest of the Arctic," may have on the destinies of the United States and the Soviet Union, "the two still standing gladiators of the Christian Era"; *A Study of History*, Vol. IX (New York, 1954), pp. 483-485.

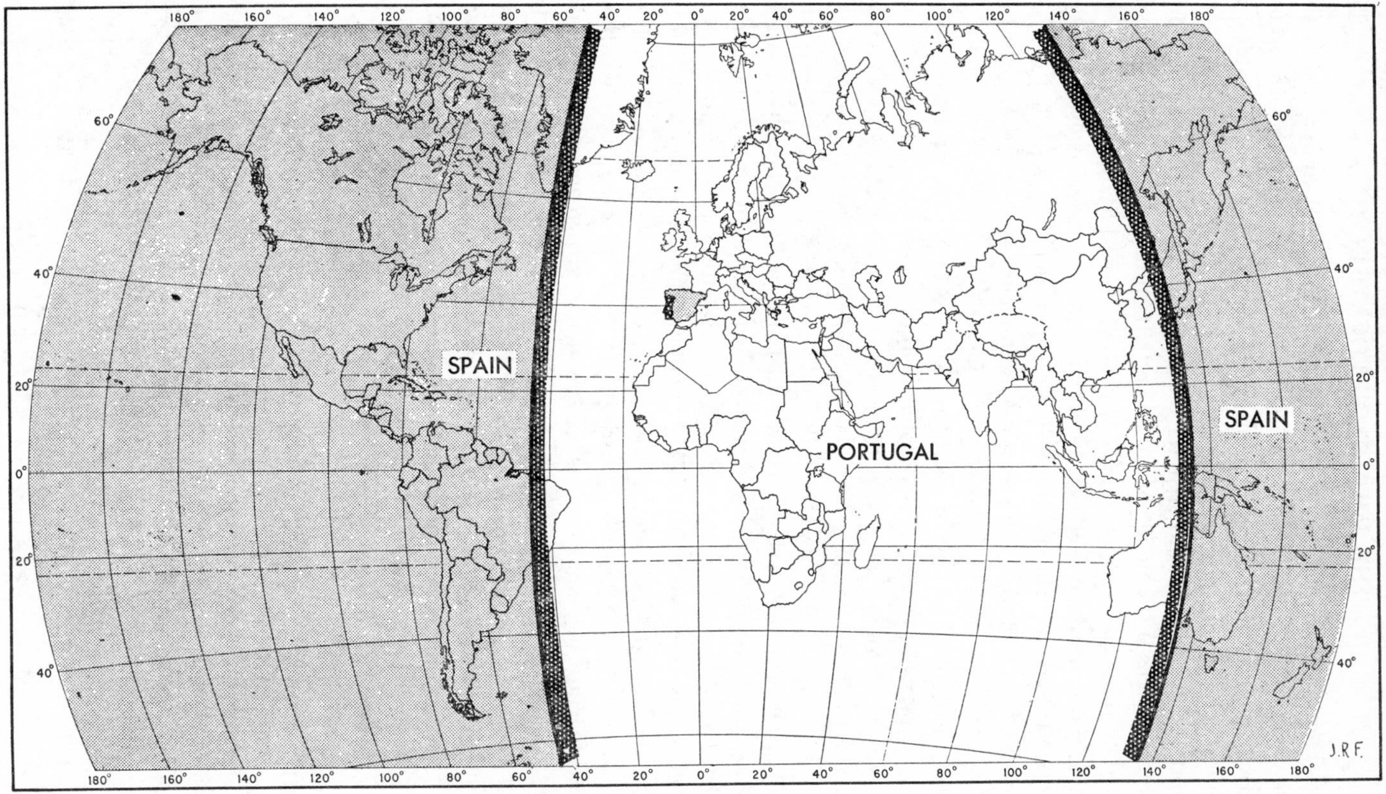

FIG. 8-12. The Partition of Tordesillas: The World Divided.

and geographical thinking throughout the world have experienced a significant trend toward revising and readjusting basic concepts of world geography. These revisions often cut across established lines of areal and continental demarcation, in order to keep pace with the shifting relationships of a continuously shrinking world. Often we find the shrinking process proceeding at such a rapid pace that the necessary adjustments in geographical thinking are sadly left behind. As a result of such cultural lags we can detect a great amount of loose thinking, especially in connection with large-space concepts, and we can trace seriously misleading political, economic, and cultural concepts to this difficulty in the redefinition of continental and other space relationships.

What is, for instance, the Western Hemisphere? Where is the dividing line between Europe and Asia? Where is the not-so-Far East, the not-so-Far North; do they assume different meanings if seen from Washington, Moscow, or London? Or, if we look at the problem in terms of the security position of the United States, what concept should be adopted for the defense of the United States—should it be continental, or based on what is called the "Western Hemisphere," or should it be global? Between these concepts there is a wide range of possibilities, from a strategy of defense based on the continental United States to an offensive projection of American strength on a global scale.[45] While we are not concerned here with the strategical problems themselves, we must realize that in order to understand them it is essential to see clearly the underlying factors of geography.

THE PARTITION OF TORDESILLAS

The present confusion may be correctly compared with that existing in 1493 when Pope Alexander VI issued his famous Bull which disregarded the basic lesson in geography that the earth is a sphere (Fig. 8-12). The Papal ruling was indeed one of the most important geopolitical decisions determining the course of world history. As the final arbiter of Christian Europe, the Pope was called upon to divide the world outside of Europe between the rival rulers of Spain and Portugal. One of his predecessors had already acknowledged Portugal's claims to the African coast when Columbus returned from his first expedition. In the Partition of Tordesillas, Pope Alexander drew the line by which the two great colonial powers of this time were assigned their spheres

[45] *Major Problems of United States Foreign Policy, 1952-1953,* The Brookings Institute (Washington, D. C., 1952), pp. 149 ff. (159).

of interest: The line was drawn from pole to pole one hundred leagues west of the Cape Verde Islands. All new discoveries west of this were to go to Spain; all the new lands east of this line were Portugal's. No provision was made for what would happen when the two should encounter each other on the other side of the globe. Under this agreement, which the two Powers formalized in 1494, slightly modifying the Bull of 1493, all of the American continents (the existence of which was then entirely unknown to everybody concerned), except for the eastern part of Brazil, were Spain's, while India and the major part of Africa were within the Portuguese sphere of influence. Greenland also would have fallen into the Portuguese sphere had that country's explorers come so far. The Portuguese origin of the name Labrador shows that they were not completely inactive in this direction. In 1606, the first Antarctic sector claim was made in the name of King Philip of Spain.[46] These man-made hemispheres continued to function until, in the seventeenth and eighteenth centuries, the British and Dutch settlers successfully put an end to this arbitrary map-making.

It is useful to recall this not-so-short-lived episode if we are to embark on the task of trying to draw a map of the world which shows the sensitive lines—the "perimeter of defense"—of the Great Powers. In so doing, we find that we need to clarify certain basic concepts.

Where is this hemisphere of ours, and where are all the others that matter? Which are the realities, and which are the myths surrounding the "continents"?

MACKINDER'S VIEW OF THE EAST AND WEST

In a memorable lecture, "The Human Habitat," which Mackinder gave in 1931, he defined what, in the world view of a geographer, are the major features of humanity and the human habitat, of the East and the West. His attempt to set in perspective some salient facts is still a classical piece of geographical definition and is quoted here at some length because it sharpens our thoughts on a subject of basic importance in the study of political geography: [47]

> The monsoon winds sweep into and out of Asia because that vast land lies wholly north of the equator and is, therefore, as a whole, subject to an alternation of seasons. Over an area of some five million square miles in the south and

[46] Martin, *op. cit.*, pp. 66, 67.

[47] H. J. Mackinder, "The Human Habitat," Records of the British Association for the Advancement of Science (London, 1931), 15 pp.

east of Asia, from India to Manchuria, and in the great adjacent islands, the monsoon drops annually a rainfall amounting on the average of years to some 18 millions of tons. Half of mankind, 900 million people [1931], live in the natural regions of this area; about 180 to the square mile. The rainfall is, therefore, of the order of some 20 thousand tons annually for each inhabitant. There is considerable traffic between the regions of this group, and there are the fisheries; in order to see it whole let us add three million more square miles for the marginal and land-locked areas. Then we shall have a total of eight million square miles, or 4 per cent of the globe surface, carrying 50 per cent of the human race. The annual increase of population may amount to some seven or eight millions, and as compared with this figure both emigration and immigration into and from the outer world are small. In the main we have here vast stable peasantries, "ascript to the globe," if we may use a medieval expression; tied to the soil; a tremendous fact of rain, sap and blood. That is the East.

The West lies in Europe, south and west of the Volga, and in that eastern third of North America which includes the main stream of the Mississippi and the basin of the St. Lawrence. Europe within the Volga boundary measures some three million square miles, and eastern North America some two million square miles. The two together are, therefore, equivalent in area of land to the group of regions which constitutes the East. If we add three million square miles for the fisheries and the oceanic belt which contains the "shipping lanes" between Europe and North America, we shall again have a total of 4 per cent of the globe's surface, and this is the main geographical habitat of western civilization. Within this area are 600 million people, or 120 to the square mile of land. Notwithstanding the oceanic break it may be regarded as a single area, for the distance from E.N.E. to W.S.W., from the Volga to the Mississippi, measures only some seven thousand miles, or little more than one-quarter way around the globe along the Great Circle. The rainfall on the land is drawn from the same source both in Europe and eastern North America; it comes mainly from the south, from the Atlantic, and is of the order of 12 thousand tons per human inhabitant per annum. There is an annual net increase of population of some four or five millions and, as compared with this, emigration to the outer world is small, for the movement of a million emigrants a year from Europe to North America in the dozen years at the commencement of this century was, of course, internal to the area.

Thus we have two areas, measuring together less than 10 per cent of the world's surface, but containing more than 80 per cent of the world's population. Outside of these areas is some 90 per cent of the world's surface, but containing only 20 per cent of the population. On some forty million square miles of land, outside the East and the West, you have an average density of population of only 10 to the square mile as contrasted with 120 on the five million square miles of the West, and 180 on the five million square miles of the East. The moisture upon the land areas, outside the Western and Eastern rain zones, varies from Sahara drought to Amazon and Congo deluge, but it is a remarkable fact that South America has upon its six and a half million square miles a population of only 10 to the square mile, or the average for the world outside West and East. This vacancy of South America and Africa may be regarded perhaps as a third great feature of the habitat of man; it must be set alongside the extraordinary and persistent self-containedness of the East and West. The increase in the world's populations outside of the "East" and the "West," even though reinforced by some immigration, is relatively insignificant. The main growths, the spread of the sheet of human blood, have been merely overflows from the anciently occupied regions into adjacent areas—into North and North-Eastern Europe, into Eastern North America, and into Manchuria—and in each case the natural frontiers of drought and frost have now been approached, except for relatively narrow outlets along the wheat belts of North America and Siberia. Even in North America the center of population has ceased to move appreciably westward.

In this continued growth of population in the East and the West in far greater actual number than in the rest of the world, we have an instance of geographical momentum. The momentum, though issuing from the past, is a fact of the present, an element in the dynamic system of today's geography.

Mackinder's daring illumination of the East and West as the globe's outstanding features of human geography displays the kind of geographical sense which draws its strength from the blending of a profound geographical and historical knowledge. To Mackinder geography was, to use his own words, "an art of expression parallel to and complementary to the literary arts . . . it ranges values alongside of measured facts. Hence outlook is its characteristic."

THE WESTERN HEMISPHERE

We shall need geographical sense—outlook—if we undertake to define the contours of what is perhaps the most important term of political geography to Americans, the Western Hemisphere.

It should be clear that hemisphere can be understood here only in a figurative meaning like the "East" or the "West." The hemisphere in a strictly geometrical sense is untouched by this discussion. It will remain an indispensable concept for the astronomer, the geodesist, and the surveyor. Here we speak of the Western Hemisphere as a household term and a myth. This Western Hemisphere is not a clearly defined concept. We associate it loosely with the Monroe Doctrine. Because of this association we are aware of its important historical and political implications, which should make it obvious that we cannot afford to define it in nebulous terms. However, if we make the attempt to trace its extent in terms of unmistakable geographical boundaries, we find ourselves immediately confronted with insurmountable barriers. We discover that, like the Holy Roman Empire, which in the words of Voltaire was neither holy nor Roman nor an empire, this Western Hemisphere is neither western nor a hemisphere. Political catchwords like "hemispheric solidarity" and "continental brotherhood" lose some of their glamour in the light of geographical facts. They must be interpreted according to what, under changing political conditions, is meant by reference to terms such as the "Western Hemisphere" or the "American Continent."

CANADA AND SOUTH AMERICA

North and South America are linked by an isthmus. That strip of land gives but the illusion of geographical contact, "because of man's odd habit of thinking that only land is a connecting element." [48] An illusion it is because there is little or no traffic along that strip of land. If Canadians, for instance, visit South America, they must travel by water or air; Canada is farther from most of South America than from Western Europe.[49] Because of this fact of geography it is logical to find that Canada has consistently refrained from direct political association with the Pan-American movement and "Hemispheric Security." The Canadian outlook has been summarized as follows: "even in mileage Canada is nearer to Europe than to South America. So remote a mass of land—unless the poorest geopolitics were to obscure the richest history—can never match that to which the sea and air give better access. From the Anglo-Russian or Franco-Russian alliances, for whose regional aims she has twice sacrificed so much, Canada abstains; under what compulsion of major policy, simple geography or common ideas should she discriminate regionally in favor of a Pan-American security pact? Her relationship with Latin America is wholly unlike her partnership in the British Commonwealth and her *entente* with the United States." [50]

Such thoughts and political conclusions are the logical expression of geographical sense among British seafaring peoples who look at the sea and at sea routes as their life arteries and highways. Only to continental and land-bound nations the sea appears as a barrier to intercourse.

THE NORTH ATLANTIC AS LINK BETWEEN EUROPE AND THE AMERICAS

In terms of geographical realities, the concept of the Americas allegedly bound together by a hemispheric solidarity is influenced by such continental thinking. It neglects the growth, during the last three centuries, of the North Atlantic Ocean as a core area of western civilization and the resulting fact that the links across it between northwestern and southwestern Europe on the east and north and South America to the west have become more important than any of the great transcontinental routes. It

[48] V. Massey, "Canada and the Inter-American System," *Foreign Affairs* (1948), pp. 693-701.
[49] *Ibid.*
[50] L. Gelber, "Canada's New Stature," *Foreign Affairs* (1946), p. 287.

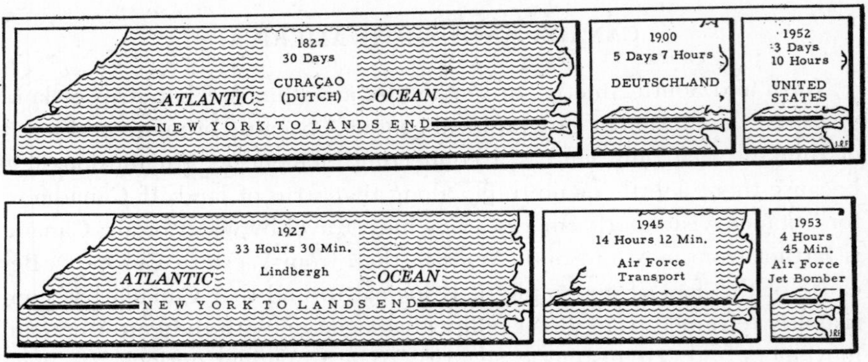

Fig. 8-13. The Shrinking of Main Water Bodies in the Light of Technological Progress (after New York Times).

is not incidental that, in stressing this basic geographical and historical trend, a British geographer, C. B. Fawcett, emphasized that "there is now in many cases a greater unity of culture and traditions, and a greater volume of intercourse, between countries on opposite shores of the Midland Ocean than between others situated on the same continent and separated by a shorter distance. Probably both Argentina and Colombia have more in common with Spain than they have with each other. Norway has more contacts with North America than with Italy. Portugal is more closely linked with Brazil than with central Europe." [51] And Portugal and Spain rank among Iceland's main customers, as the sea is not a separating barrier but a natural link which is important in their respective economies.

ECONOMICS AND THE MYTH OF THE CONTINENTS

Economic sense based on geographical realities has consistently taught that the oceans are broad highways of commerce serving to connect rather than to divide or separate. The normal exchange of bulk commodities between any two political entities with equal access to both sea and land routes has always been accomplished with the greatest ease and lowest cost by sea. In terms of "cost distances," the spatial relationships between, for instance, New York City and either continental or overseas points appear altogether different from those which present themselves if we neglect the cost factor and compare distances only.

[51] C. B. Fawcett, "Life Lines of the British Empire," in Weigert-Stefansson-Harrison, *op. cit.*, pp. 238-249.

The cost of shipping one hundred pounds of wheat by rail from Kansas City to New York in 1939 was 33½ cents to 42½ cents, while it cost only 13 cents to ship the same wheat from New York to Liverpool, a distance three times as great. In the same year it cost only $1.50 to ship a bale of crude rubber from Singapore to New York as against a cost of $1.03 to ship a similar bale from New York to Akron, Ohio by rail, even though the latter distance is only 1/25 that of the former.[52]

From these examples it is evident that, in terms of wheat and rubber distances, Liverpool and Singapore are closer to New York than are Kansas City and Akron. The significance of these relationships in economic geography has been summarized by Eugene Staley in the following manner: "Land connections, which would appear to establish easy contact between peoples on the same continent, may be barriers as well as connections, while bodies of water, appearing superficially on the map as barriers, may actually be the most important connecting links. Because this has been so distinctly true in the past, the existing patterns of culture, tradition, political affiliation, and economic interdependence which confront us in the world of today are as often oceanic as they are continental."[53] Technological progress in sea transportation, as indicated in Figure 8-13, has rapidly accelerated the shrinking process of the connecting links of bodies of water.

The most vivid illustration of the problem in its application to inter-American economic relationships was offered by Costa Rica which, "when it suffered a shortage of rice had found it cheaper to import from Saigon via Hamburg and the Panama Canal than to get it from Nicaragua, a stone's throw away."[54] Grotesque situations such as the one described here served to promote the Inter-American Highway project in which the unrealized dream of a Pan-American Railway had shifted to the more feasible goal of joining the existing roads and trails to form a continuous modern highway.[55]

[52] E. Staley, "The Myth of the Continents," in Weigert and Stefansson, *op. cit.*, p. 93.

[53] Staley, *op. cit.*, p. 96.

[54] M. E. Gilmore, "Pan-American Highway," *Foreign Commerce Weekly* (October 20, 1945), p. 42.

[55] It should be emphasized that large sections of the highway which will eventually extend from the United States-Mexican border to the southern tip of South America are still in the blueprint stage. At the lowest estimate in 1955 at least fifteen years will pass before the entire route of the Pan-American Highway will be finished. Only the Mexican section is virtually completed. The next steps are to fill gaps in the 1,590 mile road through Guatemala, Honduras, El Salvador, Nicaragua, Costa Rica, and Panama. See also p. 670 and Fig. 22-1, 2, p. 670.

A clear understanding of the role of the sea in economic terms and an application of the surrounding principles to the Western Hemisphere make it easier to appreciate the geographical reality that the North and South American continents are really overseas in relation to each other, and that, in terms of shipping distances, their great commercial centers are respectively closer to Northwestern and Southwestern Europe than they are to each other. Such an understanding, moreover, helps to explain in geographical terms why the economic, political, and cultural roots of the various American states are more closely bound to the soils of Europe than to each other. It is in the light of such geographical realities as these that we must view the attempts to define this Western Hemisphere of ours.

THE MYTHICAL BOUNDARIES OF THE WESTERN HEMISPHERE: ICELAND

A good illustration of the insurmountable difficulties confronting any attempt to draw the boundaries of the Western Hemisphere in strictly geographical terms is afforded by Iceland which, in the spring of 1956, decided to press for the liquidation of the NATO base at Keflavik, halfway between Moscow and New York and of vital importance to the Free World as it controls the northern approaches to North America (*cf.* Fig. 8-10). When, on July 7, 1941, American troops took over the protection of the island of Iceland, which at that time, and until June 1944, was still formally part of Denmark, President Roosevelt declared in a message to Congress: "the United States cannot permit the occupation by Germany of strategic outposts in the Arctic for eventual attack against the Western Hemisphere. Assurance that such outposts in our defense frontier remain in friendly hands is the very foundation of our national security."

We chose this example because it shows how, in the words of President Roosevelt and in similar pronouncements by American statesmen and military men in the years that followed, the terms "This Hemisphere" or "The Western Hemisphere" were used as if they were clear regional concepts, on the basis of which it could be defined geographically how far the United States should go in defending its security zone. Actually, Iceland is a good case in point because in recent years it has been often and vainly argued among statesmen and geographers whether Iceland is part of the Western or Eastern Hemisphere. Before, approximately, 1930 nobody doubted that because of the facts of human geography Iceland belonged to Europe.[56] From a physiographic point of view it belongs neither to Europe nor America, but is a typical oceanic island; only for geometricians was it always in the Western Hemisphere. Vilhjalmur Stefansson has suggested that one "de facto" boundary between the Eastern and Western Hemispheres should be "the middle of the widest channel" in the Atlantic Ocean between the American continents on the one hand and the European and African continents on the other [57] (Fig. 8-14). This boundary would run to the east of Iceland, but such a geographical delineation would not conform to the political boundaries of our day. The Rio Treaty of 1947 tried to redraw the boundaries of the Western Hemisphere by including in its compass the entire American land mass, the Antarctic, the Aleutians, Newfoundland and Greenland; but Iceland was left out. The reason for this omission was entirely political. At the time the treaty was drafted, the danger that these fictitious boundaries would overlap with those of the Soviet Union seemed even greater here than elsewhere.

As the map shows, the easternmost edge of Greenland extends beyond the easternmost edge of Iceland, which fact would tend to refute the popular assumption that Greenland is within the Western and Iceland within the Eastern Hemisphere (Fig. 8-15).

Suppose geographers and statesmen alike were to agree on a "middle of the widest channel" rule for determining the Atlantic boundary between the hemispheres; what then of the Pacific boundary? Stefansson's suggestion does not offer a solution because it is based on confusion of the geometrical and the metaphorical meaning of the term *hemisphere*. Thus he asserted that any hemisphere must by definition include one-half of the terrestrial globe, while overlooking the fact that such a mathematical hemisphere is always limited by "great circles." His projection of the *de facto* boundary of the Atlantic to the region of the Pacific is, geometrically speaking, not a projection but an attempt to arrive at a symmetrical construction without the indispensable axis. It would result in the inclusion within the Western Hemisphere of parts of Siberia, the islands of Micronesia and Melanesia and all of New Zealand (*cf.* Fig. 8-14).

[56] Even during the early phase of World War II, Franklin D. Roosevelt is reported to have rejected the State Department's view that Iceland was "largely" (?) a part of the Western Hemisphere. He is supposed to have based this rejection on the interesting theory that "the strain on the public idea of geography would be too severe." (B. Rauch, *Roosevelt From Munich to Pearl Harbor* [New York, 1950], pp. 194-196, as quoted in A. P. Whittaker, *The Western Hemisphere Idea: Its Rise and Decline* [Ithaca, New York, 1954], p. 160.)

[57] V. Stefansson, "What Is the Western Hemisphere?" *Foreign Affairs* (1941).

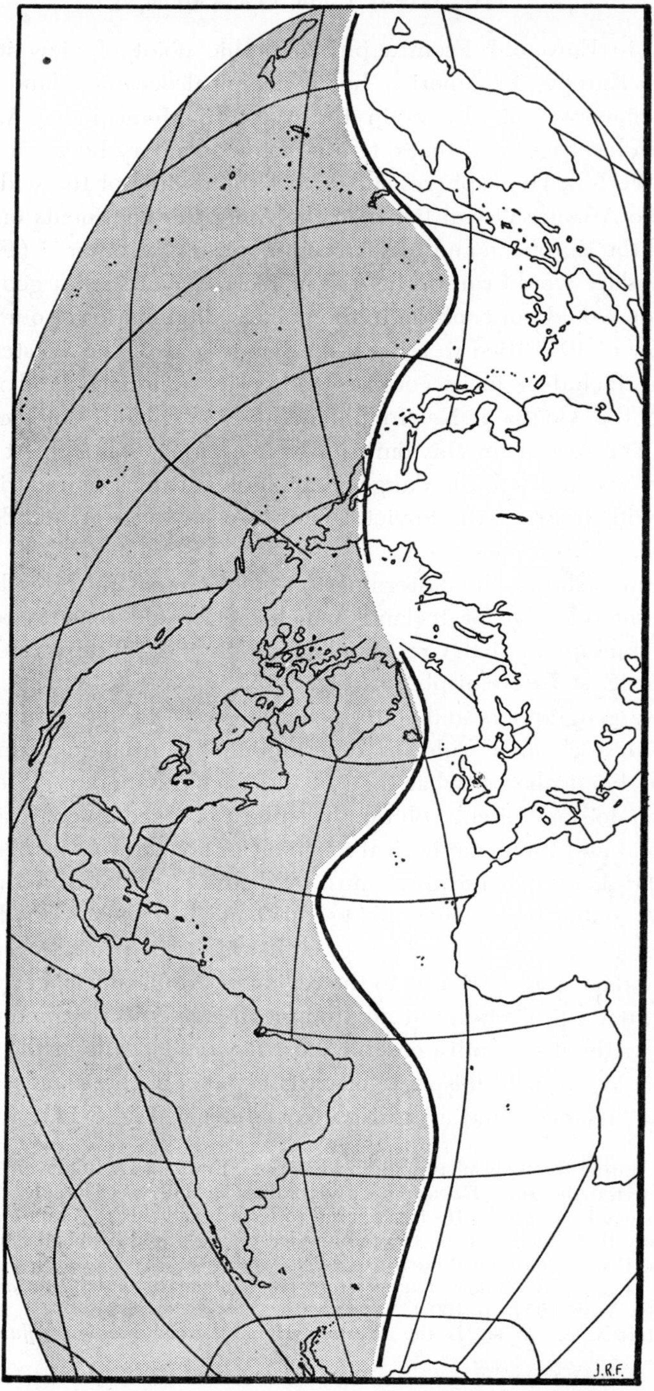

FIG. 8-14. The Boundary Between the Eastern and Western Hemispheres According to V. Stefansson.

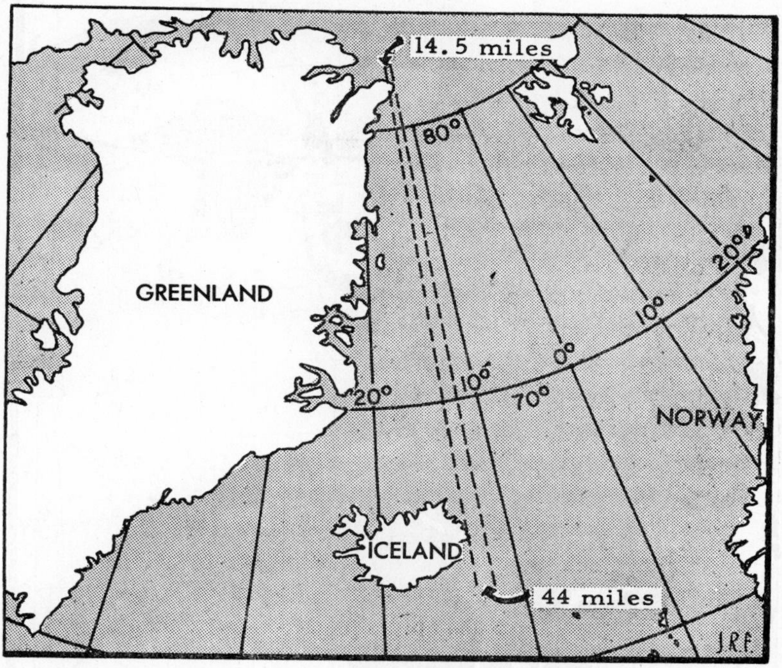

FIG. 8-15. Greenland and Iceland between the Eastern and Western Hemispheres.

THE HEMISPHERE IN MATHEMATICAL AND POLITICAL GEOGRAPHY

The confusion surrounding the proper place of Iceland on the political map of the hemispheres illustrates the fact that extreme caution is required in the use of certain types of maps for the purpose of proving points which are only seemingly geographical but are actually political. In particular, one should not confuse the metaphorical use of the term "hemisphere" with the well-established method of dividing the world into two symmetrical halves for mathematical purposes. The selective term *Western Hemisphere* for one such hemisphere defies definition in terms of mathematical geography. To grasp the term *Western Hemisphere* as one of human geography, and especially of political geography, one must be constantly aware that its human and political connotations account for the fact that its content is subject to continuous change. If one realizes this fact one will understand that it is a dangerous fallacy to confuse the Western Hemisphere clichés with the static concepts of mathematical geography. This realization is an important step toward a better

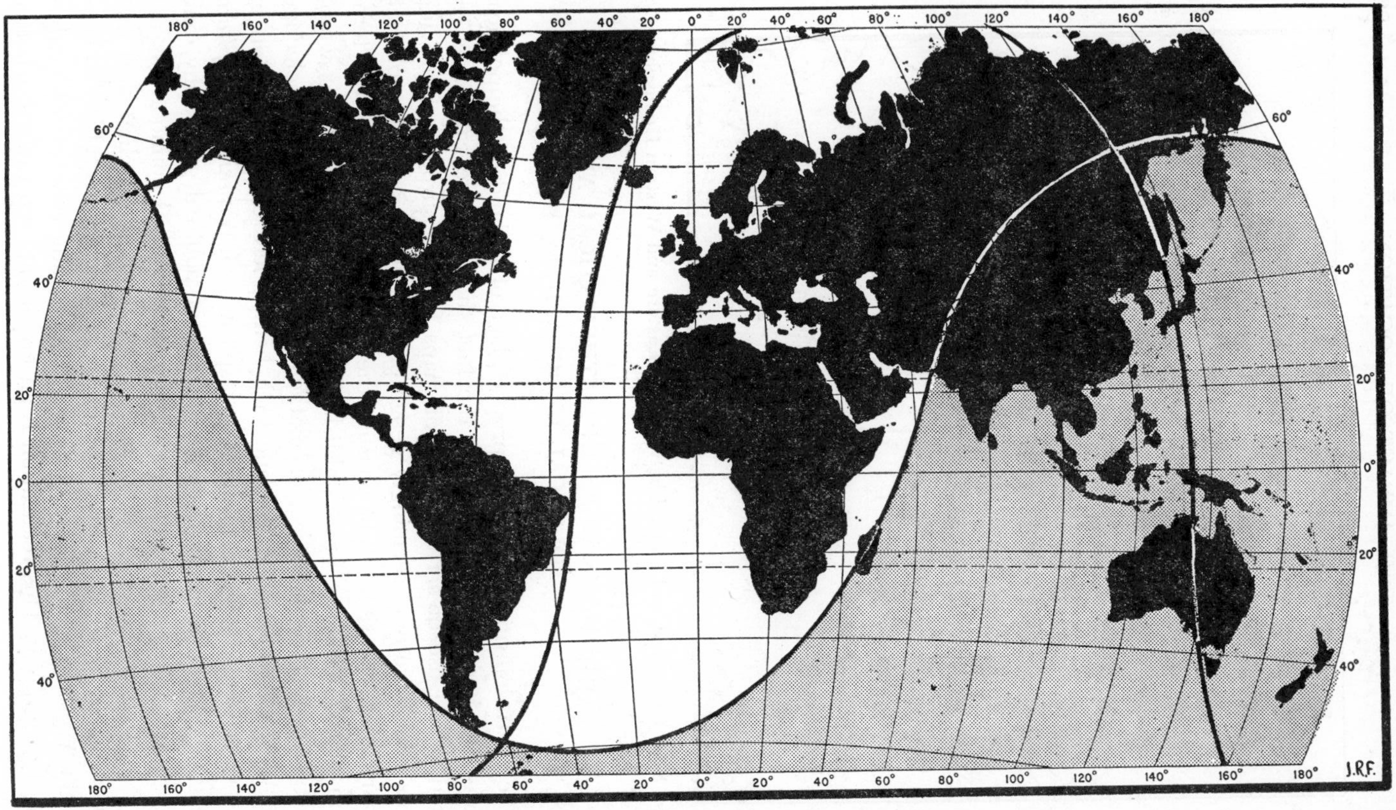

Fig. 8-16. The "American Quarter Sphere" (Boggs).

understanding of the politico-geographic factors which govern the foreign policy and the military strategy of this country.

"THE AMERICAN QUARTER-SPHERE"

In an effort to find a compromise between the mathematical and metaphorical concepts of the Western Hemisphere, S. W. Boggs [58] has offered an interesting solution. It consists in boiling down the "Western Hemisphere" to an "American Quarter-Sphere" (Fig. 8-16). Its boundaries are arrived at by taking the western half of a hemisphere centered in the Atlantic Ocean at 28° north, 31° west. The dividing center line deviates slightly from true north and south, passing through Denmark Strait, between Greenland and Iceland, and just east of the bulge of Brazil. The quarter-sphere to the west of the line contains all of continental North America, the islands to the north, even a piece of eastern Siberia, and all of South America. Sea power enthusiasts of the Mahan School would be reluctant to adopt this quarter-sphere as a useful American security zone, because its arrangements omit Iceland, most of the Aleutians, the Hawaiian chain, and Antarctica. They would further object to the exclusion of most of the Atlantic and Pacific water masses. This may serve as one more argument in favor of the thesis that no arbitrary imposition of a geometrical form on the tortured configuration of the continents will result in a usable political and geographical definition. "The atlas makers are the real creators of this artificial dilemma—they cannot free themselves from the ancient habit of dividing the world into two symmetrical halves." [59]

IDEOLOGICAL FACTORS: ARGENTINA AND THE UNITED STATES IN THE WESTERN HEMISPHERE

In addition to the geographical factors which argue against the unity of the Western Hemisphere, the objective of hemispheric integration is defeated by power factors which are economic, political, and, as a combination of both, ideological. When, in 1942, Nicholas J. Spykman analyzed the World War II realities of power relations in the Western Hemisphere, he focused his attention on United States-Argentine relations and warned that social, economic, and political forces combined with geographical remoteness to make Argentina a natural opponent of the United States

[58] S. W. Boggs, "This Hemisphere," *Department of State Bulletin* (May 6, 1945); see also his reappraisal, in 1954, in "Global Relations of the U. S.," *op. cit.* (June 14, 1954), pp. 903-912.

[59] Weigert-Stefansson-Harrison, *op. cit.*, p. 221.

and a determined resistant to United States-sponsored efforts at inter-American co-operation, whatever the surface appearance of harmony might be at any given moment.[60]

His observations of 1942 are still true today. Argentina's industrial development is blocked by deficiencies in iron and especially coal. However, her actual and, above all, potential strength as one of the greatest food-producing areas of the world has developed a proud and power-conscious feudal society which is determined to build its own power sphere in South America. Due to her distance from United States power centers, Argentina is economically and ideologically oriented toward Europe rather than to North America. Her dreams of empire as expressed during the Peron regime encompass in a "manifest destiny" area her neighbor Chile and the whole of the La Plata drainage basin, including the tributary zones in Uruguay, Southern Brazil, Paraguay, and Bolivia. The Argentinians, wrote Spykman in 1942, are determined that their state shall be the most important political unit on the southern continent and fully the equal of the United States in the Western Hemisphere.[61]

The growth of the "manifest destiny" concept in Argentina which militates against a Western Hemisphere-solidarity ideology reveals itself even more clearly if one realizes that Argentina is a white man's nation, inhabited by settlers of Spanish and Italian descent, with ethnic minorities which stem from the United Kingdom, Germany, France, and the United States. It has no Negroes to speak of and there is little evidence of Indian racial heritage. The fact that Argentina is a white man's land, a "Europe Overseas," assumes special significance if one compares its ethnic composition with that of other nations of Latin America. The contrasting population patterns of racial inheritance among, for instance, Argentina, Brazil, and Mexico, together with the related linguistic differences, defeats the very idea of a hemispheric solidarity. Looking into the future, Fred A. Carlson summed up the prospects of Latin America's racial structure as follows: [62]

> Argentina, Uruguay, southern Brazil, and the great central Brazilian plateau will become increasingly a white man's land; here the Indians will probably decrease in number and importance. The Pacific countries, Peru, Bolivia, Ecuador, and western Colombia, will become the home of an increasingly homogeneous amalgamation of the existing Spanish and Indian races, tending toward the predominance of the Indian. Chile, particularly its central valley, will remain largely white. The northern and northeastern coasts of Colombia, Venezuela, the Gui-

60 N. J. Spykman, *America's Strategy in World Politics.*

61 *Ibid.*, p. 58.

62 F. A. Carlson, *Geography of Latin America*, 3rd ed. (copyright, 1943, 1946, 1952, by Prentice-Hall, Inc., New York), pp. 15-16. Reprinted by permission of the publisher.

anas, and far north Brazil will become areas of increasingly homogeneous combinations of the prevailing white and Indian races, with considerable proportions of Negro blood, unless the Negroes come in larger numbers from the Caribbean islands. The eastern coast of Brazil north of Rio de Janeiro will remain heavily Negro, and the far interior valleys and plateaus will remain predominantly Indian. There never has been, there is not now, and probably there never will be a homogeneous race of people on the South American continent.

This racial pattern, today and in the future, with all its elements of disunity if one looks at Latin America as a whole, and with all its elements of unity if one focuses on the "white" nations of what Peron, Argentina's ex-President, called the "Southern Union," forms a formidable fundamental of Argentina's separate power sphere and of her ambition to be the nucleus of a "Greater Argentina"—the big brother in a union of nations including Bolivia, Paraguay, Uruguay, and eventually Chile and Peru.[63] Whether or not these plans will take a firm political form, the fact remains that the elements of cultural, especially ethnic and linguistic, disunity deepen the gap of geographical divides between the countries of the Western Hemisphere.

THE WESTERN HEMISPHERE AS A POLITICAL REALITY

If the Western Hemisphere is not a geographical reality, if it is far from having achieved political unity and cultural uniformity among its nations, it is still a very much alive political reality. To understand the meaning of the latter we must accept two essential concepts: (1) that we cannot define it in purely geographical terms; (2) that because it is a political concept its meaning and extent cannot remain fixed but will be constantly fluctuating. Politically the Western Hemisphere has its strongest roots in the Monroe Doctrine which is often loosely identified with the Western Hemisphere. Yet this term was not employed in President Monroe's message to the Congress in 1823, and the terms "The American continents" and "this hemisphere" were used synonymously.[64] The history of the Monroe Doctrine in recent years clearly indicates the extent to which the Western Hemisphere, as a political reality, is constantly changing, and the extent to which the two concepts are intimately associated with what the United States considers to be its major security area.

In theory the wording of the Monroe Doctrine is broad enough to cover

[63] Olive Holme, "Peron's 'Greater Argentina,' and the United States," *Foreign Policy Reports* (December 1, 1948), pp. 159-171.

[64] Spykman, *America's Strategy in World Politics*, p. 58.

both of the American continents. In practice, from 1823 to 1935, interpretations of the doctrine were applied virtually without exception to the region of the Caribbean. It was Franklin D. Roosevelt who inaugurated the idea of the multilateral extension of the doctrine when in his speech at Buenos Aires late in 1935 he declared that non-American states seeking "to commit acts of aggression against us, will find a Hemisphere wholly prepared to consult together for our mutual safety and our mutual good." Two years later, in a speech at Kingston, Ontario, Roosevelt gave assurance to the people of Canada that "the people of the United States will not stand idly by if domination of Canadian soil is threatened by any other empire."[65] By these two executive pronouncements the Monroe Doctrine was extended over a far greater geographical area than before.

The onset of World War II brought further expansions of "this hemisphere" of Monroe's. In October of 1939 the First Meeting of the Foreign Ministers of the American Republics was held and from this meeting there came the Declaration of Panama; a pronouncement clearly associated with the Monroe Doctrine and the security zone of the United States. The declaration proclaimed a "safety belt" around the American continents south of Canada. This "safety belt" ranged from approximately 300 to 1,000 miles in width and was designed to restrict naval warfare on the part of the European powers within its limits.[66] In 1940, Newfoundland and Bermuda were added to the newly-defined American security area as a part of the destroyer-bases agreement with the United Kingdom. In 1941 the area was again extended and further fortified by the occupation of Greenland. In the same year South America beyond the bulge of Brazil was effectively brought within the security zone through the negotiation of agreements with Uruguay, Brazil, and Argentina concerning the use of their ports by ships of the United States Navy. All of these political actions were taken on the basis of the Monroe Doctrine.[67]

Towards the close of World War II, the multilateralizing process begun by President Roosevelt in 1936 culminated, through the Act of Chapultepec, in the establishment of a rudimentary Pan-American defense community. This act of March, 1945 (which was not initially signed by Argentina) in effect made all of the American states co-guardians of the

[65] T. A. Bailey, *A Diplomatic History of the American People*, 4th ed. (New York, 1950), p. 740. Roosevelt later denied that his statement was meant to extend the Monroe Doctrine to Canada on the grounds that he did not interpret the doctrine as excluding Canada.

[66] *Ibid.*, p. 763.

[67] D. Perkins, "Bring the Monroe Doctrine up to Date," *Foreign Affairs* (1942), pp. 253 ff.

Doctrine, even against an American aggressor.[68] The regional collective security system first set forth at Chapultepec was formalized two years later on a permanent treaty basis at Rio de Janeiro. Article 4 of the Rio Treaty (sometimes known as the Petropolis Reciprocal Assistance Treaty, or Inter-American Treaty of Reciprocal Assistance) vividly demonstrates how far the Monroe Doctrine has been broadened since 1936 in terms of the extent to which the United States, as the major treaty power, is willing to go to defend "this hemisphere" of Monroe's. Article 4 defines in exact geographic terms the area to which the treaty applies, as follows:

> The region to which this Treaty refers is bounded as follows: beginning at the North Pole; thence due south to a point 74 degrees north latitude, 10 degrees west longitude; thence by a rhumb line to a point 35 degrees north latitude, 50 degrees west longitude; thence due south to a point 20 degrees north latitude; thence by a rhumb line to a point 5 degrees north latitude, 24 degrees west longitude; thence due south to the South Pole; thence due north to a point 30 degrees south latitude, 90 degrees west longitude; thence by a rhumb line to a point on the Equator at 97 degrees west longitude; thence by a rhumb line to a point 15 degrees north latitude, 120 degrees west longitude; thence by a rhumb line to a point 50 degrees north latitude, 170 degrees east longitude; thence due north to a point in 54 degrees north latitude; thence by a rhumb line to a point 65 degrees 30 minutes north latitude, 168 degrees 58 minutes 5 seconds west longitude; thence due north to the North Pole.

When one surveys the vast expanse of land and sea covered by the terms of this article, and considers it in terms of United States security, one finds that never before "has the Monroe Doctrine been given in practice the wide construction which its language suggests, and never before have such wide and varied activities been conducted over so large a geographical area with the object of endowing it with physical force." [69]

It would be improvident to assume that the Western Hemisphere, as a political concept, has reached the limit of its expansion. It would be equally improvident to assume that at some future time it may not contract. Its destinies are not "manifest" but are subject to the political exigencies of different times and varying power situations. It should, however, be realized that so long as the Western Hemisphere concept is predicated upon the leading political and military position of the United States, it will fluctuate as a political reality insofar and as often as geographical relationships between the United States and the rest of the world continue to change.[70, 71]

[68] Bailey, *op. cit.*, p. 837.
[69] Perkins, *loc. cit.*, p. 259.
[70] Early in 1953, an American historian, A. P. Whitaker, delivered eight lectures at University College, London, which were published in book-form in 1954 under the title "The Western Hemisphere: Its Rise and Decline" (Ithaca, N. Y., 194 pp.).

THE AMERICAN "PERIMETER OF DEFENSE"

In a sense, such expansions or contractions of the Western Hemisphere mark "the passing of the American frontier" of the nineteenth and early twentieth centuries. When ex-President Herbert Hoover, in 1946, used the phrase "perimeter of defense," which he asked to be extended by holding on to the strategic bases established during World War II, a new, and by necessity vague, term in American political geography was established. It was a fresh attempt to define, or rather to describe, the post-World War II security zone of the United States, or as many saw it, the pre-World War III zone. As before, the effort produced at best a political term, the

---

To the historian, the Western Hemisphere looks exactly like the picture which its mythical entity presents to the geographer. Whitaker holds that the Western Hemisphere idea in its original form was based on geographical concepts, political ideas, and above all an anti-European isolationism, all of which is being rejected in North-American political thought today. Whitaker also points out convincingly that the Western Hemisphere concept was, after World War II, gradually replaced by that of the "Northern Hemisphere" which more and more captured political and strategic imagination in the United States. This is well illustrated by former Secretary of State Dean Acheson's address of December 30, 1951, in which he reviewed foreign policy developments in that year. While referring half-heartedly to the Western Hemisphere as "the foundation of our position in the world," he later modified this statement by describing the position of the United States as "lying in both the Western and Northern Hemispheres." In fact, most of his address dealt with areas of the Northern and Eastern Hemispheres (Whitaker, *op. cit.*, p. 175; see also the review by G. I. Blanksten, in *The American Political Science Review* (June, 1955), pp. 536-539.

[71] After completion of this text, the authors read what seems to them a most challenging study of the problems discussed in this chapter, S. B. Jones' *Global Strategic Views* (Geog. Review, Oct., 1955) and an unpublished report by the same author on "The Conditions of War Limitation," November, 1955. In regard to the strategic concept of the Western Hemisphere, Jones probes the reality of the Western Hemisphere and its self-sufficiency and defensibility. As a typical example of the deep-rooted uncritical Western Hemisphere idea as discussed above he mentions a report by a Senate subcommittee in 1954 (see *loc. cit.*, pp. 503, 504) which, starting with the premise that "we belong in the Western Hemisphere," demonstrates the present American dependence on sources of strategic and critical materials outside the Western Hemisphere but maintains that through stockpiling, exploration, subsidization, and scientific research the Americas could be made self-sufficient for a period of war. It is held that sea lanes to South America could hug the shore and be protected from enemy aircraft or submarines. "In the last analysis land transportation can be improved." Jones attacks the notion expressed by the subcommittee that Latin America is "our own backyard." He holds that the idea of a defensible Western Hemisphere rests in part on the use of a world map centered on the North Pole. This projection greatly exaggerates east-west distances in the southern hemisphere, giving the impression that Africa and South America are far apart. The defense of South America, Jones contends, "involves the control of Africa, which probably requires the defense of Europe and the Middle East. Thus the United States cannot contract out of trans-Atlantic commitments unless it is willing to shrink into North American isolation, and even that requires that the Canadians go along with us. Whether North America has the resources for military isolation is questionable."

meaning of which was subject to constant change from the very start. To define it geographically proved, because of its quality of fluidity, as impossible as was the case in regard to the boundaries of the mythical "Western Hemisphere."

To the student of political geography, the realization of the fallacy of the Western Hemisphere concept serves also as illustration of certain more general principles in political geography. What appears to the observer as a constantly moving line, marking the contours of this, the Western Hemisphere, or of the Perimeter of Defense, depicts equally the broader areas in which, at a given time, the United States is exposed to external pressure.

UNITED STATES OUTER DEFENSE MARCHES

Arnold J. Toynbee, in his *A Study of History,*[72] devotes a chapter to the stimulus of the human environment in cases in which the impact makes itself felt in the form of continuous external pressure. That chapter he calls "The Stimulus of Pressures." In it he sets out to show that, in terms of political geography, the people, states, or cities which are exposed to such pressure fall, for the most part, within the general category of "marches." Marches are the outer provinces, or in the case of the offshore perimeter, the coastal or island defense bastions where the onslaught of the enemy is expected and where the military planners will select the sites for strategic bases. Toynbee's work is a study in contrasts, and his survey turns from the parts played by marches in the histories of the societies or communities to which they belong, to the parts played by other territories of the same societies or communities which are situated geographically in their "interiors." The "law" derived from these comparisons is that the external pressure of the human environment upon a march provides a stimulus which gives the march predominance over the interior. The greater the pressure the greater the stimulus.

It is difficult to apply this concept to the far-flung outer bastions of the United States. But what is true for a compact land area, with its defense stations distributed through the marches bordering its perimeter of defense, is also true in regard to the perimeter of defense zones which, in a shrinking world, constitute the modern marches of the United States. Whereas the march concept of old is limited to such outer provinces within the geographical limits of a national community, the new marches, in which this country organizes its outer defense net and military spheres

[72] Vol. II (1934), pp. 112-208.

FIG. 8-17. The American Perimeter of Defense: Winter, 1955.

of interest, disregard national boundaries and extend to every place where a global strategy and agreement with members of the non-Soviet community pinpoint favorable sites for strategic bases. Thus the American perimeter-of-defense march, as shown in Figure 8-17, stretches from the Caribbean bases to Newfoundland, Greenland, Iceland, the United Kingdom, Denmark, Germany, France, Spain, Italy, the Azores, Morocco, Libya, Saudi Arabia, and finally to the North Pacific, to Formosa, Korea and Japan, until the circle closes in the Aleutians and Alaska. However, the circle, as it appears in the blueprints of the military planners, is far from complete in the actual picture of the world map of early 1956, as a look at the gap in the Middle East reveals.

This perimeter extends indeed far beyond the region defined by Article 4 of the Inter-American Treaty of Reciprocal Assistance.

UNITED STATES BASES OVERSEAS

The realization that the fictitious boundaries of the "Western Hemisphere" have crumpled and that the frontiers of our national security zone lie wherever United States interests are at stake compels us to focus attention on the far-flung, yet fluctuating web of military bases outside the continental limits of the United States. Clearly the security of the United States in two World Wars could not have been assured by military bases already existing or constructed on United States territory or on territory over which the United States had been granted trusteeship rights. Rather it became an ever-growing characteristic of the American military bases system that the protection of the American mainland was entrusted to bases overseas, the sites of which were made available to the United States by its allies and friendly nations. After World War II, the fortification of the United States' perimeter of defense was continued and intensified. The greater the distance of United States outposts from its mainland, the more did they serve their twofold purpose of denying access to the American mainland to the aggressor nation and of carrying the possibility of attack close to the nerve centers of the enemy. A security system which is essentially anchored in strongholds and outposts located in foreign territory differs of course basically from one limited to strongholds within the boundaries of one power, even if that power rules as large a territory as does the United States or the Soviet Union.

The rapid pace at which technological advances in the means of warfare have progressed during the last decades makes it necessary to reexamine and redraw, in shorter and shorter intervals, the shifting boundaries of the perimeters of defense of the large powers. This rapid pace is in contrast to the gradual development of the British bases system by which the Mediterranean was slowly made a British sea: Gibraltar became British in 1704, the Maltese Islands in 1800, and Cyprus in 1878.

Before World War II, the United States did not possess a far-flung net of bases in the Atlantic arena. Its bases in the Atlantic were limited to the defense of the Panama Canal area. Equally in the Pacific arena, the pre-World War II string of bases was altogether insufficient for the defense of the American mainland. Partially developed bases were available in the Hawaiian Islands and the Philippines, and base sites existed in Alaska, Guam, Wake, Samoa, and other minor islands. Furthermore, Japanese base establishments in mandated islands neutralized United States base sites in the Western Pacific, and the provisions of the Treaty Limiting Naval Armaments of 1922 precluded the development of bases west of the 180th meridian until after 1936.[73]

After the United States entered World War II, and continuing until the present, the United States undertook to extend vastly and to solidify a system of bases overseas, and, in the case of Canada, overland, under arrangements made with that country for the establishment of a future defense frontier in Northern Canada. But the emphasis of the United States' fortification of its perimeter of defense through military bases is on bases overseas, while the U.S.S.R., in contrast, found ample compensation for the lack of opportunities overseas by establishing bases in lands directly adjacent to her, either by military occupation or through the control of and collaboration with satellite governments in those spheres of interest.

Reaching far beyond the land spheres within its own sovereign territory, the United States has established an increasingly impressive net of strategic bases overseas which, in 1945, was reported as exceeding 400 war bases of various dimensions: 195 in the Pacific area; 11 in the Indian Ocean and the Near East; and 229 in the Atlantic area (18 of which were in the North Atlantic, 67 in the Gulf of Panama and the Caribbean, 25 in the South Atlantic, 55 in North Africa and the Mediterranean, and 64 in Great Britain, France, and Germany).

The important part which military bases of all kinds play nowadays in the political geography of any major power makes it necessary to define clearly the term *base*. A "base" is not synonymous with "port." While many of the strategic bases held by the United States are located in insular areas

[73] *Major Problems of United States Foreign Policy, 1948-1949,* The Brookings Institute, 1948, p. 124 ff. The treatment of military bases in the text is largely based on this source (pp. 124-129) and on H. W. Weigert, "Strategic Bases," in Weigert-Stefansson-Harrison, *op. cit.*, pp. 219-251.

or form a beachhead in foreign territory, the term applies not only to island bases and beachheads but equally to other foreign territories available for military operations. Consequently, a complete picture of strategic bases includes overland bases, as those in Canada, and occupied territories overseas, such as was the case during and after World War II, in Germany, Austria, Italy, Japan, and Korea, as well as those bases which were established under NATO agreements.

As the history of World War II shows, military bases have been established in order to serve a number of purposes, such as the protection of shipping lanes, the establishment of fuel and weather stations, and as springboards for offensive operations.

After Pearl Harbor, the United States took vigorous steps to increase and fortify its overseas bases organization to meet actual and potential threats by the aggressor nations, both against the American mainland and the shipping lanes which constituted the life arteries connecting it with its allies. Base sites were granted by friendly nations or were seized. Not less than 134 base sites were leased in 1939 from Panama (most of which were evacuated in 1948). In the Atlantic arena, the United States was forced by the requirements of global warfare to reach out far beyond the string of bases held in Puerto Rico, the Virgin Islands, in Guantanamo, Cuba, and eight locations under British rule. Bases were acquired in Iceland, Greenland,[74] the Azores, and on some minor Atlantic islands. In all these, the United States encountered considerable reluctance on the part of the powers whose territory was affected (Iceland, Denmark, and Portugal) to grant long-term base rights.

In the Pacific, the changing fortunes of the war against Japan determined the course by which the base net of the United States was organized. When Japan surrendered, the United States was entrenched in important base positions serving the dual purpose of fortifying the defense perimeter of the United States off the Asian coast and of preventing these base areas from coming under the control of a possible enemy.[75] Among these bases are the former Japanese mandated islands. Now called the "Territory of the Pacific Islands," they were designated in November 1948 a Strategic Trusteeship area of the United Nations, with the United States as the administering authority.[76] This area consists of 650 former Japanese islands in 96 island groups in the Marshall, Mariana, and Caroline island

[74] H. W. Weigert, "Iceland, Greenland, and the United States," *Foreign Affairs* (October, 1944).

[75] *Major Problems, 1948-1949,* p. 127.

[76] H. W. Weigert, "Strategic Bases," in Weigert-Stefansson-Harrison, *op. cit.,* pp. 226 ff.

groups. The total population was in 1955 about 62,000. Among these islands, the outpost of Okinawa, an island only 400 miles from the mainland of China and less than half the size of Rhode Island, assumed primary importance.[77] In the southern Pacific, the United States acquired base sites from the Philippines Republic for a period of 99 years and secured further bases in territories under the sovereignty or jurisdiction of Great Britain, France, New Zealand, Australia, and the Netherlands.

In the Far North, the most significant base developments took place in close co-ordination between Canada and the United States, once it was recognized that the rapid growth of air power had made the North Polar regions and the Arctic Mediterranean a focus of decisive military operations (*cf.* Fig. 8-11, p. 248). While it was not the objective of this discussion to list the various bases developed since the war, and often clouded in secrecy, attention is called to the fact that for the establishment of Polar bases not only the immediate military targets of offensive and defensive action against vital areas within the United States and Canada or the Soviet Union are essential. Equally necessary are considerations aimed at establishing stations for the maintenance of navigational aids, the collection of meteorological data, aircraft tracking and warning, and air-sea rescue systems.[78] In terms of geography, the base system in the Polar regions is, from the United States' point of view, characterized by the fact that a comparison of the Soviet Union base system in the Polar areas and that of the United States shows the latter at a distinct geographical disadvantage. The Soviet Union is in full sovereign control of its bases in the North. Even there, where these bases are on territory not under the sovereignty of the U.S.S.R., the control is complete. That applies to the former U.S.S.R. bases in Manchuria (Port Arthur, Darien), as well as to those in northern Korea, which loom as an ominous threat to the life lines linking the United States and Japan. The United States' position is dependent upon a co-ordination of her base system in Alaska with bases in northern Canada, Greenland, and elsewhere.

From a structural point of view, we have to distinguish between various types of bases. Some are permanent operational bases which are fortified and garrisoned in sufficient strength to hold against a major attack; others are limited operational bases which need not be garrisoned in normal times, but can be occupied in an emergency. No such base can be evaluated, as an integral part of the over-all security system of a nation or a

[77] Formosa became an operational base for the United States Air Force after the evacuation of the Taschen Islands by the Chinese Nationalists in February, 1955.

[78] *Major Problems, 1948-1949,* p. 128.

group of allied nations, without reference to other related bases. Thus the Pacific bases, if regarded as an organic entity, can be classified as Outposts (Southern Korea, Formosa), Principal Advanced Bases (Okinawa), Main Supporting Bases (Marianas), Secondary Bases (Japan, Philippines), and Backup Bases (Aleutians, Hawaii). Geographically they can be subdivided into seven groups (including outposts which are indirectly, through treaties, part of the United States defense system): (1) the Polynesian group (Hawaii); (2) the Micronesian group (Guam); (3) the Melanesian group (New Guinea); (4) the Northern Alaskan chain (Ryukyus); (5) the offshore islands along the China coast, including Japan; and (6) the Philippine Islands; and (7) Australia and New Zealand.

In the restless years following the end of World War II, the United States had slowly and reluctantly adopted a global strategy of defense, thus repudiating conflicting defense theories which were either continental or Western Hemispheric in character. The resolution to prepare for an "offensive projection of American strength by all possible means in all possible areas,"[79] is reflected in the continuously widening perimeter of defense which consists of a systematically growing net of American and Allied military bases. Except for a significant gap in the strategic Middle East region, this system had in 1954 succeeded in drawing an iron line around the land mass of the U.S.S.R. As we have shown above, this line developed, in 1955 and 1956, serious points of stress along its perimeter. In carrying out its program, the United States took the lead in organizing groups of states for their common defense and in establishing a procedure in the United Nations that would permit collective security action to be taken upon recommendation of the General Assembly. Consequently, it would be unrealistic if one would view the perimeter of defense of the United States solely in terms of United States bases. Instead one must consider it as realization of the extensive international commitments of the United States and of the major principle of its foreign policy, of universal collective security. The result is an intricate system of regional security and of collective self-defense arrangements; military bases overseas and overland are the visible expressions of such power projection abroad.

[79] *Major Problems of United States Foreign Policy, 1952-1953,* p. 159.

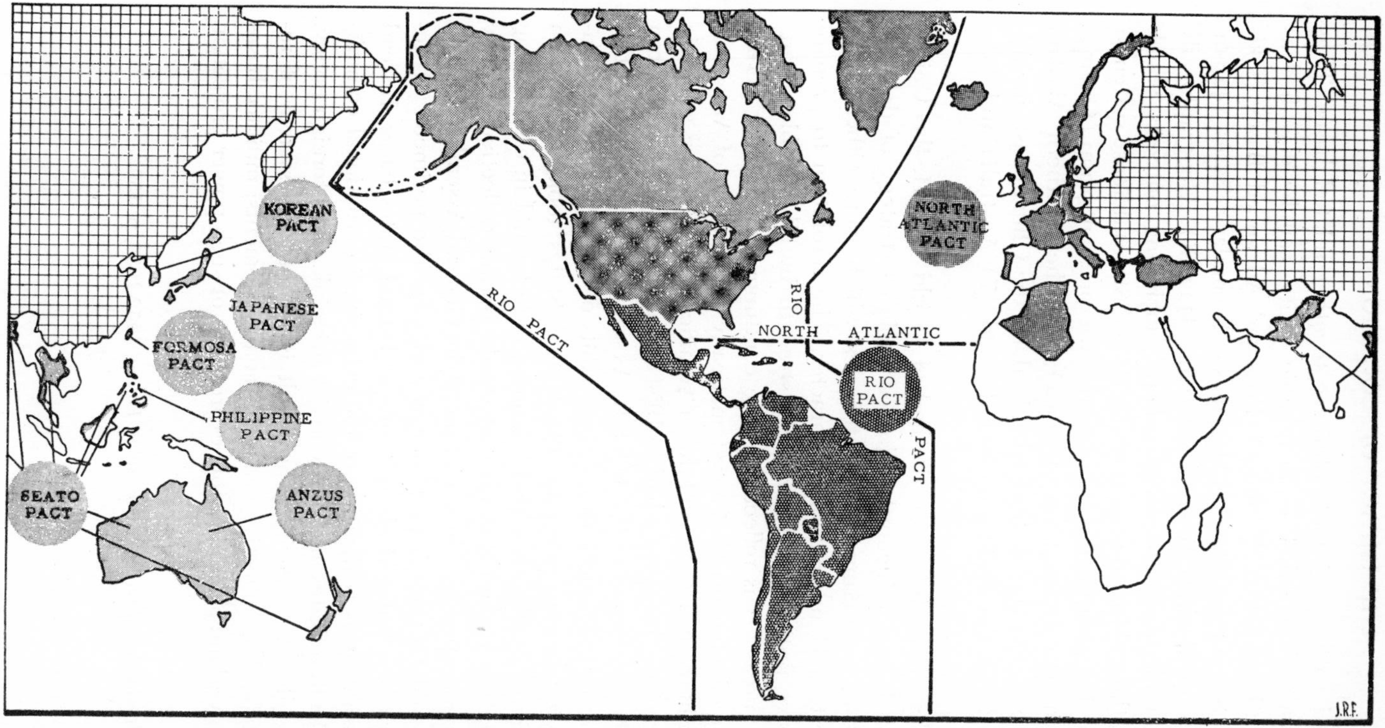

Fig. 8-18. The Western Security System. *North Atlantic Pact:* United States, Canada, Iceland, Norway, United Kingdom, Netherlands, Denmark, Belgium, Luxembourg, Portugal, France, Italy, Greece, Turkey, West Germany. *Rio Pact:* United States, Mexico, Cuba, Haiti, Dominican Republic, Honduras, Guatemala, El Salvador, Nicaragua, Costa Rica, Panama, Colombia, Venezuela, Ecuador, Peru, Brazil, Bolivia, Paraguay, Chile, Argentina, Uruguay. *Anzus Pact:* United States, New Zealand, Australia. *Philippine Pact:* United States, Philippines. *Japanese Pact:* United States, Japan. *Korean Pact:* United States, South Korea. *Formosan Pact:* United States, Formosa. *Seato Pact:* United States, United Kingdom, France, Australia, New Zealand, Philippines, Thailand.

INTERNATIONAL AGREEMENTS AS BASIS OF THE UNITED STATES DEFENSE AND SECURITY SYSTEM

The following commitments represent the basis of the American defense and security system:

Under the Rio Treaty of 1947 which we have discussed previously, the United States agreed that an armed attack on any one of twenty-one nations in the "Western Hemisphere" would be considered an attack against all and that each would then assist in meeting the attack. It is a significant limitation of the obligations, a limitation instrumental in defining the contours of important sectors of the American security belt, that it applies only within the security zone defined in the Treaty, which includes the North and South American continents and several hundreds of miles of the surrounding areas (Fig. 8-18).

The coming into being, in 1949, of the North Atlantic Treaty Organization overshadowed completely the defense system which had found expression in the Rio de Janeiro treaty of 1947. Here, too, the United States committed itself to far-reaching obligations within a defined security zone. But in linking, with the United States and Canada, nearly half the area and more than half the population of America to Western Europe, an alliance was formed which "is incompatible with the historic Western Hemisphere idea, an essential element of which was the separation of America from Europe." [80] As a comparison of the two security zones under the Rio and North Atlantic Treaties shows, these zones are not set apart but overlapping, with the North Atlantic Treaty zone in the role of an extension, however under different conditions, of the Rio Treaty security zone. The United States is obligated to regard an attack against any of the signatories within this zone as an attack against all of them. With the United States, every other signatory power is held to assist the attacked nation by taking "individually and in concert . . . such action as it deems necessary, including the use of armed forces." [81] If one follows the line indicating the extent of the North Atlantic Pact security perimeter, covering North America beyond Mexico, the North Atlantic Ocean, Western Europe (including West Germany which, while still unarmed, had joined NATO as a partner in the spring of 1955), a part of French North Africa, Greece, Turkey, and the Mediterranean, one realizes that this line falls

[80] *Ibid.*

[81] It should be noted that, as a counterpart to NATO, a Soviet military organization was established in May, 1955, which formalized corresponding obligations between the U.S.S.R. and its East European satellite states, as well as a unified military organization under a Soviet Union Commander in Chief, with its seat in Moscow.

considerably short of describing the extent of the United States perimeter of defense which relies on the military bases operated by it and friendly nations (see Fig. 8-18). To understand this discrepancy, one has to include in the picture of United States security arrangements additional obligations under the North Atlantic Treaty as well as certain regional arrangements.

If, in conjunction with the framework of complementary bilateral defense agreements, we review the geographical extent of the NATO organization as we find it established in 1955, we see that it has succeeded in establishing the fundamentals of a united western community of nations, without which, as Toynbee put it,[82] this community could not hope to survive "the siege of the West." In terms of heartland and rimland concepts, NATO has adopted the rimlands theory as a valid counterpart to strategic formulas originating in, and conditioned by the control of the Soviet heartland. If we concentrate on the North Atlantic and European arenas, as the heart of the NATO organization, we will find that they secure the vital arteries which link its members across the high seas and that they bar Soviet naval expansion and infiltration, especially by submarines. On the European mainland, the participation of the German Federal Republic paves the way for the defense of Europe which, without such participation, would remain saddled with a serious power vacuum. The West German membership in NATO will eventually bear fruit in the vital protection of the northern flank where Soviet expansion from the Baltic Sea into the North Sea must be barred. In the Scandinavian countries, Sweden's neutrality and the reluctance of Norway and Denmark to concede the stationing of foreign NATO contingents on their soil tend to weaken the structure. In the Mediterranean arena Turkey and Greece are the vital NATO rimland strongholds which stem Soviet aggression toward the Middle East, as does, among the Balkan countries, Yugoslavia. Its role is of greatest importance; in spite of its defense agreements with Turkey and Greece under the Balkan treaty of August 1954 at the time these lines are written, it can not be finally evaluated.[83] Spain, not a NATO partner but committed to the United States under a bilateral agreement, occupies highly important positions for naval and air bases, especially for the defense of the Straits of Gibraltar and North Africa.

Under the North Atlantic Pact, any attack outside the zones stipulated therein involves no other obligation than consultation. This consultative

[82] A. J. Toynbee, "The Siege of the West," *Foreign Affairs* (1955), p. 359 ff.

[83] If the Soviet Union carries out its pledge to withdraw its troops from Rumania and Hungary after the ratification of the treaty with Austria, such move would eliminate some of the major reasons for the existence of the Balkan pact.

commitment, however, is an integral and significant part of the over-all defense organizations since the interests and holdings of the United States, Great Britain, and France are on a global scale.[84]

Additional regional arrangements concluded in 1951 fortified the security position of the United States in the Pacific Arena. Under the Tripartite Security Treaty with Australia and New Zealand and the Mutual Defense Treaty with the Republic of the Philippines (expanding the 99-year military base arrangement of 1947), the United States agreed that an armed attack in the Pacific area on any one of the signatories would oblige each partner to aid in meeting the common danger. In the same year, the United States, under the Japanese Security Treaty of 1951, established the right to keep armed forces in Japan and to use them for the maintenance of peace and security in the Far East, while security arrangements with the Republic of South Korea remained in a state of fluctuation. In September, 1954, nations from far afield joined in Manila to sign an agreement aimed at stopping further Communist erosion in the wide expanse of Southeast Asia. The outcome was a broad defense organization for Southeast Asia, with its eight signatories (half of them members of the British Commonwealth), the United States, Britain, France, Australia, New Zealand, the Philippines, Thailand, and Pakistan, pledged to regard an armed attack against any of them, or against a designated treaty area, as a danger to the peace and safety of all of them. The partners are also obligated to consult on common defense measures in case such a danger arises from any other development besides armed attack from the outside, such as Communist subversion, *coup d'état,* or civil war on the Korean or Indochinese pattern. The geographical pattern of the SEATO members makes it clear that Australia and New Zealand, because of their proximity to an overpopulated Asia, are the powers most interested in increasing the military strength of the SEATO organizations.

This South East Asian Collective Defense Treaty (still called SEATO, in abbreviation of its original name, South East Asian Treaty Organization) is a much weaker structure than is NATO. This is evident from the fact that among its signatories some of the nations are missing which would be most directly threatened in their very existence by aggressive moves originating from Communist China: Indonesia, Burma, Ceylon, India, and in Indochina, Laos, Cambodia, and South Vietnam. Unlike NATO, SEATO is consultative, like the Anzus pact. Thus it falls considerably short of the more rigid NATO and in particular lacks a SHAPE as a unified military command and a combined military force; the treaty or-

[84] *Major Problems,* pp. 88-89.

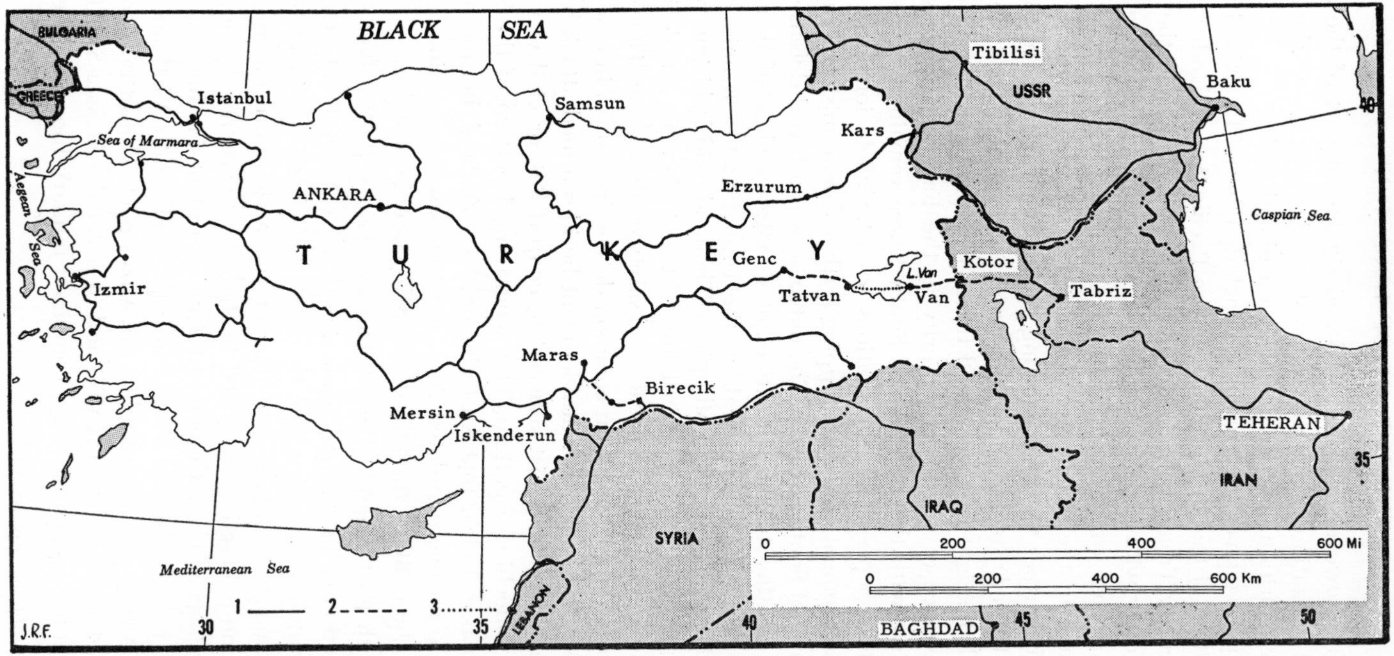

FIG. 8-19. Strategic Railroad Extension in Turkey and Iran: (1) existing railroads; (2) proposed railroads; (3) proposed lake ferry.

ganization is limited to a Council with broad functions in defense planning.

Large as the treaty area is—comprising Southeast Asia and the Southwest Pacific—its geographical limitations emphasize the fact that this structure rests on fundamentals which are temporary and far from being complete. The protected area includes not only the territories of the signatory powers but also the general area of Southeast Asia and the Southwest Pacific. A special protocol provides for the inclusion in the protected treaty area of the free part of Indochina. However, the treaty area is bounded in the north by parallel 21°30′ and thus passes south of Hongkong, Formosa, and of course Japan. In regard to these nations, direct commitments of the United States and, in the case of Hongkong, Britain, serve as substitutes for what ideally would be included in an all-embracing Pacific defense organization. With the passage by Congress of the Formosa defense resolution in January, 1955, a decisive step was taken in spelling out even more firmly the American perimeter of defense concept by defining the no-trespass line in the Formosa Strait. The resolution makes it clear to a potential enemy that there are specific areas which the United States would defend with force rather than cede, even though at the time this is written, the issue of the defense of the off-shore islands of Matsu and Quemoy looms large and ominously.

It is in the nature of a network based on regional agreements with friendly powers that its strength varies regionally and that the line which signifies the extent of the perimeter of defense is constantly changing. At present, the weakest part of the perimeter, from the United States' point of view, is along the northern tier of nations in the Middle East, between Turkey and Pakistan, with the weak links of Iran and Iraq between them (Fig. 8-19).

At the end of 1955 it appeared that some progress had been achieved in the efforts to strengthen the northern tier by laying the groundwork for a security bloc which was to include Turkey, Iraq, Iran, and Pakistan. The groundwork was laid in February, 1955, when, in the Baghdad Treaty, Turkey and Iraq agreed to establish a mutual defense organization. Britain joined the pact in April and Pakistan in September, 1955. In October, 1955, Iran announced, in defiance of the Soviet Union which protested Iran's decision sharply, that it was ready to join the defense alliance.

However, in spite of the progress made in cementing the defense line across the Middle East's northern tier, through a chain of United States-supported defense treaty organizations and in particular through the

Baghdad Pact, this 3,000-mile front appeared late in 1955 as an ominously fluctuating barrier against Soviet expansion into the Arab world. This Arab world is far from being a united bloc and the issue of "neutralism" (kindled above all by resentment against the United States' policy towards Israel), has estranged Egypt and her allies (Syria, Saudi Arabia and Yemen) which have declared their opposition to the Baghdad Pact.

From the standpoint of the United States, a strengthening of the northern tier defense arrangement has been from the beginning an integral part of a policy aimed at perfecting its over-all perimeter of defense position. The efficiency and strength of this kind of security system based on collective security principles depends entirely on the degree to which the United States will have the full co-operation of its partners. As Secretary of State Dulles pointed out in March, 1954, the bases which serve in foreign countries are in general not usable as a matter of law, and as a practical matter are not usable, except with the consent of the countries in which the bases are located. Therefore, it is implicit in the United States' security system that it operates with the consent and acquiescence of the other partners who have helped to provide the facilities which create a sort of international police system.[85] Against the Soviet bloc of Communist-controlled countries, representing a vast central land mass with a population of 800,000,000, able, because of its central position, to strike at any one of about twenty countries along a perimeter of some 20,000 miles, the United States and the nations allied with her have developed a system of bases which is an integral part and a physical expression of their collective security system.[86]

THE COLOMBO POWERS

This discussion of the politico-geographical factors surrounding the collective security system of the United States in comparison with the opposing security structure of the Soviet bloc is not meant to suggest that the political world of today can be neatly divided into two power combinations, permitting the mapping, in terms of political and military boundaries, of the Free World versus the Communist World. Such oversimplification would be grossly misleading. The political world of Southeast Asia, above all, which cannot be fitted into the not even seemingly neat balance between the Free and the Communist World, at the time these lines are written defies any attempt at integrating it, or its major nations, with any

[85] *New York Times*, March 17, 1953, p. 5.
[86] John Foster Dulles, *Foreign Affairs* (April, 1953).

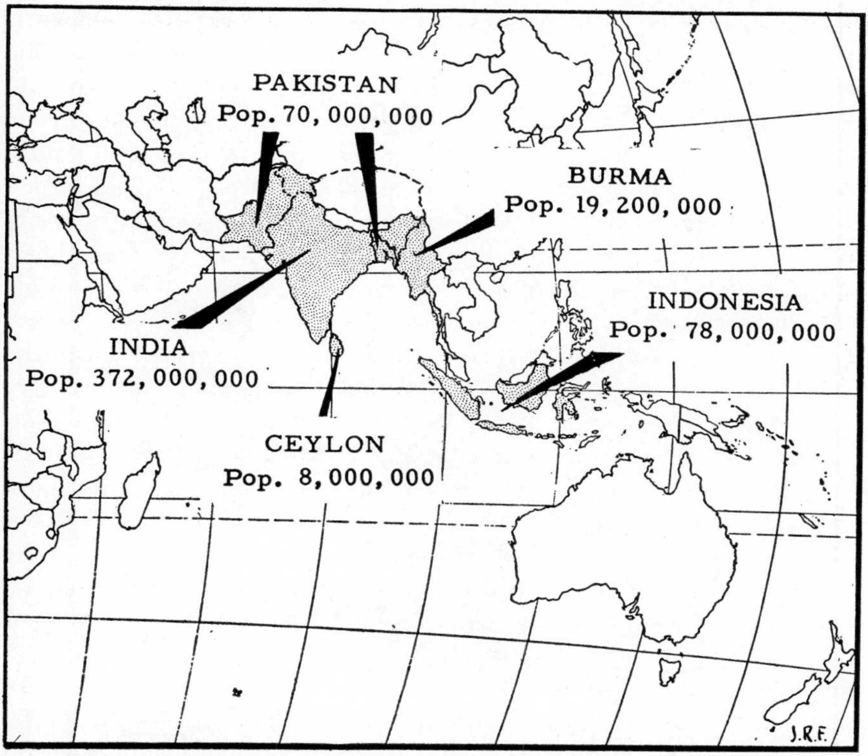

Fig. 8-20. The Colombo Powers.

degree of permanency in this scheme. In order not to be unduly impressed by the structures of base systems and regional security agreements, the importance of which for the defense system of the United States and her allied nations we have shown, we must include in our estimates the great potential power of such state systems as Pakistan, India, Ceylon, Burma, and Indonesia. In these new states, comprising a total population of about 550,000,000 (Fig. 8-20), we observe in the philosophy of the so-called Colombo Powers [87] a formative power-political grouping which cannot be identified with either the "East" or the "West." It is not, or not yet, in the nature of a bloc or firm alliance, but possesses nevertheless all the ingredients of a potential power combination which may prompt us in the fore-

[87] This group should not be confused with the economic grouping of the "Colombo Plan" which originated in 1950 for the purpose of mutual aid. At this time, the Colombo Plan embraces all Asian countries, except Formosa, South Korea, and Afghanistan, as well as Britain, Canada, Australia, and New Zealand.

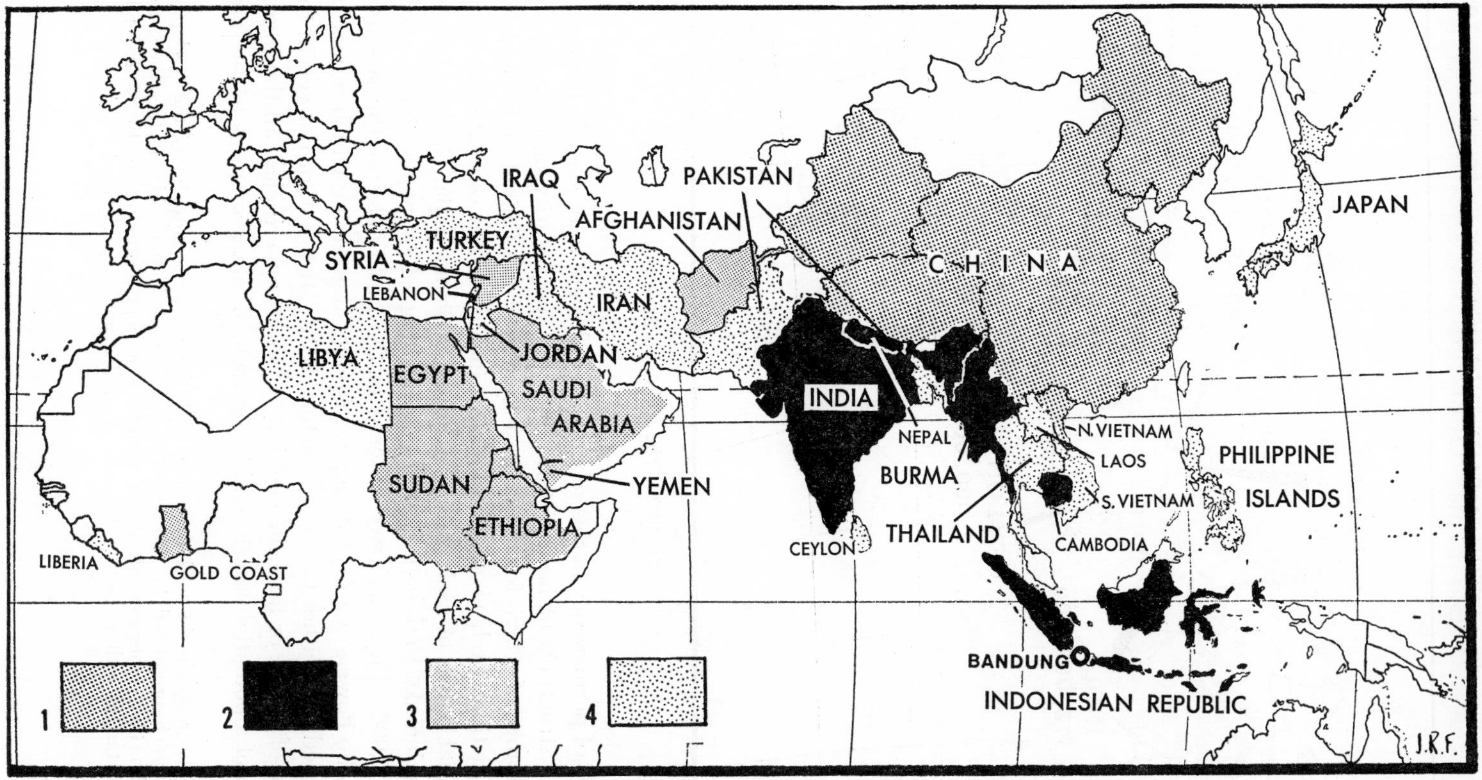

FIG. 8-21. Bandung Conference, 1955: (1) communist; (2) neutral; (3) uncommitted; (4) pro-West.

seeable future to re-draw the world map depicting the major spheres of influence of the Great Powers. Named after the city in Ceylon where the Premiers of the five members of this group first met, the Colombo Powers, while divided among themselves by many unsolved problems (as India and Pakistan) and while taking different positions in regard to their security policy toward Communist expansion (as Pakistan and Ceylon, which are considerably less neutral than were, in 1955, India, Burma, and Indonesia), these nations have in their policies enough in common to make them, and other states in Asia and Africa which they may attract in the future, the potential nucleus of a strong grouping with tangible binding features. At present, intangibles form the common base, above all the history of foreign colonial rule in which they share. Inspired by their resentment against colonialism in any form, these states are intent on determining the future course of Asian political destinies without influence from the outside. A broad extension of the sphere of nations subscribing to the general philosophy of the Colombo Plan powers has taken shape at the conference of Asian-African nations at Bandung, Indonesia. This meeting brought together delegates from twenty-nine nations comprising more than half of the world's population, and, in spite of many deep-rooted disparities in the realms of language, religion, ethnic composition, and culture, as well as differences in their political alignments and economic systems, united them by the common bond of being non-white nations who at some time in the past had been controlled by white colonial powers [88] (Fig. 8-21).

The first major combining action of the new "Anti-Colonial" bloc in the making occurred in October 1955 when the Bandung nations, aided by the Soviet groups and by scattered Latin American countries, pushed the issue of colonialism to the front of the United Nations' stage. They succeeded in having placed for general debate on the agenda of the General Assembly the questions of French Algeria and of Netherlands New Guinea claimed by the Indonesian Republic.

We cannot foresee whether and how what appears today as a loose power structure in the making will in the future affect the collective security system of the Free World and its perimeter of defense. But through the mist beclouding the future we can perceive the taking-shape of new political structures and groupings of great portent and impact. Their still nebulous contours confirm the need, so persistently stressed in these lines, for continuous re-evaluation of what on the political map of today appears seemingly as a firm and stable feature in the realm of politi-

[88] See pp. 532 ff., 551.

cal geography. Fluctuation and change are factors which enter invariably into any discussion and appraisal in the field of political geography. But certain basic factors of physical geography do not change, even though their conditioning effect on human affairs is subject to change. This general observation, which permeates all our discussions in this volume and which explains and justifies the study of political geography, has been expressed lucidly by Abraham Lincoln in his Message to Congress of December 1, 1862:

> A Nation may be said to consist of its territory, its people, and its laws. The territory is the only part which is of certain durability. One generation passes away, and another generation cometh, but the earth abideth forever. It is of the first importance to duly consider and estimate this ever-enduring part.

Part

2

THE HUMAN AND CULTURAL FACTOR IN POLITICAL GEOGRAPHY

CHAPTER 9

Population Growth and Pressure

The legal foundation of the state is its territory; but its reality exists only in its citizens—in their numbers, their distribution, their biological and demographic characteristics, their economic development, and their social institutions and cultural heritage. This chapter and the next deal with the population in terms of its numbers, distribution, movements, and demographic characteristics. Later chapters will consider cultural and economic factors in political geography.

We examine population in a study of political geography because people, like natural resources and other geographical factors germane to political power, are unequally distributed over the face of the earth. The human resources available to the several nations vary greatly both in size and quality.

Also, the human content of the national territory is forever changing, firstly, through the biological facts of birth and death and, secondly, through migrations. These changes are never exactly alike on the two sides of an international boundary. Thus there are everywhere changes in relative population and manpower that tend to shift the balance of power among the nations concerned.

Differential rates of growth create pressures against political boundaries. They create tensions in the increasing competition for the scarce resources of the earth. They provide the impetus for voluntary migrations and often the real motive in the forced expulsion or flight of refugees.

The following discussion examines these various aspects of population as an element of power and as a source of conflict. We shall first consider population *size* as an obvious element in national power. Second, we

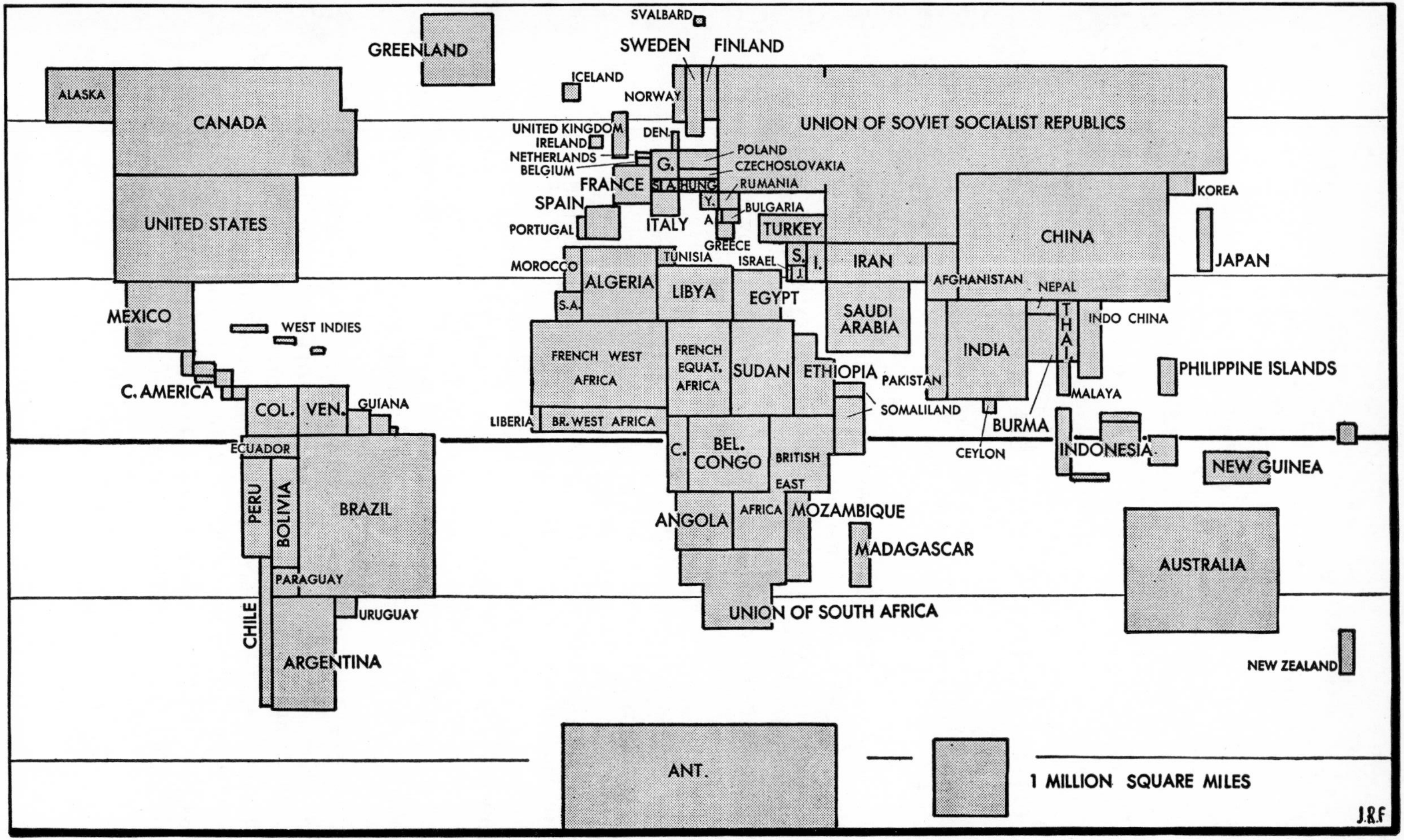

FIG. 9-1. World, Relative Land Areas (after Population Reference Bureau).

shall deal with the *distribution* of the population, which has much to do with the coherence and effectiveness of any given state or political constellation. Third, we shall consider population *growth* as a factor changing the locus and expression of power. Fourth, since numbers alone are not an adequate measure of the impact of population change, we will consider the population *structure* as a measure of the relative effectiveness of the population as the human resource base of political strength. Fifth, changes in population size and structure bring about population *pressure* against political boundaries, from areas of low economic opportunity to those of greater economic opportunity. Sixth, this pressure is released through *movement,* whether in the voluntary and primarily economically motivated migrations or in the forced migrations which pour across boundaries when the artificial dams imposed by political boundaries are breached.

A. *Size*

POPULATION VERSUS AREA

The ordinary political map of the world, and especially the Mercator projection in common use, very imperfectly reflects the real importance of the political entities portrayed. Even on an equal-area projection, which eliminates the gross distortion of the Mercator projection at the poles, Canada looms larger than the United States. Australia is larger than all of Europe west of the U.S.S.R. Argentina and India are about of equal size. The French colonies in Africa occupy a large and central position. These are facts, but for purposes of political geography, they represent only one dimension. Population is another dimension.

Figures 9-1 and 9-2 compare these two dimensions in schematic diagrams, one (Fig. 9-1) showing the nations of the world drawn in proportion to their areas, the other (Fig. 9-2), according to their population size. The first is a stylized equal-area map; in the second an effort is made to preserve the general geographical position of each country in relation to its neighbors.

The differences are striking. On the population map European countries assume a position much more comparable to their actual place in the world concentration of power. Great Britain, instead of being comparable to New Zealand or rather smaller than Madagascar, assumes its place as the most important of the British members of the Commonwealth. The map shows Asia for what it is: the principal home of mankind. Africa is shriveled to its proper proportion as the home of a relatively small percentage of humanity.

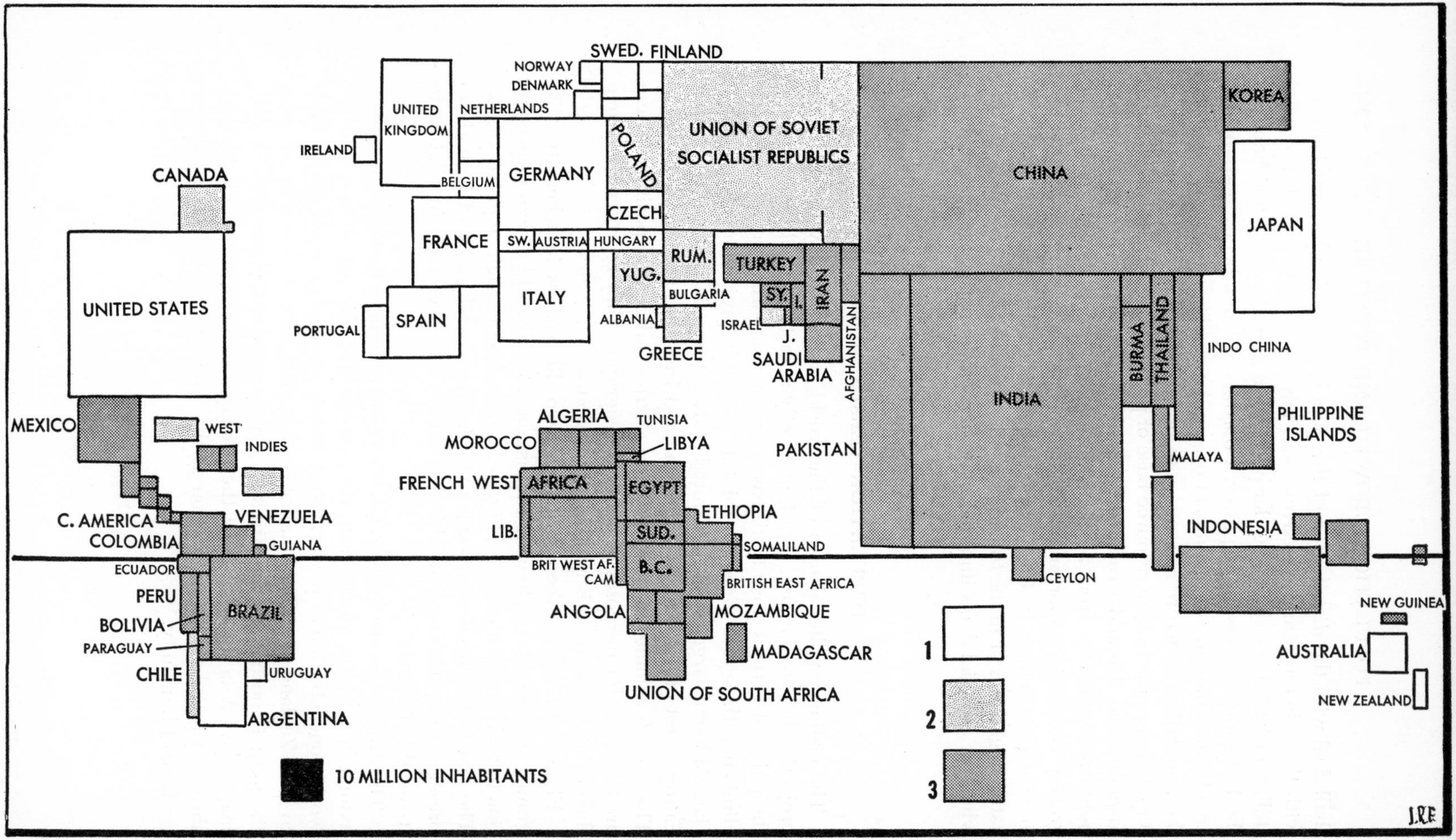

FIG. 9.3. World, Relative Population and Birth Rates: (1) under 25 per 1000; (2) 25-35 per 1000; (3) over 35 per 1000 (after Population Reference Bureau).

Few countries are even roughly comparable as shown in the two maps. The most conspicuous of these is the United States, where the population density approximates the world average. Most other countries are either much more densely or much less densely settled than the average.

NATIONAL ENTITIES

"After rechecking last year's census the National Bureau of Statistics in Peiping declared today mainland China's population, largest in the world, was 582,603,417, as of June 30, 1953." [1]

Such was the report of the first modern census taken in China. At that time the "official" figure used by the United Nations for China, including Formosa, was 463,493,000. A leading Chinese authority, Ta Chen, estimated the population of China at under 400 million before the Communist revolt. This range of some 200 million in the estimates illustrates the degree of ignorance of the true size of the population of this most populous country in the world.

There is no doubt, however, that China has the largest population in the world. If we may believe the published results of the 1953 census, China alone contains almost one-fourth of all mankind.

India, with 377 millions, is the other demographic giant of the modern world. Prior to the division of the Indian subcontinent between India and Pakistan, she was a rival to China in the sheer mass of her people.

The remaining several hundred political entities include countries of many million inhabitants and areas boasting only a few hundred persons.

After China and India come the two great continental powers, the U.S.S.R. with 200 million and the United States with 165 million. No other nation claims as many as 100 million inhabitants.

Clustered together as a third group in population size are three Asian powers of middle rank: Japan, with 89 million; Indonesia with 81 million; and Pakistan with 80 million.

The four principal powers of Western Europe are also of approximately equal population size: United Kingdom, 51 million; German Federal Republic, 50 million; Italy, 48 million; and France, 43 million.

Only one non-European country, Brazil, approximates these in size. With 58 million people Brazil is by far the most populous country in Latin America. Mexico, with 29 million, is the second Latin American country. Argentina, at the other end of Latin America, has 19 million. Spain, with

[1] Special dispatch to the *New York Times* from Hong Kong, November 1, 1954. Other population data in this section are from United Nations publications, especially the *Demographic Yearbook, 1955.*

29 million, and Poland, with 27 million, are the only other European countries with over 20 million inhabitants. There is a substantial gap between France (43 million), smallest of the world powers, and the numerous smaller nations and dependent territories.

Nigeria, with 30 million, is the largest political unit in Africa.

Five countries of Southeast and East Asia each have about 20 million inhabitants: South Korea, 22 million; Philippines, 21 million; Thailand, 20 million; Burma, 19 million; and the three Associated States of Indo-China together number perhaps 17 million.

Three Moslem countries of the Middle East each have over 20 million inhabitants: Turkey, 24; Iran, 21; and Egypt, 23. Egypt is much the largest of the Arab countries. Her population exceeds that of all the other members of the Arab League combined.

The bunching of states according to population size suggests that there may be some optimum or standard size of state under certain conditions.

The population of Asian powers is large, in keeping with the greater population of the continent. There are at least four distinct size classes of Asian states. The two giants, India and China, stand alone. Those of the second rank—Japan, Indonesia, and Pakistan—range only between 80 and 89 million. There are seven third-rank Asian and Middle Eastern powers whose populations fall within the narrow range of 19 and 24 million.[2] Aside from Afghanistan, with 12 million, the next group, including Ceylon, Taiwan, North Korea, Nepal and Saudi-Arabia, have 7 to 9 million inhabitants. Three smaller Arab states, Iraq, Syria, and Yemen, each have 4 to 5 million. The remaining Arab states—Lebanon, Jordan, and Libya—and Israel—each claim between one and two million.

The Asian and Arab states thus range themselves as follows:

MILLIONS (*population*)	NUMBER (*states*)
350-600	2
About 85 (80-89)	3
About 20 (19-24)	7
7-9	5
4-5	3
Between 1 and 2	4

The only Asian states that do not fall into these groupings are Afghanistan (12 million) and the four states in what was formerly French Indo-China. There has never been a census in the latter.

[2] Egypt, Iran, Turkey—21-24 million; Burma, Philippines, So. Korea & Thailand —19-22 million.

In Europe the pattern is apparent but less obvious:

200 million	U.S.S.R.
43-51 "	Leading Western Powers (4)
27-29 "	Spain and Poland (2)
8-17 "	Eastern European States (6)
3-11 "	Small Western Powers (10)

As noted earlier the chief Western European powers are now roughly equal in population, though the reunification of Germany would raise that country from 49 to 70 million. Among the smaller powers those of Eastern Europe are notably more populous than those of the West, which were founded in earlier periods of slower and more difficult transport and communication.

There is no comparable pattern among the political entities of Africa and of Latin America, perhaps because in both cases population size is determined as much by existing and former colonial divisions as it is by the indigenous natural regions.

Obviously population size alone, scarcely more than area, is not a sure indication of relative power. In some areas, such as Alaska, lack of population is obviously a strategic weakness. On the other hand, China and India might actually be more powerful if they had fewer people. The competition for scarce resources brought about by the sheer mass of population in these countries imposes a poverty that in many respects neutralizes mass strength. Conversely, relatively small countries, like those of Western Europe, have been able to maintain a leading power position by the effective use of their material resources on the one hand and by the maximum development of their smaller human resource through education, training, and organization.

B. Distribution

THE PATTERN OF WORLD SETTLEMENT

The illustration of population size in terms of continents and national entities, as in the preceding section, masks important aspects of population distribution as a factor in political geography. Distribution, as opposed to simple size of population, introduces a new dimension. This dimension is illustrated by Figures 9-1 and 2 which presents the world's population in relation to the major geographic and topographic features.

Perhaps the most striking fact about the spatial distribution of people is that the greater part of the world is very thinly settled or even entirely uninhabited—usually for very excellent reasons. About 40 per cent of the world's land area is no more densely settled than Alaska; that is, one person for each four square miles. Well over half the land surface of the globe is no more densely settled than Nevada, which has one and one-half persons per square mile.

The Arctic tundra of North America supports only a few thousand Eskimos, who are "concentrated" along many thousand miles of coastland. Huge interior areas are literally uninhabited. Similarly, the even larger Eurasian tundra now supports only a few thousand reindeer-herding nomads, except where mineral resources have attracted a small non-indigenous population. The sub-Arctic forest, the *taiga,* which stretches across North America and Eurasia in a belt five hundred to a thousand miles in width, has scarcely been penetrated anywhere by intensive settlement. The vast deserts and steppes of the American West, of Central Asia, of Asia Minor, of the Sahara, and of Australia have repelled close settlement over most of these enormous interior regions. Yet together these encompass close to half the land surface of the globe. This half of the world receives less than twenty inches of rainfall annually, which is usually insufficient to support profitable dry farming.

For quite the opposite reasons the Amazon and Congo Basins have resisted intensive human settlement. Here, there is too much rainfall. The tropical soils are leached of essential minerals necessary for high agricultural output. The cost of clearing jungle land is often excessive in terms of any realizable economic return.

In short, most of the world is too cold or too hot, too dry or too wet, too high or too low to provide the conditions suitable for intensive human settlement.

Most of us live in great clusters of population. Three-fourths of the world's people live in four of these clusters, those of East Asia, the Indian subcontinent, Europe, and Eastern North America. These four are roughly comparable in area and population, except that the population concentration in Eastern North America falls far below the other great centers of mankind.

East Asia (650-800 million people). This greatest concentration of humanity includes China, Korea, Japan, and the portion of Indo-China neighboring on China (Viet Minh). The high population density in North China and neighboring areas around the China Sea reflect the North Chinese origin of the civilization created by this largest mass of mankind.

The agricultural base of East Asian life is reflected in the extensive area of dense settlement. There are few major cities except in industrialized Japan. The Chinese and Korean population distribution closely follows the topography, soil, and rainfall conditions suitable for intensive agriculture. However, the lesser density in South China also in part reflects its peripheral and marginal relation to the main centers in the North. This lower density of population has in recent times led to substantially better living conditions in South China than in the North. Consequently there has been a considerable movement of the more industrious and frugal North Chinese to the South.

It is obvious that the weight of human resources in the area lies in China and not in Japan. Formerly the latter was able to profit by the lack of integration of the great Chinese mass. Until very recent times the sprawling Chinese dragon has lacked an effective head. In addition to many local and separatist tendencies, there has been a struggle between two centers of power in the core area of settlement in the North China plain.[3] This has been symbolized by the migration of the capital between Peking (literally "the northern capital") and Nanking ("the southern capital") (*cf.* Fig. 6-5, p. 154). Peking represents the traditional political dominance of China from the north, and by continental people from Central Asia. This domination was reflected in the Manchu dynasty, the last to rule China as an Empire. It is also reflected in the role of the Communists, who found their strongest roots in the land of the northern provinces. It is natural that the Communists should have revived the leadership of Peking as opposed to Nanking and the great port city of Shanghai, which were centers of commerce and foreign economic penetration. It is scarcely necessary to emphasize that implicit in the success of the Communist movement in China there was a massive repudiation of influences which have come to China via the sea, and which were so strong in the modern development of Japan. The Communists have renounced these in favor of the continental China governed from Peking.

The Indian Subcontinent (450 million people). The population of the Indian subcontinent is effectively set off from other great centers by impressive barriers of mountain and desert. Nevertheless, the Indian population cluster is somewhat less coherent in pattern than that of East Asia, and this is perhaps one reason why this cluster has never in the past served as the demographic base for a single world power. Even the great Mogul empires of the fifteenth to the seventeenth centuries were never successful in bringing the entire subcontinent under one rule.

An examination of Indian population distribution [4] will suggest why this

[3] See pp. 153 ff.
[4] Cf. O. H. K. Spate, *Geography of India and Pakistan* (London, 1954), pp. 491-493.

has been the case. The core area of India is the rich plain of the upper Indus and Ganges Rivers. Somewhat separated from this main concentration by the arid Deccan are other but smaller concentrations of population in South India. This distribution suggests a clear base for separatist tendencies in South India. These have been accentuated by the survival of Dravidian languages and influences in the South as opposed to the prevailing Indo-Aryan languages which were spread across India by successive invasions from the Northwest.

The core area of settlement stretches from the Punjab in the Northwest to Bengal in the East. As in China there is a conflicting pull between the continental foci of power, represented by New Delhi, and the economic and maritime focus of power at the mouth of the Ganges, represented by Calcutta. It is significant that Calcutta was the first British capital of India. It is still much the largest city in the country. But New Delhi represents the traditional administration of India from centers in the ecumene that are nearest the original overland sources of conquest and political power.

The highly artificial division of India and Pakistan highlights this problem. Pakistan includes the two ends of the main Indian population cluster, one in the Punjab and the other in Bengal. The western portion includes the less populous northwestern areas which however are the traditional centers of aggressive Moslem leadership in India. But the main population weight of Pakistan is at the other end, in Bengal. This is inevitably an unstable political relationship. This instability is currently pointed up by the increasing restlessness of East Bengal within the Pakistan union.

Europe (600 million people). Despite its fracture into many political entities, Europe is essentially a single cluster of population. National boundaries conceal an organized pattern of settlement reflecting economic forces older and more fundamental than present political entities. The center of European population lies in a core area including England, the Low Countries, Northern France, Western Germany, Switzerland, and Northern Italy. To the East the European settlement area reaches out across the Russian plain into Siberia, through the Balkans to West Anatolia, and across the Mediterranean to French North Africa, which is in some respects a part of Mediterranean Europe.

The pattern of European population distribution reflects history as well as contemporary fact. Originally it was Mediterranean-oriented with the densest population bordering on that Sea. Superimposed on this in the modern era has been, firstly, an Atlantic and especially North Sea orientation, which has grown out of the influence of overseas trade. In this regard we may note the heavy concentration of cities in the countries bordering on the North Sea. Secondly, there has been an eastward march of European settlement. Since 1500 probably as much new land has been firmly settled and occupied by Europeans in Eastern Europe and Asia as has been so occupied in North America. There is a great wedge of European settlement pushing across Eurasia along a narrowing base of good agricultural land. This wedge is broad at its European base, but as it pushes into Asia, it is progressively cramped by cold on the north and desert to the south.

While the European settlement area has as large a population and contains as much agricultural production area as the two great Asian clusters, it does not display as heavy rural settlement. The explanation is of course that industrialization in Europe has resulted in the rise of great cities and conurbations that together include a large part of the total population of the continent.

In Europe, even more acutely than in Asia, there is a conflict between the maritime commercial interests centered in the North Sea and the continental foci of power in Russia. In its broadest terms the East-West conflict may be thought of as a struggle between the conflicting poles of the older maritime civilization of the West and the continental interests of the East created by European settlement in the last three or four hundred years.

Eastern North America (150 million people). Eastern North America, as far west as the Rocky Mountains, is basically a mirror image of Northwest Europe. There is a concentration of population in the habitable area closest in character to that of the North Sea progenitor-countries. There is an axis of industrial urban settlement in the Northeast. This industrial area is anchored on the one side by the great metropolitan region now extending almost continuously along the coast from Boston to Washington. From this coastal base it extends westward to include the North Central States and the Great Lakes region. This is the American counterpart of the great industrial and commercial region of Northwest Europe. This industrial belt reaches from England across France and the Low Countries to include much of Germany, Bohemia, and Northern Italy.

From the industrial northeast population density declines toward the southeast (as it does toward the southwest in Europe). The Mississippi Valley is the American counterpart of the European plain. The Middle West was never settled agriculturally as densely as the European plain because its settlement occurred in competition with industrialization and the growing cityward movements of the past hundred years. The great European immigration from 1880 to 1914 was a migration from European villages to American cities rather than to the land in this country. The United States and Canada are much more urban than Europe, where agricultural settlement much antedated modern industrialization.

As compared with the other population clusters, that of Eastern North America has two tremendous advantages: (1) the region is and has been politically unified for 150 years, aside from the friendly boundary that separates out the comparatively small Canadian population; (2) the region has resources at least equaling those available to the other great population clusters and is able to utilize these resources for the advantage of a very much smaller population.

A third and less specific advantage lies in the fact that the core area centering in New York City has maintained essentially undisputed domination of the economic life of the region. Numerous political movements have reflected the emergence of continental interests in the Middle West comparable to those which have brought about the breaking off of Russia and Eastern Europe from the main cultural stream of Western Europe. These movements have been variously given the labels of agrarian, populist, isolationist, et cetera, but have never reached the strength nor the intensity to bring about a schism since the Civil War.

The West Coast of North America is of course an integral part of Anglo-America, but in terms of population geography the pattern of West Coast settlement is not closely linked to that of Eastern North America. As might be expected, it reflects an orientation toward the Pacific. Being more recently settled than Eastern North America, it is even more urban and has even less agricultural settlement and hinterland.

Australia, New Zealand, and Argentina are likewise more urbanized than Europe and for the same reasons.

As has been pointed out above, the four great clusters include three-fourths of the world's people. The remaining one-fourth are dispersed in the smaller clusters of Latin America, Africa, Southeast Asia, arid Asia, and Oceania.

Latin America. Latin America has no real population center and hence no ecumene to serve as a base for continental power on the scale of that realized by China, India, the U.S.S.R., and the U.S. The present distribution of population in Latin America has two chief features: (*a*) European settlement and influence superimposed on the ancient centers of Amerindian civilization. The ancient Aztec and Incan civilizations are still reflected in the concentrations of people in the highlands of Mexico and Central America and in the Andean intermountain valleys from Venezuela to Bolivia and Chile; (*b*) scattered African and European settlement on the Caribbean Islands and on the coasts of South America.

There has been relatively little penetration of the great lowland interior of South America. In effect there is a thin rim of settlement around a hollow interior. In some local regions of Latin America there are quite dense populations and even signs of overpopulation, as in many Andean valleys, on the islands of Santo Domingo, Puerto Rico, and certain of the other West Indies, and in El Salvador. But there is no core of population large enough to serve at this time as the assured base of a continental and world power. The political fractioning of Latin America reflects this lack.

Africa. Africa is no more densely settled than South America but it is not demographically a "hollow" continent in the same sense as South America. North Africa and Egypt are not truly African in demographic, economic, or political orientation. This area is a part of Africa by courtesy of geography rather than of culture or economics. French North Africa is of course Mediterranean in orientation but Arab in culture. Egypt and the neighboring states of the Levant form a minor population cluster that is also Mediterranean-oriented and of course older than even that of Southern Europe.

But Africa really begins beyond the Sahara. In Black Africa there are significant clusters of interior settlement and the overlay of European settlement is important only in the Union of South Africa. Politically Africa is artificially divided with regard to little more than the reconciliation of nineteenth century rivalries of European colonial powers. Consequently, there is little relationship between the distribution of population and of political organization.

With the probability that most of Black Africa will sooner or later emerge from political dependency, attention needs to be given to the possible locus of emerging African power. At the present time there would seem to be two potential competitors for leadership in the development of native African political power. In West Africa and particularly in Nigeria there is a considerable population base for political and economic power. The total population size may be deceptive, however, since there is a conflicting pull between the coastal areas, where trade and the beginnings of modern economy are concentrated, and the interior areas which are both more Moslem and more militant. A possible competing ecumene lies in the highlands of East Africa along the great Rift Valley of East Africa and on the shores of Lakes Victoria and Tanganyika. This area is now divided politically between Uganda, Tanganyika, Ruanda-Urundi, and the Belgian Congo. The Union of South Africa is thinly populated but has the only large cities and industrial centers south of the Sahara.

Southeast Asia. In Southeast Asia there are several minor centers of population focused on major river valleys such as the Irrawaddy (Burma), the Menam (Thailand), and the Mekong (Laos, Cambodia, and South Vietnam), or on islands such as Java and Luzon. In each case the cluster serves as the core area of a national entity. With the possible exception of Java, the particular ecumenes are so overshadowed by the two giant clusters in East Asia—China and India—that there is little chance for the organization of an independent political power in the area.

Dry Asia. This vast area, the traditional domain of the Moslem religion, has minor population centers in Egypt and the Levant, in the valley of the Tigris and Euphrates (Iraq), in Iran, in Soviet Asia, and even in Chinese Sinkiang. In the past this vast area has served as the geographical base for empires founded on the mobility of the nomadic horseman. Today, however, its unity lies more in the spiritual cohesiveness offered by the Moslem religion, and to a lesser extent by the community of Turkic languages spoken all the way from Constantinople to five hundred miles inside the boundaries of China. The area has proven too fragmented to provide the base for a great power in the modern world.

URBAN CONCENTRATIONS

In the previous sections attention has been called to the importance of a strong core area or ecumene to the internal strength and organization of the modern state. Related to the importance of the core area is the degree of urbanization and metropolitan concentration. The core area is usually dominated by the capital which is in the purest sense of the word the "metro-pole" and often the cultural hearth of the nation. Such cities as London, Paris, and Rome are much more than the largest cities in their respective countries. In a sense they *are* England, France, and Italy, and one cannot think of these countries as existing without these home cities. The five counties surrounding London are even called the "home" counties. There is a universal tendency for these great economic and cultural centers to attract a larger and larger proportion of the total population.

Obviously something so important in the lives of many millions of people as the growth of cities and the urban way of life must have its effect on the power and the strategic vulnerability of the nations involved. Such concentration of population has often been regarded as affecting the internal stability of the state. In the atomic age it must be presumed that external vulnerability is likewise affected by this development.

URBANIZATION AND POLITICAL STABILITY

The theory that cities are a source of instability and weakness is at least as old as Thomas Jefferson and as new as Communist revolutionary doctrine. The mobs of Paris during the French Revolution have left a profound effect on the political thought of the Western world. Later, Marx found in the cities the apotheosis of capitalism with its division between pyramided wealth and propertyless proletariat. In the present century Oswald Spengler pictured the metropolis as the ultimate graveyard of Western civilization.

In the long sweep of history it may be that modern urban society is insufficiently stable to provide the enduring social institutions and cultural traditions necessary for a lasting civilization. But in the short run, it is clear that those who fear the urban mobs as revolutionary forces have been refuted by recent history. The most urbanized countries are at the same time the most stable politically. The twelve countries having one-fourth or more of their people in cities of a hundred thousand or over is a roster of countries that have been characterized by stable governments since World War II. The single exception is Argentina.

TABLE 9-1

Degree of Urbanization: Per Cent of Population Living in Cities

	CITIES OF 100,000 AND OVER	URBAN AREAS BY NATIONAL DEFINITION [a]
Australia, 1947	51.4	68.9
United Kingdom, 1951	51.0	80.2
United States, 1950	43.7	63.7
Argentina, 1947	40.6	62.5
Israel, 1951	39.9	77.5
Canada, 1951	36.7	62.1
Netherlands, 1947	35.2	54.6
Denmark, 1950	33.5	67.3
New Zealand, 1951	32.8	61.3
Austria, 1951	32.8	49.1
Western Germany, 1950	27.1 [b]	71.1
Belgium, 1947	25.8	62.7
Japan, 1950	25.6	37.5

[a] National definitions of urban areas vary with administrative practices in the countries concerned and are therefore unreliable as a measure of urbanization. To take an extreme illustration, according to its own definitions, which include as urban all persons in communities of 500 or over, Iceland is 71.7 per cent urban and one of the most urbanized countries in the world.

[b] Excludes Western sector of Berlin.

Source: United Nations, *Demographic Yearbook, 1952* (New York, 1953), Table B, p. 11.

Conspicuously absent from this list are France, Italy, and Southern and Eastern European countries, many of which have experienced great political instability over the last fifty years.

If we take the other end of the scale, those nations having less than 10 per cent of their populations in large cities, the list generally includes countries that have not been characterized by great political stability: Bulgaria, Burma, Ceylon, Colombia, Dominican Republic, El Salvador, Haiti, India, Iran, Rumania, Turkey, and Yugoslavia. There are conspicuous exceptions, such as Turkey.

It is fair to say that in the modern world internal political stability is more likely to be found with a high degree of urbanization than in a peasant economy and society. It is precisely the countries undergoing transition from the old self-contained rural peasant world that are experiencing the most acute political disorder. Since European techniques and aspirations have now penetrated to every country of the world, there are very few if any remaining peasant societies living in premodern pattern oblivious to the disruptive influences of Western civilization.

EXTERNAL VULNERABILITY OF METROPOLISES

It is easy to draw a quick and superficial conclusion that the things that make a country effective in terms of internal organization (such as centralization in urban concentrations) are precisely the things likely to make it most vulnerable to modern warfare. Thus the existence of strong core areas focused in metropolitan conurbations is associated with internal stability, but this source of strength would seem to make the countries concerned more vulnerable to air and atomic attack.

The problem is probably not so simple and certainly is as yet unsolved. In the old days of slow military campaigns overland, the vulnerability of metropolitan capitals and of core areas could be crucial. Except for the largest countries this is less relevant now since the scope of warfare is so broad that the population and industrial concentrations in the smaller countries may be important only in relation to larger continental entities. In other words, it is now not so much the national ecumene that counts as the larger continental ecumene.

Again a nation with fewer urban centers may in fact be more vulnerable than one with many. The degree and diversification of industry in such countries as the United States and the U.S.S.R. is reflected in the existence of a great many urban concentrations. While these concentrations contain a relatively large percentage of total populations, they also represent widely dispersed industrial strength. It is not at all clear that the United Kingdom for example, with forty-two conurbations of over a hundred thousand is actually more vulnerable to complete disorganization from atomic attack than France with twenty-two.

C. *Growth*

WORLD POPULATION GROWTH

One of the most distinctive features of our age is the rapid multiplication of our species, *homo sapiens.*

The present growth of world population is unique in human history. This can be painfully demonstrated from bits of historical evidence. A little simple arithmetic will show it to be true. The present annual world population growth is estimated at well over 30 million and perhaps as high as 40 million a year. Had this *amount* of growth continued throughout the Christian era, there would now be 6.8 billions of us rather than the actual figure of about 2.6 billion. At the present *rate* of growth (which is estimated to be at least 1.2 per year) the entire population of the globe would be descended from a single couple living at the time of Christ. An Argentinian demographer has carried the illustration to its logical conclusion: if the population of two living in the Garden of Eden some six thousand years ago had increased on the average of one per cent per year the present human population would be so vast that it would have standing room only, not just on the surface of the earth but on the surface of a sphere with a radius fourteen times the *orbit* of the planet Neptune.

Obviously the amount of current population growth could never have existed before; and the present rate of growth could have existed only in brief periods of man's history.

Population growth affects political geography in two ways: (1) it never is exactly the same in any two countries, hence the demographic bases of political power are always changing; (2) it creates increased competition for the scarce resources of the earth. The first views people as a source of power and production, the second as consumers who must be fed. These two influences often work against each other. A larger population may be useful as a source of increased manpower. At the same time more people mean more competition for scarce resources. Population growth may cause a lower level of living than might be attained with a smaller population.

In this section and the following one on *Structure,* we will deal with population as a source of power. In another section, on *Pressure,* we will consider measures of population pressure, and the extent to which it is a real as against a rationalized cause of political conflict.

Population growth is often overlooked as a factor in redistribution of political power because its course is steady, undramatic, and persistent rather than immediate and self-evident. Yet in the longer sweep of history different rates of population growth have been associated with major changes in the distribution of world power. There has been an enormous population growth in every major region of the world in the modern era, but this growth has occurred very unequally among the several continents.

The expansion of world population between 1650 and 1950 is shown in Table 9-2.

TABLE 9-2

World Population Growth, 1650-1950 *
(in Millions)

	1650	1950	GROWTH 1650-1950	APPROXIMATE MULTIPLIER
Asia	330	1320	990	4
{ Europe	100	393	493	6
{ U.S.S.R.		200		
Africa	100	198	98	2
Latin America	12	165	153	14
North America	1	165	164	165
Oceania	2	13	11	6
World Total	545	2454	1909	4½

* Figures for 1650 estimated by A. M. Carr-Saunders, *World Population* (Oxford, 1936), p. 42. Figures for 1950 from United Nations *Demographic Yearbook, 1953.* All figures for 1650 and those for Asia and Africa in 1950 are highly proximate.

Now, as in all previous epochs, Asia is the principal home of mankind. In the three centuries of the modern era the Asian population has grown by a billion people.

The dynamic demographic element in modern history, however, has been the expansion of Europe.

THE EXPANSION OF EUROPE

The population of the home continent has multiplied six times. In addition some 200 million persons of European extraction are living overseas. The Europeans have thus multiplied some eight times in the past three centuries. This represents an increase from about a hundred million in 1650 to approximately 800 million persons of European extraction living in the world at the present time.[5] The population of European descent has increased from less than one-fifth of the world's people in 1650 to one-third in 1950.

The expansion of Europe relative to the rest of the world has not proceeded evenly throughout the modern era. In the broadest sense the European settlement area comprises Europe, the Soviet Union, the Americas, and Oceania. Growth in this half of the world may be compared with Asia and Africa in which continents Europeans are nowhere a majority. The comparative growth in these two areas is shown in Figure 9-5.

The population growth of Europe gained momentum in the late eighteenth century and after 1800 grew relatively much faster than in the rest of the world. Between 1800 and 1920 the population of the European settlement area gained markedly on that of Asia and Africa. Since 1920, however, two things have happened: (1) the rates of growth in the European settlement area have slowed; (2) the populations of Asia and Africa have taken a forward spurt.

Estimates made by United Nations experts for population growth in the future suggest the continuation of these trends reversing those of the last 150 years. If anything, Asia-Africa will contain a rising share of the rapidly increasing population projected for the next generation.

Let us examine the demographic expansion of Europe, and the significance of the reversal of this trend that now seems in the offing.

Population growth of European peoples has been part and parcel of the extension of European political and cultural hegemony in the world. The population of Europe has expanded three ways:

[5] The population of predominantly European descent in the world may be computed as follows. In addition to the population of Europe west of the Soviet Union, approximately 165 million of the 200 million inhabitants of the U.S.S.R. in 1950 belonged to nationalities commonly regarded as European. Of the remaining 35 million perhaps the majority live wholly or partly within the physical confines of Europe but are not conventionally regarded as of European culture. The deduction of some 15 million non-whites from the 165 million inhabitants of North America provides an estimate of 150 million of European stock in that continent. There are somewhat over 10 million persons of European descent in Oceania.

It is impossible to set a precise figure to the number of persons of predominantly European descent in Latin America. A generalization of careful analysis made in this field indicates a rough division as follows: One-third 75 per cent or more white, one-third mestizo, one-sixth Indian, and one-sixth Negroid, the latter including all persons with identifiable Negroid blood. There are perhaps 5 million persons of European descent living in Africa and Asia. Thus the European population of the world in 1950 may be summed up as follows: Europe, 393 million; U.S.S.R., 165 million; North America, 150 million; Latin America, 55 million; Oceania, 10 million; Africa and Asia, 5 million. This provides an estimated world total of 778 million. In addition there are some 70 million mestizos and mulattoes in the Americas and an unknown number in Africa and Asia.

More Intensive Use of the Home Territory. The population of Europe west of Russia has increased over 300 million since 1650. This expansion reflects both more intensive agricultural settlement and more industrialization.

It is often forgotten that much of Europe was still a frontier well into the modern era. In Roman times only the Mediterranean littoral was fully settled by modern standards. By the Middle Ages the line of mature agricultural settlement had moved northward and westward to include France and the low countries. But much of Germany and Eastern Europe remained at an early stage of agricultural settlement; Northern Europe and the Russian plain were still very thinly peopled. By the seventeenth century the "frontier" had moved far to the east and into the remote north, but there was still much unused land. Reclamation and settlement of these lands contributed to the more rapid growth of northwest and eastern Europe as compared with the Mediterranean countries.

Later, great commercial and industrial development enabled these regions to gain political and economic leadership in Europe—an accession of power made possible by the strengthening of the agricultural base and by earlier increases of population attendant on the mature settlement of the region.

The Settlement of the East. The domination of the Russian plain by the Tatars was effectively crushed about the time of Columbus. The border, or "Ukrain" moved forward into the rich black earth of the country so named. From their forests around Moscow the Russians moved out across the rich plains forbidden them earlier by their defenselessness against the horsemen of Central Asia. There followed Russian feats of exploration and settlement similar to those of the American West. Eastern Europe was still being "settled" in the eighteenth and nineteenth centuries and parts of European and Asiatic Russia even in the twentieth century. Large sections of steppe-land in the North Caucasus and Central Asia were first turned by the plow under the Communist regime. The eastward tide of settlement in Russia paralleled our own "westward movement."

The eastward movement in Russia resulted in the settlement of enormous areas by Europeans, areas now occupied by as many as a hundred million of their descendants. The impetus has expanded the boundaries of European influence effectively not only from the Don, which used to be regarded as the eastward edge of Europe, to the Urals and the Caucasus mountains, and beyond into Siberia and Central Asia. Much of Asiatic Russia is still not effectively occupied by Europeans (or by any other race).

The frontier psychology of the Soviet Union is probably one of the factors which explain Soviet expansionism.[6] One may find parallels in the "manifest destiny" of the United States, so popular a phrase in American expansion during the last century.[7] But as in our own Western movement the yearning for land is no longer so compelling as the exploitation of new industries, of mining, and of forestry in the new regions.

The Settlement of Overseas Areas. Europeans have effectively occupied (*a*) most of the habitable territory of North America north of the Rio Grande, (*b*) the temperate zones of Latin America, including Argentina, Uruguay, and Brazil south of the 20th parallel, (*c*) Australia and New Zealand. White or mestizo populations are also in majority in most of Latin America with two exceptions: first, the ancient Amerindian strongholds in the highlands of Ecuador, Bolivia, Peru, and Paraguay; and second, the British and French West Indies which were chiefly peopled from Africa. Other than within the Russian orbit, Europeans have nowhere colonized Asia unless Israel may be regarded as a European settlement. Only in French North Africa and in South Africa are there substantial footholds of European settlement on that continent. But in both cases Europeans are greatly outnumbered. In French North Africa there are about one and a half million as against approximately 18 million Moslems. In the Union of South Africa there were 2.6 million Europeans in 1950 as against 10 million non-Europeans.

It would be idle to suggest that the relative expansion of European peoples was in itself the explanation or the exclusive means of the extension of European civilization throughout the world. It is not always certain which is cause and which is effect. Did population growth in Europe both stimulate and enable the political expansion of Europe or did the political expansion of Europe provide the means for the rapid population growth of Europe? Both are undoubtedly true.

It is clear that the industrialization of Europe and its rapid population growth was in part stimulated by access to raw materials and markets in overseas countries. At the same time rapid population growth provided both the sinews and the motives for colonization and imperialist expansion. One thing is certain: the firmest influence of European expansion is in those areas that were colonized and populated by persons of European stock. The European civilization is now spreading very rapidly to all people and to all parts of the world, but the most complete migration of

[6] See the discussion of the Russian urge to the sea as a source of expansion, pp. 243 ff.

[7] See pp. 10-12.

European culture to other continents has been in those areas colonized by Europeans themselves.

POPULATION AND POWER IN EUROPE

The larger aspects of the expansion of European population have also been reflected in the specific political history of the dominant countries in the European continent and the European settlement area. In the following paragraphs, attention will be directed toward the demographic base for the successive primacy in European settlement areas of France, Germany, Britain, Russia, and the United States (*cf.* Fig. 9-3).

France. Much of the history of Europe between 1650 and 1800, revolves around France as the leading power of Europe. She was the wealthiest and in many respects the most advanced country in Europe. In the seventeenth and early eighteenth centuries France probably had the largest population in Europe, not even excluding Russia, which now has five times the population of France. This population served as a firm basis for French hegemony in Europe and for the Napoleonic conquests. But by 1800 Russia had passed France in population, and the massive size and population of that country finally destroyed French hopes for complete mastery of Europe.

The economic and political position of France in Europe has changed enormously since 1800. One element in this change is the fact that France now stands fifth rather than first in population size. She had been passed by both Germany and the United States by 1870-1871 when she suffered military defeat at the hands of the Germans; the United Kingdom passed France around 1900, or if one includes the European population of the Dominions, the British population surpassed the French about 1885; and Italy passed France about 1930. In 1939 France had only 7.3 per cent of Europe's people as compared with about 15 per cent in 1800.

Germany. The rise of Germany likewise has demographic foundations. In the Napoleonic period, Germans lived in a Europe dominated not only politically but also numerically by the French. As the result of the economic development of Germany and the population increase made possible by this development, since the middle of the last century Germans have become much the most numerous of the European peoples aside from the Russians. As the largest single group, occupying a central position in Europe, it is natural that the Germans should have sought to bring the balance of political power into line with their growing numerical and industrial importance. That this might have been achieved more effec-

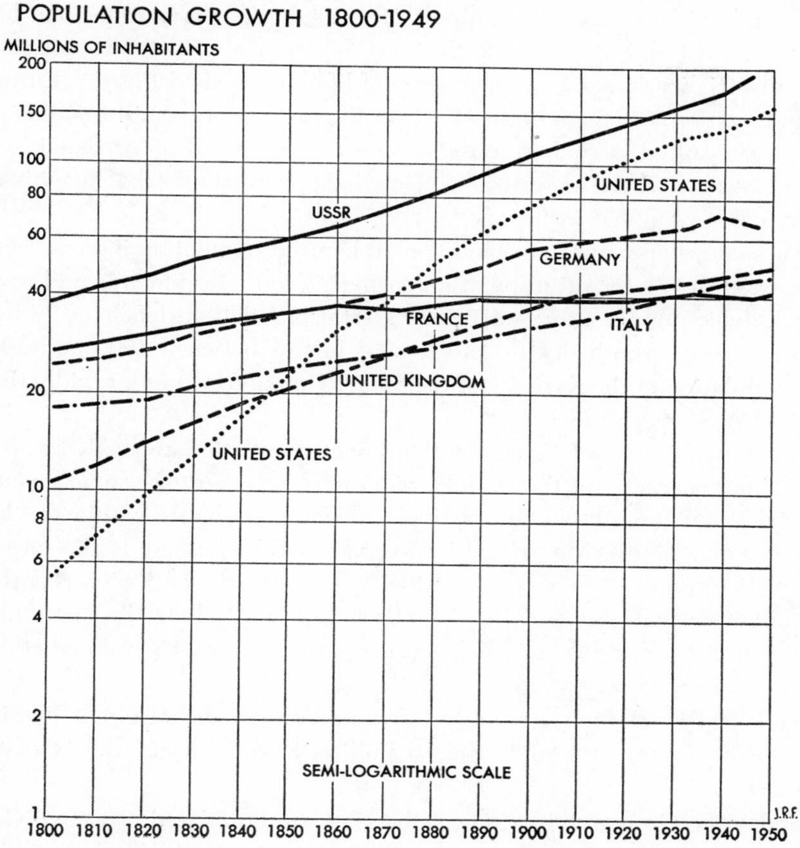

FIG. 9-3.

tively through peaceful rather than through warlike means is now unfortunately beside the point.

By virtue of its more rapid natural increase and the Nazi annexation of German-speaking areas, Germany in 1939 had 80 millions or twice the population of France and a considerably larger population than that of Britain.

Soviet Union. The populations of Eastern Europe have grown faster than those of Western Europe. At an earlier period the large population growth of this region was made possible by the fact that great areas were then in the process of initial agricultural settlement, or, put in other terms, in transition from a pastoral to a settled farm economy.

This agricultural settlement represented a superior form of land utilization, and made possible the support of a far denser population than had formerly existed. More recently the wave of material progress represented by industrialization and an urban way of life has reached Eastern Europe from its centers of origin in the West. In Russia the contrast of the old and the new resulted in such severe stress on the old social order that it was swept away and the new technical civilization was ushered in with an impetus unexampled in history.

These developments have made possible rapid population increase such as existed in Western Europe at an earlier period. Despite war and revolution, which apparently cost Russia a total population deficit of 26 millions, including both deaths and loss of births, between 1900 and 1943 the population of the territory of the Soviet Union grew more rapidly than that of Western Europe.

The very large total figure for the Soviet population conceals the cosmopolitan character of the Soviet Union, in which there are some seventy official languages. Only comparatively recently, probably within the last thirty years, has the Great Russian surpassed the German as the largest linguistic group in Europe. The 1926 census of the Soviet Union reported 78 million persons of Great Russian ethnic group. At about the same time, as reported in various national censuses, there were 85 million ethnic Germans in Europe.

By 1939 there were reported to be 99 million persons of Great Russian "nationality" as over against the 80 million inhabitants of the "Greater Reich."

Today the German minorities of the East are liquidated. The two Germanies together contain about 70 million: (50 in the Federal Republic, 18 in East Germany, and 2 in West Berlin). The U.S.S.R. now has about 200 million people of which slightly over half are Great Russians. The demographic balance has clearly swung in favor of the latter. This is the demographic basis for the eastward shift of power in Europe.

Thinking in terms of the European settlement area as a whole there has of course also been a westward migration of people and power.

The United Kingdom. Allied to the demographic expansion of Germany and of Northwest Europe has been that of Britain. Its growth has matched and if anything exceeded that of the Germans. But much more of the British population increase was drained off overseas; it established the British Dominions and it contributed the largest element in the population of the United States. While the United Kingdom has always had a smaller population in its island home than that of the German-speaking areas of

Central Europe, this metropolitan population has been effectively bolstered in influence both by the tremendous resources of the Empire and by the European population of the Dominions. If only the latter are considered as contributing to the demographic weight of the British population, this nevertheless provides a demographic base comparable to that of Germany. In 1939 this larger "British" population amounted to 70 million and at the present time it has risen to 80 million and is thus more numerous than the population of a united Germany.

The European and especially British populations that settled the United States and the British Dominions increased even more rapidly in the new environment than they did in the countries from which they came. It was this rapid growth in the United States, even more than migration, that brought about the enormous expansion of the American population. In the early nineteenth century the average American woman surviving through the childbearing period had eight children. It was this great fertility that brought about an average growth of 25 per cent per decade even when, as between 1800 and 1840, there was comparatively little immigration from Europe.

No one can say what proportion of the American population is descended from British stock, since there has been a wide mingling of European nationalities. In 1940, ninety-three million or 71 per cent of the population were estimated to be of European origin and of English mother tongue, but this figure doubtless includes a great many persons wholly or in part descended from other European stocks.

Through this rapid natural growth and by virtue of cultural assimilation of other European and African nationalities, the world population of English mother tongue has grown from perhaps 20 million in 1800 to some 225 million, leaving aside the wide use of English as a language of commerce, government, and higher education by persons of other native tongues. Whether in demographic or cultural terms this has been the most phenomenal national expansion in modern times.

As is now widely recognized, the European population, and especially that living in the heartlands of Western Europe, is not increasing as rapidly as it formerly did. As a result of the differential growth of the three great divisions of the European settlement area, the mantle of political supremacy has passed from the original homeland to the two great peripheral areas, one westward overseas and the other eastward in the great land mass of the Eurasian plain. On the horizon is the prospective great expansion of the Asian peoples.

In order to understand the basis for these great changes, both historical and future, it is necessary to analyze the dynamics of human population. These have followed a cycle of development that is sometimes called the "Vital Revolution."

THE VITAL REVOLUTION

Accompanying the Industrial Revolution has been a profound change in man's biological balance with his environment. In its initial phases this has been the increasing ability of man to cope with the age-old scourges of the four dread horsemen of the Apocalypse—famine, pestilence, war, and death.

First, the establishment of national states imposed public order and thereby greatly increased personal security from the dangers of civil strife, personal vendettas, and deaths from such mundane incidents as highway robbery, personal violence, and criminal negligence. Then the state increasingly assumed responsibility for the welfare of its citizens—through free public education, through elementary public health measures, and more recently through social security provisions and institutions. These, as well as scientific advances, brought about the reductions in deaths achieved in the more advanced countries of Western Europe during the eighteenth and nineteenth centuries.

At the same time the agricultural and industrial revolutions provided the basis for a rise in the level of living for the mass of the people. In practical terms, this meant better nutrition, clothing, housing, and new standards of personal cleanliness, all of which tended to reduce the death rate. Finally and really very recently, medical research has found answers to many serious diseases that could not previously be controlled by the usual public health procedures.

Altogether these measures have made possible the doubling of the average expectation of life at birth. For Europeans and Americans this expectation is twenty years longer than in our grandparents' generation, and forty years longer than in seventeenth century Europe. This is perhaps the greatest material achievement of our civilization.

Recently in the more advanced countries of the world there has been a parallel decline in the birth rate. But this decline in births has come later than the reduction of deaths—hence the unique population growth that is well-nigh universal today. It is natural that a decline in the birth rate should follow rather than precede the decline of the death rate in demographic evolution.

From time immemorial, human beings have had the strongest biological, social, and even religious compulsions to "increase and multiply." These compulsions have evoked persistently high birth rates throughout the world. Such reproduction was costly in terms of human wastage, since a large proportion of those born failed to achieve maturity. But high birth rates were necessary if the race was to survive the perils of life in previous ages.

The West. About one-third of the human race now exercises a substantial degree of voluntary control of family size. In a number of European countries this reduction of births had reached a point before World War II at which many persons both in Fascist and in democratic countries were becoming worried about the possibility of race suicide. The baby boom following the war dispelled the fears that people, given the means of voluntary control of family size, will necessarily fail to reproduce themselves. In fact, the wide fluctuations in the birth rate in the depression years, during the war, and in the postwar period have concealed a rather stable average family size in the West.

What matters in the long run, of course, is not the annual birth rate but the size of completed families. Recent analysis of cohort fertility—the fertility of women born in the same years and passing through life together—has given us new methods for analyzing fertility trends. Among white women born in the United States, in five-year periods beginning in 1900 and ending in 1925, the average number of children per woman has varied only between 2.3 for the women born from 1905 to 1909 and a maximum of 2.7 for those born from 1920 to 1924. The latter women of course have not completed their normal childbearing years, but it is possible to make reasonable estimates of their final fertility performance on the basis of experience thus far. These data indicate that the actual size of American families has not changed nearly as much as the annual birth rates might suggest.

Similar studies in Britain suggest that the number of children per married couple has remained remarkably stable over the last twenty-five years at about 2.2 children per couple.

It would seem that the industrial West is moving toward a new and more efficient reproduction in which low birth and death rates are roughly balanced in a new demographic equilibrium. There is every reason to suppose that the huge populations of the underdeveloped areas, given the opportunity, will respond to the same incentives that have brought about the reductions of births in the West. Neither ideology nor great cultural barriers have stopped the decline of births in a country once modern influences have reached the mass of the people. Let us illustrate this, first, from the experience of Russia, and second, from the experience of Japan.

The Soviet Union. The categorical anti-Malthusian doctrines of Communism, backed by the most comprehensive pro-natal measures existing in the world today, have apparently not been successful in checking very rapid declines in the Russian birth rate since the war. Before World War II the Russians were temporarily successful in checking the decline of births resulting from abortion in the early 1930's. This success was achieved by the simple expedient of closing down the free public abortion clinics. Since the war, however, the supplements to family wages on behalf of children and the "mother heroine medals" seem to have been ineffective in stopping the spread of the small-family pattern.

According to its official statistics, the birth rate in the Soviet Union in 1955 was 25.6 per thousand population [8] as compared with 24.6 in the United States. The Soviet figure represents a drastic decline from the prewar figure of 38 per thousand. If adjustment is made for the concentration of the Russian population in the young adult ages, the current fertility in the U.S.S.R. must be substantially below that in the United States.

Japan. The case of Japan also reveals the extent to which the small family pattern may cross cultural barriers. Once Japan became predominantly urban and industrial, the traditional forces of Oriental familism and ancestor worship apparently failed to retard the decline of the birth rate. It is interesting to note that aside from fluctuations in the birth and death rates associated with wars, the pattern of vital rates in Japan during the last thirty-five years has very closely approximated the trend of birth and death rates in England forty years earlier at a somewhat comparable stage of industrialization. By 1954 the birth rate in Japan was 20.1, well below that of the United States and rapidly approaching European levels.

The specific means used to restrict family size may differ from country to country: in Ireland, through late marriage; in Western Europe, generally, by birth control; in Japan, by abortions, which Japanese experts report now number over one million a year, despite growing efforts by the Japanese government to introduce less drastic methods of family limitation; and in Puerto Rico, and increasingly elsewhere, by post-partum sterilization of women in hospitals, at the request of the women concerned and generally following the delivery of their fourth or fifth child. Wher-

[8] *New York Times,* June 7, 1956.

ever people have become literate, urbanized, and free of the debilitating psychological and physical effects of the major epidemic diseases, the birth rate has declined.

DEMOGRAPHIC STAGES

How are these differing stages in the Vital Revolution actually reflected in population trends in the world today? In its analysis of this problem the UN has delineated five demographic types, illustrated in Figure 9-4. The first of these includes those countries in which both fertility and mortality are low. In Western Europe, rates of population growth are now generally under one per cent per year and the lowest for any major region of the world. English-speaking countries overseas are included in this category, but their higher fertility and higher rates of growth, ranging from 1.5 to 2 per cent per year, suggest that these countries are somewhat different from those of Western Europe.

Type 2 includes those areas where the birth rate has now definitely begun to decline. The death rate is now low in these regions. This situation is characteristic of Eastern Europe, the Soviet Union and temperate South America. Rates of population growth in these countries range between 1.5 and 2 per cent—that is to say, somewhat lower than in type 3.

Type 3 includes those countries that have not moved so far in the demographic transition. In these areas, which chiefly include tropical America and South Africa, birth rates remain very high but death rates are now at fairly low levels. These areas are experiencing the most rapid growth observable in the world today, generally over 2 per cent per year.

Type 4 includes those areas in which mortality, though still high, is being reduced, while fertility remains at high primitive levels. This type characterizes the Middle East, the Arab world, and most of South and East Asia. In these areas population growth is now 1 to 2 per cent per year and rising as deaths are increasingly brought under control by cheap and elementary public health measures.

Type 5, characterized by primitive levels of high fertility and high mortality, is now largely restricted to the native population of black Africa. Not long ago in human history, this was the typical demographic situation of mankind. But even in this region there is a considerable impact of the influences bringing about the Vital Revolution, especially as regards reduction of deaths.

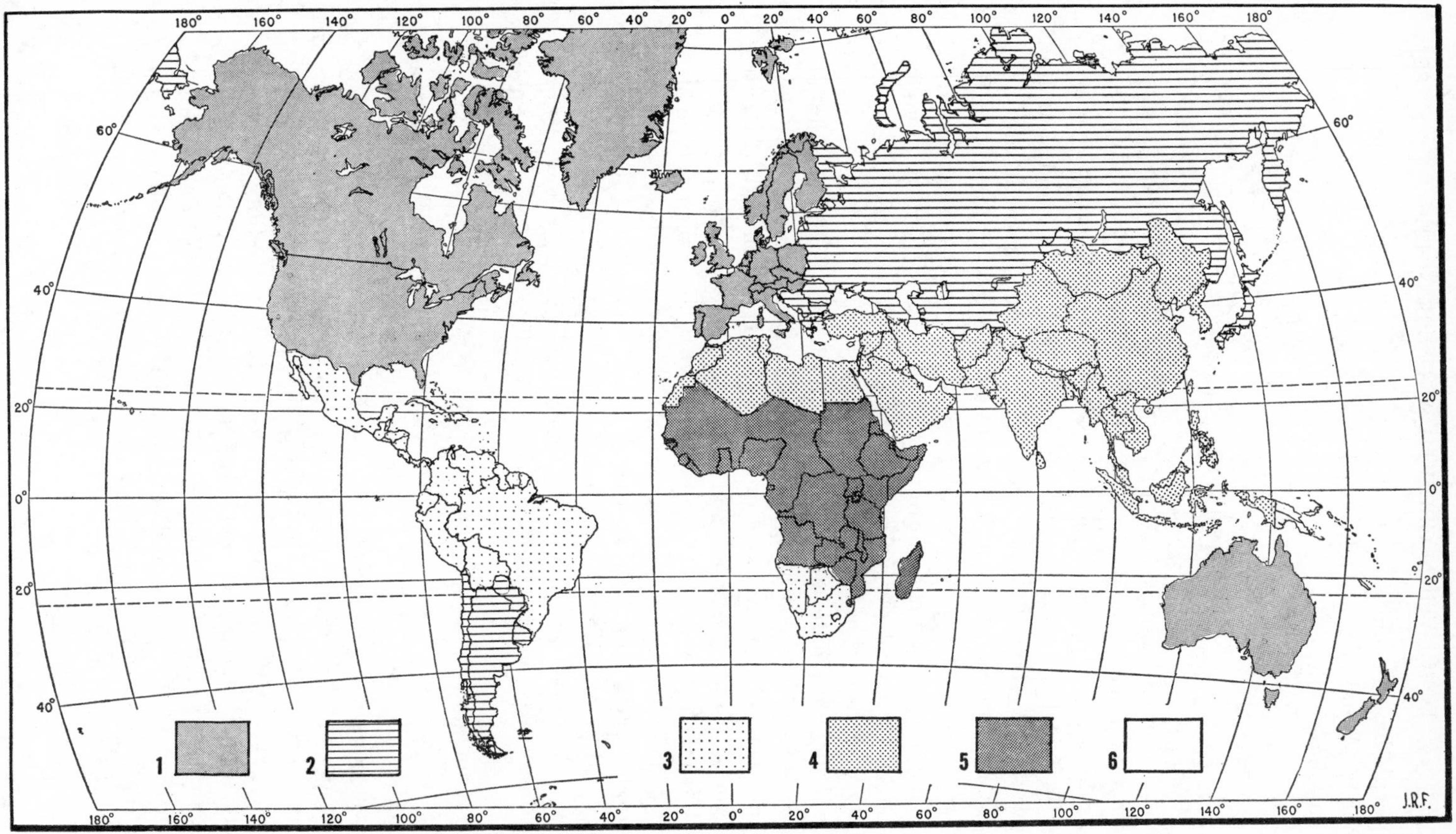

Fig. 9-4. World Regions by Demographic Type: (1) low fertility and low mortality; (2) declining fertility and fairly low mortality; (3) high fertility and fairly low mortality; (4) high fertility and declining mortality; (5) high fertility and high mortality; (6) no information.

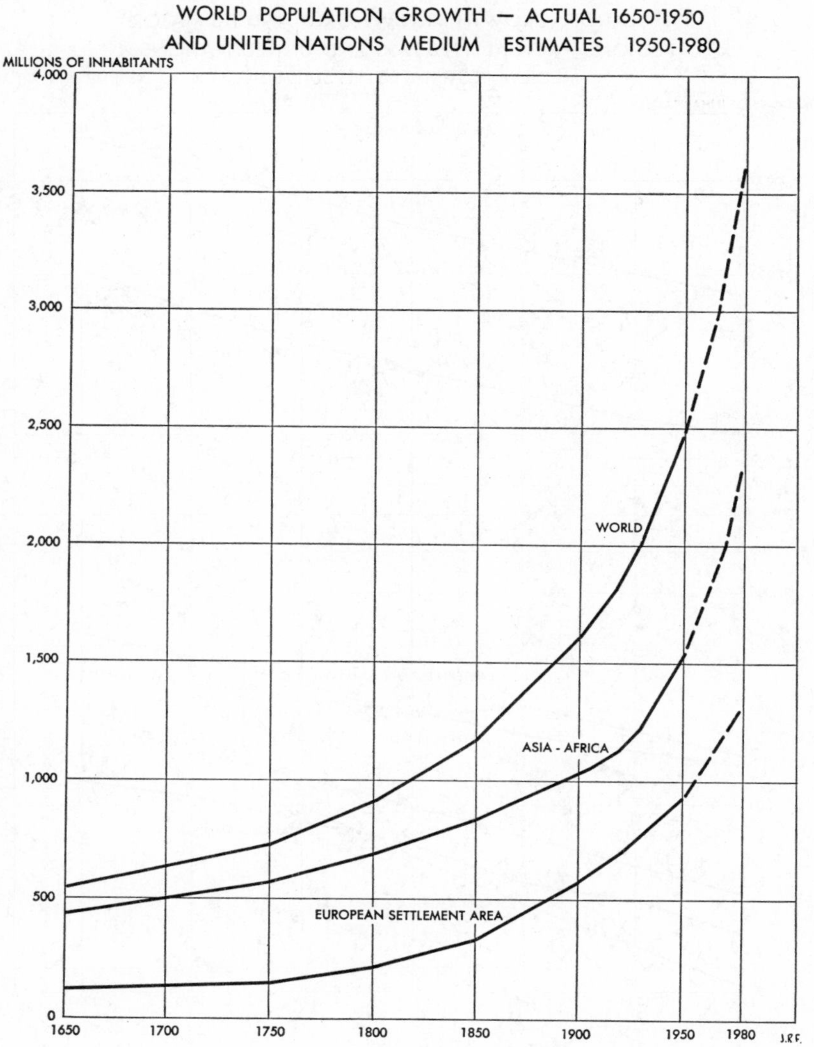

FIG. 9-5.

FUTURE POPULATIONS

What do these different trends mean in terms of future populations?

For this purpose we may use recent forecasts prepared by the Population Division of the United Nations relating to the period 1950 to 1980. Figure 9-5 is intended to give historical perspective illustrating the momentum and acceleration of *absolute* population growth in the world and

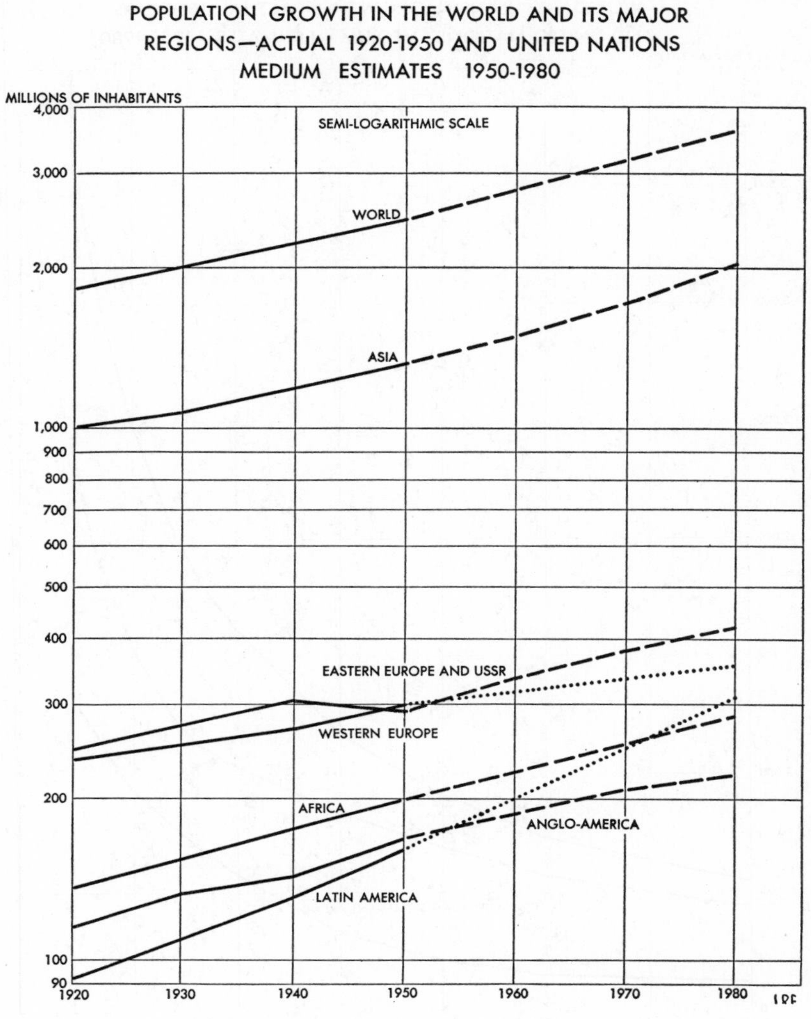

FIG. 9-6.

its two great subdivisions: Asia-Africa and the European settlement area, which includes Europe and the U.S.S.R., the Americas and Oceania. Since 1650 there has been a great expansion of the European population. In some periods this has exceeded even the absolute amount of growth in Asia and Africa, but the latter area has never lost its clear predominance in numbers. Current and foreseeable trends will widen this predominance.

The extent of this divergence will depend much on the situation in

China. Until very recently it was generally accepted that the population of China was under 500 million and that it was growing little if at all. The United Nations estimates incorporate this assumption in their forecasts. But recent reports from the first modern census in China, taken in 1953, indicate a population of not 500 million but close to 600 million increasing at 2 per cent per year. If these latter figures for China were used in the projections, the world estimate for 1980 would be close to 4 billion rather than the 3.6 billion shown on this chart.

Figure 9-6 shows the United Nations forecasts in greater detail, this time on a logarithmic scale in which parallel lines indicate equal rates of growth, rather than equal amounts of increase.

All regions are growing and will continue to grow, barring a major catastrophe. It is natural that demographic evolution should have proceeded furthest in Western Europe, the birthplace of modern industrial civilization. But despite somber predictions made a decade ago no population decline in Europe is yet in prospect. In fact there is some suggestion that the very appearance of decline, as in France before the war, will bring about reactions in public policy and private attitudes sufficient to restore a moderate rate of growth. France today has one of the highest reproduction rates in Europe.

Eastern Europe is the one major region in which the demographic losses of World War II are clearly discernible in the population curve. If very recent information on the rapidity of the birth rate decline in the U.S.S.R. and the satellite countries is accurate the United Nations forecasts for this area are too high.

In overseas Europe—in the United States, in Canada, in Australasia, and in temperate zones of South America—population growth is still rapid and above the world average. While present growth rates may not be maintained, we may expect continued growth at a less rapid pace, both from immigration and from the excess of births over deaths.

Latin America is the most rapidly growing major region. It is now surpassing America north of the Rio Grande in population. Even with an orderly demographic evolution on the pattern of Europe, it will have very rapid increase over the next generation. To the extent that weight of numbers contributes to regional importance, Latin America will play a growing role in world affairs.

But the biological fate of the species will be decided in Asia, which now, as throughout recorded history, is the principal home of the human race. Only catastrophe will prevent an enormous growth of population in Asia, a growth that is gaining momentum with each new success in public health. This is both necessary and desirable. However, the most rapid present and potential growth often is in areas least well endowed in terms of physical and cultural resources to meet the needs of an expanding population.

The United Nations forecasts a population of two billion in Asia in 1980 or 2.3 billion if we adjust for the new reports of population growth in China. We have already mentioned that almost 600 million people in China are now reported to be growing at the rate of 2 per cent or about 12 million persons, per year, the difference between the reported birth rate of 37 and the reported death rate of 17 per thousand population.

WAR AND FUTURE POPULATIONS

Finally, it must be evident that the above forecasts ignore the possibility of a major war. While we may not care to think of war as a "normal" phenomenon, it certainly is a possibility within the time span covered by these projections.

The demographic impact of modern war has been greatly exaggerated in the popular imagination. While war losses of the two World Wars seriously reduced selected populations, their impact was temporary and local, viewing the world as a whole. Their impact was negligible in retarding the forward march of world population growth. Aside from the single case of Eastern Europe one would have to look very closely on the two charts to detect any effects of the two World Wars.

This does not in any way minimize the personal tragedy or horror of war. It merely reflects the fact that the social and biological forces leading to world population growth represent basic and powerful forces that were only very temporarily checked by the two World Wars.

Another war, fought with the arsenal of horrible new weapons, might be far more disastrous to the species. But only about 5 per cent of the world's population lives in its sixty-odd urban agglomerations of over one million inhabitants. The destruction of all our major cities would not directly destroy a large part of the human race. For that matter four or five normal years of world population growth would completely replace the population of the United States and six years that of the Soviet Union. These remarks are not intended to be comforting—only to put the problem of human survival in its proper perspective.

D. *Structure*

The previous discussions have emphasized the importance of changing numbers. It is obvious that numbers alone will not determine demographic influences on national power. Obviously, populations differ in their age composition, degree of education, occupations, and other characteristics that will determine their per capita effectiveness in contributing to national power.

Figures 9-7, 8 and 9 present a comparison of age structures in countries representing different stages in demographic evolution. These charts are called "age pyramids" because of their characteristic shape.

The age pyramids of any country reflect all the things that have happened to its population for the past eighty years or more. The broadly based youthful population of India reflects both its high birth rate and its high death rate. Many children are born, but in the past, at least, these were rapidly decimated. Few survived to the upper age groups.

The age pyramid of the Soviet Union would reflect, in addition to birth and death rates, the drastic effects of war. The scars of war are obvious both in the deficits of men among survivors of military age at the time of conflict, and even more poignantly in the small numbers of the age groups born during war and revolution. But the high Russian birth rate has in the past quickly repaired such losses.

This is not happening in the United Kingdom and other Western European countries, however, where each succeeding group reaching age 15, 20, and so on, is smaller than the one that preceded it. In other words, the reservoir from which Western countries draw military manpower is receding, whereas in the Soviet Union, despite estimated direct war losses of fourteen million persons, there is a growing force of young military manpower.

In the West the situation will be changed when the children of the postwar baby boom reach military age. Furthermore the large drop in the birth rate that apparently has occurred in the Soviet Union will begin to be felt about the same time.

Consequently, present trends in military manpower heavily favor the Soviet Union in relation to the West. Trends ten to fifteen years hence may not.

A comparison of the composition of the population of several important countries is presented in Table 9-3. It may be noted that there is only a

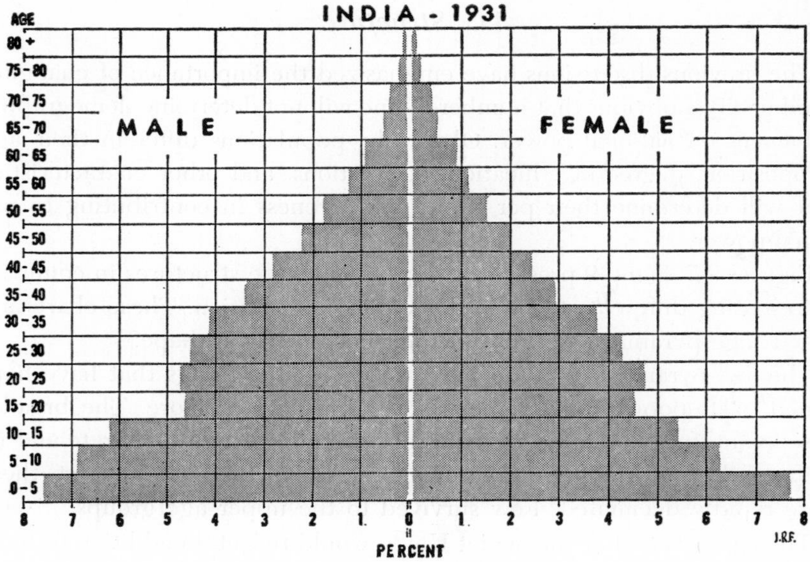

Fig. 9-7. India: Composition of Population.

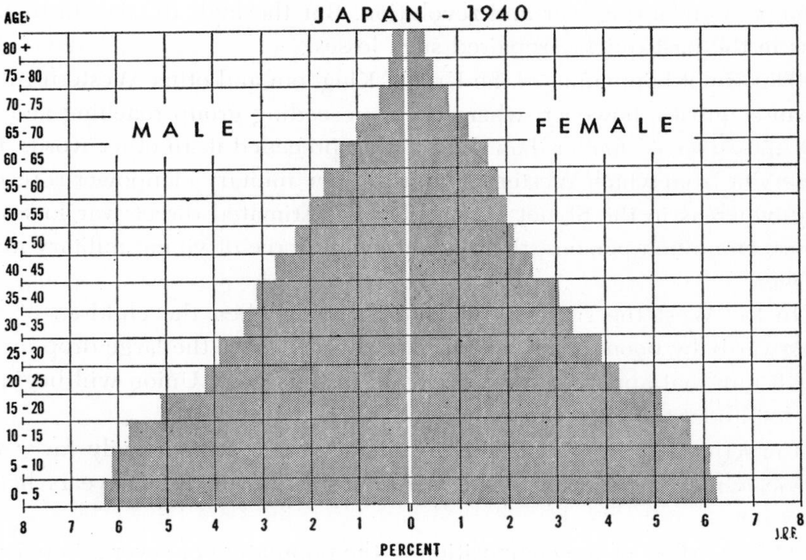

Fig. 9-8. Japan: Composition of Population.

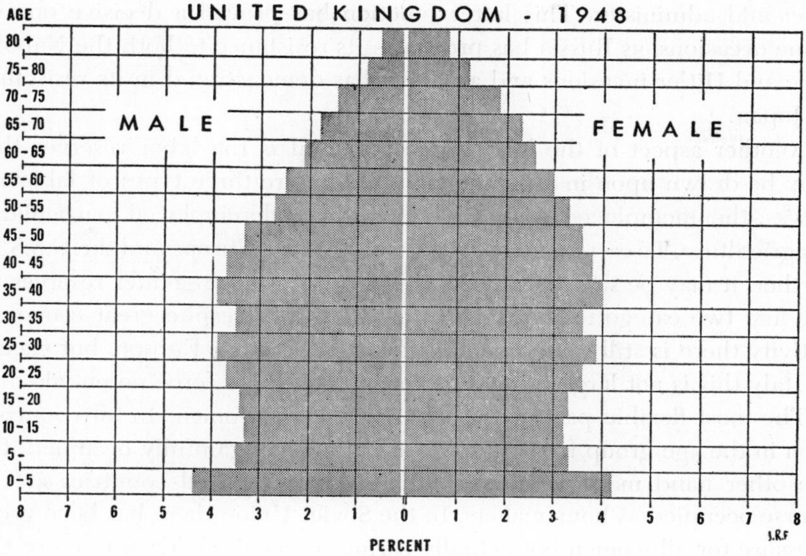

Fig. 9-9. United Kingdom: Composition of Population.

general correlation between the relative size of total populations and the size of the groups most important to military strength.

Because of their low birth rates during the depression years the United States and Western Europe have relatively small contingents of males in the most crucial military age groups at the present time. Thus while the total population of the Soviet Union is not very much greater than the combined total population of the four chief Western European powers, the number of males 15 to 24 in the Soviet Union is 5 million larger. While the Soviet population is only about 20 per cent larger than that of the United States, it has far more men at the young military ages.

On the other hand, the labor force in the Western countries is roughly proportionate to the total population. The West is therefore better off in terms of industrial manpower than it is in terms of prime military manpower. Furthermore its labor force is utilized primarily in non agricultural occupations. Despite very rapid industrialization, the Soviet population is still almost half agricultural. In the modern world, agricultural population contributes very little to the industrial potential of the country. It has value as a source of military manpower but this in turn is limited by the capacity of the economy to equip and support soldiers in the field. Defensively, of course, a large agricultural population may be difficult to conquer and administer. This latter function has proved a decisive one on some occasions, as Russia has proven in its resistance to both the Napoleonic and Hitler invasions and as China has demonstrated in its resistance to Japan.

Another aspect of the labor force potential is the labor reserves that may be drawn upon in an emergency. There are three types of labor reserves: the unemployed, housewives, and the underemployed, particularly in agriculture. To carry our comparison of Western Europe and the U.S.S.R. further, it may be said that the Western coutries have greater reserves of the first two categories but far less of the third. Despite great economic activity there is still some unemployment in Western Europe, but except in Italy this is not large in relation to the total labor force potential.

The most flexible part of the labor reserve is women. In all countries men in the age group from 15 to 59 are almost all gainfully occupied. On the other hand many women of this age group in all countries are of course occupied as homemakers. In the Soviet Union there has been great pressure for all women not actually caring for small children to enter the labor force. About two-thirds of Soviet women at ages 15 to 59 are in the labor force. There is little flexibility left for gaining woman-power in the labor force in a national emergency.

By contrast, Western countries have a very substantial reserve in women not now gainfully occupied. The proportion in the labor force is much less; in the United States only 30 per cent of women at ages 15 to 59 are in the labor force. Obviously many more than in Russia could be drawn upon in an emergency, as they were in the United States during the last world war.

The third element in labor reserve—the underemployed in agriculture—is much greater in the Soviet Union than in the West. In a few Western countries such as Italy, Spain, and Portugal, there is a substantial reserve of agricultural underemployment but nothing to compare with the Soviet Union and with Eastern Europe generally. The East has enormous reserves of farmers inefficiently employed in agricultural work who form a continuing reserve of labor for future industrialization in these areas.

These illustrative comparisons should not be given too great weight in themselves. A large population size, a large military manpower, a large and highly skilled working force are the *conditions* and not in themselves the *fact* of political power. To these ingredients must be added organization, morale, and motivation to make this potential strength kinetic.

TABLE 9-3

Manpower Comparisons, Selected Countries, 1956 *
(Rounded to Millions)

	TOTAL POPU-LATION	POPU-LATION 15-59	MALES 15-24	LABOR FORCE		
				TOTAL	NON-AGRIC.	AGRI-CULTURAL
United States	168	96	11	70	64	7
Western European Powers	195	120	14	89	67	21
United Kingdom	51	31	3	23	22	1
France	44	26	3	21	15	6
Italy	49	31	4	22	13	9
Western Germany	51	32	4	23	18	5
U.S.S.R.	200	127	19	86	49	37

* Data for the United States and the Western European powers compiled and adapted from census and official estimates of the countries concerned. Figures for the U.S.S.R. were derived from official Soviet data by the U. S. Bureau of the Census, Office of Foreign Manpower Research. The labor force figures for the U.S.S.R. apparently exclude several millions in the armed services, in labor camps, in domestic service, in the party apparatus, and in certain other categories that would be included in Western countries.

E. *Pressure*

THE GROWING POPULATION IN A SHRINKING WORLD

In previous chapters it has been noted that, geographically speaking, we live in a shrinking world. Modern transport and communication are cutting down the real distance, measured in travel time and cost, between the several parts of the globe.

Demographically speaking, the opposite is the case: we live in a rapidly expanding world. One of the most distinctive features of our age is this rapid multiplication of our species in all parts of the world.

At the same time hope is being held out that the human race as a whole, not just a single class or master race, can be freed from the degradation of grinding poverty and needless suffering. This hope is justified by technical achievements and by the rising capacity to produce. Probably the cornucopia-minded are correct in asserting that the world could meet these expectations for its present numbers. But a large part of the economic gains must each year be diverted to provide new places at the world's table rather than to improve the fare of those already here.

The "world population problem" turns out on inspection to be a series of regional and national problems. Much more important than the total resources theoretically available in the world are the specific resources available in relation to the populations of specific countries and regions. In fact even here the oft-discussed framework of the relation of people to resources offers a somewhat inadequate statement of the problem.

Quite as important as physical resources in relation to population are the crucial intervening variables that determine how effectively such resources are used and converted to meet population needs. The factors of technology, social organization, and especially political stability are quite as important in determining levels of living as the stock of physical resources.

The greatest population pressure, and the greatest growth potential, lie in the area sometimes described as Monsoon Asia, that is, non-Soviet Asia from Pakistan east to Japan. Following is a case study of the problem of people versus resources in that crucial area.

MONSOON ASIA

Half the world lives in Monsoon Asia—the poorer half. By Western standards the overwhelming majority of the population of this region live in unrelieved poverty. If sheer poverty is a measure of overpopulation, the entire area is desperately overpopulated. But the relationship between people and resources is not a simple one.

Measures of Population Pressure. Population pressure is not fully measured by "man-land ratios." These leave out a vitally important middle factor—the effectiveness with which available resources are utilized. In the broadest sense this is determined by the cultural development of the people—their motivations, their organization, and their skills. Low productivity may reflect either population pressure or backward technology. In Asia it undoubtedly reflects both. It is difficult to isolate the impact of limited resources and to measure population pressure *per se*.

Population pressure should be felt most acutely in the production of absolute essentials, and notably food. Figure 9-10 gives some measure of the prewar relationships between people, land, and food production in Asia as compared with other parts of the world. Asia was obviously heavily populated in relation to arable land. In Eastern Asia (China, Korea, and Japan) there was available only half an acre of cultivated land per person. Southern Asia was somewhat better off with .8 of a cultivated acre per person. In these terms Southern Asia was in a slightly better position than Western Europe but was at a serious disadvantage in relation to other parts of the world, particularly North America.

The different intensity of agriculture leads to quite a different comparison in terms of original calories per acre. Here Asia makes a much better showing, albeit inferior to that of Western Europe. Asia produces substantially more per acre than does the extensive agriculture of North

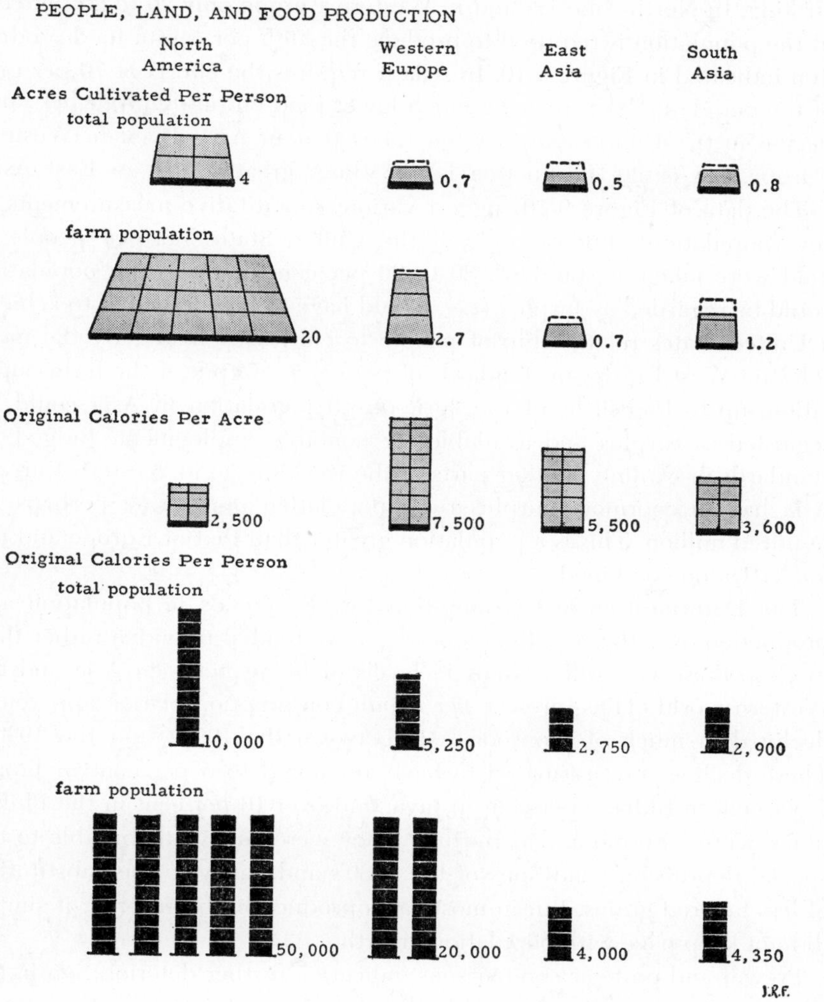

FIG. 9-10. **People, Land, and Food Production.**

America and the U.S.S.R., but, in the case of Southern Asia, less than half as much as Western Europe.

The most significant comparison is the output in relation to the population, and especially to the population in agriculture. Despite intensive agriculture, *per capita* productivity falls very far short of that in other parts of the world. This is true even in relation to Western Europe, where the crude relationships of people to cultivated land might indicate as acute a problem of overpopulation as in Asia.

The comparative productivity of persons in agriculture is particularly striking. In North America and in Western Europe only 20 to 25 per cent of the population is required to produce the high per capita food production indicated in Figure 9-10. In Asia it requires the efforts of 70 per cent of the population to produce a much lower food output. Output per farm person in the United States is ten times that in Asia. Even in Western Europe, per capita production is five times greater than in East Asia.

The data of Figure 9-10 suggest various quantitative measurements of "overpopulation." For example, if the United States ratio of people to land were taken as standard, 80 to 90 per cent of the Asian population could be regarded as surplus (*i.e.*, would have to be eliminated to achieve a United States relationship of people to cultivated land). By the more relevant West European standards of *per capita* output of the farm population, up to four-fifths of the agricultural population in Asia could be regarded as surplus and available for nonfarm employment. Judged by standards prevailing in other parts of the world, even in Western Europe, Asia has an enormous surplus rural population numbering perhaps six hundred million. This is a population greater than that of Europe and the Soviet Union combined.

The Deterioration in Consumption Levels. Trends in population and production over the past three decades have tended to widen rather than to close these vast differentials in levels of living between Asia and the Western world. Thus, prewar *per capita* consumption of rice apparently declined in much of Monsoon Asia between the 1920's and the 1930's. These declines are estimated to have amounted to 5 per cent in Japan, 7 per cent in India, 8 per cent in Java, and over 10 per cent in the Philippines, Korea, Formosa, and Burma.[9] They were partly attributable to the special depression conditions of the 1930's and partly to the substitution of less favored grains. But in most cases production did not fall; it simply did not keep pace with population growth.

Prewar and postwar comparisons indicate a further deterioration in the *per capita* consumption of food in the majority of Asiatic countries, again attributable to population growth rather than to production declines. By contrast, average diets in North and South America have undoubtedly improved and in Western Europe prewar levels are being gradually regained.

It would almost certainly seem that Asian countries would be better off as regards food consumption if they had substantially smaller populations.

[9] V. D. Wickizer and M. K. Bennett, *The Rice Economy of Monsoon Asia* (Food Research Institute, Stanford University, 1941), Ch. 10.

Even given the existing backward agricultural technology in most parts of Eastern Asia, the populations would certainly be much better fed if there were, say, one acre of cultivated land per person instead of only half an acre. Taking Asian countries as a whole and in terms of existing technology and land utilization, all are certainly overpopulated—overpopulated in the sense that the level of living would be higher if there were fewer people, other conditions remaining the same.

Possibilities of Increased Production. Fortunately we may hope that other conditions will not remain the same. To say that an area is vastly overpopulated is not to say that levels of living cannot be raised or the pressure of population ameliorated through better use of resources.

The history of Japan is particularly illuminating in this regard, since Japan is one of the most densely populated countries in the world and by many objective criteria (for example, ratio of population to arable land) the most overpopulated country. The very rapid population growth occurring in Japan prior to the war was not accompanied by deterioration of consumption levels. During the interwar period of rapid population growth the available food supply per head of population increased in quantity and quality more than at any other period in Japanese history.[10] It is true that Japan was importing rice from the colonies and that special circumstances favored Japan in its early period of industrialization. On the other hand, Japan showed a rather remarkable capacity to meet the food demands of its increased population despite very limited natural resources.

Other Asian countries may not have the great advantages earlier enjoyed by Japan in being able to find a market for industrial goods and ready sources of food imports. On the other hand, within all of these countries there are large unexploited areas which remain uncultivated owing to such factors as lack of capital, ignorance of means of effective utilization, and political instability. Thus, in India and China there are substantial areas not under the plow that would be productive with proper irrigation. In the three countries of mainland Southeast Asia (Burma, Thailand, and Indo-China) the densely populated river deltas are surrounded by large unexploited regions, substantial portions of which are suitable for various types of agriculture. In Indonesia, overpopulated Java is surrounded by thinly settled outer islands that could unquestionably support several times their present inhabitants.

[10] E. B. Schumpeter, *et. al., The Industrialization of Japan and Manchukuo, 1930-1940* (New York, 1940).

Furthermore, a comparison of rice yields in Japan and other Asian countries suggests the practical possibilities of better farm practices. Though the soil of Japan is apparently not intrinsically better for rice culture than in other major producing areas, the yields are very much larger. Japanese yields of 35 to 40 bushels of cleaned rice per acre may be compared with 25 in China and Formosa, 20 in Korea, and about 15 in India, Burma, Thailand, and Java. Higher Japanese yields are reported to be chiefly attributable to the use of better seeds and to the effective utilization of both industrial and organic fertilizers.

Or let us assume that through technological progress Asia were to achieve Western European productivity per acre. In East Asia such an achievement would increase production in that area by more than one-third and would feed two hundred million more people at present consumption levels. In South Asia the achievement of West European output per acre would double production.

Thus, as compared with the United States and even West Europe, Asia has a huge surplus farm population. But given improvements in farm practices enabling the same intensity of agricultural production as in West Europe or Japan, Asia could greatly increase her food output.

Recent Population Growth. Population pressure in Monsoon Asia is not the result of outstandingly rapid growth in this region. Historically the growth of European populations has been much more rapid. But while the latter has tended to decline, the population growth of Asia has tended to accelerate.

In the recent past, rates of growth have ranged from little or no growth estimated for China to 2 to 2.5 per cent per year in Formosa, the Philippines, and other areas undergoing especially effective public health measures. More typical of Monsoon Asia, however, is the annual rate of growth in prepartition India at 1.4 per cent between 1931 and 1941. Between 1937 and 1947 the annual growth rate of Monsoon Asia (without China) was 1.2 per cent. This may be compared with .7 per cent during the same period in Western Europe, 1.1 in North America, about 1.5 per cent in Africa, and about 2 per cent in Latin America.

In Monsoon Asia (aside from Japan) the controlling factor in population growth has been the death rate. The annual birth rate is consistently high, ranging between 35 and 45 per thousand in all countries.[11]

[11] As compared with 25 in the United States, 16 in the United Kingdom, 22 in Japan (all 1953). Official data for several of the Asiatic countries show much lower rates (India 25 in 1952), but there is ample evidence that these reflect failure to report a

In "normal" years there is an excess of births over deaths; historically this surplus was periodically wiped out by famines, epidemics, and war. In areas recently under European, American, or Japanese tutelage these periodic disasters have been progressively reduced with resultant rapid population growth. But even "normal" death rates in these areas remain high as compared to current standards in the United States. There is present a large "growth potential" realizable through further declines in the death rate.

Factors Affecting Future Population Changes. *The Potential Saving of Lives.* As in the West, declines in mortality in Asia preceded declines in fertility. Great improvement in most countries of the region has been achieved in the control of the acute and chronic contagious diseases, and great further achievements are possible with comparatively little effort. The possibilities in this regard under varying circumstances are illustrated by such experiences as those in the Philippines and Formosa, where prewar achievements in reducing the death rate were largely the result of external initiative; in Japan, where great progress was made at native initiative; and in postwar Ceylon and Japan, where startling reductions in mortality have been accomplished chiefly through the broadcast use of the new insecticides.[12] Where progress in public health has been slow or negative, the explanation is to be found in ineffective government or political disturbance (as in China, Indonesia, and French Indo-China).

---

major proportion of the births. Following are more reliable vital rates and comparison with Italian and United States data:

Vital Rates Per 1000 Population

COUNTRY	YEAR	BIRTH	DEATH	NATURAL INCREASE
China	1953	37 [a]	17 [a]	20 [a]
India	1931-41	45 [b]	31 [b]	14 [b]
Ceylon	1953	39	11	28
Malaya	1953	44	12	31
Formosa	1953	45	9	36
Japan	1953	22	9	12
Italy	1953	17	10	7
United States	1953	25	10	15

[a] As reported from a sample survey in Communist China (apparently not including areas affected by floods).
[b] Estimated from census data.

[12] In Ceylon the death rate per thousand population was cut from 22.0 in 1945 to 12.6 in 1949 and 10.9 in 1953 (chiefly through destruction of insect carriers with DDT). In Japan the death rate has been cut from prewar 17.0 (1937) to 11.6 in 1949, and 8.9 in 1953, with an annual saving of some 600,000 lives.

Such reliable evidence as does exist indicates (1) that death rates are progressively declining in most of the areas, aside from reversals occasioned by war and political disturbances, and (2) that the tempo of decline is speeding up. There is no case of general upward trend in mortality as a result of inadequate nutrition and overpopulation, despite the fact that the per capita consumption in several of the countries seems to be substantially lower than before the war. The average food supply seems to be somewhat lower but it is better distributed.

It may be argued that people are being saved from disease only to die from famine. But this point has demonstratively not yet been reached and it seems probable that in the near future it will not be reached.

Theoretically, increasing the death rate might be an effective means of reducing the rate of population growth and the pressure of population on the land. But only wars and internal upheavals may conceivably have this effect, which would be temporary in nature.

Will the Birth Rate Decline? So far as may be determined on the basis of inadequate statistical evidence, birth rates throughout the region are high—as high or perhaps higher than those prevailing in Europe and America a century ago. In Asia as in other parts of the world, high and uncontrolled fertility is an accompaniment of poverty, ignorance, and subsistence agriculture. There is no reason to suppose that this high fertility represents a native or racial characteristic, or that Asians would not be responsive to the same influences that brought about declines in the birth rate in Western countries. The difference is that, with the single and very important exception of Japan, large Asian populations have not been exposed to these influences. In the twenty years preceding World War II, the pattern of decline in the Japanese birth rate was almost identical with that experienced in Great Britain between 1880 and 1900, when that country was at a somewhat comparable period of industrialization and economic development. Similar declines in the birth rate have been noted among urban and middle class groups in India. While conservative influences are antagonistic to regulation of births in Asia, up to the present time there does not appear to be any major overt and doctrinal religious opposition.

Declining birth rates have usually been regarded as exclusively linked with industrialization and urbanization. If this were true there would be little expectation of declining birth rates in those large sections of Asia where early industrialization does not appear feasible. However, an inspection of Western experience shows that the birth rate also tends to decline with education and literacy even in the absence of industrialization. In Europe declines in the birth rate have been as closely correlated with literacy as with urbanization.[13] If this also proves to be true of Asia, it is entirely possible that declines in the birth rate may be experienced even before extensive industrialization.

The European and Japanese experience, and the fragmentary evidence for certain groups in other Asian countries, suggest that in time the birth rate will tend to fall in Asia and that the tempo of this decline will be in proportion to the rapidity of general economic and social progress on the Western pattern. However, we face the paradox that the first effects of modernization are to increase rather than decrease the rate of growth, because declines in the death rate precede those in the birth rate. This seems to be a necessary transitional stage. Controlled fertility apparently seems to be a part of the same complex of cultural factors that result in greater economic production. Anything convincing people that they can control their environment rather than accept it fatalistically will probably induce a lower birth rate.

Possibilities for Emigration. A superficially reasonable method of relieving population pressure is emigration. This was one answer of Europe to the problem and resulted in the emigration of some sixty million Europeans overseas. But, even in the exceptionally favorable situation prevailing in the nineteenth and early twentieth centuries emigration was a real solution of population pressure only in certain smaller countries and regions, such as Ireland, Scotland, and Norway.

Contemporary Asia finds herself in a very different position from Europe in the last three centuries. The desirable empty spaces of the world are already occupied or controlled by countries who would resist the immigration of large numbers of Asians.

Furthermore, there are many times as many Asians as there were Europeans during the periods of great overseas colonization. Monsoon Asia has a natural increase at the present time of at least ten million persons per year. There are no outlets for Asiatic emigration capable of absorbing even a very small fraction of this increase by peaceful means. Even if other parts of the world were to absorb these huge numbers, there is no assurance but that their places would be almost immediately taken by more rapid increase of the population at home. While a certain amount

[13] The birth rate is low in almost wholly rural countries, such as Bulgaria and the Baltic countries, where literacy is relatively high (cf. Dudley Kirk, *Europe's Population in the Interwar Years* [League of Nations, 1946], Ch. IV, p. 248).

of emigration from Asia would be desirable for various reasons, it will have symbolic rather than actual value in solving Asia's problem of overpopulation.

On the other hand, much may be expected from internal redistribution of population, especially in Southeast Asia, where there remain large areas suitable for agricultural exploitation.

The Outlook for the Next Decade. With a modicum of peace we may anticipate declining death rates in the region. In all probability these will not be matched in the earlier stages by declining birth rates. In the absence of serious political disturbances the populations of this region may be expected to increase 1.5 to 2.5 per cent per year, with a general tendency for the rate of growth to increase. Under optimum conditions, economic production must be increased by about 2 per cent per year merely to maintain the increasing population at existing levels.

The handicap of population growth to economic progress may be illustrated by reference to India and Pakistan. If the population of the Indian subcontinent grows as fast between 1950 and 1960 as it did between 1931 and 1941 and between 1941 and 1951 (15 per cent) it will rise from the present 425 million to about 490 million. This would represent an increase of 31 per cent over the prewar 1937 population.

In a carefully weighed study of the problem, Burns estimates that rice yields per acre could be increased by 30 per cent and other crops correspondingly.[14] But it would require all of this gain in the next decade merely to regain the per capita consumption of the thirties. To regain the production (and consumption) levels of the twenties would require an additional 10 per cent increase in production in the next decade, whether through higher yields per acre or through cultivation of new lands. A production increase of some 40 per cent by 1960 is necessary merely to match population growth and recapture ground lost in the past thirty years.[15]

On the brighter side of the picture is the example of Japan, which illustrates the possibility of doubling or even tripling food output through improved farm practices. While such goals are scarcely realizable in a decade, they hold out the possibility that even a rapidly growing population can be supplied with an improved diet.

To the extent that Asia is successful in promoting improved levels of living, there will initially be even more rapid population growth. But

[14] Burns, *Technological Possibilities of Agricultural Development in India* (Lahore, 1944).

[15] These figures may be pessimistic owing to the possibility that crop reporting in recent years somewhat underestimates actual production.

there is the hope that such rising levels of living will eventually be accompanied by declining birth rates and a smaller rate of growth. This is the humane solution. No matter what the rate of technological and economic progress, if the population of Asia continued to grow at the rates current and likely for the near future, population would inevitably overtake the means of subsistence and would result in a catastrophe.

THE POLITICAL SIGNIFICANCE OF POPULATION PRESSURE

The above analysis has not been optimistic. Even with the most hopeful forecasts of economic development there is no prospect whatsoever that the crowded populations of Asia can in this generation match Western levels of living. Yet this level is dangled in front of all underprivileged people as the proper standard of material life. Understandably they desire to achieve this standard and unwittingly we have encouraged them to aspire to it.

It is also only human nature that both leaders and citizens of the underdeveloped areas will attribute their difficulties in attaining the Western standard of living not to their own defects but to the fact that they have been deprived access to the territories and natural resources which Western people have appropriated for their own. Regardless of either the ethics or the logic of the situation, it seems almost certain that the human mass of the crowded areas of the world will regard this deprivation as unjust, and hence valid grounds for militant claims for more territory. This will be given further animus by the color prejudice to which they have been subjected during their colonial periods.

It seems a safe prognostication that population pressure both real and imagined will be a vital factor in the relations between the new Asian countries and the West.

At the same time, population growth in these countries consumes economic product that otherwise could be directed to better economic development. In a world where an average annual gain of 3 per cent in the national product is regarded as very large, the handicap of providing for an annual growth of up to 2 per cent or more in the population may mean the difference between success and failure—the difference between success and failure not only in the effort to raise levels of living but even more significantly in the development of political democracy.

In this sense population pressure is one of the fundamental forces militating against the free world in favor of totalitarianism.

CHAPTER 10

Migrations

MIGRATION AND HISTORY

Man's history has been described, with only slight exaggeration, as "the study of his wanderings." Some epochs of the remote past are called "periods of great migrations." This terminology presumes that at other times migratory movements were at a standstill, especially in the case of the so-called "sedentary" people. In fact, no population is ever at rest. Every epoch is a period of "great migrations." [1]

The French geographer Vidal de la Blache describes China as the scene of many obscure migrations, which taken together have changed the face of the land and the history of the world. It is no mere chance that the books containing the oldest memories of the human race, the Bible, the ancient Chinese scrolls, and Mexican chronicles, are full of accounts of migrations. There is no people without a legend of a state of unrest, of *Trieb,* to use Karl Ritter's expression, which compelled them to move from place to place until they found a final resting place "constantly promised by the divine voice, constantly held at a distance by enchantment." [2] But often what appears to be the "final resting place" in the longer span of history proves to be only a temporary refuge.

There are age-old paths of migration in natural highways provided by the physical features of the earth. Halford Mackinder in his *Democratic*

[1] E. M. Kulischer, *Europe on the Move: War and European Population Changes, 1917-1947* (New York, 1948), p. 8.

[2] P. W. J. Vidal de la Blache, *Principes de géographie humaine* (Paris, 1922), p. 70.

Ideals and Reality has vividly described how, from the fifth to the sixteenth century, wave after wave of what he termed "brigands on horseback" swept through the steppes, through the gateway between the Ural Mountains and the Caspian Sea, dealing their formidable blows northward, westward, and southward against the settled peoples of Europe.[3]

The new means of ocean transportation evolved in Europe opened a phase of the history of migration which reached its climax in the early part of this century. The study of the great transoceanic migrations and of their impact on the lands beyond hitherto unexplored ocean spaces provides the raw material of the geography of colonization and overseas empires.

More recently the conquest of the air and the great improvements in land transport have opened new avenues and means of migration. The natural barriers which formerly channeled migration are being increasingly replaced by political and other man-made barriers restricting and directing the movement of people.

ARE THERE PRINCIPLES OR "LAWS" OF MODERN MIGRATIONS?

In the perspective of centuries we see the great migrations of the past as part of vast historical processes, whether it be the decline and fall of Rome before the barbarian invaders, the Aryan invasions of India, or the European colonization of the New World. It is more difficult to perceive a pattern and direction behind migrations of the present epoch. These often seem aimless and nihilistic, in themselves a denial of order and reason. Sometimes they seem to reflect only the hatreds of those who chance to have the power to wreak their vengeance and havoc on the vanquished. Sometimes it is difficult to see meaning in so much manifest inhumanity. Yet our task in political geography is to divest ourselves (for this purpose) of moral judgments and to seek meaning and direction in the mass movements of humanity in their relation to the power of nations.

Sixty-five years ago when Ravenstein presented his famous papers on migration at the Royal Statistical Society of Great Britain,[4] the establishment of a universal law of migration seemed possible, even certain. Ravenstein's "Laws" still hold good for many purposes today, but they apply only to those movements occurring within the "rules of the game" of

[3] H. W. Weigert, *Generals and Geographers* (New York, 1942), pp. 123-125.

[4] E. G. Ravenstein, "The Laws of Migration," *Journal of the Royal Statistical Society,* 1885, pp. 167-235; 1889, pp. 241-305. Ravenstein found fixed relationships between distance of migration and the number, the age, and the sex of the migrants.

Victorian Europe. The mass migrations associated primarily with the two World Wars were entirely outside his frame of reference.

But the fact that there are new forms of migration does not mean there is no order and direction. The pattern of change itself may be more important to political geography than the orderly movements occurring within the fixed precepts of a particular epoch.

In the discussion that follows we shall seek to find the significance of modern migration movements in, first, an analysis of the types of migration, and second, in an analysis of the directions of the movement.

TYPES OF MIGRATION

There are many ways of classifying migrations—according to their degree of permanency, their intensity and volume, the human units involved, their motives, the distance traveled, and the direction of the movement. These criteria give rise to contrasts between temporary and permanent migrations; individual versus communal or tribal migrations; free versus forced movements; internal versus international and overseas migrations.

Each of these represents a different way of viewing the same phenomenon and each in its own way is relevant to problems of political geography. These dichotomies also suggest the various contrasts between the migratory movements characteristic of the nineteenth and twentieth centuries.

Thus the overseas migrations of the nineteenth and early twentieth centuries were composed of individuals and family groups, whereas the population transfers of the twentieth century were often composed of entire communities; the earlier migrations gave effect to the free and voluntary choice of individuals, whereas the war-induced transfers were motivated by fear and force; overseas migration involved continuing contacts and exchanges between the homeland and the migrants, whereas population transfers were intended to be an absolute and irrevocable uprooting from the homeland; finally, the population shifts connected with the two World Wars were chiefly continental movements associated with changed political boundaries, whereas the earlier movements were predominantly long-distance migrations overseas.

Behind these differences is a changed philosophy of the purposes and rights involved in migration. The earlier philosophy was that the individual should be free to choose his place of residence in accordance with the dictates of his conscience and the welfare of himself and his family. The modern philosophy is that individual needs and desires must be subordinated to the needs of the community as defined by the state. It can be said that migration is controlled by conscious geopolitical motivations.

It is easy to conclude that the change in type of migration is a change from order to chaos. But the great differences in the character of the two types of migrations obscure the fact that both conform to underlying forces of population pressure that determine the direction and viability of the movements.

POPULATION PRESSURE AND MIGRATION

Population pressure exists in two senses. There is the *absolute* relationship of people to resources which may, at a given stage of the arts, mean the difference between poverty and prosperity. Until very recently this was the nature of the problem in Monsoon Asia, where there existed little knowledge of better opportunities elsewhere and even less practical means of taking advantage of these opportunities. The typical Asian was a peasant who knew little about life beyond the confines of his village. In such a situation population pressure is a latent but not an active political force. There is the other and *relative* sense of differential population pressure between countries and the changes in these relationships occurring over time. To be an active force this pressure has reality only if it is known and felt by the peoples concerned. It is the latter *relative* population pressure that is significant for problems of political geography.

Relative population pressures create tensions that are either relieved through migrations or are built up against political barriers with the constant threat of explosion if these barriers are weakened. Some form of population pressure has been behind all the great migrations in history.

Population pressure that gives rise to movement is not just a matter of the mechanical density of the population. Often the great migration pressures are from areas of lesser density to higher density as was true of the barbarian invasions of the Roman Empire, of the Manchu and Mongol invasions of China, and of the Aryan invasions of India. The factor of crude density of population is relevant only as it is expressed in terms of economic opportunity.

There have been two great magnets of economic opportunity in modern Europe, which has been the source and theater of the most significant migrations in the last two centuries. The first of these was the attraction of unpeopled lands for land-hungry peoples. In the broader sense there was the opportunity for personal and national exploitation of rich natural resources in underdeveloped and relatively unoccupied countries. The second magnet was the economic opportunity offered by industrialization and commerce in the cities and industrialized regions both in Europe itself and in Europe overseas.

These two great forces in migration give us a key to the understanding, in one framework, of both the orderly migrations of the past and the seemingly chaotic migrations of the current generation. The first magnet, that of unpeopled lands, induced the great outward thrust of peoples from the older centers of population, predominantly from Western Europe but also to a lesser extent from China and India. Cutting across and in some respects directly opposing this centrifugal thrust has been the centripetal tendency reflected particularly in vast rural-urban migrations.

Most population movements in the modern world fall into a meaningful pattern if they are thought of in terms of these two great categories and in terms of the historical replacement of the first by the second.

FREE MIGRATIONS OF EUROPEANS

In the analysis that follows we will first study free migrations and especially the migrations associated with the expansion of Europe and, without recounting the details of this epic migration, attempt to point to its lasting effects and to its politico-geographical legacy in the modern world. The problem of "colonialism" has its origin in the nature of European settlement and control.

The Politico-Geographical Legacy of European Settlement. Whether colonization takes the form of permanent settlement or whether its characteristic is the establishment of sovereignty over territories providing raw materials and markets (known to the French as *colonies d'exploitation*), or whether we think of the type of colonization consisting of settler "islands" in alien lands (as, for instance, those of the Germans, Italians, and Japanese in Brazil, or the Volga-Germans in Russia before their deportation), we will always have to go back to the same common denominator explaining the sources, the strength, and the goals of colonization in a particular area. Where Europeans settled *en masse* we find a history entirely different from those colonies in which the economy was established on the extensive use of indigenous labor. The difference in terms of the political future of these areas is decisive and profound.

For our purposes it is desirable to distinguish between the various demographic manifestations of the expansion of Europe:

Overseas Areas of Predominantly European Settlement. These countries are as a group the wealthiest in the world, including the United States, Canada, Australia, New Zealand, Argentina, and Uruguay. All have in effect achieved their political independence and, with Latin American exceptions, are among the most stable politically in the world today.

Areas of European Native Amalgamation. In the greater part of Latin America European and native populations, in some cases with African infusions, are in the process of merging. The divergent percentage of European racial and cultural ingredients has resulted in a very uneven degree of development which is too often concealed by the general rubric "Latin America." The political regimes are often unstable, but culturally and politically these areas of settlement are firmly allied to the West. While the amalgamation of European and natives is most characteristic of Latin America, it also exists to a certain extent in the Philippines and in Portuguese Africa, though in these areas the European biological and cultural element is weaker than in most of Latin America.

Areas of European Settlement Where Europeans Are a Ruling Minority. This type of settlement exists chiefly in Africa. In North Africa a million and a half French rule three closely related Arab lands of 18 million inhabitants. In the Union of South Africa, 2.5 million Britains and Boers (themselves in conflict with each other) [5] hold the exclusive reins of government in a country with some 11 million nonwhites. An even smaller and less rooted white minority of fewer than 200,000 British governs an indigenous population of some 3.5 million in the British dominion of Rhodesia. These are the hard-core areas of colonialism that the colonial powers and indigenous white populations cannot relinquish without threatening the most basic welfare and perhaps even the survival of the resident whites.

Areas Governed but Not Settled by Europeans. This type of European colonization was chiefly characteristic of Asia and tropical Africa. In Asia it is dead. The Second World War greatly accelerated the development of local nationalisms and brought to an earlier end an otherwise inevitable trend against continuing European control of these areas. The vestigial remains of direct European government of Asia, whether in the Portuguese colonies, in Indo-China, or in British Malaya and Hong Kong are under the severest pressure. The same fate is clearly in store for the European colonies in tropical Africa. Already Negroes in West Africa, Nigeria, and the Gold Coast are making rapid strides toward independence. In the East African highlands the Mau Mau revolt, while unsuccessful in itself,

[5] See p. 391.

has foreshadowed the end of any prospect for permanent white control of the region.

Linguistic Islands.[6] The same drives that sent sixty million Europeans to settle overseas lands impelled the colonization of Eastern Europe by Western Europeans, particularly Germans. Rulers of Eastern Europe welcomed these settlers because of their industry and relative advancement. These newcomers chose to found their own communities and to maintain their own customs, language, and religion. Settled as units and having in their view a superior culture and higher economic status, these linguistic islands resisted assimilation. The same phenomenon occurred less frequently in overseas migration, as in the German settlements of Brazil that have maintained their language and other German characteristics for several generations. The Pennsylvania "Dutch" of the United States are such a linguistic island though now far along toward total absorption.[7] Few of these islands are likely to survive. The German *Sprachinseln* which formerly dotted Eastern Europe have been annihilated. The modern nationalisms of Europe doom such islands either to oppression or to assimilation.

Effect of Advance of Frontiers. Finally a neglected aspect of the expansion of Europe is the effect of the advance of the frontier within the new countries politically controlled by people of European stock. These internal migrations have had profound geopolitical effects particularly in the United States and the Soviet Union.

The history of the United States offers a continuous documentation of the impact of new areas which, in the overall picture of the nation, have won their place in the sun and, by achieving political maturity, have exerted their influence and that of their newly settled people upon the internal and external affairs of the Union. The "political geography" of Presidential elections may serve as illustration: until Buchanan's Presidency all Presidents came from the eastern seaboard, except for the Tennessean Jackson. From Lincoln to McKinley, the majority came from the Middle West but east of the Mississippi. Since Theodore Roosevelt, we find a greater geographical variety, but also the first Presidents from west of the Mississippi (Hoover, Truman, and Eisenhower).

[6] See the detailed discussion of linguistic factors in political geography in Chapter 11, pp. 383-403.

[7] An interesting example of such an island is that of the Russian sect of the Sons of Freedom, the Dukhobors, whose members left Russia at the beginning of the century in search of religious and political freedom and who, as squatters in British Columbia, engaged in a last-stand struggle against the Canadian government, resisting assimilation in the Canadian community.

Thus the history of internal migration in the United States offers an excellent illustration of the important principle that if the factors of instability and change motivated by internal migration are of major proportions they will redistribute power within a nation. A classical example is the decisive break which began in the United States in the 1850's, when a large-scale colonization of the Great Plains redrew the population distribution map of the country. Hitherto this had shown the European settlements clinging to the Atlantic coast, their penetration inland normally limited to a strip within a hundred miles of tidewater. The map of the population "centers" in the United States with the period between 1790 and 1950 [8] is a graphic illustration of the "Westward Course of Empire" trend which, with different connotations, is still underway. Since 1790, the center of population in the United States has not deviated more than a few miles from its original latitude, close to 39° N, but it has moved steadily westward. In a century and a half the center of population has moved about six hundred miles, at an average speed of four miles a year. The shift was particularly rapid (more than five miles a year) between 1830 and 1890. It then slowed down, especially after 1910, but quickened during World War II. The growth of California, which has continued after 1945, was and still is instrumental in drawing the country's center of population further westward.

The student of politics, both on the national and state level, will discover important changes in the composition of population groups as the result of these shifts.

The American example repeats itself in all national territories endowed with large space. The westward course of internal migration in the United States is paralleled by the many waves of migration southward, northward, and eastward which shaped the history of Russia and of the U.S.S.R. The internal geography of the Soviet Union cannot be understood without constant reference to the mass migrations and population transfers which took place during its entire turbulent history, starting with the forced resettlements of the collectivization period during 1929 and 1930 and assuming momentum again in 1932 and 1933 when mass famines starved out many villages and drove millions to the cities. As a result of planned population transfers between 1927 and 1939, the Urals, Siberia and the Far East, as well as Central Asia (in particular Kazakhstan), became the receiving centers of new waves of migration involving about five million people.[9] Since the war, migrations continue as, for instance,

[8] See Fig. 18-1, p. 572.
[9] For a detailed discussion see Kulischer, *Europe on the Move,* pp. 79-112.

to the labor camps scattered in inhospitable regions over the Soviet Union,[10] and most important, the mass movements from the villages to the towns and cities. This farm-to-town migration is rapidly turning the Soviet Union into an urbanized nation.

THE MIGRATION CYCLE IN EUROPE

Historically, mass migration from Europe has been associated with a particular stage of economic, social, and political development. It has not been a purely rational movement from the areas of lowest income or greatest physical poverty. People in such areas usually lack knowledge, means, and abilities for taking advantage of opportunities overseas. It has rather been a function of a particular stage in the transition from an essentially self-sufficient peasant economy to a modern industrial and urban economy. The sources of mass overseas migration were first in the British Isles in connection with early industrialization and the related agricultural enclosure movement. The latter dispossessed the English yeoman and the Scottish crofter and gave them impetus to seek land and fortune overseas. They were soon joined by the Irish cottager who suffered acute pressure of population on the land.

The emigration "fever," as it has sometimes been described, moved in ever-widening concentric rings as modern influences spread from their centers of origin in England, the Low Countries, and later Western Germany. The "fever" was associated with a particular stage in the transition when the horizons of life in the rural areas began to rise beyond the boundaries of the village to the world at large. New aspirations were aroused by improved communication, transportation, by free public education, and by the invasion of the money economy.

In its demographic aspects, this is also a period of transition in which improvements in nutrition, and especially simple public health precautions, were bringing down the death rate without comparable declines in the birth rate. The result was a rapid increase in population. In the relatively static agrarian economy of these areas this situation provided the push to make new vistas beyond the village boundaries even more attractive.

The way in which the migration fever spread in concentric circles across Europe, especially from west to east and from north to south, river by river, province by province, is admirably documented by Marcus Lee Hansen in his classic studies of nineteenth century migration to America.[11]

[10] *Ibid.*, p. 93.
[11] M. L. Hansen, *The Atlantic Migration* (Cambridge, Mass., 1951).

Already by 1800 economic opportunities as reported in letters by family and friends overseas were the chief motive for migration.

As economic development progressed, opportunities for employment became increasingly available in nearby factory towns and commercial centers. These offered an alternative to overseas migration. Such "intervening" opportunities characteristically resulted in a reduction in the rate of international migration which, for example, was already evident in England and Wales as early as 1860 and in Germany and Scandinavia in the 1880's and 1890's.

As is widely known, the great sources of overseas migration in the early twentieth century had already moved across Europe to the less developed rural areas of Poland, Austria-Hungary, and southern Italy. This great historic process was drastically inhibited by the first World War, by immigration restrictions in the overseas countries, and by the Russian Revolution. Indeed, it is a likely but unproved hypothesis that the blockage of movement from the east and the lack of ready outlets for populations from Eastern Europe may be related to the violence with which the East in the course of the past generation has thrown off the former economic, cultural, and political leadership of the West.

DIRECTIONS OF MIGRATORY PRESSURE IN EUROPE

By meaningful yardsticks population pressure in Europe during the past two or three generations has been greatest in Eastern and Southern Europe, much less in Northwest Europe.[12] This differential pressure has been reflected (*a*) in the predominance of peoples from these areas in overseas migration, (*b*) in the migrations from the peripheral, predominantly agricultural regions to the industrial cores of Western Europe

[12] Measures of population pressure relevant to Eastern Europe include, *inter alia,* (*a*) density of farm population on arable land, (*b*) agricultural underemployment as measured by low outputs per unit of labor, (*c*) ratios of entrants into the working ages (or the labor force) to departures from these ages through death and the attainment of retirement age. All of these applied to Eastern European countries reveal heavy population pressure before World War II.

In a very fully documented study relating to the interwar period, estimates were made of "surplus" agricultural populations (*i.e.,* agricultural underemployment) in Eastern and Southern European countries, assuming existing (1931-35) production and the European average per capita level of production for the farm population. The estimates of surplus population so derived ranged from zero (the European average) in Czechoslovakia to 50 per cent or more of all the farm populations in Greece, Poland, Rumania, Bulgaria, and Yugoslavia. The "surplus" agricultural population amounted to 4.9 million (27 per cent) in Italy; 1.4 million (12 per cent) in Spain; and 1.4 million (47 per cent) in Portugal. *Cf.* W. E. Moore, *Economic Demography of Eastern and Southern Europe* (Geneva, 1945), Table 6, pp. 63-64.

in England, Northern France, Western Germany, and the Low Countries.

In the last full decade of "free" migration from 1901 to 1910 Eastern and Southern European countries contributed 77 per cent of the overseas migration from Europe as compared with 23 per cent of "old" emigration from Northwest Europe.[13] Fifty years earlier, in the decade 1851 to 1860, less than five per cent of European emigrants were from the areas of "new" migration and over 95 per cent were from Northwest Europe.

Paralleling this change in the composition of overseas migration, there was within Europe a growing migration from the rural hinterlands to the industrial regions of Europe. There was the flight of German agricultural workers in the East to the cities and to the Ruhr. Their places were taken by Polish seasonal workers who came across the boundary for the harvests. Already before World War II large numbers of Italians, Spaniards, and Eastern Europeans were moving into France, and in the interwar period France replaced the United States as the leading destination of European migrants. This period saw the influx of Eastern Jews into Germany and this, however unjustifiably, contributed to the later violent Nazi oppression of the Jewish peoples.

Since about 1890 the prolific Eastern European peasant (usually a Slav) has been exerting economic and demographic pressure against the more urban, less reproductive Central European (usually a German), even in the face of political domination by the latter. In this he was already reversing the earlier true *Drang nach Osten* of the German peoples that drove back the Slav from the Elbe to the Niemen and established German-speaking colonies all the way across Europe to the Volga River. Already before World War I the efforts of Central European nations to strengthen their Eastern marches with Central European settlers were failures because this effort attempted to stem and reverse the tide of basic demographic and socio-economic trends. The displacement of the earlier ruling elements in the interwar years was successful because it accorded with the fundamental demographic pressures.

The demographic pressures in Eastern Europe were partially reflected in successful revolts from Western domination after World War I—revolts legitimized in the principle of self-determination and the establishment of the secession states. Then World War II broke down all barriers and released a tremendous westward thrust of the Slav. The displacement of

[13] The regions of "old" emigration include the British Isles, Germany, Scandinavia, France, the Low Countries, and Switzerland. The region of "new" emigration includes the remainder of Europe.

German by Slav has been successful because it swam with the underlying demographic pressures, just as the failures of the German in displacing the Pole were due to the fact that this effort attempted to stem and reverse the tide of basic economic and social trends.

The population pressures of Southern Europe (Italy, Spain, Portugal, and Greece) have neither been so acute nor so dramatic in results as those of the East. In terms of European averages the surplus populations were proportionately smaller, the rates of population growth historically less, than in the East. Furthermore, outlets for migration were more readily found—for Italians in France, in Belgium, in Luxembourg, and in Switzerland; for Spaniards in France; and for all, overseas. Within Italy, southern Italians found opportunities in the industrialized north and similarly within Spain the industries of Catalonia and the Basque regions met some of the needs of the surplus population in the south. Population pressure was most acute in Greece, where the exchange of populations following World War I had forced that small country to absorb a million refugees from Asia Minor. The chief locations of crowded settlement in Macedonia were also strong centers of disaffection following World War II.

Nevertheless the problem of population pressure was (and is) real. The farm product per farm worker in Italy is less than half that in France, not because the Italian farmer is less skillful or less industrious but because, on the average, he has only half as much land.[14] The situation is comparable in Portugal, worse in Greece.

The differential population pressure is accentuated by the dynamics of the labor force. In a rapidly growing population far more persons enter the labor market each year than leave through death and retirement. Italy must accommodate over 300,000 more persons in the working ages each year, while in the United Kingdom and France the population of working age is now almost stationary. These figures are certainly not unrelated to the one and a half million unemployed chronically reported in Italy since the war. Similarly Greece and Portugal, each with roughly eight million inhabitants, have had to absorb sixty to sixty-five thousand new workers each year, while Belgium (eight million) and Sweden (seven million) have each had annual increments of under ten thousand.

It should be noted that population pressure in Italy is more the result

[14] The relative figures for about 1930 on density of agricultural population per square kilometer of "arable-equivalent" agricultural land are the following: France—28.8; Italy—53.4; Portugal—49.5; Spain—34.0; and Greece—86.7 (Moore, *op. cit.*, pp. 197-204).

of past than of present growth. The current growth in Italy represents the inertia of the past, and it will disappear unless there is a sharp reversal in the present downward trend in the birth rate. The same forces seem to be at work in Spain, and are at an earlier stage in Portugal and Greece.

THE URBAN DRIFT

In all countries there has been a universal movement to the cities from the countryside. The uprooting involved in this movement was enormous —some 150 million or one-third of all Europeans were, in the interwar period, living outside the commune of their birth; over half were outside the province or department of their birth. These latter migrants particularly were persons who had moved to the towns and cities from the villages and farms.

Already by 1880 overseas migration was primarily a movement to the cities of the New World. In the United States for example 80 per cent of the foreign born represented in the 1940 census were living in urban areas as compared with only 50 per cent of the native white of native parentage.

Likewise the greater part of the migration to Australia was to the great cities of Sydney, Melbourne, and Brisbane; in Argentina the bulk of the immigration was absorbed in Buenos Aires; in Brazil the cities of Sao Paulo and Rio de Janeiro were the chief attractions; in none of these countries did large numbers of immigrants go directly to the farms or to the small towns. Within these overseas countries there was little new settlement after 1900. On the other hand, within each of these overseas countries there was a great tide of rural-urban migration. Even the westward movements in the United States after 1900 were movements primarily from Middle Western farms and small towns to the cities of the Pacific Coast.

Similarly in the Soviet Union the eastward migrations into Asia, while in one respect a continuation of the expansion of the European settlement area, were in another respect a migration from the farms of European Russia to the new industrial cities beyond the Urals.

In Western civilization the attractions of the city have come to outweigh greatly those of unsettled lands, not only because the best lands in the temperate zone have been occupied but also because the driving aspirations are those achieved only in city life.

The greatest attraction to international migrants exists where these two forces are more or less combined, as in the cities of the New World.

Thus the direction of population pressure in the Western world is from the farm and the small town to the city and especially to the cities of America. At least this is the choice of migrants in the absence of coercion and political barriers. A second choice of migrants has been the urban and industrial centers of Western Europe.

These choices were freely open to most of the populations of northwest Europe because United States quotas favored them and because major economic centers were within their territories. In part this latter opportunity was available to southern Europeans through migrations to neighboring France, and in any case there were industrial regions in Italy and Spain to absorb some of the surplus populations.

The problem was more severe and the solutions less available in Eastern than in Southern Europe. It was this demographic context in which occurred the massive population transfers set in motion by Nazi aggression, war, and postwar settlements.

FORCED MIGRATIONS

"The Nation of the Homeless." In 1952 an editorial in *The New York Times* spoke of the somber fact that "in this century the homeless form one of the great nations of the world." The displaced person is as much a symbol of this century as is the broken atom.

The dispossessed and uprooted, in the uninspired language of the bureaucracies, are classified as expellees, deportees, refugees, and displaced persons. In many cases they remain unabsorbed by the nations within whose borders they have found refuge. Yet they have changed the structure of the human and political geography of the regions in which they have settled, just as their flight or expulsion has changed the structure of the regions they have left.

The regions from which large sections of the population have been uprooted, as well as those where the refugees and the expelled have come to rest, stand out on the political map as danger zones. Vacuums have been created by the expulsion of large minorities. At the same time new irredentist agitation is created in the receiving countries. Many external and internal problems involved in the integration of the newcomers, or more often the failure to achieve such integration, confront both the nation and the international organizations concerned.

These problems of our age make it mandatory to the student of political geography to observe carefully the changes in the ethnic and national composition of nation states which are due to mass migrations and population transfers.[15]

Population Transfers in Europe. The political map of Europe and of the European lands of the Soviet orbit has undergone, since 1939, more basic changes stemming from mass population movements than the contours of changed political boundaries would reveal. The gist of the long story of migrations initiated in Europe by World War II is contained in the following chart prepared by E. M. Kulischer, which lists movements from 1939 to 1947:

TABLE 10-1 *

Redistribution of Population Produced by World War II [a]

YEARS	ROUTE	GROUP
	Transfer; Evacuation; Flight of ethnic Germans.	
1939-43	Italy (south Tyrol) to Austria and Germany	80,000 Tyrolese Germans
1944	Rumania to Germany and Austria	200,000 ethnic Germans
1944	Yugoslavia to Germany and Austria	250,000 ethnic Germans
1944	Rumania to U.S.S.R.	70,000 ethnic Germans
1944	Yugoslavia to U.S.S.R.	100,000 ethnic Germans
1944-46	Hungary to Germany and Austria	200,000 ethnic Germans
1944-45	U.S.S.R. (Russian East Prussia) to Germany	500,000 Reich Germans
1944-45	Old Poland to Germany	1,000,000 ethnic Germans (Polish citizens and transferees from other countries) [b]
1944-47	New Poland (former eastern Germany) to Germany	6,000,000 Reich Germans
1944-45	New Poland (former eastern Germany) to Denmark	100,000 Reich Germans [c]
1945-46	Czechoslovakia to Germany (partly to Austria)	2,700,000 ethnic Germans
1945-46	Soviet Zone to United States and British zones in Germany	4,000,000 Reich Germans

* Reproduced by permission of the Columbia University Press from Kulischer, *Europe on the Move.*

[a] The transfer of 230,000 Germans from Austria to Germany is not mentioned; it was partly a return of Reich Germans who had migrated to Austria after March, 1938, and partly a transfer of Sudeten German refugees comprised by the total of 2,700,000. Ethnic Germans transferred in 1939-44 to the Warteland are not listed separately. Apart from those drafted in the German army, most of them left for Germany. Se note [b]. Volga Germans are listed under Population Movements within the U.S.S.R.

[b] In 1939-44 about 800,000 ethnic Germans were transferred to the Warteland (partly to central Poland), mainly from the Baltic countries, eastern Poland, Rumania, and the southern part of the U.S.S.R.

[c] Later transferred to Germany.

[15] The reader is referred to the following sources for a comprehensive treatment of population transfers: W. S. and E. S. Woytinsky's *World Population and Production* (New York, 1953), pp. 66-110, is the most comprehensive short treatment of the subject and offers the gist of the available statistical material on individual regions. The standard works on displacements of populations in Europe are: E. M. Kulischer, *The Displacement of Population in Europe* (Montreal, 1953), and the same author's *Europe on the Move: War and Population Changes, 1917-1947* (New York, 1948), and J. B. Schechtman, *European Population Transfers, 1939-1947* (New York, 1946).

YEARS	ROUTE	GROUP
	Population Movements of Non-Germans From, Into, and Within Poland [d]	
1939-44	Poland to Germany, Austria, and Italy	275,000 Polish displaced persons
1939-47	Poland through U.S.S.R., the Balkans, and Western Europe to Great Britain	160,000 members of Polish army (including families)
1944-46	U.S.S.R. (former eastern Poland) to New Poland	1,000,000 Poles
1946	U.S.S.R. to Poland	50,000 Polish Jews [f]
1944-46	Poland to U.S.S.R.	518,000 Ukrainians, Belorussians and Lithuanians
1946	Various European countries to Poland	60,000 returned Polish emigrants
1945-47	Old Poland to New Poland	3,000,000 Poles
	Population Movements of Non-Germans From, Into, and Within Czechoslovakia	
1945-46	U.S.S.R. (Carpatho-Ukraine) to Czechoslovakia	30,000 Czechs and Ukrainians [e]
1946	U.S.S.R. (Volynia) to Czechoslovakia	33,000 ethnic Czechs
1946-47	Rumania to Czechoslovakia	30,000 ethnic Czechs and Slovaks
1946-47	Western and central Europe to Czechoslovakia	30,000 returned Czechoslovak emigrants
1946-47	Hungary to Czechoslovakia	100,000 ethnic Slovaks [g]
1946-47	Czechoslovakia to Hungary	100,000 Magyars
1946-47	Inner Czechoslovakia to the border region (Sudetenland)	1,800,000 Czechs and Slovaks
1946-47	Slovakia to Bohemia and Moravia	180,000 Slovaks and Magyars
	Population Movements of Non-Germans From and Into Yugoslavia	
1941-47	Yugoslavia to Germany, Austria, and Italy	90,000 Yugoslav displaced persons and refugees
1946-47	Yugoslavia (Istria, Fiume, and Zara) to Italy	140,000 Italians
1946-47	Yugoslavia to Hungary	40,000 Magyars [h]
1946-47	Hungary to Yugoslavia	40,000 Serbs, Croats, and Slovenes [h]
	Population Movements of Non-Germans from the Baltic Area	
1940-44	U.S.S.R. (Karelian Isthmus) to Finland	415,000 Karelian Finns

[d] Jewish refugees from Poland included below in total of 225,000 Jewish refugees from various countries.
[e] Rough estimate.
[f] Total 140,000; most went farther to west and included in total of 225,000 Jewish refugees.
[g] In course.
[h] Figures according to the exchange agreement.

TABLE 10-1 (*Cont.*)

Redistribution of Population Produced by World War II

YEARS	ROUTE	GROUP
	Population Movements of Non-Germans from the Baltic Area	
1941-44	U.S.S.R. (Estonia, Latvia, Lithuania) to Germany, Austria, and Italy	165,000 Estonian, Latvian, and Lithuanian displaced persons
1941-47	U.S.S.R. (Estonia, Latvia, Lithuania) through Germany to Belgium	35,000 Estonian, Latvian, and Lithuanian persons
1942-44	U.S.S.R. (Estonia, Latvia, Lithuania) to Sweden	30,000 Estonian, Latvian, and Lithuanian refugees
1942-43	U.S.S.R. (Estonia) to Sweden	6,000 ethnic Swedes
1943-44	U.S.S.R. (Leningrad area) to Finland	18,000 Ingermanlanders [i]
	Other Population Movements Into Or/And From Various European Countries	
1941	Bulgaria (southern Dobrudja) to Rumania	110,000 Rumanians
1941	Rumania (northern Dobrudja) to Bulgaria	62,000 Bulgarians
1946	Greece, Bulgaria, Rumania to U.S.S.R. (Soviet Armenia)	30,000 Armenians [j]
1941-45	U.S.S.R. (former eastern Poland and old Soviet Ukraine) to Germany, Austria, and Italy	150,000 Ukrainian displaced persons
1943-46	Eastern and Central Europe to Germany, Austria, and Italy	225,000 Jewish refugees
1940-45	Various European countries to Germany, Austria, and Italy	150,000 Displaced persons and refugees [e]
	Population Movements Within the U.S.S.R.	
1941	Volga region to the Asiatic part of the U.S.S.R.	400,000 Volga Germans
1941-42	Axis occupied Soviet territory to inner and Asiatic parts of the U.S.S.R.	1,500,000 Soviet citizens [k] [e]
1945-46	Southern Russia to the Asiatic part of U.S.S.R.	600,000, Crimean Tartars, Kalmyks, Chechen, and Karachai
1946	Russia proper and the Ukraine to Crimea	50,000 Russian and Ukrainian settlers [l]
1946	Dagestan to former Chechen land	60,000 Dagestan mountaineers

[i] Total 65,000; the majority returned to the U.S.S.R.

[j] Total about 100,000—about 70 per cent from non-European countries (Syria, Iran, Lebanon).

[k] Total number evacuees (partly deportees from Soviet territories) estimated at 12,000,000 of whom great majority returned.

[l] First contingent.

[e] E. M. Kulischer, *Europe on the Move* (New York, Columbia University Press, 1948), pp. 302-303.

YEARS	ROUTE	GROUP
	Population Movements Within the U.S.S.R.	
1946	Various parts of the U.S.S.R. to southern Sakhalin	50,000 Russians
1945-47	Central and western Russia proper, Belorussia, and Lithuania to Russian East Prussia	500,000 Russians, Byelorussians, and Lithuanians
1945-47	Old Soviet territory to other newly acquired western territories of the U.S.S.R.	500,000 Russians, Ukrainians, and others [e]

These mass movements in Eastern and Central Europe during and after World War II have resulted in a complete change in the ethnic and linguistic composition of some of the countries affected by these migrations as well as in a new balance of power, or lack of it, between their majorities and minorities.

Poland, for instance, is now a country virtually free of ethnic minorities. Its German minority of close to nine million before World War II has been reduced, mainly through expulsions, to approximately one to two hundred thousand,[16] most of whom live in the so-called Recovered Territories. Its large Jewish minority has been reduced, chiefly by extermination during the German occupation, to thirty to thirty-five thousand. Of the Eastern Slavic groups once residing within the boundaries of Poland the vast majority, mostly Ukrainians and Byelorussians, lived east of the Curzon line and are now outside the boundaries of Poland. Thus a country once confronted with major minority and boundary problems due to large ethnic minorities is now ethnically homogeneous.

Czechoslovakia offers another illustration of a country which, plagued by the failure to assimilate its minorities and to create a unified national state, undertook to solve its minority question by mass expulsions, affecting in particular its most thorny minority, the Germans. Numbering

[16] The estimates vary a great deal. German sources claim the existence of much larger German groups, in particular in Upper Silesia. These discrepancies show vividly the difficulties with which one is confronted in the task of defining ethnic frontiers. In border areas, such as Upper Silesia, one frequently encounters bilingual groups whose national loyalties are not clearly defined and shift with changing fortunes of war and peace. The number of bilingual Silesians is approximately one million. They are claimed by both Poles and Germans—a good illustration of the problems with which boundary-makers are confronted if attempting to draw the line in accordance with ethnic and linguistic distinctions.

FIG. 10-1. Mass Migration of Ethnic Germans into West Germany After World War II;

Expellees from:	(1)	Pomerania	891,000
	(2)	East Prussia	1,347,000
	(3)	East Brandenburg	131,000
	(4)	Silesia	2,053,000
	(5)	Danzig	225,000
	(6)	Memelland	48,000
	(7)	Estonia, Latvia, Lithuania	59,000
	(8)	Poland	410,000
	(9)	Soviet Union	51,000
	(10)	Czechoslovakia	1,912,000
	(11)	Rumania	149,000
	(12)	Hungary	178,000
	(13)	Yugoslavia	148,000
	(14)	other European countries and from overseas	274,000
Refugees from:	(15)	Soviet Zone and Berlin	1,555,000
Expellees arrived:	(16)	Soviet Zone and Berlin	4,000,000

3,300,000 in 1936, the close-knit German community of the Sudetenlands had played a prominent part in the "Protectorate" of Bohemia and Moravia during the Nazi occupation. The expulsion of 3,038,000 Sudeten-Germans under the terms of the Potsdam Agreement reduced the remaining German group in Czechoslovakia to 200,000. The vacuum created by the mass evacuation was filled by Czech settlers. But the presence of some two million Sudeten German expellees in Western Germany, clinging together in organizations which keep Sudeten German irredentism alive, makes the hastily filled vacuum appear as a zone of insecurity and a cradle of conflict. The atmosphere of insecurity is even more accentuated by the fact that the expulsion of its most troublesome ethnic group left the country still saddled with the age-old conflict between Czechs and Slovaks. Totalling 2,400,000, about one-fifth of the entire population of Czechoslovakia, the Slovaks confront the country continuously with problems of Slovak nationalism. Uneven cultural and political development between Czechs and Slovaks and a serious divergence in religious belief are factors explaining the lack of a constructive symbiosis between Czechs and Slovaks. Here we deal with a minority whose problems could not have been "solved" by migration or population transfer and whose continuous presence as a minority with an intense nationalism has so far defied all efforts to create a unified national state.

A contrasting problem is that of Germany, which was forced to receive huge masses of Germans [17] who fled or were expelled from the East as a result of World War II (Fig. 10-1). Ten and a half million or 21 per cent of the total population of the German Federal Republic of forty-nine million are expellees. These are divided into three categories: (1) some 8.4 million expellees from German provinces east of the Oder-Neisse Line now under Polish or U.S.S.R. administration, and from Czechoslovakia, Poland, Hungary, Rumania, Yugoslavia, and other countries. The largest contingents are from the former German provinces of Silesia, East Prussia, Pomerania, and Brandenburg (4,423,000), and from Czechoslovakia (1,912,000); (2) over two million persons who fled to Western Germany and are unable to return to the Eastern European areas from which they came; (3) two hundred thousand stateless and foreign refugees. Clearly the presence of a group of new citizens totalling nearly a fourth of West Germany's population confronted the country with difficult postwar adjustment and rehabilitation tasks in the process of absorbing the completely destitute millions. As a West German government source put it, the situation was about the same as if more than the total population of

[17] The figures are based on official West German estimates as of December 31, 1950.

Denmark and Switzerland combined, or if considerably more than the entire population of Australia would have been compelled to find accommodation, work, and a living in what was then (but no longer is) a totally impoverished Federal Republic of Germany.[18]

While the Iron Curtain has sealed off not only the West from the Soviet Empire but also the Soviet satellites from each other, thus bringing the mass population shifts of World War II and of the immediate postwar period to a standstill, the two Germanies separated from each other still experience a numerically reduced but continuous migration from eastern to western Germany which totalled between 1950 and 1951 about 1,800,-000 or 10 per cent of East Germany's entire population. Here, as in the lands of eastern Europe, it is still too early to evaluate the far-reaching changes which the uprooting of millions has brought to their new homelands; too early because the consolidation and assimilation process is still in progress. This statement should not detract from the fact that in some cases, however exceptional, the integration of the refugees has met with full success. A case in point is Finland which, aided by the availability of cultivable surplus land, succeeded in settling on the basis of careful planning the 415,000 Karelian Finns (about 11 per cent of its total population) who poured into Finland from territories ceded to Russia after the Russo-Finnish war of 1939 to 1940.[19]

In some parts of Western Germany the impact of the expellee groups has been so strong that it has radically changed the sociological structure of the region concerned. In national politics, the close-knit expellee groups have become power factors of great importance, affecting the strategy of the political parties and making their irredentist claims a matter of concern for the country as a whole. Furthermore the influx of refugees drastically changed the religious composition of West Germany. In the past, the map showing the geographical distribution of religions revealed a pattern of clearly discernible Protestant and Catholic areas with political leanings strongly influenced by confessional issues. The mass migrations have broken up this pattern and the denominations are much more mixed geographically than formerly.

Poland, Czechoslovakia, and Germany offer the most impressive examples in the European theatre of mass migrations in the wake of World War II. But a glance at Kulischer's list of flights and transfers of populations in Europe and the U.S.S.R. during and after World War II shows

[18] For further details, see C. D. Harris and G. Wuelker, "The Refugee Problem in Germany," *Economic Geography* (1953), pp. 10-25.

[19] See p. 241.

clearly the uprooting of the human structure of all the lands of central and eastern Europe. These wanderings differ basically from the great overseas migrations between 1870 and 1920. The war and postwar mass migrations were not motivated by the pioneer spirit of individuals and groups but by fear and coercion. The mass migrations of our time are "the flight of millions from their wrecked homes, the mass exodus of people haunted by fear, the mass shipment of human beings to destruction. Measured by the number of persons affected, these recent shifts of population have been of the magnitude of the economic migration of the whole preceding century." [20]

Population Transfers in Asia. While we have given prominence to the treatment of population movements in eastern and western Europe, it must be realized that they represent only one among numerous other equally disorganized major population displacements which originated during, or as the result of the World Wars. In 1921, Walter Duranty noted in Moscow: "One of the strangest features of Russian life today is the wanderers—wandering children, wandering soldiers, wandering families, wandering villages, wandering tribes—driven from their homes by the war or revolution to move interminably across the vast Russian plains." [21] This characterization was to hold true for many years to come and again after World War II. We find it equally true for many other danger spots on the globe, whether as the result of India's partition and the migrations this caused, or of China's flood and drought areas, resulting periodically in mass movements, or of South East Asia's migration of Chinese and Indians across international frontiers, or of Manchuria's and Japan's wandering nationals, testifying to the ambition and collapse of Japan's "Greater Asian Co-Prosperity Sphere."

Within the span of a few months, the Partition of India of August 15, 1947 prompted mass migrations "on a scale absolutely unparalleled in the history of the world." [22] The communal riots started in the Indo-Gangetic Plains, in the Punjab area which covers 55,000 square miles. Accompanied by appalling bloodshed, the final balance sheet showed in March 1948 that six and a half million Moslems had fled into West Pakistan, while about six million Hindus and Sikhs had left it. New disorders in Bengal between 1948 and 1950 started another wave of mass population move-

[20] Woytinsky, *op. cit.*, p. 110.

[21] Kulischer, *op. cit.*, p. 30.

[22] O. H. K. Spate, "India and Pakistan," *A General and Regional Geography* (London and New York, 1954), p. 110; the discussion, above, of the 1947, 1948, and consequent migrations is based on Spate's account, *op. cit.*, pp. 118-120; see also the bibliographical notes on pp. 121, 481 f.

ments, during which about three and a half million people left East Pakistan and one million Moslems entered it. What distinguishes this movement from that in the Punjab and West Pakistan is that the Bengal wave swept in one direction only until 1950, carrying Hindus on their flight from East Bengal into Indian territory; in 1950, the mass influx of these refugees generated a counterwave of Moslems into Pakistan. "The total movement is thus of the order of seventeen million," twice the population of Greater London, New York City, or Tokyo.[23] "No comparable event has ever been known."[24]

Clearly these mass migrations, and in their wake the critical tasks of rehabilitation and resettlement of the uprooted millions, have affected deeply the political, social, and cultural structure of both India and Pakistan, thus confronting the student of political geography with a radically different political and social landscape and the two countries with many problems, most of which are still awaiting solution. According to Spate's analysis, the population transfers have not perhaps modified greatly the general distribution of population, except to swell the larger towns of the north, but they have altered profoundly the communal pattern. For instance, the Indian government, in its resettlement program, has plans for eighteen new townships; by March, 1950, four million acres of reclaimed and evacuee land were allotted to 390,000 families, or a total of about two million people; the population of Delhi included in 1950 24 per cent refugees—the intrusive minorities were largely urban, which fact posed special problems to the overcrowded and unsanitary cities.[25] Thus the manifold problems of resettlement and the instability which the overflow of refugees has brought to India and Pakistan since the Partition of 1947 are still, almost a decade later, a major characteristic of the internal political geography of the subcontinent.

A mass displacement of comparable political importance was created by the warfare connected with the creation of Israel in 1948. Several hundred thousand Arabs fled or were uprooted from their homes in the territory of the new state. Since that time these refugees have been maintained in miserable camps through the largesse of an international organization created by the United Nations for this purpose.

These camps are generally located dangerously near the borders of Israel in the Gaza strip (Egypt), in Jordan, and in Syria. Very few of the

[23] London (1951): 8,346,000; New York's five boroughs (1950): 7,892,000; Tokyo (1954): 7,736,000.

[24] Spate, *op. cit.*, p. 119.

[25] *Ibid.*, p. 120.

Arab refugees have been integrated in the economies of the countries in which they live. After almost a decade of refugee life the 800 thousand Arabs under international care still hope to recover their lands. They are a persistent source of border conflict and international incidents in the troubled relations between Israel and her neighbors.

Great displacements of population are therefore not a monopoly of Europe, though it is in that continent that they have been most systematically carried through.

THE WESTWARD THRUST IN EUROPE

The preceding sections have described the forced migrations successively connected with Nazi aggressions, the war, and postwar territorial revisions. The redistribution of population incident to the second World War brought about the permanent migration of close to thirty million people, which Eugene M. Kulischer has described as probably the greatest migration in European history. In any event, it has remade the map of population and ethnic distribution in central Europe. In essence this migration has been a great westward movement induced by the collapse of Germany. Though there have been significant displacements of population affecting every country east of the Rhine, the overall pattern is of a westward push of populations before the thrust of Slavic victories in the east.

Dominating the picture is the tremendously important expansion of Slav at the expense of Teuton. In this respect European history has been turned back almost a thousand years, when Slavic settlement extended from the Baltic to the Adriatic, as far west as the present Iron Curtain. Some eleven million Germans have been forced back into the rump territory of Germandom. Almost every eastern European country has liquidated its German minority or reduced it to a small fraction of its former size. The main German settlement area has been driven back to the Oder-Neisse line.

Into the vacuum have poured millions of Slavs, particularly Poles and Czechs, who themselves have been divested of territory by the Soviet Union. Only a small fraction of this enormous movement has gone on into western Europe and overseas. The problem of economic and cultural assimilation of this enormous mass of refugees is one of the most difficult facing Europe today.

Yet from the economic point of view it is well on the way to solution.

The underlying demographic and economic pressures from East to West have been greatly reduced by the territorial changes resulting from the war. In terms of the measure of density of the agricultural population, and considering the relative change in population as compared with that of Europe as a whole in the period of 1939 to 1954, Poland has increased its relative agricultural living space about 60 per cent and Czechoslovakia by about one-fourth. In both cases this result was partly due to war deaths but chiefly to the expulsion of some thirteen million inhabitants from the present territories of these countries. Both are now better off than the European average.

The Danubian countries, on the other hand, were not so favored in the redistribution of population and their position has not been so markedly improved. In relation to European averages the Yugoslavs, Rumanians, and Hungarians are nevertheless almost certainly in a relatively better position in terms of agricultural density of population than before the war, owing to war losses and to expulsion of ethnic minorities. Quite aside from these gains, events have spared these countries the additional population pressure (relative to the European average) that would probably otherwise have occurred.[26]

The reduction of population pressure in these countries is also being promoted by (*a*) urbanization and industrialization, and (*b*) the present results of rapid declines in the birth rate that occurred in the interwar period. The one factor is increasing employment opportunities, the other is reducing the competition for available jobs and for the land. In most Eastern European countries the number of young people entering work ages (that is, age fifteen to twenty) is declining each year as a result of the fall in the birth rate that occurred fifteen to twenty years ago. This source of pressure on employment opportunities is considerably reduced.

Quite apart from its ideologies, Eastern Europe is moving into the demographic and economic situation that earlier brought relief from population pressures in Western Europe, and of course in so doing it has liquidated important minority problems.

But what of the countries that had to absorb the dispossessed of the East? In practice this means Germany since other Western countries have received far smaller contingents.

The war added one-fourth to the already crowded population of West Germany. The refugees came in enormous numbers and without resources into a land amputated by political partition and with the shattered economy of a beaten nation. The prognosis was certainly poor. But to the amazement of many observers West Germany has already gone far toward

[26] *Cf.* F. W. Notestein *et al.*, *The Future Population of Europe and the Soviet Union* (Geneva, 1944).

effective absorption of its refugees. Economic output is now far above the best achieved before the war and under Hitler. Even *per capita* income is now well above prewar levels and is increasing rapidly.

It is now clear that the presence of the refugees is actually contributing to the more sustained economic progress of Germany as compared with neighboring countries. The refugees provided a reserve of skilled, industrious labor lacking in other Western European countries where, except for Italy, early gains brought about full employment of the available labor force.

These aggregate developments do not mean that the individual refugee in Germany is better off than before the war. But they do mean that the refugee burden has not been an insuperable one and that in fact it is now being turned to advantage. The extent of this success may be measured by the fact that German leaders, far from seeking emigration outlets for "surplus" population, are now exploring possibilities for bringing in Italian and other workers to provide part of the labor needed to support rearmament.

POSTWAR MIGRATIONS AFFECTING THE EUROPEAN SETTLEMENT AREA

Since World War II there has been a substantial revival of overseas migration from Europe [27] (Fig. 10-2). Much of this is related to war displacements of population. But the publicity attending the more dramatic refugee movements has obscured the resurgence of voluntary "free" migrations such as those that peopled North America, Australasia, and large parts of South America from Europe in the last two centuries.

Since the war at least five million persons have emigrated from Europe, a mass migration exceeding the total population of Switzerland. In the average postwar year about 650,000 emigrants were recorded as leaving Europe for countries overseas, and the actual figure was undoubtedly larger. "Return" migration amounts to about one-third of this total. The identifiable net outward movement in the period 1946 to 1952 was 3.2 million or about 450,000 per year. This substantial movement represents

[27] Department of State, Office of Intelligence Research, *Survey of Overseas Emigration from Europe, 1946-51.* Unclassified Intelligence Report 6054, May, 1953. For prewar materials this summary also draws heavily on earlier studies of migration by D. Kirk; *Europe's Population in the Interwar Years* (Geneva, 1946), Chs. 4-7; "European Migrations: Prewar Trends and Future Prospects," *Milbank Memorial Fund Quarterly,* Vol. 25, No. 225 (April, 1947); and "Overseas Migration from Europe Since World War II," *American Sociological Review,* Vol. 19, No. 4 (August, 1954), pp. 447-56. Portions of the last-named article, written by Dudley Kirk and Earl Huyck, are included in the present text.

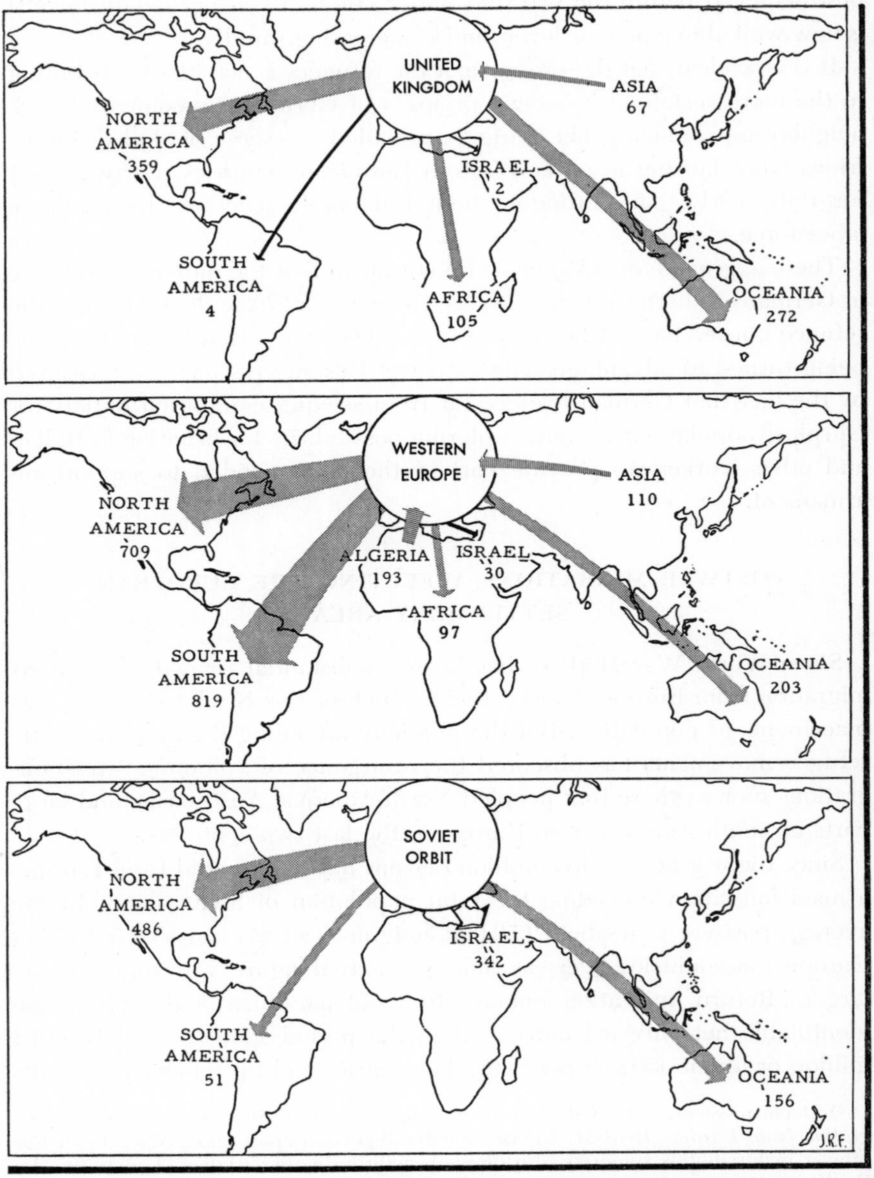

Fig. 10-2. Net Postwar Overseas Migration, Europe 1946-52 (in thousands).

the highest figures reached since the application of severe restrictive measures by the United States in the early 1920's. In gross volume it is comparable to European emigration from 1880 to 1900. It has not, however, attained the huge totals registered immediately prior to World War I.

Overseas migration drained off approximately one-eighth of the natural growth of population in Europe since the war, as compared with about one-fifth removed by the maximum movements in the years 1900 to 1914.

Much of the controversy concerning migration restrictions in the United States and other countries of immigration has revolved around the displacement of "old" migration from Northwest Europe by the "new" migration from Southern and Eastern Europe, a displacement which came to dominate overseas emigration around the turn of the century. Trends in "gross" emigration from the chief regions and countries of origin are shown in Table 10-2.

The pattern of "gross" emigration resembles that of the 1920's. The United Kingdom, Germany, Italy, Spain, and Portugal each recorded a roughly parallel emigration in the two periods, both in numbers and in percentages of the European total. Gross emigration from Eastern Europe was higher than in the 1920's but much lower than at the turn of the century. The other major difference is the new emigration from the Netherlands, which is chiefly responsible for the rise in the joint figure for France and the Low Countries.

The pattern of "net" emigration is somewhat different because of the large return migration, particularly to the United Kingdom, to the Netherlands, and to Spain and Portugal. The total net emigration by country of origin and destination is shown in Tables 10-3 and 4. The leading countries are the United Kingdom and Italy (over 600,000 each), Poland (460,000), Germany (290,000), U.S.S.R. (230,000), Spain and Portugal (180,000 each), and Rumania (160,000). Some three hundred thousand Dutch emigrated overseas since the war but these were largely offset by repatriations and other immigration from Indonesia. France was the only European country of overseas "immigration," which resulted from the mass migration of North Africans to the metropole.

As in the latter days of unrestricted migration, the leading sources were in Eastern and Southern Europe. Of the eight countries supplying over a hundred thousand emigrants since the war, six were in these regions. Certain older areas of emigration, such as Ireland and Scandinavia, were notably underrepresented. Irish emigration now goes almost wholly to Britain rather than overseas.

TABLE 10-2

Gross Overseas Emigration from Europe, 1901-52
(Annual Average in Thousands)

	1901-10	1911-20	1921-30	1931-40	1946-52 [a]
Regions of Old Emigration					
British Isles	195	183	180	32	165
Germany	27	9	56	15	40
Scandinavia	49	20	25	4	12
France, Low Countries, Switzerland	16	12	13	5	63 [b]
Regions of New Emigration					
Italy	362	219	110	26	107
Portugal, Spain	142	171	86	23	74
Eastern Europe [c]	447	271	123	34	188
Total	1,238	885	593	139	649
Percent "old" emigration	23	26	47	40	43
Percent "new" emigration	77	74	53	60	57

[a] For a number of individual countries, average for the years 1946-51.
[b] Excluding movement of Algerian workers returning to Algeria from France, estimated to average 53,000 per year in 1946-51, inclusive.
[c] Including Austria, Finland, Greece, Yugoslavia, and Soviet Orbit.

While the United States has continued to be the leading destination of European migration, it does not hold the commanding position that it did in the days of unrestricted movement, when the United States was receiving from a half to two-thirds of all European emigrants (*cf.* Fig. 10-2). Since the war the United States has played host to only about one-third (950,000) of the net movement, while Canada, Australia, and Argentina have each absorbed well over half a million. Australia in particular has been receiving immigrants at a ratio to population far exceeding that for the United States even at its greatest period of immigration. Immigration to Australia and Canada has been chiefly drawn from among British subjects and other Northwest Europeans on the one hand and displaced persons on the other, with limited numbers from other sources. Argentinian immigration has been almost wholly from Italy and Spain, with less than ten per cent of the total being displaced persons. About half of the United States immigrants were displaced persons admitted under special legislation; the remainder follow in the order of magnitude of the quotas, which favor immigrants from Northwest Europe.

The final major country of immigration is Israel, which alone in the postwar period owes its existence as an independent nation to large-scale immigration. The 370,000 Jews from all parts of Europe for whom it provided a refuge have contributed spectacularly in establishing the demographic base for the Jewish state—the new immigrants constituted 43 per cent of the total population at the end of 1951. The days of large-scale "rescue migration" appear to be over, however, for only 23,000 arrived in 1952 as compared with 191,000 in the previous year.

In the receiving country immigrants went primarily to the urban areas. Immigrants into the United States in 1952, for example, went overwhelmingly into the cities—nearly three-fifths into the big cities of a hundred thousand or over, 27 per cent into other urban areas, and only the small remainder into the rural areas. Over one-half of the 1952 arrivals in Canada went to Ontario, the most industrialized province, one-fifth went to Quebec, and only about one-sixth went westward to the prairie provinces.

Of the immigrants arriving in Australia from 1947 through 1951 only 18 per cent classified themselves as farm workers, and the flow of immigrants has gone almost exclusively to the cities. Similarly, in Israel, only one-fourth of those permanently settled had gone into agriculture. The traditional policy in Latin America of putting immigrants on the land has generally been unsuccessful, and there has been a pronounced drift to the cities in search of better employment even where initial settlement was made on the land.

Prior to World War I emigrants left Europe as individuals without governmental assistance. Since World War II, two-fifths of all European emigrants have been moved with governmental or international assistance. Despite the greater element of government control and assistance in the postwar period the self-financed, individual migrant is still the predominant type, whether in the United States or in the overseas countries as a whole. With the liquidation of the most immediate refugee problems individual migration is now a growing part of the total.

Almost all of the postwar migrants of Eastern European origin (about one million) were either displaced persons or refugees from Communism—by definition, since countries in the Soviet orbit now generally prohibit emigration except in special circumstances, such as the expulsion of ethnic Germans and of Jews from satellite countries.

Although motivated by political oppression, this movement was nonetheless in accord with underlying economic and demographic forces. The great displacements of population in Central and Eastern Europe have been successful precisely because they were in accord with population pressures from East to West. Conversely German efforts to colonize the East were unsuccessful essentially because the educated, urbanized German could not compete effectively for the land against the prolific, peasant Slav. Similarly, the displaced persons from the Soviet Union were not Great Russians but chiefly more advanced peoples thrust aside by the westward push of the Russians—the Baltic peoples, the Poles, and the Jews. In this regard the movement paralleled the "Russian" emigration of the early part of the century—actually largely a migration of these same minority peoples from the old Russian Empire.

TABLE 10-3

Net Emigration from Europe, 1946-52: Western and Southern Europe *
(in Thousands)

AREA OF IMMIGRATION	BRITISH ISLES [a]	SCANDINAVIA [b]	GERMANY	NETHERLANDS	FRANCE	ITALY	PORTUGAL	SPAIN	GREECE	YUGOSLAVIA	OTHERS [c]	TOTAL
North America												
Canada	189	11	63	63	17	61	*	1	6	12	47	470
U.S.A.	170	26	180	18	23	66	5	2	17	39	52	598
Latin America												
Argentina	1	*	9	*	2	314	7	141	*	10	5	489
Brazil	2	*	9	2	3	49	95	6	1	1	6	174
Venezuela	*	*	*	*	*	61	7	13	*	2	3	86
Other [d]	1	4	1	20	*	17	2	18	*	2	9	74
Africa												
South Africa	70	*	6	14	1	6	*	*	1	*	4	102
Other [e]	35	1	*	2	−193	−1	59	*	*	*	4	− 93
Asia [f]	−65	*	8	−111	3	2	1	*	3	8	6	−145
Oceania												
Australia	225	2	16	40	3	68	*	*	11	24	17	406
New Zealand	47	*	*	9	*	*	*	*	*	1	12	69
TOTAL	675	44	292	57	−141	643	176	181	39	99	165	2,230

[a] Including 40,000 from Ireland chiefly to U.S.A.
[b] Including Denmark (17,000), Norway (15,000) and Sweden (12,000); all primarily to North America.
[c] Including Austria (35,000), Belgium (30,000), Finland (11,000), Switzerland (19,000), generally to North America.
[d] Primarily Netherlands to Surinam, Italy to Uruguay and Peru, Spain to Cuba.
[e] Chiefly: 34,000 British to So. Rhodesia, Algerian workers to France, Portuguese to dependences (notably Angola and Mozambique).
[f] Primarily Israel—net movement of 119,000 from Indonesia to Netherlands and 68,000 from India and Pakistan to the British Isles.
* The international migration statistics presented in this table are derived from European, overseas, and international sources, all of which are in varying degrees incomplete, inaccurate, and inconsistent. Since there generally is better recording of arrivals than of departures, this table is in principle based on the statistics of the receiving country, *i.e.*, the country receiving the outward-bound migrants from Europe as immigrants, and the European country receiving the repatriates. Statistics of the country of emigration combined with those of the International Refugee Organization (IRO) and the Inter-governmental Committee for European Migration (ICEM) have been used where data of the receiving country either are not compiled, are incomplete, or unavailable (notably Argentina, Brazil, Venezuela, Indonesia, India and Pakistan). Wherever possible "country of birth" data employed in classification; elsewhere, residence or political nationality.

The free world had another type of migration of European "displaced persons." Whereas much of Eastern Europe was integrated closely into the Soviet security bloc, much of Asia achieved full independence with a displacement of the former colonial administrators. The flow back to the mother countries, particularly from India and Pakistan to the United Kingdom (110,000) and from Indonesia to the Netherlands (230,000), represented the return of long-term administrators, businessmen, their families and associates. The immigration into the Netherlands also included a number of Eurasians whose positions in Indonesia had been jeopardized by native nationalism.

TABLE 10-4

Net Emigration from Europe, 1946-52: The Soviet European Orbit (in Thousands)

AREA OF IMMIGRATION	BULGARIA	CZECHOSLOVAKIA	HUNGARY	POLAND	RUMANIA	U.S.S.R.	TOTAL SOVIET ORBIT	TOTAL WEST AND SOUTH EUROPE	TOTAL ALL EUROPE
North America									
Canada	1	10	9	77	6	31	134	470	604
U.S.A.	1	28	22	169	14	120	354	598	952
Latin America									
Argentina	*	1	3	13	1	6	24	489	513
Brazil	*	1	2	4	1	1	9	174	183
Venezuela	*	1	2	3	*	4	10	86	96
Other	*	*	1	3	*	4	8	74	82
Africa									
South Africa	*	*	*	*	*	*	*	102	102
Other	*	*	*	*	*	*	*	— 93	—93
Asia (inc. Israel)	38	22	18	121	134	9	342	—145	197
Oceania									
Australia	1	11	13	71	2	55	153	406	559
New Zealand	*	*	*	1	1	1	3	69	72
TOTAL	41	74	70	462	159	231	1037	2230	3267

But who were the majority of the European emigrants who were not displaced persons or refugees? They were individuals and families impelled by economic motives to seek their fortunes abroad in the traditional manner. Few of them sought land, which ceased to be the chief lure to overseas migrants generations ago. The typical postwar migrant was neither a farmer nor did he aspire to become one. He rather sought out and often was assisted by his relatives and friends in New York, Toronto, Sydney, Buenos Aires, or Sao Paulo. Even if he had been a farmer in Italy or Portugal his was an essentially rural-urban migration across the seas. He would indeed be foolish to exchange his status as a poor tenant on an Italian "latifundium," for example, for an even worse fate as a plantation laborer on a Brazilian "fazenda." But this in principle is what many in countries of immigration would have him do—to settle empty lands and to do jobs that natives are reluctant to undertake for sound economic reasons.

The immigrant naturally has sought his own kind, where problems of personal adjustment are fewest. If an Englishman, he followed the flag to English-speaking lands overseas. If Italian, he will be found first of all in Argentina where the Italian tongue is almost as well understood as Spanish. If Portuguese, he will be found almost entirely in Brazil and the Portuguese colonies; if Spanish, almost exclusively in Latin America. These "natural" movements still constitute the bulk of overseas migration. It is the cross-cultural refugee movements, involving major changes in language and customs, that have created the acute need for formal intervention by governments and international agencies.

Overseas emigration historically served Europe in two ways: (1) it afforded a relief from population pressure and an outlet for the discontented and oppressed; (2) it strengthened ties with overseas countries, whether these bonds were political, economic, or cultural.

The revival of emigration in the postwar period has certainly contributed to the solution of European refugee problems. The successful liquidation of the displaced persons problem was possible only through this recourse. While emigration has fallen short of objectives in some overpopulated countries, it is nevertheless contributing significantly to the solution of unemployment and underemployment in Southern Europe. For countries living in postwar austerity, such as Britain, emigration has been alternative to living under a rationed economy.

The great free migrations before World War I were an integral part of the expansion of Europe. They provided the human sinews of European colonization and empire. Where they were not an instrument of European political expansion they promoted trade, capital movements, and cultural ties that enhanced European influence in the world.

European colonization of new lands is no longer a major aspect of European migration unless the Jewish settlement of Israel could be so regarded. The vast majority of emigrants now go to areas already occupied by populations of European race. This is true even in Latin America —at least three-fourths of all European immigrants to this region went to Argentina or to the predominantly European regions of Southern Brazil.

The most important exception, aside from the dubious case of Israel, was the European immigration into Africa south of the Sahara, a net movement of at least two hundred thousand chiefly of British, Portuguese, and French administrators, entrepreneurs, and settlers in their respective territories. The Boer-controlled government of South Africa officially encourages the immigration of Dutch and Germans, but the chief effect of Boer policies has been to greatly reduce immigration from the British Isles and to stimulate a movement of British to Southern Rhodesia. In no case, however, was the migration sufficient to create a European majority even in local areas, or to change materially the minority position of Europeans in every country south of the Sahara.

The huge British emigration, 500,000 of which has gone to member states of the Commonwealth, has certainly strengthened the ties that hold together this loose association.

In fact, awareness of immigration and emigration trends within the British Commonwealth of Nations is an indispensable tool for an appraisal of its changing human structure. Since 1945, Britain has pursued a vigorous policy to encourage emigration to the overseas Commonwealth. The Commonwealth countries received an average of between 110,000 and 150,000 emigrants from Britain a year and sent to Britain 50,000 or 60,000 —including an unknown number of United Kingdom people who had changed their minds and returned.[28] Australia absorbed more immigrants than any other country. It is the only Dominion which, under a joint agreement with the United Kingdom, shares with it the entire cost of the passage of the immigrant. It is interesting to observe how the Dominions, in varying degrees, attempt to encourage the British migrant. New Zealand, for example, is particularly anxious not to dilute its Commonwealth blood. Australia tries to maintain a ratio of 50 per cent for immigrants from Britain, thus assuring a continuous predominance of United Kingdom stock (which accounted, in 1946, for over 97 per cent of its population). The remaining Australian immigrants include Italian, Polish, Dutch, German, and displaced persons. Canada displays much less preference on ethnic grounds than do New Zealand and Australia. Its course has not been a determined Commonwealth policy. Out of over a million immigrants into Canada since the end of World War II, only one-third have been British, and yet the ties with the Commonwealth have not been weakened by this fact.[29]

The countries receiving European immigration have generally profited by this movement, if for no other reason than that they have acquired a number of skilled workers and entrepreneurs without bearing the cost of their education and childhood dependency. The economic problems of

[28] "People for Export," *The Economist,* August 28, 1954, pp. 542 ff.
[29] *Ibid.*

assimilation were minimized by the high levels of economic activity prevailing in the postwar period. In the underdeveloped countries, especially of Latin America, even comparatively small numbers of European immigrants are playing a disproportionately large role, since they bring skills, work habits, and enterprise not commonly available in the less-developed countries. Only in Australia and in Israel has immigration been so large as to create serious economic maladjustments, notably in shortages of housing and other primary facilities.

With the resolution of the displaced persons problem largely through overseas migration, individual migration is again the predominant form. Such migration is now forbidden by Eastern European countries. Aside from a few intrepid individuals who successfully escape through the Iron Curtain, Eastern Europe is ceasing to be a source of overseas migration. For this reason potential migration to Israel from Europe has been greatly reduced. The leadership of that country, which is largely of European origin, is concerned about cultural inundation from areas of new Jewish immigration (from Asia and Africa) just as are the "older" European stocks in overseas countries with regard to immigrants of different cultural background.

From the problem of displaced persons, interest in sponsored European emigration has shifted to the problem of German refugees and of population pressure in Southern Europe and the Netherlands. While the German refugees are far more numerous than the displaced persons who were handled by the International Refugee Organization, they have far less impetus to emigrate, since they are now resident in a country of their own nationality. Furthermore, the rapid economic recovery in Western Germany in recent years is providing them employment opportunities. These opportunities may be often less favorable than are those for natives of Western Germany, but more favorable than they might expect to encounter in many overseas countries.

Most of Western Europe has now passed the demographic stage which brought about the great swarming of Europeans overseas in the nineteenth and early twentieth centuries. Declining birth rates in the 1930's have so reduced the numbers entering the labor force that pressure to seek opportunities abroad has been greatly reduced. In Ireland, in Scandinavia, and even in Germany there is much less pressure to migrate from demographic causes than there was a generation ago. The lower birth rates now prevailing in Southern Europe indicate that pressure from this source will also shortly recede in that region, especially in Italy, where the birth rate is now quite low—lower even than in France, the classic country of depopulation, and much lower than in the United States.

In peace, the major continuing reservoir of "normal" overseas migration in Western Europe is the underemployed rural populations of Southern Italy, Spain, Portugal, Greece, and to a less extent the Netherlands. This reservoir is declining, but its need for an outlet still poses one of Europe's most pressing economic problems. At least for the next ten years it should furnish the basis for continued overseas migration, until such time as further economic development on the one hand, and demographic trends on the other, may have resolved the problems of population pressure in these countries as they have in much of Northwest Europe.

The great overseas migrations of Europeans may well be coming to an end. Rising in their place are new pressures and new migrations.

In the United States no frontier control has yet been developed that is tight enough to seal off the two thousand miles of desert separating this country and Mexico. In its report to the President the Commission on Migratory Labor in 1952 ruefully compares the total of 65,000 displaced persons from Western Europe admitted to the United States in 1950 with the 500,000 "wetbacks" estimated to have filtered illegally across the border in that year.

Another interesting case in point, with significant social and political implications, is that of Puerto Rican mass emigration directed almost entirely at New York City. The small island (3,423 square miles) which is plagued by a high population density (646 per square mile) of a rapidly growing populace (2,210,000 in 1950, an increase of 18.3 per cent over 1940 [30]) has as a Commonwealth of the United States the advantage that it can transfer its overflow population of United States citizens to the continental United States without being hampered by immigration restrictions. As a result the influx of Puerto Ricans to New York (aided by the low flight passage rates) has reached unforeseen proportions. In 1953, 375,000 Puerto Ricans were listed in New York, which figure reflects an increase of 54 per cent over the total of 246,000 only three years earlier. Not less than 25 per cent of Puerto Rico's total population have left the island for the continent during the last two decades. The steady growth of Spanish-speaking islands within the cosmopolitan metropolis of New York provides the city government with major problems of integration of a large ethnic minority that is growing continuously, is endowed with the privileges of citizenship, and is yet far from being assimilated.

[30] *The Statesman's Yearbook,* 1953, p. 740.

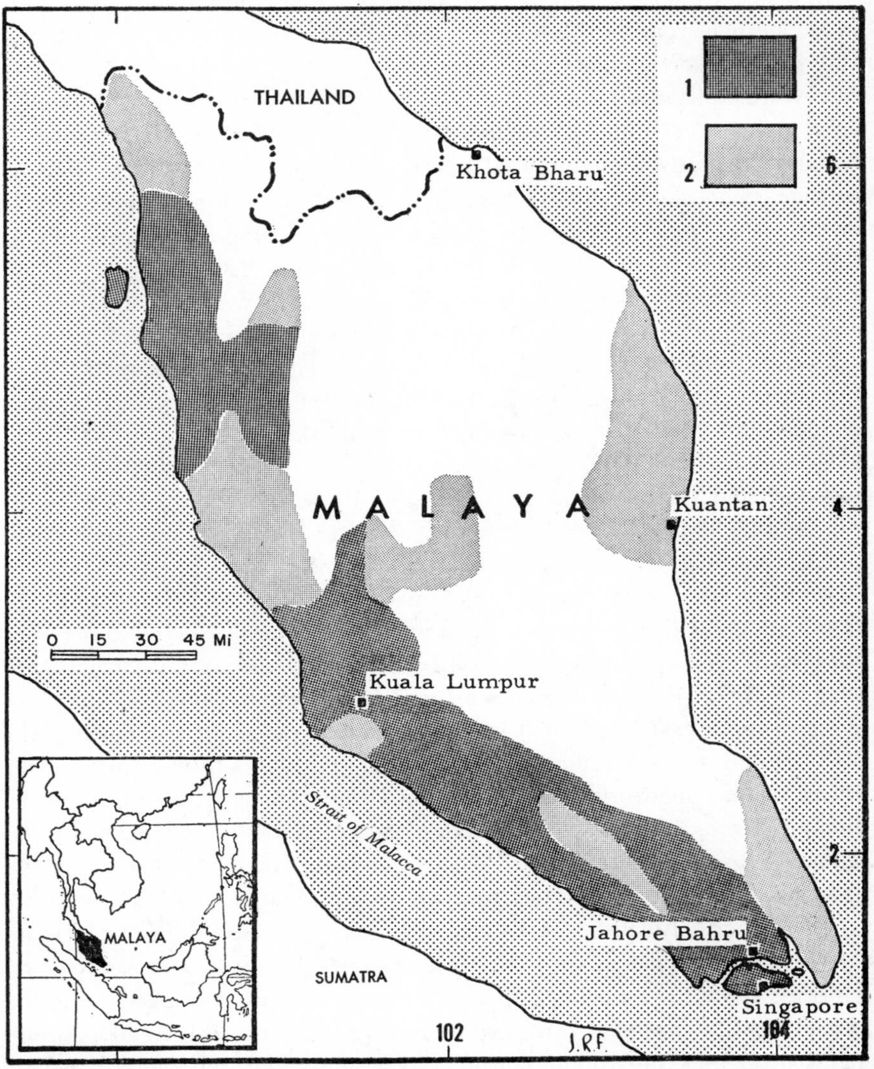

Fig. 10-3. Chinese Settlement in Malaya: (1) predominantly Chinese; (2) strong Chinese minority.

CHINESE AND INDIAN EMIGRATIONS

The primary interest of the American and European reader in overseas migration from Europe should not detract from the fact that immigration and emigration elsewhere, particularly in certain Asian territories, loom large in the political geography of the countries concerned. The following remarks, far from trying to exhaust the subject, aim only to call attention to an especially important area of structural change due to immigration, that of Chinese emigration overseas toward the peninsulas and islands of Southeast Asia.

Malaya: A Case Study.[31] Nowhere in the world do we, in this century, find as complete a change of the human geography of a territory through the impact of immigration as in Malaya (Fig. 10-3). The following observations on a territory which is a kingpin—economically and strategically—of Southeast Asia, are intended to illustrate how gradual immigration, paralleling mass migration, can lead to a decisive reversal of the ethnic structure of a country and, as a result, to important changes in its political and economic geography.

Malaya, an area of slightly more than 50,000 square miles (somewhat smaller than Florida), is situated in the southern part of the Malay Peninsula, an extension of the southeastern tip of Asia between India and China. A British colonial possession, it includes the peninsular mainland and the island of Singapore. It has a heterogeneous population of some six millions, composed of Malays, Chinese, Indians, and Europeans. The political loyalties of this population as well as their economic occupations which differ greatly between its ethnic groups, are of no small importance. Two vital commodities—tin, totaling more than a quarter of the world's output, and rubber, of which Malaya since World War II has produced 40 per cent of the world's output, have made the small territory the single largest earner of dollar exchange in the British Commonwealth and Empire; the naval and air base of Singapore commands the narrow Straits of Malacca, which is the shortest connecting link between the Indian Ocean and the South China Sea.

In this important territory we find a Chinese community which, since 1941, has outnumbered the indigenous Malay population (Chinese 2,615,000, Malays 2,544,000). The rise of the Chinese group has been rapid in the last decades, for its share of 44.7 per cent in 1947 in the combined area of the Federation of Malaya and Singapore (where the percentage

[31] F. H. Stires, *British Colonial Policy in Malaya and the Malayan Chinese Community, 1946-52,* M.A. thesis, 1953, Georgetown University; T. E. Smith, *Population Growth in Malaya* (London, 1952).

of Chinese is 77.6 per cent) compares with one of 35.2 per cent in 1921. The majority of the Chinese population have settled in the tin and rubber producing regions along the western coast of the country; 92 per cent of the total present Chinese population is located in the west coast states.[32] Since 1947, Chinese immigration has been practically stopped by the colonial administration.

Ever since the Chinese, with British permission, migrated to Malaya—at first for employment in the rubber plantations and in the tin mines—we find the human, and especially the economic and political geography of the country in a state of cleavage and the British colonial government saddled with the most complicated tasks of balancing a radically changed population. The gravity of these problems is accentuated by the fact that China has always adhered to the principle of *jus sanguinis*, according to which it viewed the overseas Chinese as citizens of China, whose activities, especially in the fields of education and of ideological loyalties, should be controlled by the homeland government.[33]

One of the main means by which the British, since 1931, have attempted to stem the Chinese tide was by the establishment of Malay Land Reservations. The late realization that the Malay people, as a race, could not compete with the far more populous other races attracted to Malaya, led to regulations under which land from the Reservation, in particular land suitable for rice cultivation, could be made available only to Malays.[34]

From whatever angle we view the human and political geography of the Malay Peninsula, we will trace the causes of its radical changes in the twentieth century and its problems of co-existence between its ethnic groups to the impact of immigration, especially Chinese immigration.

Chinese Minorities Overseas. While Malaya is the only country in Southeast Asia where the Chinese have become the dominant racial group, the problems created by Chinese immigration are shared by most other Southeast Asian countries. The total number of Chinese minorities is estimated at ten million.[35] Wherever the immigrants went, they took over

[32] In the present Federation of Malaya, which excludes the island of Singapore, the Malays form the largest single racial group (49.5 per cent), but the combined Chinese (38.4 per cent) and Indians (10.8 per cent) community is almost equally large in numbers.

[33] V. Purcell, *The Chinese in Southeast Asia* (New York, 1951), p. 359.

[34] R. Emerson, *Malaysia, A Study in Direct and Indirect Rule* (New York, 1931), p. 479. Additional problems have arisen since June 1948 when an armed rebellion of a Malayan Communist Party, composed almost entirely of Chinese, got under way. The vast majority of the Chinese community have remained aloof from this movement. For a detailed discussion see F. H. Stires, *op. cit.*, pp. 70-82, and V. Thompson and R. Adloff, *The Left Wing in Southeast Asia* (New York, 1950), pp. 210-211.

[35] Thailand: 3,000,000 (15.5 per cent), in Bangkok they constitute half of the

control of a disproportionately large share of the economy of their new country; they controlled the rice economy; they invaded successfully the retail, import and export business, industry, and banking. Their ways of life and loyalties toward their motherland left a distinctive mark on the countries in which they settled. Dislocations caused by their influx prompted a rewriting of the maps of these countries to show the social, economic, and political factors as expressed in the distribution of the indigenous and immigrant populations. Malaya offers, as we have seen, the most vivid illustration. Politically, the fact that the Chinese Communist government does not recognize the right of any Chinese national abroad to divest himself of Chinese nationality accentuates the contrast between the areas of Chinese concentration overseas and those of indigenous settlement.[36] The Indian Prime Minister Jawaharlal Nehru described this situation in 1954 as "frightening."

Indian Emigration Overseas. Of similar nature, although not as serious in their power-political aspects, are the problems created by Indian emigration overseas. For instance, Ceylon has an Indian community of about 900,000, or 13 per cent of the island's population. In 1954, negotiations between the governments of India and Ceylon were under way aimed at straightening out the involved citizenship problems of the Indian minority, and at repatriation to India of those who satisfied Indian citizenship laws. According to 1949 estimates,[37] large communities of Indians are to be found in the following countries: Burma, 700,000; Malaya, 708,000; South Africa, 282,000; East Africa, 184,000; Mauritius, 271,000 (or 63 per cent of the total population!); Indonesia, 30,000; Fiji, 126,000 (or 46 per cent of the total population); West Indies and Guianas, 406,000. In most of these areas, the influx and growth of Indian immigration, with its distinctly different economic, social, and cultural characteristics, has resulted in serious dislocations within the indigenous community. The strongest reaction took place in South Africa, leading to appeals by the Indian population to its "homeland" and to the United Nations. The history of South

---

population of 1,000,000; Indonesia: 2,500,000 (3 per cent); Vietnam: 1,000,000 (5 per cent); Cambodia: 300,000 (10 per cent); Burma: 300,000 (5 per cent); British Borneo and Sarawak: 220,000 (24.4 per cent); Philippines: 120,000 (0.6 per cent). See also L. Unger, "The Chinese in Southeast Asia," *Geographical Review* (1944), pp. 196-217.

[36] For instance, the Indonesian government announced in October, 1954, the departure of a delegation for Communist China for the discussion of the burning controversies over the double citizenship issue. Seventy-five per cent of Indonesia's Chinese minority, estimated at 2,000,000 to 3,000,000, are Indonesian citizens, whose allegiance, however, is also claimed by China.

[37] O. H. K. Spate, *op. cit.*, pp. 112-113.

African government measures aimed at restricting Indian immigration and at limiting the freedom of movement and of settlement of the Indian minority dates back to 1913 when an Immigration Act restricted the immigration of Indians in appreciable numbers. These measures paralleled those directed at the segregation of the native population. In addition to its native segregation South Africa also has a special pattern of Asian (including Indian, Goan, and Arab) communities. Indian trade is confined to certain areas; freedom of movement between the provinces is limited; land tenure and occupation of land are hedged about with legal restrictions; residential segregation is practiced. As citizens, the Indians are powerless. A report by a study group of the South African Institute of International Affairs summed up this situation in 1951 as follows: "Indians in South Africa are, to all intents and purposes, a voteless community." [38] While discriminatory measures by other African governments do not go as far as those in South Africa, the restrictions against the immigration of "non-natives" are widespread: Kenya, Uganda, Tanganyika, and Zanzibar enacted such restrictions in 1946; the Belgians tended to prevent Indian entry into the Congo; the Portuguese restricted entry into Portuguese East Africa.[39]

Such barriers frustrate very powerful underlying forces for Asian demographic expansion. Future Western policy-makers will have to take into account the results of such frustrations.

[38] *Africa South of the Sahara* (Cape Town, 1951), pp. 72-75 (74).
[39] *Ibid.*, pp. 73, 74.

CHAPTER 11

The Political Geography of Languages

A NOTE ON THE RACIAL FACTOR IN POLITICAL GEOGRAPHY

This chapter is concerned with linguistic factors as human elements of importance in the study of political geography. Language is but one of several important features of the human element in the cultural and political landscape, the geographical distribution of which invites exploration by the political geographer who will focus his attention on them. They are features which generate binding and separating forces in the lives of nations. Religion and ethnic composition are other features that must be considered. But while this book devotes a chapter to the subject of the political geography of religions, it does not include a detailed discussion of ethnic and racial factors as such. The reason must be seen in the fact that it is impossible to arrive at a satisfactory classification of the ethnic structure of states. There is no state on the world's map that is not racially heterogeneous. The waves of mass migrations, of immigration and emigration, as well as intermarriage have "resulted in such a mixture of peoples that, although ethnologists suggest various broad groupings on the basis of certain physical characteristics, there is no possibility of defining these groups by acceptable linear boundaries." [1]

On the other hand, we must be cognizant of one broad racial divide

[1] A. E. Moodie, *Geography Behind Politics* (London, 1947), p. 51; see also A. C. Haddon, *The Races of Man* (London, 1929), pp. 139 ff.

between the world of the "white man" and that of the non-white races. The contours of this ominous dividing line are as hazy as ever, but at the time these lines are written they are deepening and the boundary between the two is about to assume a new meaning in international relations. In April, 1955, a conference of twenty-nine Afro-Asian nations was held in Bandung, Indonesia, which included the widest possible variety of countries extending from Libya to Japan and encompassing more than half of the world's population. In spite of numerous separating factors in the realms of religion, language, and race, of political philosophies and affiliations, of cultural and economic systems, the nations assembled in Bandung had in common that they were, in a crude, general way, non-white and that they were suspicious of the white man's world, due to their common heritage of having been at one time or another under the control of white colonial powers. Such a division between the two worlds of white and non-white people signifies the importance of this broad racial distinction in the political geography of today.

LANGUAGE AS A MAJOR FACTOR OF UNIFICATION AND DIVISION IN THE LIVES OF NATIONS

The French Academy, about fifteen years ago, drew from numerous studies in the field of linguistics the conclusion that the number of languages still alive on this globe is 2,796. The Tower of Babel is still a reality. As the biblical story may be an echo of the problems once vexing ancient tyrants whose realms embraced countries of many languages and dialects, so language today is a vital factor in the division or unification of nations. In the creation and preservation of national consciousness, language has played a major role. Each nation strives to have a language of its own, a common language which forms the strongest unifying symbol in the life of a national community. This desire has often given rise to a national or regional consciousness so intense as to lead to separatist movements.[2] Agitations for the Breton and Catalan languages have disturbed the political equilibrium of France and Spain; in Eire, an intensified nationalism has given rise to a determined effort to revive the Irish language; in the Ukraine, one of the major obstacles to the efforts of the Kremlin in integrating this country into the U.S.S.R. has been the determined unwillingness of the Ukrainian peasantry to give up the Ukrainian language for Russian; in South Tyrol, the attempts by the Fascist Italian regime to impose the Italian language on the German-speaking population failed

[2] L. H. Gray, *Foundations of Language* (New York, 1939), p. 117.

because of the determination of the mountain people to preserve their language.

On the other hand, there are examples of nations which are unified without a language peculiar to themselves, and each without a language spoken by all the people. Switzerland is a nation with a strong and healthy national consciousness, and yet it is inhabited by speakers of German, French, Italian, and Rhaeto-Romanic, all four recognized as of equal standing. Belgium is another example of a nation linguistically divided, in this case between French and Flemish, although its unity, especially since World War II, has had to weather many a storm. Then again, we observe nations co-existing peacefully, but not united, in the face of the fact that they are linguistically almost identical, such as Denmark and Norway. Dano-Norwegian has been the literary language of Norway. But the Danes and Norwegians do not regard that fact as any reason for merging the two nations into one. Or, as one British student of linguistics remarked (and obviously with his tongue in his cheek), "English is the language of the United States of America. That is no reason for the United States to annex the British Empire." [3]

THE CASE OF INDIA AND PAKISTAN

The above examples were chosen at random to emphasize the great importance of the element of language in the internal and external politics of nations. Before we look more closely at the relationship of language and linguistic boundaries to political geography, one further example will illustrate the powerful influence the language factor still exerts in the destinies of nations, leading in this instance to a redrawing of the political map (Fig. 11-1). In India, in 1953, the new state of Andhra was inaugurated. This was the first step toward a complete remodeling of the internal political geography of the subcontinent. Of India's 450 million inhabitants, at least 250 million speak Indo-Iranian languages, while about 100 million use Dravidian tongues.[4] Actually, the picture is much more complicated: Hindi, the national language of India under the Constitution, is spoken by 42 per cent of the population. According to the government's program it is to be adopted as the official language by 1956. Besides this, 15 major languages are recognized by the Constitution, as well as 720 dialects, 24 distinct but minor languages, and 23 tribal tongues.[5] Geographically,

[3] A. C. Woolner, *Languages in History and Politics* (London, 1938), p. 10.
[4] M. Pei, *The Story of Language* (New York, 1949), p. 353.
[5] These figures are based on an Indian census published in April, 1954; *New York Times*, April 10, 1954. See also O. H. K. Spate, *India and Pakistan*, p. 125, who points out that in 1931, six languages accounted for 65 per cent of the population.

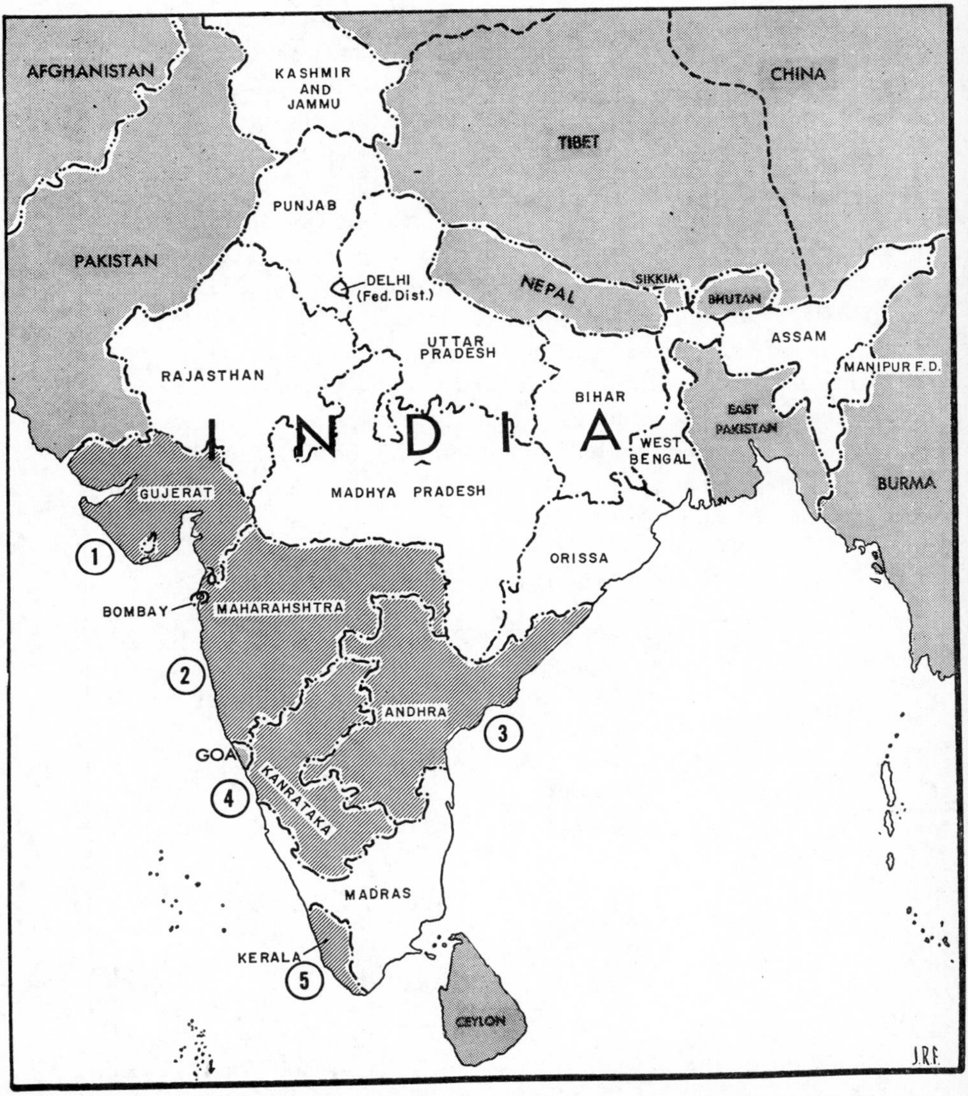

FIG. 11-1. Linguistic States of India: (1) Gujerat; (2) Maharahshtra; (3) Andhra; (4) Kanrataka; (5) Kerala (after The Economist).

the Dravidian languages are those of India's south, while the Indo-Iranian languages are spoken in the north. Between these two major competing linguistic groups lingers the official language of the recent past, English, which the Indian government is obligated to abolish within the next fifteen years. In a way, the language problems and cleavages which threaten the unity of the new state of India and divide its people in the north and south can be compared with the conflict which, a hundred years earlier, threatened the unity of the young United States.

What happened in India on October 1, 1953, when the separate state to be known as Andhra was formed for 20 million Telugu speakers of Madras, represents the surrender of India's central government to the demand that the country should redraw its internal boundaries to give a dozen major linguistic groups states of their own. The principle itself is not quite new in India. Even before 1914, when the British created Assam and Bihar out of Bengal, and the North-West Frontier Province of the Punjab, the new creations were largely, but not entirely, linguistic.[6] After independence was won by India, after the battle cry for linguistic states was no longer a demand by the Congress Party to the Colonial Government but a problem of the new Indian nation itself, it became evident to its leaders that overemphasis on linguistic factors in the redrawing of the political geography of the country threatened to foster a new concept of belonging together and of nationalism based on language, and that this strong unifying bond militated against a wider loyalty to India as a whole. It was feared that controversies over the new boundaries might upset national unity and divert the people's efforts from the more urgent economic and political problems. Yet the force of the popular demand for recognition of the language principle as a basis for a system of new Indian states had become so vehement that the wind which the Congress Party once sowed now turned into a tempest. Thus Andhra was born and a new map of India based on linguistic principles is taking shape.

In the fall of 1955, Prime Minister Nehru presented a reorganization plan for redrawing completely the political map of the federal republic of India. While its states are as administrative bodies less powerful than are the states in the United States, the cultural and linguistic differences and cleavages are much more formidable. Under the new plan, in place of the present twenty-nine states (in contrast to the quilt of seventeen provinces and about six hundred princely states at the time when independence was won by India) there would be only sixteen. Only two of them, Bombay and the Punjab, will be bilingual. Four of the large states will be Hindi

[6] "Linguistic States in India," *The Economist,* October 3, 1953.

speaking units, and Hindi is to be the national language. History will tell whether this scheme will succeed in overcoming the strong forces of regionalism and separatism at work throughout India. The strength of these forces is indicated by the fact that the Indian Congress Working Committee shortly after the new plan was presented gave in to the demands of the Marahashtrians of central and western India, who agitate for a separate Marathi-speaking state of their own, and decided to split up the present state of Bombay to form three states.[7]

In Pakistan, where many economic, ethnic, religious, and cultural factors threaten the uneasy balance between its eastern and western parts, problems having their origin in Pakistan's complicated geography of languages have become increasingly serious. The Moslem League government in Karachi tried to decree that Urdu (the Hindustani variant spoken by Moslems) be used as official language in both Pakistans. But eastern Pakistan is linguistically and culturally part of Bengal. The speakers of the Bengali tongue, who number sixty million, are more numerous than any language group in western Pakistan and their opposition against the attempt to force upon them an alien official language was violent. In May, 1954, they succeeded in transforming Pakistan into a multilingual state. Pakistan's assembly accepted a resolution declaring that Urdu and Bengali should be official languages, and in addition "such other provincial languages as may be declared to be such by the Head of the State on recommendation of the provincial legislatures." [8] English will be allowed to function as *lingua franca* until 1967.[9]

LANGUAGE AS BINDING ELEMENT

The India and Pakistan examples offer in a nutshell a picture of the multitude of significant problems with which the geography of languages confronts the student of political geography. We shall now try to define some of these problems.

There are many factors which contribute to binding communities and populations together. One, if not the strongest element in the process of cementing a nation is the possession of a common language. Race (actual

[7] A. M. Rosenthal, *New York Times,* October 23, 1955; *ibid,* October 10, 1955 and November 13, 1955.

[8] Pei, *op. cit.,* pp. 286, 346; W. G. East and O. H. K. Spate, *The Changing Map of Asia* (London, 1950), p. 123; and *Neue Zürcher Zeitung,* March 25, 1954, p. 1; *New York Times,* March 8, 1954, p. 5.

[9] The discussion of language factors in the Indian Union and Pakistan is not meant to detract from the fact that the principal cleavage in India is one of religion.

blood-affinity and, even more potent, the imagined racial community preached by the drummers of political pseudo-philosophies), ethnographic factors, the unifying force of religion, and the manifold elements of a common history and traditions—all work together in the process of amalgamation which creates and continuously recreates the substance of a nation. But language is always an essential factor, sometimes competing with religion in the order of importance.[10] A common language must always be considered a powerful bond, uniting a people within a community of ideas and ideals. Switzerland, with its four official languages, is not an exception but rather emphasizes the fact that the mosaic of each nation is so complex, the mosaic stones so different in appearance, that we cannot expect to find a general formula composed of linguistic, racial, and physical factors from which the definition of a nation or nationality can be derived.

THE LINGUISTIC FACTOR AS A BARRIER

Just as a common language cements and binds and creates a strong feeling of belonging-together, the lack of a common language will form a barrier between peoples, unless, as in Switzerland, common memories prove strong enough to challenge the factors of disunity and isolation which differences in language are apt to create.[11] In India, as discussed above, we have an illustration of the conflicting powers at work. It is still too early to say whether the unifying elements upon which the Indian government rests its claim for national unity will develop sufficient strength to offset the separating factors based on linguistic differences.

The problems with which India and Pakistan are at present confronted within their national boundaries illustrate another important factor: differences in language are not only barriers between nation and nation. Where more than one language is spoken within the national boundaries of a nation—even where different dialects prevail—the germ of not-belonging-together exists and serious problems affecting in many ways the internal geography of a nation are apt to arise. There is scarcely a nation on

[10] India offers a good illustration in confirmation of this statement. To quote O. H. K. Spate (*Geography of India and Pakistan*, p. 125): "The 'racial' element has indeed its importance—a very great importance—in the cultural history of India; it is of little practical significance today. Few Indians (and for that matter few Englishmen) could speak with any degree of scientific accuracy as to their racial origins; everyone knows what language he speaks. Next to religion language is the greatest divisive force in India (and Pakistan) today."

[11] M. Huber, "Swiss Nationality," in A. Zimmern, ed., *Modern Political Doctrines* (London, 1939), pp. 216-217.

the political map of the world without dividing factors which have their origin in linguistic differences. In each case, the nature of the problems arising from such differences has characteristics of its own and is, above all, determined by the relationship between, and the relative power of, the various language groups brought together under one nation's sovereignty. Rarely do we find cultural and political equality between language groups such as it exists in Switzerland. Mostly the co-existence between majority and minority groups, between conqueror and conquered, between colonial power and indigenous population, will accentuate the internal problems. Thus the language map which distinguishes between linguistic groups within a nation's boundaries—by showing the islands and pockets of discernible language, or on a somewhat different plane, dialect—cannot possibly do justice to the many distinctions which, nationwide, characterize the relations of language groups and thus form an integral and important part of a country's cultural and political geography.

REGIONAL CASE STUDIES

Canada. The internal political geography of Canada is distinguished by the relationship between its English element and the vigorous French group, representing more than four-fifths (about 4,000,000) of the population of Quebec, or one-third of Canada's total population of 15,000,000 [12] (Fig. 11-2). De Tocqueville's prophecy of 1830 that the French were "the wreck of an old people lost in the flood of a new nation," [13] was disproved by history. A comparison of Ontario and Quebec shows striking differences in their respective human and social geographies. There has been no melting pot. The French Canadians like to think of themselves as *les Canadiens,* and of the rest of their compatriots as *les Anglais.* In addition to cultural and linguistic and, above all, religious factors, geography has played a leading part in keeping the two nationalities alive under the same Canadian flag and preventing them from getting "lost in the flood of a new nation": set off by themselves, surrounded on three sides by the Gulf of St. Lawrence and the forested highlands to the north and south, the French Canadians are approaching their third century of agricultural and social isolation, with strong Anglo-French demarcations highlighted by linguistic divides.[14]

[12] Official Canadian statistics for 1954 show that despite occasional sharp differences between the French Canadian groups and the majority groups of English-speaking Canadians in immigration, births, infant mortality, and marriages, the proportion remains the same.

[13] J. R. Smith and M. O. Phillips, *North America,* 2nd ed. (New York, 1942), p. 72.

[14] *Ibid.,* pp. 631-639.

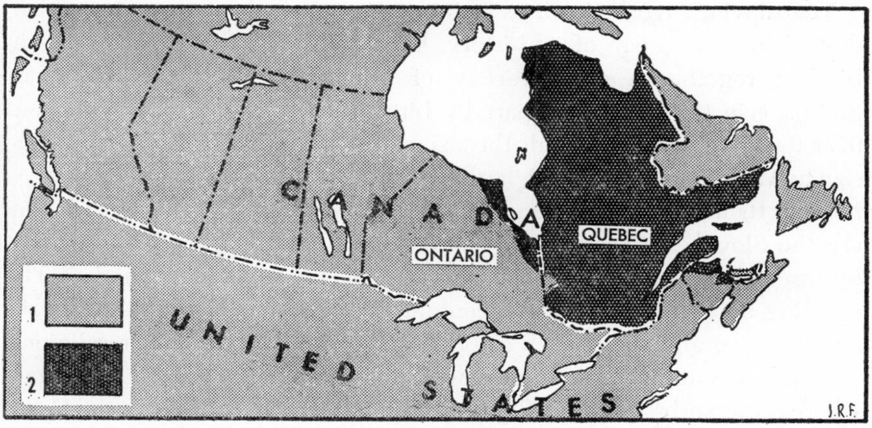

Fig. 11-2. Canada: "Les Canadiens": (1) English language area; (2) French language area.

Union of South Africa. In comparison and contrast, the geography of languages in the Union of South Africa reveals the two competing white groups, the Boers and the English, in an altogether different environmental setting. While it is true in the case of two language groups in Canada, and in the case of four language groups in Switzerland, that a more or less accurate linguistic borderline separates one linguistic group from the other, the geography of languages, with its political implications, is much more complex in South Africa. There is no clearly defined linguistic boundary line. In answer to the question put to the white population in the 1946 census as to which language they spoke at home, 57.3 per cent stated Afrikaans (language of the Boers) and 39.4 per cent English; 1.3 per cent declared themselves bilingual. In broad terms, one can observe Boer and British preponderance region-wise, with the British in the majority along the coast, in the Cape Province and, above all, in Natal, and the Boers having their strongest positions in the interior, in Transvaal, and especially in the Orange Free State. More significant than the regional divide is that between town and country. On a town-country level, the rural districts, with an Afrikaans-speaking majority of 82.4 per cent, display clearly the strength of the Boer element among the white farming population. In the cities, the ratio of 48.5 per cent English to 47.8 per cent Afrikaans reveals here the major zones of competition and conflict, complicated by the fact that English is a world language and Afrikaans a provincial tongue.[15]

[15] R. P. Hafter, "British and Boers in South Africa," *Neue Zürcher Zeitung,* June 5, 1954. In this competition between English- and Afrikaans-speaking whites, time

Yugoslavia. Yugoslavia offers an interesting example of a country which, during the short span of its history, has astonishingly well succeeded in binding together a great variety of ethnic, linguistic, and religious groups,[16] in the past torn apart by bitter feuds. Its total area of about 97,000 square miles (one-half the size of France or Spain, about the same size as Wyoming or Oregon) harbored in 1954 a population of seventeen million. Its main nationalities, comprising 87.4 per cent of the population, are the Slovenes, Croats, Serbs, and Macedonians.[17] They are set apart by three major languages: Serbo-Croat, Slovene, and Macedonian.[18] The dividing lines are even more accentuated by the fact that the Yugoslavs adopted two alphabets, each associated with one of the major religions. The Slovenes and Croats, largely Roman Catholic, use the Latin alphabet, whereas the Serbs and Macedonians, largely Serb Orthodox, use the Cyrillic alphabet, a modified form of the Greek alphabet.[19] The close link between linguistic and religious elements in Yugoslavia illustrates the blending of ethnic, linguistic, and religious factors which co-operate to distinguish groups within a multination state. Such a blending contributes to strengthening the contours of boundary lines within the state and depicting its internal cultural and political geography.

---

seems to be on the side of the latter. School statistics for 1954, as reported in the *New York Times* of January 24, 1954, show that there are twice as many Afrikaans-speaking white children in the public schools as English-speaking children (and that African Negro children far outnumber both). It is safe to predict that the English-speaking whites in most of South Africa are on the way to becoming a minority in the next generation; only the Natal coastal province and the adjacent northeastern corner of Cape Province are likely to remain as areas of English-language predominance.

[16] See pp. 431, 432, 435, 436.

[17] It should be noted that in addition to its contrasting majority groups Yugoslavia has also a highly complex minorities situation: Albanians, somewhat less than 800,000, comprise about 5 per cent of the country's total population. A look at the map reveals the precarious border situation between Albania and Yugoslavia. Since the bulk of the Albanian minority is to be found in the Kosmet border region, this fact emphasizes the problems arising out of the existence of so considerable a minority group close to the boundary of the Soviet satellite Albania. Other minorities include Hungarians (500,000), Rumanians, Czechoslovaks, Turks, and Italians. The above information is based on U.S. Department of Commerce, Bureau of the Census, *The Population of Yugoslavia* (Washington, D. C., 1954), pp. 52-55.

[18] For centuries, Macedonia has been a cradle of conflict between the nations represented today by Bulgaria, Yugoslavia, Greece, and Albania. It is of interest to note that the most recent attempt to solve the Macedonian problem has been undertaken on a linguistic basis. Macedonia is one of Yugoslavia's six autonomous republics. Of its population of about 1,200,000, some 800,000 are classified as "Macedonians," and strong efforts are made by the Belgrade government to solidify this ethnic group through the development of a Macedonian language and a folk culture of its own. For details, see H. R. Wilkinson, *Maps and Politics, A Review of the Ethnographic Cartography of Macedonia* (Liverpool, 1951), p. 165.

[19] *Ibid.*, pp. 14-15.

SUMMARY

In spite of many differences, we can describe Canada and Switzerland, or Belgium and the United Kingdom, and even Yugoslavia, as countries in which the various linguistic groups harmoniously—in spite of occasional friction—collaborate and respect each other. In contrast, in the South African Union, its colonial background, the memories of the Boer War, and the violent controversy over the Apartheid policy of the government prompt many among the Boer extremists to look upon their English-speaking countrymen as intruders and invaders.

LINGUISTIC ISLANDS AS ZONES OF FRICTION

Europe. This leads us to those political areas in which linguistic minorities, as in the case of the Germans in pre-World War II Poland and Czechoslovakia, remain an alien substance within the body politic. In these areas, the explosive conflicts caused by hostile linguistic groups led to radical solution of the problem by mass expulsions of eight million so-called ethnic Germans (whose distinguishing characteristic was the language factor) from East European countries. Often the problems resulting from the existence of "foreign" language groups within the boundaries of a nation are critically increased by the location of such linguistic islands near or along a border, thus bringing the language (or ethnic) minority close to a neighbor with whom this minority shares not only a common language but other tangible and intangible interests as well. Most of the boundary problems which vex the nations of Europe at this time are only to a small degree caused by differences over factors concerning the physical geography of the frontier zone; they arise, rather, as factors of human geography, among which the problems of conflicting linguistic and political boundaries loom large. This is true in the following active and dormant boundary disputes along the frontiers of Europe; the map of Europe which shows these zones of friction over linguistic and political boundaries illustrates how language plays a paramount role among the factors which account for the unstable political frontiers of Europe.[20]

In connection with the discussion of "dormant" disputes in Europe, in border regions where an ethnic minority is geographically close to the "motherland," mention should be made of the highly involved case of Ireland, where more English is at present spoken than Irish (which belongs

[20] List from G. W. Hoffman, "Boundary Problems in Europe," *Annals of the Association of American Geographers* (1954), p. 107.

to the Celtic group of Indo-European languages) by its three million people. To Irish nationalism the partition of Ireland will always appear intolerable, and Eire has never recognized the separation of the six Northern Counties. The language factor here is of minor importance because of the dominant position of the English language, especially in the North. Ireland is a good illustration of the importance of the religious factor in political geography: the Southern population is 94 per cent Catholic, the Northern 66 per cent non-Catholic. In a reunited Ireland the non-Catholics would amount to a little less than 25 per cent.[21] In all its complexity, the Irish problem shows the linguistic factor as only one element, and in this case not a decisive one, molding the human geography of the country.

TABLE 11-1

DISPUTED AREA	NOW CONTROLLED BY	CLAIMED BY	POPULATION TOTAL (000s)	POPULATION SPEAK LANGUAGE OF CLAIMANT—PER CENT
A. *Active Disputes*				
Dutch-German	Netherlands	Germany	9.5	100
Saar	Semi-independent France	Germany	943.	100
South Tyrol	Italy	Austria	340	60
B. *Dormant Disputes*				
N. Epirus	Albania	Greece	320	20
E. Germany	Poland U.S.S.R.	W. Germany	6,000	(close to) 100
Karelia-Viipuri	U.S.S.R.	Finland	400	?
Slovenia (Yugoslavia) Carinthia (Austria)	Austria	Yugoslavia	190	30

Linguistic Divides in Asian Frontier Zones. In the frontier zones of Asia, where nomadic people flow back and forth across the borders, the linguistic divides differ in character from those in the borderlands settled by the sedentary people of Europe. But here, too, we can observe the centripetal force of linguistic kinship which tends to consolidate people separated by political boundaries. An example is provided by the Soviet-supported efforts of Afghanistan to sponsor a Pathan nation —Pushtunistan—which would unite about seven million Pathan tribesmen now living in disputed areas of Pakistan in a state which would be domi-

[21] J. V. Kelleher, "Can Ireland Unite?", *The Atlantic Monthly* (April, 1954), pp. 58-62; I. Bowman, *The New World* (New York, 1921), pp. 30-35.

nated by the Afghanistan government and would extend that country's control over western Pakistan from the Hindu Kush range in the north to the Arabian seacoast of Baluchistan in the south. Sinkiang serves as another illustration. Here, too, the frontier between China and the U.S.S.R. is not a line but a zone. "Except for the Amur and Ussuri frontiers between the Northeastern Provinces and Siberia, the entire land frontier could be arbitrarily shifted either several hundred miles to the north or several hundred miles to the south and still affect practically no Russians and practically no Chinese." [22] Ethnically and linguistically, the frontier zone is interwoven and penetrated in both directions by Kazakh, Uiqur, and Kirghiz groups and linguistic patterns.[23]

STABILITY AND INSTABILITY OF BOUNDARIES AND THE LANGUAGE FACTOR

If one focuses attention on those sensitive spots along a political boundary where the linguistic and the political boundary fall apart, one has to distinguish between the political boundary which, in spite of lacking identity with the language boundary, has demonstrated stability in its history, and the political boundary which, cutting across a cultural landscape whose populace speaks the same language and shares the same traditions and memories of a common history, still has to pass the test of time. Typical of the first is the boundary separating Germany and Switzerland. The other extreme is exemplified by the temporary political boundary which follows the Iron Curtain and cuts a Germany which is practically without linguistic or ethnic minorities into two political units—West Germany, and the "German Democratic Republic" in what was, until 1954, the Soviet Zone of Occupation. Even though the future of Germany and its frontier is still in balance, this example shows clearly the fallacy of drawing a boundary that disregards completely the intangible factors of belonging-together that cement a nation. Such intangibles account for the unity which the United States achieved and has maintained in spite of the many separating factors which brought about the Civil War.

[22] O. Lattimore, "The Inland Crossroads of Asia," in H. W. Weigert and V. Stefansson, eds., *Compass of the World* (New York, 1949), pp. 374-394 (386).
[23] O. Caroe, "Soviet Empire," in *The Turks of Central Asia and Stalinism* (London, 1953), map after p. 272; see also pp. 32-34, 43, 255.

IRREDENTISM

The characteristic instability of the political boundary in disrupted linguistic zones (unless the boundary, as in the case of the Swiss-German frontier, has weathered the storm over a long period of history) frequently generates expansionist drives and ideologies on the part of neighboring nations. These nations tend to regard minority groups across the border speaking their own languages as akin and claim them and their territory. This is the meaning of irredentism. The term originated in Italy—*Italia irredenta* (unredeemed Italy). A political philosophy of high emotional pitch, it claimed for Italy not only neighboring areas in which Italian was spoken by a majority of the people (with Austria and Switzerland as targets), but also lands across the sea, such as Malta and the territory east of the Adriatic. In countries in which a nationalistic irredentism is rampant, we rarely find a readiness to surrender territory to a neighboring country, even though an alien language is spoken there. Thus Italy, in the heyday of its irredentist claims, did not produce proposals advocating the surrender to Switzerland and France of the German- and French-speaking districts of the Alpine valleys of Piedmont.[24] An extreme case of irredentism was presented by National Socialist Germany which started its ill-fated drive toward world domination by irredentist moves directed at the annexation of those regions along its frontier which were inhabited by a German-speaking majority: in Czechoslovakia the Sudetenlands, the Free State of Danzig, in Lithuania the Memelland, in Denmark the northern part of Schleswig, in Belgium the region of Eupen-Malmedy. The "Anschluss" of Austria belongs in the same category.

THE CHANGING MAP OF LANGUAGES: ERASURE OF LINGUISTIC POCKETS

Different from the situation of linguistic minorities residing in areas close to their linguistic or ethnic homeland is that of such minorities occupying lands surrounded entirely by territory inhabited by speakers of the language prevalent in the country to which they owe loyalty. Here the attraction and temptation which a neighboring linguistic island offers to an expansionist nation diminishes with the distance from its borders and with the separating power of "foreign" groups settled between the

[24] H. B. George, *The Relations of Geography and History*, 5th ed. (Oxford, 1924), p. 57; see also the detailed study of the borderlands of Italian language in L. Dominian, *The Frontiers of Language and Nationality in Europe* (New York, 1917), pp. 59-92.

ethnic or linguistic "homeland" and the related minority. Instead, such linguistic pockets present problems of internal political geography which, especially in those cases in which the linguistic or ethnic majority has to deal with substantial minorities, assume major proportions. The situation differs from region to region, nation to nation, and it would be a highly superficial undertaking to try and find simple formulas.

The existence of a linguistic pocket in close vicinity to the political boundary of the country in which the same language is prevalent, often leads to repressive measures against the inhabitants of the linguistic pocket. The radical solution consists in the mass expulsion of the members of minority groups who, by remaining faithful to their mother tongue and other features of their minority culture, have actually or seemingly documented their inner resistance to the state and nation to which they "belong". A more moderate solution is that of international agreements between the countries concerned aimed at an orderly population transfer or exchange. These measures and the resulting radical changes in the human and consequently political structure of many regions have assumed major and decisive proportions in the political geography of the twentieth century. Because of their importance, we shall deal with them elsewhere separately.[25] Here it must suffice to point out the quality of instability of linguistic islands, especially when their inhabitants continue to resist cultural assimilation. Strong reactions may occur by the majority against what they believe has remained a foreign element within their political entity. Much less noticeable than the effects of mass expulsions or population transfers are those changes in the political landscape of a linguistic or ethnic pocket which result from a gradual overpowering of the minority group by strong immigration movements. These usually have government support and are aimed at eventually erasing the alien island from the national map. A case in point is South Tyrol. Its German-speaking population complains that the equal rights status promised to it in the peace treaty of 1946 exists in theory only due to the fact that, since 1918, when South Tyrol became Italian, the Italian government has consistently sponsored the mass migration of Italians into South Tyrol and thus the Italianization of the region: the number of Italians has risen between 1918 and 1954 from 7,000 to 120,000.

A full understanding of the relations in political geography between linguistically dominant groups and minorities is possible only if one studies the history and historical geography of these relations. To understand, for instance, the geography of original languages in America, we

[25] See pp. 355 ff.

must be cognizant of the fact that when colonization started, America was but sparsely settled, for the most part by tribes in the hunting stage of civilization, while the few cities were subjected to ruthless extermination by the Spaniards.[26] The Inca empire builders of the Andean universal state displayed in their linguistic policy a different device of authoritarianism.[27] Having come to the conclusion that their subjects would not function as fully-equipped human instruments of a totalitarian regime unless they were equipped with some common "lingua franca"—a supplementary language of more than local currency—they selected the Quechua language and forced all the inhabitants to make themselves familiar with it. (An impressive example of the importance of a "lingua franca" as a binding element has been the choice of English as official language at the Bandung conference of twenty-eight Asian and African states in April, 1955.)

RUSSIFICATION IN THE SOVIET ORBIT

The Soviet policy toward its ethnic minorities and, as an integral part of it, the Russification of Soviet minority languages offers a significant example of an authoritarian policy aimed at changing the linguistic map of a nation's orbit and, as a result, changing also the map of its internal political geography. Enforced national conformity and ill-concealed Russification are the main characteristics of this policy.

> The history of Soviet language policy is the record of increasingly centralized manipulation and uniformalization of the "forms" of supposedly national cultures. The reins of cultural development were taken away, after the first decade of Soviet rule, from the national minority leadership, and drawn tight by Moscow. At first the aim was to sever the ties of the many cultural groups with their past and to give their cultures a fresh Soviet face; the second step was the gradual Russification of the "forms" of various cultures.[28]

As a rough approximation, one could say that the Kremlin has come full circle to imitate Tsarist policy on national minorities, the essence of which was the imposition of the Russian language, church, and culture on the non-Great Russian subjects of the empire.[29] But there are two major differences. "On the one hand, there is the fact that many scores of languages today are used in education and publishing which were not admitted by the Tsarist regime. On the other hand, the Soviets have added a new twist to the principle of Russification. The Tsarist goal had been the exclusion

[26] Woolner, *op. cit.*, p. 15.
[27] A. J. Toynbee, *A Study of History*, Vol. V (London, 1939), p. 523.
[28] S. M. Schwarz, "The Soviet Concept and Conquest of National Cultures," *Problems of Communism* (1953), pp. 41-46.
[29] East and Spate, *op. cit.*, p. 350.

of minority languages from various functions (education, literary usage); ultimately, the various ethnic groups were to end up as Russians. The Soviet regime, which has slackened this approach, has launched the Russification of languages. While supporting minority tongues in various functions, it has subjected them to an influx of Russian words and grammatical patterns, and has imposed on them Russian letters and spelling conventions." [30]

THE IMPACT OF PHYSICAL GEOGRAPHY UPON THE GEOGRAPHY OF LANGUAGES

These examples of authoritarian language policy show that there are many gradations between the extermination of minorities or their expulsion or involuntary transfer to other regions within the national boundaries and remedial measures such as the enforcing of an authoritarian language policy and a policy of linguistic *laissez faire*. Choice as well as success or failure of a government's measures are frequently conditioned by factors of physical geography. Often we can trace the survival of linguistic islands among speakers of a different tongue—or even more frequently, the survival of distinct dialects—to geographical features impeding easy communication between two areas. In the secluded southern mountains of the Appalachians, Shakespearean language survived long after it had fallen into disuse in England and in the Atlantic Coastal Plain where the mountaineers once lived. So many customs of the past survive among these people that they have well been called "our contemporary ancestors." [31] Thus mountain chains, deserts, forests, seas, as geographical features impeding communication, will lead us to innumerable locations on the world's map where from olden times linguistic pockets have remained intact and where, consequently—and in proportion to the overall national importance of these islands—problems of internal and external political geography stayed alive.

On the other hand, the relationship of physical and human geography, in terms of the political geography of languages, is not so obvious that the physiographical map provides most of the answers to the questions of why and where. By no means do linguistic boundaries always follow obvious geographical lines.[32] To claim [33] that linguistic lines of cleavage

[30] U. Weinreich, "The Russification of Soviet Minority Languages," *Problems of Communism* (1953), pp. 46-57 (47).

[31] E. C. Semple, "The Anglo-Saxons of the Kentucky Mountains," *Geographical Journal* (1901), pp. 588-623.

[32] Woolner, *op. cit.*, pp. 15-16.

[33] Dominian, *op. cit.*, pp. 2-3.

conform essentially with physical features would be a gross oversimplification of the problem. In present-day human geography these features are significant in many cases; they are not significant in many others.

For Europe, W. Gordon East [34] describes this as follows:

> . . . the lower Danube, flanked by a broad belt of marshes on its north bank, does divide Rumanian from Bulgarian-speaking peoples. The boundary between French and German passes along the wooded summits from the high Vosges. The area of the Pripet marshes separates Ukranian and Belorussian speech, and the Pyrenees effectively separate French and Spanish. Areas of scantily settled steppe and rivers which are unnavigable upstream, characterize the frontier region between Portuguese and Spanish. But, in the main, peoples and languages have negotiated physical obstacles such as mountains, rivers, highlands, and marshes. The watershed of the Alps does not neatly divide French and German from Italian; within the Alpine valleys, distinctive languages have developed in semi-isolation; neither do the eastern Pyrenees sharply divide the areas of Catalan and Provencal. As to the navigable rivers of Europe, they commonly serve to unite rather than to divide, so that the Vistula Basin forms the core region of Polish speech while that of the Rhine has become mainly Germanic, yet invaded by French on its western flank. The Danube, in contrast, presents a succession of language areas astride its valley.
>
> In lowlands and hilly country, the frontiers of language bear no obvious relationship to the relief and are clearly the expression of social forces operative long ago. Even so, former geographical features—now erased—may have been significant: thus the former Carbonnière Forest did in medieval times form a zone of separation between Flemish speech in the Scheldt Basin and French speech to the south.
>
> **THE MOVEMENT OF PEOPLES AND THE LINGUISTIC FACTOR**
>
> Europe's language map, like those of its nations and states, can be explained only in terms of historical geography, i.e., the movements of peoples, their initial settlements and subsequent colonization outwards, and their mutual reactions when brought into contact with each other. By the end of the Middle Ages the language patterns were clearly outlined; one can point to specific linguistic frontiers, notably that of French and German in the Lorraine Plateau and that of Walloon and French on the Franco-Belgian border where the boundary has changed but little during the last thousand years. And, since the end of the Middle Ages, the many migrations, colonizing efforts, and compulsory and voluntary transfers of population, especially in the last decade, have modified distributions fixed long ago.[35]

In our age of technology, more and more natural obstructions are being crossed; the impact of radio makes itself felt in the most remote hamlets. Colonization, in particular settlement colonization of the tropics, has led to the crossing of oceans by languages. It is here where historical geog-

[34] In G. W. Hoffman, ed., *A Geography of Europe* (New York, 1953), pp. 30-31.

[35] East, *op. cit.*

raphy offers the most striking examples of an immense variety of invasion forces displayed by foreign language groups from distant lands. The spread of the Greek language followed colonization. Greek cities scattered from older centers round the shores of the Mediterranean, mainly in the eastern half but also as far west as southern Italy and Marseilles.[36]

The Roman Empire carried its language far beyond the Italian peninsula, and in the Roman *colonia* (colony), where conquered lands were allotted to Roman veterans, we find the soldiers of the Roman legions and the traders introducing their own language and civilization to the barbarians.[37] Wherever Roman colonizers went, their prestige and the proud Roman civilization which they represented, as well as their close-knit and organized social community (*conventus civium Romanorum*) endowed the Roman language (and Roman law) with a privileged position.[38] Thus Latin was adopted in Western Europe, North Africa, and in Central Europe, up to the Rhine-Limes-Danube frontier zone—the outer defense curtain from Castra Regina (Regensburg) to Confluentes (Coblenz). In Western Europe the transformative force of the Roman language proved decisive and permanent. Provincial Latin conditioned the growth during the Middle Ages of languages of the Romance group: French, Provençal, Italian, Catalan, Spanish, and Portuguese. In the Swiss mountains, islands of Latin weathered the impact of centuries. In Rumania, in what once formed the Roman province of Dacia, an "inlier" of Roman speech, containing some Slav elements, remained alive.[39]

The historical geography of Roman colonization and its impact on the languages of the Romance group, however important, is only one instance of how language patterns and linguistic frontiers evolve as the result of invasions and conquests, oversea and overland colonization. The student of the history of languages and of historical geography will find here vast fields to plow, and often enough in what is scientifically no man's land. To the student of political geography this background is of great interest and in many cases, as evidenced by India, is indispensable. Here it must suffice to stress the importance of the historical events which account for the survival of linguistic islands within nations the majority of whose people are speakers of a different tongue, and also to emphasize the problems of internal and external geography generated by these language pockets.

[36] Woolner, *op. cit.*, p. 14.
[37] *Ibid.*, pp. 13-14.
[38] I. Mommsen, *Römische Geschichte,* Vol. II (1857), p. 407.
[39] East, *op. cit.*, pp. 25-26.

DIALECTS

The political geography of languages applies also to dialects, especially in regard to the internal political geography of nations. Professor Mario Pei reports that about half the students in linguistic classes who were polled as to their native tongue replied "American" rather than "English,"[40] and G. B. Shaw wisecracked in *Pygmalion* that "England and America are two countries separated by the same language." These observations and the distinctions, well known to Americans, between New England ("Yankee") and Southern American dialects bring home to the reader the importance of dialects within the framework of the geography of languages. The borderline between language and dialect is exceedingly thin and the usual distinction between a language as the accepted national form of speech and dialect as the not officially accepted form is not too helpful. In Switzerland, for instance, both German and the dialect known as Schwyzer-Deutsch are recognized officially and taught in the schools. Each language has "infinite gradations of standard tongue, vernacular, slang, cant, and jargon," and the "geographical division extends not only to regions and sections of the country, but also to towns and quarters of focus."[41] It is obvious that the use of the same dialect generates strong feelings of belonging-together among its speakers and also contributes to setting them apart from other folk groups who, while speaking and writing the same language, have a different dialect. Within a nation, the separating factors due to differences in dialect may be insignificant politically because other, unifying, factors are overwhelming. Or they may be powerful enough to build invisible walls between the various dialect groups.

To the student of political geography who attempts to trace the geographical distribution of languages on the political map and to understand the relationship of geography and language, it will thus be evident that, especially in the internal political geography of states, he cannot neglect the consideration of the unifying and separating force of dialects. When millions of so-called ethnic Germans were expelled from Czechoslovakia and Poland in 1945 and later, the problems confronting the West German government in its task of resettling the destitute expellees in the north, south and southwest of Germany were multiplied by the fact that the new German citizens spoke dialects alien to the Germans who were to receive

[40] Pei, *op. cit.*, p, 298.
[41] *Ibid.*, pp. 46-47.

the refugees in their communities. Germany itself has two great language divisions: High German and Low German, as well as numerous local variations. Its map of languages and dialects with all its political implications is, as the result of the influx of millions of ethnic-German expellees, undergoing radical changes. As settlement of compact groups of newcomers with dialects of their own becomes stabilized, new linguistic islands will be formed—islands of distinctive dialects within the national boundaries of Germany, and possessing all the characteristics of a nationality group bound together by common memories, ideals, and hopes. An interesting, although older, linguistic island of this kind within Germany is its industrial heartland, the Ruhr, with a total population of about seven million. Its mining population is composed of many ethnic groups, especially from Eastern Germany and Poland. Gradually it has assumed distinctive national characteristics of its own, and in this process has developed a new dialect, a mixture of Westphalian, East Prussian, Upper-Silesian, and High German. The speakers of the new tongue share an intangible possession which contributes strongly to the evolution of a specific folk-group within the entity of the nation.

Italy is rich in dialects which set a distinguishing pattern of human geography: Sicilian, Neapolitan, Roman, Tuscan, Venetian, and the Gallo-Italian dialects of northwestern Italy.[42]

China offers the most colorful illustration of a country divided into a large number of dialects often mutually unintelligible though falling into the broad categories of Northern and Southern [43] (Fig. 11-3). About three hundred million people speak variants of Mandarin, the dialect of northern China, now renamed *Kuo-yü* or "National Tongue"; the remaining one hundred fifty million speak widely divergent dialects, the majority of which are Cantonese, the Wu dialect of Shanghai, and the Klin dialect of Fukien.[44] Thus, while the possession of a common written language provides the Chinese with an asset making for unity, the multiplicity of dialects is a potent factor of separation which can be overcome gradually only if the northern form of the "National Tongue," as a national *lingua franca*, should be accepted on a broad national basis.[45]

[42] Pei, *op. cit.*, p. 54.

[43] Gray, *op. cit.*, p. 390.

[44] Pei, *op. cit.*, p. 371; P. M. Roxby, "China as an Entity," *Geography* (1937), pp. 1-20.

[45] H. J. Wood, in East and Spate, *op. cit.*, pp. 265-266. For a vivid description of the contrast between the Mandarin *lingua franca* and the highly diversified local dialects, see Toynbee, *op. cit.*, Vol. V, pp. 512-514.

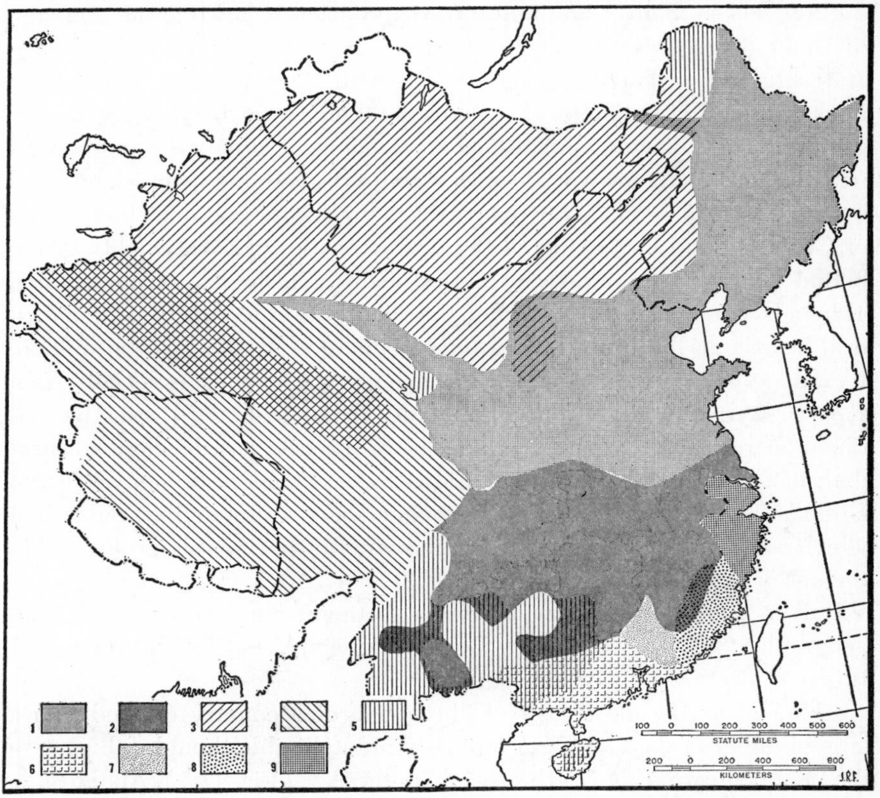

Fig. 11-3. China: Areas of Languages and Dialects: (1) Northern Mandarin; (2) Southern Mandarin; (3) Mongolian; (4) Tibetan; (5) Tribal dialects; (6) Cantonese; (7) Hakka; (8) Fukien dialects; (9) Wu dialects (after P. M. Roxby).

From the abstract point of view, the multilingual state is not ideal. Germs of disunity similar to those existing unavoidably in the multilingual state will be found in states where local dialects have remained strong enough to challenge the supremacy of the national language. In either case the student of political geography should take cognizance of these linguistic patterns which spell both unity and disunity and which therefore must be understood if one tries to evaluate the human and political geography of a nation.

CHAPTER 12

Religions: Their Distribution and Role in Political Geography

THE IMPACT OF RELIGION UPON POLITICS IN HISTORY

A few centuries ago political boundaries throughout the world coincided closely with religious boundaries. Still more important, religious differences found expression in, and were more or less temporarily settled by, political conflicts. On the other hand, political conflicts influenced religious thought and religious allegiance. At the beginning of written history the political unification of the numerous small states of the Nile valley into a unified kingdom led to the belief in a hierarchy of gods, in which the local gods became subordinate minor deities. This process has been repeated, with characteristic variations, but basically along similar lines in some other countries. Conquests led to changes in worship, because both the conquered and the conqueror shared the conviction that the god of the victorious group had proved to have greater power not only at home but even in the territory of the defeated god. Some religions required their followers to spread their beliefs by the sword. Islam is the prototype of such a religion. The spread of early Islam inevitably led to the expansion of Arab rule. In such periods a map of religious affiliations would disclose the geographical distribution and extent of political forces better than would a map of kingdoms, which would at best show short-lived dynastic combinations.

It is therefore significant for us that, in early history and even today among primitive people, the religious community precedes, and later often supersedes, the political community.[1] To see to what extent factors of the natural environment have influenced the context and the extent of religious communities, to visualize the boundaries which separate these communities—as forerunners of national communities or in competition or co-ordination with them—from other cultural or national groups is essential for the understanding of many problems of historical geography. From this perception it is but one step to the recognizing of many present-day problems of state power and conflict in which religion, and in particular organized religion, plays a part.

THE RELATIONSHIP OF RELIGIOUS DISTRIBUTION AND POLITICAL FACTORS TODAY

Periods in which the religious community was dominant alternated with periods during which politics was swayed by different motivations. Our own age is such an era, characterized by the interplay of complex and conflicting motivations. Therefore, we have to determine in this chapter whether and to what extent religious distribution coincides with political units: are such instances merely historical relics? Can and would religious distribution and loyalties affect the political map of today? If so to what extent? Can and would political changes affect religious allegiances under present-day conditions?

The first question can be approached by comparing one of the customary maps of religious distribution with a political map. For a number of reasons we have to call such a map a preliminary approximation. A large part of the globe's surface lacks reliable statistics of religious affiliation. We have only very rough estimates for the more than a quarter of humanity which lives in the Soviet Union and China. The picture is even more complicated by the fact that the available statistical sources, although they reveal certain information about the geographical distribution of organized churches, can reveal but very little concerning the religious beliefs of individuals and communities and because of this deficiency can be misleading. There is no accepted standard for reporting religious adherences. In some cases, particularly among Roman Catholics, all those baptized or even all those coming from a family of the same faith, are counted as Roman Catholics. In other churches, only those confirmed or baptized in adulthood are reported. These differences are trifling in comparison with the greater problem of how to relate the statistics of religions to the actual beliefs of individuals. For instance, in

[1] F. Ratzel, *op. cit.*, pp. 164-167.

West Germany official statistics show that 96.3 per cent of the population are Protestants or Roman Catholics—51.1 per cent Protestant and 45.2 per cent Roman Catholic. But a public-opinion sampling in 1951 indicated that only 78 per cent of the population actually "believed in God," and that only 62 per cent of these "believed in Jesus as the Son of God." In the Scandinavian countries, it is reported, Protestant pastors say that not more than one-tenth of the average parish betrays any lively interest in the church. In a poll taken in 1952 in an area of Norway where church loyalty was considered above average, 60 per cent of the young Norwegians questioned said that they were not much interested in Christianity, 14 per cent declared themselves Christians, and 25 per cent said they were well disposed toward the Christian faith. These facts contrast with the official Norwegian statistics, according to which out of a population of 3.2 million in 1946 there were only 100,000 dissidents from the Lutheran National Church. In England, where the Church of England is the center of the world-wide Anglican communion, we find that the Established Church, which baptizes some two-thirds of the children born in England, counts only 2.3 million members out of a population of 43.7 million (1951).[2] One of the few existing detailed studies on this subject shows that in a typical French provincial town, nominally almost one hundred per cent Catholic, only 15,000 of 130,000 inhabitants go to mass.[3] In an industrial environment in France it was found that only four out of 19,000 men employed in one industrial complex were practicing Catholics.[4] These facts can be paralleled for every country publishing statistics on church membership, and they should be kept in mind when using such statistics, or church distribution maps, for the evaluation of political factors.

Spain and Portugal, as well as France, appear on a church distribution map as overwhelmingly Roman Catholic countries. However, this should not lead to the conclusion that they constitute a unified bloc. It is clear that Spain's international policy is influenced strongly by religious convictions; in 1954 the Spanish government endangered much-coveted military aid from the United States rather than yield on religious principles. Spain is a country where the ruling group is firmly rooted in the Catholic faith. The allegiance of the masses to Catholicism appears to be less pronounced, as evidenced in the repeated church-burning episodes of the last 150 years. In Portugal the peasants seem to be firmer in their Catholic

[2] S. W. Herman, *Report From Christian Europe* (New York, 1953), pp. 155, 48, 49.

[3] J. Perrot, *Grenoble, Essay de Sociologie Religieuse* (Grenoble, 1953).

[4] R. F. Byrnes, "The French Priest-Workers," *Foreign Affairs,* Vol. 33 (January, 1955), p. 327.

faith. Portugal has tried, with some success, to build a corporative state following the lines laid out in the Papal Encyclical, *Quadragesimo Anno.* In France a complete separation of Church and State has taken place, and a great majority of Frenchmen seem to be Catholic only in name. A politico-religious map, in order to be useful, would have to distinguish among these three countries as three different politico-religious types: Spain, dominated by a strongly Catholic laity and adhering to traditional forms of political life; Portugal, a country where Catholicism is reshaping the social and economic life; and France, a nominally Catholic country where Catholicism has influence only upon and through one of the more important political parties. As far as Catholicism has any influence upon domestic or international policy in France, it is an indication of the strength of this party in the government of the moment rather than an indication of the fact that 99 per cent of the French population are counted as Catholics.

These examples show also that political boundaries are in certain cases good indications of the distribution of certain religious attitudes. They show also that political attitudes are influenced, both positively and negatively, by the hold religion has on the population as a whole, on a ruling group, or on the government. Of the eighty-three independent or semidependent countries of the earth (see Table I), fifty are countries where 90 per cent or more of the population belong to the same religion. This gives us a first approximation of the extent to which maps of religious affiliations and maps of political units coincide. It does not necessarily mean that the religious affiliation of a population determines its political attitudes. However, there is hardly a country containing a significant religious minority where this factor has no political significance. In some cases such religious minority status has hindered the assimilation of national groups: Armenians, Jews, French Canadians, Irish Catholics and many other groups have preserved their separate existence primarily because of religious differences. These differences are often an obstacle to intermarriage. Religious minorities sometimes form separate political parties, or as a group back the party friendliest to themselves. Poles in Germany were among the most reliable followers of the Catholic Center Party, the Lutherans in Austria of the German National Party. The Alsatians could not easily be assimilated into the main body of the French, not so much because of their German dialect but because of their strong Catholic allegiance in a religiously indifferent France.

No existing map of the distribution of religions can show an even approximately correct picture for the Soviet Union and the affiliated

Peoples' Republics. Not only has no religious census been taken in these countries for many years; we can only state with some degree of assurance that since the last census an unknown number of individuals have relinquished their original religious affiliation, and that to all appearances many young people have grown up without any real contact with a church.

THE MULTITUDE OF RELIGIOUS DENOMINATIONS

Another, though remediable and therefore minor, defect of practically all existing maps of religious distribution on a continental or world-wide scale is their oversimplification. Most maps attempt to show a broad-brush picture of the distribution of major religions, taking uniformity in doctrine rather than diversity in organization as their differentiating feature (Fig. 12-1). However, many religions are deeply split into dissenting and sometimes hostile denominations.

In the United States, we have the strongest evidence of the wide variety of Protestant churches. Two hundred and fifty-two different Protestant religious bodies were reported in 1952. While there is no unity in American Protestantism, it would be misleading to assume that the seeming disunity of the American churches as evidenced by the large number of Protestant denominations is in the nature of a serious schism. A large nucleus of 28 churches belongs to the National Council of the Churches of Christ in the U.S.A. The non-co-operative fringe contains some large conservative bodies such as the Southern Baptists and the Missouri Synod Lutherans, and some large bodies such as the Mormons and Christian Scientists, but most of the fringe is represented by some two hundred small sects which account for only 2 per cent of all Protestants. The consciousness, throughout the Western world, of the impressive unity of the Catholic Church is the indirect cause of a common misconception which assumes a similar kind of unity for other religions. This misconception is supported by the oversimplification of most maps depicting the distribution of religions. Especially where religions and political factors are closely linked, the resulting errors may lead to a distorted evaluation of the political map and of international relations as influenced by religious factors.

A case in point is the world of Islam (*cf.* Fig. 12-5, p. 426). Characteristic of the widespread ignorance (in the western world) of Islamic conditions is the now almost forgotten incident of Tangier in 1905. William II, German emperor, almost wrecked the main purpose of his Mediterranean

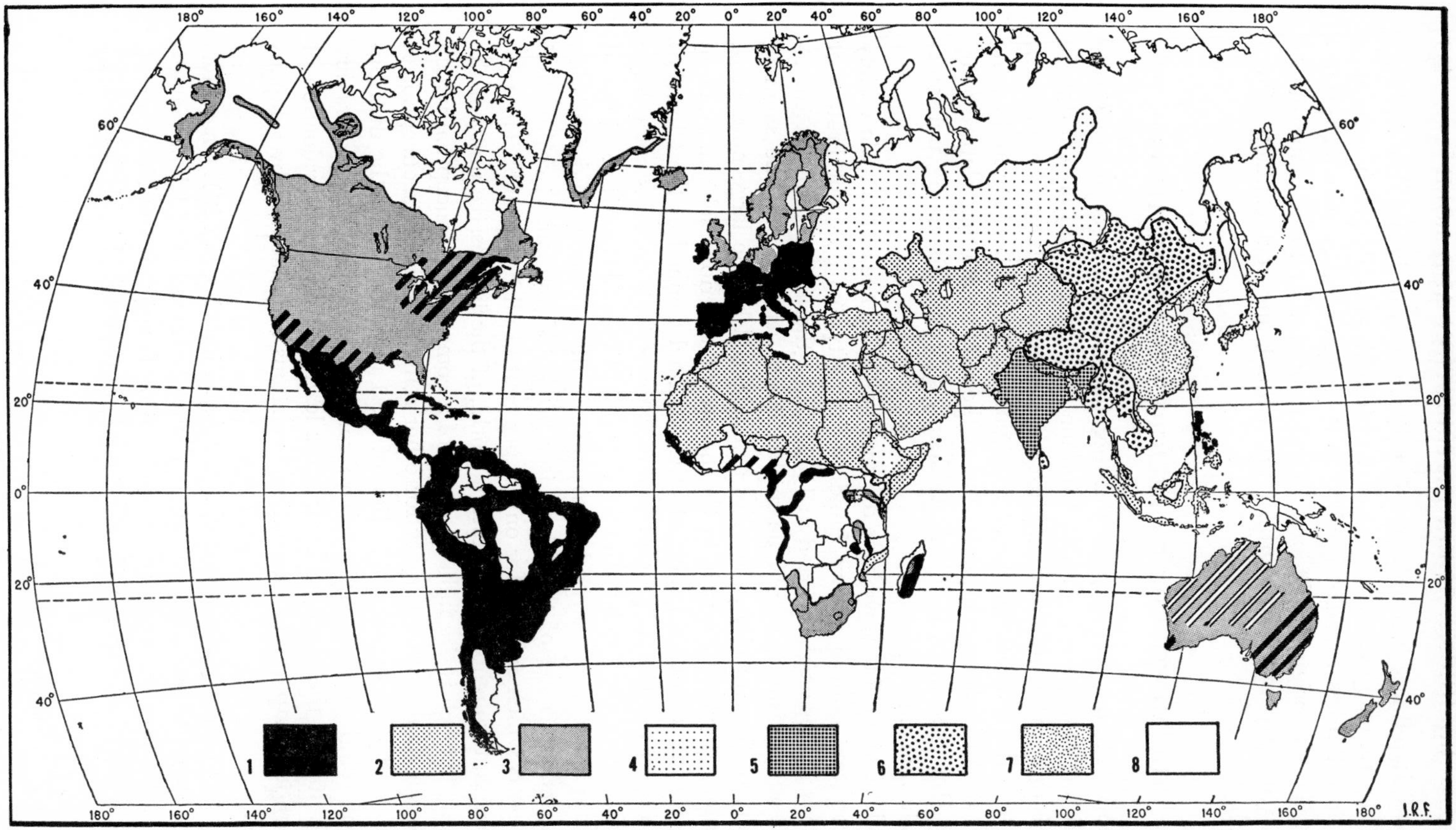

Fig 12-1. Distribution of Religions: (1) Roman Catholic; (2) Islam; (3) Protestant; (4) Greek Orthodox; (5) Hindu; (6) Buddhist; (7) Confucian; (8) others.

cruise of that year—the strengthening of his ties with Turkey—by stressing in a speech in Tangier the complete sovereignty of the Sherif of Morocco. Though the demonstration was intended against France, William did not know that the Sherif was regarded by the Grand Sultan of Turkey as a schismatic who did not recognize the Sultan's Khalifat supremacy. The Islamic world is deeply split by the hostility of Sunnites and Shiites. Iran, the only major Shiite country, is relatively unaffected by appeals from the rest of the Moslem world. Iraq is divided between these two sects, with the Sunnites more important politically. Little, remote Oman has its own Islamic denomination, seldom found outside its boundaries.

Still less known is the geographical distribution of Hindu sects in India (*cf.* Fig. 12-3, p. 420). Buddhism in Ceylon, Burma, and Thailand may be regarded as belonging to the same denomination despite the lack of common organizational ties. Tibetan or Mongolian Lamaistic Buddhism, however, is entirely different, and the Buddhism of China and especially of Japan is different again [5] and is split into many denominations, some non political, others, like Japanese Zen-Buddhism, intensively occupied with active political attitudes. These differences have never been adequately mapped—the first condition for a safe geographical approach.

The following table tries to refine somewhat the rough approximation at which a map could arrive. The data in the table are taken mainly from the *Statesman's Yearbooks* of 1953 and 1954. However, the sources of this yearbook, though presumably the best available, are of widely varying accuracy and different date.

POLITICAL AND RELIGIOUS BOUNDARIES; THEIR RELATIONSHIP

Table 12-1 shows that a majority of countries are for all practical purposes religiously uniform. It shows also that there is a surprisingly large number of countries which are unique in the religious composition of their population. The major religion of many of these countries is almost unknown to the rest of the world. The number of such countries is even larger if we include the considerable number where doctrinal uniformity may go hand in hand with separate organization. Lutheran Germany, Sweden, Norway, Denmark, Finland, and Iceland have not only separate church organizations, but they also use different languages in their serv-

[5] A. J. Toynbee, in *A Study of History* (1934-54) in many places avoids, therefore, the term *Buddhism* in favor of Mahayana when speaking of this northern Buddhism, and of the Tantric form of Buddhism when speaking of Tibetan and related forms.

TABLE 12-1

NO.	COUNTRY	RELIGION OF MAJORITY	STRONG OR SIGNIFICANT RELIGIOUS MINORITIES	REMARKS
1.	Afghanistan	Sunnitic Moslems	None	
2.	Albania	Sunnitic Moslems, 68%	Greek Orthodox–21%; Roman Catholics–9%	
3.	Argentina	Predominantly Roman Catholic		No figures available
4.	Austria	Roman Catholics–90%		
5.	Australia	Protestants–82%	Among Protestants: Anglicans–36%; Roman Catholics–18%	
6.	Belgium	Predominantly Roman Catholic		No figures available
7.	Bolivia	Roman Catholic		State religion
8.	Brazil	Roman Catholic–95%		
9.	Bulgaria	Orthodox–85%	Moslem–12%	Estimate of 1950, probably obsolete
10.	Burma	Buddhist–84%	Animists–5%; Moslem–4%; Hindu–4%; Christians–2%	
11.	Cambodja	Predominantly Buddhist		No figures available
12.	Canada	Protestants–54%	Roman Catholics–42%; among Protestants: United Church–19%, Anglicans–16%	
13.	Ceylon	Buddhists–64%	Hindu–20%; Moslem–6%	
14.	Chile	Roman Catholics–95%		
15.	China			No reliable estimate possible
16.	Colombia	Roman Catholic		State religion
17.	Costa Rica	Roman Catholic		State religion
18.	Cuba	Predominantly Roman Catholic		No figures available
19.	Czechoslovakia	Roman Catholics–77%		Estimate of 1947, probably obsolete
20.	Denmark	Lutheran–99%		
21.	Dominican Republic	Roman Catholic		State religion
22.	Ecuador	Predominantly Roman Catholic		No official figures
23.	Egypt	Sunnitic Moslem–91%	Christians, mainly Copts–6%	
24.	El Salvador	Almost exclusively Roman Catholic		No official figures

25. England and Wales	Church of England–50-65%	Other Protestant denominations more than 20%	
26. Ethiopia	Coptic Church	Moslems	No estimate possible
27. Finland	Lutherans–96%		
28. France	Roman Catholic–97%		
29. Germany (West)	Protestants–51%	Roman Catholics–45%; most Protestants are Lutherans	
30. Germany (East)	Prevailingly Lutheran		No figures available
31. Greece	Greek Orthodox–98%		
32. Guatemala	Predominantly Roman Catholic		No figures available
33. Haiti	Predominantly Roman Catholic		
34. Honduras	Predominantly Roman Catholic		
35. Hungary	Roman Catholics–66%	Protestants–27%; mostly Reformed	1941 Census, largely obsolete
36. Iceland	Lutherans–96%		
37. India	Predominantly Hindu	Moslems, approximately 10%	
38. Indonesia	Sunnitic Moslems more than 90%		
39. Iran	Shia Moslem–93%	Sunnitic Moslem–6%	Estimate
40. Iraq	Shia Moslem–57%	Sunnitic Moslem–36%	
41. Ireland	Roman Catholics–95%		
42. Israel	Jews–90%	Moslem–8%	November 1953
43. Italy	Roman Catholics–99.5%		
44. Japan	(Shinto?)		No estimates possible; state-Shinto abolished, private Shinto widespread
45. Jordan	Predominantly Sunnitic Islam		
46. Korea	(Buddhism)		No estimate of post-war conditions possible
47. Laos	Buddhists		No figures available
48. Lebanon	Christians–54%	Christians mostly Maronites; Moslem–39% mostly Sunnitic; Druzes–7%	
49. Liberia			No reliable information
50. Libya	Predominantly Sunnitic Moslem	Senussi sect of Islam	
51 Mexico	Predominantly Roman Catholic		No figures available
52. Morocco	Sunnitic Moslem–93%		Recognize the Sultan as head

TABLE 12-1 (con't.)

NO.	COUNTRY	RELIGION OF MAJORITY	STRONG OR SIGNIFICANT RELIGIOUS MINORITIES	REMARKS
53.	Netherlands	Protestants–45%	Majority of Protestants Reformed–32%; Roman Catholics–36%; no church affiliation –14%	
54.	New Zealand	Protestants–88%	Among Protestants: Anglicans–40%, Presbyterians–23%; Roman Catholics–12%	
55.	North Ireland	Protestants–66%	Among Protestants: Presbyterians–30%; Anglicans–26%; Roman Catholics–34%	
56.	Norway	Lutherans–96%		
57.	Oman	Moslem	Predominantly Qadarites	
58.	Pakistan	Sunnitic Moslem–86%	Hindu–13%	
59.	Panama	Roman Catholics–93%		
60.	Paraguay	Predominantly Roman Catholics		No figures available
61.	Peru	Predominantly Roman Catholics		No figures available
62.	Philippine Islands	Roman Catholics–83%	Filipino Church–10%; Moslem–4%	
63.	Poland	Predominantly Roman Catholic		
64.	Portugal	Roman Catholics		
65.	Rumania	Orthodox, approx. 80%	Roman Catholics–8%	Figures unreliable
66.	Saudi Arabia	Wahhabitic Moslem		
67.	Scotland	Church of Scotland (Presbyterian)–60%	Roman Catholics–12%	No official figures available
68.	Spain	Roman Catholics		
69.	Sudan	Sunnitic Moslem in the majority	Pagans	
70.	Sweden	Lutherans–99%		
71.	Switzerland	Protestants, mainly Reformed–58%	Roman Catholics–40%	
72.	Syria	Sunnitic Moslem–71%	Other Moslem denominations–12%; Alawites–10%; Druzes–3%	
73.	Thailand	Buddhists–96%		
74.	Tibet	Lamaistic Buddhists		

75.	Tunisia	Sunnitic Moslem–90%		
76.	Turkey	Sunnitic Moslem–98%		
77.	U.S.S.R.			No estimate possible
78.	Union of South Africa	(whites): Dutch Reformed Church–50%;	Anglicans–15%; other Protestant denominations–31%	
		(non-whites): Pagans, more than 60%	African Christian churches–14%; Anglicans –8%; Dutch Reformed–5%	
79.	United States	Many different Protestant denominations–60%	Roman Catholics–35%	Estimate
80.	Uruguay	Predominantly Roman Catholic		Last census of religion more than 50 years old
81.	Venezuela	Roman Catholic		No figures available
82.	Yemen	Majority of Zaiditic Moslem	Sunnitic Moslem	No figures available
83.	Yugoslavia	Serb Orthodox–50%	Roman Catholics–37%; Moslem–12%	

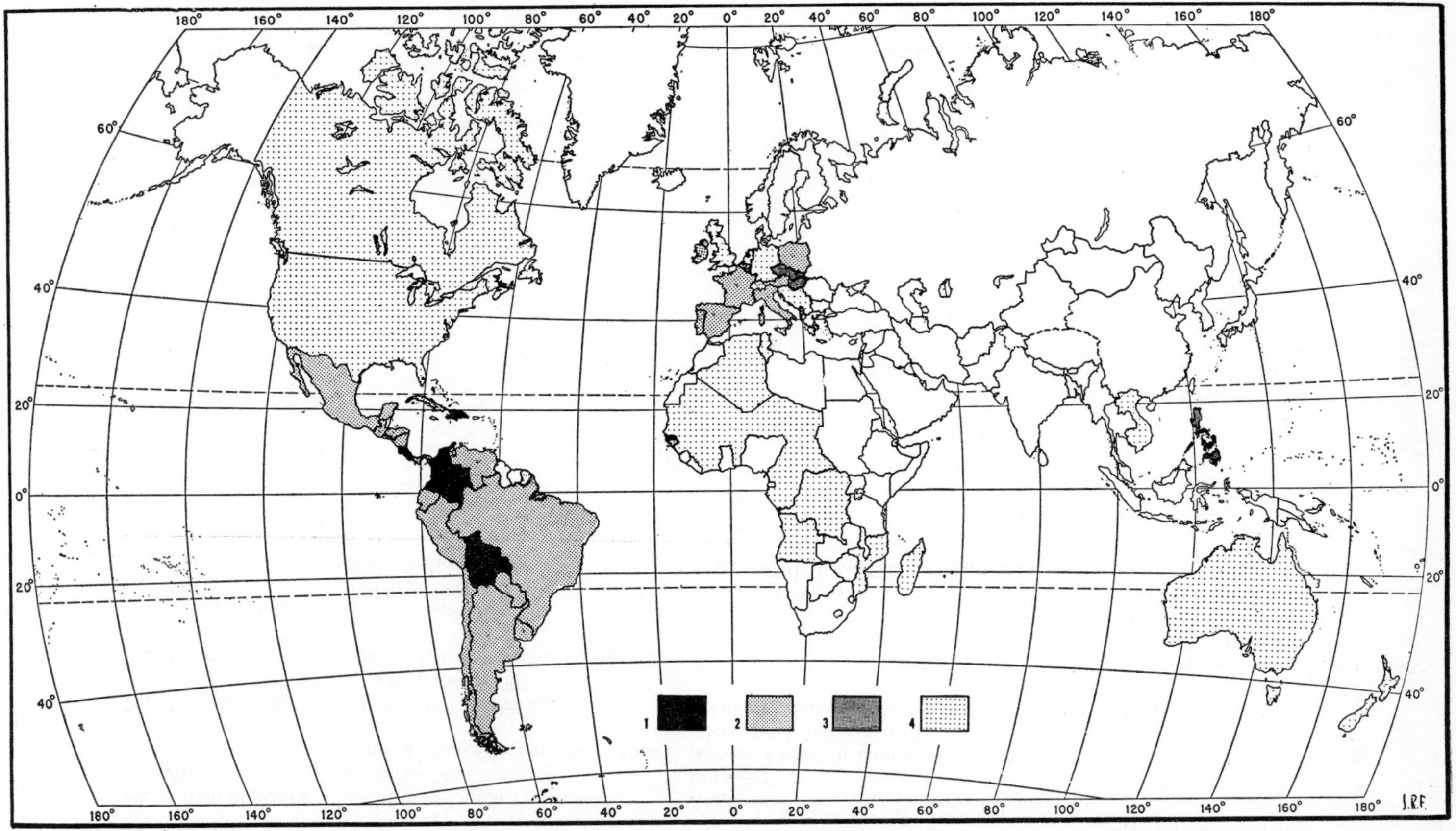

FIG. 12-2. Distribution of Roman Catholicism: (1) Roman Catholic state religion; (2) Roman Catholic predominant majority, more than 90% where figures are available; (3) Roman Catholic majority (50 to 89%); (4) Roman Catholics significant minority.

ices, making mutual exchange difficult. They may be regarded as separate units, particularly since the unifying bond of the Ecumenical Movement and the World Council of Churches of Christ has not yet the qualities of an effective movement on an international plane. It is therefore not yet tangible enough to be considered a reality in political geography.[6]

Similar considerations apply to the Buddhist "churches" of Ceylon, Burma, Thailand, Laos, and Cambodia, and their attempts to create some kind of international organization (*cf.* Fig. 12-3, p. 420).

THE ROMAN CATHOLIC COMMUNITY

The most impressive national religious grouping is that of the Roman Catholic countries (Fig. 12-2). Next in size, but much smaller, is the group of Sunnite Islamic states. Table 12-2 summarizes Table 12-1 in this respect. This table shows thirty predominantly Roman Catholic countries. The question arises as to how far these countries can be prompted to common political action by their common religion. There is no doubt that, despite their common religion, grave disagreement between them may lead even to war. The small-scale but bitter war between Costa Rica and Nicaragua in 1955 is a recent instance. There are fewer instances of common action, but more important, there are frequent demonstrations of a common attitude toward world-wide problems. It appears that even in the case of the hierarchical and well-organized Catholic Church the underlying common attitude, based on a uniform religious education, is more important than actual united leadership. This is even more conspicuous for other much more loosely organized religions. It is, however, this common attitude which enables the Roman Catholic Church to mobilize its adherents in the struggle against Communism. In countries such as Poland, Hungary, and Czechoslovakia the Catholic Church, even though forced into passive resistance, is the major obstacle to Communism. Communism seemingly benefited from the active phase of the struggle, as dramatized in the confinement of Archbishop Beran in Prague and the trial of Cardinal Mindszenty in Budapest. These victories proved so costly, however, that open persecution of Catholics lessened after Stalin's death. The Catholic Church has maintained a strong position, thus preserving for these nations some strongholds of spiritual independence and preventing a full victory for Communist totalitarian ideology. This would not have been possible without the moral backing of the entire Catholic world. In many states

[6] See pp. 421 ff.

TABLE 12-2

RELIGIOUS CHARACTER	NUMBER	COUNTRIES
Roman-Catholic countries		
(a) generally more than 90% Roman Catholics	27	Argentina, Austria, Belgium, Bolivia, Brazil, Chile, Colombia, Costa Rica, Cuba, Dominican Republic, El Salvador, Ecuador, France, Guatemala, Haiti, Honduras, Ireland, Italy, Mexico, Panama, Paraguay, Peru, Philippines, Portugal, Spain, Uruguay and Venezuela
(b) Roman-Catholic majority, dominated by Communists	3	Czechoslovakia, Hungary, Poland
Anglican churches in the majority	3	Australia, England and Wales, North Ireland
Orthodox churches in the majority, recognizing the primate of Moscow	3	Bulgaria, Rumania, U.S.S.R.
Other Christian churches		
(a) dogmatically separate churches	4	Canada (United Church), Ethiopia (Coptic), Lebanon (Maronites), and Scotland (Presbyterian)
(b) organizationally separate national churches		
(1) Lutheran	6	Denmark, Finland, Germany, Iceland, Norway, Sweden
(2) Reformed	3	Netherlands, Switzerland, Union of South Africa
(3) Orthodox	2	Greece, Yugoslavia (Serb-Orthodox)
(c) in many churches, none having a majority	2	New Zealand, United States
Sunnitic Islamic countries	11	Afghanistan, Albania, Egypt, Indonesia, Iraq, Jordan, Pakistan, Sudan, Syria, Tunisia, and Turkey
Islamic countries, having non-Sunnitic majorities or ruling groups	6	Iran (Shiites), Libya (Senussi), Morocco (Sultan head of Moslem community), Oman (Qadarites), Saudi Arabia (Wahhabis), Yemen (Zaidites)
Buddhist countries (no common organization)	6	Burma, Cambodia, Ceylon, Laos, Thailand, Tibet (northern Lamaistic branch)
Other countries	7	China, India (Hindu), Israel (Jewish), Japan, Korea, Liberia, Viet-Nam

with Catholic majorities or significant minorities, Catholic parties have sprung up and taken a strong, consistent, anti-Communist position.

Another example of the political effects of a uniform Catholic attitude is the part played by the Catholic forces in the question of internationalization of Jerusalem. The Papal policy was strongly in favor of internationalization in order to protect the many holy places in this cradle of religions. The vote of a number of Latin-American countries, apparently quite uninterested in the case in any other respect, can best be explained by their readiness to follow the wishes of the Vatican. The anticlerical government of Mexico was the only Latin-American country which instructed its delegates to cast their votes against internationalization. Also in respect to many major questions of intra-European politics, such as EDC (European Defense Community) or the Schuman plan (European Coal and Steel Community), the (Catholic) Christian Democratic parties in France, Germany, Italy, and Belgium developed essentially corresponding attitudes.

The attitude of the Catholic Church in the Spanish Civil War has been debated heatedly. There is little doubt that the volunteers on the side of Franco—as distinguished from the German and Italian contingents sent to Spain by Hitler and Mussolini—were almost exclusively Catholic, and that they were able to influence the course of politics in several countries. Mexico, on the other hand, ruled by a nominally Catholic government but one involved in a power struggle with its native hierarchy, gave active support to the Loyalist (anti-Franco) side.

This attitude of the Mexican government brings into focus the fact that not all nominally Catholic nations necessarily follow Catholic political leadership. In Mexico, the policy of the government, backed by wide circles of the population, has placed the country among the anti-Catholic Powers. Nevertheless, Catholicism is still influential. When Protestant missionary activity became intensive, Mexican governments risked conflict both with the United States and Great Britain in order to combat it.

In France the state has been involved in a struggle with the Catholic Church since the turn of the century. Laws against ecclesiastic orders were issued and enforced; the separation of Church and State became a fact. Children were not required to have religious instruction. Diplomatic relations with the Vatican were severed. At the same time, however, the French government in the Near East and Africa subsidized Catholic orders and schools and followed a course designed to identify Christianity (meaning Catholicism) and France in the minds of the natives. France's

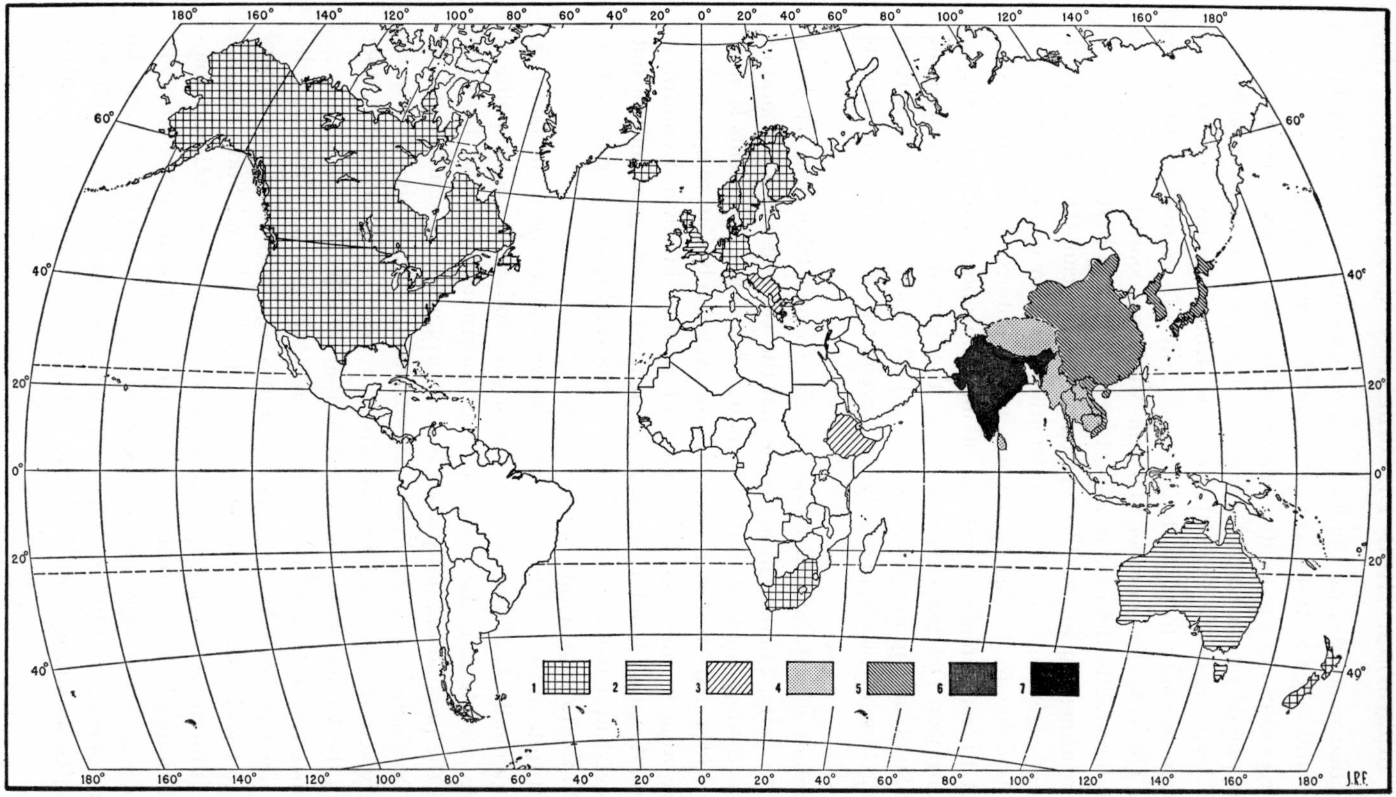

FIG. 12-3. Distribution of (*a*) Protestantism and other non-Catholic Christian Churches; (*b*) Buddhism; (*c*) Hinduism; (*d*) Judaism. (1) Protestant countries; (2) Anglican countries; (3) other Christian churches; (4) Buddhist countries; (5) Buddhism, intrinsically interwoven with other creeds; (6) Hinduism; (7) Judaism.

protectorate over Syria and Lebanon rested largely on conditions derived from France's protective position toward the Catholic Church.

All these examples point to the complex nature of the problem of religion as a motivating force in present-day politics. There is no doubt that Catholicism is such a force, but it is not a uniform force and its impact is changing from country to country. It is a function of political geography to study the distribution of Catholic Churches over the world. How strongly and under what conditions they are influential must be examined in each individual case in order to arrive at a true picture.

THE PROTESTANT COMMUNITY

If the Catholic Church, in spite of its unique and imposing unity, confronts us with difficult problems in the task of measuring the geographical distribution of its churches and of the part played by Catholicism in the realm of political geography, we find these problems multiplied if we attempt to probe the role of Protestantism (Fig. 12-3). We have already pointed out the complexity of the mosaic of Protestant denominations in the United States, with 252 Protestant churches, of which a nucleus of 28 major churches remains if we discount the smaller churches and sects. The American picture reflects the complexity of the world-wide situation of Protestantism. One must be cognizant of the major distinctions and cleavages between Protestant churches if one attempts to draw conclusions about binding or separating factors in the political field, both within a nation and internationally. In this broad discussion of religious factors, we cannot try to describe the large number of churches which have come into existence since the Reformation. The Reformation heralded a new age in which the nation-state and its specific culture emerged and became a cultural and political unit in its own right. The Protestant churches draw their distinctions not only from religious and philosophical roots but equally from this fact. The individual churches which were state churches in the Protestant countries adopted specific national, dynastic, ethnic, and linguistic characteristics that in turn contributed to the growth of the evolving nation-states. All this led to the rise of separate and competing national cultures and militated against a cultural and political unity of the West. For our purpose, the realization of this schism is necessary to avoid sweeping generalizations and faulty conclusions based on the comparison of areas and countries with "Protestant" populations. If we try to detect Protestant binding or separating elements within and between nations, we must be aware that in the northern parts of Germany and throughout the Scandinavian countries the Lutheran churches prevail, that in the Netherlands, Scotland, Switzerland, and Hungary, the Reformed or Presbyterian churches dominate, and that in England we observe an altogether different course of the Reformation leading to the formation of the Anglican Church. The separating factors are aggravated by differences of language.

While it is thus imperative to observe the distinguishing factors between the various Protestant churches in their geographical setting, we must not lose sight of the fact that the political geography of Protestantism in our time displays some centrifugal tendencies toward international reconciliation and world-wide Christian fellowship. There is a growing feeling throughout the Protestant world that a reversal of the long historical trend toward separation and division is now under way, that there is a drawing-together of the bonds of Christian fellowship. The Ecumenical Movement, a child of the twentieth century since it began in a World Missionary Conference in Edinburgh in 1910, has grown greatly in impact as the result of the tragic lessons taught by two world wars. Its last Conference, in the fall of 1954, at Evanston, Illinois, was marked by the participation of the Eastern Orthodox Churches. The hope has been expressed that this may be regarded as the first step in the eventual construction of a bridge to Russia.

In comparison with the unity and strength displayed by the world-wide organization of the Catholic Church, world Protestantism as represented by the Ecumenical Movement is still in the formative state, its membership incomplete and divided on certain questions of dogma. Above all, it is still largely a top-level movement which as yet finds no effective parallel among individual congregations or at the grass-roots level.[7] On the other hand, there are signs of a lessening of denominationalism in the United States, especially in rural areas which cannot support several churches in one community. In Europe, the common experience of churches of all denominations in their struggle, during the Third Reich, against Nazi paganism and later against Communist oppression, has served to overcome differences which in the light of common vital issues had lost their meaning. Yet a realistic appraisal of the present situation leads to the conclusion that Protestantism still remains closely identified with the culture of northern and western Europe, and that the Ecumenical Movement, while a hopeful beginning, is not yet a strong force in world affairs.[8]

[7] N. V. Hope, *One Christ, One World, One Church;* Publication No. 37 of the Church Historical Society.

[8] A. C. Murdaugh, *A Geographical Summary of Protestantism and the Ecumenical Movement.* Unpublished paper.

The conclusion at which we arrived upon viewing the Catholic Church as a motivating force in politics is equally valid in regard to Protestantism, even though the Protestant churches have no international organization comparable to that of the Catholic Church. The student of political geography cannot avoid tracing the distribution of Protestant churches throughout the world in order to detect the extent of binding and separating elements. He will have to observe closely the distinguishing factors between its member churches, despite the fact that most of them have found a common basis in the ideals and hopes of the Ecumenical Movement.

THE WORLD OF ISLAM

The Islamic nations (Fig. 12-4) have no international organization and are in this respect comparable to Judaism, Buddhism, and to some extent Protestantism. The Khalifat disappeared in the aftermath of World War I. The great pilgrims' meetings at Mecca and Medina from all over the Islamic world are no doubt an important factor in strengthening community feelings and interests.[9] However, the leading statesmen of the Islamic world rarely meet on such occasions. Nevertheless it is a fact that common attitudes on a variety of different problems exist among many Islamic countries and are a strong political reality. Good authorities still consider valid General Lyautey's famous saying that "the Moslem World is like a resonant box. The faintest sound in one corner of the box reverberates through the whole of it."

Despite all this, the Islamic world is changing rapidly, and these observations may soon lose significance. In some respects Islam is still an agglomerate of states like the Christian states at the time of the Crusades, and can be moved by an appeal to common Islamic sentiment. In many other respects a transformation to the forms of modern Western national states is progressing rapidly. In Turkey this process is practically complete and the residual Islamic consciousness seems to be on a level with that of Christian forces in Protestant Western Europe. When Communism challenged the very existence of religion in Turkestan and other Islamic areas, the Mohammedan world hardly stirred. This passive attitude can be explained in part by the cutting off of the pilgrimage to Mecca and the resulting loss of contact. Only gradually, and nowhere completely, Islamic nations are awakening to the Communist danger. Religious-national parties in Egypt, Iran, and Morocco have occasionally allied themselves with local Communist parties. The revolt of the Dungan—the Moslems of Chi-

[9] See Bowman, *op. cit.*, p. 54.

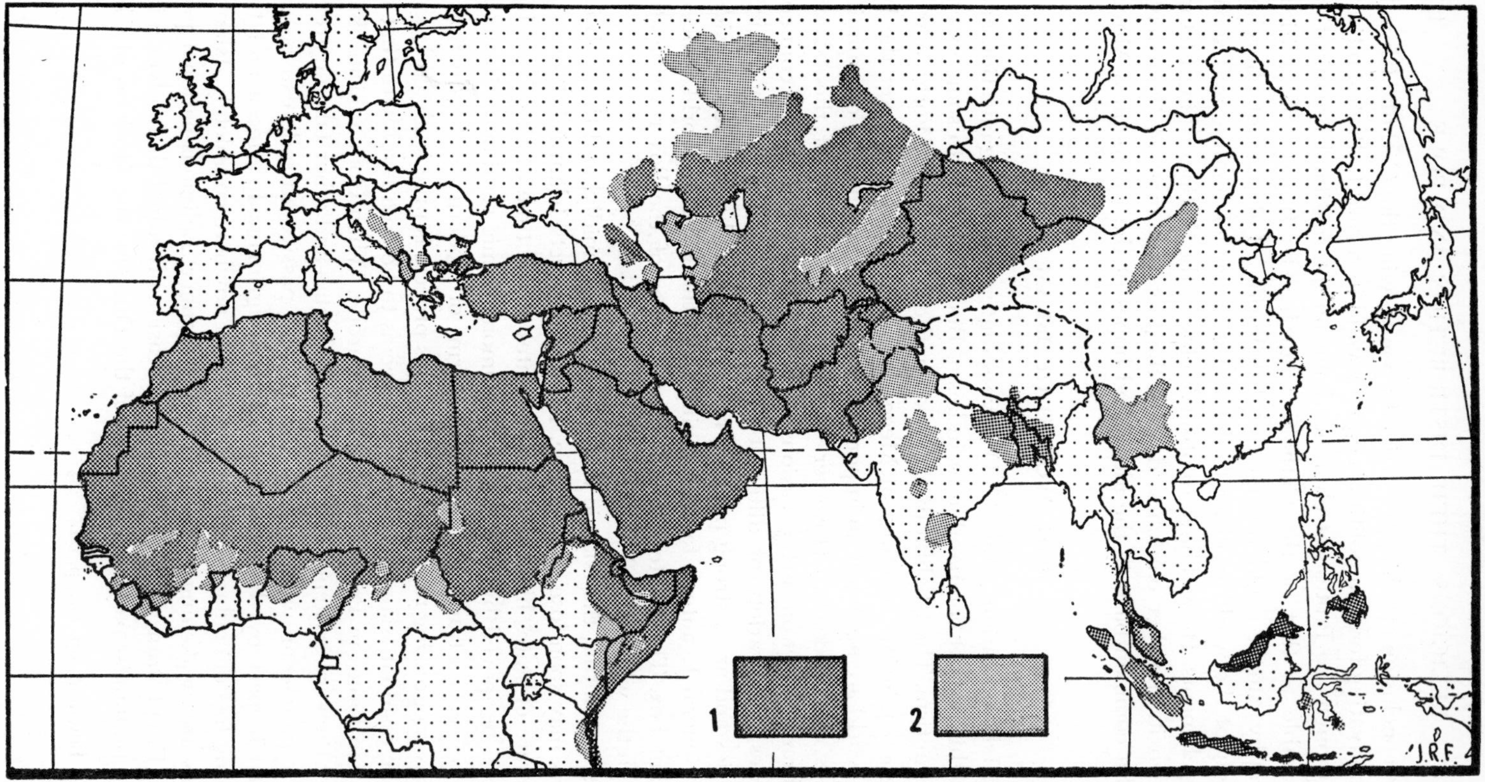

FIG. 12-4. Countries with Islamic Majorities (1) and Significant Islamic Minorities (2).

nese Kansu and Sinkiang—against the Communist regime remained practically unknown in the rest of the Islamic world and was not supported by it. On the other hand, Pakistan owes much of its success in its struggle for a separate existence to the moral support of its cause throughout the independent Moslem states. British diplomacy, recognizing the latent force of Islam, was ready to give its indispensable help to the cause of Pakistan because the British knew that by backing a Hindu-dominated unified India they would endanger their position in the entire Moslem world from Afghanistan to Libya.

This estimate of Islam by British statesmen has been confirmed by Soviet policy in Central Asia where, since 1954, the U.S.S.R. has followed a new course in its attitude toward the Mohammedans. For many years the Soviet Union wooed the Islamic countries in the Near East, especially the countries of the Arab League, and at the same time soft-pedaled its attack on religion in its own Islamic territories. It even permitted participation in the pilgrimage to Mecca. But the Islamic population, in spite of their growing indisposition toward the West, did not yield to Soviet propaganda. The Soviets then abandoned this approach and resumed their anti-religious, and especially anti-Islamic, propaganda struggle in Turkestan, thereby reorganizing Islam as a living force in the struggle for ideological and political domination. Late in 1955, a new policy toward the Islamic nations appeared to be in the making when Egypt was offered planes and weapons by the Soviet bloc. To try to evaluate the new course at the time these lines are written would be premature.

It would be a fallacy to overestimate the power of Islam in its influence on political action. The lack of an organized church comparable to the Roman Catholic Church is a significant negative factor and the symbolism to Mecca in comparison with Rome is but a weak substitute. On the other hand, common religious sentiment may prompt the Islamic countries to parallel action or attitude. Another unifying factor is the close interrelationship of religion and law in Islam.[10] Because the canon law of Islam, the Sharia, is the basis of the legal system of all of the Islamic states; with the exception of Turkey, the boundaries between these states lose a little of its divisive value as compared with other international boundaries.[11]

[10] A. T. Gibbs, *Mohammedanism* (Oxford, 1949). Every human activity has its legal aspects; therefore, an abatement of religious zeal and conviction must not lead to a comparable diminution of Islam as a legal and social bond.

[11] R. Montague, "Modern Nations and Islam," *Foreign Affairs,* Vol. 30 (1952), p. 581.

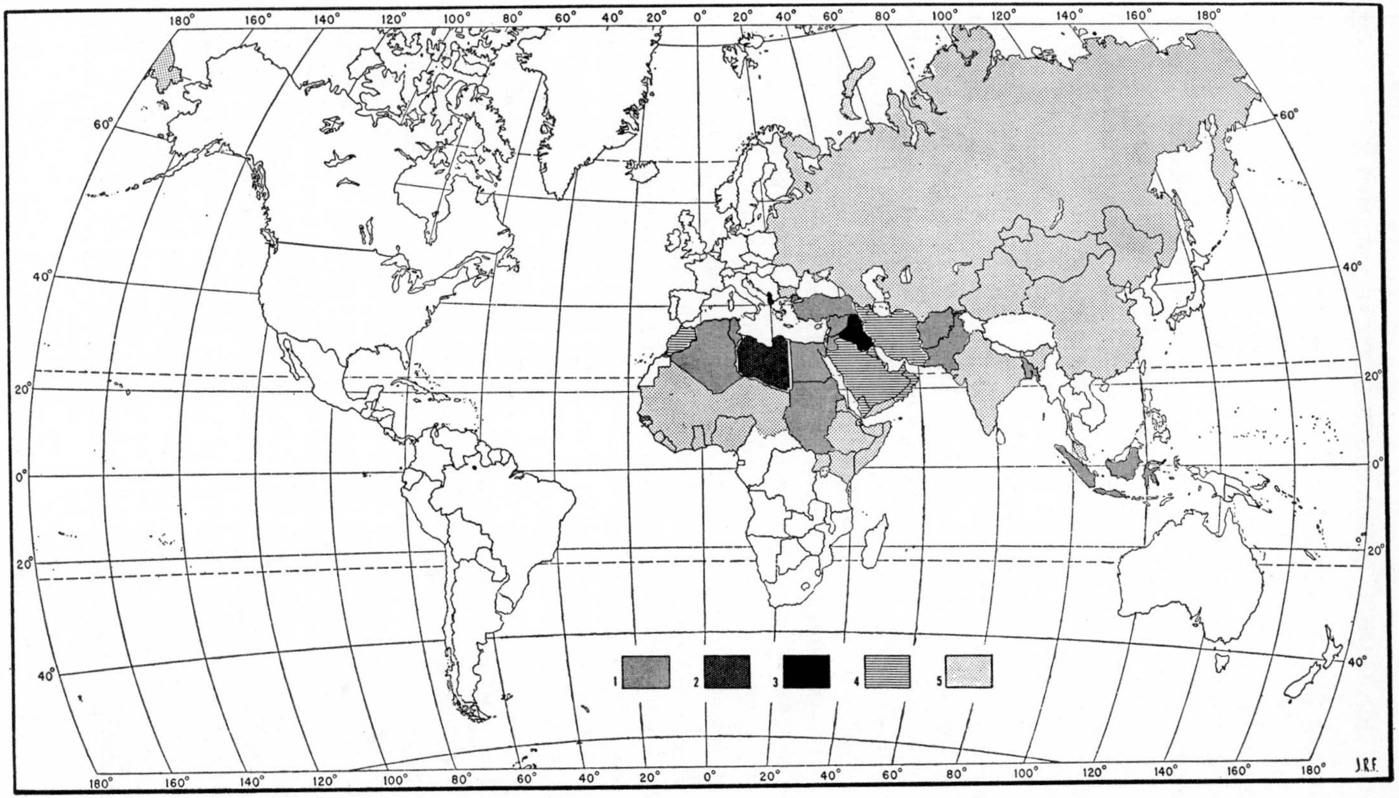

Fig. 12-5. Islamic Countries: (1) Sunnitic Islam state religion; (2) Sunnitic Moslem in the majority, but other groups ruling; (3) Sunnitic Moslem ruling, though not necessarily majority; (4) other Moslem countries; (5) non-Islamic countries with significant Islamic minorities.

THE RELIGIOUS FACTOR AND THE GREAT POWERS

Comparable to the geographical distribution of Catholicism, and to some extent Protestantism, that of Sunnitic Islam over certain parts of the world evolves as a primary factor of the political map (Fig. 12-5). However, none of the contemporary great Powers can be classified as either Roman Catholic, or Protestant, or Islamic. This reservation applies to the United States, the United Kingdom and the British Commonwealth of Nations, and, in regard to the Russian Orthodox Church, to the Soviet Union. Neither does such identification of religious distribution and state power exist in China. Even though the Catholic or Protestant or the Sunnitic Islamic countries, if we would contemplate them as units, cover an area and have populations comparable to those of the Great Powers, their political structure and influence is not on a comparable plane. In the present phase of history, as cementing factors in the process of binding nations together, religious ideologies, even where they are strongest, are of much less force than are other, nonreligious, influences.

All of the Great Powers, within their boundaries, have significant religious minorities: the United States has a strong Catholic minority, as does the United Kingdom and the English-speaking member nations of its Commonwealth. China has an important Mohammedan minority, and the same is true in regard to the Soviet Union. Among the lesser powers, France and India have strong Mohammedan groups within their borders. With the exception of the Soviet state, all these powers have been careful in their recent history not to hurt, by their foreign policies, the religious feelings of their religious minorities.

Both France and India stress the secular character of their states and the Soviet Union goes even farther in emphasizing its antireligious philosophy. Among the other great powers, especially those with predominantly Protestant populations, the fact that their map of religions discloses a checkerboard of many different faiths or denominations, excludes policies dictated solely by the ideas or ideals of one religion only. This does not mean that these nations are indifferent to the religious beliefs of their majorities. The United States and Britain are undoubtedly Christian powers, and even if we look at the extreme case of the Soviet Union, which we shall discuss later, we find that in spite of its negative attitude toward religion and the antireligious bias of its rulers, it has identified itself occasionally with the interests of the Russian Orthodox Church.

RELIGION AS A STATE-BINDING FORCE

If one looks for examples to test the thesis that religion is still a persistent political factor in the life of countries or nations, the multinational and multireligious countries which we discussed above are of much less significance than are two countries of relatively recent date which otherwise are strikingly dissimilar in most respects: Pakistan and Israel. Founded in 1947 and 1948 respectively, they are delimited primarily along lines of religious affiliation. However, that is as far as obvious similarities go. Each of these two states requires separate discussion.

Israel: A Secular State. The Jewish communities are organized on a congregational basis and have no common organizational bond, only a common religious tradition. Nevertheless, the pressure of Jewish public opinion in the United States has visibly influenced the policy of the United States toward Israeli independence. This is due not only to organized Zionist opinion, but perhaps even more to the genuine religious feelings of the non-Zionist Jews. It is the more remarkable since in Israel itself the ideology which kindled the enthusiasm of the fighters for this new state-creation is a movement of secularized and westernized Jewry. It is a national ideology which is almost indistinguishable from the national ideologies of Western Europe. While this nationalism has its religious messianic roots, they tended to be pushed into the background; Western influences favored a modern secularized Zionism which recreated Hebrew as a living language and fostered a fervent nationalism. Finally, with the acquisition of a territory all attributes of a modern national state were attained. Religion played in this process a very minor, certainly not an activating, role. The most orthodox groups, fundamentalist in the American Christian terminology, were opposed to this modern concept of a national state and some groups accepted it only after it had come into existence. But from this moment religion started to play a political role. The "religious" groups became organized in political parties and have succeeded in establishing a set of laws which reflects their convictions. The troubled boundary between Arabs and Jews, though coincident with that between religious communities, is almost exclusively a political, national, and cultural division.

Pakistan: An Islamic Nation. Altogether different is the story of the contemporaneous creation of Pakistan. National unity in its modern meaning never existed in India. However, common historical experience, the subjection under the British *raj*, molded India into a state closely resembling many western European nations before the full emergence of modern nationalism. This happened although many cultural and linguistic differences existed and still exist in India. Deep social and religious cleavages complicate the picture, such as that between Hindus and Moslems. This latter cleavage was strong enough to disrupt the emerging national unity, and in the twenties the idea of two separate states emerged and took such strong hold on the Moslems that finally no solution but partition seemed possible.

The intent to make Urdu the state language in Pakistan and Hindi in the Union of India emphasizes the linguistic factors,[12] but the national division is essentially one of religious ideologies. This is the case despite the continued existence of minorities in both countries which include many million individuals of the other faith. Under the influence of Gandhi and Nehru, India has refused to base its existence on a religious idea. There is a Hindu religious party, the Masabha, but it is of relatively minor importance. Its influence on the shaping of the Indian laws is much weaker than is that of the Israeli religious parties. It seems more successful in promoting reactionary and nationalistic, rather than distinctly religious points of its program. On the other hand, Pakistan was based from its very origin on the spiritual power and the community of Islam. Koranic law is at the basis of all its institutions. As in India, we observe in Pakistan a struggle between conservative representatives of religious institutions—in this case Islamic—and people of a more secular turn of mind. However, the primary interest to us is that the foreign policy of Pakistan is largely dictated by the concept that it is an Islamic state. This concept determines much of Pakistan's policy toward India; it led it into a community of political interests with the Arab states, though it is hardly based on a community of material interests; it has endangered its standing with its allies, the Colombo Powers—not only India, but also Ceylon, Burma, and even Islamic Indonesia; it also has helped to smooth out the inherited, dangerous conflicts with Afghanistan. While in all these international relations Islamic religious motives influenced Pakistan's attitude, there is one instance of Pakistan having made a vital political decision without reference to religious ties. The military agreement with Turkey was concluded over the protest of the Islamic Arab countries. Turkey, actually a secular state, is only nominally Islamic.

Tibet: A Vanishing Theocracy. It is difficult to find another state of the same type as Pakistan. Until quite recently Tibet was considered the perfect surviving example of a theocracy—a state where the deity not only influenced politics but, through the priests, actually ruled. In the last

[12] See pp. 385 ff.

decade many forces have been at work to unseat the Buddhist, or rather Lamaist, theocracy of Tibet. It is still too early to define the outcome of this strange struggle, although the chances appear to be slim that the old order will survive. Chinese control was imposed in 1950, and in the spring of 1954 the Indian government concluded an agreement with the Chinese Communists by which India recognized Chinese suzerainty over Tibet. Thereby India abandoned Tibet to Communist pressure and influence.

FEATURES OF ISLAM IN SAUDI ARABIA AND LIBYA

The Arab states in general have retained to the present day the character of Islamic states. However, they present a picture which is far from being uniform. In Egypt earlier, and in the small countries of southeastern Arabia only quite recently, Western secular ideas have found expression. The religious movement of the Wahhabis in the Arabian desert was a distinct reaction against the minimizing of religious concepts in life and politics. Through the alliance with and the conversion of the house of Sa'ud (rulers of Riyadh in Central Arabia), this puritanical Islamic movement became victorious. The outstanding personality of the late Abdul-Aziz ibn-Sa'ud enabled him to lead the movement to power over most of the peninsula, and at the same time to preserve its religious purity. He succeeded in this despite the necessary use of modern weapons and means of communication, despite the establishment of American oil companies on Saudi Arabian soil, and despite the use of Americans as engineers, for irrigation and agricultural projects, and as pilots. However, wars to force Wahhabism on other Moslems have ceased and it would be hard to show that Saudi Arabian foreign policy of the recent past has been dictated by its special religious bias. While no international conflict has tested whether or not the religious factor has remained a strong force in Saudi Arabian politics, modern secular ideas from the West have undoubtedly made an impression on the country, particularly since Arabs have been trained in western technology by western experts. A European authority on Arabia, H. St. J. R. Philby, himself a convert to Islam, has warned that the death of Ibn-Sa'ud may make inevitable and bring to the surface currents which have little to do with strict Wahhabism.[13]

A similar development already has gone a step farther in Libya. The Islamic sect of the Senussi was founded on puritanic principles similar to those of the Wahhabites. Hidden away in the almost inaccessible oasis of

[13] "The New Reign in Sa'udi Arabia," *Foreign Affairs,* Vol. 32 (April, 1954), pp. 453 f.

Kufra, their way of life remained unchanged until well into the twentieth century. Their intransigence was strengthened when they became the leaders and the last stronghold against the Italian conquerors of Libya. When Kufra fell to airplanes and tanks they continued the struggle from Egypt. Finally, their head, Muhammad Idris al-Mahdi al Senussi, returned with English help and became king of an independent Libya. The exigencies of the thirty-five-year struggle and lately of modern administration have tended to transform the Senussi brotherhood into a political and military organization.[14] The parliament of Libya, though still subordinate to the royal power, is capable of influencing politics to a certain degree. Its strong group of Tripolitanian members, many of them educated in Italian schools during the colonial period, are unlikely to be influenced by purely religious motivations overriding other considerations.

RELIGION AS A SUPPORT FOR MODERN NATIONALISM

So far we have discussed countries and nations where religion supplants or tries to supplant other motivations, especially the ethnic or linguistic nationalism of the nineteenth and twentieth century type. There are, however, instances where religion and ethnic-linguistic nationalism have been fused to such a degree that theoretical separation can not be undertaken. In this connection the position of the Orthodox Church and of the Roman Catholic Church in Yugoslavia deserves investigation. The show trial of Archbishop, now Cardinal, Stepinać was initiated during Tito's Stalinist phase along lines parallel to those in other satellite countries. However, it would be an oversimplification to regard it solely as an act in the attack of Communism against religion. Croatians and Serbs—and several smaller national groups—have fought for supremacy since the foundation of the Yugoslav state in 1918, indeed since 1848 within the Hapsburg monarchy. Croats and Serbs speak dialects less unlike each other than many French, Italian, German, or English dialects are unlike their standard language. The Serbs, however, have been Christianized from Byzantium, and have lived under the influence of this civilization, whether in an independent state or under Turkish rule. The Croats received Christianity from Rome, were culturally under Italian and German influence, and politically have been dependent on Hungary. The national consciousness of both nations awoke in the years of the Napoleonic wars under the leadership of theologians. The census-takers of the old Austro-Hungarian Empire refused to

[14] W. H. Lewis and R. Gordon, "Libya After Two Years of Independence," *Middle Eastern Journal,* Vol. 8 (1954), pp. 41-53 (esp. p. 51).

recognize separate languages and tabulated a Serbo-Croatian tongue. The difficulty in distinguishing nationality on the basis of the spoken language despite the existence of a fervent Serb and Croat nationalism accounts for the identification of Roman Catholics as Croats and Greek Orthodox as Serbs.[15] Thus the accusation against Cardinal Stepinać, though obviously a link in the chain of the Communist fight against religion, relied heavily on alleged activities of Stepinać on behalf of the wartime fascist Croat government and his alleged responsibility for anti-Serb atrocities. This signifies only one stage in the long-drawn struggle for the ascendancy of one of the two nations and religions in Yugoslavia. National and religious motives are inextricably interwoven.

This identification of the Catholic faith with a nationality struggling for independence is not an isolated occurrence. The best known case is that of the Irish people. Many speakers of the English tongue, among them numerous families of English descent, have become completely identified with Irish nationalism because their ancestors remained Catholics at the time of the Reformation. The number of Celtish Irishmen who at that time became Protestant was apparently much smaller. These have become indistinguishable from other English or Scotch-descended groups.

Not quite as thoroughgoing is the identification of the Reformed Church in South Africa with the Afrikaans-speaking Boer group and of the English-speaking churches with the English.[16] However, it is close enough to notice the influence of the fundamentalist creed of the Reformed Church in the Biblical concept identifying the sons of Ham with the Negroes, including the curse of Noah for this son and his descendants. The leadership of the parties advocating "apartheid" is largely in the hands of Reformed church ministers. On the other side, since the days of Livingstone, British missionaries have been in the forefront of the defenders of the rights of the native. The African natives are denominationally divided. African churches, frequently called Ethiopian or Zion churches, have more and more attracted the Christianized natives. These African churches are in some cases Christian only with great qualifica-

15 Mohammedan co-nationals are often simply referred to as such.

16 "Out of a total European Afrikaans-speaking group of 1.12 million, 1.02 million belong to the Dutch Reformed churches, whereas out of a European English-speaking group of 783,000 only 33,000 are adherents of these churches. Religion . . . deepens the cleavage . . . between Afrikaner and Briton.

In the Colored community the situation is different. About nine-tenths are Afrikaans-speaking, yet only three-tenths adhere to Dutch Reformed churches, and even in rural areas the so-called 'English-speaking' churches claim large numbers." K. Buchanan and N. Hurwitz, "The 'Coloured' Community in the Union of South Africa," *Geographic Review* (1950), pp. 405-406.

tions, as they preserve many primitive pre-Christian concepts and rites. Thus the racial-national-cultural division becomes reflected in denominational allegiance. At the same time the influence of religious leaders in the political field increases. If the nationalist policy of territorial segregation should succeed, the political map would become similar to the map of denominations.

While in South Africa primitive religions impress their stamp on allegedly Christian churches, in East Africa the conflict between white settlers and natives led in at least one instance to a revival of primitive rituals as a rallying point and a political weapon. Centered in the Kikuyu tribe of Kenya numbering over 1,000,000, the fanatical movement (Mau Mau) which started in 1952 has been a continuing problem to the British authorities and has exerted its influence on other tribes, the Moru, Embu, and Kamba, totaling well over 1,000,000. It is too early to define the contours of what at present is a fluctuating, possibly expanding area of insecurity in a region of great strategic and economic importance to Britain's position in Africa. Many elements, among them especially the growing resentment of the tribes against the *apartheid* policy of the white minority (numbering some 40,000 in Kenya), help to unify the tribal organizations in their struggle against colonial rule, but the crude and cruel quasi-religious magic of curses and charms must be seen as the main factor of cementation.

Alongside these examples should be mentioned that of Japan and its state religion, Shinto. This peculiar creed, a mixture of primitive rituals and modern concepts, was proclaimed as the state religion not to supplant other religious forms, but to create a unifying bond for all Japanese irrespective of their private religion, including private Shinto.[17] The belief in the direct descent of the Emperor from the goddess Ameratsu has been used to strengthen patriotism, devotion to the country, and to promote willingness for military sacrifice. After the defeat in World War II, state Shinto was officially abolished and the Emperor himself renounced belief in his divine descent. The opinions of different authorities about the actual hold of this belief on the Japanese are far from uniform. While some assert that even before the war state Shinto was only an outward convention, others state that it is still a real force. It seems clear that a gradual revival of Shintoism has been attempted since its collapse in 1945; however, the chief stress is on ritual and apparently Shinto has not the necessary vigor to influence political decisions.

[17] See D. G. Haring, "Religion, Magic, and Morale," in *Japan's Prospect* (Cambridge, Mass., 1946), pp. 209-59.

Nevertheless, a comparison with China shows that, although certain political attitudes almost never develop in a country whose leaders are psychologically conditioned by Confucianism, Taoism, and quietist sects of Buddhism, they occur quite naturally in a country psychologically conditioned by Shintoism and Zen-Buddhism.

RELIGIOUS INFLUENCES ON POLITICAL ATTITUDES

It was mentioned before that modern India was created as a secular state and most of its leaders repudiate any religious basis for the new state. However, the Indian struggle for independence was led by Mohandas Gandhi, the Mahatma, by means of nonviolence and nonresistance. These concepts, like most of Gandhi's doctrines, are deeply rooted in Hindu religious philosophy. So also are Nehru's international diplomatic actions thoroughly and subtly influenced by these Gandhian doctrines and Hindu philosophy.

Like Gandhi, Nehru and other Indian statesmen can be understood fully only from their Hindu background, just as even the most secularly minded politicians and statesmen of the West are unconsciously conditioned by their Christian upbringing. These factors are largely outside the field of political geography and only one observation may be added which shows the interrelationship of religious and political motivation. It is the conditioning by the great religions which accounts for the effectiveness of certain political ideologies in certain regions, and only in these regions. In this form only is religion a potent, though indirectly effective factor in many countries. Religion shapes attitudes toward human life and society, and toward the state as the politically organized form of society. The claim has been made that Presbyterianism, Islam, and Confucianism condition man for democratic forms of government. It is for the sociologist to determine the validity of such claims. The political geographer can trace only in the case of Presbyterianism that all countries in which this denomination prevails have an old and persistent tradition of democracy.

It would be wrong to point to the existence of political parties with denominational affiliations as proof for this conditioning of attitudes. It appears rather that the emergence of such political parties is a sign that in a large part of the population and in the government religion is no longer the self-evident, almost unconscious force it once was. Religious parties have emerged in Christian, Islamic, Hindu and Buddhist countries, everywhere a sure sign of spreading secularism. In Europe the emergence of Christian social, mostly Catholic parties followed in all countries the rise of nineteenth century liberalism. Despite this common origin and common religious basis there are great differences between these parties which point to the fact that religion is only one factor in their make-up.

Although religion-conditioned attitudes are universal, Christianity through its missions and backed by the prestige of Europe in the nineteenth century has the unique distinction of pervading other religions with its ethical concepts. The Jewish-Christian concept of moral superiority of monogamy is accepted in Islamic and other countries today; and so are other concepts. The most individualistic religion, Buddhism, in one of its strongholds—Burma—has begun to follow the organization of some Christian churches, and it is reported that in this new form it may be regarded as an effective force against the encroachments of Communism. In Palestine, the precarious truce between Israel and Jordan left these two countries without communication across the boundary. However, both Mohammedans and Jews are so strongly influenced by Christian ideas that at Christmas and Easter, Christians are able to cross the truce line to make the pilgrimage from the holy places in Jerusalem to Bethlehem.

POLITICAL PARTIES AND THEIR GEOGRAPHICAL DISTRIBUTION

After this digression, however pertinent, we may return to more strictly geographical problems. In the preceding paragraphs we have referred repeatedly to internal political problems. As an illustration of the problems of interest to political geography we may ask whether and how Catholicism makes itself felt in the political geography of the United States. The claim has often been made [18] that "Catholics vote more Democratic than Protestants." Actually a study of the so-called Catholic vote shows that in two political shifts—that of the Democratic victory in 1932 as compared with the Republican majority in 1928, and that of the Republican victory in 1952 as compared with Roosevelt's easy Democratic victory in 1944—the nine states with the largest Catholic populations voted in about the same manner as other states. These states are Rhode Island, which is 56 per cent Catholic; Massachusetts, 47 per cent; New Mexico, 38 per cent; New Hampshire, 35 per cent; New Jersey, 35 per cent; Louisiana, 31 per cent; and New York, Vermont, and Wisconsin, each 30 per cent.

We have mentioned the existence and importance of religious parties in discussing the cases of Israel, Pakistan, South Africa, and Yugoslavia. Yugoslavia is the only country where, during the time when it still had

[18] P. F. Lazarsfelt *et al.*, *The People's Choice,* 2nd ed. (New York, 1948).

free elections to a parliament, three parties competed for the vote appealing to religious motives. The leading Croatian party could always count on the Catholic sentiment of the Croatian peasantry, especially in opposition to the ruling Serbian group, which was Orthodox. Among the Slovenes two parties had existed since the nineteenth century, a liberal and a clerical Catholic party. The Moslems of Bosnia had founded their party only because of their position as a minority. Only the Serbian parties, in composition completely Orthodox, had no close ties with any organized religion. Today Yugoslavia is a Communist dictatorship, but as far as is known only the Orthodox Church has made its peace with the Tito government. The old antagonisms seem to persist, though underground and with different aims.

Despite the existence of several religious parties in prewar Yugoslavia, this country shares with other countries the experience that religious parties are generally the organs of the religiously-conscious part of the population in a predominantly secular state. Such a party may be the organization of a minority religion, but far more characteristic and interesting are religious parties in countries which are nominally uniform in their religion. The parties may be Catholic as in Austria, Italy, Belgium, or France; Reformed Church as in the Netherlands; Islamic as in Indonesia or Pakistan; or Hindu as the Masabha in India. In all these countries it is possible to map the area where religions and political leadership are identical, at least ideologically. Such maps are outwardly similar to the popular maps showing results of elections. They show also, however, that once such a religious party has been organized, a surprising stability results which no exclusively political group can hope to achieve. A striking example is offered by Austria. After Nazi conquest, Nazi indoctrination, and "liberation" by the Red Army, the elections gave to the religious Catholic party almost exactly the same proportion of votes as was the case a dozen years earlier; the same areas as before voted for this party. In Germany a similar phenomenon can be observed, although in that country Roman Catholicism was the religion of a minority only. The Center Party had been the Catholic party, with its strongholds in Bavaria, the Rhinelands, Westphalia, and Upper Silesia. It was distinctly a regional and minority party, nor did all of the nominal Catholics vote for it. In the whole nation Catholics were outnumbered approximately two to one by Protestants. Two major developments have basically changed this situation since 1945. The partition of Germany created a predominantly Protestant Germany in the East and improved the Catholic position in the West. In addition, over 9,000,000 Germans from countries behind the Iron Curtain, émigrés and expellees, came into the Federal Republic, a large number of them Catholics. Of the total population, according to the census of 1950, 51.1 per cent are Protestants, and 45.2 per cent Catholics. However, the former include a much larger proportion of persons whose bond with their church is very superficial. This and the internal migration has destroyed the formerly prevailing religious uniformity of the smaller political administrative units. The re-emerged religious party has declared itself no longer a Catholic, but a Christian party, though drawing most of its support from Catholics and recruiting most of its leadership from this denomination.

POLITICAL FACTORS AND THEIR RELIGIOUS IMPLICATIONS

This German example leads us to another basic question, namely, whether political changes would affect the contemporary distribution and allegiance of religions. In the case of Germany we have observed a distinctive change in the distribution pattern, resulting from the political changes since 1945. It is also generally accepted that we live no longer in a period when the principle of *cujus regio, ejus religio* (the creed of the ruler is the creed of the land) is an accepted law. Though condemned by a later more secular and religiously tolerant age,[19] this underlying principle is still active. Enforced conversion is generally condemned and is not practiced in democratic countries. But invisible and often unconscious pressures are still with us. These may lead to gradual and voluntary adjustments of church organizations, if not doctrines. In the United States the effects of such adjustments to the Civil War period can still be observed. The largest Protestant churches, the Presbyterians, Baptists, and Methodists split into southern and northern branches and this break is still not entirely healed. Almost a century earlier, at the time of the American Revolution, the Episcopalian Church split from the parent Anglican Church along political lines. Those Protestant churches which came into being as state churches, primarily the Lutheran churches, have always reflected political changes. Even the genuinely supranational and centrally controlled Roman Catholic Church could not completely escape such influences. Transfer of territory by treaty or conquest has split old-established dioceses and archdioceses. In many cases boundaries of such ecclesiastic territories were adjusted to conform with new international boundaries, though the Papal decision usually followed the political event only after some lapse of time.

[19] One of the strongest condemnations of this doctrine was voiced by Toynbee, who called it a "monstrously cynical formula" (*op. cit.*, Vol. IV, p. 221).

Apart from these administrative adjustments the Roman Catholic Church has withstood extremely well pressures to create separate national churches. A few such attempts have remained largely abortive. One of the few partly successful attempts was the creation of a "Catholic" Church in the Philippines by Bishop Aglipay as a concomitant of the awakening of national consciousness in the Islands. About 10 per cent of the population of the Philippines belong to this church. Another instance is the secession of a national Czechoslovak Church from the main body, when national feeling reached a high pitch at the foundation of this state in 1918.

This example is important for the understanding of Soviet-sponsored attempts to create national "Catholic" churches in the satellite countries with the help of schismatic priests. Only in Czechoslovakia have these attempts met with some success. The "Patriotic Priests Movement" has become a tool of Communism, with relatively broad support among the lower clergy whose material needs can be better served by the Communist state than by the oppressed Church. In another case, in the Ukraine and Rumania, the Communists succeeded in forcing the Uniate or Greek-Catholic Churches into union with the Orthodox Churches. These Uniate Churches had recognized the Pope as their spiritual head in the fifteenth century but retained their national or Greek liturgy. In pre-World War II years, they served as national rallying points for Ukrainians against denationalization attempts by Poland and Hungary. Most Uniate churches were in regions ceded during and after the war to the Soviet Union by Poland and Czechoslovakia. Thus a successful resistance to Soviet pressure for the "return" to the Orthodox Church became very difficult, psychologically and materially. It is reported that all Uniate bishops in Rumania are imprisoned.

NONRELIGIOUS IDEOLOGIES

In the present age, far more important than these attempts at forced conversion is the process of secularization. We have noted before that almost all denominational parties, from Germany to Indonesia, are arraigned not against other denominational parties, but against secular parties. We would convey a slanted picture if we did not stress again and strongly that political activity in the present age is much more under the influence of other, secular ideologies than of religious ones. The proportion of persons who only nominally belong to a church is increasing in many countries. The United States is almost unique in that the membership of all denominations has continuously increased, absolutely and proportionally, in the 150 years since religious indifference was at its peak at the time of Jeffersonian enlightenment.

Recent experience has shown that secular populations can be won over by emotionally presented ideologies. In our age these ideologies, though not religious in nature, appeal to emotions which usually respond to the religious approach. Fascism, Nazism, and especially Communism, have certain traits in common with religion. Some of these are, restriction of rational argument to specific fields, an unquestioning belief in a charismatic leader and in "infallible" books, further development of doctrine by a growing literature of commentaries which reinterpret a quasi-sacred, unchangeable text. There is also the proselytizing zeal characteristic of youthful religions, and the readiness for self-sacrifice in the service of the world mission. This accounts for a crusading spirit common to some religions and secular ideologies. It also explains the rapid and often parallel changes of both the political and religious maps in recent decades.

SUMMARY

In conclusion we find that religion is a factor which influences the attitudes and conditions the behavior of hundreds of millions of people. It thereby influences strongly the political map, even where religion as such loses its hold—its conditioning influence survives, or its place is taken by pseudo-religions. In either case, the effect of these changes finds expression on the political map. It is, therefore, rewarding for the political geographer to trace the distribution of the major religions and their organizations, and their relationship with state secular organizations. It is also rewarding to trace religious affiliations across international boundaries and to investigate their separating or binding functions. As in all other aspects of political geography, constant change and fluctuation is an integral part of the complex but stimulating picture.

CHAPTER 13

Supplement: Other Cultural Factors

LITERACY AND ILLITERACY

The reader who has followed our attempts at tracing politico-geographical factors through the medium of boundaries—ethnic, linguistic, or religious—not necessarily identical with political boundaries, will realize that these are by no means exclusive. Among other group-cementing factors of interest in the study of internal and external political geography those of literacy and illiteracy deserve special mention. But their meaning is relative—the requirements of "literacy" in the (no longer) "little red school house" in the United States differ from state to state, and often from county to county, and are difficult to compare with those in other countries. Even if one would compromise and agree on common denominators, the mapping of zones indicating the geographical extent of various degrees of literacy versus the zones of illiteracy would be a highly speculative task. To the extent that statistics on educational patterns permit such mapping, it offers a helpful tool to the student who tries to evaluate, in terms of geographical variations, the literacy achievements of groups within nations and of nations themselves.

An interesting case study along these lines was made by Ellsworth Huntington [1] who compared the literacy achievements of Iceland and

[1] *Mainsprings of Civilization* (New York, 1945), p. 127 ff. See also Huntington's attempt to measure intellectual activity by checking the percentage of non-fiction and fiction reading in public library circulation, p. 344 ff.

Newfoundland. The two islands lie 1,600 miles apart. They are of similar size, about one-third larger than Ireland. Both are thinly populated, with about 150,000 persons in Iceland and about 375,000 in Newfoundland, in contrast to about 4,350,000 in Ireland. Their ethnic composition is similar. Yet in spite of these resemblances the islands differ amazingly in cultural achievements. To name only one of Huntington's comparisons, "until recently, more than a quarter of a million Newfoundlanders had only a single public library. In Iceland, the capital alone has long had four. There are also four main regional libraries and scores of local ones, some of which are centuries old." Equally striking, and closely related to the differences in literacy, are the political and economic contrasts between the islands.

This example shows how important is the consideration of intangible elements as expressed in the vague terms *literacy* and *illiteracy* in the task of appraising all pertinent power factors of states within their physical environment. Such elements are as significant in the over-all picture as are maps showing the distribution of agricultural and mineral resources, cities, railroads, highways, inland canals, airways, or the distribution of automobiles.

Without such appraisal of literacy and illiteracy factors, educational facilities, and technical skills, the student of geography who tries to analyze the power factors and potentials of a region or country on the basis of its natural resources alone would arrive at a totally unrealistic picture. The growing opposition in underdeveloped countries of Asia and Africa to foreign influence identified with colonialism, even where it is constructive foreign aid, underlines the necessity of appraising natural resources in terms of the abilities of native populations to utilize them. As an illustration, in the Uganda Protectorate in British East Africa the great Owen Falls Dam (1954) on the Victoria Nile provides an exceptional hydroelectric power potential in the center of an important cotton-producing area. However, this large power project is part of the Protectorate's British administration. If one considers the fact that Europeans number only about 3,500 out of a total population of about 5,200,000, the question arises as to whether the native population possesses the educational and technical skills to utilize adequately its water resources, of which, as one observer put it, the country "offers a myriad of sites." [2] Professor Frank Debenham, in a study on the water resources of British East Africa, observed that "one has only to think what the Chinese or Japanese, or even

[2] *Africa South of the Sahara,* by a study Group of the South African Institute of International Affairs (Cape Town, 1951), p. 184.

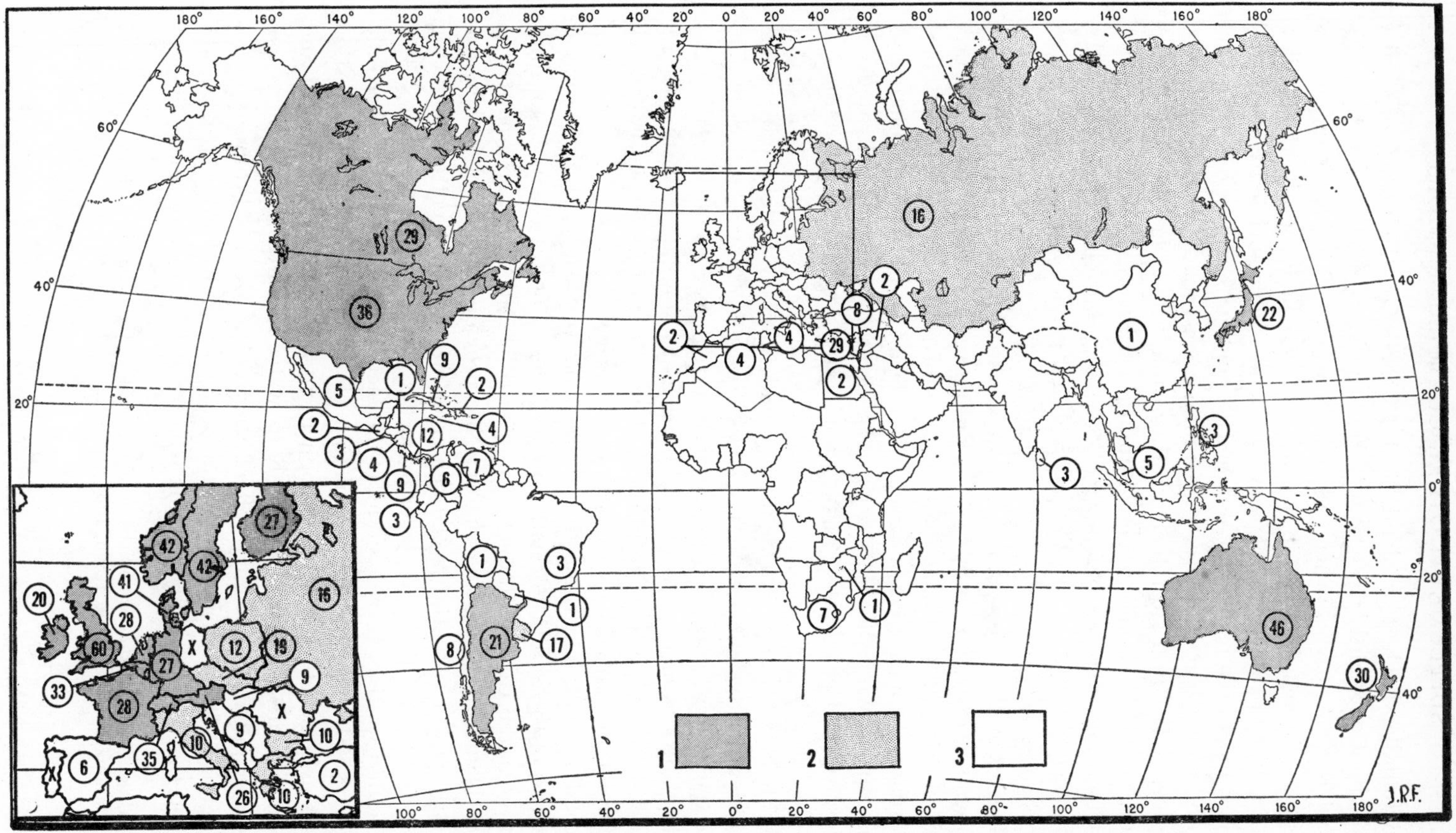

FIG. 13-1. World: Daily Newspaper Circulation per 100 Persons: (1) above 20; (2) 10-20; (3) below 10.

the Javanese, would do with such a wealth of water running past their villages at such useful gradients. Those ingenious and industrious people would have harnessed these streams to their creaking water wheels for irrigation or for grinding meal or for rough workshop power, and would have terraced their hills for maximum production." [3]

Education, knowledge, skill, and know-how are intangible power factors ranging alongside the tangible factors and are not less important than those. But to specify and to map them as one would do it in a geographical study of industries or resources is impossible. As a partial attempt at a cartographical presentation of these intangible power factors, Figures 13-1 and 2 depict newspaper circulation and frequency of radio sets on a world-wide basis; a comparison of these data permits conclusions in regard to a number of factors in the political realm in the fields of literacy, political education, and internal and external psychological propaganda.

LEGAL SYSTEMS IN POLITICAL GEOGRAPHY

The geography of the world's legal systems is a further example of how the geographical distribution of certain cohesive institutions of human society demonstrate binding or separating qualities. Of the innumerable factors which together constitute a legal system there are many which can be traced to the influence of geography. It would lead too far afield to pursue these influences. John H. Wigmore has undertaken the long-neglected task of subdividing the world map into the major legal systems. Those in existence twenty-five years ago were the Anglican, Chinese, Germanic, Hindu, Japanese, Mohammedan, Romanic, Slavic, and Soviet. For areas where no legal system had been developed, a color for Tribal Custom was added.[4] Redrawn today, this map would require a number of alterations, especially in the area of Slavic law where the extension of the Soviet orbit has carried with it the expansion of Soviet law. A sense of identity or similarity based on a law system does not promote as strongly the belonging-together concept as does the ethnic, linguistic, and religious community. However, just as these elements express, within or beyond the political boundaries of a state, the cultural traits which serve as connecting links between groups and nations, thus to a lesser but also significant degree related laws, the common adherence to principles of international law, or tribal customs serve the same purpose. Contrariwise, the line or zone which indicates where, regardless of political boundaries, the basic

[3] *Ibid.*
[4] "A Map of the World's Laws," *Geographical Review* (1929), pp. 114-120.

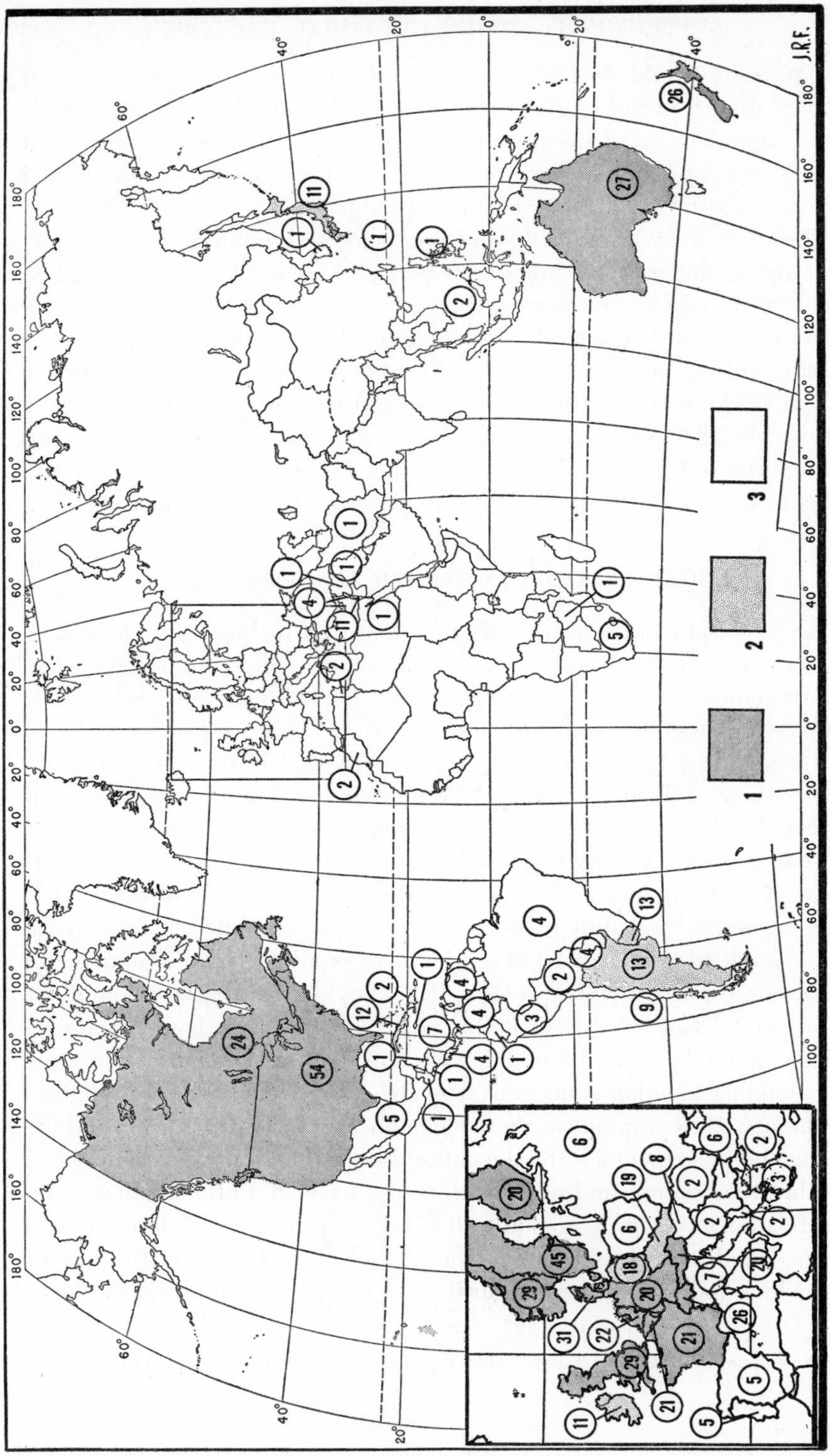

FIG. 13-2. World: Radio Sets per 100 Persons: (1) above 20; (2) 10-20; (3) below 10.

law concepts differ can be indicative of separating factors which explain characteristics of the internal and external geography of states. Quebec and Louisiana, where the Roman legal system survived, offer an illustration on the map of North America, for the internal political geography of Canada and the United States. The present struggle for survival of the Romanic-Germanic law system in the Eastern Zone of Germany depicts the crucial situation in that area. In the Mohammedan world we discover an interesting cleavage between the laws of the desert and those of the oases, as between Bedouin law and the Egyptian Penal Code. Thus the political geography of legal systems evolves as an additional aid in the task of appraising the cohesive and divisive influences and power factors among the nations.

Part

3

THE ECONOMIC FACTOR IN POLITICAL GEOGRAPHY

CHAPTER 14

The Importance of Economic Factors in Political Geography

THE RELATIVE IMPORTANCE OF LOCATION AND OTHER FACTORS

When Halford J. Mackinder read his now famous paper, "The Geographical Pivot of History" at the Royal Geographical Society on January 25, 1904, he provoked some interesting and all-too-brief comments from his friend and fellow member, L. S. Amery, later First Lord of the Admiralty and Secretary of State for India. The paper, and these comments, pose in an interesting way the problem of the significance of economic factors in political geography. Mackinder, it will be recalled, had advanced the thesis that the Asiatic steppe lands, whose horse-riding nomads had always presented a threat to Europe, would in the "closed system" of the modern world, and with the "full development of her modern railway mobility" become "the pivot region of the world's politics." Mackinder obviously did not ignore economic and social factors but he concluded that in the modern world they conferred a special advantage on land power as opposed to sea power. "Nor is it likely," he predicted, "that any possible social revolution will alter [Russia's] essential relations to the great geographical limits of her existence." [1]

[1] H. J. Mackinder, "The Geographical Pivot of History," *Geographical Journal* (April, 1904), pp. 14-16. Mackinder's emphasis on "railway mobility" is foreshadowed in the writings of the German Friedrich List who, more than a century ago, dwelt on the influence of railways upon the shifting balance of military power. See the important study by E. M. Earle on "Adam Smith, Alexander Hamilton, Friedrich List: The Economic Foundations of Military Power," in E. M. Earle, ed., *Makers of Modern Strategy* (Princeton, 1943), pp. 117-155 (148-152).

In his extemporaneous remarks Amery insisted that sea mobility was still more important to military power than railway mobility and that before long both would be supplemented "by the air as a means of locomotion." This train of thought led him to the concluding observation that ". . . to look forward a bit . . . a great deal of this geographical distribution must lose its importance, and the successful powers will be those who have the greatest industrial basis. It will not matter whether they are in the center of a continent or on an island; those people who have the industrial power and the power of invention and of science will be able to defeat all others." [2]

In retrospect it must be judged that Amery's views were the more realistic. The U.S.S.R. has become a world power not so much because of its location in the "closed heartland of Euro-Asia" as because of a profound and far-reaching social revolution which made the development of Amery's industrial power the paramount object of policy. Railways have, indeed, worked great wonders in the steppes because, as Mackinder correctly saw, "they directly replace horse and camel mobility, the road stage of development having been omitted." But their development has been slow and costly and the vast distances of the heartland are still a liability rather than an asset.

The controversy between the two men was mainly one of emphasis. Mackinder failed to foresee the advent of air power, but he did recognize in theory that other factors play their part as well as the geographical ones:

> I have spoken as a geographer. The actual balance of political power at any given time is, of course, the product, on the one hand, of geographical conditions, both economic and strategic, and, on the other hand, of the relative number, virility, equipment, and organization of the competing peoples. In proportion as these quantities are accurately estimated are we likely to adjust differences without the crude resort to arms. And the geographical quantities in the calculation are more measurable and more nearly constant than the human.[3]

Certainly once the U.S.S.R. has acquired the power of industry and science of which Amery spoke, its central location may well prove of crucial advantage in the outward extension of its piecemeal conquests. The West has already learned how costly is the task of containing a powerful aggressor at all points around this vast perimeter.

After fifty years this exchange of views still provides a needed reminder of the desirability of that bridge between the physical and social sciences

[2] Mackinder, *op. cit.*, p. 21.
[3] Mackinder, *op. cit.*, p. 17.

that Mackinder called upon the geographers to build. And the above quotation constitutes good advice for the student of political geography, especially when he addresses himself, as we do now, to the problem of the relative importance of geographical conditions on the one hand, and of the use and adaptations which various peoples make of the resources which geography provides. It suggests among other things that the service economic analysis can perform for political geography is something more than a mere cataloging of economic resources. Political geography requires more than an understanding of economic geography, or of the geographical conditions characterized in Mackinder's phrase as economic. The analysis must also relate these conditions to the "number, virility, equipment and organization" of states in order to arrive at "the actual balance of political power."

Of necessity any such analysis must have a focus. The obvious factors in any calculation of political power relationships in today's world are the states which are the centers of military and political power, the United States and the U.S.S.R., together with their allies and "satellites" on both sides. But if the balance in today's world is struck simply between these two groups of states opposing each other in the "cold war" it would be incomplete because it would ignore a large group of states hopelessly lacking in the economic and military capabilities for great power status, but which constitute a "bloc" of increasing cohesiveness and influence in world politics. These are the underdeveloped states of Asia, Africa, and Latin America. By and large these states have accepted their lot as states which are virtually defenseless against aggression from either the Sino-Soviet bloc or the other great powers. They therefore do not seek to develop more military strength than is needed to protect them from their smaller neighbors. Instead, they seek the domestic, political, and social advantages that come from economic progress. A large part of their bureaucratic energies are devoted to government-sponsored and directed measures to speed up the process of economic development. Many of them remain "uncommitted" politically because they have not, as a practical matter, been able to choose between the social and political systems represented by Communism and the democratic West.

In the conflicting attitudes of states toward wealth and economic life and their relation to national power, one can distinguish, in Mackinder's term, three sets of "competing peoples"—the industrialized states of Europe and North America, the Sino-Soviet bloc, and the underdeveloped areas of Asia, Africa, and Latin America. These three groups of states are related by two equations which are significant for today's student of political geography. One represents the relationship between the economic power of the Soviet bloc and that of the industrialized and anti-Communist West. The economic capabilities of both groups of states, though resting on radically different social foundations, are growing; how do the rates of growth compare and what do they signify for the future? The other equation represents the relationship between living standards and rates of economic growth in the industrialized states of the West and those of the so-called underdeveloped countries outside the Communist bloc. Whether the gap between the two can be narrowed, and at what rate, may determine the resistance of the underdeveloped countries to Communist propaganda and subversion, and consequently their ultimate alignment in the struggle between Communism and the democratic West.

This discussion of economic factors in political geography is essentially an attempt to estimate the quantities in these equations and their significance for the three main political groupings of the present-day world. In making the attempt we shall try in particular to show how variations in political and military power among states are related to variations in their underlying economic capabilities and how these capabilities in turn are related to geographical factors such as climate, mineral resources, and waterways. In addition we shall consider how the attempt to expand economic capabilities, either for power or welfare purposes, influences the attitudes and actions of the various states. Before proceeding to these tasks, however, the remainder of this chapter sets forth certain fundamental principles concerning the relation between economic capabilities and national power, and between physical geography and economic growth.

ECONOMIC CAPABILITIES AND NATIONAL POWER

The ability of states to afford, in the words of Adam Smith, "the great expense of firearms," [4] is nowadays so obviously a condition of national power that its analysis is essential to an understanding of international political relationships. A brief explanation of this concept of economic capability seems desirable to avoid possible misunderstanding.

In the following discussion, attention is centered on the concept of

[4] . . . In modern war the great expense of firearms gives an evident advantage to the nation which can best afford that expense; and consequently, to an opulent and civilized, over a poor and barbarous nation. In ancient times, the opulent and civilized found it difficult to defend themselves against the poor and barbarous nations. In modern times the poor and barbarous find it difficult to defend themselves against the opulent and civilized (*Wealth of Nations,* Book V, Part I, Ch. 1).

economic capabilities for military power. It is, of course, readily apparent that not all conflicting international interests are resolved by resort to war. A powerful modern state will require and use its economic capabilities in order to advance its foreign policy by means short of war, such as economic or military assistance to friendly nations. It is true that economic capabilities are seldom, if ever, as fully mobilized for other purposes as for the national defense in time of war. Moreover, in the modern world, the influence of a national state in international affairs depends ultimately on its military capabilities. Hence, political and strategic capabilities are essentially a function of the economic capabilities for war. However, the reader is asked to bear in mind that the concept of economic capabilities comprehends other purposes than purely military ones.

Economic capabilities for war may be defined as that portion of the resources of a state (usually measured by national product or national income) which it can devote to military purposes. Since the Industrial Revolution the ability of modern states to maximize their economic capabilities for war has depended on their ability to establish and maintain a position of superiority in manufacturing and technology, and to extract from the competing claims of the various private interests in the economy, sufficient resources for the national defense. As states everywhere are developing both abilities, the economic potential for war comes to be increasingly a function of the size (in terms of population and resources) of the national economy.[5]

Mere economic development (as indicated by the average standard of living, *per capita* incomes, the state of the arts, *etc.*) is an insufficient indication of national power. Switzerland, for example, has one of the highest average incomes *per capita* in the world, much higher than that of the U.S.S.R. Yet the latter, not the former, has the economic base for the massive power position that the Soviet Union in fact enjoys. Likewise, size by itself is insufficient, as the examples of China and India demonstrate. What is important is the optimum combination of size and development, of aggregate wealth or income, widely diversified as to type of commodities and services produced, and distributed in such a manner as to afford a relatively high proportion of expenditures on capital and military goods. Within fairly large limits, development has up to now ordinarily been the more important of the two factors. A smaller but developed state with relatively high *per capita* incomes (the United Kingdom or Japan) will have a surplus over and above minimum consumption and

[5] For a discussion of this point see E. Lederer's chapter on "War Economics" in H. Speier and A. Kahler, eds., *War in Our Time* (New York, 1939), pp. 206-220.

investment requirements, while a very large state with low *per capita* incomes (like India or China) may have a much smaller surplus for military and strategic purposes. When, however, such large states come under the grip of totalitarian governments, as in Communist China, the share of the national product used for military and security purpose can be forcibly enlarged. The military capabilities of such a country may therefore be expanded at a much faster rate than its over-all economic development would lead one to expect.

The acceptance of the economics of total war not only by the totalitarian states but, in theory at any rate, by almost every advanced country, and "the almost uniform development of modern technique in all countries" [6] (of which the rapidity with which the U.S.S.R. copied jet engine and atomic weapon designs is a good example) have made *aggregate resources* the most important single factor in determining economic capabilities.

RELATIVE CAPABILITIES

The relative capability of nation states has been subject to constant change, even before the advent of total war. The Netherlands was once the leading manufacturing country of Europe, and Rotterdam and Antwerp were the leading financial centers because of the wool trade. In those days Holland was a great power. In the days of the great explorations, Spain and Portugal were among the wealthiest and strongest countries in Europe. The pre-eminence of these states gave way to that of the United Kingdom. Similarly the superiority of the United Kingdom gave way in the twentieth century under the strain of two World Wars and especially with the rise of the United States and the Soviet Union. After World War II, Great Britain, although still a "big power" is no longer a first-ranking power, and this is due directly to the relative decline in her economic strength. A good illustration of this is the action of Great Britain in 1947 in turning over to the United States her commitments in Greece and asking the United States to assume responsibility for stability in that country. The government of Great Britain knew that Greece needed large measures of both economic and military assistance that the United Kingdom could no longer afford to give. This is not to say that the United Kingdom is economically weaker now than in the nineteenth century or than before the second World War. Actually, total output and exports, both in value and in physical volume, are larger than ever. But in terms

[6] Lederer, *loc. cit.*, p. 220.

of the cost of the growing responsibilities and commitments of national power, the United Kingdom's capabilities are declining.

In the new atomic age, an enormous economic base is required not only to produce atomic and other unconventional arms but to carry on the necessary scientific research and development to maintain superiority. Only three states are known to produce nuclear weapons and of these only two, the United States and the U.S.S.R., can seriously be regarded as first-ranking powers (Fig. 14-1). In fact, it is the reduction of the number of great powers to only these two which characterizes the political and strategic aspect of this new age. Both have strong economic bases compounded in each case of size (area, population, and resources) and of development (industrialization, high rates of investment, and intensive application of technology to industrial processes).

It is not intended to suggest that national power is a simple function of aggregate economic capabilities. There are variations in the social limits within which modern states can mobilize resources for military purposes. Totalitarian states can command a larger proportion of resources for extended periods than can democracies. In this way the U.S.S.R. now presents a growing threat to the peace of the world although its gross economic capabilities are less than those of the United States alone and less than those of all Western European countries combined. On the other hand, there are tangible and intangible qualities of leadership, of co-operation, of national effort and morale, which may multiply or reduce the effectiveness of the economic factors.

SHORT-RUN CAPABILITIES

Moreover, in the short run, aggregate capabilities may be less important than superiority in actual mobilized resources which give the initial military advantage and therefore may be crucial in the decisions of statesmen. In a war in which both sides would be prepared to make maximum use of the mass destructive power of nuclear weapons, the initial advantage might well prove final. On the other hand, in such a war the initial destruction on both sides might be so great as to nullify the importance of industrial output, thus leaving the issue to land and naval forces operating from prepared bases and utilizing, perhaps decisively, available stock piles.

An interesting example of how military success can be built upon existing capabilities, without reference to over-all, long-run superiority in economic potential, is provided by the effectiveness of the German stra-

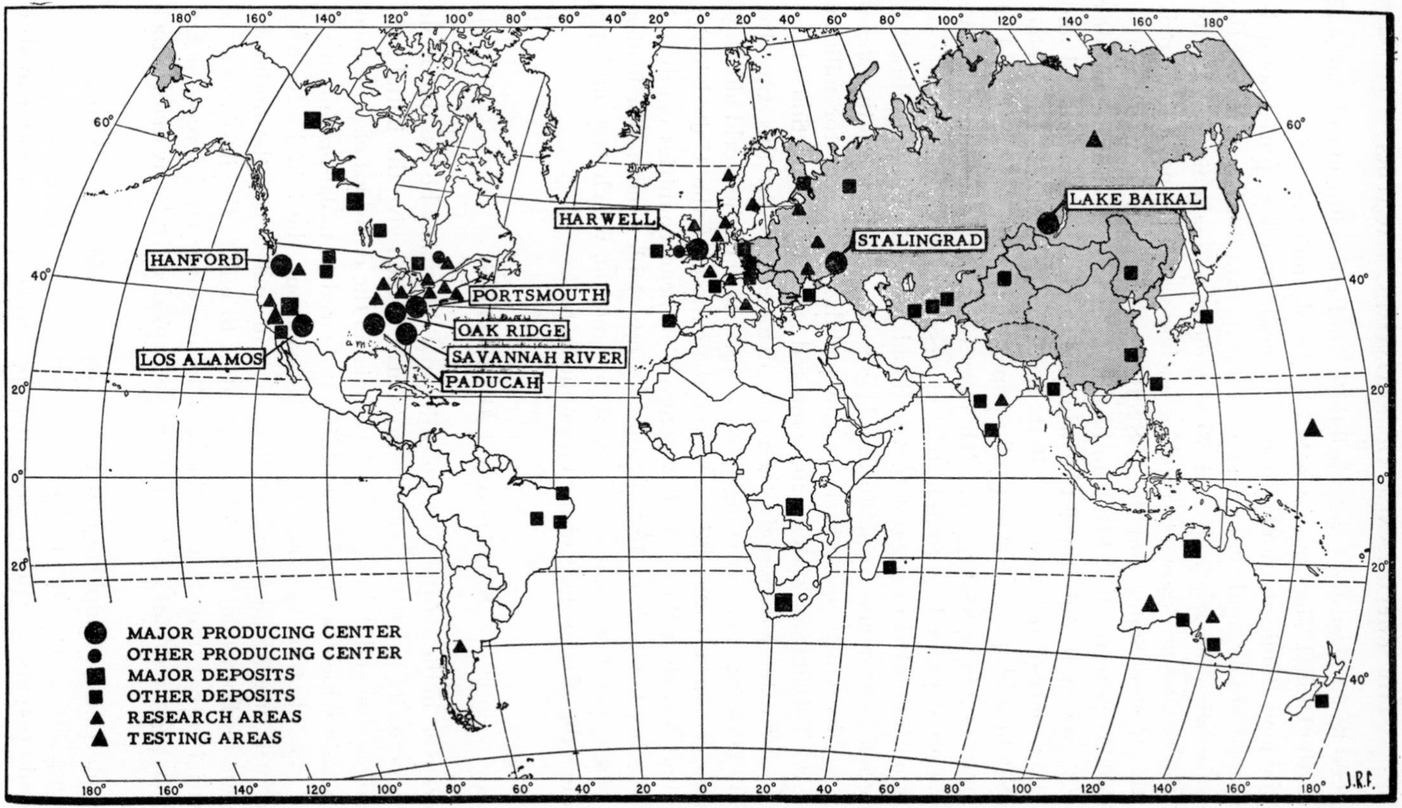

Fig. 14-1. Atomic Energy Resources.

tegic plan up to the winter of 1941. Hitler relied on more rapid mobilization of ground and air striking units of great initial power rather than on superiority in basic raw materials and industry, and he struck while his enemies were still preparing. Emphasis was placed upon a tactical air force as an instrument of the *blitzkrieg* rather than upon a strategic air force to destroy war production facilities. This plan was amazingly successful (despite the setbacks in the air over Britain) until the defeats on the Eastern Front; in September, 1941, Hitler was so confident that he directed large cutbacks in war production.

German plans for a short war were never successfully adapted to a long war. Although arms production increased by three times after early 1942, the German economy was never fully mobilized, a fact which explains its remarkable resilience to air attacks.[7] Japan's attack on Pearl Harbor was an attempt by a power with a relatively inferior industrial base to offset this disadvantage by surprise backed up by an initially superior existing force.

The Western allies, on the other hand, although tardy in their preparations for war, were much better equipped to fight a long war. They possessed a combination of a very large resource base of raw materials, labor, capital, and technological genius for converting these assets quickly to war potential. Their problem was to hold off the enemy until their resources were mobilized, after which the issue was never in doubt.

THE RELATIONSHIP OF GEOGRAPHICAL FACTORS TO ECONOMIC DEVELOPMENT

In their discussion of the relative importance of location and "geographical distribution," Mackinder might well have pointed out to Amery that location is not simply a matter of the mobility of military forces in time of war; it also establishes and determines the position of a nation with respect to those "geographical conditions" and economic resources upon which industrial power must be based.[8] It is important also to note, in support of Mackinder's thesis, that there are geographical features which, unimportant in peacetime, can critically affect the size and composition of the economic potential in wartime. One of the most graphic illustrations of this last point was provided in both world wars by Britain's dependence on sea-borne imports. The curtailment of these by submarine warfare and

[7] For a complete analysis see the United States Strategic Bombing Survey, *Summary Report,* September 30, 1945.
[8] See Chapter 7.

the military and economic cost of the convoy system placed a very large strain on the British war economy.[9]

Thus, factors such as location, size, shape, and other geographical relationships remain important determinants of political and strategic policy, while the related geographical pattern of economic development and of economic capabilities is seen to be equally pertinent.

The extent of the economic development of a region is always limited and conditioned by its natural geographical features. Some states overcome the limitations of their native environment by trade and by colonization. A few areas, rich in natural resources, still remain "undeveloped." But in general, economic development has been associated with, among other things, some favorable combination of such physical factors as climate, soil, topography, mineral resources, and waterways. The influence of these factors is not, of course, confined to economic life, but affects in a unique and organic way the growth and development of a culture. However, it is through their influence on economic life that they generally have their greatest effect on other aspects of human life. The influence of a few of the more important of these factors is considered here very briefly.

Climate and Economic Development. Climate is one of the most important geographical factors for economic development because of its effect on soils and vegetation and in turn on human life and activity.[10] Nearly half of the land on the earth's surface is in the intermediate climatic regions of the Northern Hemisphere. The economically developed regions of the world are concentrated in these regions. While there are dense concentrations of population in some of the tropical regions of Asia, Africa, and South America, *per capita* agricultural production in these areas is low and industrial production negligible. The explanation for the difference is to be found partly in the climate, through the effect of temperature and rainfall on soil and vegetation, and partly in historical and cultural factors. In tropical regions high temperature and high humidity have an enervating effect on both physical and mental activity. Rainfall, or the lack of it, and its seasonal distribution will affect the fertility of the soil and the growth of crops. In the tropical

[9] See A. P. Usher, "The Steam and Steel Complex and International Relations," in *Technology and International Relations*, Wm. F. Ogborn, ed. (Chicago, 1949).

[10] For a good brief discussion of the effects of climate on human activity see J. H. Stembridge, *The World: A General Regional Geography*, 1953, Ch. 7. For influence of climate on economic activity see L. D. Stamp and S. C. Gilmour, *Chisholm's Handbook of Commercial Geography*, 14th ed. (New York, 1954), pp. 22-52. These however, are fairly elementary. P. Gourou's *The Tropical World* (Engl. translation, London, 1953), is a much more sophisticated examination of certain aspects of the problem.

rain forests there is so much precipitation that leaching of the soil tends to deprive it of fertility. The hot desert regions like the Sahara or the great Australian desert are practically uncultivable and uninhabitable.

The geographical conditions which in the past were favorable to the growth of civilizations appear to have been different from those which exist today in association with a high degree of economic development. Marston Bates [11] has pointed out that all three pre-Columbian civilizations in the Americas, the Incas, the Mayas, and the Aztecs, were tropical in origin and did not spread far beyond the tropics. Bates cites the two extinct cultures of Ceylon and Cambodia to demonstrate that a very high level of social life and development can be attained in tropical regions. That of Ceylon depended on a remarkable system of reservoirs for storing water from the seasonal rains. It collapsed when the dykes fell into disrepair in the course of internecine wars in the thirteenth and fourteenth centuries. The Khmer Empire in Cambodia endured for five hundred years and produced a magnificent art and architecture before collapsing in the tenth century from unknown causes.

Today the regions of the tropics are among the most underdeveloped of the world. This is especially true of the equatorial rain forests, as in the Amazon and Congo river valleys. Rain falls throughout the year, temperatures are uniformly high, and the landscape is covered with a dense tropical forest. Some of the wood is valuable, like mahogany and ebony, but is difficult to reach and costly to harvest. Malaya, the Philippines, and Indonesia are in this belt but their forests are less dense because of their proximity to the sea and here conditions are more favorable to agriculture and the growth of population.

Other parts of the Tropical Zones are more favorable to man. These are the tropical grass lands and savannas and especially the monsoon lands. The former are found on both sides of the equatorial forests, in South America (Orinoco Basin and Brazilian highlands) in Africa (Sudan), in the drier parts of India, in the Philippines, and in the north and east of Australia. The temperature is uniformly high, rain falls during the summer months and the winter season is dry. These regions are primarily agricultural.

The monsoon lands are economically, as well as in many other ways, the most important of the tropical regions. With their wet, hot summers and dry winter seasons they are extraordinarily well-suited to certain types of agriculture (especially rice) and have thus become one of the most densely populated regions of the earth. The monsoon climate, which is

[11] *Where Winter Never Comes* (New York, 1953).

well marked in India, Southeast Asia, Southern China, and Northern Australia is characterized by heavy rains during summer, as winds blow from sea to land, and a dry season in winter when the winds blow in the opposite direction. In northern hemisphere monsoon lands, like India and Burma, the cool dry season lasts from November to February, the hot season from March to June, and the rainy season from June to October. In the wetter regions where the annual rainfall may be eighty inches or more, the forests resemble those of the equatorial belt and the crops include rice, tea, and jute. If the rainy season lasts as long as six to seven months, as in Pakistan, cotton and sugar cane can be grown.

Central China and Japan also receive monsoon rains and are sometimes referred to as subtropical monsoon regions. They are also among the most densely populated regions of the world.

Our own Western civilization flourished first in the Mediterranean, but its greatest development has occurred in the cooler intermediate regions where man has met the challenge of the seasons. Next to the monsoon lands of Asia, the industrial areas of Europe and the United States are the most populous areas of the world. Most of the land and large industrial areas of North America and Europe are in a cool temperate climate.

New England and the North Atlantic states are mostly in an eastern maritime type of climate, as in Manchuria, part of North China, Korea, Hokaido, and Sakhalin. Most of Western Europe and the United Kingdom are in a cooler and more humid West coast marine climate. These are usually comparatively highly industrialized regions. The former regions have a more extreme climate than the latter and are hot in summer and cold in winter, have a light to moderate rainfall, with the prevailing winds off-shore. The West coast marine-type regions are subjected to onshore westerly winds and thus have an insular climate marked by cool summers and mild winters with rainfall fairly well distributed throughout the year.

Russia's continental climate has been comparatively unfavorable to economic development, with hot summers and winter temperatures below the freezing point except in the Crimea. Over most of the country the annual rainfall is not more than twenty inches. Most of the coast line lies so far north as to be icebound for as long as six months in the year. Inland waterways are similarly affected; while the completion of the Don-Volga Canal makes possible water transportation between the Baltic and White seas in the north to the Caspian and Black seas in the south, even the southern portions of these routes are frozen for three months.

From the brief discussion given above, it will be seen that both the tropical and the intermediate regions have been found conducive to civilization. In both zones are regions which are unfavorable to life and to economic activity, the equatorial rain forests and hot deserts in the tropics and the deserts of Iran, and Gobi. The temperate deserts are more easily reclaimable through irrigation than the tropical deserts, and the tropical rain forests, of the Amazon at any rate, still more or less successfully resist human encroachment. In both the tropics and the intermediate zones there are areas of great population concentration—the tropical monsoon lands of Asia which have been almost exclusively agricultural or extractive in their development, and the industrialized regions of Europe and North America. Experience thus suggests that intermediate climates furnish the most favorable conditions for diversified economic development, including industrialization.

All the highly developed countries lie in latitudes 35° N to 70° N. This is Huntington's "very high energy" region.[12] He ascribes the high economic development of most of the countries in this zone to the invigorating effects on man of the favorable climate. Huntington eliminates relief, soil, minerals, power resources, and waterways as major factors shaping the pattern of world economic development. While a favorable climate undoubtedly has contributed to the economic progress of the developed countries, the importance attached to it by Huntington appears to be exaggerated. On the contrary, it is becoming increasingly apparent that the densely populated countries of the monsoon areas of India and China are underdeveloped precisely because the climate and other physical factors were so favorable to human life and population growth in the pre-industrial rice economies, while industrialization was possible in Northwestern Europe at least partly because the population was still relatively small in relation to land and other resources when the new era began.[13]

Soils and Vegetation.[14] Soils and vegetation are of basic importance to agriculture and forestry. If the soil of a region lacks the ability to produce agricultural and forest products it is likely that the region will be uninhabitable. Moreover the fertility of the soil is important to the industrial stages of economic development; usually a community must be able to

[12] E. Huntington, *Civilization and Climate,* 3rd ed. (New York, 1939).

[13] See especially Gourou, *op. cit.,* pp. 1-5 and 99-112; also S. Kuznet, *Underdeveloped Countries and the Pre-industrial Phase in the Advanced Countries,* an unpublished paper delivered at the World Population Conference, Rome, September, 1954. See also A. P. Usher, "Population and Settlement in Eurasia," *Geographic Review,* Vol. 10 (1930), pp. 110-132.

[14] This discussion is based to a large extent on Stamp and Gilmour, *op. cit.,* pp. 53-64); *cf.* also M. S. Anderson, *Geography of Living Things* (New York, 1954), pp. 121-168.

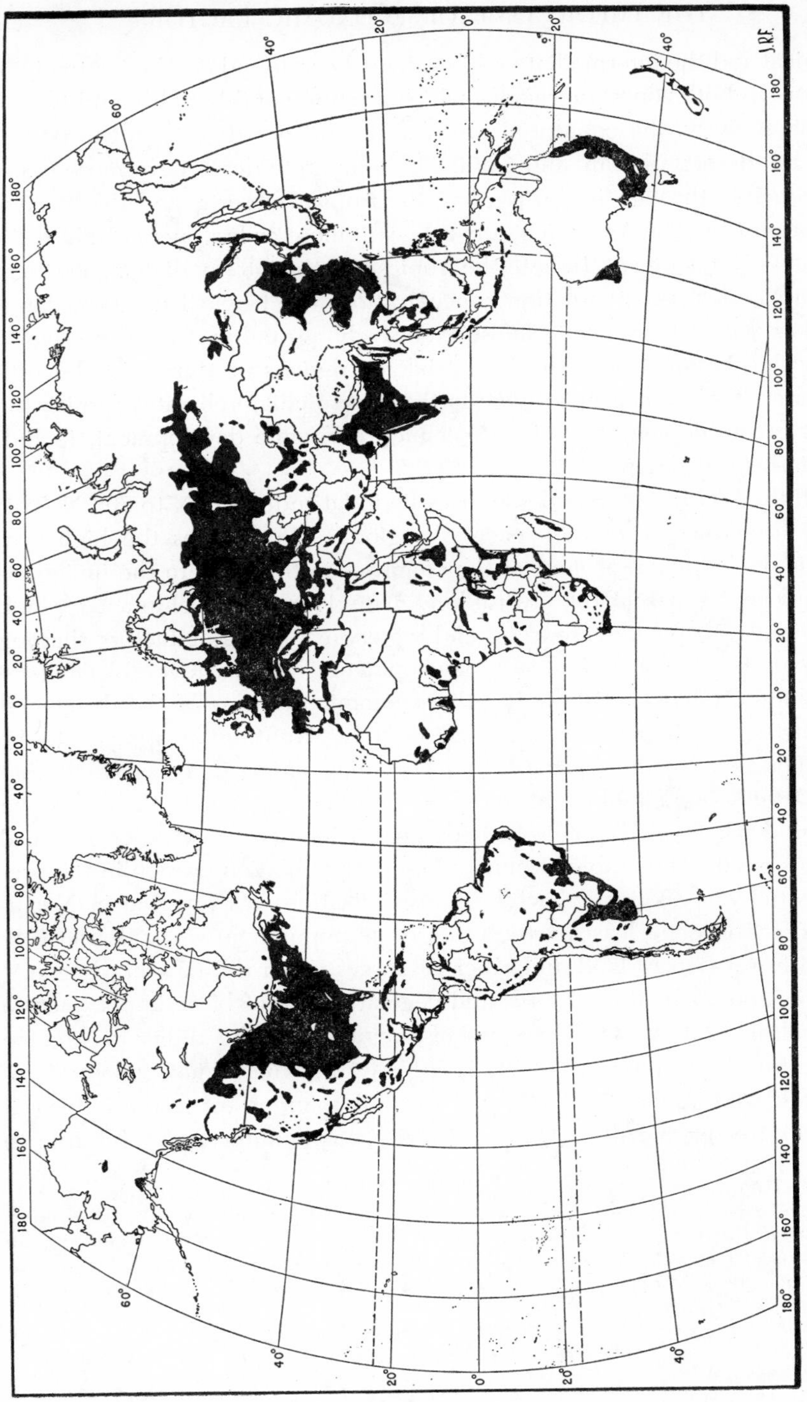

FIG. 14-2. World: Arable Land.

produce a surplus of foodstuffs in order to release part of its population to other employment before it can develop the facilities for manufacturing, transportation, and trade. This is an important part of the problem of economic development, for example, in a country like India, which has difficulty in producing enough foodstuff for its vast population. The low level of *per capita* food production is in turn partly a consequence of inability of the farmers to afford fertilization, and partly a function of mere numbers of the population, for the soil and climate throughout most of India is favorable to cultivation.

Soils and vegetation are reflections of climate. The soil of many arid lands is often very rich in minerals and only the lack of rainfall prevents the growth of grasses or crops. The great climatic regions of the world have their own distinctive soil properties, since the soil is due to the weathering of rock under different atmospheric conditions, and is subject to different effects of vegetable and animal life. However many soils are aclimatic, having within the same climatic region, numerous local variations depending on the characteristics of the parent material. Consequently the crop yield of one region may be much greater or less than that of another with the same climate.

The productivity of land for agricultural purposes depends on the fertility of the soil, and on the degree and seasonal variation of rainfall and temperature. About two-thirds of the earth's land surface is unsuited for agriculture because of insufficient precipitation and low temperature, and a large part of the balance is unusable because of topography (Fig. 14-2). About one-fifth of the land area has temperature, rainfall, and topography in the right combinations, but less than 10 per cent is fully suited for agricultural production, the proportion ranging from less than 3 per cent in Oceania to 37 per cent in Europe.[15]

Agricultural production does not vary uniformly with natural fertility and climate, because of differences in the skills of farm populations and the amounts of capital employed. The most productive agricultural regions are Northwestern Europe, the North Central and Middle Atlantic United States, the valleys of the Indus and Ganges in India and Pakistan, and Southeastern China. Smaller areas of high production are found in coastal Argentina and Brazil, the southern Ukraine, the lower Nile valley and southern Australia. Asia and Africa, although they contain more than 60 per cent of the world's population, account for just over 30 per cent of world agricultural output. Output per capita is low in Africa because

[15] W. S. and E. S. Woytinsky, *World Population and Production* (New York, 1954), p. 316, Table 154.

of primitive techniques, in Asia because of scarcity of land. Europe (including the U.S.S.R.), the Americas, and Oceania, with a much smaller population, produce 70 per cent of the world's agricultural output by value.

Agricultural production is coming more and more to depend on controlled plant food (fertilizers) and controlled water (irrigation). Farmers were once able to rely on the organic processes of animal manures and leguminous plants to restore the fertility of the soil but the intensive agriculture of today requires vast quantities of "commercial" fertilizers. World consumption of the three main commercial fertilizers, nitrogen, phosphate, and potash, in 1950 to 1951 was almost 13.5 million tons. Even with the use of such fertilizers the soil gradually becomes depleted. The destruction of agricultural soil by wind and water erosion after the natural cover has been removed is even more serious, and much good crop land, even in the United States, has been totally destroyed in this way. Topsoil that has taken thousands of years to build, has been washed away completely in two generations. Large areas of former coffee land in Brazil have been thus depleted. Erosion over the centuries in China, India, and the Middle East has destroyed millions of acres, and in the latter region, "The ruins of ancient water works explain eloquently why the land . . . is dry and sterile." [16]

Irrigation has long been employed as a remedy for the deficiency of rainfall, especially with rivers like the Nile and the Euphrates which regularly overflow their banks. Such irrigation by inundation provided not only water but fertilizing sediment which, if the floods destroyed one crop, guaranteed the success of the next. However, since water is needed most during the dry seasons, the old inundation canals have generally been replaced by dams and perennial canals. In the United States we are accustomed to irrigation works being employed to reclaim the western desert lands and forget that irrigation systems are an absolutely indispensable part of the agricultural economies of a number of ancient lands. Most varieties of rice, upon which so large a part of the world's population depends as a staple food, must be grown in irrigated fields and flooded at a certain stage of growth; if this cannot be accomplished by the rains or inundation, the water must be stored and released at the proper times. Occasionally, in some districts of India (never in all), the monsoon rains fail and famine occurs where irrigation is not practiced. In other areas, such as the Coromandel Coast of India, the annual rainfall is concentrated in a short period of a few weeks and must be stored in tanks. However,

[16] *Ibid.*, p. 479.

in the deltas of this coast, three crops of rice a year are produced in land irrigated by canals.

The necessity of irrigating rice (as well as the scarcity of arable land) has in some countries such as the Philippines, China, and Yemen produced remarkable instances of terrace cultivation. In our own time, the counterpart of these marvelous human modifications seems to be the planned development of entire river valleys to provide not only for irrigation but also for flood control, navigation, and hydro-electric power production. The most remarkable example of modern river valley development is the Tennessee Valley [17] in which, up to July 1, 1949, some $800 million had been expended for these purposes. Such measures, together with the measures to enlarge the supply or productivity of arable land by soil and forest conservation and by reclamation, take considerable time and require large investment outlays which are often beyond the means of overpopulated, underdeveloped countries.

Mineral Resources and Energy. In the period between World Wars I and II it was fashionable to interpret political rivalries in terms of the struggle for raw materials, especially minerals. Imperial powers were depicted as grasping for colonies to provide supplies of raw materials and markets for finished products. The rise of Nazism in Germany was explained in part as an aspect of the German drive to recover colonial sources of raw materials and to acquire "lebensraum." In Japan, perhaps more than in Germany, the need to expand the economy, even for peaceful purposes, was a real one. Home supplies of iron ore and coking coal were limited and petroleum was produced (in insufficient quantities) only in Japanese Sakhalin. It was against this background that Prime Minister Churchill and President Roosevelt included in the Atlantic Charter a phrase supporting the "principle" of equal access to raw materials.

The present geographical pattern of industrial development is still based largely on two minerals, coal and iron ore. In addition to its importance as a source of energy, coal is an essential raw material in the steel and chemical industries. Accordingly, one common and important geographical characteristic of almost all highly developed countries is the presence of fairly plentiful supplies of coal and iron ore, either within their own national boundaries or close at hand. Thus, while Germany is deficient in iron ore, it draws on the rich supplies of Lorraine for its steel-making industries. France, short of coal, in turn obtains supplies from the nearby Ruhr (*cf.* Fig. 17-1). Lack of coal undoubtedly was a factor retarding the development of Mediterranean Europe.

[17] See p. 579.

Today no nation has adequate domestic supplies of all minerals and very few even approach self-sufficiency. Even the United States, generally regarded as the nation most liberally endowed with natural resources, is deficient in a number of minerals including some that are essential in time of war, such as tin, nickel, and manganese. These deficiencies must be viewed in the light of our ability to stockpile large quantities of some and to devise adequate substitutes for others.[18] Similarly the U.S.S.R. and satellites, although deliberately striving for autarky (an economic potential for war not dependent on foreign supplies), import large quantities of many minerals including copper, lead, zinc, nickel, quartz crystals, and industrial diamonds. The real object of concern in both countries probably is not with its materials position in the event of a war in the relatively near future, but rather with its long-run ability to continue to supply increasing quantities of the exhaustible mineral raw materials to a rapidly growing industrial machine. In the future, the search by developed countries for mineral and other raw materials to supplement domestic supplies, rather than the search for markets or profits, is likely to be the principal incentive for the exploitation of undeveloped areas.

Much more basic to economic and industrial power than the minerals *per se*, are the sources of mechanical energy, coal, petroleum, natural gas, and hydro-power. Of these coal is the most widely used and in the actual historical development of industrialism the most important. It has been aptly said that no geographical factor is more significant in relation to the economic history of the past two hundred years than the fact that when Western man was ready to apply the steam engine to industrial power, and to make steel with coke instead of charcoal, he found enormous quantities of steam and coking coal literally under his feet, in the British Isles, in the Appalachian basin, in western and central Europe. While oil and hydraulic power have become of increasing importance as sources of energy in the twentieth century, coal is still the chief supplier of fuel and power. In 1949 nearly half of the world's energy was supplied by coal and lignite.[19] Petroleum, next in economic importance (though of prime military importance), accounted for only about 20 per cent of the world total. Petroleum and its products are, of course, easier to handle and cheaper to transport than coal. In the United States petroleum is threatening the primacy of coal as a source of energy due to the remarkable development of motor transportation. In Europe, which produces little natural oil, coal

[18] *Cf.* E. S. Mason, "American Security and Access to Raw Materials," *World Politics*, Vol. 1, No. 2, pp. 147-160.

[19] United Nations, *World Energy in Selected Years*, 1929-1950 (New York, 1952).

accounted for over 80 per cent of all energy produced, and in the U.S.S.R. over 60 per cent.[20] However, European countries are building refineries and shifting increasingly to petroleum as coal becomes more costly.

The geographic distribution of the producing petroleum reserves is quite different from that of coal, the three principal areas being (1) the Gulf Coast, Mid-continent (U.S.) and Caribbean (Venezuela), (2) the Near East (Black Sea, Persian Gulf) and (3) Far East (Indonesia). Thus a large share of today's petroleum production comes from relatively "underdeveloped" areas, from areas discovered and developed by American, British, or Dutch companies without whose capital and technical direction it could not have been produced. The geographical distribution of water power likewise does not support theories of physical determinism in explaining economic development, since water-power potential occurs in heavy concentration in many underdeveloped areas, in South America, Asia, and Africa. The highly developed countries (Fig. 14-3), the United States, Germany, Sweden, Switzerland, Japan (the United Kingdom has a very small water-potential), have all utilized their hydro-electric potential up to 40 per cent or 50 per cent or more. The availability of water power in under-developed areas poor in coal and petroleum (Brazil) should facilitate the industrial development of those areas.

NONGEOGRAPHICAL FACTORS

Geographical factors thus have generally a significant effect on the economic development of a region. Except in a few isolated instances however it is in concrete situations almost impossible to separate out and assess the importance of geographical relative to nongeographical factors. It is fairly obvious that areas like the Sahara Desert or the Canadian Arctic have been of little economic consequence to date, and may well never amount to much because of this inhospitable climate and paucity of resources. The United Kingdom could not have developed a large steel industry without coal and iron ore. The matchless resources of the United States have been a major factor in its unparalleled economic growth. For most areas, however, including the United States, the relationship between the degree of economic development and the geographic environment is much less direct than in our Sahara desert and Arctic Canada examples. Nongeographical factors have commonly been no less significant and frequently more important than the physical environment in

[20] The reasons for the U.S.S.R.'s heavy dependence on coal are given below, on p. 475 ff.

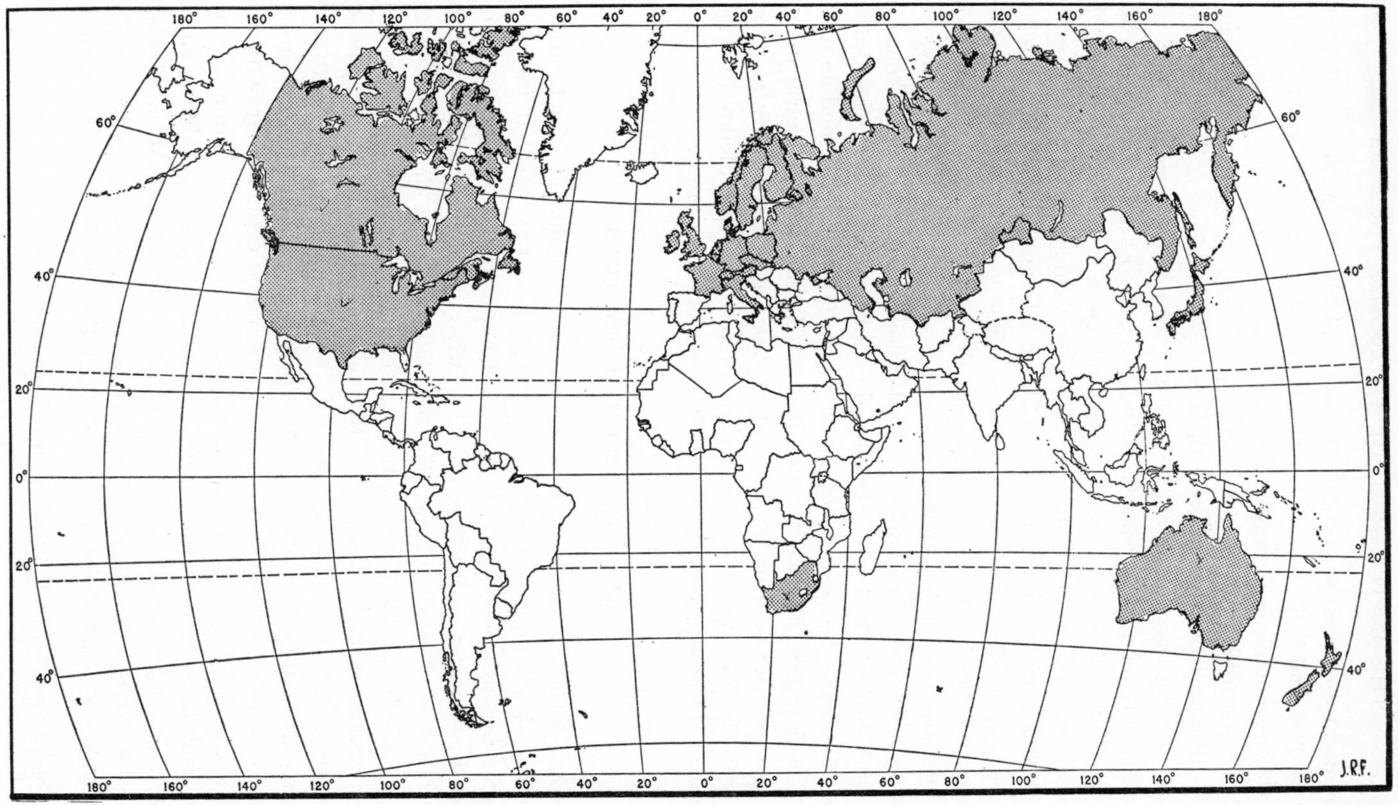

Fig. 14-3. World: Economically Developed Countries.

shaping a country's economic development. How else can we explain why countries like Switzerland and Denmark have reached much higher levels of economic development than Spain or Italy, though less well-endowed with basic resources? Or what accounted for the economic ascendency of the United Kingdom over France and Germany from the middle of the sixteenth century until almost the close of the nineteenth, despite inferior natural resources? Why was the economic development of the U.S.S.R., which is second only to the United States in natural resources, delayed until almost the beginning of the twentieth century? How and why did Japan progress so rapidly on so limited a resource base in so short a period? To answer these questions we must consider chiefly nongeographical factors.

The economic development process depends not only on the geographical environment but also on the attitude of the people toward economic progress and on prevailing social, political, economic, and legal institutions.[21] The present pattern of world economic development is largely the outgrowth of historical changes in Europe which must be traced back to the Middle Ages, and which culminated in the so-called Industrial Revolution in the eighteenth and nineteenth centuries. This was not a revolution in the sense of a sudden and radical movement of population out of agriculture into industry and a change from handicraft to machine methods of production. Rather, the industrial revolution was a speeding up of a gradual process of innovation and modernization in agriculture, commerce, and industry which had been under way in Western Europe and particularly in Great Britain since the fifteenth century. Two eighteenth century technical inventions played a major role in the Industrial Revolution. They were (1) the invention of the steam engine and its application to industry, transportation, and agriculture, and (2) the "puddling process" which made possible the widespread use of coal in the manufacture of bar iron. This change in the tempo of economic development has been described by G. N. Trevelyan in his *History of England* as follows: "Up to the Industrial Revolution, economic and social change, though continuous, has the pace of a slowly moving stream, but in the days of Watt and Stephenson it has acquired the momentum of water over a mill-dam, distracting to the eye of the spectator." [22]

The Industrial Revolution began first in Great Britain. "It was the enterprise and industry of eighteenth-century Britain that first realized the

[21] For a brief summary of the psychological and social pre-requisites of economic progress see the United Nations study, *Measures For the Economic Development of Under-Developed Countries* (New York, 1951), pp. 13-16.

[22] *History of England,* Vol. 3 (New York, 1954), p. 132.

dream of the Renaissance scientists and brought the forces of nature under human control by scientific means." The forces of nature were abundantly present in the form of coal and iron ore, but their subjection by the new scientific knowledge might have waited in vain "as was the case with Greek mechanics in the ancient world had it not been for the social initiative of British industry," an initiative which derived in turn from the moral and social ideals of Puritanism.[23] The history of this expansion illustrates the extent to which economic—indeed, all human—progress has depended on an intricate relationship of material, geographical, and cultural factors rather than on any one single set of causes. The actual balance of political power at any given time is indeed the product of all these different factors.

[23] C. Dawson, *Progress and Religion* (New York, 1938), pp. 213-215.

CHAPTER 15

The Growing Economic Strength of the Sino-Soviet Bloc

A. *The Soviet Union*

We will begin our consideration of the present world pattern of economic capabilities with the Union of Soviet Socialist Republics (U.S.S.R.) and its system of satellite states usually referred to as the Soviet bloc. It is the great increase in the economic, political, and military power of this group of states in the past three decades that, more than any other factor, accounts for the present tension in international political relationships. The name often given to this tension—the East-West struggle—suggests cultural rather than geographical issues. At the same time, the locus of Communist strength is truly in the Soviet East and China, while the pole around which the anti-Communist states cluster is the economic colossus of the West, the United States. This relationship is an especially fruitful field of study for the student of political geography because it permits him to compare the influence of geographical factors in two rapidly growing economic systems with widely differing social and political institutions. In the one, the United States, it is customary to ascribe the extraordinary progress of technology and industry to a favorable combination of abundant resources and free enterprise. In the other, the U.S.S.R., while natural resources are abundant, they were clearly only a necessary, and not a sufficient, condition of economic progress. Until the Revolution of 1917 Russia was industrially one of the most backward European states, while thereafter the country underwent the most rapid and far-reaching economic development in modern history under the force of a new economic philosophy.

One way of showing how the economic capabilities of the U.S.S.R. have increased under the Communist regime relative to those of Western countries is to compare production of important commodities and services. For example, in 1930 steel production in Russia was only one-seventh of that in the United States and less than one-fourth of the combined output of France, Germany, and Belgium.[1] In 1955 steel production in the U.S.S.R. was over two-fifths of United States output and actually exceeded the combined output of the three Western European countries.[2] If steel production in the United Kingdom is added to the three countries above, Russian steel output increased from a ratio of less than 20 per cent to over 70 per cent.

If the comparison is made with coal we find the U.S.S.R. increasing from about 10 per cent of the United States output and 8 per cent of the four Western European countries in 1930 to about 74 per cent and about 68 per cent respectively in 1955.[3] These increases suggest an extraordinary expansion in the Russian economy relative to rates of growth in the United States and Western Europe. The result is that by 1955 the U.S.S.R., with a population of 217 million, had a gross national product estimated at $149 billion or $687 *per capita* compared with $300 billion, or $891 *per capita* for the free countries of Western Europe with a population of 337 million.

GENERAL FACTORS

After the revolution of 1917, in which Finland and the Baltic states secured their independence, the new U.S.S.R. extended over an area of eight and a quarter million square miles, with a population of perhaps 170 million. The border adjustments after World War II and the reabsorption of the Baltic States increased the area to 8,708,000 square miles, as compared with 3,556,000 square miles in the United States.[4] This vast area extends over 170 degrees of longitude and more than 45 degrees of latitude, but it lies entirely in the Temperate and Arctic Zones. There

[1] W. S. and E. S. Woytinsky, *World Population and Production* (New York, 1954), Table 466, p. 1118.

[2] Department of State, *Indicators of Economic Strength of Western Europe, Canada, the United States, and the Soviet Bloc, 1955,* IR 7247, May 9, 1956.

[3] Comparisons for 1930 based on Woytinsky, *op. cit.,* Table 366, p. 870. For 1953, from Department of State, IR 7247, including West Germany only.

[4] L. D. Stamp and S. C. Gilmour, *Chisholm's Handbook of Commercial Geography,* 14th ed. (New York, 1954), pp. 493 ff.

are a number of characteristics of this land mass which are significant to its economic development.[5]

European Russia, though an enormous country, is almost entirely flat. Western Siberia, separated from Russia in Europe by the modest heights of the Urals, is a continuation of the Great European Plain, while Eastern Siberia, east of the River Lena, is a low plateau. Only the Soviet Far East is mountainous and inaccessible. Distances between cities are great, and road and rail construction is rendered difficult by the softness of the ground and the lack of stone and timber through large areas of the south. The rivers, such as the Volga which flows into the Caspian Sea, and the Dnieper and the Don which flow into the Black Sea, are adaptable to navigation, but most of the U.S.S.R. is far from the sea and has a continental climate with extremes of hot and cold. Consequently the waterways are frozen during the winter, and in Siberia, where they flow northward to the Arctic Ocean, they are usable only a few months in the year. It has often been remarked that the rivers of the U.S.S.R. run in the wrong directions (north and south instead of east and west), and the slight dependence of the U.S.S.R. on inland waterways is suggested by the fact that while nearly 70,000 miles are classed as navigable compared with 77,000 miles of railway, 85 per cent of the freight traffic is carried by rail.[6]

The U.S.S.R. has a short coast line in relation to its area, and only a few year-round ice-free seaports. This, and the lack of overseas possessions, account for the traditional lack of interest in foreign trade and shipping.

A large part of the land area of the U.S.S.R. is not suitable for agriculture. The tundra in the north is the area of permanently frozen subsoil; in the summer the ground is swampy. This land is inhabited by a few Lapps and Samoyedes with their reindeer. In the south, around the Caspian Sea and throughout Soviet Central Asia, the land is mostly desert, arable only where water is available for irrigation. Southern Russia, the Ukraine, and parts of Siberia, however, are famous for their rich black soil which is ideal for growing wheat, while the immense belt of conifer-

[5] The following discussion is limited to such geographical factors as explain the functional features of the Soviet economy as a whole, and are therefore not meant as a substitute for a study of the country's geography in its many ramifications. For this purpose see especially T. Shabad, *The Geography of the U.S.S.R.: A Regional Survey* (New York, 1951), and the bibliography on pp. 3-82.

[6] Stamp and Gilmour, *op. cit.*, p. 509; also *Trends in Economic Growth, A Comparison of the Western Powers and the Soviet Bloc,* prepared by the Legislative Reference Service of the Library of Congress, 1955 (hereafter referred to as *Trends in Economic Growth*), p. 164.

ous forests, stretching across the U.S.S.R. from the Gulf of Finland to the Pacific Ocean, contains the largest stand of virgin softwood in the world.

Thirty-four per cent of the land area of the U.S.S.R. is occupied by forest, 31 per cent by nonarable land, 11 per cent by pasture, and only 9 per cent by arable land. The country is so large, however, that this 9 per cent contains 500 million acres, compared with 353 million acres under cultivation in the United States in 1945.[7] On the other hand, even where the Soviet land can be utilized, the climate makes it difficult. Extremely severe winter weather is encountered throughout the north and center, moderating slightly in the south and southwest. There is hardly a place in the whole of the U.S.S.R. which has an average January temperature above freezing. Lumbering is hampered, livestock must be sheltered, and even in the great cultivated black earth belt the winters are too severe for fall planting of wheat. Only the production of furs in the northern forests seems to be favored by climate.

PEOPLE

The population of the present U.S.S.R. is large and growing.[8] The census for 1897 shows a total population of 125.6 million, that for 1926, 147 million, and the population total in 1955 can be estimated at 217 million. In 1926 almost 82 per cent of the labor force was agricultural. Imperial Russia was predominantly an agricultural country. Serfdom was not abolished until 1861, and in the beginning of the twentieth century most of the peasants were uneducated and unskilled. After the revolution, since the principal economic goal of the new regime was industrialization, there were two main problems. One was to find labor for the growing new industries, the other was to bring twentieth-century skills and technologies to the labor force, both industrial and agricultural. The growth of Soviet population was of some help in solving the first problem but not as much as might have been expected.[9] The average rate of population increase from 1928 to 1939 was only about 2 millions or 1.2 per cent as compared with 2.5 millions or 1.8 per cent over the period 1900 to 1914. This was the period roughly of the first and second five-year plans, in which the attendant social and cultural upheavals depressed the birth rate and raised the death rate. Again population growth was retarded in the war period, 1939 to 1950, the effects of the war on mortality and natality more

[7] Stamp and Gilmour, *op. cit.*, p. 505.

[8] See pp. 312, 315-316.

[9] W. W. Eason, "Population and Labor Force," in A. Bergson, ed., *Soviet Economy Growth* (Evanston, 1953), pp. 102 and 103.

than cancelling the "normal" population increase. However, territorial acquisitions added some twenty million persons to the Soviet population. As a result the total population, which stood at 147 million in 1926, increased to 170.5 million in 1939 and was in the neighborhood of 200 million in 1950.

However, during 1926 to 1939, when the total population increased by about twenty-three million persons, the total labor force increased by only about five million persons due to the rise in school attendance and the loss of females from the labor force which accompanied the migration of people from the farms. On balance, twenty-five million persons migrated from rural to urban areas in the period 1926 to 1939 and in January, 1939, the urban population of the U.S.S.R. was more than twice as great as it had been in 1926.[10] This movement was reflected in a marked increase in the nonagricultural labor force at the expense of the agricultural labor force. The total labor force is estimated to have been between 108.4 million and 115.5 million in 1950. The division of this labor force between agricultural and nonagricultural labor is not known but nonagricultural workers were at least 35 per cent of the total, as against 18 per cent in 1926. Projections of Soviet population to 1970 range from 244 million to 282 million, with the labor force increasing to between 135 million and 160 million.[11]

NATURAL RESOURCES

One would expect an area so vast as the U.S.S.R. to be liberally endowed with natural resources and this is in fact the case [12] (Figs. 15-1, 2). Mention has already been made of the great forests and the vast belt of black earth lands of steppes or prairies. These have permitted the U.S.S.R. to export considerable quantities of timber and wheat. The U.S.S.R. is the world's second largest cotton producer but exported only minor quantities before World War II. At present low levels of domestic consumption the U.S.S.R. can meet its own needs and those of the Eastern European Satellites. However, the U.S.S.R. is a net importer of wool and has no production of cacao, coffee, jute, and rubber.

In minerals and energy supply the Soviet Union equals or surpasses the United States in the variety and adequacy of its resources. The U.S.S.R. is estimated to possess about 23 per cent of the world's known supply of

[10] F. Lorimer, "Population Movements in Imperial Russia and in the Soviet Union," in H. W. Weigert and V. Stefansson, eds., *Compass of the World* (New York, 1945), pp. 443-460 (449).

[11] Eason, *op. cit.*, pp. 116-122, and below, pp. 483 ff.

[12] H. Schwartz, *Russia's Soviet Economy*, 2nd ed. (New York, 1954), Ch. 1.

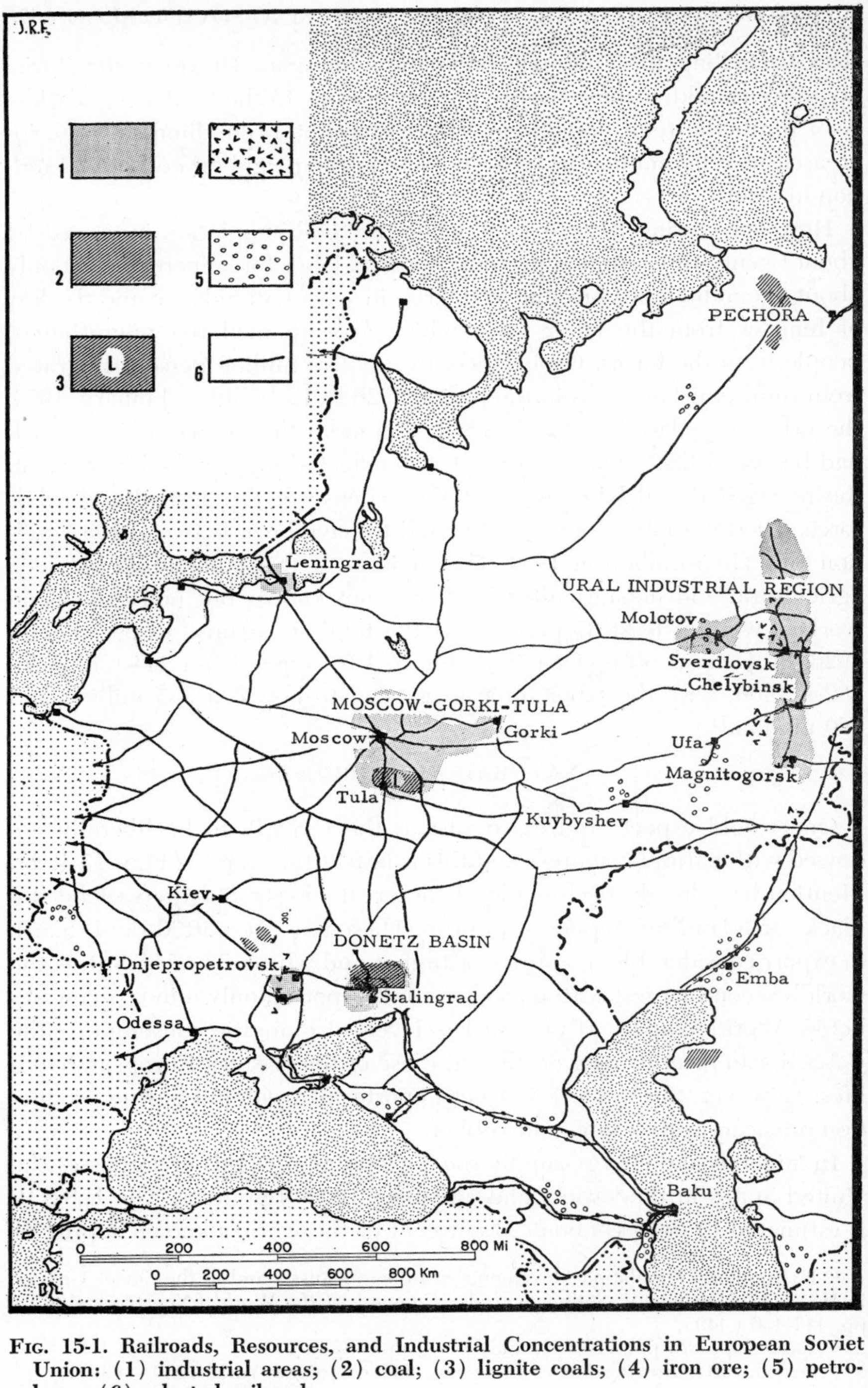

Fig. 15-1. Railroads, Resources, and Industrial Concentrations in European Soviet Union: (1) industrial areas; (2) coal; (3) lignite coals; (4) iron ore; (5) petroleum; (6) selected railroads.

inanimate energy, more than all the rest of Europe and Asia combined (19 per cent) and almost as much as the United States (29 per cent). This superiority is due mainly to coal of which the reserves are estimated at 19 per cent of the world's total, compared with 49 per cent for the United States and Canada, and 34 per cent for the rest of the world.[13] Production of coal in the U.S.S.R. increased very rapidly under the five-year plans, from 40 million tons in 1929 to 281 million tons in 1951. While the U.S.S.R. is now apparently the second largest coal producer in the world, the output of coal has barely kept up with the increasing demands of industry and transportation.[14]

In contrast, the importance of the Soviet Union as a producer of petroleum has declined. Although production had increased to 37.9 million tons in 1950, the fuel value of petroleum in the U.S.S.R. had fallen from equality with coal in 1900 to less than one-fourth, and output in relation to total world production from about 50 per cent in 1901 to about 7 per cent in 1950. The bulk of Soviet petroleum output comes from Azerbaidzhan (Baku) (*cf.* Fig. 15-1), and failure of this and other large fields to expand more rapidly is attributed to failure to obtain maximum output from small "pumping" wells, and to inadequate exploration and development of new fields. Moreover the geographical concentration of Soviet oil output in the Baku-Maikop-Grozny triangle between the Black and Caspian Seas, plus the fact that 40 per cent of the petroleum transported in the U.S.S.R. moves by rail, has put a further strain on Soviet transportation facilities.[15] However, petroleum requirements are still relatively small due to the low use of motor vehicles, and the U.S.S.R. has been able to export between 5 and 10 per cent of its annual production.

Water power, contrary to the popular impression, is not highly developed in the Soviet Union. While the potential production of hydro-electric power in the U.S.S.R. is twice that of the United States, actual output in 1937 was only one-tenth that of the United States, and only about one per cent of the potential yield. Peat and fuel wood are important sources of fuel for industry and thermal stations.

The distribution of energy resources in the U.S.S.R. is poor, nearly 90 per cent of both coal and water power being in the relatively unpopulated Asian part of the U.S.S.R. (*cf.* Fig. 15-2). Moreover, much of the coal, especially from the more accessible mines, is of poor quality and therefore uneconomical to transport over great distances. Water power utiliza-

[13] Woytinsky, *op. cit.*, p. 855.
[14] *New York Times*, March 6, 1955.
[15] Schwartz, *Russia's Soviet Economy*, pp. 234-40; also, *New York Times*, November 2, 1954, "Baku Oil Output in Sharp Decline."

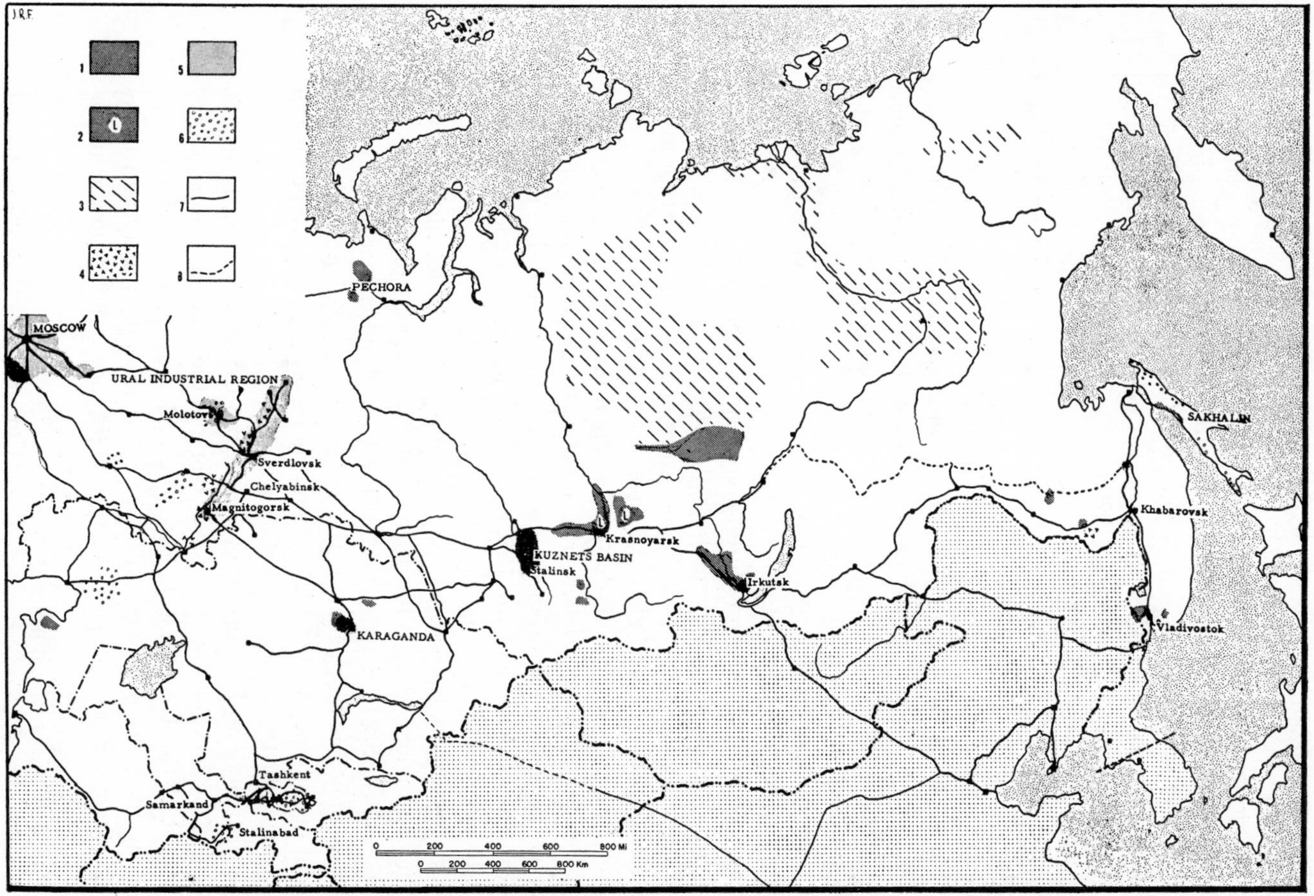

FIG. 15-2. Railroads, Resources and Industrial Concentration in Asian Soviet Union: (1) coal; (2) lignite coals; (3) unproved coal basins; (4) iron ore; (5) industrial areas; (6) petroleum; (7) railroads; (8) proposed railroads.

tion is also hampered by freezing and uneven stream flow. However, planned goals for electricity and coal output aim at equaling the present output of the United States within a decade. These goals can be fulfilled only through a vast increase in the utilization of coal and water power resources in Soviet Asia. According to the Soviet journal, *Problems of Economics,*[16] almost half of the U.S.S.R.'s coal production in 1954 originated in its eastern areas and it is expected that the proportion will rise as new sources are exploited in Soviet Asia. Similarly, the construction of future hydro-electric stations will be concentrated in eastern and western Siberia, particularly on the Angara, Yenisei, and Ob rivers.

The Soviet reserve position with regard to other minerals is very good, although extraction and processing seems to have had difficulty keeping up with expansion.[17] Before World War II the U.S.S.R. exported a number of minerals including petroleum, coal, iron ore, manganese, platinum, phosphates, and asbestos, while importing substantial quantities of non-ferrous metals and iron and steel for industrial expansion. Imports of tin, nickel, tungsten, molybdenum, and lead were stockpiled in increasing amounts. Nevertheless, on balance, mineral exports exceeded imports. During World War II the German armies overran most of the mineral-producing areas and the U.S.S.R. relied very heavily on Lend-Lease imports.

Since the war, because of the rapid increase in Soviet consumption of minerals, and perhaps because of stockpiling, the U.S.S.R. seems to have become a net importer of minerals. Principal mineral imports have been coal, uranium, zinc, cadmium, lead, arsenic, barite, bromine, fluor spar, and potash. It is important to note, however, that imports of these minerals have come largely from the European satellite countries, Poland and East Germany. Other important sources of mineral imports within the Soviet bloc are Manchuria and North Korea (pig iron, tungsten, molybdenum, lead, and zinc) and China (tungsten, tin, and antimony).

In brief, the minerals position of the U.S.S.R. is one of very large known reserves of most of the ferrous metals, fuels, and non-metallic minerals, with deficiencies in non-ferrous metals to some extent compensated for by availabilities in other parts of the Sino-Soviet bloc. Iron ore reserves are ample, although the prospect is one of increasing pig iron costs due to more extensive utilization of lower grade deposits.[18] Manganese and chromium are available for export. Evident deficiencies of the U.S.S.R.

[16] H. Schwartz, *New York Times,* September 25, 1955.

[17] See D. Shimkin's comprehensive study, *Minerals, A Key To Soviet Power* (Cambridge, 1953), especially Ch. 9.

[18] *Ibid.,* pp. 303, 304-345.

include copper, nickel, cobalt, diamonds, lead, molybdenum, uranium, tungsten, and zinc. Satellite sources are capable of reducing or eliminating the inadequacies in lead, molybdenum, uranium, tungsten, and zinc.[19] The ascertained over-all position is about as good as that of the United States, and considering that the U.S.S.R. is still in the pioneering stage of geological exploration while the United States is far advanced, the potential minerals position of the U.S.S.R.—and particularly of the Sino-Soviet bloc as a whole—is probably somewhat better.

The foregoing description has given us a bird's-eye view of the materials from which the Soviet planners are attempting to fashion an industrial base to support the political and military ambitions of the Kremlin: a vast area with a harsh climate, enormous distances to be overcome (and therefore a high proportion of productive effort expended on transportation), a growing population and an increasingly skillful labor force, tremendous supplies of timber and coal, the former hard to get at, the latter poorly distributed, adequate reserves of iron ore, and a minerals position on the whole better than that of any other world power except the United States. What use are the Communists making of these resources to develop the U.S.S.R.'s economic capabilities?

THE SOVIET ECONOMY

The expansion of the industrial economy of the U.S.S.R. under the successive five-year Plans is remarkable. Soviet official estimates, claiming a 16 per cent annual average rate of increase in national income in the period 1928 to 1937, a 19 per cent rate of growth in 1948 to 1950, and 12 per cent for 1950 to 1951 are unreliable. But even estimates by non-Soviet statisticians credit the Soviet Union with rates of growth in national income ranging from 4.5 per cent annually to 8 or 9 per cent for the period 1928 to 1937, and a comparable rate of expansion during the period 1948 to 1950.[20] Rates of growth in industrial production are conceded to be higher than for national income because of the priority given to heavy industry. Official figures show an annual rate of growth of 20.9 per cent for 1927/28 to 1937 and 23 per cent for 1946 to 1950, but Western authorities similarly believe these claims are exaggerated. The following table compares the official index of industrial production in the U.S.S.R. with recent estimates.

[19] Bergson, *op. cit.*, p. 177.
[20] *Ibid.*, p. 9.

TABLE 15-1
Average Annual Percentage Rates of Growth in Soviet Industrial Production *

YEARS	OFFICIAL INDEX	REVISED INDEX
1927/28	23.6	14.5
1932-37	18.7	16.6
1927/28-1937	20.9	15.7
1937-40	11.6	4.7
1946-50	23.0	20.5
1927/28-1950	12.5	8.9

* A. Bergson, ed., *Soviet Economic Growth* (Evanston, 1953), p. 242.

Practically no statistics of physical volume of output of any commodities have been published by the Soviet Union since the late thirties, the only direct sources of information on production being the official indices, statements of plan fulfillment and percentage increases over previous years. However, by various statistical techniques, the following indices have been constructed of industrial production in the U.S.S.R., and for related sectors of the economy.

TABLE 15-2
U.S.S.R.: Industry, Mining, and Transportation *
(1928 = 100)

YEARS	IND. PROD.	MINERALS CONSUMPTION	FREIGHT TRANSPORTATION
1928	100[a]	100	100
1932	172	171	184
1937	371	357	363
1940	430	400	422
1946	304	386	337
1950	646	586	615

[a] 1927-28.
* D. Hodgeman, *Soviet Industrial Production 1928-51* (Cambridge, 1954), p. 91.

Different rates of growth in the Soviet economy are shown in the table giving Soviet net national product by industrial origin: agriculture in 1953 showed little or no increase over 1937, while industry and transportation more than doubled.

From 1928 to 1951 coal production in the U.S.S.R. increased from 35.5 million metric tons to 282 million metric tons; crude oil production from 11.5 million metric tons to 42.3 million metric tons, electric power output from 5 million kilowatt hours to 102.9 billion kilowatt hours, pig iron production from 3.3 million metric tons to 22.1 million metric tons, crude steel production from 4.2 million metric tons to 31.4 million metric tons, and passenger cars and trucks from 600 or 700 to 364,000. By 1950, U.S.S.R. coal output was 52 per cent of that of the United States, steel production 31 per cent, electric power 23 per cent, cement production 27 per cent and woven cotton and woolen fabrics 40 to 45 per cent. "In the short span of thirty years, the Soviet Union has risen from the ranks to become the second most powerful industrial nation in the world." [21]

TABLE 15-3

The Soviet Net National Product, 1937-53 *

INDUSTRY	1937 (1)	1937 (2)	1948 (1)	1948 (2)	1953 (1)	1953 (2)
Agriculture (3)	36	100	28	86	23	102
Industry (4)	34	100	36	121	46	221
Transportation & Communications	7	100	8	120	10	211
Civil and military services	22	100	28	142	21	155
Total gross national Product	100	100	100	113	100	162

(1) Percentage of gross national product in that year, measured in 1937 factor costs (Bergson), adjusted for higher estimates of imputed land rents.
(2) Index, 1937 = 100, in same measure.
(3) Includes imputed land rentals.
(4) Includes manufacturing, handicrafts, mining, forestry, and fisheries (Soviet definition of "Industry"), plus construction.
* H. Block in *Trends in Economic Growth,* p. 284.

A large part of the increased output in the U.S.S.R. has taken the form of investment in capital goods and production for military purposes rather than increased foodstuffs and other goods for consumption. Consequently, the record of production in the latter sectors is not too impressive. A carefully constructed index of consumer goods production gives a figure of 258 for 1950 (1928 = 100), compared with 646 for all large-scale (heavy) industrial production. *Per capita* production of consumer goods in 1950 was less than twice that of 1928 because of the intervening growth in population.[22] Soviet gross agricultural production in 1940 was only 15 per cent above 1927-28 when the collective and state farm programs were started, and by 1950 had risen by no more than a further 10 per cent of 1940 output.[23]

[21] Hodgeman, *op. cit.*, Table A and pp. 128-130.
[22] *Ibid.*, p. 128.
[23] V. Timoshenko, "Agriculture in the Soviet Spotlight," *Foreign Affairs* (January, 1954), pp. 244-258.

This lopsided development of the Soviet economy is due, on the one hand, to the deliberate concentration on heavy industry in Soviet economic planning and, on the other, to both physical and institutional obstacles to the expansion of Soviet agricultural production which will be discussed later.

FACTORS IN SOVIET ECONOMIC GROWTH

The unusual growth of the Soviet economy since the 1930's seems to be due to institutional factors rather than to any favorable combination of physical factors and technology. This is suggested by the relatively slow progress of the Russian economy prior to the revolution and is confirmed by an analysis of the events that followed.

The most important factor was the decision of the Communist rulers to subordinate everything to the expansion of Soviet industry, a decision motivated by Marxist doctrine and made possible by the conditions of totalitarian rule. The mobilization of resources for investment in heavy industry was literally decreed and enforced by the state, while consumption was drastically restricted by wage control, rationing, and the sheer non-availability of many consumer goods. The high priority afforded to heavy industry and transport from the beginning accounts for the high rate of growth in the late thirties and late forties as the process began to pay dividends in output.

Second in importance was the fact that the new industrial technology had already been developed abroad and could readily be copied by importing technicians, prototypes, and plans. A large part of the high growth rate of the Soviet economy is explainable in terms of this process of catching up with the highly industrialized states of the West.

In analytical terms, the expansion of output in the U.S.S.R. can be attributed to (1) an expansion in the total labor force, (2) an increase in labor productivity, and (3) a shift in employment of labor from occupations of lower to those of higher marginal productivity. We have referred above to the growth of the labor force. Labor productivity in the U.S.S.R. also increased markedly, although by not nearly enough to explain the large increases in output. The most important component in the increase in Soviet product during the period 1928 to 1937 appears to have been the shift of labor from agricultural to nonagricultural employments where marginal productivity was higher,[24] a transfer which increased the nonagricultural labor force, on the average, by about 10 per cent annually

[24] G. Grossman, "National Income," Ch. 1 in Bergson, *op. cit.*, pp. 13, 14.

during this period. Increasing labor productivity appears to have been more important in the late thirties and in the postwar period.

In many respects the physical and geographical factors seemed to hinder rather than aid the expansion of the Soviet economy. Mention has already been made of the relatively slow rate of growth in petroleum production, and exploitation of other mineral resources has apparently run into increasing production costs and unfavorable geographical distribution of resources. The vastness of the land area and the distances to be traversed by the transportation system in the U.S.S.R. posed major problems (*cf.* Figs. 15-1, 2, pp. 476, 478). As Chauncy Harris put it:

> The negative economic role of the area looms even larger when one considers the human emptiness of most of it. Most of the people of the Soviet Union live in what is called the Fertile Triangle with its corners at Leningrad on a gulf of the Baltic Sea, at Odessa on the Black Sea, and at the Kuznetsk Basin in Siberia. The Triangle includes about one million square miles, an area roughly equivalent to the United States east of the Mississippi River. With the exception of the Caucasus and the oases of Central Asia most of the rest of the Soviet Union is relatively bare space which must be crossed by long transport lines.[25]

This factor, plus the heavy reliance on solid instead of liquid fuel, has greatly increased the share of resources that have to be devoted to transportation. The Soviet transport co-efficient (percentage of total output devoted to transportation) is the highest in the world and 40 per cent higher than in the United States.[26] This is readily seen from a comparison of ton-miles of freight carried, for example in 1953: 605 billion ton miles for the United States and 538 billion for the U.S.S.R. with less than one-third the gross national product.[27] In the twenties, Soviet planners resisted the need to expand the rail and other transportation systems because of a doctrinaire notion that transportation represented an unproductive activity. When this neglect threatened a breakdown in industrial activity, a more energetic policy was adopted, both with regard to the expansion of the system and the efficiency of operations.[28] However, the desire to minimize the resources allocated to transportation conflicted with the need to develop outlying areas containing untapped resources. The result was a decision to locate industrial development in five relatively concentrated and more or less self-sufficient regions.[29] Official theory does not

[25] *Ibid.*, p. 164.
[26] D. Shimkin, quoted in *Trends in Economic Growth*, p. 165.
[27] *Trends in Economic Growth*, Table 60, p. 171.
[28] Schwartz, *Russia's Soviet Economy*, pp. 389-404. The basic work in this field is H. Hunter's *The Economics of Soviet Railroad Policy* (Cambridge, Mass., 1949).
[29] See Fig. 14-3, p. 468.

appear to recognize that such a policy may tend to retard the over-all growth of output by limiting opportunities to reduce costs through a wider geographical division of labor.[30] The future expansion of Soviet railroads will depend on whether these policies of regional self-sufficiency and equalization remain in force. If they do not, there will be a greater need for interregional rail transportation. In a speech delivered in April, 1954, First Deputy Premier Kaganovich admitted that the regional self-sufficiency policies were being ignored and cross-hauling was occurring on a large scale because nobody "cared where goods are coming from or asked about transport costs. . . . They are all only interested in getting the goods at all." [31]

If all Soviet railway construction were regulated exclusively by Soviet economic location theory, the result would be a railway system constructed without regard to strategic requirements. While Soviet planners have perhaps not constructed exactly the kind of railway system Halford Mackinder would have expected, they have evidently taken strategic factors into account, as in the double-tracking of the trans-Siberian over its entire distance, the construction of the south trans-Siberian, and the reported construction of the Baikal-Amur (northern trans-Siberian) road. Another departure from the orthodox location theory may be evident in a program for construction of an entirely new rail network in southwestern Siberia to handle grain produced under the new "conquest of virgin lands" program to increase agricultural output and food supplies for the urban population.[32]

SOVIET FOREIGN TRADE

Soviet economic policy has always aimed at eventual *autarky* (self-sufficiency). Nevertheless imports played an important part in accelerating the rate of industrialization especially during the thirties. A brief discussion of the role of foreign trade is necessary to an understanding of the economic capabilities of the Soviet bloc.

Soviet foreign trade policy, as explained in 1934 to the Seventeenth Party Congress by Foreign Trade Commissar Rozengoltz, "meant that by

[30] For a further examination of this point see Bergson, *op. cit.*, p. 158, comments by H. Hunter on J. Blackman's paper on "Soviet Transportation" (Ch. 4); also D. Shimkin, "Economic Regionalization in the Soviet Union," *Geographical Review*, Vol. 42 (October, 1952), pp. 596-614; also Schwartz, *op. cit.*, p. 400.

[31] Schwartz, *Russia's Soviet Economy*, p. 403; also *The Tablet* (London, September 4, 1954), pp. 222-223.

[32] T. Shabad, "Soviet Adds Rails in New Grain Area," *New York Times*, May 15, 1955.

extending our economic contact with the capitalist world and introducing the latest technical innovations and speeding up our socialist construction by means of considerable imports over a definite period of time, we should prepare for the next stage—the continuation of socialist construction on the basis of a contraction of imports."[33]

Foreign trade of the U.S.S.R. expanded from virtually nothing in the first two or three years after the revolution to a peak in the late twenties and early thirties when the U.S.S.R., embarked on its first five-year plan of rapid industrialization, was desperately demanding imported capital goods. Foodstuffs (despite widespread famine in the Ukraine), timber, petroleum, and industrial raw materials were exchanged for producers' goods (machinery and equipment), on terms that became distinctly unfavorable to the U.S.S.R. because the world-wide depression affected prices of raw materials much more than the prices of finished goods. After 1931 the volume of foreign trade fell off and by 1940 the Ministry of Foreign trade was congratulating itself on the fact that the U.S.S.R. ranked second in industrial production and nineteenth in foreign trade.[34] At that time the Soviet economist Mishustin reiterated that Soviet foreign trade policy was "to utilize foreign products and above all foreign machinery . . . for the technical and economic independence of the U.S.S.R. . . . The speediest liberation from the need to import."

During World War II the liberation from imports was temporarily suspended and the U.S.S.R. received almost $13 billion worth of goods, most of it from the United States, under lend-lease arrangements. Lend-lease deliveries averaged about $3 billion annually, far greater than the highest prewar level of imports in 1931.

Analysis of the course of Soviet foreign trade in the postwar period is complicated by the paucity of data relating to trade between the U.S.S.R. and the European satellites and China. In 1953 trade between the Free World and the Communist bloc as a whole was only about one-third the pre-World War II volume of trade carried on between the two sets of countries, whereas trade within the Communist bloc was reported to be ten times the prewar volume. The principal reason for these differences is that the countries of Eastern Europe before World War II conducted most of their trade with Western Europe. Since the war their trade has

[33] A. P. Rozengoltz, *The USSR and the Capitalist World* (Moscow, 1934), p. 4, quoted by L. Herman, "The New Soviet Posture in World Trade," *Problems of Communism*, Vol. 3, No. 6 (Washington, D. C., 1954).

[34] Bakulin and Mishustin, *Statistika Vneshnei Torgovli* (Moscow, 1940), p. 299, quoted by L. Herman, *op. cit.*

been forcibly re-directed inward, to the U.S.S.R. and with one another. This is shown in the following estimates of the volume of intra-bloc trade for 1947 and 1951.

TABLE 15-4

Intra-Bloc Trade *
U.S.S.R. and Eastern European Satellites

	1947 [a]		*1951* [a]	
COUNTRY	U.S.S.R. IMPORTS	U.S.S.R. EXPORTS	U.S.S.R. IMPORTS	U.S.S.R. EXPORTS
Albania	6.5	6.5	12.0	12.0
Bulgaria	44.7	45.6	66.9	86.4
Czechoslovakia	27.9	38.9	222.5	247.5
Hungary	13.4	14.5	117.1	111.2
Poland	70.5	79.5	190.0	235.0
Rumania	19.9	29.9	119.7	122.5
E. Germany	16.0	11.0	176.0	250.0
Totals	198.9	225.9	904.2	1064.6

[a] Millions of United States dollars.
* Estimated by Leon Herman, given in H. Schwartz, *Russia's Soviet Economy,* 2nd ed. (New York, 1954), pp. 614-615.

In 1938 these countries supplied the U.S.S.R. with only $30 million of goods or 11 per cent of its total imports. In 1952 the bloc furnished over $1 billion of imports [35] or almost 70 per cent of total Soviet imports. In general this trade consists of an exchange of Soviet manufactured and semi-manufactured goods for satellite raw materials and foodstuffs. However, East Germany, Czechoslovakia, and Poland supply some machinery and transport equipment and minerals.

Trade between the U.S.S.R. and the Free World in the period 1947 to 1953 has fluctuated between $300 million and $500 million annually in imports and $250 million to $500 million in exports (current prices). Trade between the European satellites and the Free World increased to $1.1 billion in exports and $900 million in exports in 1948 and 1949. It declined to about $800 million in exports and $700 million in imports in 1953. The satellites have had a visible trade surplus which, with occasional gold sales has helped the U.S.S.R. to balance its visible trade deficit with the Free World. Details of U.S.S.R. and bloc trade are given in the following table.

[35] Official statistics of Free World countries, compiled by the United States Department of Commerce.

TABLE 15-5

Soviet Bloc Free World Trade, 1947-54 *
(Millions of United States Dollars at Current Prices)

	1947	1949	1953
Free World Exports to:			
U.S.S.R.	477	437	438
European Satellites	857	919	682
Total	1,334	1,356	1,120
Free World Imports from:			
U.S.S.R.	271	272	385
European Satellites	733	1,090	810
Total	1,004	1,362	1,195

* See footnote 35.

The volume of this trade has been limited not only by the multilateral export controls over "strategic" commodities enforced by the principal Free World trading countries operating through a Co-ordinating Committee in Paris, but also by the inability or unwillingness of the U.S.S.R. to deliver its traditional exports of grain, timber, and raw materials. Soviet offers to sell capital goods on favorable credit terms, especially to underdeveloped countries, have been until recently mostly propaganda statements.

While the foreign (East-West) trade that is permitted undoubtedly makes a contribution to Soviet economic growth, its volume is now too small in relation to Soviet production and national income to make a significant difference in the rate of this growth. The period when foreign trade made a vital and indispensable contribution to Soviet economic growth was in the late twenties and the thirties; it is too late now to expect to do much damage to the Soviet economy by export controls or other devices of economic warfare. The importance of intra-bloc trade is a somewhat different matter; although the value of this trade is roughly twice the value of the East-West trade of the European Soviet [36] bloc and it may present greater advantages to the U.S.S.R. because of its permanence, and the much greater degree of control the U.S.S.R. can exert in regard to prices, quality, and other considerations.[37]

Since 1953 the Soviet bloc has waged a new campaign of economic diplomacy in non-Communist underdeveloped areas designed to increase

[36] Economic Commission for Europe, *Economic Survey of Europe in 1954* (Geneva, 1955), Table 63, p. 111.
[37] See p. 28.

trade and other economic relations with these areas. The principal elements have been offers to purchase goods in excess supply and to supply credits and technical assistance for economic development. In some cases military equipment has been offered in exchange for raw materials like cotton.

PROSPECTS FOR FUTURE GROWTH

We have seen that the economy of the U.S.S.R. has been characterized by quite high rates of growth under the various five-year plans, rates that, if continued, would seem to make Stalin's famous production goals (50 million metric tons of pig iron, 60 million metric tons of steel, 500 million metric tons of coal and 60 million metric tons of petroleum) [38] easily attainable by 1960. A number of factors, however, suggest that recent rates of increase may not be maintained. Among these are the recent indications of a growing need for more housing, consumer goods, and foodstuffs. Housing is notoriously poor in the U.S.S.R. in terms both of quality and quantity. Even to supply the growing population over the next several decades with sufficient housing by present standards will require much larger investment in housing than the postwar rate. Housing also competes for some of the same materials and labor as investment in industry. Increased consumer goods means primarily more clothing made from scarce fibers, cotton and wool. To increase output of these "technical crops" is to add to the agricultural problem.

We have seen that gross agricultural production increased by only 23 per cent between 1928 and 1950, not enough to keep up with population growth. If a population increase to 260 million people by 1970 is assumed, this would require a 30 per cent increase in output of foodstuffs over 1950 merely to keep *per capita* consumption from falling. Despite official assurances that heavy industry and transport will continue to receive priority, it is obvious that to increase *per capita* agricultural production will require intensive efforts and probably a heavier investment than previously, since during the period 1928 to 1950 agriculture received an estimated 15 to 20 per cent of total investment with no appreciable increase in *per capita* output.[39]

The problem of expanding agricultural output is so crucial to the general outlook for the economy of the U.S.S.R. that it deserves at least a brief examination here.

[38] Speech of February 9, 1946.

[39] N. Kaplan, "Capital Formation and Allocation" in Bergson, *op. cit.*, p. 52.

Soviet agriculture suffers from difficulties of an institutional, physical, and economic character.[40] During the early thirties the Communists virtually made war on the peasants for resisting collectivization. Agricultural production declined and one-half of all the livestock were killed. There were 10 million fewer cattle in the U.S.S.R. in 1953 than in 1928, with 90 per cent of the decline being in cows.

After Stalin's death, the new regime promised better food as well as more food to a population that has long been confined to a diet of bread and potatoes. But better food means meat, milk, and lard as well as fruits and vegetables. Animal crops require several times more land and labor than vegetable food, and some of the technical crops require a subtropical climate. The area of subtropical climate is very limited in the U.S.S.R. and most of it is very dry. Recent efforts to increase the number of livestock have failed, mainly because of the scarcity of fodder but also partly because the collective farm organization is not well adapted to the intensive forms of agriculture. Moreover until recently the remuneration of collective farm members engaging in animal husbandry averaged about one-fourth of that received for the cultivation of technical crops (cotton).

Expanding the supply of food grains comes up against the fact that all the good arable land in the U.S.S.R.—according to present technology—is already cultivated, with 70 per cent in grain and with only one-third of the grain area devoted to feed grains. As a consequence, great emphasis is being placed on increasing the acre-yield of grain, and the current five-year plan (1951-55) calls for an increase of 40 per cent, an accomplishment not likely to be realized in view of past performance and the fact that 1953 and 1954 both saw poor harvests.

Among the measures that have been adopted are Stalin's "Plan for the Transformation of Nature" calling for extensive shelter belts and reforestation through the European steppes, crop rotation, and water conservation, and, more recently, Kruschev's campaign for the "conquest of virgin land" calling for the ploughing of 15 million hectares of new land per year in 1954, 1955, and 1956. This is calculated to provide 60 million tons of additional grain by 1957. The virgin land to be "conquered" is in the northern Caucasus, the Volga region, the Urals, in Western Siberia, and Kazakhstan. Kazakhstan has an area of 1,072,797 square miles, three times the size of Texas (267,000 square miles), with a population (1939) of 6,000,000, of which 1,700,000 lived in cities. The "conquest" will be organized by large state farms (Sovkhoses) rather than collective farms

[40] The discussion is based largely on Timoshenko, *op. cit.*

(kolkhoses), since state farms can be more easily set up and controlled. According to Soviet claims [41] the total sown area in Kazakhstan was 9 million hectares in 1954, and the goal for 1955 was 18.6 million; for 1956, 28.5 million hectares. There are 50,000 new houses projected for 1955 and 100,000 for 1956. All these figures illustrate an undeniably strong pressure to bring new land under the plough, especially in Kazakhstan and Western Siberia, in a task which, if successful, would extend the core areas of Soviet grain production into Soviet Asia. The goal is to create a new wheatland area with a production to rival that of the Ukraine; an eastward migration of "volunteers" from Russia and the Ukraine, and the earmarking of 120,000 tractors for this operation lend emphasis to this battle for grain.

Additional land is also being reclaimed by four big irrigation projects on the Dnieper, the Volga, the Don, and the Amu Darya rivers. These projects are expected to provide only about 15 million acres for crops, but about 55 million acres of grazing lands, mainly in the arid and desert lands north and east of the Caspian. Water from the Volga must be used sparingly because of the falling level of the Caspian Sea.

It remains to be seen how effective these measures will be. It would be an extreme and rash judgment to conclude that the problem of expanding agricultural output could not be solved by an economy whose accomplishments in other fields of output have been so considerable. The likelihood is, however, that the obstacles to be overcome will require not only larger investments in agriculture but perhaps also greater incentive payments to members of collective farms. In the process the share of output going to investment in industry might well be noticeably reduced, and the share of output represented by consumer goods increased. The net result of such developments, considering the lower average productivity in agriculture, would be to reduce the over-all rate of growth of the Soviet economy. On the other hand, higher standards of living may help to keep average industrial labor productivity up to the 1950-53 average increase of 4.5 to 5 per cent annually despite lower aggregate investment. If the productivity of agricultural labor could be raised by the new measures by about 3 per cent annually, a continuation of over-all economic growth at the rate of about 4.5 to 5 per cent is not out of the realm of probability. This would mean roughly a doubling of national product between 1953 and 1970.[42]

[41] *The Economist,* March 20, 1954, pp. 873-874; also November 3, 1954, p. 568.

[42] For the detailed derivation of this projection see *Trends in Economic Growth,* pp. 219-222.

B. *Eastern Europe—the Soviet Satellites*

The European satellites of the U.S.S.R. (*cf.* Fig. 5-6, p. 133) add 95 million people, and an area of 392,000 square miles to the mass, if not to the unity and power of the Soviet bloc. They comprise Poland, Eastern Germany, Czechoslovakia and the Balkan states: Hungary, Rumania, Bulgaria, and Albania. Compared with Western Europe, the combined industrial power of these states is not great (*cf.* Fig. 17-1, p. 540). Nevertheless, as we have seen, the productive capacity of the European satellites is significant because it is more or less at the disposal of the Soviet planners, through redirection of the satellites' foreign trade as well as by more direct political and administrative devices, and we must take account of it in any assessment of the over-all capabilities of the Soviet bloc. This is not hard to do in the gross, for we have, by virtue of recent historical data, a more accurate notion of the main economic factors of these countries than of the U.S.S.R. However there is little statistical information available for the postwar period to indicate the precise patterns and levels of economic activity in the various countries, and the volume and composition of their trade with the U.S.S.R. is likewise shrouded in official secrecy.

The over-all contribution of Eastern Europe to the economic capabilities of the Soviet bloc is summarized in the accompanying table.

TABLE 15-6

Economic Capabilities (1955) of the European Satellites *

	UNIT	EUROPEAN SATELLITES	U.S.S.R.
Population	Millions	95	217
Gross Nat. Product	Billion dollars	50	149
" " " Per Capita	Dollars	526	687
Coal Production	Million M.T.	218	330
Crude Steel Prod.	Million M.T.	14	45
Electric Power	Million KWH	74	170
Crude Petroleum	Million M.T.	15	71

* Dept. of State IR 7247.

The greatest concentration in Eastern Europe of industrial strength, as well as of population, is in Poland, East Germany, and Czechoslovakia. Albania and Bulgaria at the other extreme are almost exclusively agrarian economies with a peasant culture. Hungary and Rumania are also predominantly agricultural, but together produced about 4.5 million metric tons of crude petroleum in 1948, the last year for which Rumanian production data are available. Hungarian oil production was estimated at

500,000 tons in 1952.[43] The following table shows some of the differences in the relative economic importance of the various Eastern European countries.

TABLE 15-7

Population and Economic Activity, Eastern Europe

COUNTRY	POPULATION (Millions) 1950[a]	HARD COAL PROD. (Millions M.T.) 1951[d]	STEEL PROD. (Millions M.T.) 1951[d]	ELECTRIC POWER (Billions KWH) 1951[d]
Poland	25.0[b]	82.0	2.8	11.1
E. Germany	21.0[c]	3.2	1.5	20.8
Rumania	16.3[c]	0.3	0.7	2.5
Czechoslovakia	12.4	17.9	3.3	10.3
Hungary	9.4	1.8	1.2	3.3
Bulgaria	7.2	—	—	1.0
Albania	1.2[c]	—	—	—

[a] Economic Commission For Europe (ECE), *Growth and Stagnation in the European Economy* (Geneva, 1954), p. 237.
[b] United Nations, *Statistical Year Book,* 1953 (New York, 1953), pp. 29-30, 1950 census.
[c] *Ibid.*, estimates for 1952.
[d] ECE, *Economic Survey of Europe Since the War* (Geneva, 1954), pp. 244-246.

Before World War II foodstuffs accounted for more than two-thirds of total exports in Bulgaria and Rumania and more than one-half in Hungary. The evidence suggests that in the postwar years investment in agriculture in these countries was neglected in favor of highly publicized industrialization plans, with a consequent falling off of food production and exports. This tendency was de-emphasized after Stalin's death with results that are not yet ascertainable. Extensive land reform schemes in Eastern Europe have broken up the large estates and a relentless struggle against the more prosperous peasants (kulaks) and also those peasants suspected of anti-Communist sentiments is still in progress. In spite of widespread, mostly passive, resistance by the peasants, the Communist regimes are pressing their programs of collectivization. Throughout the satellite countries, the peasant is subject to rigid state controls in regard to production and marketing.

In other sectors of the economies of Eastern Europe, according to official claims, socialization has been carried to the extent that between 70 and 95 per cent of the value of output is being produced in the socialized sectors.

Estimates of the trade of Eastern Europe with the U.S.S.R. and data on trade with the Free World were given above. As was indicated, little is known about the precise composition of this trade. East Germany and

[43] United Nations, *Statistical Year Book,* 1953, p. 111.

Czechoslovakia, and to a lesser extent, Poland and Hungary supply metals, engineering products, and chemicals both to the U.S.S.R. and the other satellites. East Germany is an important source of uranium for the Soviet atomic energy program, as well as a supplier of electrical equipment and precision mechanical and optical products. Poland supplies coal and Hungary bauxite. The U.S.S.R. supplies raw materials and foodstuffs to Czechoslovakia and East Germany.[44]

It is reasonably clear that the volume of this trade (which until recently included some reparations deliveries from East Germany, Hungary, and Rumania) is fairly substantial and that its composition and terms are controlled by the U.S.S.R. in its favor. What is not completely clear is the extent to which the integration of the Eastern European countries with the U.S.S.R. enters into the economic planning of these countries and of intra-bloc trade. Official Soviet and satellite spokesmen have repeatedly declared that economic integration of the satellites is the aim of Soviet policy, and that investment and trade plans will emphasize the comparative advantages of the satellites to bring about an intra-bloc specialization and division of labor. According to Oleg Hoeffding,

> A writer in *Bol'shevik*, for instance, has denied any intention of turning the satellite states "separately into self-sufficient units," and affirmed division of labor among them as the objective. Each member must industrialize, with emphasis on heavy industry, but "there is no need for them to create simultaneously all branches of heavy industry, which in any event would be too heavy a task for most of these countries." Each country should develop "those heavy industries whose expansion is favored by local conditions (such as an adequate raw materials base), and those whose products are relatively scarce in the socialist camp as a whole. Of course, the range of such industries will be wider in the industrially stronger countries, e.g., Czechoslovakia, Poland and Hungary, than in Rumania, Bulgaria or Albania."[45]

Such a policy of integration may well be in conflict with overriding geopolitical and strategic considerations, according to which the U.S.S.R. may wish to keep these states viable, to levy on them for military purposes, and to keep the populations in a state of relative docility, all in order to enhance their ability to provide a defensive buffer against possible attack from Western Europe, or alternatively a staging area for a Soviet drive in the other direction. Nevertheless there is developing a fairly extensive economic interdependence between Eastern Europe and the U.S.S.R.

[44] O. Hoeffding, "Soviet Economic Relations with the Orbit" in Bergson, *op. cit.*, pp. 331-334.

[45] *Ibid.*, p. 327, the inner quotations are from an article by I. Dudinski in *Bol'shevik*, No. 19 (1950), p. 33.

C. *Communist China*

INTRODUCTION

The rise of Communism to power in China at the mid-point of the twentieth century poses some interesting problems for the student of political geography. What has the Communization of China done—what will it do—to the geographical distribution of power, not only as between "East" and "West" but also within the Soviet Bloc?

China is a country of about 3.5 million square miles and roughly 600 million people [46] compared to 9.1 million square miles and 300 million people in the European Soviet Bloc.

Is this vast area with its teeming population as significant an addition to the mass and might of Soviet power as a comparison merely of size and numbers would indicate? In modern times China had never been an effectively unified national state. Its industrial and military power remained slight, and throughout the nineteenth and the first half of the twentieth centuries China was a pawn of the Western imperial powers and of Japan. Can such a community contribute very greatly to the power of the Soviet bloc? And if, as recent evidence suggests, China under the ruthless discipline of Communism will eventually develop industrial and military resources to match its size and population, will these new capabilities be placed wholly at the service of the center of Communist power in Moscow? Or will Communism in China be subjected to the immemorial experience of other invasions—military, political and cultural—and produce a Sinicized Communism rather than a Sovietized China? In this chapter we will confine ourselves to the first question: what economic capabilities, present and potential, can China contribute to the power of Soviet Communism? In thus limiting our appraisal, however, we do not assume that these tangible capabilities are more significant than are the intangible elements affecting China's power position.

GENERAL FEATURES OF THE CHINESE ECONOMY

The China taken over by the Communists was a dual economy: one small part urban-industrial, the other and far larger part rural, peasant, agricultural. In the modern part of the economy were large coastal cities

[46] Actually 582.6 million for mainland China as of June 30, 1953, according to Peiping's National Bureau of Statistics (*New York Times*, November 2, 1954). Prior to this the generally accepted figure was around 475 million. See Chapter 9, pp. 300-301, 325.

like Shanghai, Canton, and Tientsin, but four-fifths of the population lived as peasants on small, three or four acre farms and agricultural production constituted 70 per cent of China's national income. Population density was greater than in any other part of mainland Asia except India, because of the favorable effect of the monsoon rains on the growth of vegetable crops in the eastern plain where most of the population is concentrated.

PRINCIPAL GEOGRAPHICAL REGIONS [47]

Economic activity in China shows the effect of climate and other physical features of the geography. Most of China is north of the Tropical Zone, extending from about 18° to 53° North, and most of it is mountainous. However, China has an extensive sea coast, with many excellent harbors, adjacent to which are the great alluvial plains drained by the Hwang Ho (Yellow) and Yangtse rivers. These plains extend from north of Peiping to south of the Yangtse.

South of the Great Wall "China proper" is divided into three fairly distinct geographical regions, South, Central, and North China. South China is a mountainous region with forests producing lumber, tung oil, camphor, wax, and bamboo. The warm rainy summers are favorable to a number of sub-tropical crops, such as rice, sugar cane, and cotton, which are cultivated in the alluvial valleys. Tea is grown on the mountain sides, especially in Fukien Province. Many of the people of the maritime regions are fishermen or coastal traders; some are pirates. To the west the land rises to the mountains of Tibet through limestone hills containing tin and other minerals. The principal river of this region is the Si-kiang, which rises in the plateau of Yünnan and, crossing Kwangsi Province, creates a great delta at the head of which lies Canton, a major port city where silk, woolen, and cotton goods are manufactured. It is from this area of China that most overseas Chinese have migrated, because here the environment was most favorable to population growth.

Central China is dominated by the Yangtse River, the longest of China's great rivers. In the Yangtse valley the summer rains last longer and there is a second period of rainfall in September and October. The winters, while cold, are neither so harsh nor so dry as those of North China. This

[47] For a detailed description see G. B. Cressey, *Asia's Land and Peoples,* 2nd ed. (New York, 1951), pp. 34-165, and the comprehensive bibliography on pp. 551-557; also W. G. East and O. H. K. Spate, *The Changing Map of Asia* (London, 1950), pp. 249-277; for an excellent brief summary of China's "geographical setting" see K. S. Latourette, *A History of Modern China* (London, 1954), pp. 17-23.

valley of about 700,000 square miles contains more than one-third of the population of China. In its upper regions, the Red Basin, above the Ichang Gorge, the crops include wheat, rice, millet, sugar, tobacco, and tea. In the central basins and delta of the Yangtse the land is intensively cultivated to produce wheat, rice, cotton, tea, and silk. Here also are some important manufacturing cities (Fig. 15-3): Hankow (cotton, hemp, and flour mills), Hanyang (iron and steel), Nanking (cotton, silk, and paper mills), and Shanghai, the chief entrepôt for central China, one of the largest Chinese cities, and, formerly at least, the financial center of all China. The Yangtse is navigable to Hankow for ocean-going ships.

The third principal region of "China proper" comprises the great plains of North China and the loess plateau of the northwest. This part of China is covered with the famous yellow soil known as loess, borne from inner Asia on the dry northwest winter winds. The summers are warm, with not so much rain as farther south, and the winters are very cold. Though extremely fertile, loess is porous and does not retain moisture long. The crops in this region are therefore unusually susceptible to damage by drought. The staple crops are wheat, peas, beans, and millet. This area is drained by the Hwang Ho, called "China's Sorrow" because of its disastrous flooding. The Shantung Peninsula, a hilly region lying between the old and new (1852) beds of the Hwang Ho is the most important silk-producing region in China. The Hwang Ho is not navigable by vessels of any size.

The barriers between these three districts have not been so great as to preclude cultural and political unity.[48] Great as are the distances between the farthest margins, "the space relations of Peiping, Nanking and Canton at least in terms of air travel are comparable with those of Stockholm, Prague and Rome, those of Nanking and Chunking with London and Prague." [49]

It is in the eighteen provinces of "China proper," [50] with the three main divisions just described, that the human life, culture, and economic activity of traditional China were concentrated. These eighteen provinces contain almost all of the agricultural land of China except that in the northeastern provinces (Manchuria). One authority [51] has preferred to combine "China proper" with the soy bean-kaoliang area of Manchuria and to speak of agricultural China in contrast to outer China to the west.

[48] Latourette, *op. cit.*, p. 18.
[49] East and Spate, *op. cit.*, p. 250.
[50] *Ibid.*, p. 262, for a map showing the eighteen provinces of "China proper" in relation to the outlying provinces.
[51] Cressey, *op. cit.*, p. 100.

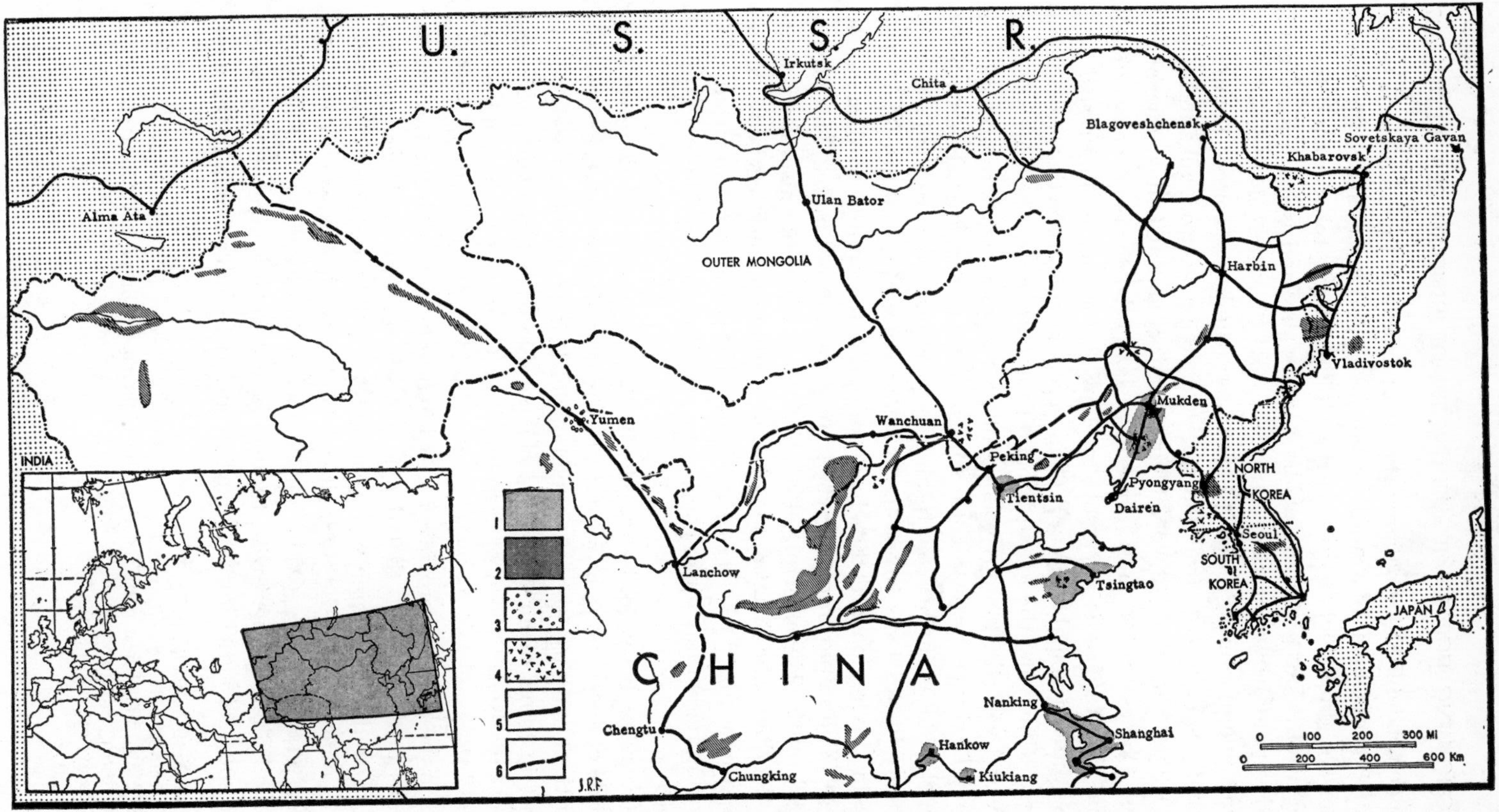

FIG. 15-3. Railroads, Resources, and Industrial Concentration of Northern China: (1) industrial areas; (2) coal deposits; (3) petroleum; (4) iron ore; (5) railroads; (6) railroads: projected and under construction.

Agricultural China is subdivided in turn into nine agricultural regions, four in the wheat, millet, and kaoliang areas of the north and five in the rice-producing regions of the south.[52] These areas include about 1,660,000 square miles, or less than half of greater China which also includes Inner Mongolia, Sinkiang, and Tibet.

The Chinese Empire in the nineteenth century possessed a number of outlying dependencies, including Manchuria, Mongolia, Sinkiang (Chinese Turkestan), and Tibet. So many Chinese migrated to Manchuria in the early part of this century that it is now overwhelmingly Chinese and is referred to as the Northeastern Provinces. Manchuria is industrially the most important region of present-day China, due to the Japanese who built railways and developed mines and factories there, finally seizing the country in 1932 and setting up a puppet state. Outer Mongolia, north of the Gobi, and the historic seat of the Mongols, broke away from China under the Republic and became the Peoples Republic of Outer Mongolia under Soviet domination. The Communists have once more established Chinese sovereignty over Tibet and Sinkiang. These enormous territories are sparsely populated and at present of little or no importance economically. However, they loom large as strategic areas, to be developed by new railways, highways, and air routes, between Soviet Central Asia and Communist China.

NATURAL RESOURCES

Since China is still primarily agricultural, its most important resource is its arable land. Over half of the area of China consists of waste (large areas are seriously eroded) or is built upon; 20 per cent is pastoral country (mostly in Mongolia, Sinkiang, and Tibet) and the remainder is about equally divided between woodland and arable land. In absolute figures, there are about 750,000 square miles of pastoral land, 325,000 square miles of woodland and 350,000 square miles of arable land. With a population of 582.6 million, there is thus about 0.38 of an acre of arable land *per capita.*[53] An earlier estimate puts the total cultivated land at 362,082 square miles, or 27 per cent for the twenty-two provinces and 425,000 square miles, or nearly 12 per cent, for all of greater China.[54] This estimate would give 0.45 acres *per capita* which by coincidence is the same as much earlier official estimates. The twenty-two provinces are the eighteen

[52] *Ibid.*, p. 96.

[53] Stamp and Gilmour, *op. cit.*, p. 613, based on Food and Agriculture Organization (FAO) reports covering 22 provinces.

[54] Cressey, *op. cit.*, pp. 89, 90, based on J. L. Buck, *Land Utilization in China* (Chicago, 1937).

provinces of "China proper" referred to above, plus the two provinces, Chahar and Jehol, of inner Mongolia and the two provinces, Tsinghai and Sikang, of eastern Tibet. These twenty-two provinces, though excluding the northeastern provinces (Manchuria), contain nearly 2 million square miles and over 80 per cent of the arable land. More than 90 per cent of the people of China live in these provinces.

While the soil, whether of the alluvial river valleys of central and south China, or of the loess plateaus of the north, is fertile and moreover is intensively cultivated, population pressure is probably high. Over-all population density for Greater China is about 167 persons per square mile based on 3.5 million square miles and close to 600 million people. This is a moderate density when compared with Japan (601), Belgium (740), or the Netherlands (830).[55] For "China proper" or "agricultural China," however, the population density would be in the neighborhood of 275 to 315 per square mile. In terms of cultivated land, however, the average density of population would be more like 1,400 persons per square mile, and in places there are over 2,000.[56]

China is between the first and second stages of demographic development, with very high birth, death, and infant mortality rates. In the past, high death and infant mortality rates together with some emigration have kept the rate of population increase low, but Communist planning will probably have to deal with a formidable rate of increase as public-health and related measures reduce the death and infant mortality rates.

China probably has very considerable mineral resources (*cf.* Fig. 15-3, p. 498), but they have been neither carefully explored nor effectively exploited. There is much excellent coal, both anthracite and bituminous, especially in the north China province of Shansi. Shansi also has very good iron ores and there are other deposits in Hupeh and Seechwan, but the largest iron ore deposits are in Manchuria and it is here that China's iron and steel industry is being developed. On the basis of iron content of ore reserves *per capita,* however, China's known reserves are extremely small in relation to other countries. Yünnan has rich copper deposits, and Hunan Province contains the world's chief deposit of antimony. Chinese tungsten production in 1950 was 11,000 tons, more than one-third of total world output. In the same year tin smelter output was only 4,000 tons out of a world total of 175,000 tons. Although little or no aluminum is produced, there are ample deposits (200 million tons) of high-grade bauxite.

[55] 1952 estimates from United Nations *Statistical Yearbook,* 1953, pp. 27-30, converted from square kilometers.

[56] Cressey, *op. cit.,* p. 86.

On the negative side, China's most serious deficiency is in oil, a situation which it shares with India.[57]

The mineral position has been summed up as follows:

> China is bountifully supplied with coal and has major reserves of antimony and tungsten. Tin and iron are available in moderate amounts, and there are small quantities of a wide variety of minerals. Copper, sulphur, petroleum, and other essentials appear very limited. China has the mineral basis for a modest industrialization, but in terms of her population she ranks well down the list of the great powers. Nevertheless, no other area on the Pacific side of Asia is better supplied.
>
> ... Few areas in the world present the basic industrial opportunities that China will seek to develop during the remainder of the twentieth century. Many of these problems rest on heavy industry and in turn upon geology. The situation is somewhat comparable to the problems of the Soviet Five-Year Plans, but unlike the U.S.S.R., China is only modestly endowed with natural wealth. It is fortunate that coal is super-abundant for it is the key to power and to chemical industry, but the shortage in iron will be serious before many decades.[58]

Per capita consumption of energy in China was less than 200 pounds, coal equivalent, in 1937, putting China among the very low energy-consuming countries, along with India, Burma, Haiti, and the Belgian Congo. Almost three-quarters of the total energy was used for heat and light, 18 per cent for industry and only 10 per cent for transport. About 57 per cent of China's energy comes from coal, 35 per cent from wood and peat, only 4 per cent from water power, and only 3 per cent from oil and gas. Northwest China is believed to contain some promising oil-bearing structures but crude oil production in China has been negligible. China is estimated to have about 22 million horse power of potential water power available 95 per cent of the time, and 41 million available 50 per cent of the time (due to uneven stream flow), but practically none of it is developed. This is less than India, Pakistan, and Ceylon together (40 million) but more than Japan (16 million).[59]

TRANSPORTATION

Before the development of rail and highway transport, the rivers and the sea coast were China's principal arteries for travel. The principal rivers, running west to east, were navigable at least by small craft for considerable distances inland, especially the Yangtse, which is navigable

[57] The two countries have also in common that they both possess large resources of coal. India, however, has the advantage that its coal is in general of better quality, is more easily accessible, and, most important, lies near its iron ore resources.

[58] Cressey, *op. cit.*, pp. 79, 85.

[59] Woytinsky, *op. cit.*, pp. 887, 935, 942-3; also Cressey, *op. cit.*, pp. 80, 81.

by river steamer as far as Chungking. In the mountainous south, human porterage was the chief other means of transport. In the north, mules and horses were used to pull wagons, and together with asses and camels, for beasts of burden. To a large extent these methods are still employed.

The railways of China were developed slowly, by foreign capital, extending inland from the treaty ports. In this way Canton was connected with Hong Kong; Nanking, Hangchow, and Ningpo with Shanghai; and Kunming (by the French) with Haiphong in Indo-China. The most extensive development was in the north where Peiping and Tientsin were linked to Manchuria and Inner Mongolia. By 1936 the Canton-Hankow railroad was completed linking the north and south positions of the system[60] (*cf.* Fig. 15-3, p. 498).

At the end of World War II mainland China had almost 17,000 miles of railway of which about 14,000 miles were serviceable. There was extensive destruction during the civil war but by 1951 reconstruction had brought the total of serviceable mileage up to about 13,500 miles.[61] Most of this mileage is single-tracked. Double-tracked lines run from Harbin to Mukden, from Mukden to Dairen and Tientsin, from Tientsin to Peiping, and from Süchow to Nanking. The highest recorded annual volume of rail freight transported by China's railways was 6.5 billion ton kilometers in 1937. In 1947 the figure was 5.3 billion ton kilometers.[62] Considering the area and population of China this constitutes a very low utilization of railway service.

In 1937 there were only some 15,000 miles of paved roads and 35,000 miles of dry-weather earth roads.

Under the Communists attention seems to have been concentrated on rebuilding the railroads and reorganizing them in the interest of greater efficiency, rather than on new construction. All railroads are now under a single administration, and the control of the Harbin-Dairen line in Manchuria was reportedly restored by the U.S.S.R. to China in 1953.[63] While the conspicuous deficiency that appears on any map of the Chinese railway system is the lack of feeder lines, the government seems bent instead on using surfaced highways. This plan, plus the difficulty and cost of rail construction in the rugged terrain of the south, and the growing potential of air transport, suggest that, except for railways constructed into the outlying dependencies for strategic purposes or to exploit new

60 East and Spate, *op. cit.*, p. 261.

61 N. Ginsburg, "China's Railroad Network," *Geographical Review* (July, 1951), p. 470.

62 United Nations, *Statistical Yearbook*, 1953, p. 297.

63 *New York Times*, January 1, 1953, p. 3.

resources, the Chinese will not embark on an overambitious railway expansion.[64]

New rail construction that is under way or may have been completed by the Communists include the line from Liuchow in the south to the Indo-China border at Chinnankuan, the line from Chungking to Chengtu projected by the Nationalists, and the extension of the Lungsi railway to Lanchow in Kansu.[65]

Plans for eventual integration of the Soviet and Chinese transportation systems (*cf.* Fig. 15-3, p. 498) call for the construction of railways west through the Kansu corridor from Lanchow through Sinkiang via Hami and Urumchi to Alma-Ata on the Soviet border; and north from Tsinin through Ulan Bator in Outer Mongolia to the Trans-Siberian at Ulan Ude. On both rail lines, considerable progress has been reported.[66] The eventual economic importance of the two rail lines, to both China and the Soviet Union, will be considerable. The Tsinin-Ulan Bator railway will shorten the journey from Pekin to Ulan Ude by more than 650 miles. The Lanchow-Alma-Ata line will open up access to the untapped mineral resources of China's North-West. It will also facilitate the movement of settlers from the over-populated eastern provinces to Sinkiang and thus promote the development of the oil, coal, lead, zinc resources of that province. The future economic importance of the two railroads, however, is overshadowed by their immediate strategic value.[67]

AGRICULTURE

The principal crops are wheat and rice, but barley, corn, millet, sorghum, and sweet potatoes are grown in large quantities. China also produces, in Manchuria, almost one-half the world supply of soybeans. The statistics on crop production in China given by FAO are for the twenty-two provinces.

That China accounts for a substantial proportion of the world supply of many of the above crops is only a reflection of the fact that China contains a large proportion of the world's population and that most of these people subsist by agriculture. Actually, their agriculture, while intensive, and employing in many cases ancient but effective methods of irrigation

[64] Ginsburg, *op. cit.*, p. 474.
[65] *Ibid.*, p. 473.
[66] See p. 498.
[67] A. White, *Recent Railroad Expansion in Soviet Asia*, unpublished (Washington, 1953); see also Ginsburg, *op. cit.*, p. 473, and East and Spate, *op. cit.*, pp. 357, 358, 585.

(about half the land is irrigated, and about a fourth is terraced, mainly for rice), is inefficient in terms of labor inputs. The average farm is small, only about four acres, and may consist of six or seven parcels. The average farm family size is approximately six persons.[68] Except for rice, sorghum, and millet yields per acre are not exceptional. There is very little mechanized equipment in use; in 1949 there were only 1,400 farm tractors in the 22 provinces. Wooden spades and hoes are common. Grain is often threshed on a stone, wheat is harvested with a sickle, and the plow is pulled by an ox or a water buffalo if the farmer is well-off, otherwise by members of the family. Hired labor accounts for only about one-fifth of the total labor performed.[69]

TABLE 15-8

Production and Yields of Principal Crops, China's 22 Provinces, 1949 *

CROP	MILLION TONS	ACRES	YIELD PER ACRE METRIC QUINTALS	PER CENT OF WORLD SUPPLY	AVERAGE WORLD YIELD METRIC QUINTALS
Wheat	20.6	52.6	3.9	12.2	3.9
Rice	44.5	45.7	9.7	29.4[a]	6.6[b]
Barley	6.6	15.3	4.3	13.5	4.4
Corn	6.5	12.3	5.3	4.6	6.5
Millet	7.1	16.2	4.3	39.7[a]	2.6[b]
Sorghum	5.4	10.8	5.1	32.1[a]	3.0[b]
Rape Seed	3.1	14.0			
Soybeans	4.9	n.a.	n.a.	34.7	n.a.
Cotton	0.4	5.3	0.8[c]	7.6	1.0[c]
Tea	12.7[d]	n.a.	n.a.	2.6	n.a.
Tobacco	0.5	1.2	4.5	13.5	4.2

[a] Excluding U.S.S.R.
[b] Excludes U.S.S.R.
[c] Tons per acre.
[d] 1948 in thousands of tons.
* W. S. and E. S. Woytinsky, *World Population and Production* (New York, 1954), based on *Yearbook of Food and Agriculture Statistics.*

The laborious character of Chinese agriculture is indicated by calculations showing that one acre of wheat requires 26 man-days of labor compared with 1.2 man-days in the United States; one acre of corn requires 23 days in China, but 2.5 days in the United States; one acre of cotton 53 days, but only 14 in the United States.[70]

Animal husbandry is unimportant save in the northwest. "It is a question, not of climate or soil, but of resources and population. The relation

[68] Cressey, *op. cit.*, p. 90.
[69] R. H. Tawney, *Land and Labour in China* (London, 1937), p. 33. This is an excellent and vivid portrayal of the rural economy of China.
[70] Cressey, *op. cit.*, p. 89.

between them has for many centuries been such that land capable of growing food for human consumption cannot be spared for raising beasts. Milk and meat will support fewer human beings than can be fed from the land which, if cattle were reared, would be required to grow fodder."[71] Such grass as does grow in the hill near the villages is needed for fuel. Only ducks, chickens, and pigs are kept by China's peasant and these subsist on waste products from the farm. Thus there is little animal manure, and commercial fertilizers are practically unknown.

These conditions, the small size of most farms, and the absence of any but primitive tools, determine the character and efficiency of Chinese agriculture. "The prevalence of minute holdings has necessitated special methods of cultivation in order to make them yield a livelihood; and these methods in turn, involving as they do, much detailed vigilance and heavy physical labor, are of a kind which can be applied only when holdings are minute . . . the Chinese farmer . . . has acquired an ingenuity which has rarely been surpassed in wringing from the land at his disposal, not indeed the most that it could yield—for the output could be increased by the use of modern methods—but the utmost possible with the resources that he has hitherto commanded. . . . It is the agriculture of a pre-scientific age, raised by centuries of venerable tradition to the dignity of an art . . . a triumph of individual skill unaided by organized knowledge. . . . But (its) economic significance has not always been appreciated, and admirers of the technical expertness of the Chinese farmer seem sometimes to forget the human cost at which his triumphs are won."[72]

And the social cost: "The Chinese farmer grows only enough food for himself and one other person outside his family. There is thus no agricultural surplus to feed an expanding urban population."[73] What is provided is not excessive. There are no aggregate data, but *per capita* food consumption is not likely to be much higher than FAO's estimate of 2,700 calories per person for all of East Asia.

INDUSTRY AND TRADE

The modern, urban-industrial sector of the Chinese economy, referred to above, developed only in a few coastal cities where western concessions and settlements were established, and in Japanese-controlled Manchuria (*cf.* Fig. 15-3, p. 498). In China proper the cotton textile industry became

[71] Tawney, *op. cit.*, p. 27.
[72] Tawney, *op. cit.*, pp. 44-46.
[73] Cressey, *op. cit.*

by far the most important manufacturing activity. In 1949 the Chinese cotton textile industry had 4.6 million spindles, the eighth-largest cotton textile industry in the world. About half the spindles are located at Shanghai, the rest at Tientsin, Tsingtao, and Hankow. About half the mills were owned by Japanese and passed into the hands of the government after World War II. China imported cotton fiber, partly because the domestic cotton has a very short staple, partly for re-export in the form of cotton piece goods and cotton rugs.

Other manufacturing enterprises, such as flour milling and food and tobacco processing were likewise concentrated in Shanghai, Tientsin, and Tsingtao. The only heavy industry to speak of was built up in Manchuria by the Japanese after 1930. Mukden became a center of armaments production, an integrated iron and steel industry was developed at Anshan, and similar expansion took place in heavy chemicals, metal processing, and railway equipment shops.[74]

There are no reliable statistics of industrial production for China. However, from a speech made by Chou En-lai in October, 1954, which compared output of the leading industries for 1954 with 1949, the following figures have been derived.

		1949	1954
Electric Power	billion kwh.	4.30	10.80
Coal	million tons	31.50	82.00
Pig Iron	million tons	0.24	3.03
Steel Ingot	million tons	0.16	2.17
Cement	million tons	0.66	4.73
Machine Made Paper	million tons	0.11	0.48
Cotton Yarn	million bales	2.40	4.60
Metal Working Machines	units		13,513

While it is not possible to verify the figures for 1954, other sources provide some light on the accuracy of the 1949 figures given by Chou En-lai. It should be remembered that economic life in many parts of China in 1949 was adversely affected by the final hostilities and dislocation of the civil war. Electric power production in 1950 was estimated at 2.2 billion kilowatt hours, about two-tenths of 1 per cent of the world total for that year. Coal production (excluding Manchuria) was 16 million metric tons in 1949 and 37 million in 1950, 1.1 per cent and 2.5 per cent of the world output excluding U.S.S.R. in those years.[75] Iron and steel production in Manchuria in 1949 was 94,000 tons of pig iron and 89,000 tons of steel,[76]

[74] Woytinsky, *op. cit.*, p. 870.
[75] *Ibid.*, p. 870.
[76] *Ibid.*, p. 1121.

figures which still reflect the removal of plant and equipment by the Soviet Union after World War II. Whichever figures are correct they indicate beyond doubt that China's industrial capabilities in 1949 were insignificant. Whether the impression of unusual growth which the figures for 1954 give can be taken as a portent of the future is discussed in another section below.

To the modern sector of the Chinese economy concentrated in the coastal cities, China's foreign trade was a source of great wealth and activity, although the total volume of trade was small in relation to China's area and population. Certain agricultural products like tung oil and pigs' bristles were exported in quantity but the biggest export item was cotton piece goods. Principal imports were raw cotton, electrical equipment and other machinery, iron and steel, chemicals and pharmaceuticals, and transport equipment. A large visible trade deficit (import surplus) was offset by a corresponding volume of remittances from overseas Chinese. Most of the trade was with the United Kingdom, the United States, and Western Europe.

THE PROSPECT FOR COMMUNIST CHINA

The description given in the foregoing pages has revealed a nation of great size and population, occupying a country not bountifully endowed with natural resources, with an underdeveloped transport system and with most of the population living so close to minimum subsistence levels as to preclude any accumulation of capital on a scale large enough to permit modernization and industrialization of the economy. How can such a country hope to wield any power in the struggle between the Communist bloc and the West, at least for a long period of time? In answering this question we should look at what the new regime has done to date, what it proposes to do, and what its problems are.

Official Chinese figures claim an impressive rate of expansion in the industrial sector of the economy since the completion of the revolution in 1949. In addition to the increases in output reported by Chou En-lai, quoted above, the Chinese Premier, in the same speech, stated that the total value of industrial production increased from 1949 to 1952 at an annual average rate of 36.9 per cent, and from 1952 to 1953 by 33 per cent. He predicted that the total value of modern industrial output in 1954 would be 4.2 times that of 1949, and the value of all output (industrial, agricultural, and handicraft) 2.2 times that of 1949. Further, Chou En-lai claimed that the ratio of modern industrial output to all output increased from 17 per cent in 1949 to 33 per cent in 1954, and the ratio of capital goods production to total industrial production from 28.8 per cent in 1949 to 42.3 per cent in 1954. State-owned, co-operative, and joint state-and-private enterprises, according to Chou, would account for about 71 per cent of total industrial output in 1954 compared to only 37 per cent in 1949.

These claims undoubtedly exaggerate the expansion going on in the Chinese economy, considering the low level of output in 1949, the well-established practice of Communist statisticians to overstate rates of growth, and the previous poverty of economic statistics in China. What probably lies behind these statements is, nevertheless, a remarkable record of reconstruction and rehabilitation of the economy, plus considerable progress in the direction of nationalization of large enterprises. The effects of war damage and civil dislocation on production had probably been eliminated by 1952, aided by good harvests in 1950, 1951, and 1952. Substantial increases in output were made in steel, cotton textiles, paper, and other consumers goods, while pig iron, coal, electric power, sugar, soybean, and wheat production remained below previous peaks.

In addition to achieving a recovery of production, the Chinese Communists may be credited with some success in bringing the industrial economy under state planning, in carrying through a large-scale program of land redistribution, and in preparing for the socialization as well as the industrialization of the economy.

In the third year of the first five-year plan it is still true to say that China's industrialization is just beginning. One writer has compared Communist China's present position with that of Japan at the beginning of the Meiji period.[77] A number of analysts have compared China's present position unfavorably with that of the U.S.S.R. at the beginning of its first five-year plan in 1928. In 1952 China has a larger industrial base than Japan had in the 1860's but much smaller than the Soviet Union's in 1928. The relation between resources and population was much more favorable in the Soviet Union. The Soviet Union had a more literate and more skilled labor force. Finally, the Soviet Union did not then need to devote so large a portion of its resources to military expenditure.

The gross national product of Communist China in 1952 was probably equivalent to not more than thirty billion dollars nor less than twenty-five billion, or roughly between 45 and 50 dollars *per capita*. Recent estimates

[77] W. W. Rostow and others, *The Prospects for Chinese Communist Society* (Cambridge, 1954), p. 320. This is a comprehensive analysis of the prospects for Chinese economic development based on studies conducted at the Center for International Studies, Massachusetts Institute of Technology.

by Alexander Eckstein include an attempt to give a breakdown of the gross national product by source and use.

TABLE 15-9

China's Gross National Product, 1952 *

BY ECONOMIC ORIGIN	PER CENT	BY USE	PER CENT
Agriculture	40.0	Household Consumption	73.0
Small scale & rural industry	15.0	Govt. Administration	4.0
Trade and Transport	24.0	Communal Services	4.0
Factory Industry and Mining	7.0	Military Expenditures	7.0
Housing	4.0	Gross domestic investment	12.0
Government and other Services	10.0		
	100.0		100.0

* W. W. Rostow and others, *The Prospects for Chinese Communist Society* (Cambridge, 1954), p. 350.

If these approximations are correct they indicate that Communist China already has mobilized a respectable proportion of total output for investment, 12 per cent as against, say 5 to 8 per cent for India. And the figure for investment excludes private investment (by the peasant, small proprietor, and so forth).

CHINESE COMMUNIST ECONOMIC GOALS

In Chou En-lai's speech to the First National People's Congress, quoted above, he declares confidently that "We shall certainly be able, in the course of several five-year plans, to build China into a strong modern industrialized, Socialist nation." There are abundant signs, however, that the Chinese officials are not blind to the obstacles that lie ahead, in the way both of industrialization and of the transition to socialism. Chou himself admits that many of the details of the first five-year plan have not been worked out, that the Chinese are inexperienced at state planning, that the industrial foundation is weak, that skilled labor is inadequate, and that industrial management is poor. He also appears to recognize that development of more, and more efficient, agricultural production is essential to provide for the rapid growth in population and for the release of manpower to the growing urban industries, and that Soviet economic and technical assistance will be indispensable.

The short-run goals that are published are nevertheless quite ambitious. The table on page 510 indicates the goals established for the first five-year Plan.

The attainment of these goals would give China a crude steel capacity equal to that of the U.S.S.R. in 1928, exceeding that of Canada, Belgium, and other small countries but considerably below the levels attained by Japan in the 1930's. The most ambitious—and dubious—features of the first five-year plan is in agriculture, calling for an increase of 30 per cent in grain output between 1953 and 1957. Consideration of these goals suggests that the factors most crucial to success or failure are likely to be found in the following: (1) the limitations of natural and human resources to growth in industrial output; (2) whether agricultural production can keep pace with population growth, and agricultural productivity keep ahead of the demands of industry for man power; (3) whether the transition to socialism will interfere with expansion of output (especially in agriculture); and (4) the gains to be had from foreign trade and Soviet aid. Let us consider each one of these factors in somewhat greater detail.

TABLE 15-10

Industrial Production Targets for Communist China *

PRODUCT	INDEX 1952 = 100	UNITS	OUTPUT 1952	TARGET [a]
Crude Steel	400	thousand MT	1,215	4,860
Rolled Steel	250	"	740	1,850
Coal	160	"	48,230	77,170
Electric Power	200	million kwh	5,700	11,400
Mining Equipment	200	n.a.	n.a.	n.a.
Metal-cutting Machinery	350	n.a.	n.a.	n.a.

[a] No exact date is given, but it refers either to the last year of the Plan, 1957, or to when the current aid agreement expires, i.e., 1959.
* Rostow and others, *op. cit.*, p. 346, from *Pravda,* September 28, 1953.

THE PROBLEM OF INDUSTRIAL GROWTH

In the present phase, because of the head start given by Japanese development, Manchuria is the key to Chinese industrial expansion.[78] In Manchuria skilled labor is more plentiful, transport is better, iron ore is found close to coal and non-ferrous metals, and steel-using industries are in operation. Manchuria has over two-thirds of known Chinese iron reserves. The Communist estimate is nearly 6 billion tons. Maximum production probably reached 5 million tons during the war. The ore is of low quality but the Japanese earlier, and more recently the Communists, claimed to have found higher-grade ores. Copper, lead, zinc, magnesium, and molybdenum are found throughout Manchuria. Manchurian coal reserves are less than a tenth of total Chinese reserves but they produce

[78] *The Economist,* September 18, 1954.

about one-half of current output. Penchihu provides the best coking coal, and together with Yentan supplies coal both for its own iron industry and for Anshan. Good quality coal is found in the Tunhua region, also near rich iron ore deposits. The coal mine in Fushun is the largest open-pit mine in the world. This coal is not of very good quality but it can be used for coking if mixed with Penchihu coal. On balance, the 1957 target of 100 million tons of coal production does not seem unlikely of attainment.

Anshan, Mukden, and Tunhua are the principal centers of industrial development. Anshan's pig iron output is reported now to be 1.6 million tons and crude steel production at 800,000 tons. Doubling of these rates, plus the addition of new plants at Tunhua, are necessary for the attainment of the 1957 steel production goal of 5 million tons.

Mukden, already the center for railway equipment, is scheduled also to be the principal location for the machine tool and other engineering industries. Chemical and engineering industries are to be developed in Harbin, Anshan, Fushun, and Penchihu. Manchuria has thus the potential for a considerable further development of metallurgy and heavy industry. The rate at which this development will go forward will depend more on the extent of Soviet assistance than on any other factor. Estimates made by Eckstein and Rostow indicate that the investment costs of the steel and electric power components of the first five-year plan would be in the neighborhood of one billion United States dollars of which about one-third would represent imported equipment that would presumably have to be supplied from the Soviet Union.[79] It is not unlikely that Soviet assistance will be concentrated in these sectors. Thus the attainment of the industrial goals by 1960 is not at all improbable.

AGRICULTURAL PRODUCTION AND POPULATION GROWTH

With the emphasis on public health and sanitation, mortality rates are now likely to decline sharply in China as they have in India, Ceylon, Egypt, and Mexico. With birth rates remaining stationary the population of China may now be expected to grow more rapidly, probably between 1 and 2 per cent per annum.[80] This means that Chinese agriculture will face the problem of expanding total output to keep *per capita* consumption the same. In addition productivity will have to be raised if man power is to be released to urban industries, and raised still further if *per capita* food consumption is to be raised from its present very low levels.

[79] Rostow, *op. cit.*, p. 348.
[80] See above, Ch. 9, p. 325.

There are, of course, two ways of increasing agricultural output: bringing more land under cultivation and increasing yields per acre. Since no more than about 15 million acres, equal to about 6 per cent of land presently cultivated, can practicably be brought to produce crops, the major reliance will have to be placed on increasing yields per acre. Substantial increases in yields are possible with the application on a large scale of commercial fertilizers. However, according to official Chinese Communist reports, production in 1952 of ammonium sulphate, one of the principal fertilizers required, was only about 350,000 tons, whereas to raise average crop yields by 25 per cent an estimated 6.5 million tons would be required. It would almost certainly take from five to ten years for production even to approach the required levels because of the high capital costs and large requirements for electricity.[81]

Other measures that may more easily be introduced, because they are labor intensive and do not require much equipment, include seed selection, pest control, flood control and water conservation, but their effect on crop yields will be more gradual and less impressive than the effects that would be expected from the widespread use of commercial fertilizers. Thus Communist China is even more likely than the U.S.S.R. to have difficulty in expanding food production to keep pace with the growth in total population and in the urban industrial population.

THE SOCIALIST TRANSFORMATION OF AGRICULTURE

It is impossible to determine what effect the program of large-scale land redistribution put in effect by the Communists has had upon output. About 30 to 40 per cent of Chinese farmers before the revolution were tenants and these now have their own plots. The state, however, is now an efficient and determined tax collector, and through the party apparatus, the mutual aid teams and producers' co-operatives may be expected to extract the food supplies needed for the urbanized areas. The incentives to more efficient crop production from land ownership may thus be eliminated. In any case, the socialist goal is collective farming, under which many of the incentives of private land ownership will disappear. There are signs that the Chinese Communists are approaching this task more circumspectly than their comrades in the U.S.S.R. whose socialist designs on the peasants inflicted damage which is still being reflected in Soviet agricultural production. "In order that agriculture may develop

[81] Rostow, *op. cit.*, p. 334.

more quickly and in a more planned way, we must gradually carry out the Socialist Transformation."[82]

By 1953 about one-half of the rural households were organized in mutual aid teams, and about 273,000 households were organized into 14,000 producer co-operatives. By 1957 some 20 per cent of all farms would be members of such co-operatives.[83] It is too early to be able to determine when the next stage, that of full collectivization, will be introduced, or at what rate it will proceed. The co-operative organization of the rural economy, together with other forms of control exercised by the state and party apparatus, is probably adequate to the needs of the regime so far as extracting the maximum share of farm output is concerned. Collectivization on the other hand will be designed presumably to organize for greater and more efficient output, and while it could take place in advance of mechanization, it is not likely in the absence of mechanization to have much effect either in increasing output or improving productivity and releasing labor for industrial employment. Collectivization may therefore be expected to proceed as and when farm machinery becomes available in significant quantities. In the meantime the goal of Chinese agrarian policy must be to hold down consumption on the farm.

The goal of a 30 per cent increase in grain output appears quite unrealistic for the reasons given above. Whatever increase is achieved, however, will not benefit the peasants remaining on the farms but is more likely to be pre-empted for the growing urban industrial population. Eckstein has constructed a model showing the growth of the Chinese economy from 1952 to 1962 in which the gross national product increases from the equivalent of $30 billion to $41.2 billion (at constant prices), or about 37 per cent, but in which aggregate expenditure on personal consumption increases only from $22 billion to $26.7 billion or 21 per cent.[84] The estimated population increase during this period is from 582 million persons to 654 millions or 12 per cent; this would indicate an increase in annual *per capita* consumption increasing from about $38 to $41. Rural consumption on the other hand is estimated in the model to increase in the aggregate from $14.7 billion to only $15.1 billion, while rural population grows from 466 million persons to 479 millions. The result is *no* increase in *per capita* consumption for the rural population.

The significance of these calculations is not that of a set of predictions

[82] Speech of Chou En-lai, October 1954.
[83] Rostow, *op. cit.*, p. 337.
[84] *Ibid.*, p. 353.

but of an attempt to express quantitatively the conditions of the kind of economic growth the Communist regime has set for the next decade. Keeping farm consumption down will help to increase industrial employment and investment; gross industrial investment in the same model increases from 4.8 per cent of gross national product to over 8 per cent and industrial output from 7 per cent of gross national product to almost 17 per cent. These projections are of course subject to a number of hazardous assumptions regarding not only the efficiency of the capital and labor recruited for the new industrial enterprises, but also and especially the course of agricultural production in the absence of consumption gains for the farmer. But the response of the Chinese peasant to the forced and unrewarded reorganization of his life and work is likely to be more important than any other single factor, both as affecting economic growth and as a test of the determination and ruthlessness of the new regime. In the light of the characteristic stubbornness of peasant resistance to change, and especially in the light of the difficulties experienced in the Soviet Union, one may conclude that while the political control of the regime is hardly in danger, its program of economic expansion has a rough road ahead.

FOREIGN TRADE AND SOVIET AID

Up to 1950 about one-quarter of China's trade was with the rest of the Soviet bloc and three-quarters was with the rest of the world. By 1954 these proportions were reversed, not so much as a result of the United Nations embargo which was imposed after the Chinese invasion of Korea, but of a deliberate policy throughout the bloc of redirecting trade inward.

In 1953 exports of Communist China to the Free World were about $434 million; imports from the Free World were about $284 million. Trade with the Soviet bloc is not reported but is probably in the neighborhood of $800 million to a billion dollars each way. In addition to its own exports to the Soviet bloc, China probably uses its visible trade surplus with the rest of the world to pay for imports from the Soviet bloc. The commodity composition of the trade probably remains much the same as before, with Communist China relying on the U.S.S.R. and the European satellites for the machinery, equipment, and manufactured goods formerly obtained from the United States, Great Britain, and Western Europe. There is little doubt that foreign trade plays an important role in China's development program since imports supply about one-fifth of the value of capital formation. The process of capital formation, in other words, to some extent takes the form of extracting an exportable surplus of raw material and agricultural commodities to pay for imports of capital goods. But increasingly China is relying on the European Soviet bloc to supply its needs for machinery and equipment, and engineering and technical services. In fact the rapid modernization of China's economy is inconceivable without such imports.

The U.S.S.R. with the European satellites, especially Poland, Czechoslovakia, and East Germany, is unquestionably in a position to supply China with a considerable quantity and variety of capital goods, which can be transported without difficulty either by sea or by means of the Trans-Siberia railway. Because China is the weaker of the two trading partners, the terms of its trade with the U.S.S.R. are probably less favorable than if it could follow a policy of buying in the cheapest market.

Soviet economic aid to China during the first four years of the Communist regime was substantial but by no means massive. Moreover, the aid consisted, apparently entirely, of credits as opposed to grant aid. In 1949 the Sino-Soviet aid agreement provided $300 millions of credits and in September, 1953, the U.S.S.R. promised to help build 141 projects, "the sinews" according to Chou En-lai, of the first five-year plan. According to unofficial reports, the September, 1953, agreement called for a ten-year aid program involving total aid equal to one billion dollars and including the $300 million provided in the 1949 agreement. Over the five-year period the annual average of economic assistance provided would be about $117 million. This would be less than 10 per cent of the average annual net industrial investment projected in Eckstein's model.[85] Most of what China requires in the way of imported capital goods from the Soviet Union will therefore have to be paid for with imports.

This is not surprising, for it would appear improbable that the U.S.S.R. would devote any considerable amount of capital resources, even against repayment, to the task of awakening the strength of China's 600 million people, when those resources are still badly needed at home. But the U.S.S.R. may well be reaching the point where it is advantageous to export certain types of capital goods in exchange for badly needed agricultural commodities. Thus, the pace of China's industrialization will depend to a large extent on its ability to expand exports of raw materials and foodstuff, either by increasing output or by restricting consumption, or by a combination of both.

[85] *Ibid.*, p. 353.

CONCLUSIONS

The Economic Potential. China is an immense country with the largest population in the world. It is a very poor country with a primitive agriculture, very little industry, an underdeveloped transportation system, and not overly well-endowed with natural resources. Its present power rests in its numbers, and its potential power in the ruthless determination of a communist dictatorship to mobilize both the people and the resources, at whatever cost, to build the economic base both for an industrialized communist state and for great power status.

Communist China's weakness lies also in its numbers in their relation to available resources, for this relationship is so unbalanced that it will be difficult to produce the surplus of agricultural output needed to feed the growing numbers of the urban industrial labor force.

It has been pointed out that to achieve the Communist economic goals the following conditions must be met: [86]

1. A high proportion of industrial output must be reinvested in industry.
2. An increasing proportion of national output must be allocated to exports in return for imports of raw materials, machinery and military equipment.
3. An increased volume of agricultural output must be allocated (*a*) to exports and (*b*) to feeding the growing urban population.
4. An increasing proportion of total output must be devoted to investment, and increases in consumption and welfare must, except for urban industrial workers, be postponed.

To meet all these conditions will be difficult. And even if they are met progress will be slow in relation to the continuing growth of the industrialized states of the West. Because of the low level of departure for China, the gap between its expanding capabilities and those of the United States and Western Europe will, in absolute terms, continue to widen for many years. In comparison, however, with other countries of East Asia, unless their development too is accelerated, the progress made by Communist China will furnish an impressive example.

The Sino-Soviet Bloc Today and in the Future

We have given this chapter the title "The Growing Economic Strength of the Sino-Soviet Bloc"; at this point we should draw the balance of our discussion on economic power factors and potentials in both the Soviet Union and Communist China to try to evaluate the factors of strength and

[86] Rostow, *op. cit.*, Ch. 15.

weakness which this bloc of the two main Communist powers of our time reveals. The Chinese-Russian alliance came into effect in February, 1950. It has proved its stability in the Korean War. The common goals of the two Communist nations have been given practical expression; in October, 1954, the two governments issued joint declarations on general questions of Chinese-Soviet relations with Japan; the U.S.S.R. agreed to evacuate the Port Arthur naval base and to transfer it without compensation to China; the Soviet-Chinese shareholding societies which were set up in 1950 and 1951 for mining and oil refining purposes were transferred by mutual agreement to China; scientific-technical collaboration and the building of the Lanchow-Urumchi-Alma-Ata railway were mutually agreed upon. In the latter case, the two governments agreed that both sides should begin the building of this line on Chinese and Soviet territory, and they also agreed to continue the plans for the building of the railroad between Tsining in China and Ulan Bator in the territory of the Mongolian Peoples Republic, which is to be linked with the railway running from Ulan Bator to Soviet territory. At the end of 1955, considerable progress had been achieved in the construction of the strategic rail links through Sinkiang and Outer Mongolia which will constitute new lines of communication between the U.S.S.R. and North and Central China, supplementing the Trans-Siberian line in the north. Such lines, when completed, will facilitate the movement of goods between China and the U.S.S.R. They will also make it much easier in time of war to move military equipment and supplies to central and southern China, on lines which would be invulnerable to naval blockade and relatively secure against airborne attacks launched from bases and naval craft off the coast of China. Eventually they will also facilitate the development of new and less exposed industrial centers in the Hinterland.[87]

It thus appears that at the time these lines are written, the links between the two nations are strong and will be further strengthened. However, in comparing the two partners we must not, in the over-all economic appraisal, lose sight of the fact that China as a partner of the U.S.S.R. appears to be in the state of infancy. Its strength lies in the future, and a comparison of, for instance, the steel and coal production data of the two countries shows the weak position of China as against that of the U.S.S.R. There is no likelihood of competitive conflicts in the near future. However, when and if these new developments lead to the appearance of an industrially and militarily strong Chinese power along the Asian boundaries of the Soviet Union, tensions and frictions may well be the conse-

[87] See p. 485, and Fig. 15-2, p. 478.

quence. They may be increased by the fact that China, whose population of close to 600,000,000 people far surpasses that of the Soviet Union with a population of about 210 million people, is and will be the strongest proponent of a persuasive "Asia for the Asians" program. This force may become a factor of ominous importance and should not be neglected in the over-all appraisal of the economic power potentials of the two Communist nations.

CHAPTER 16

Japan's Economy

In this section of the book we are attempting to assess the economic capabilities, not of all the countries of the world, but only of those major countries and area groupings whose actual or potential strength must be reckoned with in any attempt to calculate the world balance of political power. In any such attempt some attention must be given to Japan.

There are several reasons for this. In the first place, Japan has been for some time the only Asian country with the economic capabilities for great power status. Such a statement sounds surprising now that we are accustomed to think of Communist China as the major military power in the Far East. But it must not be overlooked that the military strength demonstrated by Communist China in the Korean war depended essentially on Soviet logistical support. A decade or more ago, when the cost of defeating Japan in World War II was fresh in the memories of the American people, no one thought of China as capable of creating a modern military establishment on a large scale for many years to come, while Japan had been a formidable enemy with a modern air force, a large well-equipped army and the world's third largest navy.

What has happened to alter these superficial impressions? On the one hand is the notion that Japan's economy was hopelessly crippled by war damage and the loss of empire, and that Japan's almost 90 million people, confined to the home islands, remain dependent on American aid. On the other hand is the widespread but somewhat exaggerated view that under Communism China's industrial power has grown so rapidly that economically as well as militarily China is now a modern state and one of the world's few great powers.

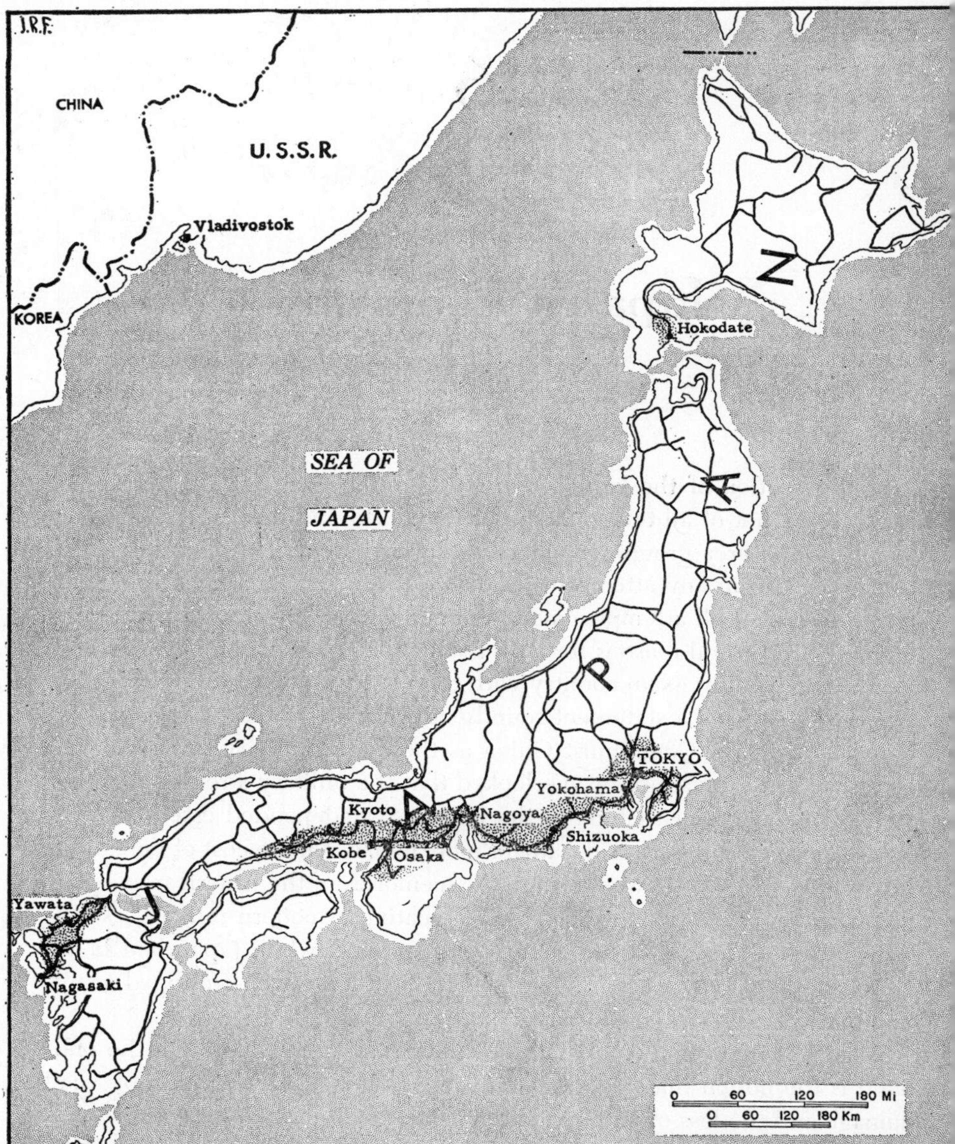

Fig. 16-1. Japan: Industrial Areas and Selected Railroads.

At present, of course, China has an overwhelming superiority in mobilized ground forces, while the sheer mass of its population constitutes a vast and perhaps unalterable advantage. Otherwise, the balance of economic capabilities still lies with Japan, as a comparison of the chief economic indicators will quickly show. With a population of around 88 million, Japan had a gross product of about $15 billion in 1952 compared with about $30 billion for Communist China's almost 600 million souls. Japan produced 43.2 million tons of coal; China 48.2 million. Japan produced 7 million tons of steel; China 1.2. Japan produced almost 52 billion kilowatt hours of electricity while China produced only 5.7 billion.[1] Moreover, Japan had an extensive road and rail communication network (Fig. 16-1), a diversified manufacturing and heavy capital goods industry, and a skilled labor force. These accomplishments combined to make Japan still the leading industrial power in Asia.

By Western standards, however, Japan had never achieved a high state of development. This is reflected in comparative *per capita* gross national product which in Japan was the equivalent, in 1954 of about $230. In the United States *per capita* gross national product was $2,280 in 1954; in the United Kingdom, $911; in West Germany, $674; and in Argentina, $650. But even with such a comparatively low level of income, Japan was once able to mobilize an impressive surplus for military and strategic purposes.

The relative abundance in Japan—as contrasted with the rest of Asia—of the things which characterize a modern industrial economy is due to the remarkable speed with which the Japanese economy was transformed after the Meiji restoration in 1868, a process which provides another reason for studying Japan's economic capabilities. This transformation was the result of a deliberate decision to modernize Japan's economy, a decision remarkable for its explicit recognition of the vital connection between economic capabilities and military power.

The Shogunate policy of isolation had been discredited, more than anything else, by the performance of western cannon in the naval bombardments of Kagoshima and Shimonoseki in 1863 and 1864, convincing proof that Japan would never be secure until the Japanese could provide themselves with modern weapons.[2] Recognition of this fact by a certain group of feudal princes led to the repudiation of the Shogunate in 1868, the restoration of the emperor, and the abolition of feudalism. The new gov-

[1] Figures for Japan from UN, Economic Commission for Asia and the Far East (ESCAFE), *Economic Survey of Asia and the Far East, 1954* (Bangkok, 1955); for China from Rostow, *op. cit., p. 297.*

[2] C. J. H. Hayes, *A Political and Social History of Modern Europe* (New York, 1929), p. 579.

ernment expressly assumed responsibility for the modernization and Europeanization of Japan. Armed forces were established on western models, and the necessary supporting industries were brought into being with the aid of government subsidies and western advisors. Neighboring islands were acquired: the northern and central Kuriles in 1875, the Bonins in 1876, the rest of the Ryukyus in 1878. Formosa was acquired in 1895 as one of the spoils of the war with China.

By 1904, only thirty-six years after the establishment of the first small arms arsenal at Tokyo, the Japanese entered the war with Russia with 6 modern battleships, 8 cruisers, 80 torpedo boats, 19 destroyers and other vessels. This war, especially the naval phase, was a decisive victory for the Japanese, and although Japan was almost exhausted at its end, it gave Japan the standing of a world power. It is true that many of the vessels of this fleet had been constructed abroad, but their possession itself is witness to a remarkable expansion of the Japanese economy, involving construction of railways, the development of ocean shipping, the creation of steel, textile, and other industries, and a rapid expansion of foreign trade.

This growth continued after the Russo-Japanese war. The population, which had been about 35 million in 1873 rose to 45.5 million in 1903, 56 million in 1920, and 73.1 million by 1940. Industrial production increased by almost five times between 1907 and 1931 and rose by a further 80 per cent between 1931 and 1937.

Japan's decisive victory over Russia encouraged further aggrandizement. Korea was annexed in 1910. Japan's role in World War I was rewarded by the mandates of the Marshall, Caroline, and Mariana islands. Manchuria was acquired in 1932, and the war against China began in 1937. Japan thus built up an overseas empire to supply it with foodstuffs and raw materials lacking at home and to provide markets in return for the products of Japanese consumer goods and light manufacturing industries. Korea supplied rice, Formosa rice and sugar, Manchuria metallic ores and soybeans, Sakhalin lumber and wood products, the Kuriles fish and other marine products. Thus did Japan's colonial policy aim at overcoming the resource deficiencies of the home islands.[3]

Much of these gains might have been preserved to Imperial Japan if not for the overconfident attack on the United States in 1941. The defeat of Japan in World War II has for practical purposes reduced Japan to the four main islands of Honshu, Kyushu, Shikoku, and Hokkaido. It is upon

[3] Cf. G. D. H. Cole, *World in Transition* (New York, 1949), pp. 462-463 for related aspects of Japanese policy.

these islands and their resources that the Japanese are trying to rebuild a viable economy and a secure state. As a result of the loss of Japan's colonial empire, Japan, with a vastly increased population, has been thrown back to the resources base which it controlled at the beginning of its expansion in the second half of the nineteenth century. In addition to this limitation, Japan has now to compete with India's slowly growing industrial capacity and with the unified military, political, and economic power of a China no longer under the influence of the West.

JAPAN'S LAND AND PEOPLE

Postwar Japan contains 147,611 square miles, about the size of California.[4] In addition to the four main islands there are hundreds of smaller islands emphasizing Japan's essentially insular character. No place is more than a few score miles from the sea and there is one mile of coastline for every 8.5 square miles of area. Living thus in the presence of the sea the Japanese, like the English, have become good sailors and fishermen and, as with the English, fish is an important item in the diet and second only to rice. Foreign trade is indispensable to the economy.

Japan is as mountainous as it is insular. The level area does not exceed 70,000 square miles and not all of this is arable. Rivers are short, steep, and generally unsuited for navigation.

Japan's location, roughly from 30° to 45° north latitude, gives it a generally temperate climate, but this statement is subject to important modifications. The islands extend about one thousand miles from southwest to northeast and are subject to both continental and marine influences. In the summer, winds from the Pacific (the summer monsoon) warmed by the Kuroshio current bring warm rainy weather; the winter monsoon from Eastern Asia, bringing cold air and moisture from the sea of Japan, is responsible for heavy snowfall in Hokkaido and northwestern Honshu. All of Japan has adequate rainfall, the seasonal and geographical distribution depending on relief and the monsoon.

On the plains, in the valleys, and on the hillsides of these narrow islands live almost 90 million people. This population is concentrated in the coastal plains, the area of greatest population extending from the Kwanto plain around Tokyo along the Pacific coast line to the Inland Sea. But wherever the land is not too steep and the soil reasonably fertile there are

[4] For a more extended discussion of Japan's geography see Cressey, *op. cit.*, pp. 166-231. The basic works are G. T. Trewartha, *Japan, A Physical, Cultural and Regional Geography* (Madison, Wisconsin, 1945), and G. H. Smith and D. Good with S. McCune, *Japan, A Geographical View* (New York, 1943).

people. Population density is almost 600 people per square mile, but since only about 13 per cent of the total area is cultivated, there are over 4,000 people for each square mile of cultivated land. About half of the labor force is engaged in agriculture and fishing, and many of those engaged in non-agricultural pursuits return to the farm during periods of unemployment. In 1947 there were 204 cities of over 25,000 people, but only six cities of over 500,000 (with a total population of 8,175,367). Although it is the chief industrial economy of Asia, Japan is still largely rural or at least non-urban in character. This is underlined by the fact that from the end of World War II to 1955 the net movement of persons from the cities to the rural districts reached a total of 4,000,000 persons.

Japan's population has undergone a rapid expansion since the end of the Shogunate. Population was fairly stable under the Tokugawa regime (1602-1867) at around 26 million, but rose rapidly after the Meiji restoration and had doubled by 1925. In 1937 the population was about 70 million, and in 1948, 80.2 million, the difference being due not so much to natural increase as to the repatriation of some 6 million overseas Japanese at the end of the war. In 1955, the population was estimated at 89 million, the latest census having been in 1950. The rate of increase is now around 1 per cent annually, much lower than in earlier decades, and Japan's population may be nearing, though it certainly has not attained, stability. Over the next decade the population may be expected to increase by 9 or 10 million.

NATURAL RESOURCES

Japan is poorly endowed with mineral resources.[5] Many minerals are present, but only a few such as coal, copper, zinc, and sulphur are present in anything like adequate quantities. The shortage of minerals is frequently cited in extenuation of Japan's expansionary adventures in the twentieth century, even though Japan's own industrial development, achieved on the basis of imported supplies of many raw materials, illustrates the falsity of the premise. Japan has no nickel, aluminum, or magnesium, and iron ore is both insufficient and of low quality. Most coking coal must be imported. Copper is Japan's most important metallic mineral and is occasionally exported; zinc is fairly plentiful and there is some production of lead, tin, and chromium.

For energy Japan has enjoyed adequate supplies of steam coal, but the best seams are nearing exhaustion and becoming increasingly costly.

[5] See the comprehensive work by E. Ackerman, *Japanese Natural Resources* (Tokyo, 1949).

Petroleum reserves are insignificant and 95 per cent of requirements are imported. A large part of Japan's total energy supply comes from hydro-electric power, but most good hydro-electric sites have already been exploited. Japan may thus be one of the first countries in which atomic power production will become economically feasible.

GENERAL FEATURES OF THE ECONOMY

In Japan, the modern industrial economy, concentrated in a few urban centers and depending on foreign trade for raw materials and markets, has been superimposed on the traditional economy in which small-scale labor, intensive agriculture, and handicraft industries, supplying the domestic market, account for a large proportion of employment. Before the Meiji restoration, Japan was almost completely independent of foreign trade, with little or no mechanized industry. Three quarters of the working population were engaged in agriculture. Textile production was a small-scale, handicraft industry. Metal production was primitive. After the opening up of Japan, the new government saw the problem of modernizing the national economy not so much as the problem of developing a surplus (as would be the case with many underdeveloped countries today) as that of converting an agricultural surplus (rice, tea, silk and silk worms) into the means to pay for imports of modern machinery and equipment. The surplus was extracted from a docile agricultural population by taxation and high rents, at first in kind but before long in money. During the early stages of Japan's development the major exports were raw silk, tea, and rice, accounting for about two-thirds of the total. As the population increased, rice disappeared from the export list, and Japan now imports large quantities of foodstuffs, but textile products—first raw silk and later cotton yarn and piece goods—provided the bulk of Japan's exports. It was not until the thirties, when Japan embarked on the creation of a war economy, that intensive development of the metal, machinery, and chemicals industries was undertaken.[6] Thus a peasant economy developed into an industrial one by first exporting the products of agriculture to obtain the machinery and equipment needed to produce light manufactured and semi-finished goods. As the export of the latter increased, that of the former declined and Japan shifted from exporting to importing food and raw materials.

This process, however, was not carried as far in Japan as, for example,

[6] See G. Allen, *A Short Economic History of Modern Japan* (London, 1946), esp. pp. 143-160.

in the United Kingdom, and a large part of Japan's working population are still engaged in agriculture. Out of a total of 41 million persons employed in 1954, about 19 million were employed in agriculture, forestry and fishing, as compared with between 6 and 7 million in manufacturing.[7] On the other hand the value of output in manufacturing (1,421 billion yen in 1953) exceeds that of agriculture, forestry and fishing (1,300 billion yen), reflecting the much greater efficiency of the modern industrial sector of the economy.

Japan's agriculture is small scale: about three-quarters of the arable land is farmed by peasants[8] whose average holding is about three acres.[9] The chief food grain is rice, grown all over the southern part of Japan and utilizing about 60 per cent of the total arable land. Japanese rice production in 1954 was about 11.8 million tons. Wheat, rye, and barley utilize about 30 per cent of all arable land. Wheat production in 1954 was about 1.5 million tons. Yields per acre are relatively high (reflecting large inputs of labor and fertilizer), and yet about 20 per cent of Japan's food grain requirements must be imported. Thus further increases in population will require imports of foodstuffs, since there is little or no remaining uncultivated arable land. Tea is another important Japanese crop and is exported in quantity to the United States. Raw silk, produced by wheat farmers, is also an important crop and once was Japan's chief export. Now it accounts for less than 10 per cent by value of Japan's total exports. Sweet potatoes are an important food crop for domestic consumption. About 1.5 million persons are employed in the fisheries, and fish is—with rice—the staple food, with a total value exceeding that of the British fishing industry. In fact, Japan leads all other countries in the number of persons engaged in the fisheries, the size of its fleets and the volume of catch.[10] Canned and frozen fish are also an important export, and the Japanese fishing fleets operate not only in Japanese and nearby waters, but seek fish and whales in distant seas. As a result, Japan is frequently involved in international conflicts arising out of actual and alleged violations of foreign territorial waters by her fishing vessels. A case in point is the fishing issue between Japan and the Republic of Korea which accuses Japan of violations of the so-called Rhee Line, a unilaterally set water boundary extending more than sixty miles from the Korean coast.

[7] United Nations, *Economic Survey of Asia and the Far East, 1954* (Bangkok, 1955), Table 12, p. 218.

[8] D. Stamp, *An Intermediate Commercial Geography* (London, 1954), Part 2, p. 409.

[9] Cressey, *op. cit.*, 196.

[10] Woytinsky, *op. cit.*, p. 727.

The industrial sector of Japan's economy includes a wide range of textiles, iron and steel products, machinery and transportation equipment, chemicals and chemical fertilizers. Emphasis however, is on textiles, which in 1953 accounted for about 30 per cent of Japan's total exports. Production of cotton yarn in 1952 amounted to 353,100 tons compared with 268,100 tons in the UK, 292,400 in West Germany, and 724,700 tons in India. Japan also produces cotton, silk and woolen fabrics, and a wide range of manufactured consumer goods such as pottery and china, glass, paper, matches, and toys. Production of some basic industrial commodities and services in 1953 is given in the table below.[11]

COMMODITY	QUANTITY	UNIT
Coal	46.5	million tons
Petroleum products	6.1	" "
Iron ore	1.5	" "
Steel Ingots and Metal	7.7	" "
Cement	8.8	" "
Electricity	55.7	billion kwh
Sulphuric Acid	4.3	million tons
Ammonium sulphate	2.0	" "
Superphosphate	1.5	" "

Industrial production in Japan is concentrated in a belt extending from Tokyo and the Kwanto plain in the east along both shores of the Inland Sea to northern Kyushu and the western entrance of the Inland Sea (*cf.* Fig. 16-1, p. 520). Small factories producing native goods—silks, lacquer-ware, toys, and Japanese paper—are still active in the villages and towns, but modern factories are concentrated in or near the large cities, especially the six largest cities of Tokyo, Yokohama, Nagoya, Kobe, Osaka, and Kyoto. Textile production is concentrated in the Kobe-Osaka region, while heavy industry tended to be concentrated in the northern Kyushu region, near the coal fields and convenient to western ports for imports of iron ore and pig iron that used to come from Manchuria.

As indicated above, the Japanese economy is heavily dependent on imports, not only of food grains and sugar but even more of raw materials such as raw cotton for the cotton spinning industry, iron ore and coking coal for the steel industry, and petroleum. In the inter-war period imports of these commodities were paid for by exports of raw silk, especially to the United States, and of cotton textiles to less developed countries in Asia and Latin America. Imports from Japanese overseas possessions such as sugar from Formosa, iron ore from Manchuria, and rice from Korea,

[11] United Nations, *Economic Survey of Asia and the Far East.*

were obtained in exchange for textiles, other consumer goods and capital equipment. This trade accounted for 42 per cent of Japan's exports in 1936. In the postwar period, the United States market for silk had dwindled, the overseas possessions were gone, and trade with the China mainland dried up, partly because of Western export controls but mainly because under the Communists China's trade was reoriented to the Soviet bloc. In addition Japanese exports encountered political barriers in many markets and increasing competition from locally produced goods. Japan's share of total world trade was sharply reduced.

During the occupation period, before Japan's export industries had recovered from the effects of the war, necessary imports (especially cotton, wheat, coal, and iron ore) were supplied by the United States to the extent of Japan's inability to pay. From 1946 to 1949 such payments, for which the United States claims partial repayment, amounted to about $2 billion. Since the end of the occupation Japan has continued to have a substantial deficit on merchandise trade account, but procurement in Japan for the account of United States troops stationed there and for the United Nations Forces in Korea has occasioned foreign exchange payments to Japan sufficient to balance Japan's accounts without further assistance. These special earnings amounted to almost $3 billion in the years 1951 to 1954 inclusive.

Roughly 40 per cent of Japan's exports in 1953 went to the dollar area, 25 per cent to the sterling area, and 35 per cent to countries with whom Japan had bilateral trade arrangements. By contrast, over 50 per cent of Japan's imports have been coming from the dollar area against only 25 per cent from the sterling area and about 20 to 25 per cent from other areas. Thus Japan's trade and payments problem is also to a large extent a dollar problem because surpluses that might be earned in trading with the sterling or other areas cannot generally be applied to offset the deficit with the dollar area.

PRESENT POSITION AND PROSPECTS

Japan's economy has made a remarkable recovery from the effects of war and postwar adjustments. Despite the 20 per cent increase in population since before the war and despite the loss of empire, industrial production is well above the prewar level. *Per capita* consumption of practically everything except possibly housing, and labor productivity are equal to or above prewar levels. Agricultural production however has not kept pace with the population increase, and present food consumption levels depend on increased imports.

As indicated above, Japan's economic problem in the short run is that of increasing exports sufficiently to balance its current accounts without the aid of special procurement expenditures by the United States. In the long run, however, the problem is that of increasing exports to pay for increased imports of foodstuffs and raw materials. It has been estimated that Japan's food grain requirements increase each year by 200,000 tons merely to feed new mouths. Without radical improvements in agricultural technology, Japan cannot meet any considerable portion of these increased requirements except through imports, since yields per acre are very high and there is relatively little unused or reclaimable land. Increased exports will require increased imports of raw materials entering into such exports. And higher levels of income will generate demands for larger and more varied diets and for other goods utilizing imported raw materials. Thus Japan must strive continually for higher levels of trade, based on increased production of exportable goods and high levels of investment.

There are good reasons for believing that Japan can restore viability and the necessary dynamism to its economy. Output has been increasing at an impressive rate and investment is maintained at a proportion of income that compares favorably with Western countries enjoying much higher *per capita* incomes. The people of Japan are industrious and thrifty as well as literate and technically skilled. While the land and labor reforms introduced under the Occupation have to some extent redistributed income progressively, Japan is relying on its own peculiar forms of private enterprise and is likely to avoid expensive or risky welfare schemes and to pursue conservative monetary and fiscal policies. Thus needed incentives to improvement and modernization of obsolete plant and equipment will likely continue to be present.

As indicated above, the big problem for Japan will lie in the field of foreign trade. Some progress has already been shown in increasing Japan's share of certain export markets, notably in Latin America. It is not as easy to see how Japan will find alternative, non-dollar, sources of imports that formerly came from the United States or mainland Asia. The natural sources of these foodstuffs and raw materials for Japan would seem to be in South and Southeast Asia, and Japan's capital goods can contribute to the development of export availabilities in these areas.

Despite Japan's industrial superiority in Asia and its not unprepossessing outlook, Japan's actual military capabilities are slight. However, Japan is recovering rapidly from what has been called the trauma of defeat and Japanese forces will undoubtedly be strengthened. Nevertheless, there is still considerable opposition to large forces, both as unrealistic in the nuclear age and as requiring diversion of resources needed for modernization and expansion of Japan's export industries.

CHAPTER

17

The Economic Capabilities of Western Europe

A. Introduction

Europe is the smallest of the continents; with an area of three and three-fourths million square miles it has only one-fifth of the land area of Asia.[1] Indeed, from the viewpoint of physical geography it is a mere extension—a peninsula—of a larger land mass to which the term *Eurasia* is properly applied. Nevertheless, because of radical differences in historical development, cultural background, and political outlook between East and West it is customary to treat the larger area as two continents, roughly separated by a boundary consisting of the Ural mountains, the Caspian Sea, the Caucasus, and the Black Sea. And, as Mackinder pointed out, in contrast with "the unbroken lowland of the east," the European peninsula is a "rich complex of mountains and valleys, islands and peninsulas." [2]

This complex is one of the three or four great centers of population and industrial activity in the world. In the nineteenth century it experienced a phenomenal expansion in population and production, and five European states (Great Britain, France, Germany, Belgium, and the Netherlands) acquired among them political control over almost all of Africa and Asia except Japan, China, and what is today the Soviet Far East. By means of education and the press, even more by reason of the prestige which ac-

[1] J. Stembridge, *The World: A General Regional Geography* (London, 1953), p. 97.

[2] H. J. Mackinder, *The Geographical Pivot of History*, reprinted with an introduction by E. W. Gilbert, Royal Geographic Society (London, 1951), p. 31.

companied the extension of European political and military sway, the cultural and political values of Europe came to dominate almost the whole world. And the world economy, with its trade and shipping, its banking and insurance services, the gold standard and related currencies, was a European creation. The nineteenth century was indeed the European age.

It is true that during the nineteenth century Russia was expanding eastward, taking over the unpeopled spaces of Siberia and creating an empire of contiguous possessions, but the full implications of this expansion, as of the westward expansion of the United States, were not realized until after the first World War. It is true also that the nineteenth century witnessed the final liquidation of the Spanish and Portuguese empires in America. Nevertheless, the last three decades of the century were a period of phenomenal territorial expansion and conquest for the European powers, and the world power of Europe was at its height at the death of Queen Victoria in January, 1901.

A few comparisons will suffice to show how vast were the social and political changes that transformed the character of Europe between 1800 and 1900 (or 1914). After remaining static for centuries, the population of Europe began to grow rapidly in the eighteenth century and even more rapidly in the nineteenth. The population of Europe as a whole was about 50 million in 1800, 246 million in 1880, and 316 million in 1910. At the beginning of the nineteenth century, as elsewhere in the world, most of the population were engaged in agricultural pursuits and lived in small towns or villages and rural areas. At the beginning of the twentieth century in most countries of northern and central Europe, the majority of people were employed in nonagricultural pursuits and lived in towns and cities. This shift of population density to the cities was a reflection of the degree of industrialization that had taken place in Great Britain, Belgium, and Germany, and to a lesser extent in France, the Netherlands, and other countries.[3]

The nineteenth century was also a period of extraordinary colonial expansion in Asia and Africa. From 1884 to 1896, in twelve years, 2.6 million square miles were added to the British Empire, bringing the total to about 11.3 million square miles in all, almost one-fourth of the land area of the world.[4] At the opening of the twentieth century Britain governed a third of the whole population of Asia. France built up an empire in Indo-

[3] See Ch. I, "Industrial Foundations of Contemporary Europe," in C. J. H. Hayes, *Contemporary Europe Since 1870* (New York, 1953).

[4] E. Halevy, *A History of the English People,* trans. by E. I. Watkin (London, 1939), Epilogue, Vol. I, p. 30.

China. The Dutch extended and consolidated their control over the East Indies and in 1914 ruled over some 54 million Asians. British, German, and French enclaves were added to that of the Portuguese in China. And the partition of Africa in the last two decades of the nineteenth century gave the British, French, Belgians, and Portuguese substantial territories. Germany belatedly carved out a colonial empire in East Africa, the Cameroons, and Southwest Africa, but lost it to the victors in the World War of 1914-18.

The importance of economic factors in any imperialist expansion is always difficult to assess and it would be foolish to try to explain the scramble for colonies by the European great powers in the nineteenth century as motivated simply by the desire for new markets, or the pressure of surplus funds seeking investment. Nevertheless there is no doubt that the leading statesmen of Europe were sufficiently impressed by popular ideas of the importance of potential colonies as markets, raw material sources, and outlets for investment to act before it became too late. Jules Ferry, French cabinet leader and champion of the cause of France's new empire, put the argument in its most extreme form: "European consumption is saturated: it is necessary to raise new masses of consumers in other parts of the globe else we shall put modern society into bankruptcy and prepare for the dawn of the twentieth century a cataclysmic social liquidation of which one cannot predict the consequences." [5]

To speak of consumption being saturated, even in the France of today, is of course absurd; whatever truth there is in Ferry's prophecy does not depend on the evident falsity of his economics. The twentieth century is witnessing, for France and other colonial powers, the United Kingdom, and the Netherlands, not a cataclysmic social liquidation, but, along with other important political and social changes, the liquidation of the colonial empires built up in the nineteenth century. Germany, we have noted, lost its empire as a result of the first World War. The Dutch lost most of their East Indies possessions after the second. Britain has surrendered India and Burma, France is losing (or has lost) Indo-China. European influence and control, except for tiny Macao and Hong Kong have been excised. Everywhere the symbols of colonialism are challenged and decried; the European age, as the title of one book suggests, is passing.

The history of European imperialism in the nineteenth century and its liquidation in the twentieth lies outside the scope of our inquiry. If our theme were the economic history of imperialism, we would analyze care-

[5] Quoted by E. Achorn, *European Civilization and Politics since 1815* (New York, 1934), p. 246.

fully the relation between these processes of expansion and contraction, on the one hand, and the underlying economic capabilities on the other. But we would find no simple, unilinear relationship. It must not be thought that the loss of empire reflects nothing more than a sapping of economic strength, the onset of economic decay. In absolute terms the economies of Western Europe are stronger, their production and consumption higher, than ever before. But it was no accident that European overseas expansion occurred after a rapid expansion in industrial production and transportation which enabled the powers to confront native rulers, in Annam and Tonkin, in Madagascar, in China, in Algiers, with overwhelming force. The Japanese learned this lesson quickly and put it to effective use themselves. Likewise it was no accident that independence came to India and Burma. Pakistan and Syria, Egypt and Indonesia, at a time when the economies of the metropolitan countries were not only recoiling under the impact of war and occupation, but facing new claims on resources from more welfare-minded citizens.

No doubt the most important factors have been in the realm of ideas and the imagination. The moral and cultural prestige of Europe tended to fall with the introduction of European ideas abroad. The submission of the Asian or African to the European's right to rule disappeared with the spread of ideas of democracy, nationalism, equality, and social justice. The basis of European superiority was destroyed when members of the subject races learned the secrets of Western science and technology and decided, rightly or wrongly, that the industrial revolution would come to their countries under their own sponsorship. But the opportunities to assert their countries' independence came at the low ebb of European economic strength in the decade after World War II.

We have merely sketched the leading role the industrialized countries of Europe played in the nineteenth and early twentieth centuries. What will be the role of Europe in the world economy of the next half-century?

Despite the loss of important overseas possessions, and even though now outdistanced by the growth of the American and Soviet economies, Western Europe has not wholly lost its dynamism. The economies of Western Europe continue to grow and in the aggregate they make a major contribution to the strength of the Free World. It is this contribution and its geographical and economic basis that we examine in this chapter.

Our method is to look first at the economic geography and the economic structure of Western Europe. With the factual information thus provided we shall then examine the dynamic factors in Western Europe's economy and their implications for the future growth of economic capabilities.

B. Geographical Features of Western Europe

Peninsular Europe would include both the countries of Western and Northern Europe and the U.S.S.R. and Eastern Europe in an unmistakable geographical unity. According to H. B. George, physical geography would divide Europe into some dozen sections: Spain (with Portugal), Gaul, the British Isles, Rhone-land, Rhineland, Italy, Balkan-land, Danube-land, North Germany, Bohemia, Russia, and Scandinavia.[6] Wright employs a simpler classification of four main subdivisions, but his Alpine-Mediterranean region would include much of Balkan-land, while East Germany, Poland, and Russia fall into his Northeastern Europe.[7] In recent years, however, it has become common to treat the whole of the U.S.S.R. separately and to exclude Russia when discussing European geography and politics. In addition, for our purposes we must limit the concept of Europe even further and focus on what is now called Western Europe, since the expansion of the Soviet bloc has engulfed the countries of Eastern Europe, the Balkans (except Greece and Yugoslavia) and the Baltic countries in a new political unity. Nor is this merely a new political dividing line cutting across a geographical unity; the countries of Eastern Europe were formerly bound by trade and cultural ties with Western Europe, and Europe formed a close-knit economic system, whereas now the cultural and economic life of Eastern Europe has been closed off from the West and its trade has been largely reoriented to the Soviet economy.

WHAT IS WESTERN EUROPE?

This division of Europe into East and West is likewise reflected in the postwar organization of political and economic life in Western Europe, for under the Marshall Plan co-operative measures to restore trade and production to normal levels, to strengthen currencies and liberalize trade, and to broaden markets, resulted in the formation of a number of new international economic planning and consultative bodies, such as the Organization for European Economic Co-operation (OEEC), the European Payments Union (EPU), and the Coal-Steel Community (CSC). Thus it is now possible for certain purposes to define Western Europe by membership in OEEC. This has an additional convenience because the OEEC is now the central source and co-ordinating agent for many of the eco-

[6] *The Relations of Geography and History* (London, 1930), p. 118.

[7] J. K. Wright, *The Geographical Basis of European History* (New York, 1928), p. 4.

nomic statistics of the member countries. More will be said of these organizations later in the chapter.

OEEC includes Austria, Belgium, Denmark, France, Federal (West) Germany, Greece, Iceland, Ireland, Italy, Luxembourg, The Netherlands, Norway, Portugal, The Saar, Sweden, Switzerland, Trieste, Turkey, and the United Kingdom. Spain is not a member of the OEEC, nor is Yugoslavia, whereas Turkey, The United Kingdom, Ireland, and Iceland are. Except for the United Kingdom these omissions and inclusions need not detain us, even though they may appear anomalous geographically, because in any case they would not greatly affect the statistical measures of economic capabilities. The British Isles, separated late in geological time from continental Europe by the straits of Dover, and strongly influenced by this geographical position, has been in the last two centuries the center of a world-wide political and economic community. Nevertheless, in this chapter the United Kingdom is considered to be part of Western Europe. Not only is this convenient because the United Kingdom is a member of OEEC and included in Western Europe for statistical purposes; the United Kingdom as a member of the North Atlantic Treaty Organization (NATO) is one of the keystones in European defense arrangements and therefore must be counted in when we are analyzing Western Europe's economic capabilities.

More important than these organizations in relation to political and strategic factors are the groupings of Western European states for military purposes. Membership in NATO therefore is another way of defining Western Europe, especially when one is measuring and comparing the capabilities of those countries co-operating in the Western European defense arrangements. This group is smaller than the OEEC group, since Austria, Sweden, Switzerland, and Ireland are members of the latter but not the former. The continental core of European defense comprises a still smaller group of countries seeking to find some basis of union or federation for defense purposes: France, West Germany, Italy, the Saar, Belgium, Luxembourg, and The Netherlands. They now constitute what is known as the Western European Union.

The Europe with which we deal in this chapter, therefore, is Europe minus Russia, the Baltic countries, Poland, Czechoslovakia, Hungary, Rumania, Bulgaria, Albania, and East Germany. In addition to the continental countries of Western Europe we shall include the United Kingdom and Ireland, Iceland (but not Greenland), and Turkey. With these exceptions, the area which we are describing has the same boundaries as the continental Europe of customary geographical descriptions: the Atlantic Ocean and the North Sea on the west, the Mediterranean on the south, and the Arctic Ocean on the north. It was always the eastern boundary which gave geographers trouble, in any case, and the boundary which has now been established by the Iron Curtain is not without a certain limited geographical sanction, for it coincides very roughly with the climatic boundary between the coastal climate of Western Europe and the continental climate of Central and Eastern Europe.[8]

Except for parts of Norway, Sweden, and Finland, Western Europe lies entirely in the Temperate Zone. But Western Europe's situation and shape influence its climate favorably, perhaps more than its latitudinal position. Its location in the westerly variable wind belt and the absence of a north-south mountain barrier mean that the moderating influence of the Atlantic Ocean is borne a considerable distance inland. Europe has the longest coast line in relation to its area of any of the continents, and no part of Western Europe is farther than 500 miles from the sea.[9] There is consequently sufficient rainfall for cultivation almost everywhere in Western Europe except the interior of Spain, and it is well-distributed throughout the year. In the west and northwest autumn rains predominate; summer rains are greatest in the eastern part of the region. In the south of Europe the mountain-sheltered peninsular countries that form the northern coast of the Mediterranean experience the dry summers and warm rainy winters associated with that name.

PHYSICAL FEATURES AND COMMUNICATION LINES

Northern Europe is separated from the Mediterranean regions by a formidable chain of mountains, the Pyrenees, the Alps, the Carpathians, and associated lesser ranges. Running south from these mountains are the folds of the Apennines, forming the backbone of Italy, and the Dinaric Alps and Pindus Mountains. North of this barrier are the central uplands including the dry Spanish meseta, the central plateau of France, the highlands of Brittany, Cornwall, and southwest Ireland, the Ardennes and the Rhine highlands, and the Vosges and Black Forest ranges on either

[8] For example, the line marking the western limit of average below-freezing surface temperatures in January (D. Stamp, *The World* [New York, 1943], Fig. 112). "The 32° F winter line runs from Iceland to northern Norway, along the coast to Denmark, south to the Alps, then east to the Caspian Sea. . . . A line from Salonika to northwest Germany will have almost all the winter rainfall of over 10 inches on the west side and that of less than 10 inches on the east—the dry continental interior." G. D. Hubbard, *The Geography of Europe,* 2nd ed. (New York, 1952), pp. 30-32.

[9] For a survey of Europe's physical geography see Stembridge, *op. cit.,* Ch. 10, and Hubbard, *op. cit.,* Chs. 1, 2, and 3.

side of the Rhine valley. North of these uplands, in turn, is the great European plain, stretching from the Atlantic Coast of France across the Lowlands and Germany, Poland, and Russia. This extensive and fertile plain not only accounts for the high proportion of arable land in Europe; it has made for an ease of communications which has facilitated the industrial expansion of northern and western Europe.[10] The plentiful and year-round rainfall provides an even flow of water in the rivers, and this plus the level character of the plain has resulted in waterways being extensively used for transportation of goods. The river systems have been extended and interconnected by canals ramifying through France, Belgium, and the Rhine valley. While most of this traffic originates or terminates at Channel or North Sea ports, two rivers connect western and central Europe with the south, the Rhone flowing into the Mediterranean at Marseille, and the Danube, navigable in normal times for over 1,500 miles from Ulm in Western Germany to the Black Sea. In recent years, however, the Danube has in its lower reaches been denied to Western European traffic by the Iron Curtain.

The terrain and climate of the United Kingdom similarly favored extensive use of inland waterways, and its coast line and location in respect to other countries of northern and western Europe provided the natural conditions for coastal and other shipping.

> The sinking of the continent by allowing the ocean to extend through the North Sea into the Baltic has opened up the heart of North-West Europe . . . the lower courses of many rivers have been converted into estuaries, at the head of which now stand some of the world's greatest ports. In the south the Mediterranean and Black Seas provided a sea-way extending more than 2,000 miles from the Atlantic while the Adriatic arm of the Mediterranean provided an outlet for the southern part of Central Europe.[11]

Altogether, the peninsular character of Europe, with its inland seas, well-developed coast lines, protected bays and harbors, and many navigable rivers constituted the basis of an extensive and economical water transport system. It is not hard to understand why foreign trade bulks so large in the economies of Western Europe.

NATURAL RESOURCES

This sketchy résumé of the "geographical conditions" of Western Europe would be incomplete without some reference to the natural resources

[10] L. D. Stamp and S. C. Gilmour, *Chisholm's Handbook of Commercial Geography,* 14th ed. (New York, 1954), pp. 316, 317.

[11] Stembridge, *op. cit.,* pp. 97, 98.

upon which the economic development of these countries rests, those "treasures of field, forest and mine bestowed upon her by a moister climate, a more varied land surface and a more complex geological past." [12]

First must be mentioned the resources of the soil and vegetation, for Europe was once largely agricultural. Most of Western and Central Europe were once covered by deciduous woodlands, long since cleared for cultivation. As noted earlier, the proportion of agricultural land is higher in Europe (37 per cent) than in any other continent. The ratio is 10 per cent in North and Middle America, 6 per cent in Asia, and 5 per cent in South America. This high proportion is due in part to the level character of the European plain, and in part to the fact that almost four-fifths of the land area of Europe receives adequate (10 inches or more annually) rainfall, as compared to one-third in North America, 30 per cent in Asia, and one-fourth in Africa. Only the South American continent compares favorably in adequacy of rainfall and its distribution.[13]

While Western Europe still depends importantly on its intensive agriculture, it is no exaggeration to say that its mineral resources are even more important, since Western Europe as a whole now imports agricultural goods and exports manufactures (Fig. 17-1). Western Europe's extensive deposits of coal and iron ore were the key to its industrial development, and are the essential base for its manufacturing industries. British coal mines still produce one-fifth of the world's coal, although the better veins have been worked out. Outside the United Kingdom, the principal coal deposits are the Franco-Belgian fields, and the Ruhr. Unfortunately, there are no coal mines of importance in southern Europe. Iron ore, however, is well-distributed in Europe, with the richest ores in Sweden and northern Spain. Most of the iron ore is produced in France, the United Kingdom, Sweden, and Luxembourg, in that order.

Production and reserves of some other important minerals are substantial, especially tungsten, bauxite, lead, zinc, mercury, and sulphur. Spain and Italy produce about two-thirds of the world supply of mercury. Italy is the second largest producer of sulphur, and Spain, Western Germany, and Yugoslavia each produce more than 50,000 tons of lead annually. Copper and tungsten are produced in moderate amounts, and nickel in small amounts. Manganese and chromite are practically all imported.

[12] Wright, *op. cit.*, p. 25.

[13] Figures on rainfall and arable land are from W. S. and E. S. Woytinsky, *World Population and Production* (New York, 1954), p. 316. For somewhat different figures and definitions see *Trends in Economic Growth*, Table 21, p. 99, based on the *Economic Bulletin for Europe*, Vol. 3, No. 2 (1951), pp. 22-23, and *Yearbook of Food and Agricultural Statistics* (Washington, 1950), Part I, pp. 13-17.

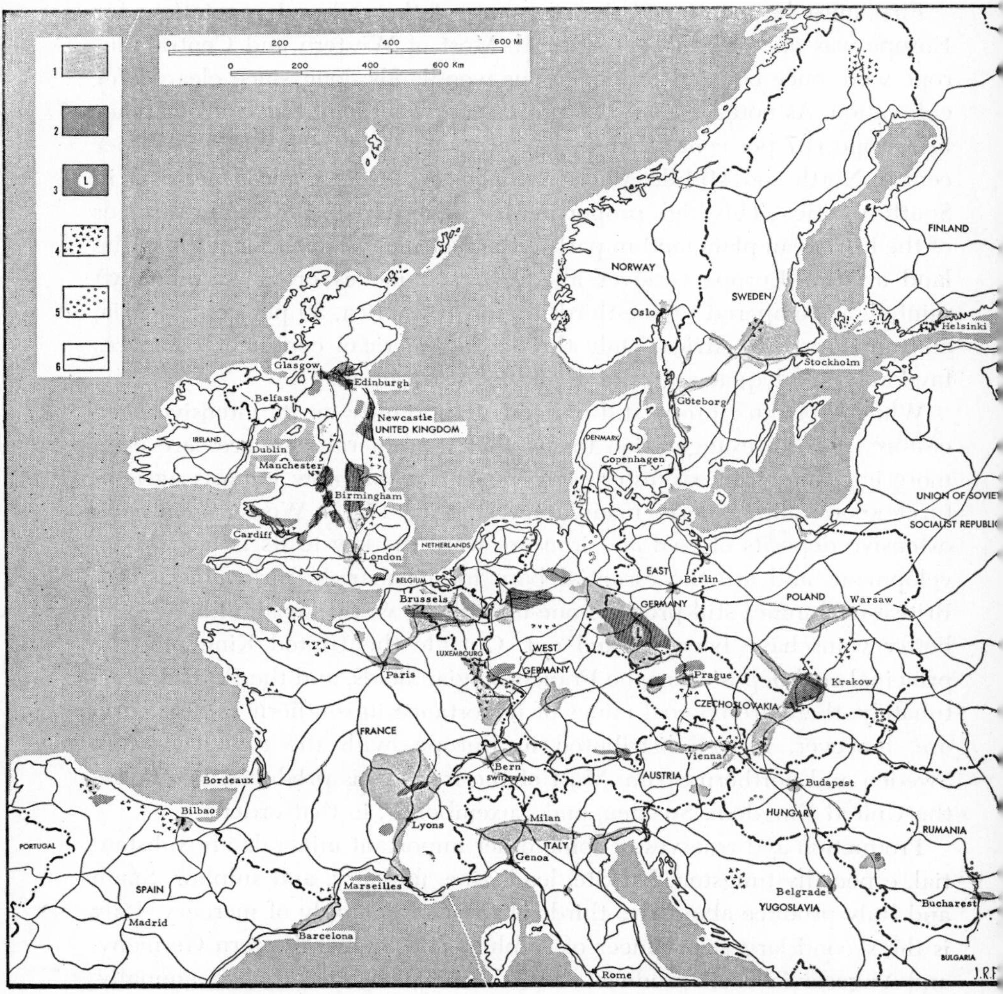

FIG. 17-1. Europe: Railroads, Resources, and Industrial Concentrations in Western Europe (1) industrial regions; (2) coal; (3) lignite coals; (4) iron ore; petroleum; (6) selected railroads.

So far very little crude oil and natural gas production have been developed in Western Europe. The poor distribution of coal and the absence of petroleum and natural gas is to some extent compensated by substantial potential and actual hydro-electrical power supplies in Italy, France, Sweden, Norway, Switzerland, and Sweden.

C. The Economic Structure of Western Europe

GENERAL CHARACTERISTICS

The group of countries we call Western Europe covers an area of 1,784,000 square miles and comprises a population of over 335 million people. It thus includes about 14 per cent of the population of the globe but only about 3 per cent of its total land area. It has an average population density of 188 persons per square mile compared with 45 for the United States, 21.5 for Latin America, 17 for Africa, and 123 for Asia. After the United States and Canada it is the most highly developed area in the world with an average gross national product *per capita* in 1955 of $891. In 1948 the combined national income of these countries was estimated at $122.6 billion or about 22 per cent of the world total.[14] Western Europe in 1955 produced 527 million tons of coal, 80 million tons of steel, 369 billion kilowatt hours of electricity, and 547,000 tons of primary aluminum. These production figures represented the following percentages of the total production of these commodities in the United States, Canada, and Western Europe combined: coal 53 per cent, steel 42 per cent, electricity 34 per cent, and aluminum 22 per cent. Western Europe's gross national product exceeds that of the entire Communist bloc; on a *per capita* basis it is almost four times as great. Western European steel and electric power production exceed production in the Communist bloc. British, Dutch, and French companies produce at home and overseas more than one and one-half times all the crude oil production in the Communist bloc. Thus the community of Western Europe possesses in the aggregate the technological and resource basis for great power status.

The economy of Western Europe as a whole is markedly industrial, with an average standard of living below that of the United States but higher than that of any other important region in the world. In the industrialized countries of Western and Central Europe a high standard of liv-

[14] Woytinsky, *op. cit.*, pp. 393, 394, and IR 7247, Dept. of State (Washington, D. C., 1956).

ing results from the use of specialized capital equipment and a skilled labor force in both industry and agriculture. The basis of the industrial life of Western Europe is a concentration of production of certain key commodities, especially coal, steel, and chemicals. Using its own production of these commodities, plus imports of other necessary raw materials, Western Europe as a whole produces a wide range of manufactured goods, both for producers and consumers, a relatively large part of which are exported to pay for imports of raw materials and foodstuffs.

Western Europe is primarily industrial also in the sense that mining and manufacturing account for larger shares of the total product than agriculture, fishing, and forestry combined. It is a food-deficit area: in 1950-52 imports of bread grain were 30 per cent of consumption, of coarse grains 21 per cent, and of sugar 36 per cent.[15] In terms of calories, Western Europe depends on imports for about one-fifth of its food supplies. However, it must not be assumed that agriculture is of no importance. The bulk of Western Europe's food requirements are supplied from within the area, and the proportion of active workers engaged in agriculture ranges from about one-fifth in northwestern Europe to about one-half in southern Europe.[16] The share of agriculture in national income ranges from between 5 and 10 per cent for the United Kingdom and Belgium to between 30 and 40 per cent for Ireland, Iceland, and Greece.[17]

ENERGY AND FUEL SUPPLY

The industrialized countries of western and northern Europe are high energy consuming countries, particularly the United Kingdom, Germany, Belgium, Norway, and Sweden.[18] Coal is still the dominant source of energy, accounting in 1950 for about four-fifths of the total energy supply.[19]

In some countries (Norway, Finland, Sweden, Italy, Austria, and Switzerland) three-quarters or more of total electricity supplies come from hydro-electric plants, but these countries were either small or their total energy consumption low relative to the larger, more industrialized

[15] Economic Commission for Europe (ECE), *Economic Survey of Europe Since the War* (Geneva, 1954), p. 170.

[16] Economic Commission for Europe, *Growth and Stagnation in the European Economy* (Geneva, 1954), Table A. 4, p. 237.

[17] *Trends in Economic Growth, A Comparison of the Western Powers and the Soviet Bloc,* Legislative Reference Service (Washington, 1955), pp. 272, 273.

[18] *Point Four,* Department of State Publication 3719, January, 1950, Appendix C-4, p. 119.

[19] ECE, *Growth and Stagnation, etc.,* p. 104.

countries, so that for Western Europe as a whole water power accounted for only 12 per cent of total commercial energy.[20]

Petroleum products and natural gas supply about 10 per cent of Western Europe's energy requirements, but petroleum production is small, amounting in 1953 to only 3.6 million metric tons, almost entirely in Western Germany and France. The resulting deficit is made up by imports of crude petroleum and petroleum products.

Assuring an adequate and expanding supply of energy in the light of coal production difficulties and the failure to find oil in significant quantities on the continent has become one of Western Europe's chief economic (and strategic) problems. See below (page 559) for further discussion of this problem.

INDUSTRY AND MANUFACTURING

The iron and steel industry is the industrial core of Western Europe. The output of the iron and steel industry is sufficient to provide for the needs of the region and to supply about three-fourths of the Free World's exports of steel products to overseas markets. Steel production in Western Europe is concentrated in four major producing areas, the United Kingdom, Western Germany, France and the Saar, and Belgium-Luxembourg (*cf.* Fig. 17-1, p. 540). While the United Kingdom has the largest production, France and Belgium-Luxembourg are the largest exporters, selling more than 50 per cent of their production abroad.

The big continental coal and steel-producing areas are interdependent. Western Germany, the largest coal and steel producer, exports coking coal and coke and imports more than half of its iron ore requirements. France is a net exporter of iron ore and imports coal and coke. Belgium-Luxembourg exports steel in large quantities but must import both iron ore and coke.

This heavy industrial base exists to support a wide range of both heavy and light manufacturing. For the countries of north and west Europe manufacturing accounts for between 25 per cent and 35 per cent of national income. For Italy also the proportion is about 30 per cent; for the other countries of southern Europe the ratio is considerably less (as 20 per cent for Greece).[21] The most important manufacturing activities in Western Europe are the engineering (machinery), textiles, and chemicals industries. These industries account for the largest share of the national

[20] See *Trends in Economic Growth,* p. 151.
[21] *Trends in Economic Growth,* Table 3.

product and employment and are most important to the strategic mobilization of economic capabilities.

Output of engineering products (machinery, electrical goods, vehicles and transportation equipment) in Western Europe in 1951 amounted to $18 billion or roughly 10 per cent of the gross national product. Of this output about $3.3 billion was exported, leaving $14.7 billion for use in Western Europe.[22] The United Kingdom and West Germany are, of course, the big producers of engineering products.

The automobile industry is an important sector in the engineering category. Motor vehicle production in 1950 was 1.6 million vehicles. In the interwar period the shipyards of Western Europe produced 80 per cent of the world's new merchant vessels, but in 1950 the share had fallen to 46 per cent.

The textiles industry is almost as important as the machinery industry although perhaps of less strategic importance. The textiles industry accounts (1950-51) for 8 per cent of all manufacturing employment in Norway and Sweden, 11 to 12 per cent in the United Kingdom, Denmark, and the Netherlands, and 18 to 19 per cent in Italy and Belgium. Exports of textiles, especially of cotton textiles, are still Western Europe's principal export.

The chemical industry is another European industry which is of first importance both economically and strategically. The chemical industry was developed in Europe in the nineteenth century and at the time of World War I Western Europe accounted for over 50 per cent of world production and over 80 per cent of world exports of chemicals,[23] to a large extent because of German leadership in synthetic dyestuffs and pharmaceutical chemicals. Subsequently, Western Europe's share of world chemical production declined because of the expansion of the chemicals industry in the United States and the U.S.S.R. However, exports of chemical products have retained their percentage share of total Western European exports.[24]

TRANSPORTATION

The countries of central and northwestern Europe (France, Belgium, Netherlands, Germany, Austria) and the United Kingdom have extensive inland water transportation systems. The United Kingdom has 4,600 miles of navigable waterway with an ingenious network of interlocking canals

22 *Trends in Economic Growth,* Table 3.
23 ECE, *Growth and Stagnation,* pp. 163-165.
24 *Ibid.*

constructed mostly in the pre-railway early nineteenth century. In 1954, the canals of the Docks and Inland Waterways Board (excluding the Manchester Ship Canal) carried only about 180 million short ton miles. France has almost 6,000 miles of navigable waterways connecting the waterways systems of the Seine, the Rhine, and the Rhone. About 11,000 craft carried more than 5 billion short ton miles in 1954.

There are about 3,000 miles of navigable waterways in West Germany, including the Rhine which is the backbone of the system. In 1954 West Germany had an inland fleet of more than 7,000 craft carrying about 8.5 billion short ton miles of freight.[25]

The Rhine flows through Europe's greatest industrial concentrations, carrying coal, coke and grain upstream, and timber, potash and iron ore downstream. It is primarily a German river, and most of the industries served by it and most of the traffic along its course are German. Yet in its delta regions the Rhine is controlled by the Netherlands and by Belgium. A net of inland canals constructed by Germany, Belgium, and the Netherlands bears witness to the competing interests of the three nations, with Germany striving, through means of port diversion, to gain an outlet to the sea which is not controlled by other states, and the Low Countries (Belgium, of course, is not directly on the Rhine) intent on channelling as much Rhine traffic as possible toward their ports. Of the German efforts directed at port diversion the Dortmund-Ems canal extension to Emden, and the Mittelland Canal, linking the Ruhr with the Elbe River, Berlin, and the Oder River are the most important. The operation of this net work, however, has been hampered by the East-West division of the country since the Midland system is in the East Zone. This had led to controversies between the occupying powers, especially in connection with the use of the canals in and around Berlin.[26]

Upstream, Switzerland and Austria share a vital interest in participation in Rhine river traffic. Both of them are landlocked. Whereas the Rhine river basin with the now very important port of Basel represents the natural outlet to the sea for Switzerland, Austria is oriented toward the Danube. A linking of the basins of the Rhine and the Danube would be of major importance since a completed and internationally functioning Rhine-Main-Danube canal would open up a new inland canal avenue from the North Sea to the Mediterranean via the Black Sea. However, thus far only the Main up to Würzburg has been fully canalized and the prospect for completion of the whole work before 1970 appears slim at the

[25] Economic Commission for Europe, *Annual Bulletin of Statistics,* 1954.
[26] See G. Hoffman, ed., *A Geography of Europe* (New York, 1953), pp. 410-411.

present time. Not only is the Danube at times beset by navigational difficulties, but the political odds created by the control of the lower Danube by the U.S.S.R. and the satellite nations of Moscow still seem to militate against the kind of international co-operation which had been carried out by the European Danube Commission on the maritime Danube (Braila-Black Sea) since 1856 and by the International Danube Commission on the fluvial Danube (Ulm-Braila) after World War I. On the basis of the U.S.S.R.-inspired Belgrade Convention of 1948, the Soviet-Satellite-Yugoslav stretch of the Danube has been controlled by the Budapest (former Galati) Danube Commission since 1949, while traffic between Germany and Austria on the one hand and the lower Danube nations on the other moves on the basis of bilateral agreements.

As other major projects for the future may be mentioned that of the canalization of the upper Rhine between the Lake of Constance and Basel and that of a Rhine-Rhone waterway which would provide Switzerland with two links to the open sea and France with an important new route to North Africa.

Despite the extensive ramification of navigable waterways in northwest Europe, the inland waterways of Western Europe, according to statistics of the Economic Commission for Europe, carry only about one-fifth of all the water and rail freight (ton miles) moved in Western Europe.[27] This is about the same proportion as obtained before World War II (1938). In the postwar period the importance of road transport has increased at the expense of rail transport but the latter remains the most important single method of internal transport for Western Europe as a whole. Motor transport in the interwar period did not increase as it did in the United States partly because motor-vehicle production was not so advanced, partly because of state regulations intended to protect the railways from motor-vehicle competition. However, road transport has made considerable progress in the United Kingdom, France, Germany, and Italy.

Railroads (*cf.* Fig. 17-1, p. 540) still transport the great bulk of domestic and particularly of international freight and passenger traffic in Europe. A certain amount of international integration already had been achieved in the nineteenth century. It comprised agreements on the (standard) gauge to be used on all principal railways between the borders of Spain and Russia, on the characteristics of railway cars and on the international transport contract. These agreements also extended to time tables for international freight and passenger trains which to a certain extent provided the framework into which the national train schedules had

[27] Economic Commission for Europe, *Annual Bulletin of Transport Statistics,* 1954.

to fit. Most of these conventions are administered by international agencies, partly governmental but largely inter-carrier organizations which, however, due to the nationalization of practically all principal railroads, have quasi-governmental character. In spite of the political division of Europe with the appearance of the Iron Curtain nearly all of these conventions and arrangements are still in force and the international organizations, such as those for car exchanges, time tables, the international transport contract, and the handling of dangerous goods, continue to operate on both sides of the Iron Curtain (excepting in most instances, however, as was the case before World War II, the Soviet Union).

Closer integration of Western European railways is being attempted now, mainly under the aegis of such post-World War II organizations as the European Coal and Steel Community, the European Conference of Ministers of Transport, and the Council of Europe. The West European countries already have pooled about 10 per cent of their freight cars, they are about to centralize their car and perhaps also locomotive purchases, and the most important rail tariffs of the Coal and Steel Community countries are in the process of being integrated.

AGRICULTURE

The relative economic importance of agriculture differs widely within the region, and the same is true of the character of agriculture in the different countries, corresponding to differences in climate, soil, density of agricultural population, size of land holdings, and agricultural techniques. "Within the area, most farming systems, apart from the purely tropical, would be found: from the rough grazings of the upland districts of Scandinavia and the northern parts of the United Kingdom to the vineyards of southern France and Italy and the tobacco fields of Greece. While single crops were often important, in general mixed farming predominated over monoculture. Farming was intensive and crop yields were well above those of the rest of the world." [28]

The principal crops are wheat, barley, corn, potatoes, sugar beets, meat and dairy products, wine, and citrus fruits. Some cotton and tobacco are grown. Crop yields for wheat and barley are about the same in Southern Europe (Greece, Italy, Portugal, and Turkey) as in the United States but are considerably higher in the other OEEC countries. Crop yields for corn are from two-thirds to five-sixths of the United States average. The de-

[28] Committee of European Co-operation, *Technical Report,* Vol. 2 (Paris, 1947), p. 21.

gree of mechanization (number of tractors per acre of agricultural land) in some countries, notably the United Kingdom, Switzerland, Sweden, Norway, West Germany, and Denmark, compares not unfavorably with that of the United States. The use of chemical fertilizers is well-advanced in northwestern Europe and is increasing in southern Europe.

Nearly all the countries are substantial importers of bread grains, although France and Spain are nearly self-sufficient and Turkey usually a net exporter. The same is true of coarse grains, except that Denmark and Finland are virtually self-sufficient while the countries of southern Europe are either self-sufficient or net exporters. France and Denmark export sugar and the Netherlands and Denmark are heavy exporters of dairy products. Denmark, Ireland, and the Netherlands export meat and meat produce and livestock (Ireland), and import vegetable products, partly for the feeding of livestock. Some of the problems involved in increasing agricultural production in Western Europe are discussed below (see pp. 549, 560-561).

REGIONAL PATTERNS

The bulk of Western Europe's population is concentrated in seven countries which account for roughly three-fifths of the population but less than a third of the total area. These are the United Kingdom, France (with the Saar), West Germany, Italy, Belgium-Luxembourg, and the Netherlands. These seven states are the core of Western Europe's economic and industrial capabilities.

These are not the most prosperous countries in Western Europe. In fact, five other countries (Norway, Denmark, Iceland, Sweden, and Switzerland) have *per capita* gross national products as high as or higher than that of the United Kingdom, which is the wealthiest of the seven states mentioned above. But these five countries account for only 20 million people and their aggregate gross product came in 1952-53 to about $20 billion. The larger group of states referred to above had a combined gross product of $143.6 billion, or three-fourths of the value of all goods and services produced in the whole of the region we call Western Europe. If the two groups of states are combined they represent about 70 per cent of the population and 85 per cent of the production.

If we look to measures of industrial power such as steel and coal production, the larger group of seven states is even more clearly apparent as the core area of Western Europe. Here is produced 90 per cent of all the crude steel, 95 per cent of the coal, and 70 per cent of the electric power for Western Europe as a whole. The railroads of these countries carry more than three-fourths of the total ton kilometers of freight transported by rail in all of Western Europe. Of the other countries only Sweden can really pretend to being an industrial power with a gross national product of over $8 billion in 1952-53 (greater than either Belgium or Holland), crude steel production of 1.8 million metric tons (Holland had less than 1 million metric tons), and electric power production more than twice as great as Belgium's and three times as great as Holland's. However, it must be noted that Sweden, because of its traditional neutrality, lies outside the framework of European defense arrangements.

The countries in which the agricultural sectors are most highly developed and production most efficient are likewise the United Kingdom and the countries of northern and western Europe. With only 24 per cent of the active population in agriculture and 28 per cent of the arable land they produce almost half of the agricultural products in all of Western Europe. The countries of southern Europe (Greece, Italy, Portugal, Spain, Turkey, and Yugoslavia) on the other hand, with more than two-thirds of the active population in agriculture and over one-half of the arable land account for only one-third of the agricultural output.[29] Thus yields are considerably lower in southern Europe and productivity per worker even less than in north and west Europe.

Agriculture in the United Kingdom is the most efficient in all of Western Europe. This is partly because of the early elimination of small holdings and the consequent low density of agricultural population, the lack of tariff protection during the last half of the nineteenth century and the early decades of the twentieth, and the wartime and postwar efforts to increase output for the purpose of economizing foreign exchange. Agricultural output in the Scandinavian countries is also relatively high both per hectare and per worker.[30]

FOREIGN TRADE

In the countries of Western Europe the principle of international division of labor is carried farther than in any other important region. In other words, with a heavy specialization in manufacturing and a concomitant dependence upon imported supplies of foodstuffs and raw materials, foreign trade is critically important to Western Europe. Roughly 10 per cent of the national income represents goods exported to pay for imports, as

[29] ECE, *Economic Survey of Europe Since the War,* p. 164.
[30] *Ibid.,* 165.

contrasted with only 4 per cent in the United States and 1 per cent for the U.S.S.R. Western Europe's imports from the rest of the world consist mainly of raw materials for Europe's manufacturing industries (51 per cent), foodstuffs and animal feed (34 per cent), and some manufactured products (15 per cent); exports to the rest of the world are mainly manufactured goods (74 per cent) with some raw materials (16 per cent) and foodstuffs (10 per cent).[31]

This high degree of reliance on foreign trade has been one of the conditions of economic progress for Western Europe, but it also has other important consequences, both economic and strategic. It not only makes the area vulnerable to disruption of shipping in time of war; it also subjects the economy to the shock of economic changes in the rest of the world, such as changes in the degree and character of demand for manufactured goods, or higher prices for raw materials and foodstuffs. Europe's prosperity and stability depend therefore not only on the efforts of Europeans but as well on the maintenance of full employment in the United States, and on a continuous expansion of supplies of raw materials and foodstuffs in overseas areas. The degree of this dependence is greater for some countries than others; in Holland, for example, 35 per cent of the gross national product is based on foreign trade.

Reference has already been made to Europe's dependence on imported food and feeding stuffs. Western Europe is also the world's largest importer of raw cotton and raw wool. Other raw materials imported in large quantities include rubber, jute, non-ferrous metals (copper and lead), sulphur, and crude petroleum.

Traditionally, Western Europe has had an adverse trade balance, that is, its exports paid for only about two-thirds of its imports from the rest of the world; and the deficit was offset by a surplus on "invisible" transactions, that is, income from shipping, insurance, and overseas investments. Now, however, as a result of the reduction in overseas investments during the war, increased indebtedness, and the larger role of United States shipping in ocean transportation, Western Europe's surplus on "invisibles" pays for a much smaller proportion of its total imports. This fact, plus the need to obtain a larger share of total imports from the dollar currency area in the postwar period, and other and more complicated factors, created the European balance-of-payments problem and its acuter manifestation known as the dollar shortage or dollar gap. More will be said about this in a later section.

[31] Organization for European Economic Co-operation (OEEC), *At Work for Europe* (Paris, 1954), p. 14; percentages are for OEEC countries in 1952.

Although the dollar problem in Western Europe's balance-of-payments should not be minimized, it should be noted that trade with the dollar area is by no means the bulk of Europe's trade. In 1953, imports from the dollar area were about 15 per cent of the total imports, and exports to the dollar area about 12 per cent of total exports, if intra-European trade is included in the total. Intra-European trade is nearly half of the total foreign trade of Western European countries.[32] However, as pointed out in another chapter, trade with Eastern Europe has been very sharply reduced.[33] Another large share (13 per cent in 1953) of Europe's trade is with the overseas territories of the United Kingdom, France, Belgium, Portugal, and the Netherlands. These territories, such as the British West Indies, Malaya, Singapore and Hong-Kong, British Africa, the French possessions in Africa and Oceania, the Belgian Congo, and others,[34] are linked to the metropolitan areas by a network of administrative and financial ties. The overseas territories constitute a common currency area with the mother country (the franc area, the Belgian monetary area, *etc.*), and tariff arrangements and import restrictions on both sides discriminate in favor of trade between the possession and the metropole. Thus in 1953, the share of the metropolitan country in the imports of the territories ranged from 30 per cent in the British territories to 65 per cent in the French, while one-third of the exports of the British and Portuguese territories, two-thirds of the French territories' exports, and over half (including re-exports) of the Belgian Congo's exports went to the metropolitan countries.

The British monetary area, called the sterling area for a variety of reasons goes beyond the British overseas territories and includes a number of independent countries. In the main these are members of the British Commonwealth, such as Australia and New Zealand, the Union of South Africa, India and Ceylon, but there are examples also of non-commonwealth sterling countries in Iceland and Iraq. Since the gold and dollar reserves of the sterling area are largely held in London, it is necessary for members as far as possible to follow concerted trade and exchange policies. Co-ordination of these policies takes place usually through periodic meetings of the finance ministers and central banking authorities of the commonwealth countries.

[32] OEEC, *Sixth Report,* Vol. 1, p. 252.

[33] See above, p. 493.

[34] OEEC, *op. cit.*, pp. 245-7, contains a convenient list of these territories. The relative size and importance of the overseas territories is to some extent indicated by the following population figures (in millions): British territories, 74; French, 53; Belgian, 16; Portuguese, 11; Netherlands, 1.5; Italian Trust Territory, 1.

D. *Dynamic Factors in the Western European Economy*

In the foregoing sections of this chapter we have seen how, in the nineteenth century, the expansion and industrialization of the European economy was correlated with the great period of European imperialism from 1870 to 1910, while in the twentieth century, after two world wars, Europe's economic pre-eminence was superseded, and its empire began to disintegrate. To cast some light upon the relation between political power and economic capabilities we proceeded to look briefly at the economic geography of Europe and the main outlines of the structure of the European economy. It is now in order to complete our examination of these problems by inquiring into the factors affecting the long-range growth of the European economy and its future prospects.

PRESENT POSITION OF EUROPE IN THE WORLD ECONOMY

No one questioned the industrial pre-eminence of Western Europe in the decade before the first World War. In 1913 Western Europe probably accounted for about one-half of the world's manufacturing output. The preceding several decades had been a period of rapid industrial expansion. Industrial production had been growing by about 3 per cent per year and about 2 per cent *per capita* annually.[35] There was unbounded confidence that the next several decades would witness more of the same. However, by 1937, Western Europe's share of total world manufacturing output was reduced to little more than one-third, and by 1954 it had shrunk to between one-third and one-fourth.[36]

This decline in Western Europe's importance was a relative one, for Western Europe's economies continued to grow after 1913 but at a slower rate. Between 1913 and 1940 industrial output grew by only about 1.4 per cent per year and 0.8 per cent per year *per capita*.[37] The United States, on the other hand, whose rate of growth even before 1913 had been more rapid than that of Western Europe, caught up during the first World War and pulled ahead during the second, while the U.S.S.R. experienced a greatly accelerated rate of growth after 1920. Today its industrial power is approaching that of all Western European countries combined.

The present and prospective relative position of Western Europe in the

[35] ECE, *Growth and Stagnation in the European Economy,* p. 56.

[36] Department of State, *Long-term Trends Affecting Western Europe's Position in the World Economy,* IR No. 6929 (Washington, 1955).

[37] *Ibid.*

world economy is not merely a question of the over-all rate of growth; it also involves the question of the growth of the relatively underdeveloped regions of southern Europe: Greece, Turkey, Southern Italy, Spain, and Portugal. Industrialization in Western Europe did not occur uniformly and even in 1913, when Western Europe's relative importance was greatest, industry was concentrated in a few countries in the north and west. The three great powers, the United Kingdom, Germany, and France, accounted for more than three-fourths of industrial output although they held only 46 per cent of the population. Their production was oriented toward export markets and was heavily weighted with capital goods.[38] Agriculture still occupied more than two-fifths of Europe's population, and the proportion was much higher in the countries of southern Europe.

This uneven pattern of economic development was in part the reflection of the uneven geographical distribution of resources, especially coal and iron ore; in part it was the result of more complex social and political influences. An understanding of these is essential to the understanding of Western Europe's prospects, which depend not only on the continuation of the present pattern and rates of growth but also on the modernization of the less-developed regions.

In analyzing the dynamic factors in Western Europe's economic position we will find it convenient to group them under two headings, internal factors and external factors. However, there are considerations that cannot neatly be ranked under either heading, especially the effect of the two great wars that were fought on European soil.

INTERNAL FACTORS: MANPOWER AND PRODUCTIVITY

Internal factors affecting the growth of Europe's economic capabilities are the size of the labor force, its distribution among employments of different productivities, and the rate at which the average productivity of the labor force increases, which in turn depends on technology, investment, and on other factors. Western Europe's population increased by about 7 per cent between 1938 and 1952 compared with a 20 per cent increase in the United States and approximately the same increase for the population within the present boundaries of the U.S.S.R. And whereas the annual increase in population for both the United States and the U.S.S.R. is estimated at around 1.7 per cent, it is slightly less than 1 per cent for Western Europe. Western Europe's labor force increased by

[38] ECE, *Growth and Stagnation in the European Economy*, p. 16.

about 10 per cent between 1938 and 1948, and at the end of 1953 was about 125 million. It was thus almost twice as large as that of the United States, although the total value of gross production was only a little more than one-half as great. The European and United States labor forces are expected to grow at about the same rate for the next fifteen years, reaching about 200 million for Western Europe and 103 million for the United States by 1970.[39] Both populations will show increasing "aging." The largest and economically most important states, France, Belgium, Germany, and the United Kingdom will not grow as fast as Western Europe as a whole. This points to one of Europe's unsolved problems of adjustment—how to transfer workers from faster-growing populations in the less-developed countries to nonagricultural employment in the more industrialized regions.

In the OEEC countries about 30 per cent of the labor force is employed in agriculture.[40] The proportion of the active population in manufacturing industry has increased over the last two decades while the active population in agriculture has declined. However, there are marked differences between different countries in the recent patterns of changes in manpower and employment. For example in the United Kingdom the population of working ages had by 1952 increased by 10 per cent over 1930, but employment in manufacturing, construction, transport, and other services increased by between 10 and 20 per cent. The offsetting declines in agriculture and mining were not enough to prevent a severe labor shortage. In France, on the other hand, alone of all the countries in Western Europe, employment in manufacturing was lower in 1951 than twenty years earlier, as was also employment in mining, construction, and transport. Employment in trade and services, however, had increased, with a consequent reduction in the average output in these occupations.

The tendency for increases in the labor force to be absorbed in trade and services rather than in industry was most marked in Italy where the total active population increase between 1931 and 1949 was 17 per cent; the increase in employment in trade and banking was 36 per cent and in other services 41 per cent. The contrast in this respect between the northern and western countries of Europe and those of southern Europe was analyzed by the Economic Commission for Europe in a way which underscores the economic factors that make for a dynamic balanced growth on the one hand, and those that produce stagnation or decay.

After noting that the agricultural population has declined in northern

[39] Population and labor force estimates from *Trends in Economic Growth,* p. 6.
[40] OEEC, *op. cit.,* Vol. 1, p. 179.

and western Europe "where industry was already dominant in 1930" and increased in the countries in which agriculture predominated, the ECE pointed out that *per capita* national income is much higher in the former countries and thus the possibilities for savings and investment are much greater. Increases in population are absorbed in industry and other urban occupations, and because *per capita* incomes are high, the proportion of increases in incomes which goes for food consumption is relatively low, and can be met by imports paid for by expanded exports of manufactures. Thus increases in the labor supply are matched by investment and economic growth, and industrial expansion is relatively easy.

In southern Europe, on the other hand, savings are low and enterprise is lacking. Government investment is inhibited by fear of inflation. A large proportion of increments to incomes goes for food, of which the domestic supply is inelastic and cannot easily be supplemented by imports because of existing pressure on the balance-of-payments. Industrial production is mostly for the home market, and is not competitive in foreign markets. Land reform only aggravates the problem: "Land reforms which increase total output on the land only slightly, and result mainly in more man-power being used for producing nearly the same quantities as before or which create too small holdings, are a poor substitute for transfer of the surplus population to industry." [41]

Thus in considerable part the future economic growth of Western Europe depends on finding more productive employment for the partially and less productively employed workers in southern Europe. In the words of the OEEC: [42]

> A surplus agricultural population may be reduced by a movement of workers hitherto employed in agriculture to other sectors; but the reduction may also be very largely achieved by the movement into other sectors of workers taking their first jobs. This movement does not necessarily involve a concentration of the population in large towns. Industries and services more or less related to agriculture may develop in rural areas. Movements from agriculture to more productive sectors have in fact been steady and rapid in the wealthiest countries, where they have contributed considerably to the improvement in standards of living; but they have been slower in other countries owing to delayed industrialisation or, since the war, to the housing shortage. Insofar as such countries are able to pursue expansionary policies, these should aim at increased industrialisation and quicker removal of the housing shortage.

Productivity per man-hour in Western European industry has been less than in the United States since the beginning of the century and is now

[41] ECE, *Economic Survey of Europe Since the War,* pp. 154, 155.
[42] *Ibid.*

between one-fourth and one-half of that in the United States. Moreover, it is not catching up, although it is increasing much more than in the Soviet Union. Between 1938 and 1954 the increase in real gross national product per man hour of employment was about 15 per cent. The increases in manufacturing industry over the best prewar years range from about 4 per cent in France and 7 per cent in Germany to 29 per cent in the United Kingdom. Increases in agriculture may have been somewhat higher. Productivity per man hour in the United States in 1954 was about 40 per cent above pre-war in industry and in agriculture has more than doubled.[43]

As contrasted with the United States, an inferior and less-balanced resource endowment in Western Europe has probably had some effect in retarding the growth of efficiency. Until relatively recently the American economy found most of its raw materials and energy at home, while the availability of land on the expanding frontier kept the price of labor relatively high and encouraged mechanization and the use of capital. These factors also contributed to a psychology of "progress" and efficiency whereas in many European countries traditional attitudes favored stability rather than change.

The nineteenth century is usually thought of as a period in which the philosophy of laissez-faire and economic liberalism prevailed, not only in the United Kingdom but across Europe. However, this is not wholly the case. The economic liberalism of the Manchester school was transplanted to the continent to thrive only briefly and was succeeded after 1875 by a growing spirit of "neo-mercantilism" under which industry, agriculture, and trade were regarded as national interests, to be protected by tariff, subsidies, licensing, and other restrictive measures.[44]

The prevalence of such attitudes toward economic progress varies among the different countries of Europe. It is probably most marked in France and least conspicuous in postwar Germany, once the stronghold of neo-mercantilism. It is not absent in the United Kingdom where, under a Labor government, what the London *Economist* called the "theory and practise of capitalism" was for a while abandoned in favor of raising the standard of living through redistribution of income.[45] This characterization of the United Kingdom as "consumption-minded" rather than capital-conscious might have been applied with equal force to almost the whole of Europe except Germany and the Low Countries.

[43] *Ibid.*, p. 61.
[44] Hayes, *op. cit.*, 32-37.
[45] *The Economist*, October 16, 1954, pp. 191-92.

SIZE OF THE EUROPEAN MARKET

An important factor in promoting efficiency in the American economy was the large size of the market and the absence of restrictions on the movement of workers and goods from one region to the other. For most Western European countries, a much larger part of their market is in other countries of Europe as well as other parts of the world. The protective tariffs of the later nineteenth and early twentieth century prevented Western Europe from taking the maximum advantage of specialization and intra-European trade. These restrictions were aggravated in the thirties by quantitative restrictions on imports and the growing practice of bilateral trade balancing. Hence one of the principal tasks of the OEEC in the postwar period has been the "liberalization" of intra-European trade. Since a larger international machinery under the General Agreement on Tariffs and Trade has been established for the purpose of reducing tariff barriers, the OEEC has concentrated on the removal of quantitative restrictions on imports of member countries from other member countries. Most progress has been made with the liberalization of raw materials imports. Some member countries have been reluctant to liberalize imports of manufactured goods for "balance-of-payments" reasons and an even greater reluctance to liberalize agricultural imports is frankly attributed by many countries to their desire to protect domestic agriculture on both social and strategic grounds.

STEPS TOWARD THE INTEGRATION OF THE EUROPEAN ECONOMY

Bilateralism has been practically eliminated from intra-European trade (except for trade with the countries of Eastern Europe) by the European Payments Union (EPU) which ensures the transferability between member countries of the Western European currencies (including sterling) received by each of these countries from the others, including the territories in their monetary areas. The importance of the EPU is shown by the fact that one-fourth of all the visible trade of the world is settled through the Union with only a very small settlement of balances in gold or dollars.[46]

Other arrangements which have been made to widen the European market include the formation of the Benelux (Belgium, Netherlands, Luxembourg) customs union and the European Coal and Steel Commu-

[46] OEEC, *op. cit.*, 139.

nity. In Benelux all customs duties (and almost all quantitative restrictions) within the area have been abolished, and a common tariff *vis-à-vis* third countries was adopted. Since its establishment in September, 1944, Benelux has weathered a number of storms and has accomplished a certain degree of economic integration. It thus becomes imperative to the student of political and economic geography to view the economic and political systems of these three member states in close union. This integration is even more significant if one considers the fact that Holland and Belgium have highly different economies. Belgium found itself in a much more favorable situation in the postwar period than Holland, which had to repair its war damages (to say nothing of damages in 1953 when flood waters engulfed 350,000 acres of land) and which had to recover from the serious shock caused by the loss of its colonial empire in the Netherlands Indies.

The European Coal and Steel Community (ECSC) has been established by a treaty as a European federal institution to pool the coal and steel resources of the six participating countries—West Germany, France, Belgium, Luxembourg, the Netherlands, and Italy. It prohibits cartels and removes barriers to the movement of coal, steel products, and workers among member countries. This treaty has created a common market without tariffs and quantitative restrictions in the most important sector of European trade and is regarded by many as the first significant step toward the unification and integration of the western European economies. It has been hailed by some as heralding the eventual establishment of a European political federation. Even if the operation of the Coal and Steel Community were only extended, as has been proposed, to other trade between the members, this would be a major accomplishment in the direction of European economic integration since the six member countries cover 450,000 square miles and include 160 million people.[47]

Still in the planning stage but likely to become a reality in the future is a Scandinavian customs union. This would unite the nations of the Nordic Council—Denmark, Norway, Sweden, and Iceland—in an organization which, following the successful model of the Scandinavian Airlines System, would bring about joint enterprises in such industries as steel, chemicals, and textiles. Thus, as a first step towards a customs union, the necessary conditions for a common market in certain goods would be created.[48]

[47] For further information see Foreign Operations Administration, *Monthly Operations Report,* June 30, 1954; also OEEC, *op. cit.,* pp. 137-138.

[48] *The Economist,* 1954, pp. 671-672.

Although the result of all these measures has been to expand intra-European trade well beyond the expectations entertained at the beginning of the Marshall Plan in 1948, when no significant increase was expected, the share of intra-European trade in the total foreign trade of Western European countries remains about the same as in the prewar period. It is clear that a marked expansion in regional trade relative to trade with the rest of the world will require more intensive programs.

SPECIAL PROBLEMS—ENERGY

Coal production in Western Europe has not increased above the prewar level and presents a serious structural problem. Up to World War I, Western Europe as a whole was a net exporter of energy in the form of coal and coal bunkers, mainly from the United Kingdom. After World War I, and especially since the 1930's, the tendency has been towards stability or even contraction in the demand for coal due to the substitution of other fuels and water power, and to increased efficiency in the use of solid fuels. Depletion of the better seams has tended to increase costs and it has been difficult to obtain increases in productivity. It is not likely that further improvements in the utilization of coal will be sufficient to offset the failure of output to rise. Stagnation in the coal-mining industry has created considerable problems in a number of communities, but especially in the United Kingdom where the mines are old, deep, scattered, and difficult to mechanize, and where mounting costs and the drift of miners into other occupations has tended to keep production below even the reduced demand. This has prompted the government to embark on the most ambitious program for producing electricity from atomic reactors that any country has yet devised.

Coal production in France, similarly, although slightly above the prewar level is still below the production target of 60 million tons set by the Monnet five-year plan. France has 40,000 fewer miners than in the thirties, and costs are mounting. Despite the growing use of petroleum, the demand for coal in Europe may for some time tend to outstrip European production and to require imports. As a result discussions have begun both in the Coal and Steel Community and in the OEEC looking toward the development of a unified atomic energy program to supplement conventional sources of energy.

Western Europe's difficulty in expanding coal production is compounded by the failure to find petroleum in any considerable amounts. However, the United Kingdom, France, and other OEEC countries have for balance-of-payments reasons expanded their own refinery capacity with a view to reducing imports of products in favor of increased imports of lower cost crude petroleum. Imports of products into the United Kingdom, France, Germany, Italy, and the Netherlands, for example, fell from 17.5 million tons in 1948 to 12.9 million tons in 1951, while in the same period the same countries increased their imports of crude petroleum from 15.4 million tons to 51.2 million.[49] In 1953, for the first time, some net exports of refined products took place; Western Europe imported 8.2 million tons of products and exported 9.4 million tons (in addition to intra-European trade of 16.6 million tons).[50]

Western Europe's petroleum requirements are increasing at a rate of 10 to 15 per cent annually. The refineries of Western Europe are almost wholly dependent on crude oil from the Middle East producing countries such as Iran, Kuwait, Iraq and Saudi Arabia. The crude oil is transported to the Eastern Mediterranean by pipeline or through the Suez canal and then generally by tanker to the refining centers. This dependence on Middle East oil to supply Europe's rapidly growing energy demands, and the apparent vulnerability of transportation arrangements in the area is one of the reasons why Western European countries, especially the United Kingdom and France, are anxious to preserve peace in that region.

AGRICULTURE

By 1953-54 agricultural output in Western Europe (OEEC countries) had risen to 129 per cent of the best prewar levels, which is an increase of about 14 per cent on a *per capita* basis. A number of factors contributed to the increase, among them increased use of fertilizers and machinery, seed selection, and better livestock production methods. Perhaps most impressive is a 16 per cent increase in livestock products compared with prewar levels, accomplished despite a 30 per cent reduction in imports of feed.[51]

As indicated earlier, however, there is in many continental Western European countries a great need for improved productivity in agriculture, and for the release of manpower to other employments. A number of factors appear to be interfering with more efficient land utilization and productivity. An important obstacle is the very considerable fragmentation of agricultural land (small average size of plots), averaging from less than

[49] ECE, *Economic Survey of Europe Since the War,* pp. 298-99.
[50] *The Economist,* November 20, 1954, p. 674.
[51] OEEC, *op. cit.,* p. 55.

one hectare in Belgium, Switzerland, and West Germany, to two or three in the Netherlands, southwest France, and Spain. However, the averages do not tell the whole story. About six million hectares of farm land are estimated by the Food and Agriculture Organization to be in need of consolidation in West Germany and Italy, and as much as nine million in France and twelve million in Spain.[52]

Another obstacle to more efficient agriculture is the high degree of government protection, expressed in tariff and quantitative restrictions on imports. Aside from imports of cereals, sugar, fibers, and vegetable oils, most "Western European countries have chosen . . . to protect and maintain their agricultural structure composed of millions of small farmers, reserving for them virtually the whole of the market for animal products and most of that for vegetables and fruits."[53]

The desirability of liberalizing and enlarging the European market for agricultural products and promoting greater specialization has been recognized by members of the OEEC. Proposals have been made for the creation of a "green pool," a federal institution similar to the Coal-Steel Community to integrate the markets of member countries and relax restrictions on the sale and movement of agricultural products among them. These proposals have been dropped but further consideration is being given to the matter under auspices of the OEEC.[54]

EXTERNAL FACTORS AFFECTING WESTERN EUROPE'S ECONOMIC GROWTH

As noted above this division into internal and external factors affecting Western Europe's economic outlook is somewhat arbitrary because the two sets of factors contain forces acting on one another in a reciprocal relationship. Thus, the depression of the early thirties with its adverse effect on the demand for, and prices of, foodstuffs and raw materials helped to motivate primary producing countries to shift resources in the direction of their own industrialization. The consequences of this in the period after World War II are seen in reduced export availabilities of primary products from these countries and a shift in their demand away from consumer goods, especially textiles, which are one of Western Europe's (and the United Kingdom's) most important exports, in favor of an

[52] *Trends in Economic Growth*, p. 109.

[53] United Nations Food and Agriculture Organization, *European Agriculture—A Statement of Problem* (Geneva, 1954), p. 2.

[54] *Trends in Economic Growth*, p. 110. See also *Economic Survey of Europe Since the War*, pp. 233, 234.

increased demand for capital goods of the latest design, especially from the United States. The position of Western Europe in the world economy has undergone a number of such changes since 1913 and these changes are sometimes called structural changes to denote their deep-rooted and irrevocable character.[55]

To trace these changes and their manifold interrelationships carefully would require an extended discussion going beyond the scope of this chapter.[56] However, the principal trends can be delineated adequately if we examine (*a*) the long-term change in the share of Western Europe in world trade and some of the reasons therefor, and (*b*) the trade and payments position of Western Europe in the decade after World War II. At this time, the effects both of certain structural changes and of the disorganization of the war combined to create a situation in which Western Europe's receipts from abroad, particularly of dollars, were quite insufficient to maintain a reasonable level of imports.

DECLINE IN WESTERN EUROPE'S SHARE OF WORLD TRADE

Along with the decline of the relative importance of the Western European economy after World War I went a decline in Western Europe' share of total world trade. In terms of total world exports Europe's share shrank from more than 50 per cent before World War I to 45 per cent in the interwar period and to about 35 per cent in 1948-50.[57] Another way of expressing this change is in terms of shares in total trade: trade between non-European countries, which was only 25 per cent of total trade in the period 1909 to 1913, rose to 40 per cent in the period 1925-38, and to 50 per cent in 1948-50. At the same time intra-European trade declined from about one-third of total world trade to about one-fifth.

Most of this decline in the interwar period represented a loss of exports by the three big European trading nations, the United Kingdom, Germany, and France, whose share of total European exports fell between 1913 and 1938 from about 64 per cent to 52 per cent.

The most obvious explanation for the declining importance of Western Europe in world trade was the growing importance of other trading nations, particularly the United States and Japan. An important factor contributing to this development, especially with regard to the United States but by no means the only one, was the interruption caused to Europe's

[55] ECE, *Economic Survey of Europe Since the War,* p. 10.

[56] See *ibid.,* Chs. 2, 6 and 7, also ECE, *Growth and Stagnation in the European Economy,* especially Chs. 2 and 9.

[57] ECE, *Growth and Stagnation in the European Economy,* pp. 168-170.

trade by two world wars. In the interwar period, moreover, there were important shifts in the commodity pattern of world trade, which may be summarized by saying that (as percentages of total imports) the demand for textiles and miscellaneous manufactures fell, the demand for metals and chemicals was relatively stable, while the demand for machinery and transport equipment (including motor cars) rose. The declining volume of textile exports from Western Europe attributable to the growth of domestic textile production in overseas areas and to increasing competition from Japan, the United States, and India (that is, textile exports from Europe were a declining proportion of a shrinking total trade), was especially injurious to the trade of the United Kingdom, Germany, France, Belgium, and Switzerland. On the other hand, the benefit of the increased demand for machinery and transport equipment went largely to the United States.

The relationships described merely suggest what a more detailed analysis would show: that the European countries because of the effects of World War I and of various rigidities in their industrial systems reacted only very slowly in the interwar period to large and rapidly moving changes in the commodity pattern of world demand. After 1938 the evidence suggests that the indicated adaptations were being made; in any case by 1950 Western Europe had regained its 1938 position in total world trade, and after 1950, in particular by virtue of the rapid expansion of German exports, had recovered even more lost ground.[58] Moreover, the United Kingdom, France, and Germany have regained their 1913 relative positions in total European exports.

EUROPE'S POSTWAR PAYMENTS PROBLEM

While there is therefore some reason to think that Western Europe has the capability of recovering some of its former pre-eminence in world trade, there remain certain structural imbalances in the pattern of world trade, in part the legacy of World War II, which continue to confront Western Europe with the elements of the "dollar problem." Even before World War II Western Europe had a deficit on current account with the dollar area[59] estimated at about $2 billion in 1953 prices. In the general system of convertible currencies and multilateral settlements which then prevailed, this deficit was made up with dollars earned by European exports to third areas having dollar surpluses resulting, for example, from

[58] OEEC, *op. cit.*, p. 93.
[59] The United States, Canada, Mexico, Venezuela, Colombia, the Caribbean and Central American Republics, and the Philippines.

rubber and tin sales from Southeast Asia and gold sales from South Africa.

After World War II a number of factors combined to make it difficult to achieve balance in Western Europe's external accounts and next to impossible to impose balance in the dollar accounts. These factors, in effect, operated to reduce Western Europe's real income and to make it necessary to expand commodity exports very considerably while economizing to the maximum on imports. Very briefly the new factors were the following:

Western Europe's capital position deteriorated very badly as a result of the war. Long-term investments, especially in the United States, had been sold. Large sterling debts were incurred during the war to obtain wartime goods and services in India, Egypt, and other countries, and large dollar debts were incurred by the United Kingdom and France in 1946 and 1947. Revenue from shipping, insurance, and other commercial and financial services was adversely affected by new competition, while overseas military expenditures for the United Kingdom and France were greatly increased. The greatest burden of all was that imposed by the shift in the terms of trade which because of reduced export availabilities of foodstuffs and raw materials increased the prices of imports relative to the prices of Western Europe's exports.

Meanwhile partly as the result of the war and partly as the result of political, social, and technological changes, the supplies of raw materials and foodstuffs from the dollar area increased while similar supplies from the sterling area and other non-dollar sources tended to decline. Thus wartime demands stimulated production of foodstuffs in North America, aluminum from the dollar area increased in importance relative to sterling area tin and lead, imports of dollar petroleum increased. At the same time in many countries inflation and population increases swelled domestic consumption at the expense of exports, and resources were shifted away from the production of foodstuffs for export to industrial development—as notably in Argentina and Australia. These developments all tended to shift Europe's imports from non-dollar to dollar sources but without any corresponding rise in receipts from the dollar area. Most of the wartime and postwar increase in imports of the United States was in commodities originating in the Western Hemisphere, such as coffee, timber and paper, aluminum, and petroleum.

THE MARSHALL PLAN

As a consequence of these developments, unless Western Europe was to cut its imports below the levels needed to maintain employment and production, a deficit in the dollar balance-of-payments was inevitable—a deficit beyond the capacity of Western European countries to finance from their scanty reserves of gold and dollars. It was this situation which led to the Marshall plan under which the United States financed the dollar deficit in Western Europe's balance-of-payments during the period 1948-52 and permitted some reconstitution of Western Europe's gold and dollar reserves.

The dollar problem has temporarily disappeared although there are grounds for believing that it has not been completely excised. The chief factor in its disappearance is the large volume of dollar payments to Western Europe resulting from military expenditures in connection with the stationing of United States forces in Europe, and United States procurement of military goods and services. A high proportion of these expenditures, it is true, may become a fairly permanent feature of United States participation under NATO in the arrangements for the defense of Western Europe. In the absence of these payments, however, and with the termination of United States economic assistance to Western Europe, the dollar-payments position of Western Europe would once again be somewhat precarious. In the long run, strength in the European payments situation depends on the continued expansion of exportable supplies of foodstuffs and raw materials in non-dollar areas. The loss of colonial possessions and the reduced ability of the metropolitan countries of Western Europe to influence the character of overseas economic development through capital exports, coupled with the drive for industrial development and autarky in the primary producing countries makes the long-run outlook at best uncertain.

E. Summary and Conclusions

Western Europe has lost its former position of industrial and commercial supremacy and with this loss has gone a decline in her world-power position and a significant loss of colonial possessions. However, the prospect is not one of unrelieved stagnation or decay. The favorable endowments of climate, geography, and natural resources remain, as does the heritage of unparalleled cultural, scientific, and technical achievement. The population and labor force are growing although not as rapidly as in the United States or the U.S.S.R. There are encouraging possibilities for greatly strengthening the European economy through modernization of agriculture and widening of the European market. The principal obstacles to the future and continuing growth of Europe's economic capabilities lie in the sphere of external economic relations. Europe must expand its exports of manufactured goods in third areas in competition with those of the United States (and Japan) in order to command the growing amounts of raw materials and foodstuffs that will be needed. These areas must in turn continue to offer for sale to Western Europe on reasonable terms the needed foodstuffs and raw materials. Purchases by Western Europe of raw materials and foodstuffs from the dollar area must be kept within the limits set by Western Europe's ability to earn dollars (*a*) by exports of goods and services to the protected United States market, (*b*) by exports of manufactures to dollar-surplus primary producing countries (as Malaya), and (*c*) through United States military expenditures in NATO countries.

Since 1950 the evidence has increasingly demonstrated Western Europe's capacity to make the indicated adjustments. Even if this progress is sustained, however, there is little likelihood of Europe regaining the relative economic capabilities on which its world supremacy at the end of the Victorian age was founded. There is, moreover, every indication that the over-all economic capabilities of the Soviet bloc, which are now not far exceeded by those of all Western European countries combined, will in the next two decades surpass them. The importance of Western Europe's economic capabilities, then, must be viewed in the light of the contribution they make to aggregate Western capabilities rather than in themselves. To the extent, therefore, that power relationships continue to depend on relative economic capabilities (as opposed to new factors introduced by the possession of nuclear weapons), Western Europe's future lies not in an independent course but is bound up with the fortunes of the Western alliance.

CHAPTER 18

The United States and Canada

A. *The United States*

The United States occupies a dominant position in the world economy. With only about 6 per cent of the world's population it accounted for almost 40 per cent of the world's output of goods and services in 1954. This was almost twice the production of all of Free Europe or of the entire Soviet bloc, including Communist China.

By virtue of its great economic strength the United States plays a major role in world economy. In 1954 the United States accounted for 20 per cent of the world's exports and 14 per cent of its imports. The United States is the world's largest creditor nation and the principal supplier of capital for overseas investment. It is little wonder, therefore, that this country's domestic and foreign economic policies are of vital concern to other countries.

The enormous economic capabilities of the United States largely account for its position as the leading world power. World War II demonstrated the awesome military force which these capabilities are able to support. In 1944 at the peak of the war effort the United States produced 45 per cent of the armaments of all the belligerents. The United States was truly the arsenal of democracy. The resources of the United States have become an important instrument of national power in peace as well as in war. They have been used on a lavish scale to restore the war-devastated economies of friendly as well as former enemy powers and to bolster up the economic and military strength of the Free World. Economic power is of course only one of the ingredients of national power, but in the hands of the United States it has become a major instrument of statecraft.

As with other areas, geographical factors cannot entirely explain the course and pattern of United States' economic development. Nonetheless, this chapter suggests that favorable geographical factors such as rich natural resources, climate and terrain, and world location have been more important for the economic development of the United States than for any other nation except possibly the Soviet Union.

GEOGRAPHY AND PEOPLE

Geography. The United States, with a land area of roughly 3 million square miles, is the third largest nation in the Western Hemisphere; Canada is the largest and Brazil is the second largest. It is bounded in the north by Canada, in the south by Mexico, and includes most of North America between 30 degrees and 49 degrees north latitude. "Separated by some 3,000 miles of the Atlantic Ocean from Europe, with its international problems, and by 5,000 miles of the Pacific Ocean from the countries of eastern Asia . . . the U.S.A. has tended until recently to isolate herself from commitments overseas. . . ." [1] Its relative isolation from other major centers of power has of course been a great strategic advantage to the United States, since the danger of foreign invasion was virtually eliminated. As a result, the United States, like the United Kingdom in an earlier era, was until recent times able to avoid involvement in costly and destructive foreign wars and to devote its major energies to peaceful pursuits. However, progress in weapons development, the collapse of the historic balance-of-power system in Western Europe, and the emergence of Communist Russia, are factors which are rapidly eliminating the advantage of virtual insularity formerly enjoyed by the United States.

Though exceeded in size by the U.S.S.R., China, Canada, and Brazil, the United States has a more favorable physical environment than any of these countries. Virtually all of the United States falls into Ellsworth Huntington's "very high energy" zone where the climate is believed to be most invigorating for human endeavor. The proportion of productive land area is much greater in the United States than, for example, in the U.S.S.R. or Canada where large regions lie in the Arctic Zone, or in Brazil, with its vast tropical rain forest of limited economic value. The great size of the United States, its distribution over wide latitudes, and the modifying influence of mountains and two oceans produce a wide variety of climates

[1] L. D. Stamp and L. S. Suggate, eds., *Geography For Today,* Book 3, "North America and Asia," 4th ed. (London, 1954), p. 119.

and a corresponding diversity of crops. "Rocks of almost every geological age furnish in abundance almost every kind of mineral. . . ." [2] Size has contributed to the economic growth of the United States in another important respect. Products move freely without interference of tariff barriers over a market area of 3 million square miles with more than 160 million consumers. As a result the United States enjoys the large economic benefits to be derived from a high degree of regional specialization and the economies of large-scale production. Free Europe, by contrast, with an area smaller than the United States and a population of over 300 million, comprises seventeen sovereign states administering fourteen separate tariff systems each operating to prevent the most efficient utilization of the area's resources. A wide domestic market also has reduced the dependence of the United States on foreign trade, thus making it less vulnerable to foreign economic developments.

Four main physical divisions may be distinguished in the United States. Virtually all of the western part of the country, except for a narrow strip of lowland along the Pacific Coast, comprises the western highlands. These extend from Mexico into Canada and consist of a series of plateaus and hills interspersed with high mountains. The plateaus are cut off from rain-bearing winds from the Pacific by high mountains so that the region is generally dry. While large irrigation projects have made farming practical in some of the interior basins, agriculture is generally limited to the lowlands and valleys near the coast. Elsewhere in this region, despite the growth of manufactures in recent years, stock raising, forestry, and mining are of major importance. The latter two activities have been favored by an abundance of mineral and forestry resources and large low-cost hydro-electric power development.

Next come the great interior plains or lowlands. A continuation of the Canadian prairie provinces, they extend to the Gulf of Mexico and have a maximum breadth of 1500 miles. Within this zone, the upper Mississippi Valley and the Great Lakes region constitute the heart of the North American continent. Fertile alluvial and glacial soils, an abundance of coal, metals, and water power, and a well-developed water and railway network have made this the most important agricultural and industrial region in the United States.

East of the great plains are the eastern highlands or Appalachians. Much lower in elevation than the western highlands, the Appalachians roughly parallel the Atlantic Coast, extending from Maine to Alabama. The northern Appalachians contain the richest coalfields in the United

[2] *Ibid.*, p. 164.

States and account for almost three-quarters of the total output. These coalfields form the basis of the heavy industry complex in the northeastern and north-central part of the United States.

The fourth major physical division is the coastal plain bordering the Gulf of Mexico and the Atlantic coast. This region is broad at the Gulf and narrows toward the north where the Appalachians reach almost to the sea. First settled by the original colonists, parts of the eastern lowlands have remained the most highly developed and densely populated regions in the United States.

While the river system played an important role in the development of the United States up through the first half of the nineteenth century, its significance was reduced by the fact that the principal rivers flow in the opposite direction to the main stream of commerce, which is east and west. Thus the Mississippi system, largest in the United States and third largest in the world and navigable for thousands of miles, flows north and south entering the Atlantic through the Gulf of Mexico. Rivers entering the Atlantic between the St. Lawrence River and the Gulf are small and of limited direct value to navigation. However, they form estuaries and harbors in their lower courses endowing the Atlantic coast with excellent seaports like New York and Baltimore. The one east-west water route of major significance is the St. Lawrence-Great Lakes system which connects the heart of North America with the Atlantic Ocean. This system will become of increasing importance with the completion of the St. Lawrence Seaway described elsewhere in this chapter.

People. The population of the United States as reported by the 1950 census numbered 150.7 million. The United States is not considered to be overpopulated in the sense that the pressure of numbers on natural resources is an obstacle to continued economic expansion. The population is increasing at a rapid rate and by April 1, 1956 had reached an estimated 167.4 million. Between 1948 and 1952 the annual rate of increase was 1.76 per cent as compared with 0.9 per cent for Free Europe and 1.5 to 1.7 per cent for the Soviet Union.[3] The present rapid growth of population is due almost entirely to natural increases. During the decade 1940 to 1950 immigration accounted for less than 5 per cent of the growth in population and in the previous decade for less than one per cent. This is in sharp contrast with the period 1850 to 1910 when immigrants accounted for anywhere from 27 per cent to 55 per cent of the increase in population

[3] Joint Committee on The Economic Report, *Trends Toward Economic Growth, A Comparison of Western Powers and The Soviet Bloc* (Washington, D. C., 1955), p. 6.

in a single decade.[4] Between 1820 and 1951 more than 40 million immigrants entered the United States, of whom an estimated 30 million remained. The abandonment of a liberal immigration policy after World War I sharply reduced the influx of immigrants. In 1953 net immigration of less than 150,000 was below the authorized quota level.

The proportion of the total population which the foreign-born white population represents has fallen progressively since the end of the nineteenth century. In 1950 foreign-born whites were 7 per cent of the total population as compared with almost 15 per cent in 1890. Negroes, descendants of the original slaves, accounted for 10 per cent of the total population in 1950 as compared with almost 16 per cent a century earlier. Other races including North American Indians represented only about one-half of one per cent of the total.

Average population density in 1950 was 50.7 persons per square mile. Greatest densities are in the industrialized and urbanized northern and eastern states. The New England, Middle Atlantic, and East North-Central states had an average population density of 178 per square mile in 1950. These fifteen states with 15 per cent of the land area of the United States had more than half the total population. Most thinly-populated are the Mountain and West North-Central states with average densities of 5.9 and 27.5 persons per square mile respectively.[5] Rational considerations such as economic opportunities, cultural advantages, and climate have had an important effect on the distribution of population. However, the prewar National Resources Committee study showed that "historical accident and differential reproduction rates have played a far larger part in determining population distribution in this country than is generally supposed. The sheer size of our land area, its geographical diversity, and the variety of cultural patterns controlling our interests and attitudes have served to intensify the force of these irrational factors." [6]

The population of the United States shows a high degree of mobility.[7] The two main channels of movement have been (1) westward and (2) away from the farms to urban industrial centers (Fig. 18-1). A measure of the extent of the westward movement is indicated by the fact that between 1790 and 1950 the center of population of the United States moved

[4] J. F. Dewhurst and associates, *America's Needs and Resources* (New York, 1955), p. 51.
[5] *Ibid.*, p. 69.
[6] U.S. Government Printing Office, *The Problems of a Changing Population* (New York, 1938), p. 37.
[7] See pp. 168, 169.

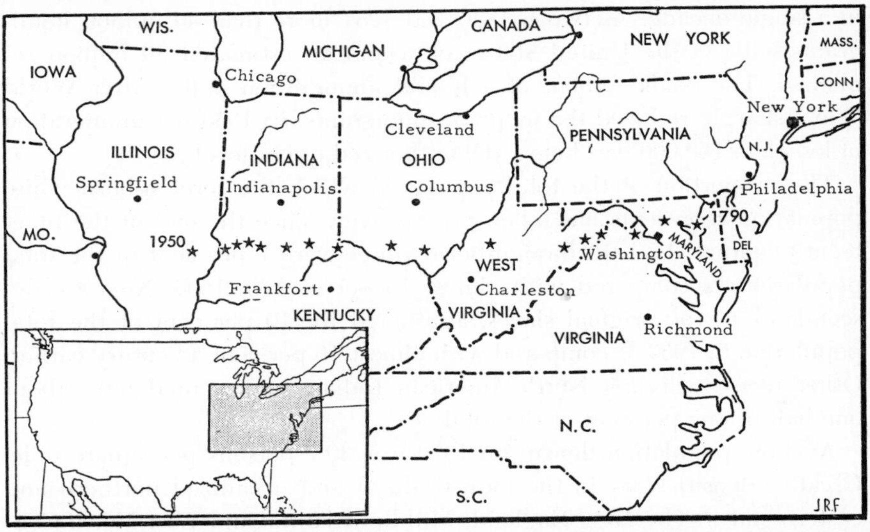

Fig. 18-1. The Westward Course of the United States as Shown in the Ten-year Shift of the Population Center, 1790-1950.

from its original location east of Baltimore to a point near Olney, Illinois, 686 miles west and 30 miles south. This westward movement is a continuing one. Between 1940 and 1950 the center of population moved a distance of 42 miles west and 7.6 miles south. Greatest relative growth has occurred in the Pacific states and Mountain states which in 1950 accounted for 13 per cent of the total population as compared with 5.4 per cent in 1900. Between 1940 and 1950 the population of the Pacific states increased 48.8 per cent and the mountain states 22.3 per cent as compared with the national average of 14.3 per cent. Increasing economic opportunities resulting from the wartime expansion of industry and the postwar boom have added impetus to the movement of population to the Pacific states in the past decade, especially to California.

Like the westward movement of population, the movement of persons from the farm and rural areas to urban centers has been going on since Independence. In 1790 only about 5 per cent of the population of the United States was classified as urban. By 1950 almost 58 per cent of the population was urban (living in communities of 2500 persons or more).[8] Between 1890 and 1950 the proportion of the population living in cities of 100,000 or more rose from 15.4 per cent to 29.3 per cent. This progressive decline in the rural population reflects the great increase in the rela-

[8] W. S. and E. S. Woytinsky, *World Population and Production* (New York, 1953), p. 124.

tive importance of industrial activity over the past century or more, and the reduced relative importance of agriculture.

RESOURCES

The United States has a rich and varied natural resource base (Fig. 18-2). In contrast with most other developed nations, these resources were adequate until quite recently to satisfy the bulk of this country's food and industrial raw material needs and to provide a sizeable surplus for export. Thus in 1900 the United States produced a 15 per cent surplus of materials other than food and gold.[9] However, by the decade of the forties this surplus had become a deficit as a result of the unsatiable and rapidly-rising demands of American industry. According to the report of the President's Materials Policy Commission "there is scarcely a metal or a mineral fuel of which the quantity used in the United States since the outbreak of the First World War did not exceed the total used throughout the world in all the centuries preceding." [10] With less than 10 per cent of the population of the Free World, the United States consumes almost half the volume of materials produced. Thus we find that by 1950 the United States had a 9 per cent materials production deficit (excluding food and gold) and the projected possible deficit for 1975 is estimated at 20 per cent. This trend accounts in considerable measure for the growing United States interest in developing new foreign sources of supply for minerals and fuels and explains why the bulk of United States overseas investment since the war has been going into mineral development.

Agricultural Land. Agriculture is the major exception in the United States changing materials picture. This country's agricultural resource base currently yields all major food and agricultural raw material requirements except tropical products like rubber, coffee, and sugar, and in addition provides sizeable surpluses for export. According to the President's Materials Policy Commission, the United States should have no great difficulty in meeting the projected 38 per cent increase in consumption of agricultural products by 1975 on the basis of existing land-use now in farms. "This can be done by improving or upgrading the use of much land now in farms and by bringing in new land only to offset any farm acres that will be taken out for urban and other uses." [11]

According to the 1950 Census, the cropland of the United States totaled

[9] The President's Materials Policy Commission, *Resources for Freedom,* Vol. 1, *Foundations for Growth and Security* (Washington, D. C., June, 1952), p. 2.

[10] *Ibid.,* p. 3.

[11] *Ibid.,* Vol. 5, *Selected Reports to the Commission,* p. 70.

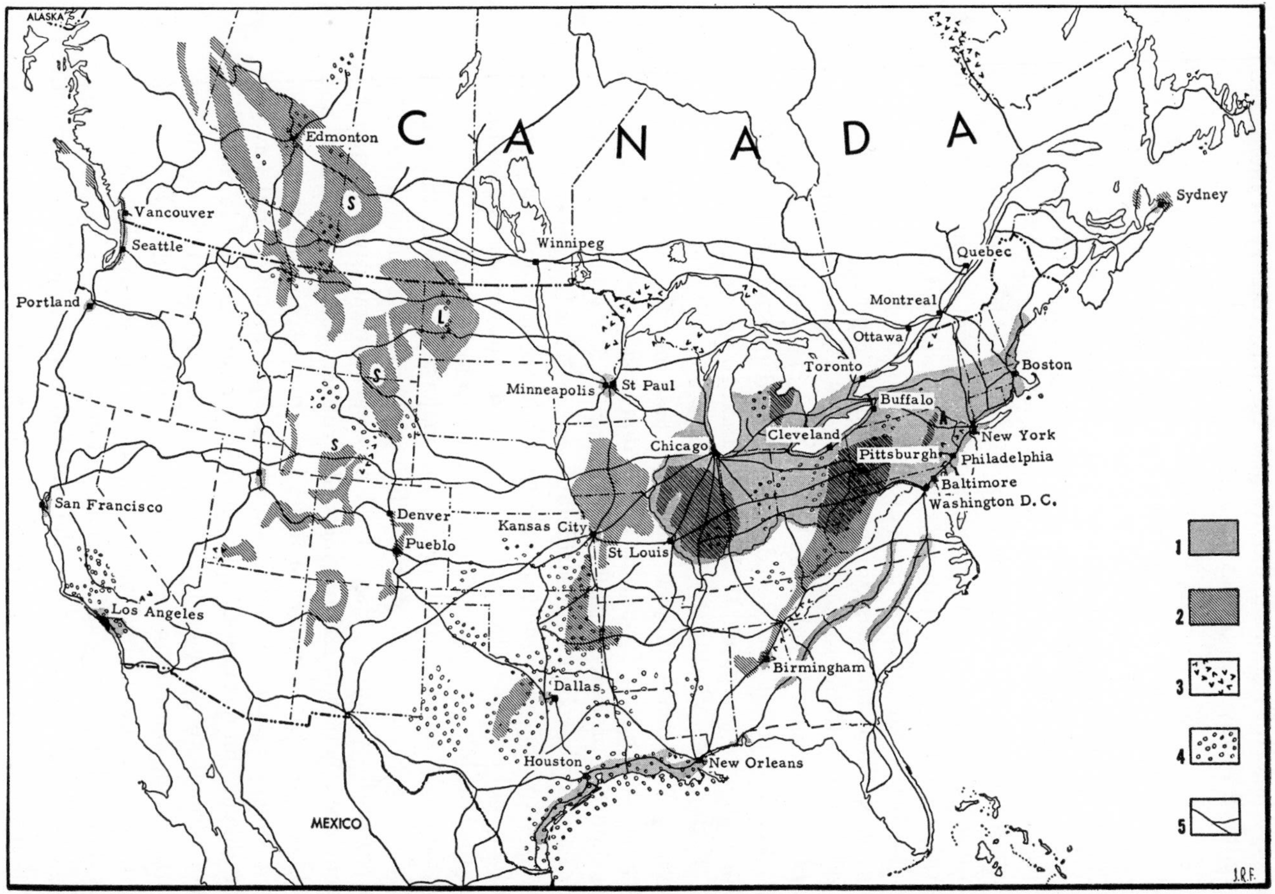

FIG. 18-2. Anglo America: Railroads, Resources and Industrial Concentrations: (1) industrial area; (2) bituminous coal (A–anthracite; S–sub-bituminous; L–lignite); (3) iron ore; (4) petroleum (oil and gas fields); (5) selected railroads.

409 million acres or somewhat more than two and a half acres per person. While this is considerably less than the 555.9 million acres estimated for the U.S.S.R. by the Food and Agriculture Organization of the United Nations, the difference may be more apparent than real. Severe climate and inferior soils in a number of regions operate to materially reduce the productivity of Russian croplands. Colin Clark has estimated that the U.S.S.R. has only about 70 per cent of the "standard farmland" of the United States.

Forests. One-third of this country's land area or 622 million acres is in forest land. However, of this area only 460 million acres is suitable for the growing of commercial timber. Despite this large acreage the United States has shifted from an exporter to an importer of lumber, largely because of the failure to build up productive stock. However, it is estimated that forest land presently available would be ample to cover requirements under a proper forestry management program.[12] A recent report of the United States Forest Service shows that in 1955, the United States for the first time in its history was growing more timber than was being removed by cutting or destruction.[13]

Minerals. Despite the substantial inroads made into reserves and the growing importance of mineral imports the United States still meets the bulk of its requirements from domestic sources. Thus in 1950, United States mineral production, excluding gold, was approximately 90 per cent of apparent consumption. Reserves of many of the important minerals are still abundant. Table 18-1, prepared by the President's Materials Policy Commission, lists the major industrial minerals in three groups according to the adequacy of known United States' reserves. Metals shown as deficient in reserves in relation to expected future needs are further broken down according to prospects for improving supplies by discovery of new deposits, beneficiation of low-grade ores, and replacement by synthetics or substitutes.

The Commission's study indicates that the possibilities of increasing reserves in most of the deficient categories are still considerable. It points out that "geologists agree that the United States still possesses vast hidden mineral resources." [14] The principal unknown factor is the cost of exploiting these resources. Technological progress has been important in the past in permitting the use of lower-grade reserves and there is every reason why this should be so in the future. Furthermore, it should be

[12] *Ibid.*, p. 37.
[13] As reported in the *Wall Street Journal*, October 27, 1955.
[14] *Ibid.*, Vol. 5, p. 27.

TABLE 18-1

Domestic Supply Position of Selected Mineral Materials *

1. *Known Economic Reserves Adequate For Well Over 25 Years*

Magnesium	Molybdenum
Coal	Phosphate
Potash	Lime
Salt	Sand
Clay	Gypsum
Borax	Bauxite
Feldspar	

2. *Known Economic Reserves Inadequate*

a. Discoveries geologically likely though not necessarily adequate:

Copper	Lead
Zinc	Uranium
Vanadium	Tungsten
Antimony	Petroleum
Natural Gas	Sulfur

b. Beneficiation progress expected:

Iron	Aluminum
Titanium	Beryllium
Thorium	Oil from Shale
Fluorine	Graphite

c. Synthesis progress expected:

Oil from Coal	Gas from Oil

3. *Little or No Known Economic Reserves, Significant Discoveries Not Expected*

a. Beneficiation progress expected:

Manganese

b. Synthesis progress expected:

Industrial Diamonds	Quartz Crystals
Sheet Mica	Asbestos

c. Significant beneficiation or synthesis not expected:

Chromium	Nickel
Tin	Cobalt
Platinum	Mercury

* The President's Materials Policy Commission, Vol. 1, *Foundations for Growth and Security* (Washington, D. C., June, 1952), *Resources for Freedom*, p. 26.

pointed out that even if such reserves should prove to be relatively high cost, the resultant drain on the United States economy is not likely to be excessive. In 1950, the total value of all metals consumed in the United States was roughly $2 billion or less than one per cent of the Gross National Product. At present the United States employs only 4.5 per cent of its total manpower to produce crude materials other than food.[15] Tech-

[15] *Op. cit.*, p. 69.

nological developments in beneficiation and synthesis promise to increase the reserves of a number of important minerals at relatively moderate cost increases. Thus while the United States may exhaust its reserves of high-grade, low-cost iron ore of the Lake Superior region in the next twenty-five years, it has huge reserves of taconite with 25 to 35 per cent iron ore content. On the basis of methods of concentration now being developed, it is estimated that the use of these ores would raise the cost of pig iron only about 5 per cent.[16] Proved recoverable oil reserves in the United States at the end of 1954 of 29.6 billion barrels represented only about eleven years' consumption at the then prevailing rate, and still undiscovered reserves were estimated to amount to only about 35.9 billion barrels. However, it is estimated that 500 billion barrels could be produced, at higher cost of course, from synthetic shale deposits. Large-scale oil production from huge coal reserves is also possible.

This is not to suggest that the United States has no reason to be concerned about its future resource position. The problem of increasing reserves is more than a matter of higher costs. Market forces alone cannot always be depended upon to bring about the required expansion. Long-range planning and various measures requiring direct government intervention may be necessary. Minerals are finite and exhaustible resources. Even if current estimates of United States' reserves are on the low side, serious deficiencies could develop, if not in twenty-five years, then in fifty years, if proper steps are not taken now. Fifty years is not a long time in the life-span of a nation.

The United States has always been deficient in such important minerals as chromite, cobalt, industrial diamonds, nickel, and manganese. As shown in Table 18-2 domestic production of these minerals in 1949 was 10 per cent or less of domestic consumption. The same table also shows the considerable decline that has occurred since 1935 to 1939 in this country's relative self-sufficiency in copper, lead, and zinc. The figures in Table 18-2 need to be interpreted with caution regarding what they imply for the strategic security of the United States. As noted above, imports in some cases reflect cost considerations rather than absolute shortages. Where serious deficiencies exist as in the case of minerals like nickel and tin, the building up of strategic stockpiles affords considerable insurance against serious wartime deficiencies. Furthermore, in a national emergency substantial cutbacks in nonessential consumption can be made. Then, of course, there is a wide range of possibilities in the area of con-

[16] The President's, Materials Policy Commission, *op. cit.*, Vol. 2, *The Outlook for Key Commodities*, p. 5.

servation, standardization, and substitution. Finally, it should be noted that most of the imported minerals come from Western Hemisphere sources which greatly reduces the threat of enemy takeover and the problem of maintaining lines of communication. For these reasons, even though being cut off from foreign sources of supply in wartime would present difficult problems of adjustment for the United States, the over-all effect on its war effort would be very minor.

TABLE 18-2

Relative Self-Sufficiency of U. S. in Minerals, 1935-39 and 1949 *

MINERAL	SELF-SUFFICIENCY: RATIO OF DOMESTIC PRODUCTION TO DOMESTIC CONSUMPTION (PER CENT)	
	1935-1939	1949
Antimony	12	24
Asbestos (long fiber)	5	8
Chromite	1	[a]
Coal:		
Anthracite	102	113
Bituminous and Lignite	103	98
Cobalt		11
Copper	107	70
Diamonds (Industrial)	0	0
Iron Ore	94	95
Lead	90	69
Magnesium	160	97
Manganese	6	9
Mercury	67	25
Molybdenum	294	113
Nickel	2	1
Petroleum Crude	109	94
Phosphate Rock	151	115
Platinum Metals	32	12
Potash	64	104
Sulfur	128	139
Tin	[a]	[a]
Tungsten	32	58
Zinc	94	74

[a] Less than 0.5 per cent.
* *Statistical Abstract of the United States, 1952*, p. 693.

Water Power. Water power is much less important as a source of energy in the United States than coal, oil, or gas. In 1950 it accounted for only about five per cent of this country's production of commercial energy, as against roughly 43 per cent for coal, 32 per cent for oil, and 20 per cent for gas. Although the United States possesses only about 5 per cent of the world's hydraulic resources, it produces roughly 30 per cent of all the hydro-electric energy. Untapped hydraulic resources are estimated at about four times what is presently being utilized.

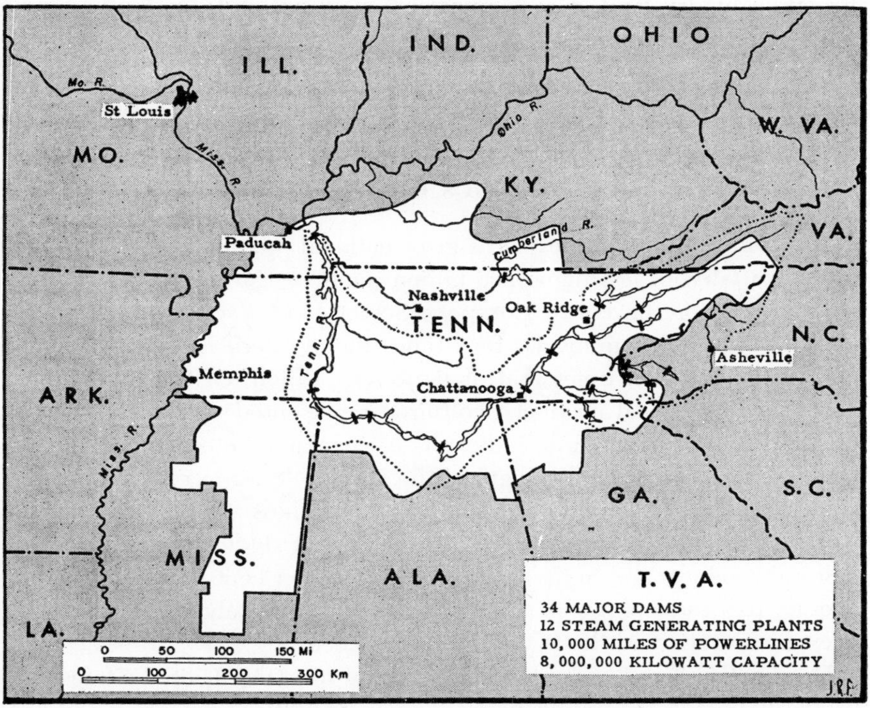

Fig. 18-3. Regional Extent of TVA Activity.

Despite the relatively minor position of hydro-electric power in the total energy picture, it has been an important factor in the development of certain regions of the United States, especially where combined with irrigation and flood control. The most notable of such multiple purpose projects is the government-financed Tennessee Valley Authority,[17] one of the world's major engineering projects (Fig. 18-3). Here power development was secondary to the primary purpose of creating a nine-foot channel for navigation from Knoxville to the mouth of the Tennessee River, and for the prevention of floods. Other objectives included erosion control, reforestation, and rural rehabilitation. TVA has had a major impact on the economy of the Tennessee Valley. The well-being of the farm population has been greatly improved and a major impetus was given to the development of manufactures. Other notable multi-purpose schemes are the Columbia and Colorado River projects. Both have provided low-cost power for industries in the Pacific Northwest as well as water for the

[17] See p. 663.

irrigation of dry land. The Tennessee Valley authority and other large multi-purpose projects have brought the Federal Government into the power business in competition with private utilities. The resultant clash of interests has had and will continue to have important political repercussions.

CHARACTERISTICS OF THE ECONOMY

In 1954 the United States had a gross national product of $360.5 billion, as compared with less than $200 billion for Free Europe and only about $175 billion for the entire European Soviet bloc. *Per capita* income of almost $2300 per annum was four times the Western European average and four and a half times that of the Soviet Union. Of the total United States gross national product two-thirds represented personal consumption expenditures. All major indicators of economic potential point to the overwhelming economic strength of the United States in relation to other countries. The United States accounts for almost 40 per cent of the world's output of manufactures. It is the largest single producer of agricultural products and minerals; it produces 40 per cent of all commercial energy. Its production of crude steel is only moderately less than that of Western Europe and the Soviet Bloc combined.

During the first hundred years of its history the United States was primarily an agricultural economy. The availability of extensive and rich agricultural lands was a highly dynamic factor in the expansion of the economy during this period. It attracted much needed immigration. Agriculture provided the surplus required to feed an increasing urban industrial population and was a primary source of savings and investment. Despite the rapid growth of industry, agriculture still contributed 50 per cent more to national income than manufacturing in the decade 1869 to 1879 (see Table 18-3 below).

It was not until 1890 that manufacturing surpassed agriculture as the principal source of income. By 1953, manufacturing was almost six times as important as agriculture. The fall in the relative contribution of agriculture to total output has been accompanied by a still sharper decline in the proportion of the gainfully employed persons engaged in agricultural pursuits. In 1870 more than 50 per cent of the total United States' labor force was in agriculture. By 1953 the proportion had declined to less than 10 per cent. The other most striking change in the composition of the country's national income has been the increasing contribution of government. This is a result of a long-run trend reflecting the growing complexity of economic and social life requiring increasing government responsibilities.

Total output in the United States has been increasing at a rapid rate. Between 1938 and 1953 gross national product in constant prices rose roughly 120 per cent as against an increase of about 40 per cent for Free Europe and 62 per cent for the Soviet Union.[18] However, these differences reflect to an important degree the fact that the United States was spared the destructive effects of World War II. Thus between 1948 and 1953 the increase in United States production was only 27 per cent as against 21 per cent for Free Europe. In the same period United States output increased only about two-thirds as rapidly as that of the U.S.S.R.

TABLE 18-3

National Income by Major Industrial Divisions
1953 and 1869-1879 *
(*Percentage Distribution*)

INDUSTRY	1953	1869-1879 (AVERAGE)
Agriculture, forestry and fishing	5.5	20.5
Mining	1.8	1.8
Construction	4.9	5.3
Manufacturing	32.0	13.9
Wholesale and retail trade	17.2	15.7
Finance, insurance, real estate, *et cetera*	9.3	11.7
Transportation and other public utilities	8.5	11.9
Services	9.4	14.7
Government	11.4	4.4

* Data for 1953 taken from United States Department of Commerce, *Survey of Current Business,* February, 1955, and for 1869-79 from United States Department of Commerce, *Historical Statistics of the United States 1789-1945* (Washington, D. C., 1945), p. 13.

The economic supremacy of the United States reflects the relatively high productivity of American industry and agriculture. Productivity in the sense of output per man-hour was substantially higher in the United States before the war than in Europe as a whole, and this lead has been extended in the postwar years.[19] Again much of the difference since the war reflects the damage and dislocation caused by the war to European industry and agriculture. Since the war man-hour productivity in the United States has been increasing at a rate of 3.5 per cent per year. Currently, this means that the United States is adding $13 billion annually to its output of goods and services. A study of 31 industries for the period 1935 to 1939 found average output per man-hour in the United States to be approximately 2.8 greater than in the United Kingdom where

[18] *Joint Committee On The Economic Report, op. cit.,* p. 2.
[19] Organization For European Economic Co-operation, *The Report of the OEEC,* Vol. 1 (March, 1955), p. 55.

it was roughly the same as in Germany and Sweden.[20] Output per man-hour in agriculture in the United States increased by approximately two-thirds between 1935-39 and 1951. The increase for Western Europe as a whole in the same period was probably about one-fifth.

Favorable geographical factors alone, including resources and climate, do not explain the high output *per capita* in the United States. Environmental factors clearly affect productivity but their significance tends to decline as a country becomes more highly developed. Rich resources are of particular importance during the earlier stages of a country's economic growth because of the strong attraction they can exert on capital and labor. The discovery of gold in California is an excellent example, as is petroleum development in Texas. Subsequently, such factors as technology, organization, management, worker skills, incentives, and the like tend to overshadow resources in importance. More than anything else it is probable that the high productivity of the United States results from the efficiency of the methods it has developed to exploit its natural resources rather than from the relative abundance of these resources themselves. Of particular importance has been the substitution of mechanical energy for human energy. This explains why *per capita* consumption of commercial energy in the United States of 7.51 metric tons per year coal equivalent is the highest in the world. Indirectly the abundance of natural resources in the United States, particularly agricultural land, was an important factor in the substitution of mechanical labor for human labor. Free land competed with industry for labor during most of the nineteenth century, thereby tending to force wages up. There was thus a considerable incentive for industry to economize in the use of labor and to substitute machinery wherever possible.

MANUFACTURES

United States industry is both extensive and diversified. In addition to being the world's leading manufacturing nation, the United States can produce virtually all of its requirements of manufactures at costs equal to, if not lower than, those of foreign countries. Production of durable goods is slightly more important than of consumer goods. The principal industries in terms of their contribution to national output are machinery and transportation equipment, primary metals and fabricated metal products, textile products and apparel, food and kindred products, and chem-

[20] L. Rostas, *Comparative Productivity in British and American Industry* (London, 1948).

icals in that order. Output in a number of major industries is quite highly concentrated in a few firms. Thus in 1947, four firms produced 40 per cent or more of the output of the following industries:

1. Motor vehicles and parts
2. Meat packing
3. Steel works and rolling mills
4. Organic chemicals
5. Cigarettes
6. Copper rolling and drawing
7. Soap and glycerin

While natural advantages have largely determined the location of a number of important industries, other influences such as historical factors or the location of consumers often have been of equal if not greater significance. Thus the continued importance of industry in the states bordering the Atlantic is to an important extent the result of history (*cf.* Fig. 18-2, p. 574). This region happened to be settled first and its industry therefore got an earlier start than in the rest of the country. This is not to deny that the east coast possessed a number of natural advantages by way of resources, proximity to the sea when ships were the chief means of communication, closeness to Europe, and others. However, today, many of these advantages no longer exist. The development of the automobile industry in Detroit came about largely because this area had been the site of the horse-drawn carriage and wagon industry. On the other hand, the location of the steel industry together with its supporting industries can be attributed in large measure to the presence of abundant coal and iron ore fairly nearby and cheap water transport for the movement of bulky raw materials. The development of the aluminum industry in the Pacific northwest was largely determined by the availability of cheap hydro-electric power.

Three regions, New England, the Middle Atlantic states, and the East North Central states, accounted for more than two-thirds of all United States' manufactures in 1952. The other principal manufacturing regions are the South Atlantic and the Pacific states. While the North Central and Northeastern states dominate the industrial landscape, important regional shifts have been under way for some time, both westward and southward, following the general trend of population movements. The most significant changes have been the increased relative importance of manufactures in the West South Central and Pacific states. This shift has been accompanied by a gradual decline in the relative importance of New England and the Middle Atlantic states. Between 1939 and 1952, the share of total manufactures for these two regions declined from roughly 39 per cent to 34 per cent. The high costs of labor and power and the absence of sufficient compensating advantages have been important factors in this shift.

AGRICULTURE

Despite its declining economic importance in relation to manufactures, agriculture has been a major element of strength in the economy of the United States. Twice in the space of twenty-five years United States agriculture was equal to the task of greatly expanding output to meet the large wartime requirements of this country and its allies. After both wars, United States exports of foodstuffs prevented widespread starvation and suffering in war-devastated Europe and the Far East.

The United States is in the enviable position of being the world's most industrialized state and at the same time of being able to easily meet all of its essential food and agricultural raw material needs. In addition the United States normally produces more agricultural products than it consumes and therefore has a surplus for export. Agricultural imports are limited to tropical products like rubber, silk, tea, coffee, spices, and bananas. Only the U.S.S.R. of the other major powers approximates the favorable agricultural position of the United States, but as described in Chapter 15, it is experiencing increasing difficulties in meeting its needs.

An outstanding characteristic of United States' agriculture is its high productivity. This was impressively demonstrated during World War II. From 1939 to 1944 the volume of agricultural output increased 25 per cent with only a 6 per cent increase in crop acreage and an actual decline in farm employment. Greater use of fertilizers and increased farm mechanization, combined with favorable weather, all contributed to bringing about the increase. Most United States' farms are moderately large. In 1945, approximately 45 per cent of all land in farms fell in the 50 to 499 acre size category. Two-thirds of the cropland harvested was by farms in this size range. Approximately 40 per cent of all farm lands were in farms of over 1000 acres. However, most of this acreage was used for livestock raising and dairying, since the percentage of cropland harvested was less than 14 per cent. Tenancy is declining in the United States. In 1930, 42 per cent of all farms were tenant-operated. By 1945 the percentage had declined to about 30 per cent.

Favored by many different types of climate the United States produces a wide variety of crops ranging from semi-tropical products like rice, sugar cane, cotton, and oranges, to typical Temperate Zone crops like wheat, rye, and corn. Up until the mid-1920's farm receipts from sales of crops exceeded income from livestock and livestock products. By 1950 receipts from livestock products were 25 per cent higher than from crops. This shift resulted in part at least from the rise in income levels and the resultant increased demand for high-protein foods. The principal crops were cotton, fruits and vegetables, food grains, feed grains, tobacco, and oil-bearing crops. Livestock represents more than half of the value of livestock and livestock products, while dairy products, poultry, and eggs account for most of the remainder.

The two principal agricultural regions are the West North Central and the East North Central states. Together these two regions accounted for approximately 45 per cent of the value of cash farm receipts in 1949. These states are the major cereal, livestock, and dairying regions of the United States. Texas, Mississippi, and Arkansas are the major cotton-producing states. The South Atlantic states, primarily the Carolinas and Virginia, produce two-thirds of the tobacco. The Pacific states, notably California, produce the largest share of fruits, nuts, and vegetables.

The productiveness of American agriculture has created difficult economic and political problems both here and abroad. Largely as a result of the inability of the farm industry to adjust to the loss of export markets following the recovery of foreign agriculture after World War I and World War II, the United States has had a serious surplus problem for three or more decades. Because of the system of Congressional representation, United States farmers enjoy much greater political strength than their numbers suggest. Consequently, strong political pressures have been exerted to reduce the burden of surpluses on farm prices and incomes. The result has been a succession of measures, starting with the Federal Farm Board of 1929, to restrict output and subsidize farmers. Despite the expenditure of billions of dollars in farm aid, only limited progress has been made toward solving the problem of surpluses, chiefly because of the difficult political issues involved. In the course of its efforts to support farm prices, the United States Government through the Commodity Credit Corporation has accumulated billions of dollars of surplus farm products. Various measures have been taken in recent years to dispose of these surpluses abroad by sales at less than world-market prices and tie-in arrangements with foreign aid programs. While the legislation governing such sales specifies that they should not interfere with the regular commercial exports of other friendly powers, this is often difficult to avoid. A number of countries like Canada, Australia, New Zealand, and Argentina that depend heavily on agricultural exports have expressed serious concern about the effects of the surplus disposal programs on their sales in foreign markets.

TRANSPORTATION

The United States is served by the most extensive and probably one of the most efficient transportation systems in the world. The development of this system closely paralleled and at the same time was a major factor in promoting the growth of the United States' economy. The vast distances dividing the country were for a time as much or more of a hindrance than an asset to economic development. The transportation system by helping to bring about political and economic unification laid the basis for the present high degree of regional economic specialization which characterizes the United States.

The backbone of the United States' internal transportation system is a vast rail network of roughly 225,000 miles of line which in 1953 handled 40 per cent of the world's railway freight traffic [21] (*cf.* Fig. 18-2, p. 574). Important also is the unexcelled highway system of more than 2 million miles of hard-surfaced roads used by 53 million passenger cars and trucks, about two-thirds of the Free World total. Of rapidly increasing significance are pipelines for the carriage of petroleum and natural gas, and air transport for passenger travel. While inland waterways have lost their earlier pre-eminence they are still significant for the movement of low-cost bulk commodities and are likely to become of greater importance with the completion of the St. Lawrence Seaway described below.

Natural as well as technological factors have had an important influence on the development of transport in the United States. During the early period of the country's history, highways were the main arteries of commerce and travel. Lack of public roads led to extensive construction and use of toll turnpikes by private companies, particularly between 1800 and 1820. Most of the early roads ran in a north to south direction, in part at least because of the difficulties of traversing the Alleghanies. One of the most notable exceptions was the famous Cumberland Road which followed the valley of the Delaware River through the mountains. By 1838 the Cumberland Road extended from Cumberland, Maryland to Vandalia, Illinois. After it was opened to Wheeling in 1818, the Cumberland Road became a major thoroughfare between the east and the west. Its economic significance is suggested by the fact that the time required to travel from Baltimore to Wheeling was reduced from eight to three

[21] United Nations, *Statistical Yearbook*, 1954, p. 289.

days.[22] In general, highway transportation was very expensive, so that it was not economical to produce agricultural products or exploit mineral resources any great distance from the market. Consequently, the rich resources west of the Alleghanies were of limited economic value.

With the appearance of Robert Fulton's steamboat in 1807 inland water transport gradually began to assume increasing importance. During the second quarter of the nineteenth century the Ohio and the Mississippi Rivers were the principal arteries of commerce in the Middle West. In 1840, New Orleans was the fourth largest port in the world.[23] The era of canal-building, ushered in by the completion of the Erie Canal in 1825, gave a major impetus to inland water transport. The Erie played an important role in the opening of the West and in establishing the commercial supremacy of New York. The Canal which extended from Buffalo to Albany over a distance of 364 miles provided a cheap all-water route from the east to the west, diverting considerable traffic that formerly went down the Mississippi to New Orleans. It gave New York a great advantage over Baltimore and Philadelphia in trade with the west. The financial success of the Erie Canal started a veritable orgy of canal-building with highly unfavorable financial consequences for a number of states.

While the railroad era began in 1830, it was not until after the Civil War that the railway succeeded the steamboat as the chief carrier of domestic traffic. At the same time, with the completion of the first transcontinental line in 1869, the shift in the main flow of traffic from north and south to east and west that had begun with the construction of the Erie Canal was completed. The railways maintained their supremacy unchallenged until World War I. Since then heavy inroads into the railways' commanding position have been made by motor transport, pipelines, and most recently the airplane.

Table 18-4 below clearly indicates the rapid decline in the relative importance of rail transport for the movement of freight traffic during the past quarter-century, and the rapid rise in the importance of motor vehicles and oil pipelines. While the volume of air freight in 1953 totalled 400 million ton miles, it was still less than one-tenth of one per cent of all freight traffic. The importance of this traffic is greater than its magnitude suggests, however, because of its speed and flexibility. The decline in rail passenger traffic has been even more marked than for railway freight. By 1952 the railroads accounted for only 50 per cent of all passenger traffic

[22] D. P. Locklen, *Economics of Transportation*, 3rd ed. (Chicago, 1947), p. 82.
[23] *Ibid.*, p. 72.

of common carriers as compared with 98 per cent in 1915, while the proportion of bus and airplane transport had increased to 31 per cent and 18 per cent respectively. However, passenger transportation by private automobiles of 500 billion passenger miles was roughly four times greater than that of all common carriers. In addition to its great impact on the transportation use pattern, the phenomenal growth in the ownership and operation of private automobiles has had a significant influence on the living habits of the population. The automobile has been a major factor in the growing movement of city workers into the suburbs. It has contributed to the decentralization of industry and the decline of the small rural town.

TABLE 18-4
Distribution of Intercity Freight Traffic
1926-1953 *

TRANSPORT AGENCY	PER CENT DISTRIBUTION 1926	1950	1953
Railroads	77.1	58.7	51.7
Great Lakes, rivers, and canals	15.7	16.2	16.9
Trucks	2.8	12.4	17.4
Oil Pipelines	4.4	12.7	14.0
Total:	100.0	100.0	100.0

* Data for 1926 and 1950 were taken from J. F. Dewhurst and associates, *America's Needs and Resources* (New York, 1955), p. 263, and for 1953 from Interstate Commerce Commission, *Monthly Comment on Transportation Statistics,* October 15, 1954.

The rail system of the United States is very unequally distributed. The number of lines and the density of traffic is greatest in the industrial east (see Fig. 18-2). In 1950, states like New Jersey, Pennsylvania, and Illinois had more than twenty miles of railway per square mile of territory; at the other extreme Nevada and Arizona had less than two miles. Similar differences exist with respect to state highway systems. Unlike most countries the United States rail system is privately-owned and operated.

Most of the inland waterway traffic moves on the Great Lakes and on river systems like that of the Mississippi and canals such as the New York Barge Canal. Great Lakes traffic consists chiefly of grain, iron ore, and coal. A wide variety of cargo moves on the Mississippi including sugar, cotton, and rice. While the relative importance of inland water transport has been fairly stable for some time, the completion of the St. Lawrence Seaway is likely to increase its role.

The Great Lakes and the St. Lawrence River provide an all-water route from Duluth, Minnesota, to the Atlantic Ocean, a distance of more than

2,000 miles (*cf.* Fig. 6-11, p. 166). However, deep-draft ocean navigation cannot now go beyond Montreal. The United States and the Canadian Governments for many years have sought to develop the St. Lawrence-Great Lakes route jointly so as to enable deep-draft ocean-going vessels to reach the Great Lakes. Agreement finally was reached in 1954. When the project is completed during 1958, ocean-going vessels of up to 20,000 tons will be able to sail into the heart of the American continent. The resultant reduction in transportation costs and increased water traffic should bring widespread benefits to the mid-west. Costly transshipments of grain from the mid-west to foreign destinations will be eliminated. It is estimated the cost of shipping wheat from Duluth to Montreal will be cut by one-third.[24] The steel industry, which is 70 per cent located on the Great Lakes, will be able to bring in ore directly by sea from the rich Labrador-Quebec mines instead of transshipping it by rail or to smaller ships as at present. The Department of Commerce has estimated the Seaway will handle 35 million tons of ore *per annum*. The Seaway is expected to bring about a big increase in general traffic between lake ports and foreign ports. It will be of great strategic significance in wartime since it will reduce the open sea route from the United States to the United Kingdom by 1,000 miles. It has been estimated that when the Seaway is completed it will carry more tonnage than the Suez and Panama Canals combined. Clearly the Seaway will not be an unmixed blessing. Eastern railways and ports may be heavy losers.[25]

Brief mention should be made of coastwise and ocean-going shipping. In 1953 the United States had 462 vessels aggregating 5 million deadweight tons actively engaged in coastwise shipping. Freight carried by this fleet equalled about 13 per cent of that originated by the railroads. The bulk of this traffic was petroleum and petroleum products and to a much lesser extent coal and coke. The opening of the Panama Canal in 1914 greatly stimulated coastwise shipping between the east and west coasts. The economies of an all-water route from the east coast to the west coast has made it advantageous to move cargo from as far west as Chicago to New York or Philadelphia for shipment to the Pacific Coast via the Panama Canal. In 1953 the active United States flag fleet engaged in foreign trade numbered 629 vessels aggregating 7,390,000 deadweight tons. American flag vessels in 1953 carried 39 per cent of the country's imports and 29 per cent of its exports. The total United States' merchant marine is more than double the active fleet. In 1953, some 1836 vessels with a

[24] *The Economist,* August 28, 1954, p. 664.
[25] See also pp. 165 ff.

deadweight tonnage of 18.4 million were in reserve. In 1952, the tonnage of the United States merchant fleet, both active and inactive, was 40 per cent of the world total.

FOREIGN TRADE

Although the United States is the world's largest trading nation, it is much less dependent on foreign trade for its economic well-being than any other major power except the U.S.S.R. This dependence is not only small but is also declining. Since World War II the ratio of imports to gross national product has been 3.3 per cent or less, as compared with about 4.5 per cent after World War I. The corresponding ratio in the case of exports is close to 4 per cent. These low ratios are in marked contrast to those for the United Kingdom or Japan, for example, where foreign trade is equal to 20 and 30 per cent respectively of the gross national product.

Important reasons for the small and declining place of foreign trade in relation to total United States production is the richness of the country's natural resources and the efficiency and diversity of its industry. These resources have enabled the United States to feed its growing population and to provide the raw materials for its rapidly expanding industry without a corresponding increase in imports of primary materials. In addition, United States industry can produce virtually all of the country's requirements of manufactures, and trade policies have tended to restrict the entry of competing foreign imports. Various other factors have operated to increase United States self-sufficiency, such as the development of synthetics like rayon for natural silk, synthetic for natural rubber, more efficient use of raw materials, and so on. Despite the future prospect of a rapid growth of United States raw material imports, it is not expected that total imports will rise as rapidly as total production.

The increasing self-sufficiency of the United States economy partly explains the postwar dollar difficulties of the rest of the world. As described in Chapter 16, foreign countries, particularly Western Europe, became increasingly dependent on the United States for imports, particularly of basic foodstuffs and raw materials. However, exports to the United States and other dollar countries did not rise correspondingly. Hence the large balance-of-payments deficits of the rest of the world with the United States. During the period 1946 to 1953 these deficits aggregated $32.5 billion or more than one-fifth of the value of United States exports of goods and services.[26] As a part of its policy to help the economic recovery of

[26] Commission on Foreign Economic Policy, *Staff Papers* (Washington, 1954), p. 15.

the war-devastated world, and to build up the strength of its allies to resist communism, the United States extended net foreign aid of $41 billion between 1946 and 1953 to cover the trade deficit.[27] Since 1953, the dollar problem has been reduced to manageable proportions, although the dollar position of certain countries is still precarious. This explains the continuing concern abroad about United States foreign economic policies, particularly with respect to imports.

It should be recognized that foreign trade is more important to the United States economy than the low ratio of this trade to total output might suggest. As pointed out in the section on resources, the country is heavily dependent on foreign sources for a number of important and in some instances highly strategic raw materials. Foodstuffs like coffee, cocoa, and sugar, which are considered important to the United States standard of living, come wholly or in large part from abroad. In the case of exports, a number of products, particularly agricultural commodities and machinery, depend heavily on foreign markets (see Table 18-5 below).

TABLE 18-5

Exports of Selected Commodities as Percentage of U. S. Production *

AGRICULTURAL COMMODITIES (1949-51 AVERAGE)	PER CENT	NON-AGRICULTURAL COMMODITIES (1951)	PER CENT
Rice	42.6	Rolling mill machinery and parts	34.9
Cotton	39.0	Tractors	22.6
Wheat	33.5	Sewing machines and parts	22.3
Tallow	33.3	Textile machinery	21.6
Grain Sorghum	29.5	Printing machinery and equipment	17.5
Soybeans	25.1	Oilfield machinery, tools and parts	17.3
Tobacco	25.1	Office appliances	16.3
Lard	22.0	Motor trucks and coaches	15.6
		Agricultural machinery (except tractors)	11.7

* Commission on Foreign Economic Policy, *Staff Papers* (Washington, 1954), p. 5.

As is typical of highly-industrialized countries the United States imports chiefly crude and semi-manufactured products and exports mostly manufactures. In 1953, imports of crude materials, crude foodstuffs, and semimanufactures were 70 per cent of all imports. In the case of exports, finished manufactures were 70 per cent of the total. Unlike most industrialized countries, the United States also is an important exporter of both foodstuffs and crude materials. Exports of crude and manufactured food-

[27] *Ibid.*, p. 40.

stuffs and of crude materials were 9 per cent and 11 per cent respectively of total exports in 1953.

In addition to accounting for the largest share of world trade the United States is the world's leading creditor nation and exporter of capital. At the end of 1952 United States private and governmental investments abroad totaled $37.5 billion.[28] By contrast, the United States was a debtor nation before World War I. During the period from 1948 to 1952 net new capital outflow, public and private, and reinvested earnings of United States-owned subsidiaries, averaged over $2 billion *per annum.*

The postwar years have brought marked shifts in the geographical pattern of United States trade. In 1953, 55 per cent of this country's imports came from Canada and Latin America as compared with 32 per cent prewar. Exports to Canada and Latin America increased to 38 per cent of the total against 32 per cent prewar. Imports from Western Europe declined from 24 per cent in 1937 to 20 per cent in 1953. Exports excluding military aid to the same areas fell from 27 to 17 per cent. Trade with the rest of the world, chiefly the independent non-sterling countries in Asia and Africa, also has fallen off substantially. The increased significance of imports from Canada and Latin America reflects the growing role of these areas as suppliers of crude materials and foodstuffs. At the same time raw materials like tin, jute, and silk, supplied by Asian countries, declined in importance. The fall in European exports partly reflects the reduced importance of United States imports of manufactures and partly the displacement of such imports by Canada. The expansion of United States exports to areas like Canada and Latin America has resulted to an important extent from the displacement of former European suppliers of these areas.

FUTURE ECONOMIC PROSPECTS

Projecting future economic growth trends is at best a hazardous undertaking. Nonetheless it is a reasonable prediction, barring unforeseen disasters such as a general war involving widespread physical destruction, that the United States will maintain and probably increase its absolute economic superiority for some time in the future. If this country's annual rate of economic growth is no greater over the next two decades than the average rate of the past century (3 per cent), total output by 1975 will be more than double that of 1950, or roughly $570 billion. This figure could well be on the low side, however, in view of present rapid technological

[28] *Ibid.*, p. 79.

advances making for increased productivity, such as automation, and the fact that prolonged depressions in the past kept the rate lower than it otherwise would have been. While the United States economy is still not depression-proof, it is generally believed that with present improved techniques of control, business fluctuations will not be severe in the future. The United States Joint Committee on the Economic Report has estimated the potential rate of growth of this country's national output at 4 per cent per year over the next decade.[29] The maintenance of this rate until 1975 would produce a United States gross national product of $728 billion in 1950 prices. As mentioned in Chapter 15 the rate of growth of the U.S.S.R. economy until the 1970's is expected to be higher than that of the United States, possibly 4.5 to 5 per cent *per annum*. These rates would give the U.S.S.R. a gross national product of $300 billion to $350 billion by 1975, as compared with roughly $100 billion in 1950. Thus while the ratio of United States output to that of the U.S.S.R., will be less than at present, the absolute superiority of the United Sates will be increased whether its rate of growth is 3 per cent or 4 per cent *per annum*.

Canada

No description of the economic capabilities of the West would be complete without at least a brief look at Canada. Though greatly overshadowed by the United States, Canada, with a population of only 16.5 million in 1954, now ranks sixth among the industrial nations of the world. She is also a leading exporter of industrial raw materials and foodstuffs. During the past decade or so Canada has been developing at a spectacular rate. If present economic growth trends continue, Canada may well emerge during the next generation as the fourth or fifth industrial power.

Canada's economic development has been paralleled by a corresponding growth in her international status. Although a member of the British Commonwealth of Nations, Canada is an independent and sovereign nation and pursues her own vigorous foreign policy. Canadian troops fought with United Nations forces in Korea. As a NATO country Canada, like the United States, in addition to providing armed forces has made sizeable contributions in the form of mutual aid to other member countries.

Common economic and strategic interests as well as close cultural ties have made for increasing Canadian-United States dependence and co-

[29] "Potential Economic Growth of the United States During the Next Decade," 83rd Congress, 2nd session, Washington, 1954.

operation. Canada is both the best customer and chief supplier of the United States. United States capital has been a major factor in Canada's economic development. Canada occupies a highly strategic position from the point of view of the security of the United States in today's era of long-range bombers and atomic missiles, since most of the great circle routes from the United States and Europe pass over Canada. Millions of Canadians have crossed the border to become American citizens.

GEOGRAPHY AND PEOPLE

Canada is the second largest country in the world with a total area of 3.8 million square miles. It embraces all of the northern half of the North American continent except Alaska, Greenland, and the French islands of St. Pierre and St. Miquelon. However, cold climatic conditions limit the habitable area of Canada to less than 10 per cent of the total as compared with more than 50 per cent for the United States. With the incorporation of Newfoundland in 1949, Canada now comprises ten provinces and the Yukon and Northwest Territories.

The geography of Canada is similar to that of the United States in many important respects. Western Canada, like Western United States, is characterized by rugged mountains and plateaus. The interior plains of the Canadian prairie provinces are an extension of the Great Plains and lowlands of the United States. In the east Canada has its mountainous and hilly Appalachian region which includes all of the eastern provinces. The largest physiographic division of Canada is the Laurentian shield, a vast V-shaped area of 1.8 million square miles which extends from the interior plains to the coast of Labrador. This region is marked by rugged slopes of rocky hills broken by river valleys and is the source of most of Canada's mineral wealth. Between the Appalachians and the Shield are the St. Lawrence lowlands—a plain of low relief extending from Quebec City to Lake Huron, a distance of 600 miles.[30]

Most major Canadian rivers, except the St. Lawrence, are of limited utility for transportation since they flow away from the more settled regions to the cold northern waters. Thus the Nelson-Saskatchewan flows into the Hudson Bay and the Mackenzie-Athabaska flows into the Arctic. However, the St. Lawrence and the Great Lakes afford an unequalled inland navigation system, extending for a distance of 2,000 miles through the most highly developed regions of Canada.

According to the 1951 Census, Canada had a population of just over

[30] Stamp and Suggate, *op. cit.*, pp. 155-158.

14 million. The population is increasing at the rapid rate of more than 2 per cent *per annum,* chiefly as a result of natural increase, but partly through immigration and amounted to 16.5 million in 1954. Immigration has increased significantly since the war, mostly because of highly prosperous economic conditions. United Nations population experts have estimated that Canada's population should reach 20 million by 1980.

The two basic stocks of Canada's population are French and English (*cf.* Fig. 11-2, p. 391). The French are primarily the descendants of the original seventeenth and eighteenth century colonists. Of the 1951 population of 14 million, 4.3 million were of French extraction and 6.7 million British. Other Europeans number 2.5 million. The remaining population consists mostly of Indians and a few Eskimos. The large French minority has been a source of considerable social and policital friction throughout Canada's history. Most Frenchmen still speak their mother tongue and observe the customs and laws of their ancestors. "Not even 189 years of British rule have changed them. The difference between a French and a British Canadian is greater by far than between a British Canadian and an American." [31]

Population density (*cf.* Fig. 2-9, p. 48) is low, averaging 3.92 persons per square mile in 1951. The cold and inhospitable Northwest and Yukon territories which account for almost 40 per cent of the area of Canada had a population density of only about 2 persons per 100 square miles while the average density in the provinces was only 6.6 persons per square mile. Climatic factors keep most of Canada's population in the south. Half of Canada's population lives in a narrow band, 100 to 125 miles from the Canadian-United States border, and 90 per cent live 200 to 225 miles from the border. Two-thirds of the population live in the provinces of Ontario and Quebec.

Until fairly recently the movement of population from east to west in Canada closely paralleled that of the United States. Thus between 1871 and 1951 the proportion of Canada's total population living in the western provinces of Manitoba, Alberta, Saskatchewan, and British Columbia increased from less than 2 per cent to 26 per cent. This movement was greatly stimulated by the completion of the transcontinental railway in 1885 which opened up the rich agricultural lands of the west. While the population of British Columbia has continued to increase relative to the rest of the country during the past decade, that of the prairie provinces has been declining, reflecting the falling relative importance of agricul-

[31] K. Munro, "Now Canada Comes of Age," *New York Times Magazine,* March 30, 1952; see also p. 390.

ture. In recent years there has been a tendency for the population to move in a more northerly direction. The chief stimulus for this movement has not been opportunities in agriculture, like the movement to the west, but rather the growth of mining activity. The quest for and exploitation of mineral deposits has created dozens of new towns virtually in the wilderness. One example is the town of Kitimat, a hundred miles south of the Alaskan border, which is the site of the largest aluminum expansion project in the Free World. Four years ago Kitimat was an Indian fishing village. Today it has a population of 5,000 and by 1959, when the project is completed, it is expected to have 20,000.[32] Another settlement has mushroomed at the Burnt Creek iron ore mine project on the Quebec-Labrador boundary, 360 miles north of Seven Islands on the Gulf of St. Lawrence. Or again, the discovery of vast uranium deposits at Blind River in the Ontario wilderness is changing and has changed a slumbering lumber town of 3,000 people into a thriving community of 15,000 persons in a few years. While the movement northward has been hampered by the lack of rail and highway transport, it has proceeded much more rapidly than otherwise would have been possible as a result of the availability of air transport. Thus mining operations began at Burnt Creek with equipment flown in by air one year before the railroad from Seven Islands was completed.

RESOURCES

Canada's rapid economic growth of recent years has been based to a very important degree on the exploitation of the country's rich natural resources (*cf.* Fig. 18-2). Canada is still in the stage of economic development where the exploitation of its natural resources can significantly affect the entire economy. Thus the iron ore deposits of Ungava and northern Quebec "are directly responsible for the railways now being constructed from the St. Lawrence and the 'opening up' of new lands. The past three years have seen a significant change in the whole of Canada's economy through the Alberta oil strikes."[33] Since Canada's natural resources are still relatively undeveloped, their exploitation is likely to have an important influence on the pattern of economic growth for some years to come. Canada's frontier is still an expanding one and probably her greatest need is more people. Some authorities have estimated Canada could support a population of 100 million.[34]

Agriculture. Though less well-endowed than the United States with

[32] L. D. Stamp, *Our Undeveloped World* (London, 1953), p. 122.
[33] *Ibid.*, p. 122.
[34] Stamp and Suggate, *op. cit.*, p. 184.

land suitable for agriculture, despite its greater area, Canada's agricultural land base is nonetheless more than adequate in relation to its population. United Nations estimates place Canada's arable land area at 93 million acres (1950), or more than 6 acres *per capita*. Unoccupied but potentially productive agricultural land exceeds 170 million acres. Like the United States, Canada should experience no difficulty for the foreseeable future in feeding its growing population and at the same time providing a sizeable volume of exports.

Forest. Canada's forest resources are among the richest in the world. They are the basis of Canada's vast timber and pulp and paper industry which for some time has exceeded all other industries in importance. Canada produces more than one-half the world's newsprint and is a major producer and exporter of wood pulp and timber. The country's total lumber stand on accessible and inaccessible land is about two-thirds that of the United States. However, roughly 45 per cent of this stand is at present inaccessible, against 10 per cent for the United States.[35] The trees are predominantly softwood, and these enjoy the widest general demand.

Minerals. Canada possesses an abundance of mineral and fuel resources. Although production is still small, Canada's reserves of high-grade iron ore are among the largest in the world. Copper, nickel, lead, zinc, uranium, and asbestos reserves are more than adequate to cover future needs for some years to come and are exploited primarily for export. Like the United States, Canada's principal mineral deficiencies are in the ferro-alloys—chromium, manganese, tin, tungsten, and molybdenum.

Canada has large reserves of high-grade bituminous coal suitable for coking. However, these reserves are located mainly in the maritime and prairie provinces and in British Columbia, and not in the industrialized provinces of Ontario and Quebec. Transportation savings make it more economical for these two provinces to buy coal from nearby United States sources, which explains why Canada is a large net importer of coal.

Since 1947, large reserves of oil and natural gas have been discovered in western Canada. Proved reserves now amount to less than one per cent of the Free World total. However, expert geologists estimate potential reserves may amount to as much as 50 billion barrels or more than 10 per cent of the present reserves of the Free World.[36] While Canada now imports about half of its petroleum requirements, it should achieve sta-

[35] The President's Materials Policy Commission, *op. cit.*, Vol. 5, p. 53.

[36] H. M. H. A. Van Der Valk, *The Economic Future of Canada* (New York, 1954), p. 54.

tistical self-sufficiency in a few years. Locational factors, however, will make it economical for Canada to continue to import some petroleum. At present many gas wells have been closed in Canada for lack of markets, but in time the construction of pipelines to major consuming areas will help to overcome this problem.

Large areas of Canada enjoy an abundance of cheap hydro-electric power. Canada ranks after the United States in installed hydro-electric capacity. Low-cost hydro-electric power has been an important factor in Canada's industrial development. It has compensated to an important extent for the lack of coal in industrialized Ontario and Quebec. It has been the basis for the development of Canada's huge aluminum as well as other electro-metallurgical industries, and has been extremely important to the growth of the pulp and paper industry which is a large user of electric power. So far only about one-quarter of Canada's hydro-electric resources have been developed. Large untapped sources are still available for exploitation in British Columbia, Manitoba, Northern Ontario, Quebec, and Labrador.

GENERAL ECONOMIC CHARACTERISTICS

As mentioned previously production in Canada has been growing at a rapid rate, almost doubling between 1939 and 1951. Average *per capita* gross national product in 1953 was roughly $1,600 or more than twice the average of Free Europe. Though less industrialized than the United States, Canada's industry greatly exceeds agriculture in importance. In 1952 manufactures accounted for 29 per cent of the net domestic product as against 14.2 per cent for agriculture.

As in any rapidly developing country agriculture has been declining in relative importance for some time. At the beginning of the century 40 per cent of Canada's labor force was engaged in agriculture and by 1951 the percentage had declined to 19 per cent. The relative contribution of agriculture to total output has also been falling but to a lesser extent. The prairie provinces, like the great plains of the United States, are Canada's principal agricultural region. Their main crop is wheat, although the trend is toward greater diversification. Canada produces enough wheat to feed 100 million people. The chief crops in the maritime provinces are potatoes and apples, while in Ontario and Quebec mixed farming predominates. Like the United States, Canada has had an agricultural surplus problem for some years.

Employment in industry outnumbers employment in agriculture two to one. The principal industries are pulp and paper, food processing, and non-ferrous smelting and refining respectively. Production of more complex industrial products such as machinery and equipment tends to be limited by the small size of the Canadian market. Ontario and Quebec account for roughly 80 per cent of all manufactures. The industrial predominance of these two eastern provinces owes much to the availability of cheap hydro-electric power, their proximity to the high-quality coal of the eastern Appalachian region of the United States, and the superb inland water transport system of the St. Lawrence River and the Great Lakes. American investors have a large stake in Canadian industry. It has been estimated that United States-controlled industrial enterprises represent about one-third of the total investment in Canadian industry.[37] Total United States investments in Canada amounted to $8 billion in 1952.

Canada's prosperity is heavily dependent on foreign trade. Approximately one-quarter to one-fifth of the country's gross national product derives from exports. Moreover exports are primarily processed raw materials like foodstuffs, wood products, pulp and paper, and metals, and are somewhat lacking in diversification. As a result Canada is relatively vulnerable to external economic developments though by no means to the same degree as the typical underdeveloped country. Finished manufactures, chiefly machinery and equipment, are Canada's principal imports. Since World War II the United States has replaced the United Kingdom as Canada's principal trading partner. In 1953, some 59 per cent of Canada's exports went to the United States and 74 per cent of its imports came from the same source.

OUTLOOK

Canada's future economic prospects are considered to be highly favorable. Its population and economic growth rates are among the most rapid in the Free World, and it has an abundance of natural resources. One authority in a recent study estimated that Canada might have a gross national product of $80 billion in 1952 prices by 1980.[38] This estimate may well be on the high side. Nonetheless there is good reason to believe Canada will continue to develop more rapidly than most other industrialized nations and that it will emerge before the end of the century as one of the world's leading economic powers. In this process it has been prophesied by the Governor of the Bank of Canada that "Canada would

[37] *Ibid.*, p. 124.
[38] *Ibid.*

be very much less dependent on its export trades, much more highly developed in its secondary and tertiary industries, that it would have repatriated much of the ownership of basic industries now held in the United States, and that the process of the next twenty years would be increasing 'Canadianization' rather than 'Continentalization.'"[39]

[39] *The Economist,* May 28, 1955, p. 746.

CHAPTER 19

The Challenge of the Underdeveloped Areas

GENERAL ECONOMIC CHARACTERISTICS

The term *underdeveloped* has a number of connotations. Here the term is used to describe countries that are unable to provide what they consider to be acceptable levels of living for the mass of their populations. If we arbitrarily take a figure of $300 *per capita* as a minimum acceptable annual income, we find that countries which fall into the underdeveloped category account for most of the free world's population and land area. In 1953, with a population in excess of one billion, the underdeveloped countries had 70 per cent of the peoples of the non-Communist world. Their land area is also roughly 70 per cent of the total. They are to be found in all hemispheres and on every continent, but primarily in Asia, Africa, and Latin America (*cf.* Fig. 14-3, p. 468).

As might be expected, given the wide differences in their natural and cultural environments, the underdeveloped areas have extremely diverse economies. Despite these diversities, the underdeveloped areas share enough common characteristics to permit meaningful generalization about their economies, which are more directly affected by geographical factors than are those of the more highly developed areas, especially the industrialized and urbanized countries. To understand the basic features of their economic systems, especially those rooted in the relationships of man to his natural environment, is a prerequisite for the understanding of the economic and political geography of the underdeveloped countries.

The greater the degree of their underdevelopment, the greater is the interrelationship of economic and political factors in their human geography.

The outstanding characteristic that the underdeveloped countries have in common is of course their poverty. Most of the population live at, or close to, bare subsistence levels. Average *per capita* incomes amounted to roughly $70 in 1949 compared with $690 for the more developed regions and $1,450 for the United States.[1] Inequality in the distribution of income between underdeveloped and developed countries is no less marked than that between individuals within a single country. Of an estimated national income among Free World countries of $460 billion in 1949, the developed countries accounted for $350 billion or roughly 75 per cent. In other words, the developed countries with 30 per cent of the population of the non-Communist world accounted for more than three-quarters of the total output of goods and services.

Despite the efforts of the underdeveloped countries to accelerate their economic growth, the gap between incomes in the underdeveloped and the developed countries continues to increase. According to Professor Simon Kuznets, this process has been going on for more than a century.[2] The indications are this gap will continue to widen for the indefinite future. The reasons are partly the low economic growth rates in many underdeveloped areas but primarily the fact that these rates apply to a much lower absolute base than in the case of the industrialized areas.

Low living standards are evidenced by inadequate diets, primitive housing, poor health, and low levels of education. Most of the inhabitants of the underdeveloped areas have a daily *per capita* food supply of less than 2,200 calories per day, or 20 per cent below what is considered the minimum for health and efficiency. This compares with 3,000 calories or more for the industrialized countries. These calorie differences do not take into account qualitative differences: for example, consumption of animal proteins in the underdeveloped areas is one-fourth of that in developed countries. Endemic and other diseases are common and undermine seriously the vitality of the people. In many of these countries, the geography of diseases is an integral part of their economic and political geography: wherever there is the tsetse fly, sleeping sickness may bar social and political development. Almost every African native is infested with some type

[1] United Nations, *Per Capita Incomes of Seventy Countries—1949* (New York, October, 1950).

[2] "Underdeveloped Countries and the Pre-Industrial Phase In the Advanced Countries: An Attempt at Comparison," delivered before the United Nations Population Conference in Rome, September, 1954.

of intestinal worm, and over large areas a great proportion of the people suffer from malaria, plague, yaws, and syphilis.[3] However considerable progress has been made in coping with these diseases during the past 15 years in East and Central Africa. Birth and mortality rates are high and life expectancy is low. In the underdeveloped areas as a whole, expectation of life at birth is less than 35 years as against 60 years in the developed regions. Approximately two-thirds of the male population are illiterate, compared with 5 per cent in developed countries. The worker force is lacking in specialized training and skills. Although it is impossible to measure in reasonably accurate statistical terms the degree of literacy and technical skills in underdeveloped areas, it must be realized that these factors are of considerable significance in evaluating the usefulness, actual and potential, of the resources of an area to man and his political organizations.[4] The differentiation in literacy and skills itself defies analysis, at least in many of the areas with which we are concerned (*cf.* Fig. 13-1, 2, pp. 442, 444). These difficulties, however, only underline the need for exploration of the intangible factors by trying to equate the human and the natural resources of such an area within political boundaries.

Agriculture is the principal economic activity. More than 60 per cent of the people in the underdeveloped areas depend on agriculture for a livelihood compared with 30 per cent or less in industrialized countries (see Table 19-1). Thus with respect to the distribution of the labor force, the underdeveloped countries stand where the developed countries stood a hundred to a hundred and fifty years ago. Many rural areas are on the bare fringe of the money economy. Farmers produce primarily for their own use and exchanges frequently involve barter.

Land is scarce relative to population in many underdeveloped areas. As a consequence, average farm holdings are generally very small, usually less than what is considered the minimum for efficient operation. Many areas have semi-feudal agricultural systems characterized by large estates. Large estates are widespread in the Caribbean, throughout South America, in South East Asia, in Ceylon, and in parts of East Africa.[5] Tenancy commonly associated with large estates is often characterized by high rents and insecurity of tenure. In certain areas, notably Africa south of the Sahara, communal tenure is the most common form of land ownership.

The underdeveloped countries account for less than 10 per cent of the

[3] "Annual Medical Report for Kenya (1928)," as quoted in W. Macmillan, *Africa Emergent* (London, 1938), pp. 30-37.

[4] See pp. 499-501.

[5] United Nations, *Land Reform* (New York, 1951), p. 18.

Free World's industrial output. Industry is confined largely to the processing of raw materials for export and the manufacture of consumers goods for domestic consumption. In many areas industry is controlled by foreign investors and its impact on the total economy is peripheral. Handicrafts still account for a considerable share of the manufacturing output in many areas. Only a few countries have any heavy industry, and crude steel production is less than 3 per cent of the Free World total.

TABLE 19-1

Proportion of World Population in Agriculture, 1949 *

AREA	TOTAL POPULATION (MILLIONS)	AGRICULTURAL POPULATION (MILLIONS)	AGRICULTURAL POPULATION AS PERCENTAGE OF TOTAL
North America [a]	163	33	20
Europe	391	129	33
Oceania	12	4	33
South America	107	64	60
Central America [b]	50	33	67
Asia	1,255	878	70
Africa	198	146	74
WORLD TOTAL	2,176	1,287	59

[a] United States and Canada.
[b] Includes Mexico.
* United Nations, Food and Agriculture Organization, *Yearbook of Food and Agriculture,* 1950, p. 16.

Productivity per worker in agriculture and industry is low. Yields per person in agriculture in 1947-48 were well below the world average and far less than in the United States or in Western Europe (see Table 19-2).

TABLE 19-2

Productivity of Agricultural Population by Continents, 1947-48 *

CONTINENT	YIELDS PER PERSON IN AGRICULTURE (METRIC TONS)
World Average	0.42
North and Central America	2.57
South America	0.48
Europe	0.88
Oceania	2.38
Asia	0.22
Africa	0.77

* Food and Agriculture Organization of the United Nations, *Monthly Bulletin of Food and Agricultural Statistics,* Vol. 2, No. 9 (September, 1949).

Various factors account for this low productivity, including underemployment of labor, lack of equipment, backward technology, limited use of fertilizers, use of inferior land, and unfavorable climate. The limited use of mechanical energy is indicated by the fact that consumption of commercial sources of energy in underdeveloped areas is one-sixteenth or less that in the United States. Underemployment of labor is particularly significant in the densely populated countries of Asia where lack of alternative opportunities leads to overcrowding of farms. The following data on income of workers in manufacturing and handicrafts for selected countries in 1948 indicates that productivity per industrial worker in underdeveloped countries, compared with developed countries, is even less favorable than in agriculture.[6]

World	$ 910
United States	4110
Canada	3000
United Kingdom	1450
Middle America	720
South America	520
Turkey	400
Africa	265
India	200

Communications and transportation facilities are poorly developed. For example, in 1951, the highly developed countries, the United States and Canada had over 300 telephone instruments in use per 1000 population as against 2 instruments per 1000 in the underdeveloped countries. Most underdeveloped areas are inadequately serviced by any form of transportation. Whereas the United States and Canada moved about 6,000 ton miles of freight *per capita per annum* in 1951, the underdeveloped countries generally carried less than 130 tons *per capita*. The number of motor vehicles in use in the underdeveloped areas in relation to population was less than 3 per cent of that in the developed countries.[7]

Two or three primary products generally account for the bulk of all exports. Export earnings are extremely volatile because of wide cyclical swings in the world market demand for such products. Thus the economies of the underdeveloped countries are highly vulnerable to external market forces over which they have relatively little control. A United Nations' study showed average annual fluctuations of 35 per cent in pro-

[6] W. S. and E. S. Woytinsky, *World Population and Production Trends and Outlook* (New York, 1953), p. 1013.

[7] United Nations, *Statistical Yearbook*, 1954.

ceeds from exports of a number of important primary products during the first half of the twentieth century.[8]

With the notable exception of Latin America, the rate of economic growth in many underdeveloped areas in recent decades has barely kept pace with the increase in population. As a result, *per capita* real incomes have remained almost stationary at a time when they have been rising rapidly in the industrialized countries of the West.

Many serious obstacles stand in the way of the efforts of the underdeveloped countries to speed up their rate of economic development. Low incomes leave only a relatively small margin for savings and investment. The rate of capital formation in most underdeveloped areas is just about adequate to keep up with the population growth, hence any significant increase in the rate of domestic capital formation would require a reduction of existing low living standards. Not many governments of underdeveloped areas have the requisite administrative skills to divert more production from consumption into investment, and might well be unwilling to assume the attendant political risks.

Lack of domestic savings can of course be compensated by infusions of capital from abroad. The amount required to induce a satisfactory rate of economic growth in the underdeveloped areas would be extremely large. A group of experts appointed by the Secretary-General of the United Nations estimated that capital imports of more than $10 billion per year would be required to raise *per capita* incomes in the underdeveloped areas by 2 per cent *per annum.*[9] This compares with the current flow of not much more than $1 billion *per annum.*

Lack of capital is by no means the only obstacle to economic progress. In many areas economic development will require fundamental changes in the social and economic structure of society and massive efforts to raise levels of education. Many parts of Africa, for example, are only just emerging from tribal forms of society where land is held in common and the experimental or scientific attitude is virtually unknown. Other societies in parts of the Middle East and Latin America are still semi-feudal in their essential characteristics. Wealth and power are associated with the ownership of land rather than success in industry and trade. Absentee ownership and farm tenancy are widespread, thereby reducing incentives to improve existing inefficient farming methods. Much wealth is wasted in conspicuous consumption. Moreover, many members of the ruling classes

[8] *Relation of Fluctuations in the Prices of Primary Commodities to the Ability of the Under-Developed Countries to Obtain Foreign Exchange* (July 5, 1951).

[9] United Nations, *Measures for the Economic Development of Under-Developed Countries* (New York, May, 1951).

are resistant to economic progress because of the threat that it poses to their power and prestige.

Governments are frequently inefficient and corrupt, and political instability and civil disorder may be endemic. As a result, the atmosphere of confidence about the future which is essential to sustained economic progress is often lacking.

Many underdeveloped areas lack an entrepreneurial class capable and willing to exploit the advances of modern technology. Investors tend to favor commercial ventures offering high and quick returns. Consequently, the development of many of the basic services required for economic growth, such as power, transport, and communications, is generally inadequate.

Demographic factors (*cf.* Fig. 9-2, p. 296) pose serious obstacles to economic development. Most of today's highly developed countries had low rates of population increase during their pre-industrial periods. Rapid population growth came after they began to develop. By contrast, a number of underdeveloped countries—the Philippines, Thailand, Malaya, Ceylon, Bolivia—have rates of population increase double those of the developed countries at a comparable stage of development. This imposes a heavy investment burden on the limited savings of these countries to support the increments to their populations. Certain areas, notably South Asia, face both overpopulation and the prospect of a rapid rise in the rate of population growth. India's population, for example, probably exceeds the optimum relative to its resources. Increments to the labor force, therefore, mean lower returns per worker because of the necessity of having to exploit progressively inferior resources. Inferior resources can be offset by improved technology, but this requires increased amounts of capital per worker and thereby raises the cost of economic development.

Better public health measures are expected to bring about a substantial lowering of death rates in the years immediately ahead without a corresponding decline in birth rates. As a result, India's annual rate of population increase for example might rise to about 2 per cent in the next decade or so as compared with about 1.25 per cent each year since the war. This will mean a yearly addition to the population of about 8 million persons. Where population is rising at the rate of one per cent annually it has been estimated that a country must have real savings equal to 4 per cent of the national income to maintain *per capita* incomes. With a 2 per cent increase in population, the rate of savings would have to reach 8 per cent per year. Thus some overpopulated countries may well face the problem of having to run faster simply to stand still. Moreover, if the experience of industrialized countries is any guide, it will take some decades before declining birth rates significantly reduce population growth. Unless the overpopulated countries are able to accelerate this planned reduction, they may face a serious population explosion.

Even the above brief and incomplete discussion indicates that the underdeveloped countries face many hurdles in their efforts to industrialize. Many of these obstacles were surmounted only gradually by the western industrialized countries. Whether the process can be telescoped rapidly enough to satisfy the aspirations of the underdeveloped areas still remains to be seen. In any case, the achievement of economic progress "will make enormous demands on intelligence in planning, honesty and ability in execution, and on discipline within the community." [10]

THE CHALLENGE OF ECONOMIC BACKWARDNESS [11]

Economic backwardness and mass poverty in many regions of the world and among large numbers of people are not recent phenomena. Wide differences in living standards between the industrialized countries of the West and the underdeveloped countries of Asia, Africa, and Latin America have existed for a century or more. Up until the last decade or so, this situation had no significant international political implications. The underdeveloped areas played an important but largely passive role in the struggles of the great powers to acquire territory. They were valued largely as sources of food and raw materials to meet the growing needs of the industrial states and as markets for finished manufactures. The industrialized countries showed a minimum concern for the welfare of the underdeveloped areas. Although the latter became increasingly restive and resentful of their role as "hewers of wood and drawers of water," they were for the most part too weak economically and politically to do much about it.

Particularly since the end of World War II, the underdeveloped countries have moved from the periphery to the center of the world political arena. Two factors largely account for this. On the one hand, the political and economic control of the Western powers over the less developed areas has declined sharply, partly because of the weakness of Western Europe and partly because of the growing strength of the movement for national self-determination and social justice in the backward countries. As a result, we have witnessed since 1947 the voluntary withdrawal of the

[10] *Ibid.*, p. 89.

[11] For a fuller treatment of this subject see E. Staley, *The Future of Underdeveloped Countries* (New York, Harper & Brothers, 1954).

British from India, Burma, Ceylon, and Pakistan. We have seen the forced retirement of the Netherlands from Indonesia and France's surrender of a part of Indochina and her declaration of the independence of Morocco and Tunisia. Britain and France face growing political turmoil and unrest in certain of their African dependencies. There has been a progressive weakening of the political and economic influence of the major industrial powers in the Middle East and to a much lesser extent in Latin America. On the other hand, we have had the breakdown of the traditional balance-of-power system in international relations and the polarization of political power around the two superstates, the United States and the U.S.S.R. After a brief period of co-operation during and immediately following World War II, relations between the United States and Russia rapidly deteriorated. By 1948 the threat of Communist expansion and Russian ambitions for world supremacy became increasingly clear.

Soviet strategy appears to be gradually to isolate the United States by cutting off country after country from the Free World, bringing each into the Communist camp. While the Communists have been willing to resort to naked aggression on a limited scale to achieve their aims, as they did in North Korea and Indochina, their favored weapon has been internal subversion and infiltration. Mass propaganda, false promises, threats, and trained revolutionaries are widely used by the Communists to attract adherents to the Soviet fold. Economic and political unrest are exploited wherever they exist. The Russians made strenuous efforts to undermine Western Europe after the war by capitalizing on the economic stagnation, social unrest, and disillusionment which affected the entire area. These attempts were frustrated in large measure by the success of the United States'-sponsored European Economic Recovery Program. Billions of dollars of United States aid were effective in helping to rehabilitate war-devastated Western Europe and in removing the principal causes of economic and social discontent.

More recently the threat of Communist penetration has taken a new course. Thwarted in the more highly developed industrialized countries of the West, the Communists now appear to be directing their main attack against the underdeveloped areas. Their efforts already have succeeded in bringing into the Soviet orbit the East European satellites and mainland China with a combined population in excess of 700 million. The menace of Soviet expansion in the underdeveloped areas probably represents a much more serious challenge to the Free World than Communist penetration of Western Europe. Political and economic conditions in many of the underdeveloped countries are ideal for Soviet exploitation.

The governments of most of these countries are weak and inexperienced. Poverty and mass discontent are widespread. Most backward areas have had a long heritage of political and economic domination by the Western industrialized powers. Consequently they are extremely suspicious if not hostile toward the West. Soviet propaganda plays on these suspicions in order to discredit the West and to drive a wedge between the independent underdeveloped areas and the Free World. The postwar years have brought a rising tide of expectations among backward peoples for economic betterment. Millions in the underdeveloped areas have become aware of their depressed economic status and are no longer willing to sit back idly and do nothing about it. They are determined to try to achieve higher living standards. This ferment among the peoples of the underdeveloped areas has been graphically described by Eugene Black, President of the International Bank for Reconstruction and Development, as follows: [12]

> Perhaps the most powerful single force shaping the course of history in our time is the awakening consciousness of the underprivileged masses of the people that the conditions of poverty, ill-health and ignorance in which they live are not preordained and their deep conviction that they have a right to the opportunity to earn a better living for themselves and a better future for their children.

The awakening of the backward areas was dramatically demonstrated by the convening of the Bandung Conference of Asian and African States in April, 1955 (*cf.* Fig. 8-21, p. 288). The final communiqué of the conference placed major emphasis on the urgency of promoting economic development in the Asian-African regions.

The desire of the underdeveloped countries for economic progress is of course motivated by other considerations in addition to the wish to improve living conditions. Important also is their concern about security and national prestige. Like Japan and Turkey before them, the governments of many underdeveloped countries, particularly in the newly independent ones, recognize that political independence has limited significance if they are too weak militarily to prevent foreign interference in their domestic affairs or to defend themselves against external aggression. Economic progress is viewed as an essential step in the development of military strength. Countries like India which aspire to leadership among Asiatic peoples realize this will require the building-up of their economic and military strength.

[12] *Summary Proceedings,* Fifth Annual Meeting of the Board of Governors, Washington, D. C., November 30, 1950.

Although to some extent an irrational consideration, the prestige factor also is significant as a motive for economic progress among underdeveloped countries. Most backward areas are extremely sensitive about their inferior economic status. They view economic progress and in particular industrialization as essential if they are to gain acceptance and respect in the community of nations. The preoccupation of the underdeveloped countries with problems of economic growth is strongly reflected in the proceedings and discussions within the United Nations. It has led to the establishment under United Nations auspices of special study groups to examine the economic problems of regional groupings of countries such as the Economic Commission for Latin America, and the Economic Commission for Asia and the Far East. Most underdeveloped countries have in recent years prepared detailed plans to speed their economic growth and have established special government agencies to implement these plans. Some of these plans are soundly conceived, others are highly visionary. In many cases, however, their fulfillment is very uncertain because of financial limitations as well as the many other serious impediments to economic growth which were described elsewhere.

Economic backwardness is only one of a number of issues which the Communists seek to exploit in the underdeveloped areas. Other sources of discontent subject to Communist manipulation include peasant resentment against the wealthy estate owners, Soviet claims of Western racial intolerance, and the anti-imperialist theme. Thus while economic progress in underdeveloped countries is likely to reduce the danger of Communist penetration, it by no means eliminates the risk.

Lack of economic progress can be expected to increase discontent among the masses who though politically inarticulate expect better things. This discontent undoubtedly will be exploited by Communist agents and their supporters in an effort to undermine existing governments which are at least neutral in the East-West struggle if not allied with the democratic West. Many governments of underdeveloped countries have been greatly impressed by the rapid economic progress achieved in the U.S.S.R. and its satellites. If their present efforts to develop fail, they may be tempted to follow the Communist solution. "Under total dictatorship, the accumulation of capital is straightforward for, even if standards are low, saving can be enforced by starving the marginal people. Russian 'kulaks' yesterday, Chinese peasants today, have been taught to pay with their lives for the program of industrialization. . . . But modernization is achieved. The methods are there. This fact constitutes perhaps the chief attraction of Communism to backward peoples everywhere." [13] This is why the economic backwardness of the underdeveloped areas now presents such a grave challenge to the Free World. The threat of Communist penetration and even takeover is of course not equally great in all underdeveloped areas. Most vulnerable would appear to be the countries of Asia on the fringes of the Communist bloc. Though Communists are active in Africa and Latin America, their efforts in these regions pose less of a problem for the West. Nonetheless these regions do show considerable political and social instability in part at least because of unsatisfactory economic conditions. Communist-inspired or not, this growing unrest in the underdeveloped areas is a threat to the security of the Free World.

THE INTERESTS OF THE FREE WORLD IN THE UNDERDEVELOPED AREAS

Strategic. It is of great importance for the security and economic welfare of the Free World that the presently uncommitted underdeveloped areas do not fall into the Soviet camp. Many underdeveloped areas occupy highly strategic geographical positions across lines of communication important to the Free World both in peace and in war. The Suez Canal in the Middle East, which links the eastern Mediterranean and the Indian Ocean, is a case in point. Underdeveloped areas provide bases which are essential links in the West's air offensive and defensive systems. They are significant as assembly areas and supply bases for troops and materiel in time of war and as fueling stations for naval and cargo vessels. Control of these areas by unfriendly powers would greatly weaken the defensive and offensive military capabilities of the West.

The underdeveloped areas are a vast source of manpower which if effectively mobilized could greatly increase the military capabilities of the Communist bloc. Such areas now outside the Soviet orbit have a population of over one billion persons. Of this number over 700 million live on the periphery of the Communist sphere in the Middle East and in South and Southeast Asia. These are the regions now most vulnerable to Communist subversion. If they were to go Communist, the population of the Soviet bloc would be almost doubled, thus giving the bloc an overwhelming superiority over the West in manpower.

Sheer numbers alone obviously do not make for economic and military

[13] B. Ward, "One Answer to the Challenge of Africa," *New York Times Magazine*, October 31, 1944.

power. If they did, many underdeveloped countries would be first-rate powers. The quality and leadership of the population is more important than numbers. The populations of the underdeveloped areas are deficient in health, literacy, and in technical skills. They frequently lack strong and effective leadership. However, the recent experiences of the United Nations forces in Korea, and of the French in Indochina demonstrate that Communist leaders can mobilize these peoples into effective fighting forces within the brief period of a few years. Even in their present stage of economic development the underdeveloped countries, particularly in Asia, thus have major military potentialities.

Economic. The United States and the other industrialized countries of the Free World are heavily dependent on the underdeveloped areas for raw materials and this dependence is expected to increase rapidly. According to the President's Materials Policy Commission, the United States drew on foreign sources for 9 per cent of its raw material needs in 1950. The corresponding figure for other Free World industrialized countries is considerably higher. Most of these raw materials came from the underdeveloped areas. By 1975, the President's Commission estimates that imported raw materials will represent from 15 to 25 per cent of United States' requirements and a much higher proportion of Japan's and Western Europe's. Many of these raw material imports are items of considerable strategic importance. According to the International Development Advisory Board, "Of all of the imported items which are of sufficient military importance to be included in our stockpiles, 73 per cent are drawn from these areas [underdeveloped]." [14] The Board concluded that "The loss of any of these materials through aggression, subversion or social collapse, would be the equivalent of a grave military set-back." [15]

The underdeveloped areas are the major trading partners of the industrialized countries of the West. In the years 1948 to 1950, approximately half of the foreign trade of the United States was with the underdeveloped regions. For Western European countries, the percentage was almost 70 per cent in 1950.[16] This trade, by promoting international economic specialization and division of labor, has contributed materially to raising living standards in both the industrialized and the underdeveloped countries. It is essential for the economic viability of countries like Japan and the United Kingdom, which are particularly dependent on foreign trade.

The industrialized countries have other important economic interests

[14] *Partners in Progress*, a Report to the President by the International Development Advisory Board, March, 1951, p. 5.

[15] *Ibid.*, p. 46.

[16] *Ibid.*, pp. 6-7.

in the underdeveloped countries. Among these are very substantial investments. The return on these investments finances a large proportion of the traditional import deficits of countries like the United Kingdom or the Netherlands. The underdeveloped areas are an important source of earnings for services like shipping, insurance, and banking. They earn scarce dollars for European affiliates and provide many commodities which otherwise would have to be purchased for dollars. They provide all sorts of special and valuable economic advantages to individual Western countries such as tariff preferences and monopoly rights to exploit mineral resources.

Communist expansion in underdeveloped countries typically has resulted in a progressive decline in the penetrated area's economic relations with the West. Foreign investments are expropriated without compensation to the rightful owners. Thus the Chinese Communists took over an estimated billion dollars in properties belonging to United Kingdom nationals. Trade with the Free World contracts sharply.[17] In 1951, the volume of Western Europe's trade with the European satellites, including East Germany, was only about 20 per cent of prewar. Trade between Red China and the Free World also has declined very significantly since the Communist takeover. Trade of the satellites with each other and with the Soviet Union, on the other hand, has shown a more than corresponding increase. Before World War II trade between the U.S.S.R. and the eastern European countries and China was almost nonexistent, and between the satellites themselves was of very limited significance. By 1951, however, it is estimated that intra-bloc trade accounted for 80 per cent of total-bloc trade.[18] This represents a tenfold increase in the volume of intra-bloc trade.

Part of the decline in trade between the West and the Communist bloc, and in particular with Communist China, has resulted from the application of Western security controls. In large measure, however, it is the result of deliberate Soviet policy. Soviet foreign trade policy is governed more by security than by economic considerations. The Russians seek to maximize intra-bloc trade and to reduce dependence on outside supplies to a minimum. This policy of economic autarchy is designed to limit the vulnerability of the Soviet bloc to the cutting off of foreign sources of supply in the event of war.

Practical considerations necessarily have limited and will probably con-

[17] *Economic Bulletin for Europe,* Economic Commission for Europe, Second Quarter, 1952.

[18] *Ibid.*

tinue to limit the extent and speed with which satellite economies are integrated into the Soviet bloc. One very important consideration is the fact that many underdeveloped areas have supplies available for export substantially in excess of the bloc's immediate requirements. For example, the bloc could not use all of Iran's oil in the foreseeable future and the same would be true for Malayan rubber. At the same time, the bloc's capabilities for supplying the machinery and equipment required to promote the economic development of the backward areas is limited. Under these circumstances, continued trade with the West would still be advantageous.

Such Communist-controlled supplies, however, would be highly unreliable. They could be cut off at any time for political or other reasons or might be used as a lever to force political concessions. They might be supplied at relatively unfavorable terms to Western buyers. Soviet trade is conducted through state trading corporations and their bargaining power is generally much stronger than that of private individual traders in the West.

So far the over-all adverse economic effects on the West of Communist expansion in the underdeveloped areas has been fairly moderate. Certain countries have been harder hit than others. Japan is an example of a country whose trading position has been most seriously affected by Communist expansion. Before the war more than 30 per cent of Japan's trade was with the Chinese mainland and North Korea. By 1954 this was reduced to a trickle. Loss of China both as a source of raw materials and as a market for exports is an important obstacle, though by no means the only one, to Japan's becoming self-supporting. Moreover, the Japanese economy is particularly vulnerable to any further Communist expansion in the Far East. At the present time roughly 35 per cent of Japan's foreign trade is with South and Southeast Asia as against 20 per cent prewar. If this region fell into the Communist bloc, Japan would find it almost impossible to achieve economic self-support except by coming to terms with the Communists.

The Soviet economy probably has gained more than the West has lost as a result of the expansion of the Communist orbit. There is considerable evidence to indicate Russian exploitation of the satellites. Moreover, if the satellite economies are able to maintain anything like the high rates of growth they claim to have achieved under the Communists, the result would be a considerable over-all strengthening of the bloc economy relative to the West. According to official Communist statistics, rates of economic growth in the eastern European satellites have averaged 10 to 20 per cent a year during the 1950's.[19] This compares with quite low rates of growth in many underdeveloped regions outside of Latin America. Official Chinese figures claim that 15 per cent of the gross national product was budgeted for investment in 1954. If true, this would give China a level of investment almost twice that of neighboring South and Southeast Asia which has roughly the same total population. In the absence of a rapid speeding up of economic growth in South and Southeast Asia, China could in the foreseeable future become the dominant economic power in the Far East.[20]

Regardless of the outcome of political trends in the underdeveloped regions, their efforts to develop more rapidly are creating and will continue to create major problems of economic adjustment for the industrialized countries. These problems largely derive from the determination of the underdeveloped areas to diversify their economies and to reduce their dependence on exports of a few primary products. This distrust of relying on production of primary products stems in part from the drastic deflation of raw material prices during the 1930's and also the tendency of the underdeveloped countries to associate raw-materials production with colonialism and foreign domination. As a first step in this process of diversification, almost all underdeveloped countries are attempting to meet at least some part of their requirements for the simpler types of manufactures such as textiles, shoes, soap, matches, and other consumer goods. This has cut sharply into the markets of the large traditional exporters of consumer goods like the United Kingdom and Japan. It has necessitated significant and costly shifts in the structure of their export industries to accommodate the reduced relative importance of consumer-goods exports. In some instances, notably India, underdeveloped countries since the war have become major competitors of industrialized countries for export markets. In 1950 India, with exports of 118 thousand tons of cotton cloth, was the world's largest exporter, exceeding Japan and the United Kingdom by a considerable margin. The rise of India as an important and efficient textile producer partly explains why Japan's exports of cotton goods are only 40 per cent of prewar. Today we find Lancashire, which rose to eminence as the world's leading textile center largely on the basis of its markets in the underdeveloped areas, asking the British Government for tariff protection against Indian textiles.

The measures taken by the underdeveloped countries to industrialize and diversify their economies are partly responsible for the fact that the

[19] United Nations, *Economic Survey of Europe in 1953* (Geneva, 1954).
[20] See Chapter 15, pp. 509-518.

industrialized countries are unable to import food and raw materials on as favorable terms as before the war. A number of countries deliberately have pursued economic policies designed to encourage the expansion of industry at the expense of primary production. Often the favored industries are impractical and are able to withstand foreign competition only under an umbrella of high protective tariffs. Argentina is one of the most notable examples of a country which pursued this type of policy after World War II. The result was a sharp decline in export availabilities and higher prices for foodstuffs to Argentina's traditional market, the United Kingdom. Subsequently Argentina reversed its shortsighted policy of neglecting agriculture when the decline in its export earnings threatened to jeopardize its entire development program. Although such extreme policies favoring industrialization have been abandoned by most underdeveloped areas, the distrust of primary production persists.

Even where the advantages of promoting primary production are recognized, many obstacles are placed in the way of expanding output by the underdeveloped countries. These include various prohibitions and limitations imposed on foreign investors, such as restrictions on the convertibility of capital and earnings or the requirement of majority local participation in the ownership and management. Then there is the frequent threat of nationalization or expropriation without adequate compensation. Many underdeveloped countries are unwilling to allow foreign capital to participate in the exploitation of their natural resources even though they lack the capital and technical know-how to do it themselves. Where foreign capital is welcomed, the underdeveloped areas are insisting on a larger share of the profits and are demanding more adequate compensation for local labor. All of these factors, combined with the fact that the best and most accessible resources are being consumed, suggest that primary products will be available from the underdeveloped areas on progressively less favorable terms.

ECONOMIC AID IN THE STRUGGLE FOR THE UNDERDEVELOPED AREAS

Since World War II the industrialized countries of the West and in particular the United States have shown a growing concern about the economic problems of the underdeveloped areas. In part this interest is based on humanitarian considerations and in part on a recognition that the material well-being of the advanced countries is heavily dependent on the economic health of the underdeveloped countries. More importantly, however, it reflects concern about the security of the Free World. Poverty and lack of economic progress are recognized as important causes of the growing political instability and social unrest in the underdeveloped areas making them fertile breeding places for Communist subversion.

This view of the relationship between economic development and subversion has found widespread expression in official and semi-official documents dealing with United States foreign economic policy. Thus the International Development Board in its report to the President states: [21] "To achieve lasting peace, security, and well-being in the world we must join forces in an economic offensive to root out hunger, poverty, illiteracy and disease. The issue really is one of economic development versus economic subversion. Soviet imperialism is seeking to chop off country after country, to leave us in isolation."

One of the principal weapons employed by the West to counter the danger of political instability and Communist subversion in the underdeveloped areas has been economic and military aid. Here because of its much greater industrial capabilities the West enjoys a strong advantage over the U.S.S.R. Most of the aid extended by the West has been provided by the United States. The economies of the other major industrial powers have been too weak since the war to support contributions on anything like the U.S. scale. Nonetheless aid from other countries has not been inconsequential. Under its Colonial Development and Welfare Act, the United Kingdom provided 140 million pounds sterling from 1945 to 1954 to assist in colonial development. An additional 80 million pounds is to be provided for the next 5 years. In addition, the European metropoles, particularly the United Kingdom, France, and Belgium, have been making sizable investments in their colonies to promote economic growth. To an important extent these investments were made possible by direct U.S. aid to Europe.

During the period July 1, 1945 to June 30, 1954, direct U.S. economic aid to the underdeveloped areas in the form of grants and credits exceeded $5 billion (see Table 19-3). With the recovery of Western Europe, economic aid to the underdeveloped areas has represented an increasing share of total aid. In 1953 U.S. economic aid to the underdeveloped areas of roughly $1.2 billion represented almost half of all U.S. economic aid. In 1955 to 1956 it is estimated the proportion will be more than two-thirds.

The U.S.S.R. by contrast appears to have extended relatively limited

[21] *Partners in Progress* (Washington, D. C., March, 1951).

assistance to the underdeveloped countries, except to China, and its European satellites and much of this has been military aid. It was not until 1953 that the U.S.S.R. made a contribution of $1 million to the United Nations technical assistance program. More recently, however, there have been signs that the U.S.S.R. may step-up its economic offensive. The most notable example in this campaign to date has been Soviet penetration of Afghanistan. A reported 500 Russian technicians were in Afghanistan in 1955 helping in the country's economic development.[22] When Pakistan closed its Afghan border and imposed an economic blockade against Afghanistan as a result of an incident in March 1955 arising out of the Pushtunistan dispute, the Russians were quick to capitalize on the situation. They offered the Afghans an alternate transit route to the Pakistan Port of Karachi through Soviet territory. An agreement was signed authorizing the landing of Afghan imports at Black Sea ports and their carriage by rail at subsidized rates to the Soviet-Afghan border. Early in 1955 the Soviet Union signed an agreement to build a million-ton steel plant for India on very favorable terms. In addition to supplying arms to Egypt in 1955 the Russians also said they were willing to help finance the High dam on the Aswam, a 10 year $1,300 million project. It also is increasing its efforts to arrange bilateral trade agreements with the underdeveloped areas purchasing products like Egyptian cotton or Burmese rice which in 1955 were in serious oversupply. In some instances it has offered to extend long-term credits. With its growing industrial strength the U.S.S.R. could become a formidable competitor against the West in an economic offensive to gain political capital among the underdeveloped regions.

TABLE 19-3

U. S. Non-Military Grants and Credits to Underdeveloped Areas July 1, 1945 Through June 30, 1954 * a

AREA	TOTAL	NET GRANTS	NET CREDITS
Near East and Africa	$ 860	$ 598	$ 262
South Asia	389	123	266
Southeast Asia	1,173	962	211
Korea and Nationalist China	2,035	1,907	128
Latin America	906	207	699
Total	$5,363	$3,797	$1,566

[a] In millions.

* Excludes aid given dependent areas through United States grants or loans to the mother countries. Also excludes aid by the United States through international organizations. United States Department of Commerce, *Foreign Grants and Credit by the United States Government,* June, 1954.

[22] *New York Times,* November 15, 1955.

Point Four. Assisting the economic development of the underdeveloped areas can be said to have become a definite part of United States foreign economic policy with the adoption of the so-called Point IV program in 1950. The name Point IV derives from the famous fourth point of President Truman's inaugural address of January 20, 1949, in which he called for "a bold new program for making the benefits of our scientific advances and industrial progress available for the improvement and growth of underdeveloped areas."

This proposal resulted in the Act for International Development which authorized technical assistance programs to the underdeveloped areas under both bilateral and United Nations multilateral arrangements.

Point IV is essentially a long-range program intended to lay the basis for gradual economic and social progress in the underdeveloped areas. Its main emphasis is on the supplying of basic technological and scientific services and the training of foreign nationals rather than on the provision of capital. Capital goods are a small fraction of the technical services component. The expectation is to gradually create a favorable atmosphere for private investment.

The United States bilateral technical assistance program is considerably larger than the United Nations multilateral program. United States appropriations for technical assistance in the fiscal year 1954 amounted to $118 million. This compares with $40 to 50 million at the disposal of the United Nations and its specialized agencies. In August, 1953, over 1,500 permanent American technicians and several hundred local-contract and temporary technicians were serving abroad under United States bilateral programs. In addition, almost 1,500 awards had been made to foreign trainees. This compares with approximately 1000 experts and 1375 trainee awards under the United Nations program.[23]

Efforts in the field of technical assistance have concentrated on agriculture, health, education, public administration, and resource development. Remarkable results have been achieved in many of these vital areas. In some countries, malaria has been eliminated and infant mortality sharply reduced. In others, improved agricultural methods have brought significant increases in yields. At the same time, however, the gains from technical assistance have given rise to some serious new problems. Improved farming methods have released agricultural workers for industrial employment where opportunities in industry are still lacking. Or again, reduced death rates have aggravated the problem of population pressure.

[23] Commission on Foreign Economic Policy, *Staff Paper* (Washington, D. C., February, 1954), p. 74

Probably the chief criticism levelled at the program is that it can be expected to achieve results only very slowly; too slowly perhaps in the critical areas most vulnerable to Soviet expansion. Economic development requires capital as well as technical know-how if advantage is to be taken of the new knowledge. This capital has not yet been forthcoming in adequate amounts from private sources. The problem has been met to a limited extent in the United States by special assistance programs which depart from the philosophy of Point IV. The International Bank for Reconstruction and Development as described below also has made a contribution to the capital needs of the underdeveloped areas. Although the technical assistance programs have won many friends for the West, they generally have not lived up to the expectations of the underdeveloped areas for outside aid.

The International Bank for Reconstruction and Development. The International Bank was established primarily for the purpose of assisting "its member countries to raise production levels and living standards by helping to finance long-term productive projects, by providing technical advice and by stimulating international investment from other sources." [24] Of its 57 members, 39 are in the underdeveloped category. Although membership is open to all countries no Soviet-bloc country now belongs and no loans have been extended outside the Free World.

Since the start of its operations in 1946 until July, 1954, the Bank has loaned almost $1 billion to the underdeveloped countries. Roughly half went to Latin America, one-quarter to South and Southeast Asia, and the remainder to Africa and the Middle East. Most of the loans went to finance vital services, such as transportation, electric power, telecommunications, and irrigation, which have not attracted adequate private capital. In addition, Bank technicians have furnished a number of underdeveloped countries with valuable assistance in preparing development projects and programs. Although the contribution of the International Bank to the underdeveloped areas has been considerably more significant than the total amount of loans extended suggests, it has not satisfied their desire for external loans. In general the underdeveloped areas feel that the loan requirements of the Bank are too rigid. They have campaigned for the creation of subsidiary international loan agencies with lower standards.

Atoms-for-Peace. Few proposals in recent years have done more to fire the hopes of the underdeveloped areas for accelerated economic growth

[24] *International Bank For Reconstruction and Development*, 1946-53 (Baltimore, 1954).

than President Eisenhower's dramatic atoms-for-peace plan laid before the United Nations on December 8, 1953. As an outgrowth of this proposal, steps are being taken to establish an International Atomic Energy Agency, and the United Nations in the meantime invited 84 nations to participate in an international conference on the peaceful uses of atomic energy at Geneva in August, 1955. Atoms-for-peace has been widely interpreted as a simple prescription for the economic difficulties of the underdeveloped areas. Visions have been conjured up of a vast source of cheap electric power which will usher in a new era of economic growth in the underdeveloped areas.

Such extravagant expectations are hardly warranted for the foreseeable future. In the first place the President's proposal is necessarily limited in its scope. It does not provide for large atomic power plants. The 120 kilograms of fissionable material which is being contributed to the program by the United States and the United Kingdom would not fuel one large power plant. The plan by and large calls for an exchange of training facilities and information and the use of radioactive by-products of atomic fission in agriculture, industry, and medicine. The fissionable materials contributed by the participating countries will be used to fuel small research reactors. Thus the program is intended primarily to train personnel and promote applied research in the peaceful uses of atomic energy. This is certainly a requisite first step for virtually all underdeveloped countries which have few or no qualified personnel and no technical facilities for handling fissionable materials.

In the second place, and more important for the underdeveloped areas, are the limitations which economic considerations are likely to impose on the peaceful applications of atomic energy. It is now technically feasible to construct electric power plants fueled with fissionable materials. However, such power is high cost and appears likely to remain so over the next decade or so. Any cost advantage which nuclear power is to enjoy over conventional power must derive from savings in fuel costs. Fixed costs of plant and equipment for nuclear power plants are expected to run 50 per cent higher than for conventional plants, and operating and maintenance costs may be twice as high. Lower fuel costs alone cannot result in drastic reductions in electricity costs. Fuel costs in modern thermal plants in the United States, for example, account for at most one-half of electric power generating costs and only about one-fifth of the average price paid by consumers.

The outlook for the next decade or two, therefore, is that nuclear power plants will be competitive only with conventional thermal plants burning relatively high-cost coal or petroleum. They will not be competitive with most hydro-electric plants now in existence or with plants which can be built on fairly favorable sites. The latter fact will limit the economic use of nuclear power plants in underdeveloped areas for some time to come. Most underdeveloped countries with growing power requirements still possess substantial unexploited hydraulic resources capable of producing very low cost power. A major reason for the failure of power supply to keep pace with requirements in a number of underdeveloped countries is the shortage of capital. The much higher capital costs of nuclear power plants would therefore be a deterrent to the introduction of nuclear power even in areas handicapped by high fuel costs. The problem of size is also relevant. The demand for power in underdeveloped regions frequently does not warrant the construction of large power stations. While atomic power plants are flexible as regards size, the smaller they are the less economical they become.

The above considerations are expected to limit the use of atomic power plants in backward areas to regions which lack cheap local fuel and are remote from good hydro-electric sites. However, even if technological progress permits the construction of nuclear power reactors at substantially lower costs than now anticipated, the resultant power savings will not be a major stimulus to economic growth. The reason for this is simply that power represents a relatively small share of the total cost of most industries. In the United States the cost of electricity represented only 1.7 per cent of the value added by manufactures for all industry in 1947. For a number of industry groups the ratio was between 2 and 4 per cent. Electric power is an important cost factor primarily in such industries as aluminum, ferro-alloys, and chemicals.

This is not to minimize the significance of atomic power for the underdeveloped areas. World energy consumption is making rapid inroads into the world's reserves of coal, petroleum, and natural gas. As lower cost reserves are exhausted, fuel costs can be expected to gradually rise. Consequently, fissionable materials are likely to become of increasing importance over the long run as a source of energy. Over the short run, the greatest benefits to be derived by the underdeveloped areas from atoms-for-peace may well result from developments in the use of radio-active isotopes in industry, medicine, and agriculture.

CHAPTER

20

Southwest Asia

Southwest Asia (also called the Middle or Near East) is an area of very limited over-all economic capabilities. It is nonetheless a region of great economic and strategic importance to the Free World by virtue of its vast low-cost oil reserves and its geographic location. Linking three continents, Southwest Asia stands astride vital air and water routes connecting Europe, Asia, and Africa. It controls two of the most vital water links in the world: the Straits connecting the landlocked Black Sea and the Mediterranean, and the Suez Canal joining the Mediterranean and the Indian Ocean. All through history this crossroads of the world has been a key factor in the strategic calculations of the major powers. It was a pivotal area in the defense of India and Africa in World War II. As a critical buffer zone between Europe and Africa on the one hand and the U.S.S.R. on the other, Southwest Asia is now of major strategic importance to the defensive system of the West. At the same time, much of the area is subject to serious social, political, and economic unrest. There are few stable governments in Southwest Asia capable of controlling the rising tide of nationalism and revolt against economic oppression. Arab-Israeli relations and inter-Arab feuds are a constant threat to the stability of the area. The Israel-Arab conflict has created a critical refugee problem. The recent Soviet sale of arms to Egypt has created a new challenge. All of these developments taken together constitute a serious danger to the position of the Free World in this area.

AREA AND POPULATION

As defined here, Southwest Asia comprises ten independent states and a number of small sheikhdoms and protectorates. With an area of 2.1 million square miles it is greater in size than Europe, excluding the U.S.S.R., and approximately two-thirds the size of the United States. The total population, however, is less than 70 million and average population density is only 32 persons per square mile. The latter figure is not very meaningful, however, since much of the region is unfit for human habitation or is unpeopled except for nomads. A few countries like Israel and Lebanon are fairly densely populated (see Table 20-1).

Southwest Asia is an area of high birth rates and declining though still high death rates. During the period of 1940 to 1950 average population growth in Southwest Asia was 1.35 per cent per year. Population growth rates are accelerating and according to United Nations' estimates may reach 1.83 to 2.32 per cent per year by 1980. This would give Southwest Asia a population of 99 to 106 million by that time.

TABLE 20-1

Southwest Asia: Area, Population, and Population Density, 1953

COUNTRY	AREA [a] (SQUARE MILES)	POPULATION [b] (THOUSANDS)	POPULATION DENSITY (PER SQUARE MILE)
Aden Colony	80	150	1,875
Aden Protectorate	122,000	650	5.3
Bahrein	231	112	484
Iran	629,344	20,253	32
Iraq	168,114	4,882 (1952)	29
Israel	8,108	1,650	198
Jordan	37,264	1,360	36
Kuwait	8,000	150	19
Lebanon	4,016	1,353	337
Muscat and Oman	82,007	550	6.7
Qatar	8,500	20	2.3
Saudi Arabia	617,700	7,000 (1952)	11.3
Syria	70,014	3,535	50.4
Trucial Oman	5,792	80	13.8
Turkey	296,185	22,461	75.8
Yemen	75,290	4,500 (1952)	59.8
Total	2,132,645	68,706	32.2

[a] United Nations, *Statistical Yearbook*, 1953.
[b] United Nations, *Population and Vital Statistics Reports*, Series A, Vol. 7, No. 1 (New York, January, 1955).

GEOGRAPHY AND CLIMATE

Southwest Asia divides into two fairly distinct physical areas. In the north and northeast are the high plateaus of Anatolia and Iran, enclosed by rugged mountain ranges, and having average elevations of 4,000 feet. Narrow coastal belts fringe these plateaus along the Caspian and Black Seas in the north and along the Aegean and Mediterranean Seas in the west and southwest. The remainder and largest part of Southwest Asia (approximately two-thirds) forms a vast level plain which gradually slopes upward to form the highlands of Saudi Arabia overlooking the Red Sea and the Gulf of Aden.

Although Southwest Asia is located largely in tropical latitudes, it shows wide variations in climate. The coastal regions of the Mediterranean are hot in summer and wet and cool in the winter. The Anatolian and Iranian plateaus are generally characterized by cold winters and hot dry summers. Their fringing littoral regions are wet and warm. Arabia, except for the southwest which has a monsoon climate, has cold winters and little or no rainfall.

The one outstanding climatic characteristic of Southwest Asia is its aridity. Almost all of Arabia, much of Iraq, and most of eastern and central Iran are desert. Rains exceeding 24 inches annually are largely confined to the areas bordering the Black and Caspian Seas in the north and the Aegean and Mediterranean Seas in the west and southwest. Most of the region has less than 8 inches of rain and over half has less than 4 inches. The significance of this lack of moisture for raising food, which is the principal economic activity of the region, is apparent in view of the fact that wheat will not grow without irrigation where rainfall is less than 8 inches.

The aridity of Southwest Asia has had a major influence on economic activity in the area and on the distribution of population. Population density is closely correlated with rainfall. As a result, the region is characterized by numerous, relatively small, cultivated pockets separated by extensive desert area. Although large areas of Southwest Asia lack sufficient moisture for growing crops, they do support vegetation for pasturage. Thus a considerable portion of the total population, possibly one-seventh, is nomadic and is engaged in the raising of livestock.

RESOURCES

In terms of its area, Southwest Asia is relatively poor both in good agricultural land and in mineral resources with the notable exception of oil (Fig. 20-1). Most of the region is mountain, desert, or swamp. The Food and Agricultural Organization of the United Nations classified roughly 8 per cent of the land area as arable as compared with more than 23 per cent in the United States. This is not to say that the area lacks potentialities for further economic development. Despite a somewhat limited resource base, much of Southwest Asia is underpopulated and can support a considerably larger number of people at higher levels of living, provided these resources are more effectively exploited. Best situated resource-wise are Syria, Iran, Iraq, and Turkey. Some countries, like Israel, Lebanon, and Jordan, have serious population problems. Large oil reserves offer "at least six countries the first chance for centuries to break out of the rut of poverty, and to organize a rise in standards of living and education that will be sudden and decisive enough to outstrip the lusty local tendency to a high birth rate." [1] Nonetheless even in the most promising areas economic growth in Southwest Asia may continue to be slow. Technical skills will have to be acquired. The proportion of total production devoted to investment will have to be greatly increased. And most important in a number of countries major institutional and social changes will have to come about to establish the necessary preconditions for sustained economic growth.

Agricultural Land. Compared with the rest of the continent, Southwest Asia's resources of arable and potentially productive land area in relation to the population are relatively favorable. As shown in Table 20-2, arable land amounts to roughly 1.7 acres *per capita* and ranges from less than half an acre in Lebanon to approximately 2 acres in Syria, Iran, and Turkey. By comparison, cultivated land in industrial United States is more than 2.5 acres per person, whereas in primarily agricultural economies like Australia, New Zealand, or Uruguay and Chile it is more than 4 acres *per capita*. Because of poor methods of cultivation, a sizable portion of the arable land lies fallow every year to restore its fertility. In Iraq, large tracts of arable land have become saline because of poor drainage, resulting in a serious drop in yields.

Estimates of potentially productive land suggest that the area under cultivation can be more than doubled or that Southwest Asia could grow enough foodstuffs to feed twice its present population at existing diet levels, assuming no changes in farm methods. However, the estimate of potentially productive land must be considered more as a theoretical maximum rather than as a figure likely soon to be achieved. Only a few countries—Syria, Iraq, and Turkey—offer some possibilities for increased

[1] *The Economist,* July 2, 1955, p. 16.

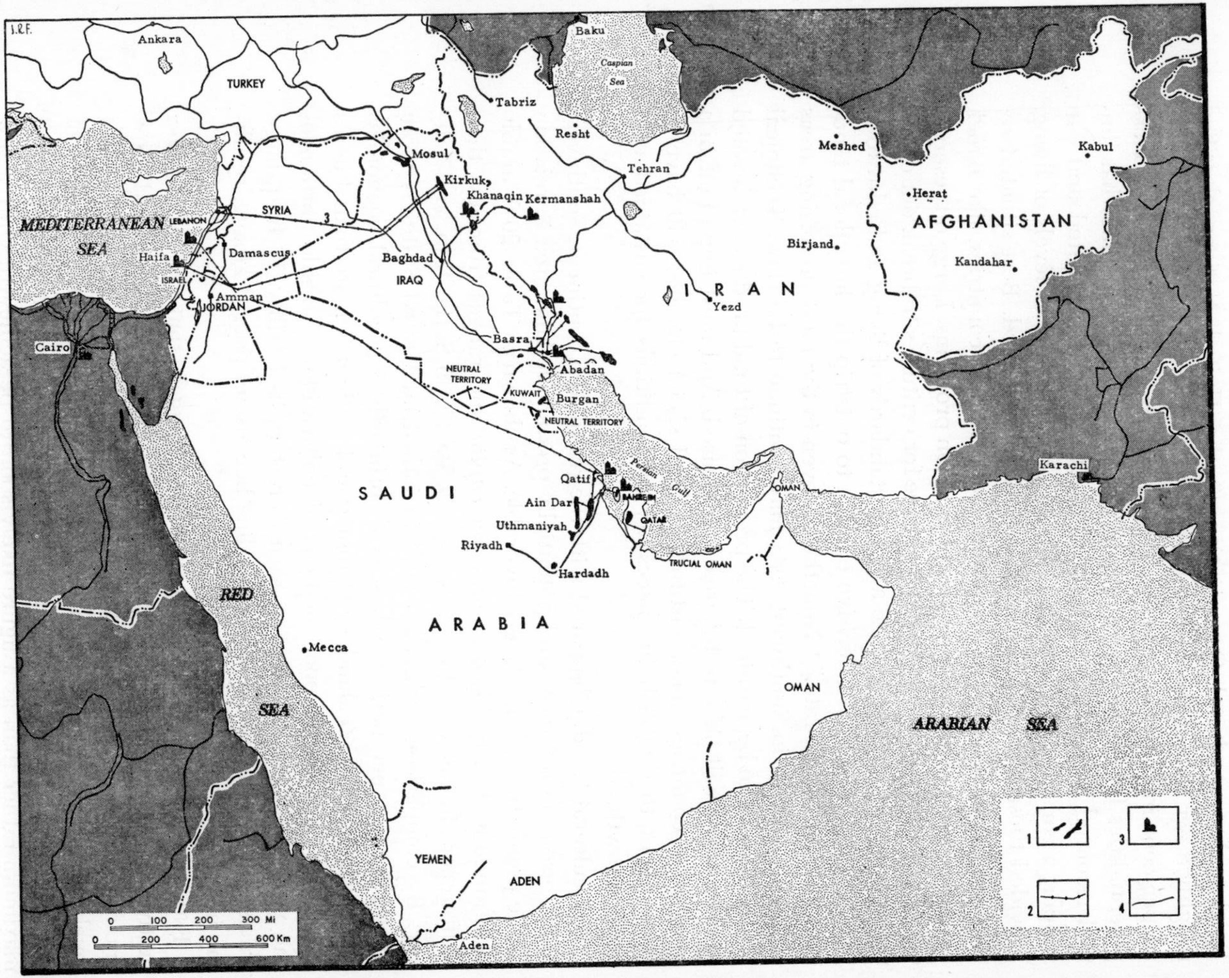

Fig. [illegible] Middle East Oil Fields and Pipelines: (1) oil; (2) pipelines; (3) refineries; (4) railroads.

dry farming. Most of the potentially productive land, although inherently fertile, would require expensive irrigation and drainage projects and extensive transportation development. Iran, Iraq, and Syria are fortunate in having large rivers which can be harnessed to supply water. Thus the International Bank for Reconstruction and Development in its economic survey of Iraq concluded that much of the soil is inherently fertile and "with ample water, manpower, and implements, the area under cultivation might be almost tripled." [2] Again, the Joint United States-Syria Agricultural Mission in its 1946 survey concluded that a series of irrigation projects drawing on the Euphrates and its tributaries might permit an additional 2 million acres to be put under intensive cultivation. If this were done these areas could not only feed their growing populations but also produce considerable food for export. One of the main problems is to mobilize the required capital. An additional difficulty is that some water-development schemes, such as the proposed Jordan Valley project, cut across national boundaries and require the co-operation of nations highly distrustful of each others' intentions—in this case, the Arab states on one hand and Israel on the other.

TABLE 20-2

Arable and Potentially Productive Land *

COUNTRY	PERIOD	ARABLE LAND (THOUSANDS OF ACRES)	ARABLE LAND PER CAPITA (IN ACRES)	POTENTIALLY PRODUCTIVE (THOUSANDS OF ACRES)
Aden Protectorate	1947	272	0.4	. . .
Iran	1950	41,414	2.0	81,543
Iraq	1951	5,777	1.2	29,900
Jordan	1947	1,186	0.9	. . .
Lebanon	1950	692	0.5	. . .
Israel	1951	981 [a]	0.6	. . .
Syria	1950	8,737	2.5	9,578
Turkey	1949	37,707	1.7	. . .
Total		96,766	1.7	121,021

[a] Total agricultural area including permanent meadows and pastures.
* United Nations, Food and Agriculture Organization, *Yearbook of Food and Agricultural Statistics*, 1952, Vol. 6, Part 1.

Oil. Oil is one resource Southwest Asia possesses in great abundance (*cf.* Fig. 20-1, p. 628). Indeed the location of the world's richest oil reserves in Southwest Asia accounts in large part for the great interest of the major world powers in this region. In 1953 Southwest Asia's proven re-

[2] *The Economic Development of Iraq* (Baltimore, 1952), p. 1.

serves of crude petroleum of 8.3 billion metric tons amounted to roughly 53 per cent of the world total, or 63 per cent if the Soviet bloc is excluded. These reserves were two and a quarter times larger than those of the United States. Moreover, these reserves yield very low-cost oil. It costs the Anglo-Iranian Oil Company less than 15 cents to produce a barrel of crude oil as compared with 70 cents in Venezuela and $1.70 in the United States.[3] As shown in Table 20-3 a few countries, principally Iran, Iraq, Kuwait, and Saudi Arabia, account for the bulk of these reserves.

TABLE 20-3

Southwest Asia: Estimated Proven Reserves of Crude Petroleum by Country in 1953 *
(in millions of metric tons)

COUNTRY	QUANTITY	PER CENT OF WORLD TOTAL
Bahrein	40.9	neg.
Iran	1,722.3	11.05
Iraq	1,470.6	9.44
Kuwait	2,444.3	15.69
Qatar	163.2	1.05
Saudi Arabia	2,426.51	15.57
Turkey	11.1	neg.
Total Southwest Asia	8,278.9	52.80
United States	3,809.6	24.45
Venezuela	1,380.5	8.86
World Total	15,580.4	100.0

* *World Oil*, August 15, 1954.

The magnitude of these reserves is suggested by the fact that they would meet total United States' requirements at present rates of consumption for a period of more than thirty years. Moreover, these proven reserves by no means represent the total oil resources of the region. While these reserves have been expanding rapidly as a result of continued exploitation and drilling activities, much of the potential oil-bearing land of the region is still untapped. Thus estimated petroleum reserves increased by more than 25 per cent between 1951 and 1953. A more recent estimate made for the U.S. Joint Congressional Committee on Atomic Energy placed Southwest Asia's crude oil reserves in 1956 at 230 billion barrels or more than double the previous accepted estimate.[3a] It is ex-

[3] *The Annals*, Vol. 294 (July, 1954), p. 152.

[3a] *Background Material for the Report of the Panel on the Impact of the Peaceful Uses of Atomic Energy* (Washington, D. C., 1956), p. 92.

pected that Southwest Asia's reserves will continue to increase in absolute terms and will become relatively more important as reserves in other areas, particularly the United States, are used up. By 1956, Southwest Asia's share of the Free World's oil reserves had increased to 75 per cent.

Other Mineral Resources. Our knowledge of Southwest Asia's other mineral resources suffers from the fact that much of the region has never been adequately surveyed. Except for petroleum, however, the area appears to be poor in mineral resources. Turkey, the only country in the region with the coal and iron ore required to support heavy industry, is the one exception. The region's deficiency in minerals is suggested by the low output figures given in Table 20-4.

TABLE 20-4

Output of Minerals, 1939, 1943, 1945, 1948 to 1952 *
(thousands of metric tons)

COUNTRY AND MINERAL	1939	1943	1945	1948	1949	1950	1951	1952
Iran:								
Iron oxide	10		0.2	5	11	7		
Iraq:								
Salt	11	23	15	14				
Israel/Palestine:								
Potash (K_2O content)	32	47	45	50				
Salt	9	18	20	5	9	7	2	
Lebanon:								
Salt		7	7	8	9			
Saudi Arabia:								
Gold (kilograms)	4.97	1326	1181	2300	2079	2059		
Syria:								
Salt	14	12	15	8	21	22		
Turkey:								
Antimony (content)	0.7	—	—	0.5	0.5	1.3	2.2	
Boracite	15.2	—	5.0	5.3	7.1	9.8		
Copper (smelter production	6.7	9.7	9.9	11.0	11.3	11.7	17.5	19.1
Chrome ore (Cr_2O_3 content	92	76	72	140	217	202	287	
Emery	10	7.8	2.2	7.9	8.9	1.2		
Iron ore (Fa content)	155	59	82	121	136	143	143	195
Manganese ore (Mn content)	0.9	1.1	2.0	3.3	11.1	15.8	24.7	
Coal	2696	3166	3720	4023	4183	4360	4730	4863
Lignite	185	625	725	1010	1272	1203	1255	1374
Quicksilver	13.6	6.4	5.4	0.9	—	—		
Salt	240	266	254	266	318	310	273	
Sulphur	2.6	3.4	4.6	2.6	3.1	6.0	7.4	

* United Nations, Department of Economic Affairs, *Review of Economic Conditions in the Middle East 1951-1952* (March, 1953), p. 122.

Turkish reserves of 500 million metric tons of bituminous coal and over 125 million tons of sub-bituminous coal are ample to cover the country's foreseeable needs. Most of these reserves are of coking quality as required for steel-making. Iron ore reserves, however, are relatively small, amounting to 15 to 35 million metric tons with an iron content of 65 per cent. Lower-grade ore also has been found. Turkey has large reserves of high-grade chromium and is now a major world supplier. Turkey's copper reserves are estimated at from 4 to 8 million tons. A large number of small manganese deposits are also found in Turkey.

Although a variety of minerals have been found in other parts of Southwest Asia besides Turkey, they generally have been low in quality and limited in amount or located in inaccessible areas. In many instances not enough information is available about these deposits to tell whether they will warrant commercial exploitation.

EXTENT AND CHARACTER OF ECONOMIC DEVELOPMENT

Southwest Asia is in no sense an economic unity. Quite the contrary. Economic ties between the countries of Southwest Asia are minor. The chief reason for this is that their economies are essentially competing rather than complementary. The limited economic relationships between the countries of Southwest Asia is indicated by the fact that intra-regional trade is only about 5 per cent of total trade. This compares with 30 per cent for the rest of Asia and more than 50 per cent for Western Europe.

All of the countries of Southwest Asia except possibly Israel are underdeveloped. Average annual *per capita* income of the region in 1949 was only about $125. Only a few countries, notably Turkey, Lebanon, and Israel, have *per capita* incomes appreciably higher than the average. Low incomes are reflected in diets for most of the area, which are inadequate from a nutritional point of view and malnutrition is quite widespread. During the period 1946 to 1949 the calorie content of food supplies available for human consumption in Iran and Iraq was less than 2000 per person per day.[4]

Agriculture is the principal economic activity and supports the bulk of the population. For most countries 75 per cent or more of the employed population works in agriculture and animal husbandry. Except for Turkey the area has no heavy industry. Manufactures are confined largely to the production of consumer goods and the processing of foodstuffs.

[4] United Nations, Food and Agriculture Organization, *Current Developments of and Prospects for Agriculture in the Near East, 1951.*

Production per worker in agriculture and in industry by Western standards is low. During the five-year period 1947 to 1951 productivity in agriculture was only 62 per cent of the world average and roughly 20 per cent of that of North America. Productivity in industry as compared with developed countries is even less favorable than in agriculture.

Fuel and power consumption, which is one of the best measures of economic development, was less than 0.50 metric tons (coal equivalent) per person in 1949. This compares with 7.32 metric tons for the United States and more than two and a half metric tons for most Western European countries.

Literacy levels with few exceptions are very low. In most countries less than 10 per cent of the population over ten years of age can read.

Southwest Asia's exports consist largely of food and raw materials and its imports of manufactures. For most countries two or three commodities frequently account for a high percentage of the value of all merchandise exports. As a result their economies are highly vulnerable to foreign market forces over which they have little or no control. Merchandise imports are greatly in excess of exports. The deficit is financed largely from earnings on oil sales, foreign grants and loans, and donations and remittances.

While a few countries like Turkey and Israel have enjoyed moderate economic progress in recent years, the area by and large suffers from economic stagnation. Savings and investment are low and are just about adequate to meet the needs of the rising population. Much of the income of wealthy potential savers goes into luxurious living. As a result living standards have shown little or no improvement in the past decade or more. While many countries in the region have embarked on programs to speed up their economic development, progress to date has been slow. Except in the case of the oil-producing countries lack of capital has been a major obstacle. The rich oil-producing countries have been plagued by many other problems such as inefficient governments, political instability, and the resistance of the ruling classes to major social and economic changes.

AGRICULTURE

Most of the agricultural land of Southwest Asia is devoted to the production of wheat, barley, maize, and rice for domestic consumption. Except for a few years following World War II the area traditionally has had a cereal surplus, with the large exports of Turkey, Syria, and Iraq exceeding the deficits of the rest of the region. Cash crops such as citrus fruits, cotton, sugar, oil-seeds, tobacco, dates, and olive oil have been of increasing importance with the development of transportation and the growth of export markets. Some areas, particularly on the Arabian Peninsula, because of the poverty of the soil will support only pastoral nomadism. But the numbers of people involved are comparatively few.

Cultivation is typically small-scale, the average family working a plot of five to seven acres. Methods of cultivation are extremely primitive and largely account for low yields per worker of one-eighth to one-quarter those in Western Europe or the United States. Despite the lack of water, modern irrigation methods have been introduced only on a limited scale except in Iraq, Iran, and Israel. Farm implements are chiefly hand tools and animal-drawn equipment. Very little power equipment is employed except on the larger estates. In 1952, it was estimated that the number of tractors in use in Iran, Iraq, Lebanon, Syria, and Turkey totalled less than 37,000. Almost 90 per cent of these were in Turkey.[5] Fertilizer consumption is negligible in most countries and is not even sufficient to replace a small fraction of the nutrients extracted from the soil through cultivation.[6] Only a few countries use high-yield seed varieties and every year crop yields are substantially reduced as a result of pests and disease. For example, it is estimated that 15 per cent of Iran's total agricultural production is lost through insects, rodents, waste, and spoilage.[7]

A number of irrigation and multipurpose projects of the TVA variety have been planned or proposed to improve agricultural conditions in Southwest Asia. Among these is the previously mentioned Jordan Valley Development scheme, which is strongly supported by the United States Government because of the contribution it will make toward relieving the Arab refugee problem. The plan as prepared under the direction of the United Nations would irrigate 234,000 acres of land in Israel, Jordan, and Syria, much of which could then produce crops the year round. In addition, the scheme would produce 65,000 kilowatts of electric power. Iraq has vast flood control and irrigation works already under way which when completed will nearly double the present area of irrigated land.

The extensive discussions held between the countries interested in the Jordan Valley project illustrate the difficulties of obtaining agreement on river schemes involving international rivers. In this case four countries lay claim to the waters of the Jordan. Even in the most favorable political atmosphere, reaching agreement on such questions as to how the available waters are to be divided, sharing of costs, and where the dams and

[5] United Nations, Food and Agriculture Organization, *Agriculture in the Near East* (November, 1953), p. 52.

[6] *Ibid.*, p. 57.

[7] Department of State, *Agriculture In Point 4 Countries,* Part 4 (August, 1952).

power installations should be located is difficult. In the case of the Jordan Valley Development project these difficulties have been greatly magnified by the bitterness of Israeli-Arab relations. To minimize or eliminate the need for direct Arab-Israeli negotiations, it has been proposed that the project be placed under international administration and supervision. Whether or not arrangements can be worked out so that the project can go forward is still uncertain.

Extreme inequalities in the ownership of land are an important cause of rural poverty and a major source of political and social unrest in many parts of Southwest Asia. Except in Israel, in Jordan, and in parts of Lebanon and Turkey, the principal form of tenure is that of large estates cultivated by tenants, many of whom are share-croppers. Thus in Iran an estimated 90 per cent of the rural population are tenant share-croppers.[8] A few absentee landlords (including the Shah), religious endowments, and the government own most of the land. Large holdings of tribal sheikhs and other wealthy individuals are also the general rule in Iraq. According to a recent United Nations study, "landlords supply little capital to agriculture and exact excessive rents from tenants, who enjoy little security. In spite of some improvement in recent years, agricultural credit facilities are inadequate, and the peasants pay high rates of interest to money-lenders. Many measures of reform are needed, security of tenure and wider opportunities of ownership and further development of the co-operative movement, among others."[9] Only Turkey, with its land-reform policy initiated in 1945, has taken effective action to develop peasant proprietorship. In Israel, farming settlement is primarily communal or co-operative.

INDUSTRY

Except for petroleum, industry is relatively unimportant in Southwest Asia in terms of the numbers employed and the contribution to national output. Only Turkey and Israel have made significant strides in the direction of greater industrialization. And only in Israel is the contribution of industry to national income greater than that of agriculture. Light industries producing textiles and possessing foodstuffs for domestic consumption predominate. Handicrafts still account for a large proportion of the area's output of manufactures. Turkey with its modest iron and steel industry is the only country in the region with any heavy industry.

Turkey's industrialization has occurred largely at government initiative

[8] *Ibid.*, p. 12.

[9] United Nations, *Progress In Land Reform* (New York, 1954).

and was largely motivated by the desire to strengthen the power of the state. Government banks own and operate about three-fourths of Turkey's industry. Despite its comparative progress Turkey is still a long way from being an industrialized state. Only 8 per cent of the labor force are in industry as against 64 per cent in agriculture. Turkey's crude steel output of roughly 150,000 tons *per annum* is only one-third that of Yugoslavia.

Israel's industrialization, in contrast with that of Turkey, has been brought about largely through the initiative of private entrepreneurs. Light metals and machinery and food processing are of greatest importance.

As in agriculture, productivity in industry is very low by Western standards. The reasons are largely the same as in agriculture. They include insufficient and inadequate industrial equipment, lack of competent supervisory personnel and poorly trained workers, inadequate supplies of locally produced raw materials, and so on.

PETROLEUM INDUSTRY

The petroleum industry is by far the region's most important industry. Production of petroleum has expanded rapidly in Southwest Asia since the war, largely in response to the great increase in world consumption. In 1953 the area produced 121.7 million metric tons of crude oil or roughly 18 per cent of the world total—or 20 per cent if we exclude the Soviet bloc. Table 20-5 shows the region's crude oil output by countries for the years 1948 and 1950 through 1953.

TABLE 20-5

Southwest Asia: Crude Production by Country, 1948 and 1950-53 *
(thousands of metric tons)

COUNTRY	1948	1950	1951	1952	1953
Bahrein	1,496	1,511	1,508	1,510	1,506
Iran	25,270	32,259	16,844	1,348	1,366
Iraq	3,427	6,479	8,690	18,850	28,200
Kuwait	6,400	17,291	28,327	37,631	42,654
Quatar	—	1,636	2,370	3,296	4,003
Saudi Arabia	19,260	26,301	37,476	40,698	41,566
Turkey	3	17	19	22	28
Total Southwest Asia	57,742	88,613	97,566	105,707	121,673
World Total	470,000	525,000	592,000	623,000	666,000
Southwest Asia's Share of World Total	12.3	16.9	16.5	17.0	18.4

* United Nations, Department of Economic Affairs, *Summary of Recent Economic Development in the Middle East 1952-53* (New York, 1954), p. 17.

The sharp drop in Iranian output during and after 1951 reflects the virtual stoppage of oil operations during the dispute between Anglo-Iranian Oil and the Iranian Government over nationalization of the industry. It is estimated that in 1953 crude productive capacity in Iran and elsewhere in the region was at least 50 million tons, or roughly 40 per cent more than actual production.[10]

Refinery Capacity. Most of the oil produced in Southwest Asia is shipped out of the region as crude oil. In 1950, before the shutting down of the Abadan refinery in Iran, which is the largest in the world (*cf.* Fig. 20-1, p. 628). Southwest Asia's output of refinery products aggregated about 40 million tons or 9 per cent of the world total. In 1952 refinery output was down to 23.6 million tons or to slightly less than 4 per cent of the world total. In 1952 the annual crude charging capacity of the refineries of the region exceeded 50 million tons and was gradually being expanded. Output of major refineries products by countries for the period 1950-52 is given in Table 20-6.

TABLE 20-6

Southwest Asia: Output of Major Refinery Products by Countries, 1950-52 *
(thousands of metric tons)

COUNTRY	1950	1951	1952
Bahrein	6,841	8,040	8,621
Iran	24,665	12,807 [a]	1,332 [a]
Israel	187	707	805 [b]
Kuwait	1,101	1,203	1,326
Lebanon	394	420	461
Saudi Arabia	4,825	7,395	7,971
Turkey	5	6	5
Total	40,521	33,224	23,607

[a] Partly estimated.
[b] Estimated.
* United Nations, *op. cit.*

Ownership of the Petroleum Industry. Subsoil rights to oil in Southwest Asia are almost universally vested in the State. However, except for Iran, which nationalized the properties of Anglo-Iranian oil in 1950, exploitation of Southwest Asia's oil resources is predominantly in the hands of foreign enterprises. In 1953, American companies controlled about 60 per cent of the area's output, British and British-Dutch companies 35 per cent, and French concerns 5 per cent. These foreign oil concessionaires operate under profit-sharing agreements with the local governments. While the

[10] *Ibid.*, p. 46.

exact details of these agreements vary from country to country, they uniformly provide for an equal sharing of the net operating revenues of the oil company. In 1954 the Iranian Government turned over the operation of its oil industry to a consortium of foreign companies.

Economic Significance of Petroleum to Southwest Asia. The Southwest Asian oil producing countries derive very significant economic benefits from petroleum. These benefits are primarily indirect and are represented by oil company royalties and other payments to the local governments, local expenditures of the oil companies for labor and supplies, employment, and so on. It is estimated that in 1952 the operations of the oil companies contributed as much as two-fifths to the combined national income of Saudi Arabia, Kuwait, Iraq, Qatar, and Bahrein. Before nationalization 10 per cent of Iran's national income came from the oil industry. Although petroleum is the principal source of energy in the region, only a small fraction of total production is consumed locally. In 1952, Southwest Asia's consumption of petroleum amounted roughly to 6.5 million metric tons, or about 5 per cent of production. Exports including bunkering fuel exceeded 97 million metric tons in 1952.

The largest economic benefits derived from oil are represented by direct payments of oil companies to the local governments. These payments consist of royalties, taxes, dead rent and certain other items. In 1953 they amounted to roughly half a billion dollars and in 1954 to about $700 million.

Local employees of the oil companies in 1951 numbered more than 100,000. Wage payments to these employees plus company purchases of local materials and supplies make an important contribution to economic activity in the areas where the oil companies operate.

As a result of their large incomes from oil the petroleum-producing territories of Southwest Asia have been afforded an important means of financing much needed economic development. So far, however, only a few, notably Iraq and Kuwait, have taken advantage of this opportunity. A good part of the income is still being dissipated by individual rulers on personal expenditures.

Importance of Southwest Asia's Oil to the Free World. Southwest Asia is the world's most important exporter of petroleum. The bulk of its exports go to Eastern Hemisphere markets. In 1953, Free World countries outside of the Americas obtained about 70 per cent of their petroleum requirements from Southwest Asia, while the proportion for Western Europe exceeded 90 per cent. Although American companies accounted for the largest share of the region's output, the United States obtained only about 3 per cent of its requirements from this source. Thus while American oil companies have a significant economic stake in Southwest Asia's oil resources in terms of investment and revenues, the United States economy is not now dependent upon oil from this area. For Western European countries, by contrast, Southwest Asia's oil is of vital importance. It is doubtful whether sufficient oil could be obtained from alternative sources to meet Western Europe's needs except possibly over a long period of time and at great cost. Moreover, such oil as could be obtained elsewhere would be more expensive, would have to be paid for largely with dollars, and would impose a heavy drain on Western Europe's balance-of-payments position. Finally, Southwest Asia's oil is an important source of earnings particularly for the British and the Dutch.

In the event of a war, Southwest Asia's oil would be of vital importance to the Free World. Western Hemisphere supplies alone would be wholly inadequate to meet the essential civilian and military requirements of the United States and its Allies.

In the years ahead, Southwest Asia's oil is likely to become of increasing economic importance to the United States as consumption continues to rise and reserves eventually dwindle. So far, despite frequent pessimistic predictions that United States' crude oil reserves would soon be exhausted, new discoveries have outpaced production. However, this cannot keep up indefinitely. In fact, during the past five years United States demand for crude has started to exceed production. If, as estimated by the Paley Commission, United States demand for petroleum by 1975 is double the 1950 amount, dependence on foreign supplies, particularly from Southwest Asia, will be much greater than now.[11]

COMMUNICATIONS

Southwest Asia, which is a land bridge connecting three continents, is a vital link in the world communications network. Its present significance dates in considerable measure from the opening of the Suez Canal in 1869. As a result Southwest Asia has become a cornerstone of the highly important Suez Canal–Red Sea–Strait of Bab-el-Mandeb water route which enables vessels up to 45,000 tons to pass directly from the Eastern Mediterranean to the Red Sea and Indian Ocean.

This route is followed by virtually all shipping from Europe to the Far East and Australia. It is of major importance to all maritime powers, and

[11] The President's Materials Policy Commission, *Resources For Freedom* (Washington, D. C., June, 1952), p. 107.

in particular to the United Kingdom, with its large economic interests in South Asia and the Far East. The economic advantages of this route are demonstrated by the fact that the distance from London to Bombay via the Suez Canal is 4,500 miles less than by the Cape of Good Hope route. The resultant savings in transportation costs contributed significantly to the growth of trade between Europe and Asia. The Red Sea-Suez Canal water route has assumed increasing significance in recent years with the large movements of petroleum from the Persian Gulf.

The Suez Canal greatly outranks in importance all other international canals in terms of volume of traffic handled. In 1952 over 86 million net registered tons of shipping moved through the Suez Canal as compared with 34.5 million tons for the Panama Canal. The largest share of this traffic has always been and continues to be British. It is not surprising that the British had grave misgivings about relinquishing its control over the Canal Zone to Egypt. The United States now ranks second to the United Kingdom, largely because of oil shipments from Saudi Arabia.

André Siegfried has described the significance of the Suez Canal as follows: [12]

> Of all the great roadways of the world, the sea road to India via the Isthmus of Suez is probably the most important, for it joins East and West Asia and Europe,—that is, the two most thickly populated continents having the most ancient civilizations. The Isthmus itself, by virtue of its geographical position, has always been a focal point, but its greatest significance dates from the opening of the Canal, in 1869, at a time when Europe was triumphantly expanding, thanks to the industrial revolution and steam navigation. The rapid pace of industrialization could not have kept pace without access to raw materials from the outermost parts of the earth and the opening of new markets for manufactured goods. And the introduction of America to the Far East in the Twentieth century further enlarged the role of this intercontinental route. If the Canal is blocked or its efficiency impaired the whole Western World is affected.

While not a great international water route like the Suez Canal, the Straits are of considerable economic and strategic importance because they provide the only water passage between the Black Sea and the Mediterranean. Concern over control of the Straits has always been important to the U.S.S.R. because of the otherwise landlocked position of Southern Russia. This explains why Russia has consistently sought to obtain the right to uninterrupted passage through the Straits in peace and war.

Southwest Asia's oil pipelines are also of great international economic

[12] "The Suez: International Roadway," *Foreign Affairs*, Vol. 31, No. 4 (July, 1953), pp. 604-618; see also p. 241.

significance [13] (*cf.* Fig. 20-1). Most important are the two large-diameter pipelines from Saudi Arabia and Iraq to the Mediterranean. The pipeline from Saudi Arabia, completed late in 1950, stretches from the oilfields of Saudi Arabia, through Jordan and Syria, to Sidon in Lebanon. This thirty to thirty-one-inch pipeline, with a length of 1,720 kilometers and a present throughput capacity of 15.5 million tons a year, required an investment of $230 million. The Iraqi pipeline, with diameters of twenty-six, thirty, and thirty-two inches, and a length of 895 kilometers, has a normal throughput capacity of 13.5 million tons a year. The line was completed in 1952 from Kirkuk field in Iraq to Baniyas in Syria; it required a total investment of about $115 million.

In addition to these lines, the pipeline systems of several oil producing countries were expanded during the past three years. In Iraq, a pipeline of twelve to sixteen inches, with a length of 120 kilometers, was laid between the Zubair field and Fao on the Persian Gulf; it has a crude carrying capacity of 2.6 million tons annually. This line was finished late in 1951; in 1952 plans were laid to construct a parallel line with a diameter of twenty-four inches. There was another plan, also, to construct a pipeline of twelve and three-quarter inches, with a length of about 220 kilometers, capable of carrying 1.3 million tons of crude petroleum a year from Ain Zalah to the main Iraqi pipelines near Shuraimiya. The construction of a sixteen-inch pipeline from Kirkuk to Haifa, which was interrupted in 1948, was not completed. Another parallel twelve-inch pipeline from Kirkuk to Haifa, which was shut down in 1948, remains closed. In Saudi Arabia, the pipeline system was expanded in 1951 by 76 kilometers of new pipelines with a capacity of nearly 14 million tons of crude petroleum a year. During the past three years additional pipelines were laid in Iran, Kuwait, and Qatar. Expansion of oil handling facilities also included construction of storage and harbor facilities in the new oil ports of Sidon, Baniyas, and Fao, as well as expansion of existing facilities in Iran, Kuwait, Qatar, and Saudi Arabia.

The rapid growth of international air transport also has contributed to the importance of Southwest Asia in the world communications network. Southwest Asia is an essential transit area on the international air routes between Europe and the Far East, the United States and the Far East, and Europe and Cape Town. At the present time a large number of different international air routes cross Arabia. Air transport also has contributed significantly to the improvement of local communications.

[13] United Nations, *Review of Economic Conditions in the Middle East 1951-52*, Ch. 3, "Petroleum," pp. 53-66.

The principal rail systems of Southwest Asia (*cf.* Fig. 20-1) were developed by foreign powers primarily for strategic and political reasons and have only limited international or domestic economic significance. In 1951 the quantity of freight moved *per capita* was only about 2 per cent of that of the United States. There are two main systems. One extends from Europe via Turkey to Egypt and the Persian Gulf. The other starts at the Arabian Gulf, crosses Iran in a north northeastern direction and reaches the Caspian Sea near the Soviet border. Both systems were linked during the war but are now separated. During the war the Trans-Iranian railroad was of great significance in moving American supplies from the Persian Gulf to the Soviet Union. The railroad from Basra to Turkey via Baghdad also was important during World War II for the movement of cargo to Turkey, since the Mediterranean was virtually closed to Allied shipping.

CHAPTER 21

South and Southeast Asia

A POWER VACUUM

South and Southeast Asia is largely a power vacuum perilously close to the Communist bloc and a primary target of Communist expansionist ambitions. Before World War II the entire region except Thailand and Afghanistan was under direct foreign domination. India, Burma, Malaya, Borneo, and Ceylon were controlled by the United Kingdom; Indonesia by the Netherlands; Indochina by France, and the Philippines by the United States. After World War II most of the area became independent but none of the newly formed states have as yet achieved any real political and economic strength. Some of the governments of the area are weak and inexperienced; a number of countries are beset by serious internal disorders. Limited progress has been made in breaking with the misery and poverty of the past. As a result discontent and frustration are probably a greater threat to the political stability of South and Southeast Asia than of any other underdeveloped area. At the same time Communist influence has greatly increased in Asia as a result of the consolidation of Chinese Communist power on the mainland. It is not surprising therefore that Communists have been making a major effort to expand their influence over the area by propaganda, economic blandishments, infiltration, and outright conquest.

Vital interests of the Free World are threatened. South and Southeast Asia have more than one-quarter of the world's total population and almost 40 per cent of the population of the Free World. The area is an important source of raw materials as well as a market for exports. It occupies a highly strategic geographical position on the periphery of the Asian land mass. It dominates important air and sea routes and controls major air and naval bases. The control of the area by unfriendly powers would endanger the entire Western Pacific defensive system. This threat to its vital security interests accounts in part at least for the West's large-scale economic and military aid to the region. Thailand, Pakistan, and the Philippines have joined the West as parties to the Manila Pact and Pacific Charter of September, 1954, to protect the area against both open armed attack and internal subversion. Most of the region, however, is as yet uncommitted and is making every effort to remain neutral. Whether such a neutral course will be possible remains to be seen. In any case there appears to be no early prospect of a relaxation of Communist efforts to win the area.

AREA AND POPULATION

Despite its diversity South and Southeast Asia has an essential unity which sets it apart from the rest of Asia. Its unifying characteristics include similarities in geographic structure, climate, economic activities, culture, and history. With an area of more than 3.5 million square miles South and Southeast Asia is larger than the United States. In contrast with other hot wet regions which typically are thinly peopled, South and Southeast Asia is one of the most heavily populated areas in the world. It had an estimated population of approximately 650 million in 1953, or one quarter of the world total on 6 per cent of the earth's surface. This compares with 170 million on the 11.5 million square miles of hot wet regions outside Asia.[1] South Asia, the largest and most populous of the two regions embraces an area of more than 1.8 million square miles and has more than 450 million people. The principal countries of South Asia are India, Pakistan, Ceylon, and Afghanistan. (See Table 21-1.) Other political units include independent Nepal and Bhutan and small Portuguese enclaves. Pakistan comprises two territories separated by a distance of nearly 1,000 miles. This unique political phenomenon arose out of the provisions of the Indian Independence Act of 1947 which ended British rule in India and provided for the establishment of the Dominion of India and the Dominion of Pakistan. The political boundaries of the new states were fixed primarily along cultural—especially religious—and linguistic ethnic lines. Areas predominantly Hindu became Indian and Moslem areas Pakistan. They make little economic or geographic sense. The distribution of the two religions in former British India was such as

[1] P. Gourou, *The Tropical World* (London, 1952), p. 2.

to result in a divided Pakistan state. Of the two zones which make up what has now become the Republic of Pakistan, East Pakistan with 42 million people crowded in an area one-sixth the size of West Pakistan is the most important.

TABLE 21-1

South and Southeast Asia: Area Population and Population Density of Principal Countries, 1953

COUNTRY	TOTAL AREA [a] (SQUARE MILES)	POPULATION [b] (THOUSANDS)	POPULATION DENSITY (PER SQUARE MILE)
South Asia			
Afghanistan	230,888	12,000 (1951)	52
India	1,269,591	372,000	293
Pakistan	365,893	75,842 (1951)	207
Ceylon	25,330	8,155	321
Southeast Asia			
Burma	261,600	19,045	73
Thailand	197,659	19,556	99
Indochina	272,355	30,000	110
Malaya	52,286	6,829	131
Indonesia	735,268	78,163 (1952)	106
Philippines	115,600	21,039	182

[a] United Nations, *Statistical Yearbook*, 1953.
[b] United Nations, *Population and Vital Statistics Reports*, Series A (New York, January, 1955).

Southeast Asia has an area of roughly 1.6 million square miles and a population of more than 200 million. It includes Laos, Cambodia, Viet Nam, Burma, and Thailand on the broad Indochina peninsula, Malaya on the narrow Malay peninsula, and the Indonesian and Philippine archipelagoes east and southeast of the mainland. Viet Nam was divided by a provisional military demarcation line as a result of the Geneva Conference of July 1954. The northern part comprising 60,000 square miles and roughly 13 million people is controlled by the Communist Viet Minh. Free Viet Nam has a republican form of government.

South and Southeast Asia has an average population density of almost 200 persons per square mile. This is very high for a predominantly agricultural region, exceeding a number of industrialized countries including the United States. Population densities vary widely from country to country. In general the Indian subcontinent is overpopulated while Southeast Asia is underpopulated. Almost half of India's population lives on 14.5 per cent of the total area with a density of 755 to the square mile. However, Southeast Asia has some of the most densely populated agricultural regions in the world. Java and Madura (Madoera) in Indonesia for example, have more than 1,000 inhabitants per square mile and the Tonkin Delta in North Viet Nam more than 1,100.

Most of the people of South and Southeast Asia live in villages and small market towns. The number of persons living in cities of more than 50,000 is only a small fraction of the total population. Rural settlements tend to be highly concentrated in the river valleys, deltas, and low-lying plains like the Ganges Valley in India, the Red River and Mekong deltas of North Viet Nam and Cambodia, the Menam delta of Thailand, and the Irrawaddy delta of Burma.[2] Population density in these areas reaches 2,000 per mile. Adjacent areas are often quite sparsely populated for a variety of reasons including the cultural habits of the natives, less favorable soils and malarial infestation. Thus the outer islands of Indonesia have a population density of under 60 persons per square mile as compared with Java and Madura's 1,100. Except for Tonkin, Annam, and fringe areas along the coast, the Indochinese peninsula's population density is under 25 persons per square mile.

South and Southeast Asia is characterized by high birth rates and declining but still high death rates. Population is currently estimated to be growing at a rate of somewhat more than 1.25 per cent per year in South Asia as against 1.6 per cent in Southeast Asia. Declining death rates according to United Nations estimates may raise the growth rate to as high as 1.83 to 2.32 per cent *per annum* by 1980. This would result in a population in excess of 1 billion in 1980.

GEOGRAPHY AND CLIMATE

South Asia lies entirely north of the equator and half of the Indian subcontinent lies outside the tropics in the Temperate Zone. Except for the northern tip of Burma all of Southeast Asia is in the Tropical Zone extending to 10 degrees above the equator. The Indian subcontinent has the following three main geographic divisions: [3] (*a*) The northern mountain wall with elevations of more than 3,000 feet, (*b*) a lowland alluvial area with an elevation of generally under 500 feet which extends in a band 120 to 200 miles wide completely across northern India, east and west, and has an area of 300,000 square miles,[4] and (*c*) the plateau of the Indian peninsula with an area of about one million square miles and ele-

[2] United Nations, *Economic Survey of Asia and the Far East* (New York, 1950), p. 36.

[3] L. D. Stamp, *Asia: A Regional Geography,* 11th ed. (London, 1952), pp. 13-14.

[4] J. E. Spencer, *Asia East by South* (New York, John Wiley & Sons, 1954), p. 4.

vations of 3,000 to 1,000 feet sloping from the West to the East. Between the Eastern and Western edges of this plateau are narrow coastal plains.

The northern mountain barrier has served in many ways to keep India a land apart. For all practical purposes India is accessible only by sea and by air. It has no rail connections with other countries of Asia. The lowland alluvial plain is one of the most fertile areas on the earth's surface, which largely accounts for its dense population. The peninsula has poorer soils and less favorable water conditions for irrigation than the alluvial plain. Here population is concentrated mainly on the coastal plains.

Southeast Asia like India displays considerable variation in its physical features. In general the terrain of the region is hilly and mountainous. Much of the territory of Indochinese peninsula and Thailand is wild and rugged. Mountain ranges extend throughout the length of the Malayan peninsula into Indonesia. As a result Malaya has few stretches of level ground and no less than two-thirds of Java is upland or mountainous. The ruggedness of the terrain makes overland transport extremely difficult, so that water transport is of primary importance. Much of the soil is infertile and is covered with dense equatorial forest. Swamps and marshes are frequent along the coast. Scattered throughout the area, however, are fertile regions of lowland with large stretches of alluvial soil which, as mentioned above, are the chief centers of population. Other fertile areas, chiefly in the Philippines and Indonesia, have resulted from ash of extinct volcanoes mixing with the soil.

The climate of South and Southeast Asia is tropical even though roughly half of the Indian subcontinent is outside the tropical belt. The reason for this is that the Himalayas form a great climatic barrier that protects India from the cold winter winds of Central Asia.

South and Southeast Asia is predominantly a monsoon zone. Summers are the rainy season almost everywhere, except in the equatorial regions where seasonal differences are less marked and rain is fairly abundant at all times. In the region of the monsoons expanding hot air creates low pressure areas on the mainland each spring. In early June moist air moves landward from the sea to equalize the pressure. As the air moves across the land it brings rain for a period of almost four months. The monsoons account for 80 to 90 per cent of the total precipitation. During other seasons there is very little rain. The amount of rainfall varies widely from region to region depending chiefly on differences in relief in relation to wind direction.

The monsoon plays a vital role in South and Southeast Asia's agriculture. For example, 80 per cent of India's crop land depends on the monsoon for water. It feeds large rivers for irrigation. It permits a fairly long growing season. If the monsoon fails, as it periodically does, famine may ensue.

ECONOMIC AND STRATEGIC SIGNIFICANCE

South and Southeast Asia plays an important role in the world economy. In 1953, the region accounted for roughly 6.5 per cent of the total value of Free World trade. It is a major producer of a number of so-called "key materials," notably natural rubber, tin, mica, titanium, and manganese.[5] (See Table 21-2 and Fig. 21-1.) Most of the region's output of these products is exported and represents a large share of the requirements of Western Europe and the United States. The area is also a dominant or large world supplier of many other important raw materials and foodstuffs.

TABLE 21-2

South and Southeast Asia: Relative Importance as Producer of Key Materials *

COMMODITY	SHARE OF FREE WORLD OUTPUT (1950)	COUNTRIES
Natural rubber	89 per cent	Malaya, Indonesia, Ceylon, Thailand
Tin (metal)	62	Malaya, Indonesia, Thailand
Mica	46	India, Pakistan
Titanium	30	India, Pakistan
Manganese (ore)	26	India, Pakistan
Graphite	11	Ceylon
Bauxite	7	Indonesia
Petroleum	3	Indonesia

* The President's Materials Policy Commission, *Resources For Freedom,* Vol. 1 (Washington, D. C., June, 1952), pp. 98-100.

It supplies the bulk of the Free World's requirements of jute and burlap, manila hemp, tea, copra and coconut oil, and varying amounts of a large variety of other tropical products such as lac and other gums, spices, palm oil, sugar, and quinine. The economic vulnerability of the West to the loss of these supplies has been reduced as a result of the development of synthetics, more efficient utilization of materials, the opening up of alternative sources of supply, and the accumulation of strategic stockpiles. Nonetheless the economic burden of such a loss would still be considerable.

South and Southeast Asia is of particular economic importance to the former European colonial powers, especially the United Kingdom and the

[5] The President's Materials Policy Commission, *Resources For Freedom,* Vol. 1 (Washington, D. C., June, 1952), pp. 98-100.

Netherlands. While independence has operated to circumscribe the economic activities of foreign nationals in South and Southeast Asia, it has not radically altered the area's traditional pattern of trade. As before the war the largest share of South and Southeast Asia's trade is with the metropoles or affiliated currency areas. India, Pakistan, Burma, and Ceylon have remained members of the sterling area. Laos, Cambodia, and Viet Nam are in the franc area, and the Philippine peso is linked to the dollar. Malaya is the United Kingdom's largest source of dollar earnings. Singapore, in its outstanding *entrepôt* role for the region, is a large source of service income for British concerns.

Japan's economic well-being, as a result of the loss of its empire, is much more dependent on South and Southeast Asia than before World War II. South and Southeast Asia now provides a market for almost 40 per cent of Japan's exports, and supplies approximately 30 per cent of its imports. As mentioned in Chapter 16, Japan's serious postwar balance-of-payments difficulties would become almost hopeless if trade with South and Southeast Asia were cut off.

The importance of South and Southeast Asia to the security of the rest of the Free World hardly requires more than brief mention. If the area fell under the control of unfriendly powers the United States outer defenses in the Pacific would be seriously breached. A path to Australia would be opened across the discontinuous land bridge of the Indonesian Islands. British control of the Indian Ocean which is vital for the defense of Southwest Asia and Africa would be jeopardized. Finally, if the manpower and resources of the area were effectively organized by a ruthless authoritarian power, as the Communists have done in China, the balance of world power might in time overwhelmingly shift against the West.

RESOURCES

South and Southeast Asia's over-all resource picture in relation to area and population is not too favorable. With a population in excess of 600 million, average density in 1953 was roughly 220 per square mile or almost five times the world's average. As described elsewhere, areas of greatest population pressure are the Indian subcontinent and Java. Much of Southeast Asia, by contrast, is underpopulated with large areas of potentially productive land available for cultivation.

The region's heavy population density is not offset by any unusual endowment in other natural resources. South and Southeast Asia's mineral resources, while fairly diversified, appear to be modest. They warrant no particular optimism regarding the potentialities of the area for industrial development.

Agricultural Land. Comparison of population with arable or actual land under cultivation is of course much more meaningful than comparison with total land area since only part of the land is usable for the growing of food and raw materials. As shown in Table 21-3, South and Southeast Asia with less than one acre of cultivated land per head of population, is at the bottom of the world scale with respect to arable land *per capita.*

TABLE 21-3

Areas of Cultivated Land Per Head of Population *

ACRES PER HEAD	
2½ or more	North and South America, Australia, New Zealand, Eastern Europe (except Czechoslovakia), U.S.S.R.
1 to 2	Western and Central Europe, except Switzerland, Holland, and Belgium
Marginal	Czechoslovakia, Austria, Italy, Western Germany
Below 1	United Kingdom, Belgium, Holland, Switzerland India, China, Japan and much of Southeast Asia, Egypt

* J. Russell, *World Population and World Food Supplies* (London, 1954), p. 16.

Moreover much of the land is lacking in nitrogen and phosphate and is without dependable water. Even the countries of Western and Central Europe, which are much more highly industrialized and depend on imports to cover many of their requirements for food and agricultural raw materials, have up to two and one-half times the land area *per capita* of South and Southeast Asia. Because of its low *per capita* farm area the only way the region can come close to feeding itself is by producing an almost wholly vegetarian diet. Animal food production requires much more land than vegetable food. An acre of land will yield up to 3000 pounds of bread or 10 tons of potatoes but only 100 to 200 pounds of meat.[6] By force of necessity, therefore, South and Southeast Asia must devote most of the cultivated area to cereal production.

As shown in Table 21-4 the quantity of arable land varies considerably from country to country ranging from a low of about one-third of an acre in Indonesia to more than one acre for Burma. These differences should not be taken too literally, however, because of possible inaccuracies in the country's classification of what constitutes arable land. Double-cropping in some areas also affects the significance of the figures.

[6] *Ibid.*, p. 16.

TABLE 21-4

South and Southeast Asia: Arable and Potentially Productive Land Per Capita *

COUNTRY	PERIOD	ARABLE LAND (MILLIONS OF ACRES)	ARABLE LAND PER CAPITA (IN ACRES)	POTENTIALLY PRODUCTIVE (MILLIONS OF ACRES)
India [a]	1950	324.5	0.87	98.4
Pakistan [b]	1948	51.2	0.68	22.2
Ceylon	1951	36.3	0.44	2.8
Afghanistan	1948	6.2 [c]	0.52	6.9
Philippines	1951	16.5 [d]	0.78	12.2
Indonesia	1947	27.2	0.35	
Malaya	1951	5.2	0.76	2.4
Burma	1950	21.1	1.10	19.3
Indochina	1951	18.7 [d]	0.62	21.9
Thailand	1949	11.7 [e]	0.84	
Totals		518.6	0.81	

[a] Including all of Kashmir.
[b] Excludes Baluchistan.
[c] Excludes fallow.
[d] Total agricultural areas including permanent meadows and pastures.
[e] Main crops only.
* United Nations, Food and Agricultural Organization, *Yearbook of Food and Agricultural Statistics,* 1952, Vol. 6, Part 1.

Even if all of the so-called potentially productive land of the region was brought into cultivation, the amount of arable land *per capita* would still be only slightly more than one acre. In point of fact, however, much of this land, particularly in India, can be reclaimed only at great cost. Only the Philippines, Burma, Indochina, and Thailand still have large unexploited areas of good agricultural land. China with its teeming millions may be sorely tempted to move into these areas sometime in the future in order to relieve the growing pressure on its strained land resources.

Mineral Resources.[7] Exact knowledge of the mineral resources of South and Southeast Asia is lacking, since the area has not yet been adequately surveyed. However, the geology of the region is sufficiently well-known as to make any sensational new mineral discoveries unlikely (Fig. 21-1). Coal and lignite reserves amount to less than 5 per cent of the world total, petroleum reserves to less than 2 per cent, and water power reserves to about 15 per cent. The only metals found in significant amounts in relation to the world total are tin, manganese, bauxite, iron ore, and titanium.

[7] The materials used in this section were taken from United Nations, *Development of Mineral Resources In Asia and The Far East* (Bangkok, 1953).

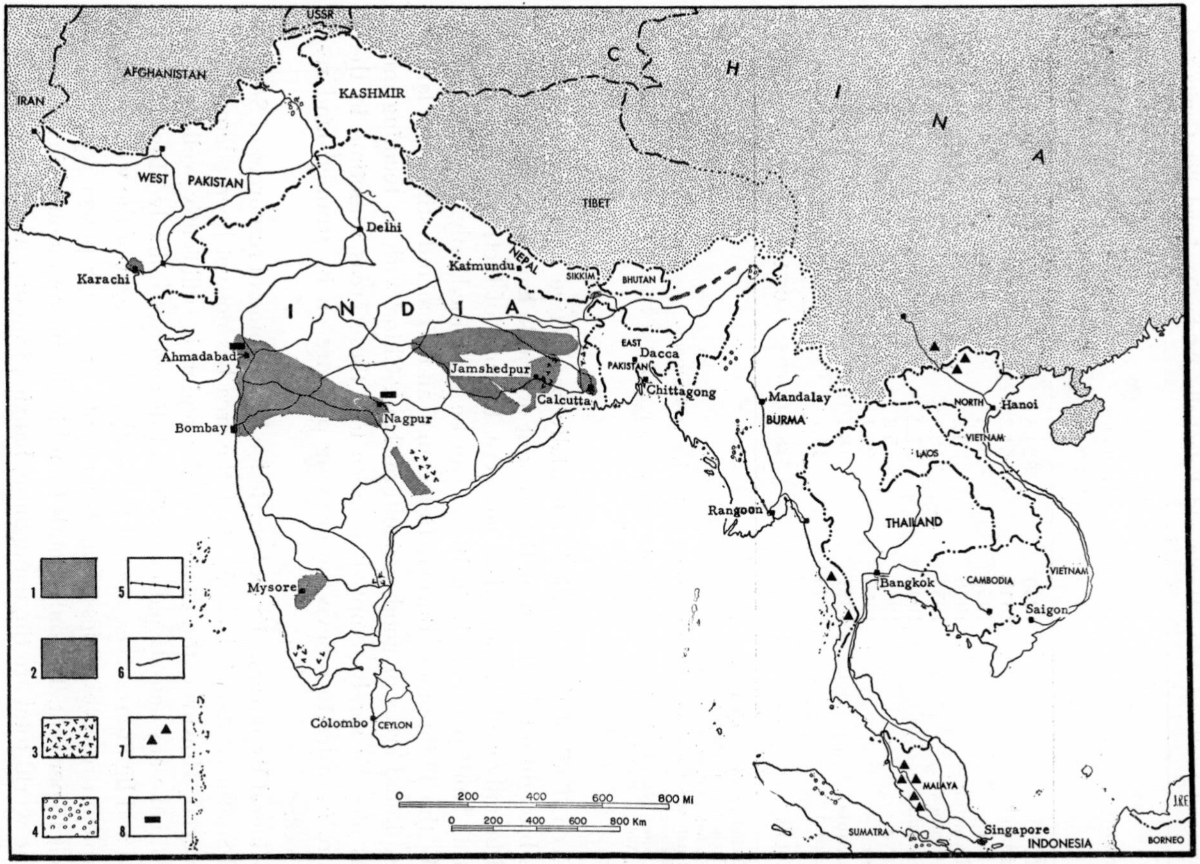

FIG. 21-1. Southeast Asia: Railroads, Resources and Industrial Concentration: (1) industrial areas; (2) coal; (3) iron ore; (4) petroleum; (5) oil pipelines; (6) railroads; (7) tin; (8) manganese.

Only India has the iron ore and coal reserves required to support a large steel industry. India has immense iron ore reserves estimated at 10,000 million tons, of which as much as half has an iron content of 60 per cent. India also has the bulk of the area's high-grade coal, including coking coal, although here its reserve position is much less favorable than with respect to iron ore. Reserves are estimated at 5,000 to 6,000 million tons, of which, however, less than 1,000 million tons is of coking quality. Much of this reserve is now inaccessible and coking coal could become a problem with a rapid speed-up in India's industrialization. While coal is found in most of the other countries of the area, much of it is poor quality, chiefly lignite. Indonesia and the Philippines have large iron ore reserves, but these have a high nickel and chromium content which has to be eliminated before the ore can be of any commercial value.

The area is well-provided with such ferro-alloys as tungsten, manganese, and titanium and is moderately endowed with reserves of molybdenum, chromium, and vanadium. Except for tin, South and Southeast Asia is deficient in non-ferrous metals. Limited amounts of antimony are available in most countries. Small quantities of copper are to be found in the Philippines, India, and Burma. Lead and zinc reserves still remain untapped in Burma.

Both India and Indonesia have the bauxite reserves required to establish an aluminum industry, provided cheap power can be provided. Rich magnesite reserves have also been identified in both countries. Ceylon has sizable reserves of high-grade graphite and India of muscovite bloc mica. No significant amounts of uranium-bearing mineral deposits have been discovered but the region abounds in beach sands containing monazite, which after uranium may be the most important source of fissionable materials. The area is deficient in native sulphur required for a chemical industry but has some pyrites and gypsum.

Petroleum is found in significant quantities in Indonesia, British Borneo, and Burma, although known reserves are small in relation to the world total. Indonesia's oil reserves of about one billion barrels are roughly 1 per cent of the world total. Burma's petroleum supplies will be just about sufficient to cover its growing needs.

While many parts of the region lack adequate coal and petroleum, virtually every country, and in particular India, has a huge water power potential which has been almost untouched. These hydraulic resources are not always located in areas where the need for power is greatest and their development will require large-scale investments. Nonetheless they could meet a sizable share of the region's future electric power needs.

BASIC ECONOMIC CHARACTERISTICS

The most pervasive economic characteristic of South and Southeast Asia is its poverty. With more than one-quarter of the world's population, the area accounts for only about 6 per cent of total production. Levels of living everywhere are at or close to minimum subsistence levels, averaging less than $75 *per capita.* As a result only a very small margin of production can be spared for investment. For much of the region the level of investment is just sufficient to take care of the growth of population so that living standards are stationary or increasing only very slowly.

The economy of South and Southeast Asia is predominantly agricultural. The rural population represents anywhere from 70 to 90 per cent of the total. Industrial development has been limited and outside of India has been confined chiefly to mining, the processing of primary products for export, and small-scale (including handicraft) production of consumer goods for domestic use. Manufacturing and construction for most countries of the region account for less than 15 per cent of national income as compared with 50 per cent or more for agriculture. Before the war a considerable share of the capital required for financing industrial development was provided by overseas investors, principally European. Now most of the capital is mobilized locally, in large part by the governments. Except for the Chinese, however, the number of foreigners directly engaged in the economic activities of the region was relatively limited. The overseas Chinese, by contrast, are of considerable numerical importance in Southeast Asia, especially in Malaya, the Philippines, and Thailand. They play an economic role considerably greater than even their numerical importance suggests through their extensive control of the retail and export-import trade of the area. The success of the overseas Chinese and their dual-citizenship status has aroused considerable resentment among local people and governments, and has generated a variety of legislative enactments designed to curb their activities.

While large plantations producing mainly commercial crops for export occur in some parts of the region, most farming is of a small-scale subsistence variety. The typical farm unit is only 2 to 5 acres as compared with 140 acres in the United States, and is too small to permit the farmer and his family to eke out more than a bare existence. In a number of areas the size of the peasant's plot will not even support a bare subsistence. The principal crops are rice and other grains which are largely consumed on the farm. Commercial crops produced for export include rubber, tea, rice, copra, jute, cotton, and manila hemp. Productivity in agriculture is low.

Population pressure is acute over much of the area including India, Cambodia, Laos, Viet Nam, South Burma, and in Java and Madura. Moreover, these pressures have been intensified in recent years as modern improvements in public health and sanitation have reduced the death rate without a corresponding decrease in the birth rate. Since there are very few opportunities in industry, rural overcrowding, progressive fragmentation of farms, and underemployment in agriculture is commonplace. In India, for example, it has been estimated that rural unemployment and underemployment may be as high as 80 million.[8]

Economic relations between the countries of South and Southeast Asia are limited by the fact that their economies are more competitive than complementary. All export mostly food and raw materials. Since there is little industrialization within the region the raw materials exports go principally to Japan and non-Asiatic markets. It was the complementary character of the Japanese and Southeast Asian economies which partly inspired Japan's efforts in World War II to construct its "Greater East Asia Co-Prosperity Sphere." Trade within the region is limited primarily to movements of rice from the surplus to the deficit areas, and exports of textiles from India.

Exports lack diversification. Two or three products account for two-thirds or more of the exports of most countries in the area. These exports are typically subject to wide fluctuations in price and volume depending on foreign market conditions. The result is equally wide movements in the export earnings and levels of income of these countries.

INDUSTRIAL DEVELOPMENT

The very limited character of South and Southeast Asia's industrial development is strikingly revealed by the fact that in 1948, the region accounted for an estimated 1.5 per cent of world mining and manufacturing production.[9] This was only about one-third of the industrial output of Japan and less than that of Belgium. India with 1.2 per cent of the world total accounted for the bulk of the area's output of minerals and manufactures.

The dominant position of India (*cf.* Fig. 21-1, p. 652) and the small

[8] "India—Progress and Plan," *The Economist,* January 22, 1955.
[9] United Nations, *Monthly Bulletin of Statistics,* April, 1951.

TABLE 21-5

South and Southeast Asia: Industrial and Mineral Production, 1952

COUNTRY	COAL *	ELECTRICITY (MN KWH)	PETROLEUM CRUDE *	IRON ORE *	CRUDE STEEL *	TIN CONCENTRATES (TONS)	COTTON YARNS *	COTTON FABRICS (MN METRES)	CEMENT *
India	36,804	6,192	—	3,984	1,608	—	656	4,212.0	3,600.0
Pakistan	600 [a]	300	180	—	—	—	—	159.6	538.8
Ceylon	—	120	—	—	—	—	—	8.4 (Mn sq. metres)	—
Indonesia	960	—	8,520	—	—	37,956	—	—	—
British Borneo	—	—	5,112	—	—	57,744	—	—	—
Philippines	—	552 (Manila)	—	1,164	—	—	—	6.0	316.8 [d]
Malaya	324 [a]	960	—	1,073	—	—	—	—	—
Burma	—	—	—	—	—	960	2	—	—
Thailand	—	60 [b]	—	—	—	9,624	—	—	247.2
Indochina									
Viet Nam	852	228	—	—	—	286 [c]	—	—	220.8
Cambodia	—	24	—	—	—	—	—	—	—

[a] Malaya: lignite only. Pakistan: including lignite.
[b] Bangkok electric works only which accounted for 82 per cent of total generation in Thailand in 1951.
[c] Includes Laos.
[d] Production Cebu Portland cement only.
* Thousands of tons.

amount of industrialization in the rest of the area is further highlighted by the production data shown in Table 21-5. In 1952, India's coal production was twelve times that of the rest of the region combined and its output of electricity roughly three times as great. It had the only steel industry. Its textile industry not only dwarfed that of the rest of South and Southeast Asia but has become a major factor in the world export market. Only India produces heavy machinery and equipment like locomotives and railway cars. It has the only significant chemical industry. Despite its considerable industrialization relative to the rest of the region, India's economy is still overwhelmingly agricultural. Factory employment in manufactures and mining in 1952 amounted to only about 2.5 million workers. In 1950, mining and manufacturing and construction accounted for only 15 per cent of the net domestic product as against 50 per cent in agriculture. *Per capita* consumption of commercial energy was 0.10 metric tons coal equivalent, or only one-eighth that of Japan. Moreover, light industries are of major importance. Thus in 1952, approximately two-fifths of the entire industrial labor force of India was employed in the cotton and jute mills.

In the other countries of South and Southeast Asia, factory industry consists chiefly of plants processing agricultural and mineral products mainly for export. These include rice mills in Burma, Cambodia, Laos, Viet Nam, and Thailand, oil refineries in Indonesia, tin smelters, vegetable oil and rubber processing plants in Malaya, and sugar and coconut oil mills in the Philippines. In addition, most countries of the region manufacture a considerable variety of consumer goods like ceramics, glass, matches, soap, cigarettes, paper and canned foods. All have small-scale metal-working industries capable of making simple tools and equipment and of doing repair work. In all countries including India handicrafts still account for a considerable share of total output of manufactures.

Relative to its area and population South and Southeast Asia has a poorly developed inland transportation system. Only India, which accounts for about two-thirds of the length of railway lines for the entire region, can boast of a reasonably well-developed and efficient rail system. The development of this network has contributed significantly to India's economic and political unification. It has been an important factor in facilitating the movement of food from surplus to deficit areas in times of local crop failures, thereby greatly reducing the frequency and severity of famines which have plagued India in the past. But even in India, the railway network is by no means adequate to service the country's growing requirements. Freight movements frequently involve carriage both by rail and coastal vessel, resulting in costly loading and unloading charges, because of the overburdened rail system. The exploitation of valuable mineral resources has been handicapped by the inability of the rail system to move the ore from the mines.

Elsewhere in South and Southeast Asia water transport both inland and coastal has played a much more significant role than land transport in the region's economic development. In Burma the "linear build of the country, traversed by the Irrawaddy, has meant an easy development of water transport. Native traffic in considerable volume has flowed along the Irrawaddy, the Chindwin, and the Sittang for centuries, as well as along the whole coastal fringe." [10] Similarly in Thailand the waterways have long carried the bulk of the local transportation. Coastal shipping is the primary form of transport in the Philippines and Indonesia. Intra-regional transport is almost wholly by sea since rail or highway connections between countries, except as between India and Pakistan, are either very inadequate or wholly lacking. A considerable amount of this traffic is moved by small coastal vessels. A few countries have developed their own merchant marines. India has a merchant fleet of almost half a million gross registered tons of vessels larger than 100 tons. Its shipyards are capable of building large oceangoing ships. Pakistan and the Philippines have merchant fleets of between 150,000 and 200,000 gross registered tons.

Because of poor land connections the development of civil aviation in South and Southeast Asia has been very rapid since the war. Air freight expressed in ton-kilometers increased fourfold in India from 1948 to 1952. Large though less spectacular increases were registered in other countries of the region. Most of the countries of South and Southeast Asia have established their own airlines.

AGRICULTURE

The pattern of agriculture in South and Southeast Asia shows considerable diversity. Most widespread is permanent or sedentary farming which involves the intensive cultivation of a given plot of land on a semi-subsistence basis. Shifting subsistence agriculture is practiced on a much more limited scale, chiefly in the rougher uplands, and accounts for 5 to 10 per cent of the area under cultivation in most countries. This migratory form of cultivation involves the clearing and planting of plots of land for a period of two or three years until the fertility of the soil is greatly

[10] J. E. Spencer, *Asia, East by South* (New York, 1954), p. 218.

reduced and then moving on and repeating the process in a new site. Finally, there is cash-cropping, largely for export, both by small individual farmers and large plantations.

Food crops account for roughly three-quarters of the acreage under cultivation in all South and Southeast Asia countries except Malaya and Ceylon. Of the food crops grains, chiefly rice, are of overwhelming importance. Wheat, maize, millet, and sorghum are grown in significant amounts only in India and Pakistan. Grains supplemented by potatoes, pulses, and sugar are the backbone of the native diet.

Although growing food is the principal economic activity of South and Southeast Asia, the area has experienced great difficulties since the war in expanding food output as rapidly as population. In 1953-54 *per capita* food production was 10 per cent below prewar levels, whereas in North America and Western Europe it was higher by 19 per cent and 7 per cent respectively. Before the war South and Southeast Asia had a sizable grain surplus, mostly rice. Thailand, Burma, and Indochina, Asia's rice bowl, with exports of milled rice in excess of 6 million metric tons met the import requirements of the traditional grain-deficit countries, India, Ceylon, Indonesia, and Malaya, and in addition exported more than 2 million tons outside the region. Since World War II South and Southeast Asia has been a large grain-deficit area partly as a result of the reduced availabilities of rice from the "rice bowl" countries and partly because of the increased requirements of the traditional deficit countries. In 1953 this deficit still exceeded 2.5 million metric tons. In the past few years most of the countries of South and Southeast Asia have come to recognize the serious nature of their food position, and have given increasing attention to the problem of expanding food supplies. These efforts have achieved a fair measure of success and have sharply reduced the region's grain deficit from the 1951 peak levels. The present food position of the area is however still precarious. With the population of South and Southeast Asia increasing by more than 10 million persons annually, the area cannot afford to relax its efforts to expand food output.

As mentioned elsewhere, South and Southeast Asia also produces a wide variety of tropical products, chiefly for export. For most countries, with the notable exception of Ceylon and Malaya where the ratio is much higher, the acreage given to commercial crops is about 10 to 15 per cent of the total. Approximately 90 per cent of the world's supply of natural rubber comes from South and Southeast Asia. Other products of which the area is major world supplier include vegetable oils, fibres, spices, and tea (see Table 21-6).

TABLE 21-6

South and Southeast Asia:
Selected Agricultural Exports As Percentage of World Total

COMMODITY	PERCENTAGE SHARE (1952)	PRINCIPAL EXPORTERS
Sugar	7 per cent	Philippines
Copra	75	Philippines, Indonesia, Ceylon
Groundnut oil	77	Pakistan, India
Linseed oil	22	India
Coconut oil	63	Philippines, Ceylon
Palm oil	32	Indonesia, Malaya
Castor oil	50	India
Tea	90	India, Ceylon, Indonesia
Pepper	75	India, Indonesia, Borneo
Cotton	12	Pakistan, India
Raw jute	95	Pakistan
Abaca	80	Philippines

Reference already has been made to the low productivity of agriculture in South and Southeast Asia. Yields per unit of land are considerably below other countries employing intensive agricultural methods. The production of wheat per acre in India and of rice throughout the region is barely one-third that of Japan. Cotton yields per acre in India and Pakistan are one-third to two-thirds those in the United States. Yields per worker in agriculture as compared with more developed countries are still lower.

Many factors contribute to these low yields. The use of inferior and unirrigated soils is of major importance. Other factors include the inadequate use of fertilizers, the lack of mechanical equipment, the land tenure system, overcrowding, and unscientific farm methods.

South and Southeast Asia as mentioned above is largely dependent for its water supply on the relatively brief monsoons. The amount and reliability of the monsoon rains varies widely from season to season in many areas causing wide fluctuations in crop output. Considerable precipitation is lost as a result of the rapid run-off of torrential downpours and large areas are subject to flooding. Extensive recourse has been had to irrigation and drainage projects to meet the problem of ensuring the proper amount of water at the right time. Dykes are widely employed to contain the flood flow. Much land is irrigated by artificial canals leading from dammed-up rivers. Tanks and reservoirs in the upper reaches of many rivers have been used for centuries to store water for irrigation purposes. Wells also are tapped for subsurface water. In recent years some countries, notably India, have embarked on vast multi-purpose projects of the Tennessee Valley Authority type which will provide flood control and irrigation for millions of acres as well as electric power.

In 1950 more than 81 million acres of land in South and Southeast Asia were irrigated. This represented roughly 25 per cent of the area under principal crops. Any significant increase in agricultural output in the area, particularly in India, will require a large expansion of irrigated crop lands. This fact generally has been recognized with the result that most development plans give a high priority to irrigation projects. In the first two years of the five-year development plan which was started in 1952, irrigation was extended to 2.25 million acres in India. Thailand has a major irrigation project under way at Chainat which will provide regular water supply to an area of 2.4 million acres.

The development of the Bhakra-Nangal canal irrigation system in India has been a major source of international friction between India and Pakistan.[11] On July 15, 1954, Prime Minister Mohammed Ali of Pakistan described the opening of the canal as a "potential threat to peace in the subcontinent." [12] According to Pakistani engineers the 677 mile Bhakra-Nangal irrigation system, by diverting water from the Sutlej river which flows into Pakistan, will dry up the canals which irrigate Pakistan's 5,000,000 acre granary in the Punjab Province. After long and often bitter negotiations India agreed to help Pakistan finance the development of alternative water sources in accordance with recommendations made by the International Bank for Reconstruction and Development.

Fertilizer consumption in South and Southeast Asia is extremely low. In 1951 to 1952, South and Southeast Asia with 50 times as much arable land as Japan consumed only about one-quarter as much nitrogenous fertilizer. Fertilizer plants are being constructed in a number of countries to meet the deficiency but a tremendous gap still remains to be filled.

Animal power, chiefly buffaloes, provides the main source of farm energy. Farm implements are of the most primitive types. In 1949, India and Pakistan together employed an estimated 10,000 tractors in agriculture or fewer than in Finland.

The land tenure system by weakening incentives is a serious obstacle to raising productivity in agriculture. Farm tenancy still exists on a considerable scale in many parts of the region. In 1950 over two-thirds of the farming population of India were tenant cultivators and agricultural laborers. Tenancy is a serious problem in South Vietnam and in the newly

[11] See p. 100.
[12] As reported in the *New York Times* of July 16, 1954.

settled lower Menam delta in Thailand. About 35 per cent of the farming population of the Philippines were tenants in 1950. In densely populated Central Luzon, tenancy occurs on about 88 per cent of the cultivable land. Rents are high, usually half or more of the gross produce. Tenants have little incentive to improve their farms (1) since most of the increase in output is usually siphoned off by the landlord in the form of higher rents, and (2) they often have no security of tenure. While legislation has been passed in a number of countries to reduce tenancy and correct some of its worse abuses, the governments are hampered in carrying out these measures by a lack of funds to reimburse landlords and resistance of landholders.

Most of the farming population is permanently debt-ridden. Since their land affords them only a bare hand-to-mouth subsistence, they have no reserve of capital to meet emergencies like crop failures, deaths, weddings, and so on. Loans are usually only available at exorbitant interest rates ranging, up to 100 per cent *per annum,* from landlords or moneylenders, since no satisfactory systems have been developed to provide rural credit on reasonable terms. Once a farmer falls under the grasp of a moneylender he very rarely escapes and he frequently ends up a tenant on his own land.

These are only some of the more serious features of the land tenure system in South and Southeast Asia. It is small wonder therefore that the system breeds improvidence and inefficiency. No less serious than the adverse economic effects of the land tenure system are the disruptive political effects. Inequitable land tenure systems have been important sources of agrarian unrest in a number of countries in the region, the two most outstanding examples being the Philippines and Communist Vietnam. The promise of land reform is an issue which has great appeal to the tenant who cherishes the opportunity to own his own piece of land. It is not surprising therefore that "land for the peasants" is one of the most potent propaganda weapons of the Communists in many parts of South and Southeast Asia.

FUTURE ECONOMIC PROSPECTS

The countries of South and Southeast Asia are very conscious of their depressed economic status and are making serious efforts to break with the poverty of the past. Virtually all governments have prepared blueprints outlining programs covering a period of years to accelerate their country's economic growth. All except Afghanistan are members of the

Colombo Plan,[13] created in January, 1950, to provide a framework for international co-operative effort in promoting the economic development of the region. Members outside South and Southeast Asia are Great Britain, the United States, New Zealand, Australia, Canada, and Japan. The Colombo Plan arrangement is essentially an informal one. It has no authority over individual members. Its primary purpose is to provide a vehicle for the exchange of information as to the status and progress of the national development programs in South and Southeast Asia. It also serves as a channel for aid furnished by some member countries outside the area. Thus in 1950 Australia pledged approximately £ A 31.25 million to countries of South and Southeast Asia through the Colombo Plan and Canada appropriated $133.4 million through 1955-56. Some technical assistance is exchanged by member countries under a Technical Co-operation Scheme.

The individual national economic development programs generally cover a three-to-six-year period. They are fairly modest in their objectives. They call for a gradual increase in the rate of investment, an increase in total production somewhat more rapid than the growth of population, and only very moderate increases in *per capita* consumption. In almost every case the government has been assuming a major responsibility for new investment (generally 50 per cent or more of the total). Major emphasis is on agriculture and basic services like electric power and transportation.

For some countries these development plans are still only paper plans, and little progress has been made in implementing them, largely because of unsettled internal political conditions as in Indonesia or Viet Nam. Where countries have made substantial progress, notably in India, Burma, the Philippines, and Thailand there nonetheless have been delays because of programming difficulties, shortages of qualified senior personnel, and similar problems. Lack of adequate resources to finance investment has been a major bottleneck in virtually every country. This lack of capital may well be the most intractable obstacle to sustained economic progress in the region.

The problem of inadequate resources may be less serious in the foreseeable future for Southeast Asia than for South Asia. Southeast Asia except for Indonesia is still relatively underpopulated. It produces a large food surplus and still has sizable areas of good agricultural land to be opened up. Government profits from exports of rice have provided and can continue to provide a good source of income to finance development

[13] See pp. 286-289.

projects. In South Asia, in India and Pakistan, the situation is different. The pressure of population on resources is already great and there is relatively little room for expansion. Yet population is rising at the rate of 1.5 per cent *per annum* and may increase to 2 per cent in another decade as a result of expected reduction in the death rate. Living standards are so low that it is extremely difficult to divert more resources from consumption to investment. If the goals of India's first five-year plan, ending March 1956, were to be met on schedule, savings would still only represent about 7 per cent of total production. This is only slightly more than enough to meet the needs of the expanding population. The Indian picture is by no means all dark. India possesses a stable government and an efficient and honest civil service. It is showing a strong determination to speed up its economic growth. Its mineral resources will support a substantially higher level of industrial output than at present. Agricultural productivity is low and offers substantial opportunities for improvement. The Government is one of the first to officially support programs to control population. Whether these positive factors will be sufficient to overcome the considerable obstacles to India's economic development, particularly the shortage of capital, remains to be seen.

Pakistan from its inception as an independent nation has been confronted with much greater obstacles to economic growth than India. It has had to face the serious handicap of being divided into two widely separated parts (*cf.* Fig. 2-3, p. 35). It received the smallest share of former United India's natural resources and administrative and technical skills. It had to shoulder the heavy costs of a huge refugee problem. Under the circumstances it is not surprising that Pakistan's economic progress has been slow. It is still too early to tell whether or not Pakistan can establish a solid economic base from which sustained economic growth can proceed.

Communist China, starting from a considerably lower level than India, has achieved a relatively high rate of savings and investment in a few years if its official statistics can be accepted as reliable. But Communist China is an authoritarian state with a ruthless disregard for human needs and values. The essentially democratic countries of South and Southeast Asia cannot readily impose greater sacrifices on the mass of the population without running grave political risks. But if the region fails to achieve economic growth by democratic methods, it may in desperation decide to emulate the Communist pattern. This is the danger which confronts the Free World in South and Southeast Asia.

CHAPTER 22

Latin America

Latin America's economic and strategic importance to the Free World at the present time, particularly to the United States, derives largely from its role as a major supplier of essential foodstuffs and raw materials, as well as from its location in relation to vital lines of communication, such as the Panama Canal and the Caribbean Sea. Economic relations between the United States and Latin America are a frequent source of friction. However, politically it is aligned with the West, although it is not free from or immune to Communist penetration, as the Guatemala experience showed. It makes little military contribution to the Free World system of collective security because of its limited capabilities.

Latin America's importance lies chiefly in its rapidly growing potential. Its population is growing faster than that of any other region in the world. If present demographic trends continue Latin America could have a population of 500 million within the next fifty years, or double the anticipated population of the United States and Canada.[1] Latin America is the one major underdeveloped area in the Free World which is undergoing rapid economic development and where the prospects for continued economic growth are favorable. Moreover the desire for economic improvement is one of the most powerful forces operating in Latin America today. If present trends continue, Latin America is bound to play an increasing role in world affairs by virtue of the sheer growth of its population and expanding economic capabilities.

[1] Report to the President, *United States–Latin American Relations,* Department of State Bulletin (November 23, 1953).

AREA AND POPULATION

Latin America extends for a distance of more than 6,000 miles from the Rio Grande, separating the United States and Mexico, to Cape Horn at the southern extremity of Argentina. Including the West Indies it embraces an area in excess of 8 million square miles or two and two-thirds that of the United States. Latin America's population in 1953 of approximately 172 million about equalled the combined populations of English-speaking Canada and the United States. It includes twenty republics and a number of European colonial possessions in the West Indies and the Guianas. This chapter will deal primarily with the independent countries of Latin America, since the colonies are much closer politically and economically to the old world than to the Western Hemisphere.

Latin America is thinly populated with an average density of 22 persons per square mile. With 19 per cent of the habitable land area of the world it has only about 7 per cent of the world's population. Among the major regions of the world, only Australia and Africa have a lower population density. Wide variations from this average are found from country to country and as between different regions in the same country. At one extreme is Haiti with more than 300 persons per square mile and at the other Paraguay with less than 10. (See Table 22-1.) A very few rural areas, such as the Barbados in the British West Indies, have population densities similar to those found in South and Southeast Asia. Even among the most-thickly peopled areas population density rarely exceeds 125 per square mile and usually is less. In general, Middle America (Mexico, Central America, and the Caribbean Islands) is more thickly populated than South America. For an underdeveloped region Latin America shows an unusually large concentration of population in urban centers. Five cities have populations of one million or more and thirty-nine have populations between 100,000 and one million [2] (*cf.* Fig. 6-3, p. 150).

The population of Latin America shows great racial diversity. The main components are Indians, whites, and Negroes. The absence of strong inhibitions against mixed marriages has resulted in the widespread mingling of these three groups, so that today more than half the population of Latin America is of mixed heritage, or mestizo. Only two countries, Argentina and Uruguay in the temperate zones, have predominantly white populations. Elsewhere the proportion of peoples of unmixed European ancestry is generally less than 15 per cent. Pure-blooded Indians are a

[2] P. E. James, *Latin America,* rev. ed. (New York, 1950), p. 7.

majority in Ecuador, Peru, Bolivia, Paraguay, and Guatemala. Negroes predominate on most of the Caribbean Islands. Natural factors such as climate have been important in contributing to the low proportion of whites to the total population, particularly in the tropics. Spanish and Portuguese colonial policies which favored quick exploitive returns rather than permanent settlement also had some effect.

TABLE 22-1

Latin American Republics: Area, Population and Population Density, 1953 *

COUNTRY	AREA (SQUARE MILES)	POPULATION (000)	POPULATION DENSITY (PER SQUARE MILE)
Venezuela	352,141	5,440	15.4
Colombia	439,825	12,108	27.5
Ecuador	105,510	3,924	37.2
Peru	506,189	9,035	17.9
Bolivia	416,040	3,107	7.5
Chile	286,396	6,072	21.2
Paraguay	150,516	1,496	9.9
Argentina	1,072,745	18,393	17.1
Uruguay	72,172	2,525	34.9
Brazil	3,286,169	55,772	16.9
Mexico	758,550	28,053	36.9
Guatemala	42,044	3,049	72.4
El Salvador	13,176	2,052	155.7
Nicaragua	57,144	1,166	20.4
Honduras	59,160	1,564	26.3
Costa Rica	19,238	881	45.7
Panama	28,575	864	30.2
Cuba	44,217	5,807	131.3
Dominican Republic	19,129	2,291	119.7
Haiti	10,700	3,227	301.6
Total	7,739,637	166,825	Av. 21.5

* United Nations, *Statistical Yearbook,* 1954.

Population is growing most rapidly in Middle America and tropical South America where birth rates are high and death rates are already fairly low. During 1949 to 1951 the average annual rate of population growth of mainland Middle America was 2.87 per cent. No figures are available in the same period for tropical South America but during 1940 to 1950 the average annual growth rate in this area was 2.23 per cent. Growth rates are lower, under 2 per cent *per annum,* in temperate South America where fairly low death rates are accompanied by declining birth rates. United Nations projections suggest the possibility of a Latin American population in excess of 300 million by 1980.

GEOGRAPHY AND CLIMATE [3]

Geographical factors have had important economic and political effects on Latin America's development. Latin America is part of what is loosely termed "the Western Hemisphere." [4] However, while the Panama Canal has linked the entire west coast of South America as well as its northern territories with both coasts of the United States, the southeastern shore from Cape São Roque to the Plata river region is almost as close to Europe as to the United States, and is much nearer to Africa than to either.[5] Roughly 95 per cent of South America lies east of New York City. The fact that South America juts so far out into the Atlantic has helped to promote economic, cultural, and political relations with Europe. It is only in the past quarter-century that Latin America's cultural relations with the United States have become closer than with Europe. At the same time South America's extreme southerly position has had an over-all inhibiting effect on its relations with the rest of the world because the main streams of commerce have been east and west.

Although Latin America extends from roughly 33 degrees north latitude to almost 55 degrees south latitude, approximately three-quarters of it lies in the tropics. The main reason for this is the triangular shape of South America which tapers off sharply below the tropic of Capricorn.

Latin America exhibits wide differences in topography and climate which in turn have significantly affected the pattern of economic development and settlement. Middle America, connecting the United States and South America, is predominantly mountainous with few extensive flat areas. Plains and lowlands are largely limited to narrow strips along the coasts and certain rivers. Slopes are gentler and coastal areas broader in the east than in the west so that the orientation of commerce eastward has been facilitated. The topography of Central America has been an important fact in the failure of the area to achieve greater political and economic cohesiveness. In the Caribbean, Cuba is relatively level while the Dominican Republic and Haiti have the rugged and mountainous terrain of the mainland. Northern Mexico to the tropic of Cancer is arid or semi-arid. Further south rainfall is more plentiful though still inadequate in many places. The Gulf and Caribbean coasts are wetter than the Pacific coast. No part of Cuba is deficient in moisture but semi-arid areas are found in Haiti.

[3] Based largely on P. E. James, *Latin America,* rev. ed. (New York, 1950).
[4] See p. 258.
[5] L. L. Bernis, *The Latin American Policy of the United States* (New York, 1943), Ch. 1.

While most of Middle America is close to or in the Tropical Zone, the high elevation of much of the region has a significant moderating effect on the temperature. Mexico City, 7,500 feet above the Pacific and Guatemala City 5,000 feet above it, even though in the tropics, have a climate most of the year like spring in Southern California 15 to 20 degrees to the North. With few exceptions, the highlands are the areas of greatest population density in Middle America even though low-lying but potentially richer agricultural lands are available, as in the Gulf region of Mexico. Undoubtedly the invigorating climate of the high plateau as compared with the hot unhealthy lowlands has contributed to this pattern of settlement.

South America divides from West to East into three main longitudinal zones (1) the cordilleras of the Andes, (2) the lowland belt and (3) the plateaus of Guiana and Brazil. The Andes form a high mountain belt 100 to 400 miles wide extending from the Caribbean in the North to the tip of Tierra del Fuego in the South. Over most of this distance the Andes rise close to the coast leaving only very narrow coastal plains. These mountains have been a major obstacle to the development of communications with the rest of the continent and have served to retard the west coast's economic development. The west coast has few good harbors but the opening up of the Panama Canal played a vital role in reducing its economic isolation. Arable land is limited to coastal valleys and high plateaus between the mountains.

The lowland belt, which includes the Orinoco, and Amazon river valleys, and the Chaco and Pampas plains, is almost continuous from the mouth of the Orinoco to the northern border of Patagonia. It embraces roughly half the area of South America. Much of this area has few people, particularly in the hot humid tropical latitudes. The lowland plains meet the Guiana and Venezuelan highlands in the North and the Brazilian highlands in the east. The former are remote from the coast and relatively unexplored. The latter which extends through most of the length of Brazil at an elevation of 1,000 to 3,000 feet support the bulk of the country's population and again illustrates the attraction of cooler highlands in tropical regions.

One other significant physical feature of South America is its vast river system. The Amazon, with a drainage basin of almost three million square miles, is the largest river in the world. The Orinoco to the north drains an area of possibly four hundred thousand miles. However, fluctuations in water levels, rapids or falls, and other obstacles have impaired the usefulness of these and other rivers for water transportation.

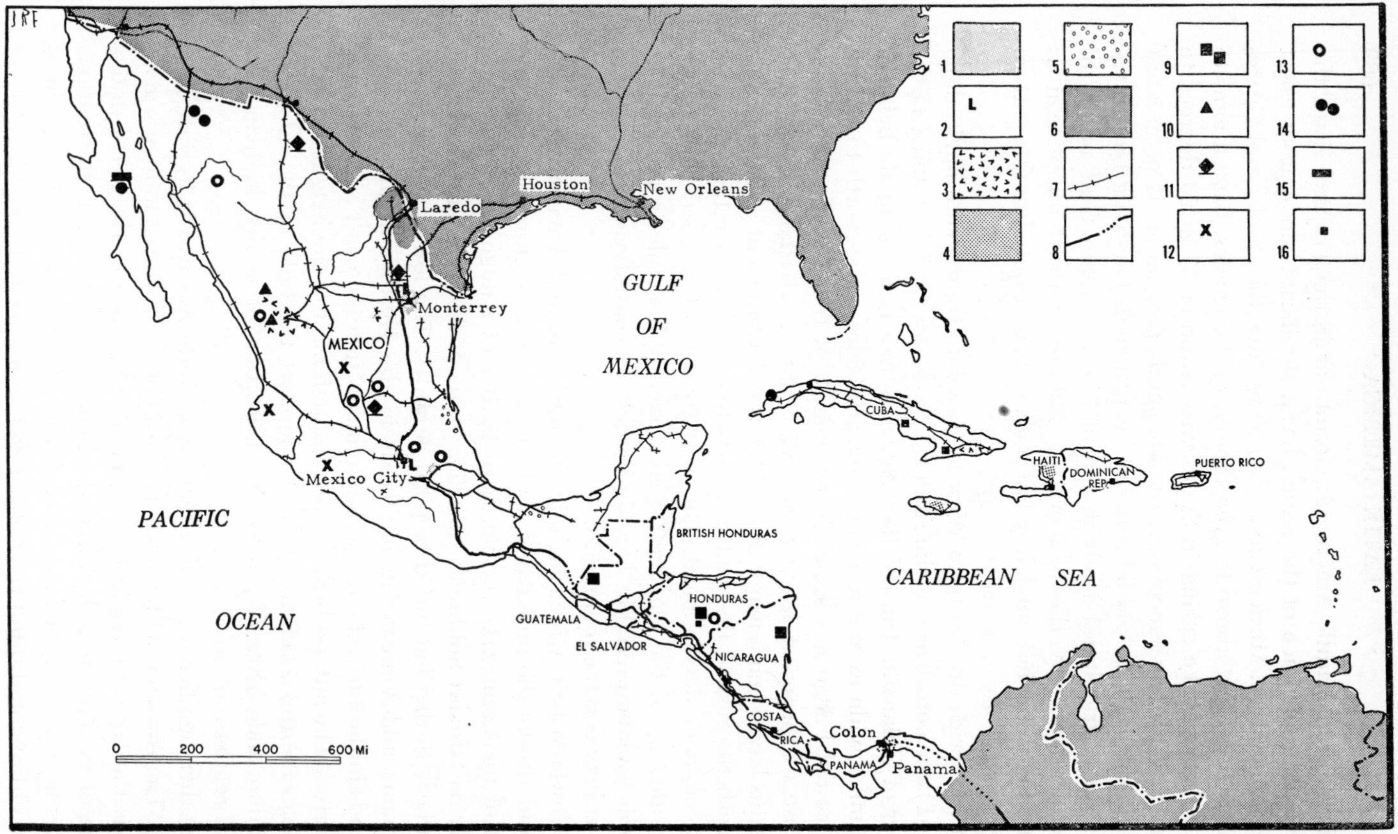

FIG. 22-1. Central America: Resources: (1) industrial areas; (2) steel mills; (3) iron ore; (4) aluminum; (5) oil; (6) coal; (7) railroad; (8) Pan-American Highway; (9) gold; (10) tin; (11) lead and zinc; (12) mercury; (13) silver; (14) copper; (15) manganese; (16) chromite.

Altitude and shape exercise important influences on the climate of South America. High altitudes as in Middle America counteract the effect of latitude in the tropical regions. Thus, on the east coast, the Brazilian highlands produce relatively cool climates for a distance of 400 to 600 miles inland in an area ranging from the Tropic of Capricorn to within ten degrees of the equator. Quito, the capital of Ecuador, though almost on the equator, with an elevation of 9,000 feet has an average monthly temperature of 54 degrees Fahrenheit. The tapering shape of South America exposes the climate of the southern part of the continent to the moderating influences of the ocean. As a result, temperatures are much less extreme both in summer and winter than for the same latitudes in North America.

Tropical South America generally has an abundance of rainfall and in some areas, like the Amazon lowlands, has an excess. Arid or semi-arid conditions obtain in Northeast Brazil and in the coastal areas of Ecuador, Peru, and the Atacama desert of Northern Chile. Central and Southern Chile have an ample supply of rainfall, while on the eastern side of the Andes, in Argentina, arid and semi-arid conditions prevail over most of the area.

RESOURCES

Latin America probably is the best-endowed of the major underdeveloped regions with respect to physical resources (Figs. 22-1, 2). Except for most of the West Indies and certain Central American countries like El Salvador, where the pressure of population on resources is acute, the area is underpopulated. Arable land *per capita* is two or three times greater than in South and Southeast Asia and exceeds most countries in Africa. Moreover, unused but potentially productive land is at least 50 per cent of the arable land area. Latin America has large reserves of many of the most important minerals required to support an industrial economy. It has vast untapped water power resources. Its major deficiency is coal. There is little doubt that Latin America's resource base will support a much larger population than at present and at rising living standards, provided the capital can be mobilized to effectively exploit these resources.

Agricultural Land. According to World Food and Agriculture Organization statistics, arable land and unused but potentially productive land represent about 5 per cent of the total area of Latin America. The number of cultivated acres is roughly 1.3 *per capita.* The cultivation of potentially productive land would raise this figure to about 2 acres *per capita.* This figure is probably on the low side, in that considerable land now classed as "permanent meadows and pastures" could be used to raise crops. Individual countries show wide variations from the average in cultivated land *per capita.* (See Table 22-2.) The best-endowed countries are Argentina, Chile, Paraguay, and Uruguay in the mid-latitudes. The humid Pampa of Argentina is one of the best-endowed meat and grain producing areas in

TABLE 22-2

Latin America: Arable and Potentially Productive Land *

COUNTRY	PERIOD	TOTAL ARABLE LAND (INCL. FALLOW AND ORCHARDS) (000 ACRES)	ARABLE LAND PER CAPITA (1953 POP.)	TOTAL UNUSED BUT POTENTIALLY PRODUCTIVE (000 ACRES)
Venezuela	1951	6,672	1.23	583
Colombia	1950	6,029[a]	0.5	...
Ecuador[b]	1949	7,413	2.16	5,752
Peru	1950	3,954	0.44	...
Bolivia	1938	845	0.3	...
Chile	1942	8,238	1.36	...
Paraguay	1947	3,830[c]	2.56	...
Argentina	1948	74,130	4.03	...
Uruguay	1951	5,046	2.0	...
Brazil	1947	46,541	0.8	72,390
Mexico	1951	37,065	1.32	22,239
Guatemala	1950	3,553	1.17	...
El Salvador	1950	1,349	0.66	...
Nicaragua	1949	1,678	1.44	7,786
Honduras	1951	2,001	1.29	...
Costa Rica	1950	872[d]	1.0	...
Panama	1951	608	0.7	...
Cuba	1946	4,868	0.84	62
Dominican Republic	1946	1,680	0.73	...
Haiti	1947	1,137	0.35	...
Total		217,509	Av. 1.30	

[a] Excludes fallow.
[b] Excludes Oriente Province.
[c] Total agricultural area.
[d] Excludes holdings of less than 0.7 acres.
* United Nations, Food, and Agricultural Organization, *Yearbook of Food and Agricultural Statistics,* 1952, Vol. 6, Part 1.

the world.[6] The possession of this rich natural resource was an important factor in the more rapid economic development of Argentina than of other parts of Latin America. While Latin America has a relatively favorable land base as compared with other underdeveloped areas, it is nowhere nearly as well-endowed with good soils as the United States. In

[6] P. E. James, "An Assessment of the Role of the Habitat as a Factor in Differential Economic Development," *American Economic Review,* Vol. 41, No. 2 (May, 1951), pp. 231-238.

the United States 23 per cent of the total land area is arable or potentially productive, while the number of acres cultivated *per capita* of population is about 4. The main reason for the substantially lower ratio of cultivable land in Latin America is the existence of vast tropical rain-forest areas like the Amazon and the Orinoco.

The Amazon Valley is almost equal in size to the United States and accounts for roughly two-fifths of all of South America. Yet it supports a population of under 4 million. Despite the variety of its still largely unexploited natural resources, it has yet to be demonstrated that the area can support a large population at satisfactory levels of living. The sparse population cannot be explained by the hot humid climate alone since regions in similar latitudes of South and Southeast Asia are among the most densely populated in the world. Approximately two-thirds of the Amazon Valley consists of rough foothills and mountains which are extremely difficult for man to penetrate. This territory virtually rings an almost flat inner basin of about one million square miles. Transportation is less of a problem in this inner area because of its vast system of interconnecting waterways. However, here the only soils suitable for intensive cultivation are the flood-plains. A study made in 1952 indicated that only 3 to 4 per cent of the inner basin is subject to inundation.[7] Lands beyond the flood-plain, despite their dense tropical vegetation, have almost no mineral nutrient reserves. When cleared and cultivated they lose their fertility in one or two years. The lands above the flood-plain therefore offer little attraction to the farmer, since they require shifting cultivation and will yield him only a bare subsistence. Their most economic use may be for raising tropical tree crops like palm oil. The trees of the forest themselves are of limited commercial value because of the absence of dense stands of single species, particularly conifers.

Of the 30,000 to 40,000 square miles of flood-plain only about 500 square miles are cultivated. This area could therefore support millions of additional population. However, it would yield them only the same meager subsistence as the rice-grower in the rich delta regions of Asia, since the farm family can cultivate only a few acres with the limited equipment at its disposal. Large-scale operations would require heavy capital investments in dykes, drainage systems, and pumps. Thus, Fairfield Osborn concludes, the Amazon Valley "might eventually accommodate forty or fifty million persons at the bare subsistence stage now prevailing."[8] An alternative might be the development of extensive plan-

[7] F. Osborn, *The Limits of the Earth* (Boston, 1953), p. 142.
[8] *Ibid.*, p. 145.

FIG. 22-2. South America: Resources: (1) coal; (2) iron ore; (3) aluminum; (4) oil; (5) railroad; (6) Pan-American Highway; (7) mercury; (8) silver; (9) copper; (10) vanadium; (11) manganese; (12) platinum; (13) tin; (14) tungsten; (15) gold; (16) lead and zinc, (17) uranium; (18) diamonds.

tation operations like the Ford Company rubber plantation established in the 1930's. The failure of the Ford project, however, suggests that the high costs of attracting the required labor may make it difficult to produce commercial crops in the area at competitive world prices.

Countries in the mid-latitudes possess the greatest possibilities for expanding agricultural output. "The permanent pastures of the Pampas might become very much more productive through the increased use of the plough and the introduction of a rotation system based on the occasional cultivation of the land and improved varieties of grass and herbage plants, especially alfalfa." [9] In the tropics there are large unused areas suitable for cattle raising. Increased crop production, however, will depend in considerable measure on more irrigation.

Minerals. (*Cf.* Fig. 22-1, 2.) Latin America has many minerals in more than adequate quantities. It has a very significant share of the Free World's reserves of such essential minerals as iron ore, copper, lead, zinc, bauxite, petroleum, tin and tungsten (see Table 22-3).

TABLE 22-3

Latin America: Share of Free World's Reserves of Selected Minerals *

MINERAL	PERCENTAGE SHARE	PRINCIPAL COUNTRIES
Iron ore (50 per cent Fe content or more)	40 per cent	Brazil, Venezuela, Chile, Mexico
Manganese (45 per cent mn or above)	10 per cent	Brazil, Cuba
Copper (contained metal)	38 per cent	Chile
Lead (contained metal)	11 per cent	Peru, Argentina, Chile
Zinc (contained metal)	9 per cent	Argentina, Peru, Mexico
Tin (contained metal)	10 per cent	Bolivia
Antimony (contained metal)	77 per cent	Bolivia, Mexico
Bauxite (contained metal)	38 per cent	West Indies, Brazil, Surinam
Tungsten (contained metal)	18 per cent	Bolivia, Brazil, Peru
Native sulphur	48 per cent	Chile, Mexico
Mercury	4 per cent	Mexico
Petroleum	12 per cent	Venezuela, Mexico, Colombia, Peru

* The President's Materials Policy Commission, *Resources For Freedom,* Vol. 11, Ch. 23 (Washington, June, 1952).

Other minerals found in Latin America include platinum, vanadium, nickel, bismuth, and fluorspar. Uranium has been found in a number of countries. Mexico and Brazil appear to be the best-endowed with mineral

[9] F. L. McDougall, "Food and Population," *International Conciliation,* No. 486, publication of the Carnegie Endowment For International Peace (New York, 1952). p. 572.

resources. In general, however, the economic significance of Latin America's mineral resources has been reduced by virtue of their distance from industrial centers, the inadequate transport system, and the shortage of power. This is especially true in the case of Brazil.

The little coal found in some countries of Latin America is generally low-grade and not suitable for coking. Countries having the greatest energy requirements such as Argentina and Brazil frequently also lack sufficient petroleum as an alternative source of power. As a result they are heavily dependent on imported fuels. Such imports have been absorbing a growing share of their limited foreign exchange earnings, thereby restricting imports of capital equipment for economic development. Brazil and Argentina are seeking to solve this problem by expanding domestic oil production. Favorable geological formations suggest the existence of large oil reserves in both countries. The development of Latin America's vast water power resources can also provide needed energy. The hydraulic resources of Brazil alone are estimated to exceed those of the United States. However, hydro-electric projects require large investments of capital. Furthermore, there is no substitute for coal in the making of blast furnace products and open hearth steel and in the manufacture of certain heavy chemicals, or for petroleum for highway transportation. Some relief from the coal problem may be provided as shipments of Latin American iron ore to the United States expand. Vessels which otherwise might proceed from the United States in ballast can carry coal at low transport costs.

ECONOMIC AND STRATEGIC IMPORTANCE

Latin America is of greater significance in the world economy than any of the other major underdeveloped regions. In 1953 it accounted for approximately 10 per cent of the total value of world trade. It is of particular importance as a trading partner of the United States. Latin America takes one-fifth of all this country's exports and supplies one-third of our imports. It thus accounts for a substantially larger share of United States trade than all of continental Western Europe and the United Kingdom. It is more important as a market for United States exports than Asia, Africa, and Oceania combined.

Latin America is a major world producer of a wide variety of industrial and agricultural commodities (see Table 22-4), most of which are shipped abroad. Many of these commodities are strategic in character; some thirty items on the United States' strategic stockpile list come from Latin America. Latin America provided 20 per cent or more of the total United

States supply (1952) of such metals as copper, lead, zinc, manganese, vanadium, beryllium, antimony, and cadmium. It furnishes various other strategic metals like tin and tungsten in lesser but important amounts. More than 55 per cent of this country's imports of crude petroleum and iron ore come from Latin America and over 90 per cent of our aluminum imports. Latin America is of particular importance to the United States as a source of essential supplies in wartime, since (1) it is less vulnerable to enemy takeover or destruction, and (2) lines of communications with Latin America are easier to maintain and protect than with other overseas areas.

TABLE 22-4

Latin American Republics:
Share of World Production of Selected Raw Materials, 1952 *

INDUSTRIAL COMMODITY	PER CENT	AGRICULTURAL COMMODITY	PER CENT
Tantalite	52.4	Henequen	98.1
Bauxite	46.2	Coffee	83.3
Beryllium	46.2	Cocoa beans	25.1
Silver	36.8	Sugar cane and beet	15.5
Bismuth	34.7	Sisal (1951)	24.3
Antimony	34.4	Flaxseed	21.4
Petroleum	18.9	Wool	15.0
Tin, mine	18.9	Cotton	12.5
Zinc, mine	16.0	Cottonseed (1951)	12.3
Fluorspar	15.1	Abaca (1951)	10.9
Tungsten	12.9	Cattle (number)	10.1
Graphite	12.7	Hogs (number)	9.8
Manganese	7.2	Corn	9.0
Molybdenum	7.4	Wheat	3.9
Mercury	5.8	Peanuts (1951)	2.3
Platinum–group metals	4.9		
Nickel	4.7		

* Foreign Operations Administration, *Report on the Economic Situation in Latin America* (Washington, D. C., August, 1954), p. 91.

Large amounts of foreign capital, particularly United States capital, are invested in Latin America. At the end of 1953, almost $7 billion, or roughly one-third of all United States private investment abroad, were in Latin America.[10] These yielded a return of roughly $1 billion annually. Despite the large investments, Latin-Americans are inclined to feel that the United States has not shown sufficient concern about their development problems. They are particularly resentful about the large amount of United States aid given Europe and Asia as compared with Latin America. They feel they are too much taken for granted. Other major

[10] United States Department of Commerce, *Survey of Current Business* (May, 1954).

investors, notably the United Kingdom and France, substantially reduced their investments in Latin America during the interwar period. British investments as of 1951 were down to about $700 million.[11]

The strategic importance of Latin America is of course not limited to its role as a supplier of essential materials. Middle America is on the doorstep of the United States. Therefore any threat to the security of the area is a direct threat to the security of this country. The Caribbean countries guard the approaches to the vital Panama Canal. Parts of Latin America can provide valuable air and naval bases to protect American lines of communication as they did in World War II. At the present time Latin America has only very limited military capabilities to contribute to the defense of the Free World. But it is an area experiencing very rapid population growth and considerable economic expansion. An area which may have as many as 500 million people by the year 2000 necessarily will play an increasingly important role in the international political arena in the coming years.

BASIC ECONOMIC CHARACTERISTICS

Probably the most significant feature of the Latin American economy has been its rapid rate of growth. Latin America is not stagnating like many other underdeveloped regions. During the decade ending in 1953 *per capita* gross national product for the region as a whole has increased at a rate of more than 2.5 per cent *per annum.* This compares with the growth of *per capita* income of 2.1 per cent *per annum* in the United States during the period 1869 to 1952. Rates of investment averaged close to 15 per cent of gross national production over the period or only slightly less than in the more highly developed areas. While certain favorable and probably nonrecurring factors contributed to this impressive record of growth, this postwar experience indicates elements of underlying strength in the Latin American economy.

Latin America is nonetheless still poor. In 1952 average *per capita* gross national product was only about $250. While this is considerably more than South and Southeast Asia's $75 per person it is far below the $2,000 for the United States. Wide variations from the average obtain from country to country (see Table 22-5). Argentina and Venezuela with per capita incomes in excess of $425 approach the lower end of the scale for industrialized countries. Five countries with incomes of less than $100

[11] Pan-American Union, *Foreign Investments In Latin America: Measures For Their Expansion* (Washington, D. C., 1954), p. 10.

per person are close to being on a par with the most impoverished underdeveloped areas. Moreover, since incomes are distributed very unequally in Latin America, most of the population has substantially lower incomes than indicated above. In addition to low incomes, Latin America portrays all the other typical characteristics of underdeveloped regions. Diets are inadequate in a number of countries, productivity is low, educational facilities are grossly inadequate, and illiteracy is widespread. The over-all death rate is roughly 50 per cent higher than in the United States, and in many countries large segments of the population suffer from endemic debilitating diseases.

TABLE 22-5

Latin America: Per Capita Gross National Product, 1952 *
(in 1950 $ U. S.)

Argentina	430	Guatemala	163
Bolivia	66	Haiti	62
Brazil	217	Honduras	149
Chile	296	Mexico	222
Colombia	215	Nicaragua	139
Costa Rica	198	Panama	362
Cuba	406	Paraguay	56
Dominican Republic	171	Peru	96
Ecuador	90	Uruguay	295
El Salvador	167	Venezuela	452

* Foreign Operations Administration, *op. cit.*, and United Nations, Department of Economic Affairs, *Economic Survey of Latin America, 1953* (New York, 1954).

Latin America is still a predominantly agricultural economy in terms of employment of the labor force. Moreover, the organization of agriculture is largely feudal in character with large estates taking up the greater part of the cultivable land throughout the region. Of a total active population in 1953 of 33.9 million, almost 60 per cent was engaged in agriculture.[12] Only Argentina has a larger labor force in industry than in agriculture. However, industry because of its greater productivity accounts for a larger share of total output than agriculture.

Almost all countries are highly dependent on proceeds from exports of a few primary products to finance necessary imports. Thus in 1952 coffee accounted for 60 per cent of the value of Brazil's exports, copper for 56 per cent of Chile's, sugar for 70 per cent of Cuba's, petroleum for 98 per cent of Venezuela's, and coffee for 54 per cent of Central America's. This high degree of specialization explains the intense interest of Latin Americans in international commodity stabilization arrangements for their

[12] United Nations, Department of Economic Affairs, *Economic Survey of Latin America, 1953* (New York, 1954), p. 23.

main exports. Intra-regional trade is small, amounting to less than 10 per cent of total trade. The principal reason is that the economies of the region are largely competing rather than complementary. An additional factor is the poor transport connections between countries.

TRANSPORTATION

Few countries in Latin America, except possibly Argentina, Chile, Uruguay and Venezuela, and parts of Brazil and Mexico, can be said to have reasonably well-developed transportation systems (*cf.* Figs. 22-1, 2). The lack of modern means of transport over most of Latin America is a serious impediment to the region's economic growth. In many parts of Latin America, such as Ecuador, "mountainous terrain cuts off rich agricultural regions from population and industrial centers . . . Better highway rail, harbor, inland waterway, and air transportation facilities will often create conditions which would make possible the development of mining, manufacturing, agricultural and other enterprises . . ." [13] While development of transport is a paramount need in Latin America, efforts to overcome this handicap are severely hampered by the heavy costs imposed by such natural obstacles as the eastern plateaus, the vast Tropical Zone, and the rugged Andes.

Although the few developed rail networks are limited to the mainland east coast and Cuba, the railways account for the bulk of the internal traffic of most Latin American countries. The rail systems of most countries are short and rarely interconnected. They frequently were constructed for the primary purpose of carrying raw materials, usually minerals, from the interior to the ports for overseas shipment. Few lines run north and south. Only in several countries do rail lines have international connections, like the trans-Andine lines between Chile and Argentina. A serious obstacle to the development of both national and international connections, in addition to the terrain, is the absence of standardized gauges. In an effort to promote Western Hemisphere railway development, the American Republics have established a Pan-American Railway Congress Association.

Highway transport has been of growing significance in recent years and in a few countries, notably Mexico, rivals the rail system in importance for the carriage of interurban freight. An important reason for the rapid growth of road transport is the low density of population in many areas. As a result the volume of traffic frequently is not sufficient to war-

[13] Department of State, *United States–Latin American Relations* (December, 1953).

rant the high costs of constructing railroads. By and large the highway system is poor. Only a small percentage of the roads have all-weather surfaces and paved highways are largely confined to urban centers and their environs. During the rainy season many roads are impassable. As with railroads, natural obstacles impede the development of highways.

Despite Latin America's excellent river system, inland water transport in most countries generally moves no more than about 10 per cent as much cargo as the railways. Inland navigation has great potentialities, however, and could become of increasing importance in the interior as South America is developed. Thus ocean-going vessels up to 7,000 tons can navigate the Amazon up to Manaus, a distance of almost 700 miles from the Atlantic, while vessels half that size can navigate to the Peruvian port of Iquitos, a distance of almost 2,000 miles. Furthermore, water transport is much cheaper than land transport. It costs less to move cargo six thousand miles by ship from Callao, Lima's port, through the Panama Canal and up the Amazon to eastern Peru, than over the 500-mile trans-Andes highway from Lima to Pucallpa on the Ucayali river.[14]

Most traffic between Latin American countries is moved by coastal shipping. Some countries, chiefly Argentina and Brazil, have sizable coastal fleets. In addition, the twenty Latin American Republics in 1952 had more than 9 million dead-weight tons of ocean-going vessels of 1,000 tons or more. Of this amount, however, approximately 6 million tons were Panamanian and Honduran vessels owned by United States interests. If these are excluded Latin America's ocean-going fleet is about 3 per cent of the world total. It accounts for only a small percentage of Latin America's total overseas trade. Two countries, Paraguay and Bolivia, are landlocked. In the case of Paraguay, all its exports and imports must pass through Argentina. As a result, Paraguay has been under continual pressure from Argentina.[15]

INDUSTRIAL DEVELOPMENT

Manufacturing has expanded much more rapidly in Latin America since the war than other economic activities. Between 1945 and 1952, manufacturing output including construction increased at the rate of 6.9 per cent per year as compared with 2.7 per cent for agriculture and 4.8 per cent for total production. In 1952, manufactures and construction accounted for roughly 28 per cent of total production as compared with

[14] Osborn, *op. cit.*, p. 126.
[15] See also p. 197.

less than 24 per cent for agriculture. However, manufactures exceeded agricultural output in only three countries, Argentina, Chile, and Mexico (see Table 22-6). These countries together with Brazil, Colombia, and Venezuela account for 90 per cent of Latin America's industrial output.

TABLE 22-6

Latin America: Relative Importance of Manufactures in Selected Countries, 1952 *

AREA	MANUFACTURING AND CONSTRUCTION (PER CENT OF TOTAL OUTPUT)	AGRICULTURE (PER CENT OF TOTAL OUTPUT)	OTHER ACTIVITIES (PER CENT OF TOTAL OUTPUT)
Latin America	27.9	23.6	51.5
Argentina	34.3	29.0	36.7
Chile	24.7	15.7	59.6
Mexico	20.3	18.2	61.5

* United Nations, *Economic Survey of Latin America, 1951-52.*

A number of countries, notably Bolivia, the Caribbean and Central American Republics, and Panama and Paraguay have experienced relatively limited industrial development. In part at least their problem has been the small size of the domestic market. This has led the governments of Central America to study the possibilities of developing new activities based on an integrated regional market. A meeting of the Ministers of Economy held at Tegucigalpa in August 1952, agreed on the principles involved in reciprocity and singled out potential industries where these principles could be applied.[16] Thus far, however, no real progress has been made toward the goal of regionalization of industry. Industrialization probably has gone further in Argentina than anywhere else in Latin America despite that country's deficient mineral and power base. Whereas private enterprise predominates in Latin America, the governments of many countries are a major source of investment funds. Thus at the present time roughly half of all new capital expenditures in Argentina, Venezuela, and Mexico are made by the Federal Government.

As in other underdeveloped regions, industrial output consists in large part of consumer goods for the domestic market, although the processing of foodstuffs and the refining of copper, lead, and zinc for export are of some importance. Capital goods industries do not account for more than 15 per cent of Latin America's industrial output. However, Latin America

[16] Economic Commission for Latin America, Committee of Ministers of Economy on Economic Co-operation in Central America, *Report of the First Sessions.*

has a sizable and growing steel industry. In 1954, Brazil, Chile, and Mexico had a combined output of crude steel in excess of 2.0 million metric tons. New mills were about to be opened in Colombia, Argentina, and Peru. Argentina's San Nicolás steel mill on the Paraná River will have a steel ingot capacity of 588,000 metric tons. Argentina, Mexico, and Brazil have mechanical transforming industries of considerable importance, producing machinery, motors, railway rolling stock, home appliances, and other products, while Mexico and Brazil also have motor vehicle assembly plants. The production of construction materials, particularly cement, lime, and wood, is important in a number of countries. Progress also has been made toward establishing a basic chemical industry.

Latin America's industrial development has been hampered by the lack of basic services, particularly electric power and, as described elsewhere, transport. Electric power is frequently so short that in some countries it has had to be rationed. These deficiencies have prevented the establishment of new enterprises and impeded the efficient operation of existing ones. Private capital has contributed little to meeting the shortage in basic services because of the investment habits of local capitalists. Much of Latin America's new investment goes into fields like speculative commercial ventures and luxury urban construction which contribute relatively little to development. Consequently a good deal of the responsibility for providing these services has been assumed by the governments. However, the amounts of capital required are large and commonly exceed the resources of the governments.

AGRICULTURE

With the exception of the few countries noted above, agriculture is the principal economic activity in Latin America. Although not land-poor like Southeast Asia, Latin America nonetheless has a major land tenancy problem. In the Caribbean and South America, the large estate dominates the agrarian structure. The large estate is characteristic of all countries except parts of Costa Rica, El Salvador, Haiti, and Mexico. For Latin America as a whole, individual landholdings in excess of 15,000 acres account for about 50 per cent of all agricultural land.[17] In Argentina 85 per cent of the privately owned land is in estates larger than 1,250 acres while 80 per cent of the farm population own no land. Plantations are important in some regions, chiefly in Central America and the Caribbean but do not

[17] United Nations, *Land Reform: Defects in Agrarian Structures as Obstacles to Economic Development* (New York, 1951).

dominate the economy as a whole. The bulk of the rural population of Latin America consists of small tenants, landless laborers, and small landowners of subsistence farms with very low living standards. In many countries the relationship between the tenant and the landlord is feudal in character. In return for the right to cultivate a small piece of land the tenant devotes a specified number of days' labor per week on the estate. As in Southeast Asia, the large estate, except for the plantation which practices intensive cultivation, is a serious drag on productive efficiency. Moreover, large estates devoted to grazing result in serious under-utilization of land. Countries like Colombia and Venezuela, which have ample land resources to be self-sufficient in foodstuffs if more intensive cultivation was practiced, have to import food to feed their populations. "The pattern of land utilization is . . . the reverse of what market conditions and natural resources require. The hillside land, which is best suited for pasture and woodland, is intensively cultivated for subsistence crops by hoe culture which destroys the top soil, while the valley floors, more suited for arable cultivation are used for grazing." [18] Thus . . . "the combination of very extensive agriculture and a high degree of concentration of ownership prevents a fuller utilization of land resources and an expansion of food production for local needs, and it depresses the living standard of the majority of the farm population." [19]

In addition to its adverse economic effects, the system of land tenure in Latin America as in other underdeveloped areas is a serious source of social tension. It is considered the most fundamental issue in the social, economic, and political life of Ecuador, Peru, and Bolivia. Political opportunists periodically exploit the land problem in order to enlist broader peasant support for their policies. The most recent example was the expropriation of large estates and the distribution of land, albeit limited, to the peasants by the Communist-dominated Arbenz Government in Guatemala prior to its overthrow in June 1954. Where extensive foreign ownership of plantations exists, as in Guatemala and other parts of Central America and the Caribbean, the tensions created by the land tenure problem are frequently heightened. In the West Indies, the plantation economy has created "strikes, riots, the burning of canes, and in some colonies even an uncertainty from year to year whether the state of labour relations will permit the whole crop to be taken off." [20]

Only two countries in Latin America have instituted broad agrarian

[18] *Ibid.*, p. 20.
[19] *Ibid.*, p. 49.
[20] W. A. Lewis, *Issues in Land Settlement Policy*, a report to the Caribbean Commission West Indian Conference, 1950.

reform programs, Mexico as early as 1915 and Bolivia in August 1953. Reform measures periodically have been introduced in a number of other countries but nothing much has come of them to date. The major obstacle is of course the resistance of the powerful landholders. This problem was described by the Government of Chile in response to a United Nations questionnaire on land reform as follows: [21]

> Owing to the economic and political structure of the country, land reform in Chile is difficult to carry out. Land holders who would be affected by any action of an economic, political, administrative, legal or social nature will vigorously oppose its implementation, and their political and economic influence is very powerful. In spite of this, the necessary conditions are being created in Chile to initiate a land reform policy, which will have to be introduced gradually, in other words, with due safeguards but with determination.

While modern methods of cultivation are being rapidly introduced in a number of Latin American countries, the techniques of the peasant farmer are still primitive. His principal tools are the hoe and the machete. The use of fertilizers is quite limited. Thus far the employment of modern equipment, scientific techniques, and the use of fertilizers is largely confined to the large plantations and estates.

Before the war, the growing of food and agricultural raw materials for export was almost as important as for domestic consumption. For the period 1934 to 1938 agricultural exports averaged roughly 45 per cent of total agricultural output.[22] Growing local requirements resulting from the expansion of population, rising incomes, and general economic development have radically changed this relationship. In 1953, agricultural exports represented only about one-third of total production. While the volume of Latin America's agricultural output in 1953 was approximately one-third higher than before the war, virtually all of this increase was retained at home.

Despite the growth of agricultural output, production has not been satisfactory in relation to the growth of population. On a *per capita* basis total agricultural production and food production in 1953-54 were still below prewar. This lag in agricultural production has resulted in considerable measure from the preoccupation of most Latin American governments in the postwar years with programs to speed up their industrialization. Ill-considered government policies were adopted which favored industry at the expense of the agricultural sector of the economy. Only in the past year or two, with population increasing at a rapid rate, has

[21] United Nations, *Progress in Land Reform* (New York, 1954), p. 43.
[22] United Nations, *Economic Survey of Latin America, 1953*, p. 135.

it been recognized that agriculture is no less important than industry for Latin America's economic development. A number of countries, notably Argentina, Chile, Mexico, and Brazil, are now actively attempting to stimulate agricultural output by means of various incentives and aids to farmers. These policies are already beginning to bear fruit.

Table 22-7 gives the production of the principal agricultural crops cultivated in Latin America and the importance of these crops in world trade. Latin America is a dominant area in the exports of tropical products like sugar, coffee, bananas. It is an important supplier of meat, cacao, cotton, and wool. Exports of grains are much less important than before the war, in large part because of reduced output and export availabilities from Argentina.

TABLE 22-7

Latin America: Production and Exports of Agricultural Production

COMMODITY	PRODUCTION[a] (MILLION METRIC TONS) 1948-50 (AV.)	1952-53 (PROV.)	EXPORTS AS PER CENT[b] OF WORLD TOTAL 1952
Bread grains	8.6	10.8	3.6 (1952-53)
Maize	14.6	17.7	15.4 (1952-53)
Potatoes	4.8	5.0	neg
Cassava	15.5	15.9	neg
Sugar (raw equivalent)	12.2	12.4	63
Bananas	6.5	7.5	79
Cacao	0.26	0.24	23
Coffee	1.85	1.98	82 (1952-53)
Cotton	0.79	1.08	17
Hard fibers	0.25	0.24	22
Wool (clean basis)	0.18	0.20	15
Meat	5.69	5.54	33

[a] United Nations, FAO, *The State of Food and Agriculture*, 1953, Part 2 (January, 1954), p. 71.
[b] United Nations, FAO, *Yearbook of Food and Agricultural Statistics*, 1953, Vol. 7, Part 2.

FUTURE ECONOMIC PROSPECTS

Latin America's long-term economic development prospects appear to be much more favorable than for most other underdeveloped regions. Except for the lack of coal the region has a relatively rich resource base both in agricultural land and minerals. Although the population is increasing rapidly, the region as a whole is underpopulated, so that greater numbers should contribute to increasing returns in productive activities. Moreover, the area already has demonstrated a substantial capacity for rapid economic growth over the past decade or more. In the process many of the traditional social and institutional obstacles to economic development have been broken down. The stage of Latin America's economic growth and development has been likened in many respects to that of the United States during the latter half of the nineteenth century.[23]

Nonetheless, the area faces many difficult economic problems. There is the need to maintain a proper balance between industrial development and the production of primary products. As described above, a number of Latin American countries in their haste to industrialize have tended to neglect the production of agricultural products and minerals. Since these products are the primary source of export earnings needed to finance imports of capital equipment, the result has frequently been to delay rather than speed up economic development. In some cases countries which could readily feed themselves have been sizable food-deficit areas. This same sense of urgency has commonly led governments to embark on projects beyond their financial capabilities. Frequently this has caused widespread inflation, thereby inhibiting productive investment and creating friction between employers and wage earners. Many uneconomic industries have been fostered by excessive protection and subsidies. More investment is required in basic services like transport, communications, and power. This calls for a change in the attitude of investors who now favor speculative ventures with high quick returns. Managerial skills are short in many fields. Most importantly, the level of investment needs to be raised. While savings and investment have been relatively high in Latin America as compared with other underdeveloped regions, they have been inadequate to the task at hand. Raising the rate of investment in the absence of large infusions of capital from abroad will be a slow process, however, given the present low level of incomes. Yet many Latin American countries, obsessed with fear of foreign exploitation, pursue economic policies which operate to keep out much needed capital from abroad.

For the foreseeable future it appears unlikely, even if the above problems can be met, that *per capita* gross national product will increase at a faster rate than the 2.5 per cent of the past decade or so. This would raise *per capita* gross national product to about $500 in 28 years, which is within 15 per cent of the present-day average *per capita* gross national product of Western Europe. With a prospective population at that time of more than 300 million people, Latin America could thus be an area of considerable economic capabilities.

Clearly the extent and the pattern of Latin America's economic development is likely to vary widely from country to country. Certain Cen-

[23] Foreign Operation Administration, *Report on The Economic Situation in Latin America* (Washington, D. C., August, 1954), p. 5.

tral American countries and most of the West Indies with their limited resources and dense populations are likely to advance less rapidly than the average. The rich agricultural resources of the southern republics of Latin America, and their lack of iron ore and coal, suggests that this area will not achieve the degree of industrial specialization of Western Europe.[24] Tropical Latin America, particularly Brazil and Venezuela, also lacking in coal, has vast iron ore reserves and a tremendous water power potential. Its resource base, therefore, offers greater possibilities for the development of industry than the rest of the region. Climatic factors, lack of skilled labor, and the high cost of capital, however, may well delay this development until some time in the more distant future. In the meantime tropical agriculture and mining are likely to be of continuing importance.

[24] A. J. Brown, *Industrialization and Trade,* pamphlet published by The Royal Institute of International Affairs (London, September, 1943), p. 23.

CHAPTER 23

Africa: The Last Stand of Colonialism

Africa is the last of the large colonial areas, with roughly 70 per cent of its territory under some form of foreign control. However, this vast continent is showing increasing signs of restiveness under foreign tutelage. "Africa is headed for great political changes. The trend of events is inexorably toward an adjustment in relations between the native population and its European rulers." [1] Violent disorders already have broken out since World War II in a number of territories, particularly in French North Africa and British East Africa. Growing local disturbances in Algeria have developed because of dissatisfaction with the speed of French political and economic reforms. In British East Africa, resort to violence is largely a result of native frustration over policies of white supremacy. So far, Belgian and French colonies south of the Sahara have been spared these difficulties as a result of their paternalistic economic policies and the absence of color discrimination. In some areas local aspirations for greater freedom have been met by substantial political concessions, as in the Gold Coast, Nigeria, and the Anglo-Egyptian Sudan. Whether the necessary concessions will be made elsewhere in time to avoid widespread political and social disturbances remains to be seen. Such a development clearly would be damaging to the strength of the Free World because of the importance of a politically stable and friendly Africa as a source of many strategic materials, as a safeguard to

[1] C. W. de Kiewiet, "African Dilemmas," *Foreign Affairs* (April, 1955), pp. 444-457.

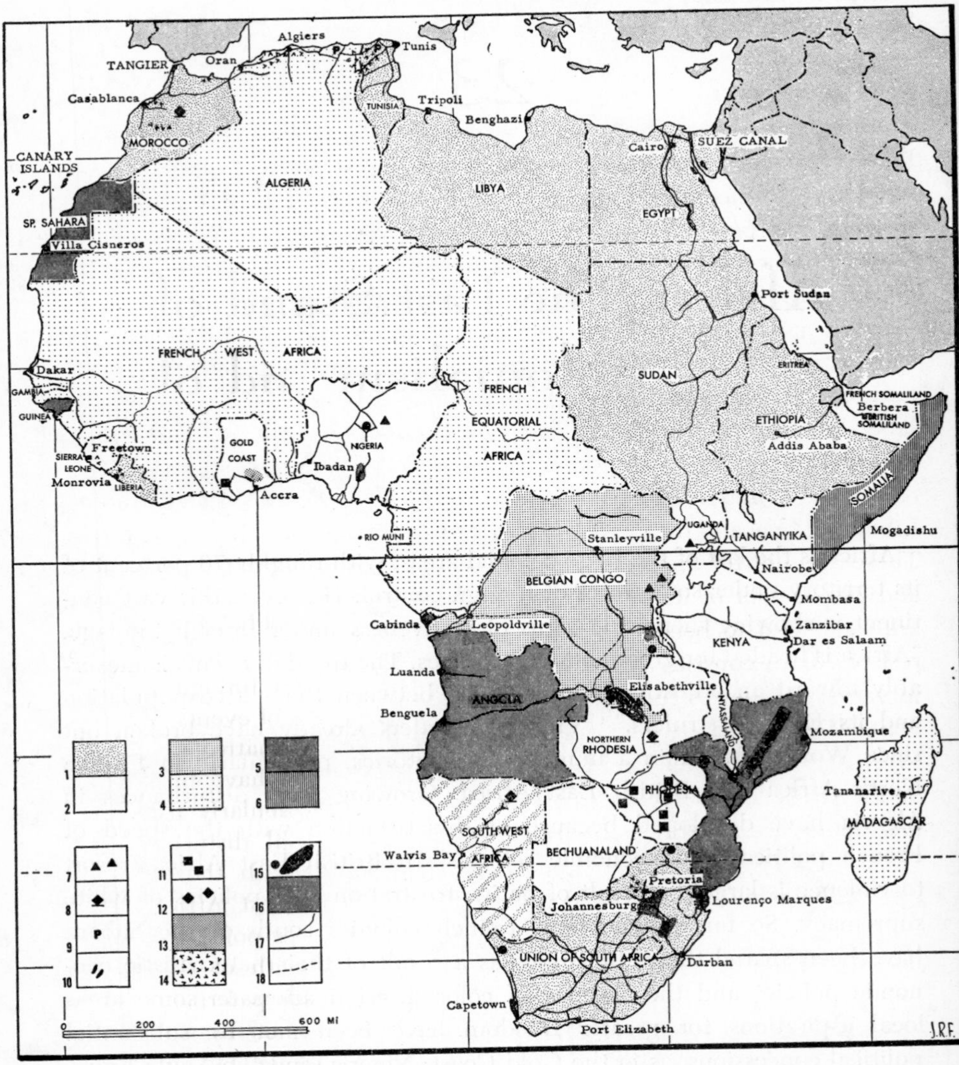

FIG. 23-1. Resources, Railroads and Political Structure of Africa: (1) independent; (2) British colonies; (3) Belgium colonies; (4) French colonies; (5) Portuguese colonies; (6) Italian mandate; (7) tin; (8) lead and zinc; (9) phosphate; (10) petroleum; (11) gold; (12) diamonds; (13) aluminum; (14) iron ore; (15) copper; (16) coal; (17) railroads; (18) proposed railroads.

the security of Allied naval and air bases on the continent, and as a protection for key lines of communication in time of war.

AREA AND POPULATION

Africa, with an area of 11.7 million square miles, is exceeded in size only by Asia (including Asiatic U.S.S.R.). Its distance north to south is 5,000 miles and its maximum breadth is 4,600 miles. Although Africa embraces more than 20 per cent of the surface of the earth, its estimated population of 212 million (1953) is less than 9 per cent of the world total. Average population density is slightly more than 18 persons per square mile. Only Oceania among the continental areas is more thinly populated. The sparseness of Africa's population has been a serious hindrance to the area's economic growth, leading to the prevailing wasteful system of migrant labor, limiting the development of the domestic market, and frustrating the construction of an economic transport and communications system.

Only six countries in Africa (Figure 23-1)—Egypt, the Sudan, Ethiopia, Liberia, Libya, and the Union of South Africa—are politically independent. These account for approximately 26 per cent of the continent's total area and 29 per cent of its population. Tunisia, Morocco and the Gold Coast are scheduled to become completely independent in 1956 or 1957. The rest of Africa consists of non-self-governing territories and dependencies in varying stages of transition toward self-government which, except for South-West Africa are under the jurisdiction of European countries. South-West Africa, a former mandated territory, is controlled by the Union of South Africa. The percentages of African territory controlled by European metropoles are roughly as follows:

COUNTRY	PERCENTAGE OF ALL AFRICA
France	37[a]
United Kingdom	28[b]
Belgium	8
Portugal	7
Italy	2
Spain	1

[a] Including Tunisia and Morocco.
[b] Including the Gold Coast.

The borders separating individual African territories are almost wholly artificial in the sense that they show little or no relationship to ethnic or geographic factors. Boundaries cut through tribes and separate natural geographic regions. The extent and configuration of most African territories largely reflect the success of the respective European metropoles in carving out their claims. As one writer has aptly pointed out, African "boundaries of territories were, and are, no more than the result of conference and negotiation by statesmen in Europe, by whom, 40 and 50 years ago, African human geography was unknown and economics little understood. Frontiers were drawn with a ruler on a blank map, or by give and take about the unknown, in Western foreign ministries . . ." [2]

Despite its predominantly colonial status, Africa has been of minor importance as an outlet for European immigration. Climate and closely related health problems have been the main obstacles to European settlement, but modern technology and new developments in public health could overcome these drawbacks. Persons of European descent living in Africa number only about 5.5 million, or less than 3 per cent of the total population. Most of these live in the more temperate and disease-free regions of the continent. Approximately 3 million are to be found in the Union of South Africa, less than 2 million in Mediterranean Africa. The balance is located chiefly in East and Central Africa, attracted by the relatively favorable climate and the presence of considerable mineral wealth. In addition, Africa south of the Sahara has an important non-African minority of Syrians, Lebanese, and Indians and Pakistani. This group is engaged largely in commerce and is a target of considerable native antipathy.

Population density varies widely from country to country (see Table 23-1) and is strongly influenced by geographic factors. In interpreting the low average densities it must be recognized that many parts of Africa are virtually uninhabitable. Thus Egypt is more than 95 per cent desert and in terms of productive land has a density in excess of 2,000 per square mile. However, few areas of Africa are overpopulated in the sense that there is a continuous supply of surplus labor. Except for Egypt and mining centers in Southern and South-Central Africa, there is a close correlation between population and mean average rainfall.[3] Tropical Africa shows much greater population density than comparable areas of South America. Gourou suggests that differences in the accessibility of the two continents may account for these variations; the greater navigability of the Amazon as compared with the Congo made it easier for Europeans to penetrate the Amazon valley and to inflict damage on the native population by spreading disease, by slave hunts, and by instituting

[2] C. G. Haines (ed.), *Africa Today* (Baltimore, 1955), p. 20.
[3] W. Fitzgerald, *Africa*, 4th ed. (New York, 1942), p. 108.

serfdom.[4] Unlike Latin America, Africa has few urban concentrations of population.

TABLE 23-1

Africa: Area, Population and Population Density of Principal Countries

COUNTRY	AREA[a] (000 SQ. MI.)	POPULATION 1953[b] (000)	POPULATION DENSITY (PER SQ. MI.)
Algeria	846.1	9,367	11.0
Sudan	967.5	8,820	9.1
Belgian Congo	905.0	12,154	13.4
Egypt	386.0	21,935	57.0
Ethiopia	409.3	15,000 (1951)	36.7
French Equatorial Africa	969.1	4,492 (1952)	4.6
French West Africa	1,835.0	17,435 (1952)	9.5
Gold Coast	78.8	4,062	51.5
Kenya	225.0	5,851	26.0
Liberia	43.0	1,648 (1949)	38.3
Libya	706.6	1,500	21.2
Madagascar	227.7	4,464	19.6
Morocco	150.2	8,220	54.7
Mozambique	297.7	5,895	19.8
Nigeria	338.6	30,000	88.6
Northern Rhodesia	290.3	2,020	6.9
Southern Rhodesia	150.3	2,260	15.0
Tanganyika	362.4	8,069	22.3
Tunisia	60.2	3,630	60.3
Uganda	94.0	5,343	56.9
Union of South Africa	472.7	13,153	27.8
Other	1,880.6	27,379	14.5
Total	11,696	212,697	Av. 18.2

[a] United Nations, *Statistical Yearbook,* 1952.
[b] United Nations, *Population and Vital Statistics Reports* (New York, October, 1954).

Three distinct demographic regions may be identified in Africa. Northern or Mediterranean Africa is characterized by high birth rates and declining though still high death rates. Recent rates of population increase in this region have been estimated by the United Nations at 1.56 per cent *per annum* and may reach a "medium" rate of 1.86 per cent by 1980 as death rates continue to fall.[5] Middle or intertropical Africa is characterized by both high birth and death rates. Satisfactory estimates of population growth in this area are limited by the poverty of information. The United Nations considers one per cent as a "medium" figure for the present rate of population growth, with an upper limit of 1.5 per cent and a lower limit of 0.5 per cent. In the absence of more definite mortality

[4] P. Gourou, *The Tropical World* (London, 1952), p. 125.
[5] United Nations, *Framework For Future Population Estimates, 1950-1980, By Regions* (1954).

trends, it was estimated that growth rates over the next twenty-five years in this area would continue about as at present. The third demographic area is Southern Africa, with high birth rates and fairly low death rates. Here the current rate of population increase is estimated at 2.15 per cent *per annum* with a projected "medium" rate of 2.32 per cent by 1980. The total population of Africa is projected at roughly 300 million by 1980.

GEOGRAPHY AND CLIMATE

Geographic factors probably have had a more significant effect on Africa's general development than on that of any other continent. The continent's forbidding physical characteristics go a long way toward explaining the late opening up of the area south of the Mediterranean littoral.[6] The hot humid interior is infested with virulent tropical diseases. The coast has few good harbors and the rivers do not provide easy access to the interior because of water falls and rapids near the coast. Only the Congo has a deep water estuary. Extremely rugged topography impedes travel north and south. It is not surprising, therefore, that Africa's real contact with the outside world, except in the climatically more favorable extreme north and south, did not begin until the closing decades of the nineteenth century.

Africa is the most tropical of all continents, with almost four-fifths of its total area lying in the tropics. It is bisected by the equator and has roughly the same climate zones in the north and south. Most of Africa is a plateau with elevations of from 1,000 to 4,000 feet, flanked by mountain chains in the extreme northwest and on the southern margins of the Cape. Elevations are highest south of the equator, particularly in the east, making for more temperate climatic conditions than in the north. The plateau's edge is close to the seaboard so that Africa has very narrow coastal plains. The shore line lacks indentations and except in the Mediterranean there are few natural harbors. Ocean depths descend abruptly save off the Mediterranean and extreme southern coasts. As a result there is a lack of feeding grounds for fish, and fishing plays a negligible role in the life of the people.

Four major climate zones may be distinguished. The first is the area approximately 5 degrees north and 5 degrees south of the equator which is hot, humid, and has rain throughout the year. This region, which extends for a distance of 400 miles on each side of the equator, is covered by a dense tropical rain forest. The next zone, extending roughly from 5

[6] Lord, Hailey, *An African Survey*, 2nd ed. (New York, 1945).

degrees to 15 degrees north and south of the equator, is also hot and humid but receives all of its precipitation in the summer. This area, which is 600 to 800 miles wide on each side of the Equatorial Zone, is the tropical grassland or park-savanna region. The vegetation consists primarily of scrub forest and coarse grass 5 to 12 feet high. Ocean currents and mountains modify the characteristic climate of these two zones. Kenya, Tankanyika, Uganda, Nyasaland, and Mozambique in East Africa have quite equable climates except in the low-lying coastal regions. Elevations of more than 4,000 feet produce climates not unlike the Andean plateau of Colombia. At Nairobi, which is almost on the equator but has an elevation of 5,500 feet, the highest average monthly temperature is 66 degrees and the lowest 58 degrees. These are the only regions in tropical Africa which have attracted European settlers in any numbers, giving rise to serious conflicts of interest between the whites and the natives.

The third zone is the hot desert which extends between 15 degrees and 30 degrees north and south of the equator. Temperatures are high throughout the year and there is virtually no precipitation. North of the equator this zone includes the Sahara desert which extends from the Atlantic Coast to the Red Sea and has an average width of 800 miles. The Sahara has an area almost equal that of the United States and except for occasional oases is only suitable for nomadic herdsmen. The Sahara has been a major barrier to the spread of ancient Mediterranean cultures to the south, and has been an important factor in Middle Africa's backwardness. South of the equator, desert conditions are repeated only in South-West Africa. The southeast trade winds bring rain, precipitated by the South African plateau, to the eastern part of the subcontinent.

The fourth zone covers the area beyond 30 degrees north and south of the equator and includes the Mediterranean littoral of Morocco, Algeria, and Tunisia in the north and the southwestern corner of the Union of South Africa. Here the climate is typically Mediterranean, not African, with mild rainy winters and hot dry summers. The Atlas range in the northwest precipitates moisture from winds blowing from Europe and the Atlantic, thereby making the land between the mountains and the sea habitable. East of Tunisia, in the absence of such mountains, the sea and the desert come together for most of the 800 miles of Libya's coastline. Here again the desert has presented a significant obstacle to direct cultural exchange between Egypt and the French North African littoral. As pointed out in the United Nations *World Economic Report 1949-50*, "North Africa, bordering on the Mediterranean, and separated from the rest of Africa by the vast wastes of the Sahara desert, is by history and geography closely associated with southern Europe, of which in an economic sense much of it forms an integral part." Although a part of Africa geographically, South Africa is cut off from the rest of the continent by the formidable barriers of the Karoo desert and the southern mountain ranges.

RESOURCES

Widely divergent views prevail as to Africa's economic potential. In part at least these differences stem from the fact that the area's resources have been only partially assessed. On the basis of presently available information it would appear that Africa is by no means "a promised land." Like most predominantly tropical regions, Africa's resource base is seriously deficient in many important respects. Soils are much poorer in essential minerals and humus than in temperate regions. They erode rapidly and decline in fertility under constant cropping. Desert and poor scrub land cover nearly one-third of the continent and the desert is slowly spreading south. Africa is less healthy than regions in the temperate belt. Much of Africa's vast tropical forest area contains species of little or no worth. Although a major world source of many important minerals such as copper, gold, manganese, and uranium, Africa is deficient in coal, iron ore, and petroleum. It does, however, have a vast untapped water power potential, which has given rise to a number of ambitious plans for hydroelectric power development. One of these, which the Central African Federation has decided to undertake, would involve the damming of the Zambesi River at Kariba gorge and would be larger than Boulder Dam. Cheap power and industrialization offer one solution of the pressure of the increasing native population on the land.

Agricultural Land. According to statistics compiled by the Food and Agriculture Organization, Africa, with approximately 7 per cent of its total area classified as arable land, has the lowest ratio of cultivable land of all continental regions except Oceania. Nonetheless arable land (including fallow and orchards) in relation to population appears to be considerable, averaging 2.8 acres *per capita* for the continent as a whole (see Table 23-2). There are of course a number of countries with substantially less than this average, the most outstanding being Egypt with less than one-third of an acre *per capita*. The population is also pressing on the land in French North Africa and Kenya. The high average figure is generally misleading on other grounds. Water supply is inadequate or unreliable in many areas. Furthermore, a considerable proportion of the arable land continually lies fallow in tropical Africa. Since tropical soils rapidly lose their fertility under constant cropping, shifting cultivation as in the uplands of Southeast Asia is the traditional method of native farming. A piece of ground will be planted for only a few years, and as its fertility is exhausted it will be abandoned and permitted to relapse into forest or savanna. After the lapse of a certain number of years the fertility of the exhausted land is at least partly restored and it is cleared and used again.

TABLE 23-2

Africa: Arable and Potentially Productive Land in Selected Areas *

COUNTRY	PERIOD	TOTAL ARABLE LAND (INCL. FALLOW AND ORCHARDS) (000 ACRES)	ARABLE LAND PER CAPITA (1953 POPULATION)	TOTAL UNUSED BUT POTENTIALLY PRODUCTIVE (000 ACRES)
Algeria	1951	15,686	1.7	. . .
Sudan	1951	5,888	0.7	. . .
Belgian Congo	1951	121,079	10.0	. . .
Egypt	1951	6,056	0.3	1,633
Ethiopia	1951	27,181	1.8	19,768
French Equatorial Africa	1950	74,130	16.5	. . .
French West Africa	1950	24,710	1.4	
Gold Coast	1951	13,121	3.2	
Kenya	1948	3,954	0.7	
Liberia	1948	4.480	2.7	6,721
Madagascar	1947	12,355	2.8	618
Morocco	1950	19,609	2.4	18,557[a]
Mozambique	1948	4,942	0.8	
Southern Rhodesia	1951	3,825	1.7	
Tanganyika	1948	7,413	0.9	
Tunisia	1951	9,496	2.6	
Union of South Africa	1951	19,028	1.4	
ALL AFRICA		600,453	Av. 2.8	

[a] Includes rough grazings.
* United Nations, Food and Agriculture Organization, *Yearbook of Food and Agricultural Statistics*, 1952, Vol. 6, Part 1.

This shifting system of agriculture requires many more acres to support a family than under a permanent system where a single plot can be cultivated continuously. According to Stamp, the practice of shifting cultivation in Nigeria should allow seven years of fallow for each year of cultivation. This would mean that the average family of 3.6 persons cultivating an average plot of 2 acres needs 16 acres of land to support itself.[7]

A few countries like Ethiopia have rich and fairly accessible lands available for exploitation. In general, however, under existing agricultural techniques arable land *per capita* in Africa is not plentiful. On the con-

[7] L. D. Stamp, "Land Utilization and Soil Erosion in Nigeria," *Geographical Review* (1938), p. 35.

trary, with the expansion of population the supply of arable land over much of the continent is becoming increasingly inadequate, and many areas are experiencing growing difficulties in satisfying their food requirements. A considerable area of Africa is more suitable for pastoral than for crop-raising pursuits. However, large regions in the park-savanna country are infested with the tsetse-fly and cannot be used for livestock raising until immunization against sleeping sickness is developed. Then Africa south of the Sahara could become one of the major grazing areas of the world.[8]

Forest Resources. Forests cover 25 per cent of the total area of Africa and exceed those of Latin America in extent. However, Africa does not compare with Latin America as a storehouse of tropical timber since only 40 per cent of the forest area is productive forest. Moreover, of this productive share roughly 60 per cent is inaccessible.[9] Until very recently the continent traditionally was a deficit area in forestry and forest products. Almost all African forests are of hardwood varieties and commercial outlets have been found for only a limited number of species. In 1948 Africa produced only between one and two per cent of the Free World's output of industrial wood. It has been estimated that production will barely keep pace with growing requirements over the next two or three decades.

Minerals. Although Africa has a number of serious mineral deficiencies her mineral resources in many categories are equal or superior to those of any other continent (*cf.* Fig. 23-1). The presence of these minerals has been a major incentive to European intervention in Africa and has significantly affected relationships between the native populations and Europeans. Africa leads the world in reserves of copper, cobalt, chromite, manganese, uranium, industrial and gem quality diamonds, and phosphate rock (see Table 23-3). Reserves of bauxite, antimony, tin, asbestos, and rare metals such as columbium, tantalum and platinum are more than adequate. While not in the strategic-metal category, Africa's gold fields are the richest in the world and have played a vital role in financing South Africa's economic development. The richest mineral regions are the Union of South Africa, South-West Africa, Southern and Northern Rhodesia, and the Belgian Congo.

Of the non-ferrous metals the two principal deficiencies are lead and zinc. More significant, however, are the lack of mineral fuels and iron ore. Africa depends on external sources for about one-sixth of its energy sup-

[8] F. Osborn, *The Limits of the Earth* (London, 1954), p. 85.

[9] The President's Materials Policy Commission, *Resources For Freedom,* Vol. 5 (Washington, D. C., June, 1952), p. 55.

plies.[10] Egypt has the only productive oil resources and these represent less than a fraction of one per cent of total world reserves. Africa has the smallest coal reserves of any continent. Proved reserves of coal in Africa have been estimated at 2 per cent of the world total and probable reserves at 4 per cent.[11] The bulk of these reserves are in the Union of South Africa and Rhodesia. Most of the known deposits are of poor quality and occurrences of coking coal are few. In contrast with its limited coal reserves Africa is estimated to have 40 per cent of the world's water power resources, or four times the potential of North America. Lack of fuel resources will be a handicap to industrialization in many parts of Africa in the absence of large-scale electrification. Africa's iron ore reserves amount to somewhat less than 15 per cent of the world total and most of these have less than 50 per cent iron content. These iron ore reserves are found chiefly in the Union of South Africa, in Southern Rhodesia, and in French West Africa. On the basis of the presently known occurrences of coal and iron ore, only the Union of South Africa and Southern Rhodesia have the raw material resources necessary to support a significant iron and steel industry.

TABLE 23-3

Africa: Reserves of Selected Minerals as Percentage of Free World Total *

MINERAL	PER CENT	PRINCIPAL PRODUCING AREAS
Copper	40	Belgian Congo and Northern Rhodesia
Manganese (av. grade 45%)	38	Union of South Africa, Belgian Congo, Morocco
Manganese (av. grade 25%)	20	Morocco, Belgian Congo
Chromite	80	Union of South Africa and Southern Rhodesia
Phosphate rock	70	French North Africa
Diamonds	95	Belgian Congo and Union of South Africa
Cobalt	90	Belgian Congo, Northern Rhodesia
Lead	6	Morocco, Nigeria
Zinc	5	Belgian Congo, Morocco

* The President's Materials Policy Commission, *Resources For Freedom,* Vol. 2 (Washington, D. C.).

ECONOMIC AND STRATEGIC IMPORTANCE

Africa's over-all international economic importance is not proportionate to its population and area. In 1953, Africa accounted for less than 7 per cent of world trade. Nonetheless the continent was a very important

[10] United Nations, *Review of Economic Conditions in Africa* (New York, February, 1951), p. 106.
[11] *Ibid.,* p. 107.

if not a major factor in the foreign trade of a number of European colonial powers. In 1953, France, Portugal, the United Kingdom, and Belgium-Luxembourg conducted 30 per cent, 25 per cent, 15 per cent, and 10 per cent respectively of their total foreign trade with Africa. Most of this was with their colonies. The largest share of the foreign trade of the African dependencies is engrossed by the European metropoles. In 1953, the share of the foreign trade of the dependent territories with their respective mother countries was as follows: [12]

DEPENDENCY	SHARE OF EXPORTS TO METROPOLE	SHARE OF IMPORTS FROM METROPOLE
British [1]	53	47
French [2]	63	67
Belgian	56	40
Portuguese	24	40

[1] Includes Gold Coast.
[2] Includes Tunisia and Morocco.

The economic importance of the dependencies to the metropoles is of course not limited to trade. A significant share of the overseas investments of France, the United Kingdom, and Belgium have been made in Africa. These investments are highly productive and profitable, are important earners of foreign exchange, and provide the metropoles with essential foodstuffs and industrial raw materials. Estimates of the United States Department of Commerce place total book value of American direct investments in Africa, exclusive of Egypt, at $458 million at the end of 1952.

Africa is a major producer of a large number of industrial raw materials and foodstuffs, chiefly for export. The most important of these are listed in Table 23-4. Not included is uranium, for which no production figures are available because of security reasons. However, Africa—principally the Belgian Congo and the Union of South Africa—is believed to be the world's largest producer. The Union of South Africa produces more than half of the Free World's output of gold. Most of this gold is shipped to the United Kingdom and makes an important contribution to meeting the sterling area's hard-currency needs.

Brief mention needs to be made of North Africa's locational importance by virtue of its position astride the vital Mediterranean and Suez passageway to the Indian Ocean and the Far East. As mentioned in Chapter 19 this route is of great commercial and strategic significance to the Free World and in particular to the United Kingdom and the Far East. "Because of its geographical relationship to the highways of the

[12] Compiled from United Nations, *Direction of International Trade,* Series T, Vol. 5, No. 8 (New York).

Mediterranean, to the Atlantic and the Indian Oceans, and to the oil fields of the Middle East, Africa would immediately become part of the global front line in the event of war." [13] The experience of the past war demonstrated the great strategic importance of North Africa as a logistical springboard in any military operations against southern Europe. The area has a string of airbases which form a vital part of the Free World's first line of defense against Soviet aggression. North Africa's strategic importance is enhanced by virtue of its highly defensible position between the desert and the sea.

TABLE 23-4

Africa: Share of Free World Output of Selected Raw Materials, 1950

MINERAL	PER CENT	AGRICULTURAL	PER CENT
Manganese (ore)	54	Groundnuts	20
Copper (metal)	24	Coffee	13
Antimony (metal)	25	Cocoa	66
Cobalt (metal)	87	Cotton	13
Tin (metal)	19	Sisal[a]	50
Industrial diamonds	87	Palm oil[a]	69
Chrome (ore)	45		
Asbestos	12		
Graphite	10		
Phosphate rock	35		

[a] Per cent of world exports.

GENERAL ECONOMIC DEVELOPMENT

Africa is the most backward of the major underdeveloped regions. With more than 8 per cent of the world's population, it accounts for only about 2.5 per cent of the world's production. All of this vast continent with the exception of the Union of South Africa falls into the underdeveloped category. Nonetheless, significant regional variations are to be found in the pattern and degree of economic development. Broadly speaking, three major zones of economic development can be identified. The first is North Africa, which embraces the Mediterranean countries from Morocco in the west to Egypt in the east and has a population of roughly 40 million. As pointed out elsewhere, this area except for Egypt is really an extension of the European Mediterranean economy. As a result of its longer exposure to European influences, North Africa is generally more advanced than the rest of Africa. The second and by far the largest economic region is Middle or Intertropical Africa, which extends roughly

[13] de Kiewiet, *op. cit.*, p. 447.

from 30 degrees north latitude to the Union of South Africa. This area with a population of 140 million is only beginning to emerge from almost complete dependence on subsistence pursuits to participation in various forms of activities involving money exchange. According to Albion Ross in his series of articles on Africa, published in *The New York Times,* middle Africa "is filled with people still in the childhood stage of the human race . . ." [14] Finally, there is the Union of South Africa which, at least in the European sector, has most of the characteristics of a highly developed western economy.

Poverty and disease are endemic in Africa. Food shortage is widespread and much of the population is undernourished and too weak to resist tropical disease. The limited statistical data available suggest that the bulk of the population has incomes below $75 *per annum* (see Table 23-5) and in some areas incomes are falling. Thus *per capita* income in

TABLE 23-5

Africa: Per Capita National Income of Selected Countries *
(in U. S. Dollars)

COUNTRY	YEAR	AMOUNT
Belgian Congo	1951	63
Egypt	1950	121
Gold Coast	1950	102
Kenya	1952	52
Nigeria	1950-51	67
Northern Rhodesia	1952	89
Southern Rhodesia	1952	151
Tunisia [a]	1952	100
Uganda	1952	53
Union of South Africa	1952	272

[a] *Revue D'Économie Politique* (Paris, March-April, 1954).
* United Nations, *Statistics of National Income and Expenditure,* Series H, No. 6 (New York, August, 1954).

Egypt today is considerably less than it was in the 1920's. Incomes are distributed very unevenly between natives and Europeans. Thus, Frenchmen in North Africa are generally considered to enjoy living standards equal to, or higher than, in metropolitan France ($880 *per capita* Gross National Product in 1954). The relatively small white populations of the Union of South Africa have higher average incomes than in most European countries. Accordingly, average incomes of native peoples in countries where Europeans play a significant economic role are substantially less than shown. An economic middle class is virtually unknown in native

[14] *New York Times,* October 24, 1954.

Africa south of the Sahara, except possibly in the Belgian Congo and the Gold Coast. Incomes in Nigeria, which is a predominantly native agricultural economy, probably are fairly representative of the mass of Africa's population.

Agriculture is the principal economic activity with about three-fourths of the population of the continent as a whole dependent on farming for a livelihood, as compared with about 60 per cent for South America. In most countries agriculture accounts for 40 to 55 per cent of the national income. Except for the Union of South Africa, manufacturing generally accounts for 10 per cent or less of total production. Again, outside of the Union, most progress in the development of secondary industry has been achieved in French North Africa, chiefly Algeria, Egypt, the Belgian Congo, Kenya, and Southern Rhodesia. Handicraft industries are of some significance in parts of West Africa, particularly the Gold Coast and Nigeria. Manufactures follow the typical pattern for underdeveloped areas, with primary emphasis on consumer goods industries like textiles, food packing, and the processing of raw materials for export. The production of minerals accounts for a significant percentage of total output in a few countries like the Belgian Congo, Northern and Southern Rhodesia, and of course the Union of South Africa. Most industrial and commercial enterprises are controlled by non-indigenous elements. For example, a 1952 census of business in Tunisia showed that 90 per cent of the commercial and industrial establishments employing more than 50 persons were owned by non-Tunisians.

Although the scope of the money economy is gradually widening in Africa as more of the native population exchanges its production or labor for cash, subsistence agriculture is still of primary importance, particularly in the middle region. The United Nations has estimated that in all territories of Middle Africa, except the Gold Coast, subsistence farming accounts for approximately 60 per cent or more of the total land area cultivated by the native population.[15] In many areas like French West Africa, Kenya, and Southern Rhodesia, the percentage exceeds 80 per cent. The same United Nations study estimates that 60 per cent of the adult male population is engaged in subsistence production. In certain areas like French West Africa, the Gold Coast, and Nigeria, cash earning chiefly takes the form of cash cropping. In others like Kenya and Southern Rhodesia, wage earning is the chief source of native money income. In some territories like the Belgian Congo, money incomes are derived both from

[15] United Nations, Department of Economic Affairs, *Enlargement of the Exchange Economy in Tropical Africa* (New York, 1954), p. 13.

cash cropping and wage earning. Wage earning activities are in various stages of transition from intermittent employment for wages combined with subsistence farming to complete dependence on wages. The growth of the wage-earning class has been greatest in areas like Kenya, Northern Rhodesia, and Southern Rhodesia where the pressure of the population on the land has forced natives to seek alternative means of earning a livelihood. Nonetheless labor remains scarce in many parts of Africa, and the movement of labor to the towns and mines frequently impairs agricultural output.

Production methods in agriculture among the native populations are extremely primitive. Yields per acre and per man are the lowest of all the continents. Food crop yields per acre are only about 60 per cent of the world average. Most natives employ no more efficient tool than the hoe. While a few are learning to use the plough, its general employment in many regions is impossible because the tsetse fly precludes the use of draft animals. Outside of a few areas like Egypt and French North Africa conservation of water and the use of fertilizers is rare. Agricultural output also suffers from the fact that many parts of Africa are subject to periodic drought and famine.

Like other underdeveloped regions, exports of a few primary products account for the preponderant share of total exports in most countries. Thus in 1952 cotton accounted for 87 per cent of the value of Egypt's exports, copper for almost 90 per cent of the value of Northern Rhodesia's exports, and cocoa for 60 per cent of the Gold Coast's exports. As a result, levels of income are subject to wide fluctuations depending on external market conditions. Intra-African trade is small. In 1948 only 13 per cent of Africa's exports were intra-regional.[16] The chief reasons for this low figure are (1) the exports of most of the territories are competing rather than complementary, (2) trade is largely oriented overseas because of the strength of colonial ties, and (3) transport and communications are very poor.

Africa has a poorly developed transport system. Human porterage is still of importance in tropical Africa for the movement of goods over short distances. Relatively few areas outside of French North Africa and the Union of South Africa are adequately served by rail, road, or river communications (*cf.* Fig. 23-1, p. 690). Lack of transport is a major obstacle to the development of most of Africa. In 1949, the total length of Africa's rail network (excluding Egypt) was only about 39,000 miles, of which

[16] "Summary of World Trade Statistics," *United Nations Statistical Papers*, Series D, No. 2 (New York, April, 1950).

roughly one-half was concentrated in French North Africa and the Union of South Africa.[17] Railway development, particularly in Middle Africa, occurred largely in response to the need to transport minerals from the interior to the coast for export abroad (*cf.* Fig. 7-6, p. 186). In many cases the servicing of agricultural communities is thus largely fortuitous. Internal crosswise rail development is insignificant. "Such transcontinental connections as the Cape to Cairo Railway or the Trans-Saharian were partially built or projected to serve national and imperial schemes and not necessarily to respond to strictly economic criteria."[18] Few highways in tropical Africa are hard-surfaced and most are impassable during the rainy season. Natural obstacles, such as falls and rapids close to their mouths, and seasonal fluctuations in the flow, place severe limitations on the use of Africa's rivers for transportation purposes. Except for the Nile and Congo river systems, river transport is largely limited to the navigable lakes like Nyasa and Victoria.[19]

CONTRASTING COLONIAL POLICIES

Marked differences are to be found in the colonial policies which the European metropoles pursue in their African dependencies. Very frequently these policies reflect strong geographical influences. The British officially proclaim the primacy of the interests of the native populations and seek to encourage the development of self-government in their territories. In the Belgian colonies a paternalistic attitude toward the native population still governs colonial policy and the emphasis is on efficiency and maximum returns for the mother country. Neither the native nor the white populations have political rights. Preparation for self-government is viewed as a goal for the more distant future after the natives have been civilized. Portugal's colonial policies are somewhat similar, except that Angola and Mozambique are considered overseas provinces of Portugal rather than colonies. French policy looks toward the gradual integration of its African dependencies into the French Union on a basis of common citizenship and unified political institutions as in Algeria. In the case of Tunisia and Morocco, however, the French are being compelled to grant independence outside the framework of the French Union.

British policies have brought dependencies like the Gold Coast and Nigeria, well along the path toward self-government. This process has

[17] United Nations, *Review of Economic Conditions In Africa* (New York, 1951).
[18] Haines, *op. cit.*, p. 129.
[19] Hailey, *op. cit.*, p. 1541.

been facilitated by the absence of any significant numbers of European settlers in these territories, thereby minimizing the inevitable clash of interests between the natives and the whites. However, these same conditions do not obtain in many parts of British Central and East Africa. Here more favorable climatic conditions have attracted moderate numbers of white settlers, who favor a policy of white supremacy. The result has been increasing social tensions and in certain instances serious physical outbursts like the Mau Mau disturbances in Kenya described elsewhere.

British policy has favored the federation and consolidation of its African territories. The first move in this direction has been the creation of the Central African Federation in 1953 comprising Northern and Southern Rhodesia and Nyasaland. Political considerations figured most importantly in the establishment of the Federation, but the desire to create a more cohesive economic unit combining three essentially economically interdependent political units was a contributory factor. While the white minorities favored the Federation, it was bitterly opposed by the natives in all three territories. They fear that the resultant improvement in economic conditions will attract additional white settlers and add to the pressure on the natives. Conflicting racial interests block a proposed similar federation of Uganda, Kenya, and Tanganyika. Efforts to organize tropical Africa along regional lines to take into account natural resources and communications are a recognition of the limitations of the original colonial boundaries.

Thus far Belgian policies in the Congo have been highly successful in maintaining political stability. Unlike the Union of South Africa and British East Africa, the Congo has no color bar. Natives are permitted and encouraged to train for and occupy skilled positions. The size of the white population is limited and there are few permanent settlers. Political rights of both whites and natives are barred as noted above, although the Belgians are planning to give the right to everyone to vote in municipal elections. Just how long this situation can continue is uncertain. There is the periodic pressure from Belgian groups who want to send out large numbers of white settlers to the Congo. If these efforts were realized the result could be a breakdown of the present system and the development of conditions similar to those in some British territories. Then there is always the possibility that the growth of native self-government in neighboring territories will generate similar pressure in the Congo.

In French West Africa political conditions are still relatively tranquil, but as in the Congo there is always the prospect that growing native aspirations for self-government will intensify. In French North Africa, with its sizable European minority, the conflict of interests between the natives and whites and the growing demands of the natives for greater political and economic freedom created a highly explosive political situation. As a result France has been forced to agree to grant independence to Morocco and Tunisia and certain economic and social reforms to Algeria. Portuguese territories enjoy relative political stability as a result of strict government controls, the small white population, and the fact that the process of modernization has not gone very far due to the limited resources for economic development at the disposal of the Portuguese government.

AGRICULTURE

Since World War II, total agricultural output in Africa as well as output of foodstuffs has increased somewhat more rapidly than the population. This has permitted some raising of the very low prewar *per capita* levels of food consumption as well as a considerable expansion of exports. However, most of the improvement in diets probably has been limited to the Union of South Africa and the more prosperous cocoa and mineral-producing regions. Africa produces the bulk of its essential food needs, although the margin between supplies and requirements is narrowing. Thus, whereas Africa before the war had an export surplus of cereals of about three-quarters of a million tons *per annum,* it is now running a slight deficit largely because of Egypt's sizable imports and reduced surpluses from French North Africa.

Principal Crops. Africa displays considerable variation from region to region with respect to the principal crops, production for the home market and for export, methods of cultivation, and farm agricultural organization. In French North Africa the principal food crops are wheat and barley, in Egypt wheat, corn, and rice. South of the Sahara wheat is of almost negligible importance except in the Union of South Africa. Root crops, millets, sorghum, pulses, and maize are of greatest significance. Root crops are particularly important in tropical areas. In certain territories, the proportion of cultivated land devoted to the production of export crops represents a large percentage of the total. The Gold Coast with 45 per cent is a notable example. Countries where the area under crops mainly for export range between 20 and 30 per cent include Egypt, French Equatorial Africa, and Uganda. In some areas high prices for export crops have reduced production of food for local consumption. This could create serious food deficiencies in periods of rapidly declining export prices. (The principal agricultural exports were given in Table

23-4.) Although Africa is believed to have significant potentialities for increasing meat production, cattle-raising is presently of only limited economic significance. In tropical Africa a major limitation, as mentioned earlier, is the widespread presence of the tsetse fly. Purely nomadic tribes are found chiefly in the savanna region on the southern border of the Sahara.

Land Tenure. Although landlordism is much less of a problem in Africa than in other underdeveloped regions, the continent nonetheless faces serious difficulties in certain areas arising out of existing land tenure arrangements. Communal tenure is the most widespread form of agricultural organization in Africa south of the Sahara. While it manifests itself in a variety of forms communal tenure has a number of common features. "Land is held on a tribal, village, kindred or family basis, and individuals have definite rights in this land by virtue of their membership in the relevant social unit. Hence, title to land has a communal character and it is usufructuary, rather than absolute."[20] Subsistence shifting-cultivation usually is associated with communal forms of land tenure.

A number of developments that vary in importance from region to region are breaking up this traditional system of land tenure and cultivation. Shifting agriculture, as described on page 697, requires a plentiful supply of land. However, with the growth of population the pressure of numbers on the land has made more intensive methods of cultivation necessary. This has frequently led to overcropping and soil exhaustion. It has forced increasing numbers of natives to seek employment on European-owned plantations and in industry as an alternative or supplementary source of income. This process has been intensified by the earlier colonial land alienation policies. In French Equatorial Africa and the Belgian Congo vast territories were declared vacant by the state and turned over to private concessions. This resulted from a misunderstanding of the fact that seemingly vacant lands were in fact cultivable tribal areas lying fallow. Subsequently the concessions originally granted were considerably reduced and government policies were adopted to encourage native freeholds. In the Union of South Africa, Kenya, and Northern Rhodesia, reserves of land were set aside for the native population. However, these reserves were wholly inadequate under existing methods of cultivation.

The shortage of land and the reserve system has been a major cause of Kenya's Mau Mau uprisings. Roughly 4,000 white settlers occupy the

[20] United Nations, *Land Reform* (New York, 1951).

12,000-square-mile fertile belt of the green highlands of Kenya where Negroes cannot acquire land. By contrast the Kikuyu tribe of 1,250,000 persons is restricted to 2,000 square miles. Land hunger is intense. The pressure of population on this limited area has made it necessary for about 200,000 natives to work on plantations and in other employments on the white reserve. This is back of the Mau Mau's determination to drive the white man out.

The growth of cash cropping by which land acquires a commercial value is also contributing to the break-up of the communal system of land tenure. This process has gone further in Uganda and the Belgian Congo where the desire to exploit land for commercial purposes has promoted widespread individual forms of land ownership. Also important has been the growing demand for labor resulting from the expanding production of minerals and agricultural products for export. A growing number of natives have abandoned subsistence agriculture to become industrial and agricultural wage earners.

In certain parts of Africa, particularly eastern central and southern, there has been some development of plantation agriculture mainly by Europeans. Crops consist mostly of export products such as sisal, sugar, coffee, tobacco, and rubber. Because of the early difficulties of attracting native labor some of these plantations were developed by immigrant labor. The most notable example was the use of Indians on the Natal sugar plantations. After serving their period of indentured service many of these Indians stayed on in Natal to engage in market-gardening and retail trade. This has given rise to a color problem in the Union of South Africa second only to that of the Negro problem, a problem which has been the cause of serious strictures between the Union of South African Government and the Government of India.

In French North Africa and Egypt individual ownership in property is well developed and landlordism is a problem. Thus in Tunisia, the French hold 25 per cent of the land devoted to crops although they represent less than 7 per cent of the population. Moreover, these are the most fertile and best-watered lands. Natives generally farm small uneconomic plots. This situation may well change if the French pull out in the face of growing local instability and pressures. Until the land reform law of September, 1952, one-half of one per cent of Egypt's population owned one-third of the land in holdings of 50 acres or more. Another one-third of the land was owned by 5 to 6 per cent of the population in plots of 5 or more but less than 50 acres. The remaining one-third was controlled by

94 per cent of the landowners in plots averaging under one acre.[21] Under the land reform program almost 600,000 acres of land are to be taken from 1,758 landowners and distributed to 250,000 families over a period of five years.[22] While the program has improved the lot of the peasant families affected, it by no means has destroyed the wealthy land-owning class or solved the basic problem of land hunger.

For most of Africa, however, the poverty of the natives is chiefly a result of the primitive methods of farming, which lead to food shortages and land exhaustion, rather than the system of land tenure. One promising approach to the introduction of better farming and better land use is the so-called settlement scheme. "They are . . . the means of settling either land reclaimed from bush and waste, or reclaimed from aridity by irrigation, or land lately used by Africans to the point of exhaustion and rehabilitated by proper fallowing, manuring and similar treatment, and then laid out in proper holdings, bunded strip cropped or otherwise treated to prevent soil erosion, etc. and settlement by peasants." [23] An outstanding example is the Gezira Scheme in the Sudan which embraces one million acres with irrigation canals. The Scheme is a partnership between the government and the peasant who share the profits and the responsibilities for maintaining the land. The government furnishes the land to the peasant in forty-acre plots on a long-term lease basis and is responsible for the supply of water. It also provides qualified agricultural managers, mechanical equipment, fertilizers, and marketing facilities. The peasant on his part is required to observe proper methods of cultivation. Through their representatives the peasants have assumed an increasing role in running the project. The Gezira Scheme has been highly successful and similar projects have been established in a number of other territories. The settlement scheme would appear to offer considerable opportunities for improving the lot of the native populations.

LONG-RUN ECONOMIC PROSPECTS

Since World War II government-sponsored long-range economic development plans have been drawn up for most African territories and in many areas these plans are now being implemented. In the case of the dependent territories a large proportion of the funds is being provided by the metropoles. By and large these plans provide for investments

[21] Department of State, *Agriculture In Point Four Countries,* Part 4, *Near East and Independent Africa* (August, 1952), p. 1.

[22] *New York Times,* October 20, 1955.

[23] United Nations, *Progress In Land Reform* (New York, 1954), p. 107.

which are unlikely to attract private capital and yet are fairly basic to the achievement of any real economic progress. The principal categories of investment include irrigation, transportation, social services like education, health, public housing, and measures to increase agricultural productivity. While the programs seek to stimulate production of primary products required by the metropole they show much more concern for the welfare of the native population than earlier colonial policies. Despite these plans there is still no evidence of a significant acceleration of economic growth in most parts of Africa.

Before economic development can proceed very rapidly in Africa among the native populations, more resources will have to be shifted from subsistence to exchange activities and productivity will have to be greatly increased. Otherwise the incentives and the means of providing surpluses required to feed workers in industry and to accumulate capital will be lacking. New techniques of farming will have to be developed to counteract the declining productivity of the soil and permit settled agriculture. The failure of the Tanganyika Groundnut Scheme is a good example of the difficulties of introducing new methods of cultivation in tropical regions even where large-scale financial backing is available. A fundamental attack will have to be made against the problem of disease. There are many obstacles to the development of industry. An entrepreneurial class will have to develop. A disciplined and trained labor force has to be established. Levels of literacy will have to be raised. Even the present limited development programs are greatly hampered by the lack of skilled workers and adequately trained administrators. Then there is the problem of native-white relations in some areas. Thus, much of Africa has a considerable way to travel before it faces the no less serious problem of capital shortage. Very few of the native economies have the capacity to mobilize significant amounts of capital for investment. While the present expansion of basic services under government auspices will attract private capital into industry, mining, and agriculture, not much of this capital is likely to move into the native economy. Thus the native economies may benefit from the present programs only indirectly. There are some exceptions, of course, like the Gold Coast which has accumulated large sums for development through its cocoa stabilization fund, and the Belgian Congo with its profitable mineral export industries. Some countries, like Egypt, may be unable to expand output rapidly enough to keep pace with the growth of population. For most of the region, however, economic development is likely to be slow and production of foodstuffs and industrial raw materials will continue to predominate. Perhaps the outlook for Africa is well summed up in the following statement by Albion Ross in his previously mentioned series of articles on Africa: [24]

The drama of the Americas will never be re-enacted here unless the findings of the geographers, soil scientists and the like are all wrong. The theory of the "dying continent" is probably regarded today by African soil scientists as somewhat of an exaggeration but they grant that it contains a vital element of truth. The native will need all of his African heritage as the generations go by and will be lucky if it can support him in decency.

[24] *New York Times,* October 26, 1954.

Index

The Index is not meant to list every geographical place name mentioned in the text. Rather, it attempts to list subject matters, place names, and names of persons which have been given substantial treatment; even with this limitation, the great variety of subjects covered in the text precludes a complete indexing.

ONE WORLD DIVIDED

1956

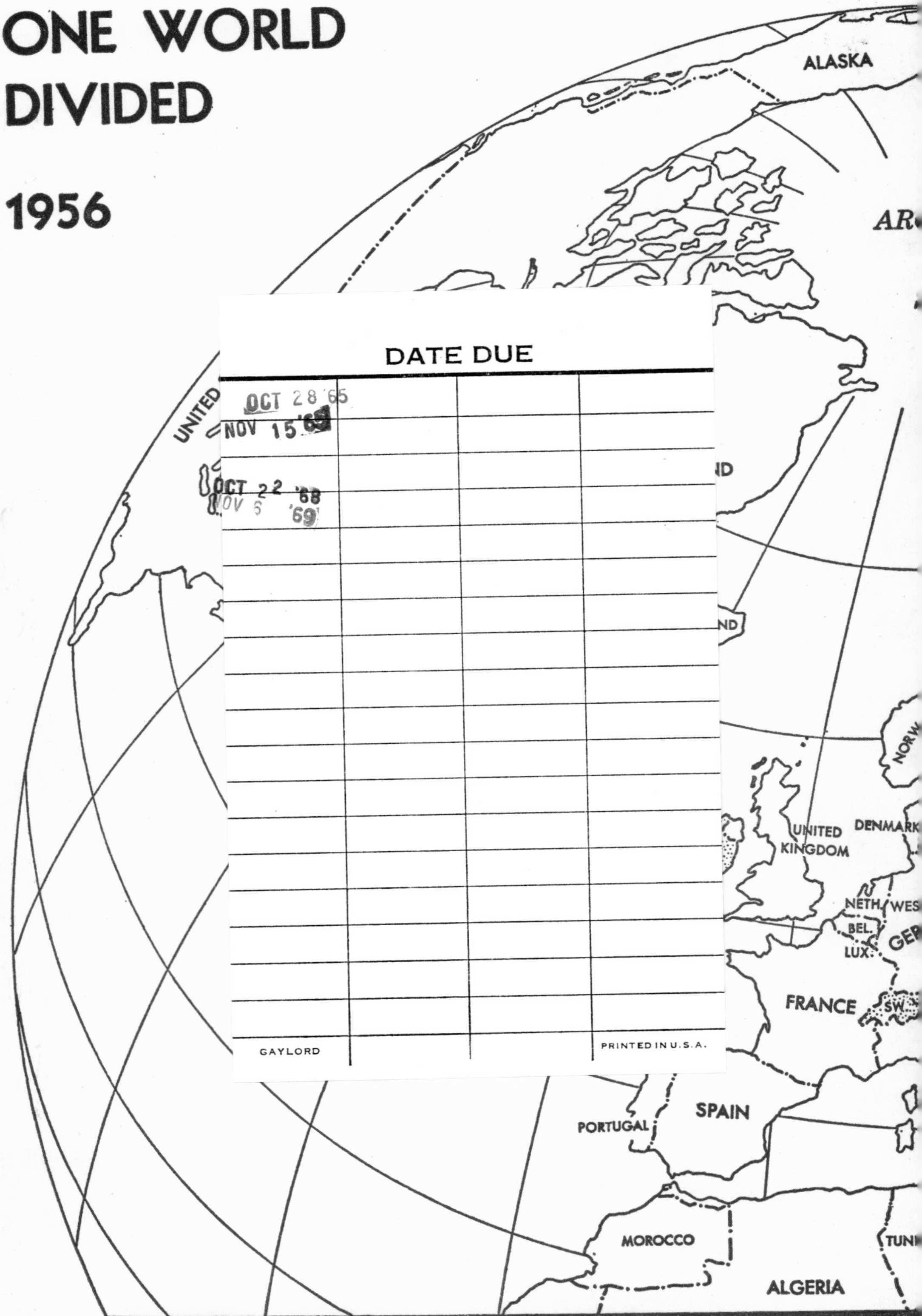

Neutralist Nations and Nations Not Participating in Western Defense Pacts